SOUTHWEST

Road Trip

TIM HULL

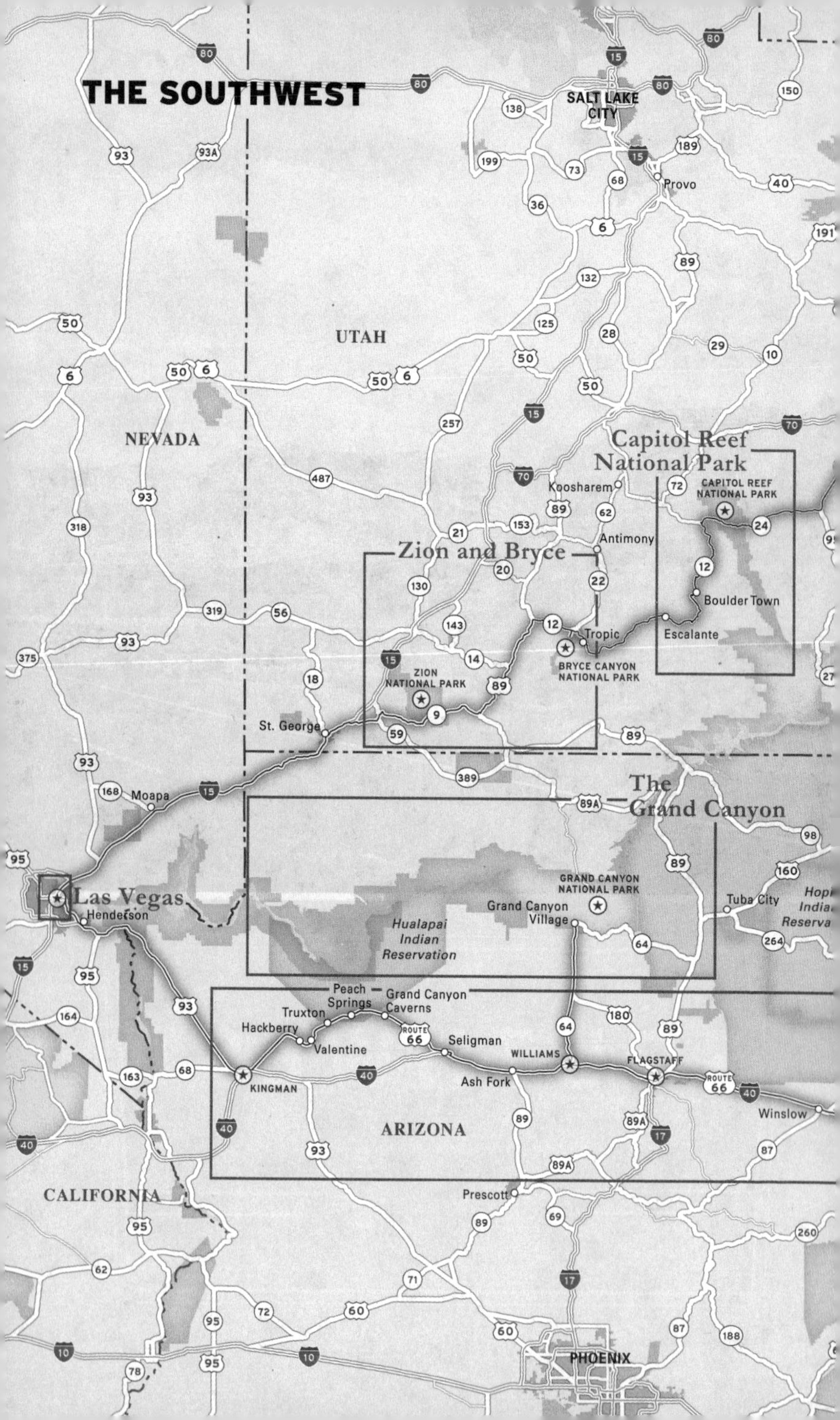
THE SOUTHWEST
SALT LAKE CITY
Provo
UTAH
NEVADA
Capitol Reef National Park
CAPITOL REEF NATIONAL PARK
Koosharem
Antimony
Zion and Bryce
Tropic
Boulder Town
Escalante
BRYCE CANYON NATIONAL PARK
ZION NATIONAL PARK
St. George
Moapa
The Grand Canyon
GRAND CANYON NATIONAL PARK
Grand Canyon Village
Tuba City
Hopi Indian Reservation
Las Vegas
Henderson
Hualapai Indian Reservation
Peach Springs
Grand Canyon Caverns
Truxton
Hackberry
Valentine
Seligman
WILLIAMS
FLAGSTAFF
KINGMAN
Ash Fork
Winslow
ARIZONA
CALIFORNIA
Prescott
PHOENIX
ROUTE 66

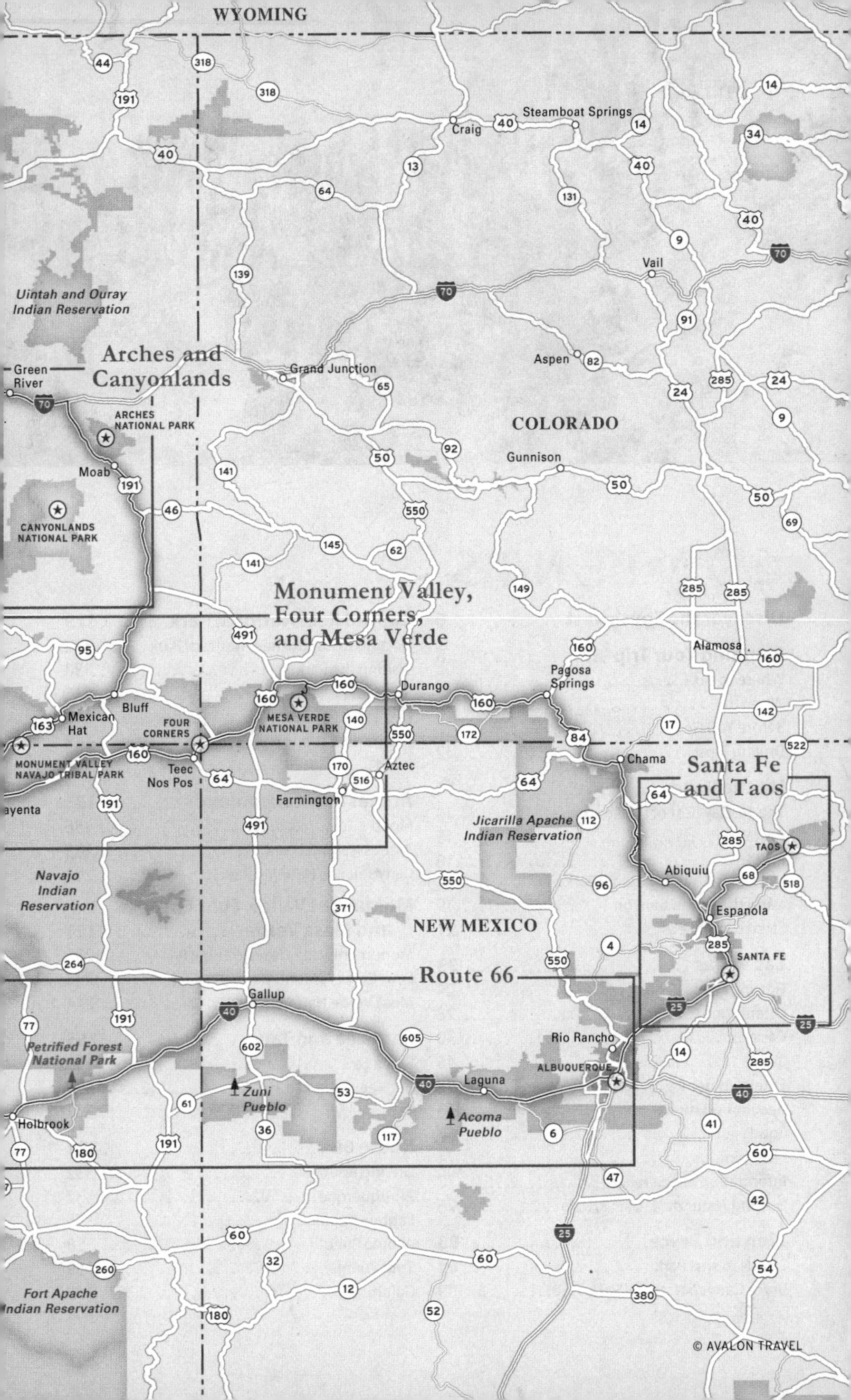
WYOMING
COLORADO
NEW MEXICO
Arches and Canyonlands
Monument Valley, Four Corners, and Mesa Verde
Santa Fe and Taos
Route 66
Uintah and Ouray Indian Reservation
Green River
ARCHES NATIONAL PARK
Moab
CANYONLANDS NATIONAL PARK
Craig
Steamboat Springs
Vail
Aspen
Grand Junction
Gunnison
Alamosa
Durango
Pagosa Springs
Bluff
Mexican Hat
FOUR CORNERS
MESA VERDE NATIONAL PARK
MONUMENT VALLEY NAVAJO TRIBAL PARK
Teec Nos Pos
Kayenta
Aztec
Farmington
Chama
Jicarilla Apache Indian Reservation
Abiquiu
TAOS
Espanola
SANTA FE
Navajo Indian Reservation
Gallup
Petrified Forest National Park
Holbrook
Zuni Pueblo
Laguna
Acoma Pueblo
Rio Rancho
ALBUQUERQUE
Fort Apache Indian Reservation
© AVALON TRAVEL

CONTENTS

Discover the Southwest 6

Planning Your Trip 8
Where to Go 8
When to Go 10
Before You Go 10
Driving Tips 12

Hit the Road 14
The 14-Day Best of the Southwest 14
Best Views 15
Best Hikes 18
Las Vegas, Utah's National Parks, and the Grand Canyon 19
Stretch Your Legs 21

Las Vegas 23
Getting to Las Vegas 24
Orientation 28
Casinos 30
Sights 45
Entertainment 53
Accommodations 63
Food 67
Shopping 74
Information and Services 77
Getting Around 78

Zion and Bryce 83
Zion National Park 84
Bryce Canyon National Park 109

Capitol Reef National Park 129
Getting to Capitol Reef National Park 132
Visiting the Park 133
Sights 135
Recreation 142
Accommodations 148
Food 151

Arches and Canyonlands 153
Moab 156
Arches National Park 189
Canyonlands National Park 201

Monument Valley, Four Corners, and Mesa Verde 231
Monument Valley Navajo Tribal Park 235
Four Corners Monument 243
Mesa Verde National Park 244

Santa Fe and Taos 255
Santa Fe 256
Between Santa Fe and Taos 290
Taos 301

Route 66 331
Driving Route 66 332
Albuquerque 332
Laguna Pueblo 356
Acoma Pueblo 358
Zuni Pueblo 359
Gallup 362

Petrified Forest National Park 368
Holbrook 371
Winslow and Vicinity 372
Flagstaff 375
Williams 395
Ash Fork 398
Seligman 399
Grand Canyon Caverns 401
Peach Springs 402
Truxton and Valentine 402
Hackberry 402
Kingman 403

The Grand Canyon 411
Getting to the Grand Canyon 415
Visiting the Park 419
The South Rim 425
The North Rim 445
The Inner Canyon 450
Grand Canyon West 456

Essentials 463
Getting There 463
Road Rules 465
Visas and Officialdom 469
Travel Tips 470
Health and Safety 474
Internet Resources 477

Index 481

List of Maps 495

DISCOVER
the Southwest

The great American road trip finds its wild side in this mysterious landscape. You'll rise from arid red rock fairylands, through river-cut canyons to the high and mighty evergreen forests, and then descend again—sometimes in one scenic stretch of road. You'll pass through small towns and villages happily ensconced in a plateau time warp, when colorful billboards marked oases in the desert and freedom could still be found on the back of a Harley.

Bring your hiking boots, your trusty camera, and a water bottle, but leave your preconceptions at home. Follow these twisting two-lane highways with an open mind and an open heart, and you will discover the unexpected and the impossible: the neon-lit hedonism of Las Vegas and the otherworldly hoodoo forests of Bryce Canyon; the unspeakable beauty of the Grand Canyon and the dreamy adobe charm of Santa Fe. Wander among the glowing red cliff dwellings and the eroded sandstone monuments to uncover something about beauty, history, time—and perhaps even yourself.

Come to the Southwest and get lost ... or found.

124
HISTORIC
NEW MEXICO
66
ROUTE

PLANNING YOUR TRIP

Where to Go

Las Vegas

Rising out of the desert like a high-tech oasis, Las Vegas is an adult playground of **casinos, bars, buffets, over-the-top shows,** and **plush hotels.** Dig a little deeper to find fine food, a flourishing arts scene, and local hangouts in the shadows of **The Strip.**

Zion and Bryce

Zion National Park presents stunning contrasts, with barren, towering rock walls deeply incised by steep canyons containing a verdant oasis. Zion is so awe-inspiring that the early Mormons named it for their vision of heaven. **Bryce Canyon National Park** is famed for its red and pink hoodoos, delicate fingers of stone rising from a steep mountainside.

Capitol Reef National Park

In Capitol Reef National Park, the Fremont River carves a magnificent canyon through **Waterpocket Fold,** offering hikers a leafy, well-watered **sanctuary** from the park's otherwise arid landscapes.

Arches and Canyonlands

In vast **Canyonlands National Park,** the Colorado River begins to tunnel its mighty—and soon to be grand—canyon through an otherworldly landscape of red sandstone. The beauty is more mystical at **Arches National Park,** where hundreds of delicate arches provide windows into the solid rock. High-spirited **Moab** is a recreational mecca, known for its **mountain biking** and comfortable, sophisticated dining and lodging.

Monument Valley, Four Corners, and Mesa Verde

A sculptor couldn't have carved the **red sandstone** buttes, arches, and spires at **Monument Valley Navajo Tribal Park.** The **cliff dwellings** at **Mesa Verde National Park,** built in naturally worn alcoves high up in the canyon walls, are ancient stone masterworks. On the way between these two spots, stop at **Four Corners National Monument** and twist your body into four states at once.

Santa Fe and Taos

Santa Fe, New Mexico's picturesque capital has a human scale and a golden glow (partly from the loads of money spent here). **Museums** are a major draw—for state history, folk art, and more—as are the scores of **galleries.** Taos melds artists, spiritual seekers, and ski bums—plus centuries-old Spanish and American Indian families. Make time to enjoy the **creative atmosphere,** cultivated in coffee shops and restaurants.

Route 66

Peaceful nostalgia, the ruins of a bygone heyday, and a **quirky road culture** pervade the sections of Historic Route 66 between **Albuquerque,** New Mexico, and **Kingman,** Arizona. It's possible to spend the whole drive watching the ever-changing scenery of **high-desert plains,** lava fields, ancient villages, and **petrified forests.**

The Grand Canyon

A mile-deep slice into the **Kaibab Plateau,** the Grand Canyon defies easy description. Stare in awe at the **colorful layers** from the canyon's edge—or descend deep into the canyon to meet its creator: the mighty **Colorado River.**

Clockwise from top left: Las Vegas; turquoise jewelry for sale in Santa Fe; Hackberry General Store along Historic Route 66.

When to Go

The national parks and the other sights on the Colorado Plateau are open year-round, but **spring, summer,** and **early fall** are the best and the busiest seasons for a visit. During the **high season from May to September,** the parks—especially Grand Canyon, Zion, and Arches—are crowded with vacationing families and international tourists.

In the higher elevations like Bryce Canyon, Grand Canyon, Mesa Verde, and Taos, **winter** is **cold and snowy.** These spots are much more sedate, though still steadily occupied, and prices are much lower in some areas. The **Wetherill Mesa** section of Mesa Verde and the **North Rim** of the Grand Canyon are both **closed during winter.**

Perhaps the best time to come to the Southwest is **mid-September to early October.** You'll find the major sights a bit less busy since school is in session. The days are mostly warm in the low country and moderate in the highlands, while the nights are generally cool and pleasant at low elevations and brisk and refreshing up high. And of course, the sky everywhere is big, blue, and cloudless.

Before You Go

The easiest places to **fly** into are **Las Vegas** and **Albuquerque.** Flying into Las Vegas will orient your road trip as described in this guide and is the best starting point for a shorter trip heavy on Utah's national parks and the Grand Canyon. Flying into Albuquerque is the best option for a trip dedicated to discovering Santa Fe, Taos, and Route 66, which will take you right past the Grand Canyon.

You could also fly into Phoenix's **Sky Harbor International Airport,** rent a car, and drive 2.5 hours north to start your journey at Grand Canyon National Park's South Rim.

Book **hotels** and **rental cars** in advance for the best rates and availability, especially in the summer, which is high season for travel. If you plan to rent a car in one city and return it in another, you should expect to pay an additional fee, which can be quite high.

High-season travelers should also plan ahead for the **big-name attractions.** Reservations are essential at the **campgrounds** and **lodges** at **Grand Canyon National Park.** With just one lodge each and limited campsites,

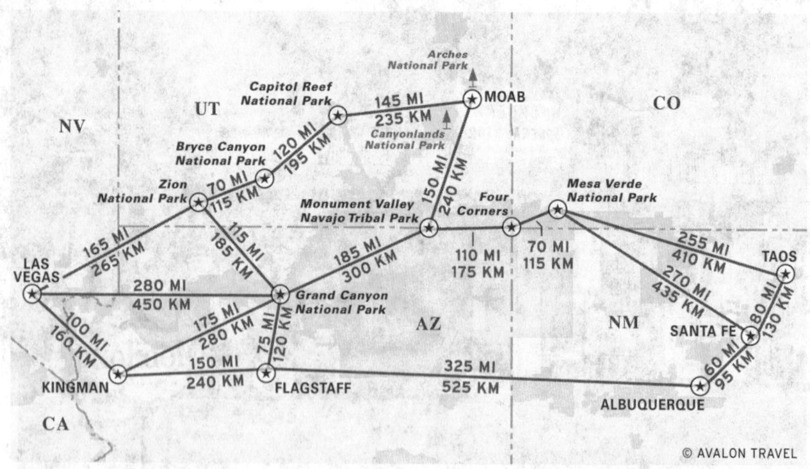

Clockwise from top left: Ten Thousand Waves spa in Santa Fe; Wigwam Motel near Route 66 in Holbrook; Havasu Falls, Grand Canyon West.

reservations are also a must for **Zion National Park, Bryce Canyon National Park,** and **Mesa Verde National Park.**

During the summer high season, it's essential to make reservations in advance for accommodations in the small towns that surround these popular parks, including **Springdale** near Zion, **Tropic** near Bryce, and **Tusayan** near the Grand Canyon's South Rim.

If you want to **hike** or **ride a mule** down into the Grand Canyon for an overnight stay or **raft** the roiling rapids of the Colorado River, start planning at least **six months** out.

Coming to the United States from abroad? You'll need your **passport** and possibly a **visa.**

Bring **layered clothing.** Expect **desert heat** in the summer in Las Vegas, the inner depths of the Grand Canyon, and at lower elevations in southern Utah, such as Moab and Arches National Park. Also be prepared for cooler temperatures: Nights, even in the summer, turn cool above 7,000 feet, where several of the great parks on this route sit. Remember this when visiting the Grand Canyon, Bryce Canyon, and Mesa Verde. For much of the Southwest, mid-to-late summer is the rainy season, so you might encounter intermittent afternoon thunderstorms and find yourself in need of **rain gear.**

Driving Tips

Las Vegas has a lot of traffic, especially on Thursday and Friday evenings. The **Nevada Department of Transportation** (www.nvroads.com) has information on current road conditions.

Expect **high summer temperatures** driving around Las Vegas. Heat can also be a problem on the routes to and from the Grand Canyon, Zion, and Moab. Make sure your car has sufficient **engine coolant** and working **air-conditioning** and take along plenty of **drinking water.**

Utah's scenic Highway 12

You may also encounter **thunderstorms** in this area from July to mid-September, which can lead to road flooding. Never enter a running wash. Contact the **Nevada Department of Transportation** (877/687-6237, http://nvroads.com), the **Arizona Department of Transportation** (dial 511 in state, www.az511.gov), the **Utah Department of Transportation** (dial 511 in state, www.udot.utah.gov), the **New Mexico Department of Transportation** (dial 511 in state, www.nmroads.com), and the **Colorado Department of Transportation** (dial 511 in state, www.cotrip.org) for each state's road conditions.

Though not exactly backroads, the routes on this trip are mostly **two-lane highways** rather than bustling interstates. During the summer high season you will encounter groups of **motorcyclists** and **RVs** inside the national parks and along the roads on the Colorado Plateau, Historic Route 66, and the High and Low Roads from Santa Fe to Taos. Also keep an eye out for the occasional long-distance bicycle gang. You may encounter **wildlife** along these roads, especially at night or early in the morning and inside Grand Canyon and Mesa Verde National Parks.

Many of the roads in this region pass through **Indian reservations,** on which you should never drive off-road or even off the main roads without first getting permission to do so. While on the vast Navajo Nation, which crosses portions of Arizona, Utah, and New Mexico, keep an eye out for livestock crossing the road.

While there are **gas stations** and other services throughout the region, in some areas they are few and far between. Never let your tank go below half full and always keep extra water and food in your vehicle. Bring a **hard copy of a map** instead of relying on your phone or GPS. The best map of the region is AAA's Indian Country map. **Cell phone service** is likely to be spotty on the reservations, in the national parks, and in the more remote corners.

HIT THE ROAD

The 14-Day Best of the Southwest

You can hit the top destinations of the American Southwest in **two weeks** by driving in a loop of roughly 2,000 miles. The day-by-day route below begins in Las Vegas, but you can just as easily start in Albuquerque or Flagstaff if that works better for you. For detailed driving directions for each leg of this road trip, see *Getting To...* at the beginning of each chapter. All mileage and driving times are approximate.

Day 1

LAS VEGAS

It's easy to fill a day with fun in Las Vegas. Walk the Strip and get acclimated to this adult fantasy world, sip drinks by the pool at **Harrah's,** or splurge on a room at the **Bellagio.** Catch a showing of Cirque du Soleil's Beatles-themed ***LOVE*** in the evening and grab a late-night meal at **Rose. Rabbit. Lie.** For more suggestions on how to spend your time in Vegas, see page 31.

Days 2-3

ZION AND BRYCE

165 miles / 3 hours

Grab a coffee from **The Egg & I** to wake up for the drive to **Zion National Park.** Leave Las Vegas at 8am to reach Zion by 11am. The **165-mile** drive to the **Springdale entrance** takes about **three hours;** however, traffic, especially in summer and on weekends, can make it much longer.

Explore **Zion National Park** to see iconic attractions like **Court of the Patriarchs** and the **Emerald Pools.** Make reservations ahead of time to spend the night in the comfort of the **Zion Lodge** or at the park's **South Campground** or **Watchman Campground.**

Make the **70-mile, 1.5-hour** drive to **Bryce Canyon National Park.** Hike the **Navajo Loop Trail** or head to **Fairyland Canyon,** where worthwhile hikes include the **Fairyland Loop Trail.** Stay the night at the **Lodge at Bryce Canyon** (make reservations in advance) or camp at **North Campground** or **Sunset Campground.**

Day 4

CAPITOL REEF NATIONAL PARK

120 miles / 2.5 hours

Wake up for the drive to **Capitol Reef National Park,** a scenic **120-mile, 2.5-hour** drive from Bryce Canyon. Leave by 7:30am and arrive by 10am, and check in at the **Capitol Reef Inn and Café** in Torrey or the park's **Fruita Campground.**

Take the park's **21-mile** round-trip **scenic drive (1.5 hours)** to **Capitol Gorge.** Leave your car in the parking area and take the two-mile round-trip hike into Capitol Gorge to see the petroglyphs, pioneer registry, and natural water tanks.

Day 5

ARCHES AND CANYONLANDS NATIONAL PARKS

145 miles / 2.5 hours

Get an early start for the **145-mile, 2.5-hour** drive to **Moab,** the gateway city to Arches and Canyonlands. Once you drop your bags off and get a bite to eat in town, head to **Arches National Park,** which is **five miles** (**10-minute** drive) away. Drive to **The Windows** trailhead and stroll around the easy paths leading to four arches.

It's a **25-mile, 40-minute** drive to **Canyonlands National Park** from Arches. Stop at **Green River Overlook** and the **Grand View Point,** and hike the short, easy **Grand View Trail.**

It's a **30-mile, 45-minute** drive back to Moab from Canyonlands. Stay at the **Best Western Canyonlands Inn** or the **Gonzo Inn,** and have dinner at the **Desert Bistro.**

Best Views

Whether you're looking across a canyon, down from a mountain, or off the rooftop bar at a high-rise hotel, a stunning view can make you feel like you're on top of the world.

Las Vegas

- **Stratosphere Tower:** The thrill rides on the observation deck are hair-raising, but head to the 107th floor and its namesake 107 Lounge for a quieter view—with cocktails (page 30).
- **Mandarin Bar:** For unforgettable views of the Strip, visit this sleek, up-scale bar on the 23rd floor of the Mandarin Oriental (page 64).

Zion and Bryce

- **Court of the Patriarchs Viewpoint:** Zion's favorite viewpoint features three towering, jagged red-rock peaks with skirts of greenery, called Abraham, Isaac, and Jacob (page 93).
- **Sunrise Point:** This is the ideal place in Bryce to watch the sun climb over the great canyon's hoodoo forest (page 115).

Capitol Reef

- **Panorama Point:** It's said this area has some of the clearest air in the United States, which enhances the sweeping view of Capitol Reef and the Henry Mountains (page 135).
- **Goosenecks Overlook:** Watch a humble creek meander through the starkly beautiful canyon that it has been carving for eons (page 135).

Arches and Canyonlands

- **Green River Overlook:** Watch the mighty Green River, a shock of color contrasting with the hard, red land, snake its way across the plateau (page 209).
- **Grand View Point:** See Canyonlands spread out before you from high up on the Island in the Sky (page 211).

Monument Valley, Four Corners, and Mesa Verde

- **Monument Valley Navajo Tribal Park Visitor Center:** Take in the otherworldly view of Monument Valley from a high patio (page 238).
- **Sun Point View:** Stop at this Mesa Verde overlook for a classic view of Balcony House, the largest cliff dwelling in North America (page 250).

Santa Fe and Taos

- **The High Road to Taos:** There are several great views on this drive through the mountains from Santa Fe to Taos (page 295).
- **Rio Grande Gorge:** Just outside of Taos, the Rio Grande flows through an 800-foot rift, offering dizzying views from above (page 312).

Route 66

- **Tawa Point Viewpoint:** A stop along the road moving through Petrified Forest National Park, this is the best spot to view the Painted Desert (page 369).

Grand Canyon

- **Mather Point:** The most-visited viewpoint in the Grand Canyon is this classic panorama, which includes a quarter of the massive canyon below (page 434).
- **Yavapai Observation Station:** Hanging off the Grand Canyon's South Rim, this museum puts your first glimpse of the canyon into context with interpretive exhibits (page 434).

Days 6-7

MONUMENT VALLEY, FOUR CORNERS, AND MESA VERDE

150 miles / 3 hours

It's an almost **three-hour** drive of **150 miles** from Moab to **Monument Valley Navajo Tribal Park.** Spend an hour or so driving the dirt road through the valley, stopping at the various pull-offs and viewpoints. Get a closer look at these huge natural sculptures along the short **Wildcat Trail.** Stay the night in **Kayenta** or **Mexican Hat.**

It's **110 miles (two hours)** to **Four Corners Monument** from Monument Valley. Stop for the requisite photo of yourself in four states at once, and peruse the creations of the Navajo vendors and artists.

From Four Corners, it's **70 miles** (nearly **two hours**) to the central part of **Mesa Verde National Park** (one hour to the entrance and about 40 minutes up the mesa). Head to the **Chapin Mesa Archeological Museum,** tour **Cliff Palace** and **Spruce Tree House,** and hike **Petroglyph Point Trail.** Stay the night at the park's **Far View Lodge,** or at one of the hotels in nearby **Cortez** or **Mancos.**

Day 8

MESA VERDE TO SANTA FE

270 miles / 5.5 hours

After a good night's sleep, head out for **Santa Fe.** Including the road down the mesa, the **270-mile** drive takes about **5.5 hours.** Take **US 160** to **Pagosa Springs,** where you can soak for a while in one of the 18 pools at **The Springs Resort.** From Pagosa Springs take **US 84** to get to downtown Santa Fe.

Days 9-10

SANTA FE AND TAOS

Walk around the central **Santa Fe Plaza,** shopping and chatting with the artists selling wares on the sidewalks. Tour the **New Mexico Museum of Art** and check out the **Cathedral Basilica of St. Francis of Assisi.**

Have lunch at **Tia Sophia's,** then head over to the **Canyon Road art galleries.** Have dinner at **Café Pasqual's** and stay the night at **La Fonda.**

Grab a coffee from **The French Pastry Shop** to wake up for the drive along the **High Road to Taos.** Leave Santa Fe by 8am to reach Taos by 10:30am, but allow more time to visit the villages along the scenic route. The **80-mile** drive to Taos takes at least **2.5 hours.**

Tour **Taos Pueblo,** then make your way to the center of town and walk around **Taos Plaza.** Check out the **Taos Art Museum** and the **Kit Carson Home and Museum.** Eat at **Abe's Cantina y Cocina** and return to Santa Fe on the **Low Road to Taos (70 miles, 1.5 hours).**

Days 11-12

ROUTE 66 TO WILLIAMS

370 miles / 5 hours

It's an hour's drive **(65 miles)** on **I-25 South** to get to **Albuquerque** from Santa Fe. Once you get to town, check out **Petroglyph National Monument** and ride the **Sandia Peak Tramway.** Head out of town in the afternoon and drive **Historic Route 66** for **140 miles (two hours)** to **Gallup,** staying the night at the equally historic **El Rancho Hotel.**

The next morning, drive **Historic Route 66/I-40** for **70 miles** to **Petrified Forest National Park.** Leave Gallup by 8am to reach the park by 9am and spend a few hours driving south along the park road.

From the park road's southern terminus, drive **50 miles** (about **one hour**) west to **Winslow** and have lunch at La Posada's **Turquoise Room.** Drive **60 miles (one hour)** on I-40 to **Flagstaff** and wander around its historic downtown.

Continue **35 miles** (just over **30 minutes**) on I-40 to **Williams.** Check in to the **Lodge on Route 66,** walk the town's

Clockwise from top left: Monument Valley's red buttes and spires; two essential New Mexican accessories; Sandia Peak Tramway.

Best Hikes

Zion and Bryce

- **Emerald Pools Trails:** These short and popular trails lead to spring-fed pools, trickling miniature waterfalls, and striking views of Zion Canyon (page 98).

- **Queen's Garden and Navajo Loop Trails:** An easy path that descends into Bryce Canyon and winds among the hoodoos below the towering cliffs (page 118).

Navajo Loop Trail, Bryce Canyon

Capitol Reef National Park

- **Fremont River Trail:** This climb to an awe-inspiring viewpoint includes a stroll through orchards (page 146).

- **Capitol Gorge:** Walk through a sandy gorge, its red walls etched with petroglyphs and the names of Mormon pioneers (page 147).

Arches and Canyonlands

- **Delicate Arch Trail:** Follow the photographers across the slickrock to stand beneath the park's most improbable and inspiring arch (page 197).

- **Grand View Trail:** This short rim hike features amazing views of Canyonlands and the meeting of the Colorado and Green Rivers (page 211).

Monument Valley, Four Corners, and Mesa Verde

- **Wildcat Trail:** Walk the arid red valley around famous West Mitten Butte in Monument Valley (page 241).

- **Petroglyph Point Trail:** Hike along a forested ridge, high above a canyon, to a well-preserved panel of petroglyphs (page 251).

Santa Fe and Taos

- **Gavilan Trail:** Explore the forest high above Taos on this steep hike to a mountain meadow (page 319).

- **El Salto Falls:** In Arroyo Seco, experience caves and waterfalls via a short hike (page 319).

Route 66

- **Long Logs Trail:** Witness the remains of a Triassic forest on this flat trail at Petrified Forest National Park (page 371).

- **Humphreys Peak Trail:** On your way through the forest outside Flagstaff, hike up to the highest point in Arizona (page 388).

Grand Canyon

- **Rim Trail:** An easy 13-mile trail, this all-day hike showcases the grandeur of the South Rim (page 436).

- **Bright Angel Trail:** Descend into the Grand Canyon for a few hours—or spend the night at Phantom Ranch near the Colorado River (page 436).

Route 66-centric main strip, and have dinner at **Pancho McGillicuddy's.**

Day 13

GRAND CANYON

Enjoy a break from your car by taking the **Grand Canyon Railway** from **Williams** to **Grand Canyon National Park.** Take in the views from the **Rim Trail** or descend into the canyon on the **Bright Angel Trail.** Get an appetizer or a drink at the historic **El Tovar Hotel** before taking the train back to Williams. For dinner, indulge in a prime cut of meat from **Rod's Steak House.** For more suggestions on how to spend your time in the Grand Canyon, see page 420.

Day 14

ROUTE 66 TO KINGMAN; RETURN TO LAS VEGAS

240 miles / 4 hours

Have a big breakfast at the **Pine Country Restaurant** in Williams. Head west on **I-40** for the **20-mile, 20-minute** sprint to **Ash Fork,** the starting point for a **50-mile (one hour)** section along **Historic Route 66.** Stop and tour **Grand Canyon Caverns,** peruse the gift shops in **Seligman,** and grab snacks at the **Hackberry General Store,** another **50 miles (one hour)** west. Next, continue another **30 miles (45 minutes)** along lonely Route 66 to **Kingman.**

In Kingman, tour the **Historic Route 66 Museum.** If you don't want to end your trip just yet, stop along the **110-mile, two-hour** drive between Kingman and Las Vegas for a tour of **Hoover Dam.**

Back in **Las Vegas,** check in to the **Cosmopolitan** or the **Wynn** and take a well-deserved rest from the road and relax by the pool before your flight home the next day.

Las Vegas, Utah's National Parks, and the Grand Canyon

In just **one week** and approximately **1,100 miles,** you can experience many of the Southwest's most famous attractions. If you have more time, it's well worth adding another day to each of the main stops. Mileage and driving times are approximate.

Day 1

LAS VEGAS

After you fly in, check in and leave your bags at **Aria** or **Mandalay Bay,** then head out to explore the Strip. Go for steak at **N9NE** at The Palms or gastropub fare at **Culinary Dropout** at the Hard Rock Casino, then catch a showing of Cirque du Soleil's **O** at the Bellagio. Don't stay out too late—you'll be rising early and hitting the road.

Day 2

ZION AND BRYCE

165 miles / 3 hours

Get an early start for the **165-mile, three-hour** drive to **Zion National Park.** Leave by 8am to arrive by 10:30am. Explore Zion for about three hours, having lunch at **Zion Lodge** and hiking the **Riverside Walk.**

After lunch, drive **70 miles (1.5 hours),** to **Bryce Canyon National Park.** Explore the rim at spots like **Inspiration Point,** take a short hike below the rim on the **Queen's Garden Trail,** and watch the sunset over the canyon. Stay and eat in the park's **Lodge at Bryce Canyon** or in nearby **Tropic.**

Day 3

CAPITOL REEF

120 miles / 2.5 hours

Get up early and head out for the **120-mile, 2.5-hour** drive to **Capitol Reef National Park.** Leave by 8am to arrive by 10:30am. Bring a picnic lunch with you and take the **21-mile scenic drive (1.5 hours),** then hike the 2.5-mile **Fremont River Trail** to Miners Mountain viewpoint.

ONWARD TO MOAB

145 miles / 2.5 hours

Drive **145 miles (2.5 hours)** to **Moab.** Stay at the **Best Western Canyonlands Inn** or the **Gonzo Inn** and have dinner at the **Desert Bistro** or **Eddie McStiff's.**

Day 4

ARCHES AND CANYONLANDS

Drive **five miles (10 minutes)** to Arches National Park. Stop and see **The Windows** and hike three miles round-trip to **Delicate Arch.**

Drive **25 miles (40 minutes)** to the **Island in the Sky District** of **Canyonlands National Park** and explore viewpoints like **Shafer Canyon Overlook.** Hike the short **Grand View Trail,** then head back to Moab for a relaxing night.

Day 5

MOAB TO SOUTH RIM GRAND CANYON

330 miles / 6 hours

It's a **330-mile, six-hour** drive on US 191, US 163, then US 160 from Moab to **Grand Canyon National Park's South Rim.** The route crosses much of the western Navajo Nation and passes right through **Monument Valley Navajo Tribal Park.** Take a few hours to explore the park. Time your trip to have lunch at the **Blue Coffee Pot Café** in **Kayenta,** about 30 miles south of Monument Valley.

From Kayenta, take US 160 West to US 89 South, then AZ-64 West to the **Desert View entrance** of the Grand Canyon. Spend the night at **El Tovar** or the **Bright Angel Lodge.**

Day 6

SOUTH RIM GRAND CANYON

Walk along the park's **Rim Trail** for outstanding, accessible views of the canyon. In **Grand Canyon Village,** stop into the **Hopi House** to see Native American art and the **Lookout Studio,** where you can use telescopes set up on the outdoor terrace to get better views of canyon features. Get a meal at the **El Tovar Dining Room** or **The Arizona Room.**

Day 7

GRAND CANYON TO LAS VEGAS

280 miles / 4.5 hours

The **280-mile, 4.5-hour** drive from Grand Canyon back to Vegas moves along **I-40** between **Williams** and **Kingman.**

To follow **Historic Route 66,** exit the interstate at **Ash Fork,** about **15 miles (20 minutes)** west of Williams. (This will add 20 miles and 30 minutes to the drive.)

In Kingman, stop at **Mr. D'z Route 66 Diner** for lunch. Afterward, jump back on the road for the **110-mile, two-hour** drive back to Las Vegas.

Stretch Your Legs

Pagosa Springs, Colorado, has the deepest hot spring in the world.

Quick roadside pullovers recharge your batteries and fight road weariness. The Southwest Road Trip loop is flush with worthwhile roadside attractions, like caverns, ruins, and hot springs.

Las Vegas to Zion

Don't risk missing the spectacular **Virgin River Gorge** (page 28) while you're driving through it at 75 mph. Pull over and visit the Virgin River Canyon Recreation Area to see it in all its glory.

Zion to Bryce Canyon

Take time out from driving to tour the **Maynard Dixon Living History Museum** (page 87), where you'll see the great painter's charming home and studio and his unique impressions of the landscape.

Bryce Canyon to Capitol Reef

Learn about Ancestral Puebloans and their architecture at the **Anasazi State Park Museum** (page 133).

Capitol Reef to Moab

At Utah's first national monument, **Natural Bridges National Monument** (page 161), see a few of Mother Nature's wonders.

Moab to Monument Valley

See the ruins of a Chacoan great house at **Edge of the Cedars State Park Museum** (page 161).

Both **Goosenecks State Park** (page 236) and **Valley of the Gods** (page 236) offer stunning views of the Utah landscape.

Mesa Verde to Santa Fe

Stop at **Pagosa Springs** (page 258), a wooded resort town along the San Juan River, to soak your road-weary bones in the world's deepest natural hot spring.

Las Vegas
Las Vegas seduces the senses, indulges the appetite, and sparks the imagination. An oasis of flashing marquees, feathered showgirls, chiming slot machines, and endless buffets, Las Vegas is a monument to fantasy.
UT
NV
AZ
CA
Zion National Park
165 MI/265 KM
3 HOURS
Grand Canyon National Park
280 MI/450KM
5 HOURS
LAS VEGAS
100 MI/160 KM
2 HOURS
Kingman
56
14
93
15
18
59
95
164
ROUTE 66
68
163
40
© AVALON TRAVEL

The chance at fortune has lured vacationers into the southern Nevada desert ever since the Silver State legalized gambling in 1931.

At first, the cowboy casinos that dotted downtown's Fremont Street were the center of the action, but they soon faced competition from a resort corridor blooming to the south on Highway 91. The burgeoning entertainment district reminded Los Angeles nightclub owner Billy Wilkerson of Sunset Boulevard in Hollywood, so he dubbed it "The Strip," and together with Bugsy Siegel built the Flamingo, the first upscale alternative to frontier gambling halls. Their vision left a legacy that came to define Las Vegas hotel-casinos. Las Vegas has gone through many reinventions in the decades since—from city of sleaze to Mafia haven, family destination, and finally upscale resort town.

Today, each megaresort offers more to do than many small cities. Under one roof you can indulge in a five-star dinner, attend spectacular productions, dance until dawn with the beautiful people, and browse in designer boutiques. If there's still time, you can get a massage and ride a roller coaster too. The buffet, a fitting metaphor for this city with an abundance of everything, still rules in the hearts of many locals and visitors, but an influx of celebrity chefs is turning the town into a gastronome's paradise to rival Paris, New Orleans, New York, or Tokyo. Similarly, cutting-edge performers such as Blue Man Group and Cirque du Soleil have taken up residence.

So pack your stilettos, string bikini, money clip, and favorite hangover remedy, and join the 35 million others who trek to Sin City every year to experience as many of the Seven Deadlies as they can cram into their vacation time. No one back home has to know you've succumbed to the city's siren song. After all, "What happens in Vegas . . . "

Getting to Las Vegas

From Zion National Park

165 miles / 3 hours

The relatively short, **165-mile** drive from Zion National Park to the Las Vegas Strip traverses Utah's lush and temperate Dixie region, negotiates the dramatic Virgin River Gorge, and ends in the Mojave Desert. Traveling primarily along **I-15 South,** the trip shouldn't take more than **three hours.** Rise early in Zion and you'll be gambling by noon.

Leaving the park, join **UT-9 West** and drive for nearly 20 miles. At the intersection with UT-17, turn left to follow UT-9, passing through the town of Hurricane. After 15 miles, get on **I-15** going **south** toward St. George. The interstate leads right into Sin City after another 130 miles.

Along the way, the road runs alongside and crosses over the **Virgin River,** and cuts through the **Virgin River Gorge** (milepost 13-22). The curvy road demands special attention from the driver, who will no doubt have to contend with the oohing of passengers while trying to keep eyes on the road and off the scenery.

Scenic Detour

Since the drive from Zion to Vegas is comparatively easy and short, consider adding a **70-mile, two-hour** scenic detour through the Moapa Valley and Lake Mead, for a total drive of **200 miles** and **four hours.**

About 110 miles south of Zion on **I-15,** take the exit for **NV-169 (exit 93)** toward Overton, then turn left to get on **NV-169 South.** NV-169 leads through the Moapa Valley and, after 20 miles, into **Lake Mead National Recreation Area** ($10 per car). Continue on **Northshore Road (NV-167)** for 45 miles as it moves past breathtaking

Highlights

★ **Caesars Palace:** Caesars Palace carries on the Roman Empire's regality and decadence with over-the-top excess (page 35).

★ **Fremont Street Experience:** Part music video, part history lesson, the six-minute shows are a four-block-long, 12-million-diode, 550,000-watt burst of sensory overload (page 45).

★ **Mob Museum:** Explore what some old-timers still refer to as "the good old days," when wiseguys ran the town, meting out their own brand of justice (page 47).

★ **Gondola Rides:** Just like the real Grand Canal, only cleaner, The Venetian's waterway meanders along the Strip, with gondoliers providing the soundtrack (page 49).

★ **Secret Garden and Dolphin Habitat:** At The Mirage's twin habitats, the tigers, lions, and leopards can be seen playing impromptu games and the bottlenose dolphins never resist the spotlight (page 49).

★ **High Roller:** The world's largest observation wheel overwhelms the senses with driving music, videos, and unmatched views of the Strip (page 50).

★ **Las Vegas Springs Preserve:** The city's birthplace, these natural springs now display the area's geological, anthropological, and cultural history along with what may be its future: water-conserving "green" initiatives (page 52).

★ **Atomic Testing Museum:** Visit a fallout shelter and measure your body's radioactivity at this museum that traces the military, political, and cultural significance of the bomb (page 52).

★ ***LOVE:*** Cirque du Soleil's magical mystery tour features artistry, acrobatics, and Beatles music in a surreal examination of the Fab Four's legacy (page 55).

desert scenery and the shores of shrinking Lake Mead. Keep your eyes out for desert bighorn sheep. At the intersection with **Lake Mead Parkway/NV-564,** turn right to get onto the parkway and bid farewell to the lake. After about seven miles, you'll drive through Henderson. In another two miles, NV-564 becomes **I-215.** Follow I-215 for 10 miles, then take **exit 12A** for **I-15 North.** In less than five miles, you'll be immersed in the Strip.

Stopping in Overton

Twelve miles off I-15, Overton is a compact agricultural community that makes a good pit stop on the way to Lake Mead. Overton's downtown is strung along several blocks of NV-169, also known as Moapa Valley Boulevard and Main Street.

The town offers two strong lunch options. **Sugars Home Plate** (309 S. Moapa Valley Blvd., 702/397-8084, 7am-9pm Tues.-Sun., $9-25) serves $7.50 bacon and eggs, $8-10 burgers, including the Sugar Burger, a cheeseburger with Polish sausage, and homemade pie. There's also a sports bar with bar-top video poker and sports memorabilia. Just a block away, **Inside Scoop** (395 S. Moapa Valley Blvd., 702/397-2055, 11am-8pm Mon.-Sat., 11am-7pm Sun., $10-25) has filling sandwiches and 30-plus ice cream flavors. The baked potatoes come with whatever toppings you can imagine.

The **Plaza Motel** (207 Moapa Valley Blvd., 702/397-2414, $50-60) provides basic guest rooms and a jumping-off point for visits to Valley of Fire State Park and Lake Mead.

From the Grand Canyon

From the West Rim

120 miles / 2.5 hours

The good news is that the West Rim is the closest canyon point to Las Vegas—only about **120 miles,** or **2.5 hours,** even with the big detour south around the White Hills. The bad news is there's almost nothing to see along the way.

From Meadview, take **Pierce Ferry Road** 40 miles down past Dolan Springs.

Best Hotels

★ **Wynn:** No castles, no pyramids. Opting for class over kitsch, substance over splash, the Wynn is a worthy heir to "Old Vegas" joints (page 32).

★ **Harrah's:** It may seem middle-of-the-road, but its location puts it in the middle of the action (page 34).

★ **Bellagio:** All the romance of Italy manifests through dancing fountains, lazy gondola rides, intimate bistros and—in case the spirit moves you—a wedding chapel (page 38).

★ **Cosmopolitan:** Part Museum of Modern Art, part *Cabaret* Kit Kat Klub, this center-Strip resort blends visual overload with sensuous swank (page 40).

★ **Aria:** The centerpiece of City Center makes no concessions to old-school Sin City, choosing an urban feel accentuated by marble, steel, glass, and silk (page 40).

★ **Mandalay Bay:** Let the conscientious staff and serene elegance of this end-of-the-Strip hotel take you away from Vegas's pounding hip-hop and clanging slot machines (page 43).

★ **Golden Nugget:** A Strip-style resort in the otherwise staid downtown district, the Nugget features a waterslide surrounded by a shark-filled aquarium (page 44).

★ **Mandarin Oriental Las Vegas:** Splurge for environmentally friendly luxury at this LEED-certified hotel (page 64).

Turn right to pick up **US 93 North** and continue for 50 miles, until US 93 becomes **I-515.** Follow I-515 for about five miles, then take **exit 61** for **I-215 West.** Continue on I-215 for about 10 miles, then take **exit 12A** for **I-15 North,** and the interstate will lead to the Strip in less than five miles.

From the South Rim

280 miles / 5 hours

The South Rim is **280 miles** from Las Vegas, a **five-hour** drive. Most summer weekends, you'll find this route crowded but manageable, unless there's an accident. From Grand Canyon Village, take **US 180/AZ-64 South** for 60 miles to **Williams.** Turn right to join **I-40 West** and continue for 115 miles to **Kingman,** a good **stopping point.** (For more information on Kingman, see page 403.)

From Kingman, jump on **US 93 North** for 80 miles, after which the highway becomes **I-515.** In about 10 miles, take **exit 61** for **I-215 West.** Continue for another 10 miles, then take **exit 12A** for **I-15 North.** It's another five miles on the interstate to the Strip.

From Kingman (Route 66)

100 miles / 2 hours

To get to Las Vegas from Kingman, Arizona, it's a **100-mile, two-hour** drive. Join **US 93 North** and, after 75 miles, turn right, following signs for US 93 North. After five miles, US 93 North joins with **I-515 North.** After another five miles, take **exit 61** for **I-215 West.** Drive on I-215 for 10 miles, then take **exit 12A** for **I-15 North** toward Las Vegas. To reach the Strip, take the exit for **Flamingo Road** after less than five miles on I-15.

By Air

More than 900 planes arrive or depart **McCarran International Airport** (LAS, 5757 Wayne Newton Blvd., 702/261-5211, www.mccarran.com) every day, making it the sixth busiest in the country and 19th in the world. Terminal 1 hosts

Best Restaurants

★ **The Egg & I:** You can order something other than eggs—but given the name, why would you (page 68)?

★ **Mon Ami Gabi:** Order the baked gruyére and a baguette and channel your inner Hemingway for a traditional French bistro experience (page 71).

★ **Culinary Dropout:** This creative gastropub takes its comfort food very seriously. The soft-pretzel fondue appetizer will have you dreaming of melted cheese (page 72).

★ **RM Seafood:** Soft lines and brushed metal accents evoke a glittering sea while the menu reflects Chef Rich Moonen's advocacy of sustainable fishing practices (page 72).

★ **N9NE:** You *have* to get the steak, but make sure others in your party order the gnocchi and the lobster ravioli, so you can sneak bites from their plates (page 72).

★ **Rose. Rabbit. Lie.:** Order six or eight small plates per couple, and let the sultry torch singers and rousing dancers play on as you nosh the night away (page 73).

★ **Le Thai:** The best of Las Vegas's impressive roster of Thai restaurants, Le Thai boasts playful interpretations of traditional Thai cuisine in a trendy yet unpretentious atmosphere (page 73).

★ **Phat Phrank's:** The no-frills presentation keeps the focus on the food: California- and New Mexico-inspired variations of traditional Mexican fare (page 74).

Stretch Your Legs

The short section of I-15 through the **Virgin River Gorge** (Zion-Las Vegas drive, milepost 13-22) is dramatically scenic, but it's also a bit more twisty and technical than the average stretch of interstate. This portion of I-15 is actually in Arizona, a lonely corner of the state called the Arizona Strip, and it's a sight to behold.

You can't really see it and drive it at the same time, unless you want to do both poorly. Take the exit for Cedar Pockets (exit 18) to **Virgin River Canyon Recreation Area** (www.blm.gov/az, $8), a BLM-managed campground and trailhead, for the perfect spot to get out of the car and take in the scenery of the Virgin River and its great gorge. Look for the **Virgin River Gorge Nature Trail,** an easy 0.2-mile stroll with a view of the canyon in all of its glory.

domestic flights, while Terminal 3 has domestic and international flights.

McCarran Airport provides easy transfers to the Las Vegas Strip using **shuttle vans, buses,** and **rental cars.** Limousines are available curbside for larger groups. A **taxi ride** from the airport to the Strip (15 minutes) or downtown (20 minutes) runs no more than $25. A $2 surcharge is assessed for pickups from the airport, and there is a $3 credit card processing fee. It's cheaper and often faster to take the surface streets from the airport to your destination rather than the freeway, which is several miles longer.

Orientation

Las Vegas Boulevard South—better known as the Strip—is the city's focal point, with 8 of the 12 largest hotels in the world lining a four-mile north-south stretch between Tropicana and Sahara Avenues. Running parallel to I-15, this is what most folks think of when someone says "Vegas."

The **Lower Strip**—roughly between the "Welcome to Fabulous Las Vegas" sign and Harmon Avenue—is a living city timeline. The Tropicana is here, providing a link to the mobbed-up city of the 1960s and 1970s. Camelot-themed Excalibur, completed in 1990, and the Egyptian-inspired Luxor, which opened in 1993, serve as prime examples from the city's hesitant foray into becoming a "family" destination in the early 1990s. Across from the Tropicana, the MGM Grand opened in 1993 as a salute to *The Wizard of Oz.* One of Vegas's first destination hotels, it was also one of the first to abandon the family market, bulldozing the adjacent theme park in favor up upscale condos. City Center puts the mega in megaresort—condos, boutique hotels, trendy shopping, a huge casino, and a sprawling dining and entertainment district—that cemented the city's biggest-is-best trend. The Lower Strip seems made for budget-conscious families. Rooms are often cheaper than mid-Strip. There are plenty of kid-friendly attractions (even a roller coaster).

The **Center Strip** is between Harmon Avenue and Spring Mountain Road. If the Lower Strip is a longitudinal study, the Center Strip is a cross section of the varied experiences today's visitors can choose. The well-heeled can sip martinis at Caesars Palace; the flat-stomached can flaunt it at the Cosmopolitan's Marquee Day Club; and the rubber-necked can marvel at the Eiffel Tower, fountains, volcanoes, and whimsical floral displays. Center Strip and its patrons share Type-A personalities. The casinos are packed tight, and though the sidewalks can become masses of humanity on weekend nights, all the temptations are within walking distance.

Ranging from Spring Mountain Road

The Strip

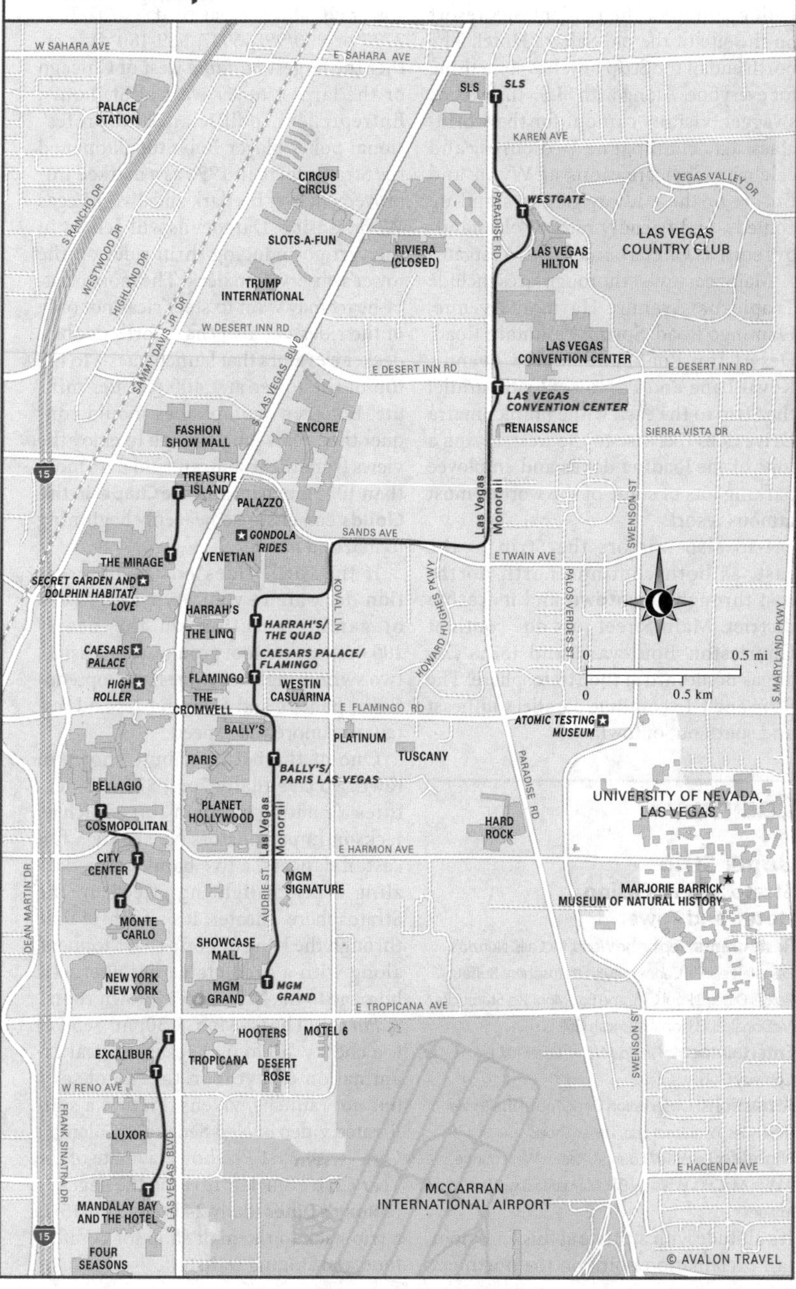
W SAHARA AVE
E SAHARA AVE
SLS
SLS
KAREN AVE
PALACE STATION
CIRCUS CIRCUS
VEGAS VALLEY DR
WESTGATE
LAS VEGAS COUNTRY CLUB
LAS VEGAS HILTON
SLOTS-A-FUN
RIVIERA (CLOSED)
TRUMP INTERNATIONAL
S RANCHO DR
WESTWOOD DR
HIGHLAND DR
SAMMY DAVIS JR DR
W DESERT INN RD
E DESERT INN RD
LAS VEGAS CONVENTION CENTER
LAS VEGAS CONVENTION CENTER
RENAISSANCE
SIERRA VISTA DR
FASHION SHOW MALL
ENCORE
S LAS VEGAS BLVD
TREASURE ISLAND
PALAZZO
GONDOLA RIDES
SANDS AVE
THE MIRAGE
VENETIAN
E TWAIN AVE
SECRET GARDEN AND DOLPHIN HABITAT/ LOVE
HARRAH'S
HARRAH'S/ THE QUAD
THE LINQ
CAESARS PALACE
CAESARS PALACE/ FLAMINGO
HIGH ROLLER
FLAMINGO
WESTIN CASUARINA
THE CROMWELL
E FLAMINGO RD
ATOMIC TESTING MUSEUM
BALLY'S
PLATINUM
TUSCANY
PARIS
BALLY'S/ PARIS LAS VEGAS
BELLAGIO
UNIVERSITY OF NEVADA, LAS VEGAS
COSMOPOLITAN
PLANET HOLLYWOOD
HARD ROCK
E HARMON AVE
CITY CENTER
MGM SIGNATURE
MARJORIE BARRICK MUSEUM OF NATURAL HISTORY
MONTE CARLO
SHOWCASE MALL
NEW YORK NEW YORK
MGM GRAND
MGM GRAND
E TROPICANA AVE
HOOTERS
MOTEL 6
EXCALIBUR
TROPICANA
DESERT ROSE
W RENO AVE
LUXOR
E HACIENDA AVE
MCCARRAN INTERNATIONAL AIRPORT
MANDALAY BAY AND THE HOTEL
FOUR SEASONS
Las Vegas Monorail
KOVAL LN
HOWARD HUGHES PKWY
PALOS VERDES ST
SWENSON ST
PARADISE RD
S MARYLAND PKWY
AUDRIE ST
DEAN MARTIN DR
FRANK SINATRA DR
15
0
0.5 mi
0
0.5 km
© AVALON TRAVEL

to the Stratosphere, the **Upper Strip** received a shot of much-needed exuberance with opening of the opulent SLS resort on the site of the old Sahara Hotel. The north end of the Strip now has something for everyone, Along with SLS's throwback swagger, visitors can opt for the world-class art, champagne pedicures, and celebrity chef creations at Wynn and Encore or the midway games, stand-up comedy, and friendly rates at old stand-bys such as Circus Circus and Westgate.

Major east-west thoroughfares include Tropicana Avenue, Harmon Avenue, Flamingo Road, Spring Mountain Road, Desert Inn Road, and Sahara Avenue. Koval Lane and Paradise Road parallel the Strip to the east, while Frank Sinatra Drive does likewise to the west, giving a tour of the loading docks and employee parking lots of some of the world's most famous resorts.

I-15 also mirrors the Strip to the east, as both continue north-northeast through **downtown** and its casino district. Main Street juts due south at Charleston Boulevard and joins Las Vegas Boulevard at the Stratosphere. The Strip and I-15 continue parallel southeast and south out of town.

Casinos

Upper Strip

Stratosphere Casino, Hotel, and Tower

Restaurants: Top of the World, McCalls, Nunzio's Pizzeria, Fellini's, Cannery 108, Stratosphere Buffet, Roxy's Diner, 8 Pool Café and Bar, Mookies, Starbucks, McDonald's, El Nopal Mexican Grill

Entertainment: *Pin Up*, *MJ Live*, Level 107, L.A. Comedy Club

Attractions: Observation Deck, Top of the Tower thrill rides, Roni Josef Spa, Tower Shops

Nightlife: Level 107 Lounge, Radius Wet Lounge, Airbar, McCall's Whiskey Bar, Margarita Bay, CBar, Images

It's altitude with attitude at this 1,149-foot-tall exclamation point on the north end of the Strip. Depending on how nitpicky you want to be, the **Stratosphere Tower** (2000 Las Vegas Blvd. S., 702/380-7777 or 800/998-6937, $69-180 d) is either the largest *building* west of Chicago or the largest *tower* west of St. Louis. Entrepreneur, politician, and professional poker player Bob Stupak opened the Stratosphere in 1996 as a marked improvement over his dark and dive-y Vegas World Casino. Daredevils will delight in the vertigo-inducing thrill rides on the tower's observation deck. The more faint-of-heart may want to steer clear not only of the rides but also the resort's double-decker elevators that launch guests to the top of the tower at 1,400 feet per minute. But even agoraphobes should conquer their fears long enough to enjoy the views from the restaurant and bars more than 100 floors up, and the **Chapel in the Clouds** can ensure a heavenly beginning to married life.

If the thrill rides on the observation deck aren't your style, get a rush of gambling action on the nearly 100,000-square-foot ground-floor casino, two swimming pools (one has a tops-optional policy), and a dozen bars and restaurants more your speed.

One of the better tribute shows in town, ***MJ Live*** (daily 7pm, $74-104) features a rotating roster of three Michael Jackson impersonators backed by a full cast of dancers, a live band, and a dazzling array of lighting effects in the Stratosphere Theater. It's a faithful tour through the King of Pop's chart-toppers, along with a predictable but energetic homage to his Jackson 5 Motown roots.

Pin Up (Thurs.-Mon. 9:30pm, $65-76) is a cheeky (all four cheeks), musical examination of a year in the life of sexy, but not raunchy, vixens. Picture a soft-R-rated video of Neil Sedaka's "Calendar Girl," with 2011 Playboy Playmate of the Year Claire Sinclair turning the pages.

Roxy's Diner (daily 24 hours, $10-15) is a trip back to the malt shop for comfort food and singing waitstaff.

Two Days in Las Vegas

Day 1

Pick a hotel based on your taste and budget. We suggest **The Linq** (page 35), close to the High Roller observation wheel, fine dining, hip watering holes, and rocking live music venues.

Get your gambling fix for a few hours before heading across the street for brunch at The Mirage's **Cravings Buffet** (page 34). It operates on a familiar theory, with separate stations highlighting different cuisines. After the gorge-fest, you'll be ready for a nap, and you'll need it. This is Vegas; no early nights for you!

Couples should start the evening off with a romantic dinner at Paris's **Mon Ami Gabi** (page 71). For a more modest meal, the eponymous offering at The Venetian's **B&B Burger & Beer** (page 32) hits the spot. If you only have time for one show, make it ***LOVE*** (page 55) at The Mirage. The show is a loose biography of the Beatles' creative journey, told by tumblers, roller skaters, clowns, and the characters from John, Paul, George, and Ringo's songs—Eleanor Rigby, Lucy in the Sky, and Sgt. Pepper.

Day 2

Celebrate the kitsch and class of vintage Vegas. Head downtown to stock up on Elvis sideburns and Sammy Davis Jr. sunglasses before loading up on eggs Benedict and 1970s flair at the **Peppermill Restaurant & Fireside Lounge** (page 68). While it's daylight, make your way to the **Neon Museum and Boneyard** (page 47), the final resting place of some of Las Vegas's iconic signage. And while you're in the neighborhood, witness the rise and fall of the Mafia in Las Vegas at the **Mob Museum** (page 47).

Back at the hotel, change into your glad rags and beat it over to the Tuscany's Copa Room. Order up a neat bourbon and watch Sinatra try to make it through a rendition of "Luck Be a Lady" while Dino and Sammy heckle and cut up from the wings in ***The Rat Pack Is Back*** (page 57). Then get out there and gamble into the wee hours! For a chance to rub elbows with celebrities, head over to **XS** (page 32) at Wynn. Expect celebrity DJs, a major party, and steep prices.

SLS

Restaurants: Katsuya, Bazaar Meat, Cleo, Ku Noodle, Umami Burger, 800 Degrees, Northside Cafe, The Perq

Nightlife: Foxtail, Sayers Club, Center Bar, Monkey Bar

On the site of the legendary Sahara Casino, **SLS** (2535 Las Vegas Blvd. S., 855/761-7757, $149-249 d) targets the swanky sophisticate market. Its management team, SBE Entertainment Group, built its reputation with exclusive restaurants, nightclubs, and boutique hotels in the ritziest destinations in the country—Beverly Hills, South Beach, and Manhattan. SLS incorporates those proven nightspot and restaurant brands, channeling Rat Pack cool through a modern lens, aiming to be a major player in Vegas. Despite the connections and the proven formula, SLS has been a tough sell in Las Vegas, but SBE's deep pockets and a rebounding economy bode well for its eventual success.

Three towers offer standard rooms of 325-435 square feet. All boast 55-inch televisions, soft pastel accents, and 310-thread-count sheets atop BeautyRest mattresses. The all-suite Lux Tower attracts resort visitors with luxurious peekaboo showers and the hotel's signature Saints and Sinners snack box. World Tower rooms take aim at business travelers, with extra seating areas, work desks, and infinity sinks. Story Tower is for the urban crowd, featuring big beds as center points for socialization.

Chef Jose Andres doesn't want guests at **Bazaar Meat** (Sun.-Thurs. 5:30pm-10pm, Fri.-Sat. 5:30pm-11pm, $65-120) ordering a huge bone-in rib eye, rack of lamb, or inch-thick tuna steaks. He wants you to try them all. His Spanish-influenced meat-centric dishes are meant to be shared with everyone in your party. The restaurant's decor reinforces that aim with long communal tables, open cooking stations, and a small gaming area.

Sayers Club (Sun.-Wed. 7pm-11pm, Thurs.-Sat. 7pm-3am, $11) bills itself as a live-music venue. There's plenty of live indie pop, folk, and psychobilly bands on weekends, but with lots of open space and an industrial-warehouse feel, it's a natural environment for DJs. The go-go cages, platforms, and poles seem imported en masse from L.A.'s Hollywood Boulevard.

Wynn Las Vegas/Encore

Restaurants: Andrea's, Botero, Country Club, Lakeside Seafood, Mizumi, Sinatra, SW Steakhouse, Tableau, Wing Lei, Allegro, The Buffet, Drugstore Café, La Cave, Red 8, Society Café, Terrace Pointe Café, Wazuzu, Zoozacrackers

Entertainment: *Showstoppers, Le Rêve,* Michael Monge

Attractions: Lake of Dreams, Wynn Golf Course, Penske Wynn Ferrari

Nightlife: XS, Surrender, Encore Beach Club, Eastside, Encore Lobby Bar, Parasol Down, Parasol Up, Tower Suite Bar, VDKA

An eponymous monument to indulgence, ★ **Wynn** (3131 Las Vegas Blvd. S., 702/770-7000 or 888/320-9966, $259-500 d) marked the $2.5 billion return of Steve Wynn, "the man who made Las Vegas," to the Strip in 2005. Wynn invites fellow multimillionaires to wallow in the good life and the hoi polloi to sample a taste of how the other half lives: Gaze at Wynn's art, one of the best and most valuable private collections in the world, or drool over the horsepower at **Penske Wynn Ferrari,** the dealership Wynn partly owns. If you're not in the market for a $250,000 ride, logo T-shirts, coffee mugs, and key chains are also available.

Never one to rest on his laurels, Wynn opened the appropriately named Encore Tower next door in 2008. Red must be his favorite color, because the casino area is awash in it. The twins' opulence is matched by the resort's Tom Fazio-designed golf course, open to hotel guests only, of course. Although guests come to explore the privileges of wealth, they can also experience the wonders of nature without the inconvenience of bugs and dirt. Lush plants, waterfalls, lakes, and mountains dominate the pristine landscape.

In addition to the gourmet offerings, don't miss the dim sum at **Red 8 Asian Bistro** (11:30am-midnight Sun.-Thurs., 11:30am-1am Fri.-Sat., $20-30).

Wynn-Encore's formal sophistication belies its location on the site of the old Desert Inn with the unself-conscious swagger Frank, Dino, and Sammy brought to the joint. Both towers boast some of the biggest guest rooms and suites on the Strip, with the usual although better-quality amenities and a few extra touches, like remote-controlled drapes, lights, and air-conditioning. Wynn's guest rooms are appointed in wheat, honey, and other creatively named shades of beige. Encore is more colorful, with the color scheme running toward dark chocolate and cream.

Center Strip

The Venetian

Restaurants: AquaKnox, B&B Burger & Beer, B&B Ristorante, Bouchon, Buddy V's, Café Press, Canaletto, Canonita, Canyon Ranch Café, Carlo's Bakery, Casanova, db Brasserie, Delmonico Steakhouse, Grand Lux Café, Grimaldi's, Lobster ME, Noodle Asia, Otto Enoteca Pizzeria, Prime Burger, Public House, Tao Asian Bistro, Tintoretto Bakery, Trattoria Reggiano, Yardbird, Zeffirino, Food Court (Bella Panini, Café Pan, Chicken Now, Chipotle, Johnny Rockets, Panda Express, Social Life Pizza, Subway, Wasabi Jane)

Entertainment: *Lipschtick*

Attractions: Madame Tussauds Las Vegas, Gondola Rides, Streetmosphere

Nightlife: Tao, Tao Beach, Bellini Bar, Rockhouse, Bourbon Room, V Bar, Oculus

While Caesars Palace bears little resemblance to the realities of ancient

Rome and Luxor doesn't really replicate the land of the pharaohs, **The Venetian** (3355 Las Vegas Blvd. S., 702/414-1000 or 866/659-9643, $209-349 d) comes pretty close to capturing the elegance of Venice. An elaborate faux-Renaissance ceiling fresco greets visitors in the hotel lobby, and the sensual treats just keep coming. A life-size streetscape with replicas of the Bridge of Sighs, Doge's Palace, the Grand Canal, and other treasures give the impression that the best of the Queen of the Adriatic has been transplanted in toto. Tranquil rides in authentic gondolas with serenading pilots are perfect for relaxing after a hectic session in the 120,000-square-foot casino. Canal-side, buskers entertain the guests in the **Streetmosphere** (various times and locations daily, free), and the **Grand Canal Shoppes** (10am-11pm Sun.-Thurs., 10am-midnight Fri.-Sat.) entice strollers, window-shoppers, and serious spenders along winding streetscapes. Don't miss the magicians at Houdini's Magic Shop, and treat yourself at Barney's New York.

After you've shopped till you're ready to drop, **Madame Tussauds Las Vegas** (10am-8pm Sun.-Thurs., 10am-9:30pm Fri.-Sat., adults $30, ages 4-12 $20, under age 4 free) invites stargazers for hands-on experiences with their favorite entertainers, superheroes, and athletes. Then you can dance the night away at **Tao** (10pm-5am Thurs.-Sat., lounge daily 5pm-1am).

Fine dining options abound, but for a change, try the lobster ravioli or traditional pizza and pasta dishes in the bistro setting of **Trattoria Reggiano** (11am-11pm Sun.-Thurs., 11am-midnight Fri.-Sat., $20-30).

The Venetian spares no expense in the hotel department. Its 4,027 suites are tastefully appointed with Italian (of course) marble, and at 650 square feet, they're big. They include sunken living rooms and luxe Roman tubs.

The Palazzo

Restaurants: Café Presse, Canyon Ranch Grill, Carnevino, CUT, Dal Toro, Espressamente Illy, I (heart) Burgers, JuiceFarm, Grand Lux Café, Hong Kong Café, LAVO, Legasse's Stadium, Morels, Sushisamba, Table 10
Attractions: Grand Canal Shoppes, Atrium Waterfall
Nightlife: Laguna Champagne Bar, Double Helix, LAVO Lounge, The Label, Salute Lounge, Fusion Latin Mixology Bar, The Lounge at Sushisamba

The lobby at **The Palazzo** (3325 Las Vegas Blvd. S., 702/607-7777 or 866/263-3001, $199-339 d), The Venetian's sister property next door, is bathed in natural light from an 80-foot domed skylight focused on a faux-ice sculpture, bronze columns, and lush landscaping. Motel 6 this ain't. Half of the 100,000-square-foot casino is smoke-free, part of The Palazzo's efforts in achieving energy efficiency and environmentally friendly design.

Las Vegas has carved out a niche as a bachelorette party central, and **LAVO** (5pm-midnight daily) is well-positioned to treat the bride-to-be and her entourage in the style to which they hope to become accustomed. With decor reminiscent of a library, LAVO pours top-shelf booze amid subdued lighting, first editions, and burnished leather. LAVO recently added the Casino Club, a sort of high-class speakeasy. Waiters deliver premium bottles, appetizers, and even full dinner directly to your personal gaming table.

The Palazzo is a gourmand's dream, with a handful of four-star establishments. A refreshing counterpoint to dark, woody steak houses that seem to spring up in Vegas, **Carnevino** (noon-midnight daily, $45-70) is light and bright, with snootiness kept to a minimum. That does not mean Chef Mario Batali skimps on quality. He selects the best cuts and refrains from overwhelming them in preparation. Salt, pepper, rosemary, and a little butter are all that's required.

Accommodations are all suites, with Roman tubs, sunken living rooms, and sumptuous beds that would make it tough to leave the room if not for the lure of the Strip.

The Mirage

Restaurants: Tom Colicchio's Heritage Steak, Fin, Morimoto, Stack, Portofino, Samba Brazilian Steakhouse, BLT Burger, California Pizza Kitchen, Cravings Buffet, Carnegie Delicatessen, Paradise Café, Pantry, Blizz Frozen Yogurt, The Roasted Bean, Starbucks

Entertainment: The Beatles *LOVE*, Terry Fator Boys II Men, Aces of Comedy

Attractions: Secret Garden and Dolphin Habitat, Aquarium, Mirage Volcano, Atrium

Nightlife: 1 Oak, Revolution Lounge, Rhumbar, High Limit Lounge, Heritage Steak Lounge, Japonais Lounge, The Sports Bar, Dolphin Bar, Bare Pool Lounge, Lobby Bar, Stack Lounge

While grand and attention-grabbing, **The Mirage** (3400 Las Vegas Blvd. S., 702/791-7111 or 800/627-6667, $129-300 d) was the first understated megaresort, starting a trend that signifies Las Vegas's return to mature pursuits. This Bali Ha'i-themed paradise lets guests bask in the wonders of nature alongside the sophistication and pampering of resort life. More an oasis than a mirage, the hotel greets visitors with exotic bamboo, orchids, banana trees, secluded grottoes, and peaceful lagoons. Dolphins, white tigers, stingrays, sharks, and a volcano provide livelier sights.

1 Oak (10:30am-4am Tues. and Fri.-Sat.) has two separate rooms with bars, DJs, and crowded dance floors. With dark walls and no lighting, 1 Oak makes no excuses for providing a sinful, sexy venue for the beautiful people to congregate.

The Mirage commands performances by the world's top headliners, but **The Beatles *LOVE*** packs 'em in every night. It's a celebration of the Fab Four's music, but even more an exploration of classic Beatles tunes come to life. Acrobats, roller skaters, clowns, and specialty acts conjure up the Walrus, Nowhere Men, and Lovely Rita.

The Mirage's guest rooms have tasteful appointments and some of the most comfortable beds in town. The standard 371-square-foot rooms emit a modern and relaxing feel in browns, blacks, and splashes of tangerine, mauve, and ruby.

Harrah's

Restaurants: Ruth's Chris Steak House, Flavors, the Buffet, Oyster Bar, Ice Pan, Toby Keith's I Love This Bar & Grill, Fulton Street Food Hall, Starbucks

Entertainment: *Million Dollar Quartet, Menopause the Musical,* The Improv Comedy Club, Mac King Comedy Magic Show, Big Elvis, *X Country*

Nightlife: Carnaval Court, Numb Bar, Piano Bar, Signature Bar

Seemingly unwilling to engage in the one-upmanship of its neighbors, ★ **Harrah's** (3475 Las Vegas Blvd. S., 800/214-9110, $55-165 d) has been content instead to carve out a niche as a middle-of-the-action, middle-of-the-road, middle-of-the-price-scale option. But with The Linq pedestrian thoroughfare with bar, shops, and huge observation wheel behind its property, Harrah's may find itself thrust into hanging with the cool crowd, whether it wants to or not.

Carnaval Court, outside on the Strip's sidewalk, capitalizes on the street-party atmosphere with live bands and juggling bartenders. Just inside, Vegas icon **Big Elvis** (2pm, 3:30pm, and 5pm Mon., Wed., and Fri., free) performs in the **Piano Bar,** which invites aspiring singers to the karaoke stage Monday through Wednesday evenings, and dueling twin sister keyboardists take over each night at 9pm.

Don't miss ***Million Dollar Quartet*** (5:30pm and 8pm Mon. and Thurs., 7pm Tues., Fri., and Sun., 6:30pm Wed., $71-97), which recreates the serendipitous star convergence-jam session with Elvis, Carl Perkins, Jerry Lee Lewis, and Johnny Cash. Even 60 years later (and with actors portraying the icons) the magic is still palpable. It's even kid-friendly!

The country superstar lends his name and unapologetic patriotism to **Toby Keith's I Love This Bar & Grill** (11:30am-2am Sun.-Thurs., 11:30am-3am Fri.-Sat., $15-25). Try the fried bologna sandwich.

★ Caesars Palace

Restaurants: Bacchanal Buffet, Rao's, Nobu, Gordon Ramsay Pub and Grill, Old Homestead Steakhouse, Payard Patisserie & Bistro, Serendipity 3, Mesa Grill, Beijing Noodle No. 9, Restaurant Guy Savoy, Searsucker Las Vegas, Café Americano, Sushi Roku, Forum Food Court (Smashburger, Phillips Seafood Express, Earl of Sandwich, Graeter's, Tiger Wok & Ramen, Difara Pizza, La Gloria)
Entertainment: *Absinthe,* Matt Goss
Attractions: *Fall of Atlantis* and *Festival Fountain Show,* aquarium, Appian Way Shops, Forum Shops
Nightlife: Omnia, Fizz, Cleopatra's Barge, Seahorse Lounge, Numb Bar & Frozen Cocktails, Lobby Bar, Spanish Steps, Vista Cocktail Lounge

Rome would probably look a lot like Las Vegas had it survived this long. **Caesars Palace** (3570 Las Vegas Blvd. S., 866/227-5938, $175-300 d) has incorporated all the ancient empire's decadence and overindulgence while adding a few thousand slot machines. Caesars opened with great fanfare in 1966 and has ruled the Strip ever since. Like the empire, it continues to expand, now boasting 3,348 guest rooms in six towers and 140,000 square feet of gaming space accented with marble, fountains, gilding, and royal reds. Wander the grounds searching for reproductions of some of the world's most famous statuary. The eagle-eyed might spy Michelangelo's *David* and Giambologna's *Rape of the Sabines* as well as the Brahma Shrine. The casino is so big that the website includes a "slot finder" application so gamblers can navigate to their favorite machines.

Cleopatra's Barge (5pm-3am daily), a floating lounge, attracts the full spectrum of the 21-and-over crowd for late-night bacchanalia. Carmine and gold accents only add to the decadence. A live band and the Dirty Virgins dancers back **Matt Goss** (9:30pm Tues. and Fri.-Sat., $75-144) and his original compositions and interpretations of the Great American Songbook.

All roads lead to the **Forum Shops** (10am-11pm Sun.-Thurs., 10am-midnight Fri.-Sat.), a collection of famous designer stores, specialty boutiques, and restaurants. Not all the shops are as froufrou as you might expect, but an hour here can do some serious damage to your bankroll. You'll also find the ***Fall of Atlantis*** and ***Festival Fountain Show*** (hourly 10am-11pm Sun.-Thurs., 10am-midnight Fri.-Sat., free), a multisensory, multimedia depiction of the gods' wrath.

If you (or your wallet) tire of Caesars's high-on-the-hog dining, nosh on British pub food at **Gordon Ramsay Pub and Grill** (11am-11pm Sun.-Thurs., 11am-midnight Fri.-Sat., $25-40). When in doubt, you can never go wrong with the fish-and-chips.

With so many guest rooms in six towers, it seems Caesars is always renovating somewhere. The sixth tower, Octavius, opened in 2012. Most newer guest rooms are done in tan, wood, and marble. Ask for a south-facing room in the Augustus and Octavius towers to get commanding vistas of both the Bellagio fountains and the Strip.

The Linq

Restaurants: Guy Fieri's Vegas Kitchen and Bar, Chayo Mexican Kitchen & Tequila Bar, Hash House a Go Go
Entertainment: *Divas Las Vegas,* Mat Franco
Attractions: Auto Collection, O'Shea's
Nightlife: Yes, 3535, Fat Tuesday, Catalyst, TAG Lounge and Bar

At **The Linq** (3535 Las Vegas Blvd. S., 800/634-6441, $89-210 d), rooms are sleek, stylish, and smallish, at 245-350 square feet. Pewter and chrome accented with eggplant, orange, or aqua murals evoke vintage Vegas. Other amenities include marble countertops, 47-inch flat-screen TVs, and iPod docks. But the hotel is really just a way to stay close to all the Gen X-focused boutiques, bars, and restaurants in the adjacent outdoor promenade.

The high point of this pedestrian-friendly plaza is **The High Roller,** the highest observation wheel in the world, but there's plenty more to warrant a stop.

Brooklyn Bowl (5pm-late daily, $15-30) has you covered on eat, drink, and be merry, combining dozens of beer taps with delectable noshes and live entertainment. The cuisine at **Guy Fieri's Kitchen and Bar** (8am-midnight Sun.-Thurs., 8am-2am Fri.-Sat., $20-35) is gourmet bar food, with sashimi tacos and truffled french fries.

Vegas icon and locals' favorite **O'Shea's** (24 hours daily) brings back the kegger party, with all its lowbrow frivolity. Cheap drafts, heated beer pong challenges, and Lucky the Leprechaun keep the festivities raging well into the wee hours.

America's Got Talent winner **Mat Franco** (7pm Thurs.-Tues., additional matinee 4pm Sat., $46-90) combines jaw-dropping production illusions with how'd-he-do-that close-up tricks. His easygoing banter and anything-to-please attitude ensure it's never the same show twice.

Flamingo

Restaurants: Center Cut Steakhouse, Paradise Garden Buffet, Jimmy Buffett's Margaritaville, Carlos N Charlie's, Beach Club Bar & Grill, Club Cappuccino, Food Court

Entertainment: Donnie and Marie, *Legends in Concert, X Burlesque*, X Comedy – *Uncensored Fun*, Jeff Civillico: *Comedy in Action*

Attractions: Wildlife Habitat

Nightlife: It's 5 O'Clock Somewhere Bar, Garden Bar, Bugsy's Bar

Named for Virginia Hill, the long-legged girlfriend of Benjamin "don't call me Bugsy" Siegel, the **Flamingo** (3555 Las Vegas Blvd. S., 702/733-3111 or 800/732-2111, $80-150 d) has at turns embraced and shunned its gangster ties, which stretch back to the 1960s. After Bugsy's (sorry, Mr. Siegel) Flamingo business practices ran afoul of the Cosa Nostra and led to his untimely end, Meyer Lansky took over. Mob ties continued to dog the property even after Kirk Kerkorian bought it to use as a training ground for his pride and joy, the International (now the Westgate). Hilton Hotels bought the Flamingo in 1970, giving the joint the legitimacy it needed. Today, its art deco architecture and pink-and-orange neon beckon pedestrians and conjure images of aging Mafiosi lounging by the pool, their tropical shirts half unbuttoned to reveal hairy chests and gold chains. And that image seems just fine with the current owner, Caesars Entertainment, in a Vegas where the mob era is remembered almost fondly. Siegel's penthouse suite, behind the current hotel, has been replaced by the **Flamingo Wildlife Habitat** (8am-dusk daily, free), where ibis, pelicans, turtles, koi fish, and, of course, Chilean flamingos luxuriate amid riparian plants and meandering streams.

Guests can search for their lost shaker of salt in paradise at **Jimmy Buffett's Margaritaville** (11am-2am Sun.-Thurs., 11am-3am Fri.-Sat., $20-30) while people-watching on the Strip and noshing on jambalaya and cheeseburgers.

The Flamingo transformed many of its guest rooms into Fab Rooms in 2012, but the older Go Rooms are actually more modern, dressed in swanky mahogany and white with bold swatches of hot pink. The rooms are only 350 square feet, but boast high-end entertainment systems. Suite options are just as colorful and include 32-inch TVs, vintage art prints, padded leather headboards, and all the other Vegas-sational accoutrements.

Rio

Restaurants: Royal India Bistro, Hash House a Go Go, Village Seafood Buffet, Martorano's, VooDoo Steakhouse, Búzio's Seafood Restaurant, KJ Dim Sum & Seafood, Wine Cellar & Tasting Room, All-American Bar & Grille, BK Whopper Bar, Pho Da Nang Vietnamese Kitchen, Sports Deli, Carnival World Buffet

Entertainment: Penn & Teller, Chippendales, The Eddie Griffin Experience, *X Rocks*

Attractions: VooDoo Zip Line, Masquerade Village

Nightlife: VooDoo Rooftop Nightclub & Lounge, Masquerade Bar, IBar, Flirt Lounge

A hit from the beginning, this carnival just off the Strip started expanding almost before its first 400-suite tower was complete in 1990. Now with three towers and 2,500 suites, the party's still raging, with terrific buffets, beautiful people-magnet bars, and steamy shows. "Bevertainers" at the **Rio** (3700 W. Flamingo Rd., 866/746-7671, $89-180 d) take breaks from schlepping cocktails by jumping on mini stages scattered throughout the casino to belt out tunes or gyrate to the music. Dancers and other performers may materialize at your slot machine to take your mind off your losses.

While topless dancers and hard rock are the premise of every strip club in town, the focus at ***X Rocks*** (10pm Thurs.-Sun., $62-95, 18 and over) is on the choreography and props, rather than the flesh (yeah, right!). Comedian John Bizarre yuks it up between routines. The dancers and the Chippendales hang out at Sin City Sundays at **VooDoo Lounge** (8pm-2am Sun.-Thurs., 8pm-3am Fri.-Sat.), 51 stories up. If that's not enough physical perfection for you, **Flirt Lounge** (6:30pm-midnight Sun.-Tues. and Thurs., 6:30pm-1am Fri.-Sat.) and its easy-on-the-eyes waiters keep the Rio's Ultimate Girls Night Out churning.

Búzio's (5pm-10pm daily, $25-45) has great crab-shack appetizers and buttery lobster and steak entrées.

All of the Rio's guest rooms are suites—a sofa and coffee table replace the uncomfortable easy chair found in most standard guest rooms. A dressing area separate from the bathroom makes night-on-the-town preparations easy. Rio suites measure about 600 square feet. The hotel's center-Strip location and room-tall windows make for exciting views.

Lower Strip

The Palms

Restaurants: N9NE Steakhouse, Lao Sze Chuan, Nove Italiano, Alizé, 24 Seven Café, Bistro Buffet, Café 6, Hooters, The Eatery
Entertainment: The Lounge, Brendan Theater
Nightlife: Ghostbar, Social

The expression "party like a rock star" could have been invented for **The Palms** (4321 W. Flamingo Rd., 866/942-7770, $110-175 d). Penthouse views, uninhibited pool parties, lavish theme suites, and starring roles in MTV's *The Real World: Las Vegas* and Bravo's *Celebrity Poker Showdown* have brought notoriety and stars to the clubs, concert venue, and recording studio. The 2,500-seat **Pearl Concert Theater** regularly hosts rock concerts. **Ghostbar** (8pm-late daily), 55 floors atop the Ivory Tower, treats partiers to vistas of the Strip and night sky. Eclectic entertainers play **The Lounge** (24 hours daily): comedy tonight, heavy metal cover bands tomorrow, and funky soul next week.

Andre Rochat's **Alizé** (6pm daily, $50-90) is the quintessential French restaurant: authentic fare, a cognac cellar, snooty clientele, sophisticated decor, and top-of-the-world views.

The Fantasy Tower houses the fantasy suites, while the original Ivory Tower offers large guest rooms. They're sleek, with geometric shapes and a designer mural, but their best features are the feathery beds and luxurious comforters that make it easy to roll over and go back to sleep, even if you're not nursing a hangover. The newest tower, Palms Place, is part of the Las Vegas "condotel" trend. Its 599 studios and one-bedrooms, restaurant, spa, and pool offer opportunities to recuperate from the partying.

Bellagio

Restaurants: Jasmine, Le Cirque, Michael Mina, Picasso, Prime Steakhouse, Fix, Lago, Todd English's Olives, Noodles, Yellowtail, Harvest by Roy Ellamar, Circo, Sensi, The Buffet, Café Bellagio, Pool Café, Café Gelato, Palio, Snacks, Jean Philippe Patisserie
Entertainment: Cirque du Soleil's *O*
Attractions: The Fountains at Bellagio, The Conservatory, Bellagio Gallery of Fine Art, public art
Nightlife: The Bank, Hyde, Lily Bar & Lounge, Petrossian Bar, Baccarat Bar, Pool Bar, Sports Bar Lounge

With nearly 4,000 guest rooms and

suites, ★ **Bellagio** (3600 Las Vegas Blvd. S., 702/693-7111 or 888/987-6667, $200-320 d) boasts a population larger than the village perched on Lake Como from which it borrows its name. And to keep pace with its Italian namesake, Bellagio created an 8.5-acre lake between the hotel and Las Vegas Boulevard. The view of the lake and its **Fountains at Bellagio** (3pm-midnight Mon.-Fri., noon-midnight Sat.-Sun.) are free, as is the aromatic fantasy that is **Bellagio Conservatory** (24 hours daily). And the **Bellagio Gallery of Fine Art** (10am-8pm daily, $14-19) would be a bargain at twice the price—you can spend an edifying day at one of the world's priciest resorts (including a cocktail and lunch) for less than $50. Even if you don't spring for gallery admission, art demands your attention throughout the hotel and casino. The glass flower petals in Dale Chihuly's *Fiori di Como* sculpture bloom from the lobby ceiling, foreshadowing the opulent experiences to come. Masatoshi Izumi's *A Gift from the Earth,* four massive basalt sculptures representing wind, fire, water, and earth, dominates the hotel's main entrance.

The display of artistry continues but the bargains end at **Via Bellagio** (10am-midnight daily), the resort's shopping district, including heavyweight retailers Armani, Prada, Chanel, Tiffany, and their ilk.

Would you like not only to eat like a gourmand, but to cook like one too? **An Executive Chef's Culinary Classroom** ($135) is your own private Food Network special. The resort's chefs provide step-by-step instructions as guests prepare appetizers, entrées, and desserts at their own workstations.

Befitting Bellagio's world-class status, intriguing and expensive restaurants abound. **Michael Mina** (5pm-10pm Mon.-Sat., $50-80) is worth the price. Restrained decor adds to the simple elegance of the cuisine, which is mostly American beef and seafood with European and Asian influences.

Bellagio Conservatory

Traditional Asian dishes are the specialty at **Noodles** (11am-2am daily, $15-20), if you're in search of something more affordable. Don't miss the weekend lunch dim sum, especially the shrimp dumplings with bamboo shoots.

Bellagio's tower rooms are the epitome of luxury, with Italian marble, oversize bathtubs, remote-controlled drapes, Egyptian-cotton sheets, and 510 square feet in which to spread out. The sage-plum and indigo-silver color schemes are refreshing changes from the goes-with-everything beige and the camouflages-all-stains paisley often found on the Strip.

Paris Las Vegas

Restaurants: Burger Brasserie, Mon Ami Gabi, Martorano's, Hexx, Gordon Ramsay Steak, Eiffel Tower Restaurant, Café Belle Madeleine, La Creperie, JJ's Boulangerie, Le Café Ile St. Louis, Le Village Buffet, Yong Kang Street
Entertainment: *Jersey Boys*, Anthony Cools
Attractions: Eiffel Tower
Nightlife: Napoleon's Lounge, Le Cabaret, Le Central, Le Bar du Sport, Gustav's, Chateau Nightclub & Rooftop

Designers used Gustav Eiffel's original drawings to ensure that the half-size tower that anchors **Paris Las Vegas** (3655 Las Vegas Blvd. S., 877/242-6753, $120-250 d) conformed—down to the last cosmetic rivet—to the original. That attention to detail prevails throughout this property, which works hard to evoke the City of Light, from large-scale reproductions of the Arc de Triomphe, Champs Élysées, and Louvre to more than half a dozen French restaurants. The tower is perhaps the most romantic spot in town to view the Strip; you'll catch your breath as the elevator whisks you to the observation deck 460 feet up, then have it taken away again by the lights from one of the most famous skylines in the world. Back at street level, the cobblestone lanes and brass streetlights of **Le Boulevard** (8am-2am daily) invite shoppers into quaint shops and "sidewalk" patisseries. The casino offers its own attractions, not the least of which is the view of the Eiffel Tower's base jutting through the ceiling.

The **Paris Theatre** hosts headliners. **Anthony Cools—The Uncensored Hypnotist** (9pm Tues. and Thurs.-Sun., $49-82) cajoles his mesmerized subjects through very adult simulations.

You'll be wishing you had packed your beret when you order a beignet and cappuccino at **Le Café Ile St. Louis** (6pm-11pm daily, $15-25). While the look and feel are French sidewalk café, the menu tends toward American.

Standard guest rooms in the 33-story tower are decorated in a rich earth-tone palette and have marble baths. There's nothing Left Bank bohemian about them, however. The guest rooms exude little flair and little personality, but the simple, quality furnishings make Paris a moderately priced option in the middle of a top-dollar neighborhood. Book a Red Room if modern decor is important to you.

Cosmopolitan

Restaurants: Beauty & Exxex, Blue Ribbon Sushi Bar & Grill, China Poblano, D.O.C.G., Estiatorio Milos, Holsteins, Jaleo, Overlook Grill, Rose. Rabbit. Lie., Scarpetta, Secret Pizza, STK, The Henry, Va Bene Caffè, Wicked Spoon

Attractions: Lucky Cat, public art

Nightlife: Rose. Rabbit. Lie., The Chandelier, Vesper Bar, Book & Stage, Bond, Queue Bark, The Neapolitan, Marquee Nightclub & Day Club

Modern art, marble bath floors, and big soaking tubs in 460-square-foot rooms evoke urban penthouse living at ★ **Cosmopolitan** (3708 Las Vegas Blvd. S., 702/698-7000, $280-440 d). Because it's too cool to host production shows, the resort's entertainment schedule mixes DJs of the moment with the most laid-back headliners (Bruno Mars and John Legend have graced the stage). **The Chelsea** hosts mixed martial arts cards regularly.

That nouveau riche attitude carries through to the restaurant and nightlife offerings. **Rose. Rabbit. Lie.** (6pm-midnight Wed.-Thurs., 6pm-1am Fri.-Sat., $80-150) is equal parts supper club, nightclub, and jazz club. Throughout the evening bluesy, jazzy torch singers, magicians, tap and hip-hop dancers, and a rocking, if a touch loud, sound system keep the joint jumping. If you go for dinner, order 5-6 small plates per couple. Make one of them the sweet corn royal. **Vesper Bar** (24 hours daily), named for James Bond's favorite martini, prides itself on serving hipster versions of classic (and sometimes forgotten) cocktails. Possibly the best day club in town, **Marquee** (11am-6pm) on the roof, brings in the beautiful people with DJs and sweet bungalow lofts. When darkness falls, the day club becomes an extension of the pulsating Marquee nightclub.

Aria

Restaurants: Aria Café, Bardot, BarMasa, Blossom, the Buffet, Carbone, Five50, Herringbone, Javier's, Jean Georges Steakhouse, Jean Philippe Patisserie, Julian Serrano, Lemongrass, Pressed Juicery, The Roasted Bean, Sage, Starbucks, Tetsu

Entertainment: Cirque du Soleil's *Zarkana*

Attractions: Public art, Crystals

Nightlife: Alibi, Baccarat Lounge, High Limit Lounge, Lift Bar, Lobby Bar, Pool Bar, Sports Bar

All glass and steel, ultramodern ★ **Aria** (3730 Las Vegas Blvd. S., 702/590-7757, $210-500) would look more at home in Manhattan than Las Vegas. Touch pads control the drapes, the lighting, and the climate in Aria's blueberry- or grape-paletted guest rooms—one touch transforms the room into sleep mode. A traditional hotel casino, Aria shares the City Center umbrella with **Vdara,** a Euro-chic boutique hotel with no gaming.

Guests are invited to browse an extensive public art collection, with works by Maya Lin, Jenny Holzer, and Richard Long, among others. **Crystals,** a 500,000-square-foot mall, lets you splurge among hanging gardens. Restaurants fronted by Julian Serrano and Michael Mina take the place of Sbarro's and Cinnabon.

Culinary genius Masa Takayama guarantees that the bluefin at **BarMasa** (5pm-11pm daily, $25-40) goes from the Sea of Japan to your spicy tuna roll in less than 24 hours.

Hard Rock

Restaurants: 35 Steaks+Martinis, Culinary Dropout, Fu Asian Kitchen, Mr. Lucky's, Nobu, Pink Taco, Juice Bar, Fuel Café, Pizza Forte

Entertainment: The Joint, Vinyl, Soundwaves

Nightlife: Rehab Pool Party, The Ainsworth, Center Bar, Sidebet Draft Bar, Luxe Bar, Midway Bar

Young stars and the media-savvy 20-somethings who idolize them contribute to the frat party and spring break mojo at the **Hard Rock** (4455 Paradise Rd., 800/473-7625, $170-320 d) and the spring-break atmosphere poolside. While the casino is shaped like an LP, if your music collection dates back to wax records, this probably isn't the place for you. The gaming tables and machines are located in the "record label," and the shops and restaurants are in the "grooves."

Contemporary and classic rockers regularly grace the stage at **The Joint** and party with their fans at **Rehab Pool Parties** (11am-dusk Fri.-Sat.).

The provocatively named **Pink Taco** (11am-10pm Sun.-Thurs., 11am-midnight Fri.-Sat., $15-25) dishes up Mexican and Caribbean specialties.

Several rounds of expansion have brought the resort's room count to a Vegas-respectable 1,500. Guest rooms are decorated in mint, cinnamon, or gray, and include stocked minibars, Bose CD sound systems and plasma TVs, as befitting wannabe rock stars.

New York New York

Restaurants: Tom's Urban, Nine Fine Irishmen, Shake Shack, Gallagher's Steakhouse, Il Fornaio, Chin Chin Café & Sushi, Gonzalez y Gonzalez, America, 48th and Crepe, Nathan's Hot Dogs, New York Pizzeria, Broadway Burger Bar, Quick Bites, Village Street Eateries
Entertainment: Cirque du Soleil's *Zumanity*, Brooklyn Bridge buskers, dueling pianos
Attractions: Hershey's Chocolate World, Big Apple Coaster & Arcade
Nightlife: Coyote Ugly, The Bar at Times Square, Center Bar, Pour 24, Big Chill, High Limit Bar, Lobby Bar, Chocolate Bar

One look at this loving tribute to the city that never sleeps and you won't be able to fuhgedaboutit. From the city skyline outside (the skyscrapers contain the resort's hotel rooms) to laundry hanging between crowded faux brownstones indoors, **New York New York** (3790 Las Vegas Blvd. S., 866/815-4365, $130-230 d) will have even grizzled Gothamites feeling like they've come home again. Window air-conditioners in the Greenwich Village apartments evoke the city's gritty heat.

The **Big Apple Coaster** (11am-11pm Sun.-Thurs., 10:30am-midnight Fri.-Sat., $14) winds its way around the resort, an experience almost as hair-raising as a New York City cab ride, which the coaster cars are painted to resemble. **Big Apple Arcade** (8am-midnight daily) has games of skill and luck, motion simulators, and rides.

Dueling pianists keep **The Bar at Times Square** (1pm-2:30am Mon.-Thurs., 11am-2:30am Fri.-Sun.) rocking into the wee hours, and the sexy bar staff at **Coyote Ugly** (6pm-2am Sun.-Thurs., 6pm-3am Fri.-Sat.) defies its name.

New York New York's 2,023 guest rooms are standard size, 350-400 square feet. The roller coaster zooms around the towers, so you might want to ask for a room out of earshot.

MGM Grand

Restaurants: Joel Robuchon Restaurant, L'Atelier de Joël Robuchon, Tom Colicchio's Craftsteak, Hecho en Vegas, Shibuya, Fiamma, Michael Mina Pub 1842, Emeril's New Orleans Fish House, Wolfgang Puck Bar & Grill, Grand Wok and Sushi Bar, Crush, Hakkasan, Avenue Café, Stage Deli, Corner Cakes, Food Court, MGM Grand Buffet, Tap Sports Bar, Starbucks, Centrifuge, Blizz Frozen Yogurt & Dessert, Cabana Grill, Project Pie
Entertainment: Cirque du Soleil's *Kà*, David Copperfield, Jabbawockeez, Brad Garrett's Comedy Club
Attractions: CSI: The Experience, CBS Television City Research Center
Nightlife: Centrifuge, Rouge, Lobby Bar, Wet Republic Ultra Pool, Hakkasan Night Club, Whiskey Down, West Wing Bar

Gamblers enter **MGM Grand** (3799 Las Vegas Blvd. S., 888/646-1203, $130-250 d) through portals guarded by MGM's mascot, the 45-foot-tall king of the jungle. The uninitiated may feel like a gazelle on the savanna, swallowed by the 171,000-square-foot casino floor, the largest in Las Vegas. But the watering hole, MGM's 6.5-acre pool complex, is relatively predator-free. MGM capitalizes on the movie studio's greatest hits. Even the hotel's emerald facade evokes the magical city in *The Wizard of Oz*.

Boob tube fans can volunteer for studies at the **CBS Television City Research Center** (10am-8:30pm daily, free), where they can screen pilots for shows under consideration by the network and its competitors. And if your favorite show happens to revolve around solving crimes, don some rubber gloves and search for clues at **CSI: The Experience** (9am-8pm daily, age 12 and up $31.50, not recommended for children under 12). Three crime scenes keep the experience fresh.

MGM Grand houses enough top restaurants for a week of gourmet dinners. If you only have time (or budget) to try one, make it **Shibuya** (5:30pm-10pm Sun.-Thurs., 5:30pm-10:30pm Fri.-Sat., $75-120). The sushi and sashimi will draw the eye, but you do yourself a disservice if you don't order the pork belly.

Standard guest rooms in the Grand Tower are filled with the quality furnishings you'd expect in Las Vegas's upscale hotels. The West Tower guest rooms are smaller, at 350 square feet, but exude the swinging style of an upscale Hollywood studio apartment crammed with a CD and DVD player and other high-tech gizmos; the 450-square-foot rooms in the Grand Tower are more traditional.

Tropicana

Restaurants: Bacio Italian Cuisine, Biscayne, Beach Café, South Beach Food Court
Attractions: Xposed!
Entertainment: Rich Little, *Raiding the Rock Vault*, Illusions Starring Jan Rouven, Laugh Factory
Nightlife: Tropicana Lounge, Lucky's Sports Bar, Coconut Grove Bar

When it opened at in 1959, the **Tropicana** (801 Las Vegas Blvd. S., 888/381-8767, $140-200 d) was the most luxurious, most expensive resort on the Strip. It has survived several boom-and-bust cycles since then, and its decor reflects the willy-nilly expansion and refurbishment efforts through the years. Today, the rooms have bright, airy South Beach themes with plantation shutters and light wood, 42-inch plasma TVs, and iPod docks.

The beach chic atmosphere includes a two-acre pool complex with reclining deck chairs and swim-up blackjack. After a slow start, Las Vegas is now quite LGBT friendly. As the sign says, "Welcome to FABULOUS Las Vegas." The Trop is leading the way. On summer Saturdays (noon-7pm) the pool deck hosts **Xposed!**, a gay pool party with sand volleyball, go-go dancers, and trendy DJs.

The time-capsule premise is a bit tired, but the music in ***Raiding the Rock Vault*** (8pm Wed.-Mon., $59-99) is a rollicking nostalgic look at the rock era, from the British Invasion and free love, through disco and Vietnam protests to '80s hair bands and the rise of commercialism.

Luxor

Restaurants: Tender Steak & Seafood, Rice & Company, Public House, T&T Tacos & Tequila, More Buffet, Pyramid Café, Backstage Deli, Food Court, Blizz, Burger Bar, Ri Ra Irish Pub, Slice of Vegas, Hussong's Cantina
Entertainment: Criss Angel: *Believe*, Carrot Top, Blue Man Group, *Fantasy*
Attractions: *Bodies... the Exhibition*, *Titanic* artifacts
Nightlife: LAX, Centra, Aurora, Flight, High Bar, PlayBar

Other than its pyramid shape and name, not much remains of the Egyptian theme at the **Luxor** (3900 Las Vegas Blvd. S., 877/386-4658, $89-220 d). Much of the sarcophagus-and-scarab decor was swept away. In its place are upscale and decidedly post-pharaoh nightclubs, restaurants, and shops. Many are located on the sky bridge between Luxor and Mandalay Bay. What remain are the large, 120,000-square-foot casino and 4,400 guest rooms in the pyramid and twin 22-story towers. You can also see the largest atrium in the world, an intense light beam that is visible from space, and inclinators—elevators that move along the building's oblique angles.

There is a story line in Criss Angel's ***Believe*** (702/262-4400 or 866/983-4279, 7pm and 9:30pm Wed.-Sat., 7pm Sun., $65-142), but it's really just framework for the magician's mind-freaking illusions and engaging personality. The **Atrium Showroom** (702/262-4400 or 800/557-7428) is home to ***Fantasy*** (10:30pm daily,

$42-65), a typical jiggle-and-tease topless review with some singing and comedy thrown in, and comedian and prop jockey **Carrot Top** (8pm Wed.-Mon., $60-71).

Old-school touches such as chandeliers and red leather sofas contrast the young and flat-bellied guests at **LAX** (5pm-late Wed. and Fri.-Sat.).

Staying in the pyramid makes for interesting room features, such as a slanted exterior wall. Stay on higher floors for panoramic views of the atrium below. Tower rooms are newer and more traditional in their shape, decor, and amenities.

Mandalay Bay

Restaurants: Aureole, Border Grill, Burger Bar, Charlie Palmer Steak, Citizens Kitchen & Bar, Crossroads at House of Blues, Fleur, Kumi, Lupo, RM Seafood, Rivea, Stripsteak, Bayside Buffet, Beach Bar & Grill, House of Blues Foundation Room, Hussong's Cantina, Mizuya, Noodle Shop, Raffles Café, Red Square, Ri Ra Irish Pub, RX Boiler Room, Sea Breeze Ice Cream and Juices, Slice of Vegas, Sports Book Grill, Veranda, Yogurt In, Starbucks
Entertainment: *Michael Jackson ONE*
Attractions: Shark Reef
Nightlife: Light, Daylight Beach Club, Bikini Bar, Evening Call, Eyecandy Sound Lounge, Fat Tuesday, House of Blues Foundation Room, Minus 5 Ice Lounge, Orchid Lounge, Press, Skyfall Lounge, Verandah Lounge, 1923 Bourbon Bar

Enter this South Pacific behemoth at the southern tip of the Las Vegas Strip and try to comprehend its mind-boggling statistics. ★ **Mandalay Bay** (3950 Las Vegas Blvd. S., 877/632-7800, $150-300 d) has one of the largest casino floors in the world at 135,000 square feet. Wander into Mandalay's beach environment, an 11-acre paradise comprising three pools, a lazy river, and a 1.6-million-gallon wave pool complete with a real beach made of five million pounds of sand. There's also a tops-optional sunbathing pool deck. You could spend your entire vacation in the pool area, gambling at the beach's three-level casino, eating at its restaurant, shopping for pool gear at the poolside stand, and loading up on sandals and bikinis at the nearby Pearl Moon boutique. The beach hosts a concert series during summer.

When you're ready to check out the rest of the property, don't miss **House of Blues** (hours vary by event), with live blues, rock, and acoustic sets as well as DJs spinning dance tunes.

Mandalay Place (10am-11pm daily), on the sky bridge between Mandalay Bay and Luxor, is smaller and less hectic than other casino malls. Unusual shops such as The Guinness Store, where fans can pick up merchandise celebrating their favorite Irish stout, share space with eateries and high-concept bars like **Minus 5** (11am-2am Sun.-Thurs., 11am-3am Fri.-Sat.), where barflies don parkas before entering the below-freezing (23°F) establishment. The glasses aren't just frosted; they're fashioned completely out of ice.

An urban hip-hop worldview and the King of Pop's unmatched talent guide the vignettes in ***Michael Jackson ONE*** (7pm and 9:30pm Fri.-Tues., $69-160). Michael's musical innovation and the Cirque du Soleil trademark aerial and acrobatic acts pay homage to the human spirit.

Sheathed in Indian artifacts and crafts, the **Foundation Room** (5pm-late daily) is just as dark and mysterious as the subcontinent, with private rooms, a dining room, and several bars catering to various musical tastes.

Vegas pays tribute to Paris, Rome, New York, and Venice, so why not Moscow? Round up your comrades for caviar and vodka as well as continental favorites at **Red Square** (5pm-10pm Sun.-Thurs., 5pm-11pm Fri.-Sat., $35-50). Look for the headless Lenin statue at the entrance.

Standard guest rooms are chic and roomy (550 square feet), with warm fabrics and plush bedding. Get a north-facing room and put the floor-to-ceiling windows to use gazing the full length of the Strip. The guest rooms are big, but nothing special visually, but the baths are fit for royalty, with huge tubs, glass-walled showers, and king's-and-queen's commodes. To go upscale, check out the Delano boutique hotel; for very upscale, book at the Four Seasons—both are part of the same complex.

Downtown

Binion's

Restaurants: Top of Binion's Steakhouse, Binion's Deli, Binion's Café, Benny's Smokin BBQ & Brews, Cowgirl Up Cantina, Whiskey Licker

Before Vegas became a destination resort city, it catered to inveterate gamblers, hard drinkers, and others on the fringes of society. Ah, the good old days! A gambler himself, Benny Binion put his place in the middle of downtown, a magnet for the serious player, offering high limits and few frills. **Binion's** (128 Fremont St., 702/382-1600) now attracts players with occasional $1 blackjack tables and a poker room frequented by grizzled veterans. While Binion's and the rest of Las Vegas have been overtaken by Strip megaresorts, the little den on Fremont Street still retains the flavor of Old Vegas, though the Binion family is no longer involved. Harrah's bought the place in 2004.

The hotel at Binion's closed in 2009, but the casino and restaurants remain open, including the **Top of Binion's Steakhouse** (5pm-10pm daily, $30-55), famous for its Fremont Street views and aged black Angus.

Golden Nugget

Restaurants: Vic & Anthony's, Chart House, Grotto, Lillie's Asian Cuisine, Red Sushi, Cadillac Mexican Kitchen & Tequila Bar, Buffet, The Grille, Claim Jumper, Starbucks

Entertainment: Gordie Brown

Attractions: Hand of Faith, Shark Tank

Nightlife: Rush Lounge, Gold Diggers, H2O Bar at the Tank, Claude's Bar, Ice Bar, Bar 46, Cadillac Tequila Bar

Considered by many to be the only Strip-worthy resort downtown, the ★ **Golden Nugget** (129 E. Fremont St.,

Fremont Street Experience

800/634-3454, $89-179) has been a fixture for nearly 70 years, beckoning diners and gamblers with gold leaf and a massive gold nugget. Landry's, the restaurant chain and new Nugget owner, has embarked on an ambitious campaign to maintain the hotel's opulence, investing $300 million for casino expansion, more restaurants, and a new 500-room hotel tower.

If you don't feel like swimming with the sharks in the poker room, you can get up close and personal with their finned namesakes at the **Golden Nugget Pool** (9am-6pm daily, free), an outdoor pool with a three-story waterslide that takes riders through the hotel's huge aquarium, home to sharks, rays, and other exotic marine life. Bathers can also swim up to the aquarium for a face-to-face with the aquatic predators, or schedule a **guided tour** (1:30pm Wed., $30). Waterfalls and lush landscaping help make this one of the world's best hotel pools.

Gold Diggers nightclub (9pm-late Wed.-Sun.) plays hip-hop, pop, and classic rock for the dancing pleasure of guests and go-go girls.

When checking in, pause to have your picture taken with the **Hand of Faith,** a 62-pound gold nugget. Rooms are appointed in dark wood and warm autumn hues.

Sights

Downtown

★ Fremont Street Experience

With land at a premium and more and more tourists flocking to the opulence of the Strip, downtown Las Vegas in the last quarter of the 20th century found its lights beginning to flicker. Enter the **Fremont Street Experience** (702/678-5777), an ambitious plan to transform downtown and its tacky "Glitter Gulch" reputation into a pedestrian-friendly enclave. Highlighted by a four-block-long canopy festooned with 12 million light-emitting diodes 90 feet in the air, the Fremont Street Experience is downtown's answer to the Strip's erupting volcanoes and fantastic dancing fountains. The canopy, dubbed Viva Vision, runs atop Fremont Street between North Main Street and North 4th Street.

Once an hour between dusk and 1am, the promenade goes dark and all heads lift toward the canopy, supported by massive concrete pillars. For six minutes, visitors are enthralled by the multimedia shows that chronicle Western history, span the careers of classic rock bands, or transport viewers to fantasy worlds. Viva Vision runs several different shows daily.

Before and after the light shows, strolling buskers sing for their supper, artists create five-minute masterpieces, caricaturists airbrush souvenir portraits, and costumed (sometimes scantily) characters pose for photos. Tipping is all but mandatory. Fremont Street hosts top musical acts, including some A-listers during big Las Vegas weekends such as

Downtown Las Vegas

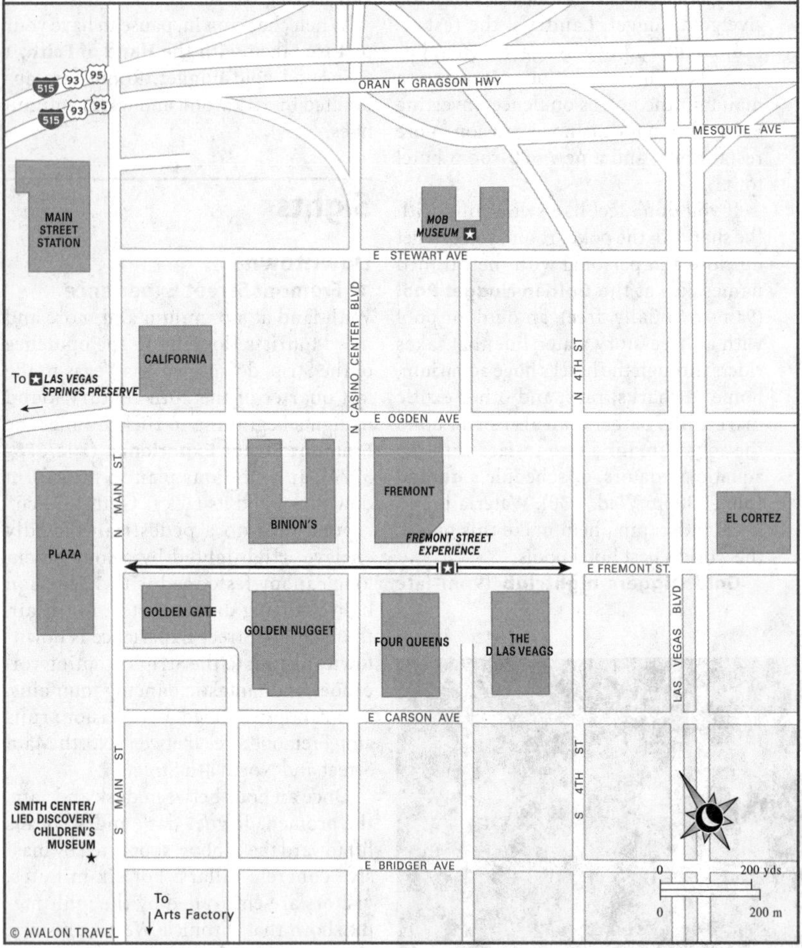

National Finals Rodeo, NASCAR races, and New Year's. The adjacent Fremont East Entertainment District houses quirky eateries, clubs, and art galleries.

Las Vegas Natural History Museum

Las Vegas boasts a volcano, a pyramid, and even a Roman coliseum, so it's little wonder that an animatronic *Tyrannosaurus rex* calls the valley home too. Dedicated to "global life forms . . . from the desert to the ocean, from Nevada to Africa, from prehistoric times to the present," the **Las Vegas Natural History Museum** (900 Las Vegas Blvd. N., 702/384-3466, 9am-4pm daily, adults $10, seniors, military, and students $8, ages 3-11 $5) is filled with rotating exhibits that belie the notion that Las Vegas culture begins and ends with neon casino signs.

Visitors to the Treasures of Egypt

gallery can enter a realistic depiction of King Tut's tomb to study archaeological techniques and discover golden treasures of the pharaohs. The Wild Nevada gallery showcases the raw beauty and surprisingly varied life-forms of the Mojave Desert. Interactive exhibits also enlighten visitors on subjects such as marine life, geology, African ecosystems, and more.

The 35-foot-long T. rex and his friends (rivals? entrées?)—a triceratops, a raptor, and an ichthyosaur—greet visitors in the Prehistoric Life gallery. And by "greet" we mean a bloodcurdling roar from the T. rex, so take precautions with the little ones and the faint of heart.

Neon Museum and Boneyard

Book a one-hour guided tour of the **Neon Museum and Boneyard** (770 Las Vegas Blvd. N., 702/387-6366, 9am-4pm and 7:30pm-9pm daily, adults $18-25, students, seniors, and veterans $12-22) and take a trip to Las Vegas's more recent past. The boneyard displays 200 old neon signs that were used to advertise casinos, restaurants, bars, and even a flower shop. Several have been restored to their former glory. The **visitors center** (9:30am-8pm daily) is housed in the relocated scallop-shaped lobby of the historic La Concha Motel. You can skip the boneyard and take a free self-guided tour of nine restored signs displayed as public art. Note that the neighborhood can be sketchy.

Lied Discovery Children's Museum

Voted Best Museum in Las Vegas by readers of the local newspaper, the three-story **Lied Discovery Children's Museum** (360 Promenade Pl., 702/382-5437, 9am-4pm Tues.-Fri., 10am-5pm Sat., noon-5pm Sun., $14.50) presents more than 100 interactive scientific, artistic, and life-skill activities. Children enjoy themselves so much that they forget they're learning. Among the best permanent exhibits is *It's Your Choice,* which shows kids the importance of eating right and adopting a healthy lifestyle. Exhibits show kids creative ways to explore their world: drama, cooperation, dance, and visual arts. The Summit is the playground jungle gym on steroids—13 levels of slides, ladders, tubes, and interactive experiments.

Mormon Fort

The tiny **Mormon Fort** (500 E. Washington Ave., 702/486-3511, 8am-4:30pm Tues.-Sat., $1, under 12 free) is the oldest building in Las Vegas. The adobe remnant, constructed by Mormon missionaries in 1855, was part of their original settlement, which they abandoned in 1858. It then served as a store, a barracks, and a shed on the Gass-Stewart Ranch. After that, the railroad leased the old fort to various tenants, including the Bureau of Reclamation, which stabilized and rebuilt the shed to use as a concrete-testing laboratory for Hoover Dam. In 1955 the railroad sold the old fort to the Elks, who in 1963 bulldozed the whole wooden structure (except the little remnant) into the ranch swimming pool and torched it. The shed was bought by the city in 1971.

Since then, a number of preservation societies have helped keep it in place. The museum includes a visitors center, a re-creation of the original fort built around the remnant. A tour guide presents the history orally while display boards provide it visually. Your visit will not go unrewarded—it's immensely refreshing to see some preservation of the past in this city of the ultimate now.

★ Mob Museum

The **Museum of Organized Crime and Law Enforcement** (300 Stewart Ave., 702/229-2734, http://themobmuseum.org, 10am-7pm daily, adults $20, seniors, military, and teachers $18, age 11-17 $14, under age 11 free) celebrates Las Vegas's Mafia past and the cops and agents who finally ran the mob out of town. The museum is located inside the city's downtown post office and courthouse,

Grand Canyon Tours from Vegas

Nearly a dozen tour companies relay visitors from Vegas to and through the Grand Canyon via a variety of conveyances—buses, airplanes, helicopters, off-road vehicles, and rafts. Coupons and discounts for online reservation and off-season bookings are plentiful; it is not uncommon to book tours at less than half the rack rates listed here.

Grand Canyon Tours

Grand Canyon Tours (702/655-6060 or 800/222-6966, www.grandcanyontours.com) packs plenty of sightseeing into its bus tours ($80-200), which can include the Grand Canyon Railway or Hualapai Ranch. Helicopter tours ($275-408) cut down the commute, leaving more time at the canyon and allow an earlier return. Choppers skim over Hoover Dam, Lake Mead, the Black Mountains, and the Strip during the 1.5-hour flight. Stops can include the Grand Canyon Skywalk, Grand Canyon West Ranch, and the canyon floor.

Look Tours

Look Tours (4285 N. Rancho Dr., 702/749-5715 or 888/796-4345, www.looktours.com) also offers bus tours (6am-10pm daily, $80-115) and an overnight trip via fixed-wing aircraft ($160-309). Do-it-yourselfers can rent an SUV from Look (7am, 8am, or 9am daily, $170 pp, 2-person minimum) for a leisurely 24-hour exploration of the West Rim.

Maverick Helicopter Tours

Maverick Helicopter Tours (6075 Las Vegas Blvd. S., 702/261-0007 or 888/261-4414, and 1410 Jet Stream Dr., Ste. 100, Henderson, 702/405-4300 or 888/261-4414, www.maverickhelicopter.com) shuttles its customers to the canyon via spacious, quiet Eco-Star helicopters (daily 7am-4:30pm, $619) and partners with Pink Jeep Tours for a guided road tour to the West Rim followed by a slow descent to the bottom of the canyon (daily 6am-5pm, $395).

SweeTours

SweeTours (6363 S. Pecos Rd., Ste. 106, Las Vegas, 702/456-9200 or 877/997-9338, http://sweetours.com) offers several packages ($169-385), which include options for travel by bus, SUV, helicopter, and boat.

appropriately the site of the 1951 Kefauver Hearing investigating organized crime.

Displays include the barber chair where Albert Anastasia was gunned down while getting a haircut, and an examination of the violence, ceremony, and hidden meanings behind Mafia "hits," all against a grisly background—the wall from Chicago's St. Valentine's Day Massacre that spelled the end of six members of Bugs Moran's crew and one hanger-on. Bringing Down the Mob displays the tools federal agents used—wiretaps, surveillance, and weapons—to clean up the town.

Downtown Arts District

Centered at South Main Street and East Charleston Boulevard, the district gives art lovers a concentration of galleries to suit any taste, plus an eclectic mix of shops, eateries, and other surprises. The **Arts Factory** (107 E. Charleston Blvd., 702/383-3133), a two-story redbrick industrial building, is the district's birthplace. It hosts exhibitions, drawing classes, and poetry readings. Tenants include a toy shop, a yoga studio, a roller-skate store, a *tres-chic* bistro, and galleries and studios belonging to artists working in every media and genre imaginable. One downstairs space, **Jana's RedRoom** (11am-7pm Wed.-Sun. and by appointment) displays and sells canvases by local artists.

Virtually all the galleries and other paeans to urban pop culture participate in Las Vegas's **First Friday** (5pm-11pm every month 1st Fri.) event, but otherwise galleries keep limited hours, so if there's something you don't want to miss, call for an appointment.

At the southern edge of the District, browse the edgy, often avant-garde displays at **Blackbird Studios** (1551 S. Commerce St., 702/782-0319) and neighboring Circadian Gallery, with its aggressive, brooding expressions and impressionistic studies by Daniel Pearson.

Center Strip

Madame Tussauds Las Vegas

Ever wanted to dunk over Shaq? Party with the dudes from *The Hangover*? Leave Simon Cowell speechless? **Madame Tussauds Las Vegas** (3377 Las Vegas Blvd. S., 702/862-7800, www.madametussauds.com/lasvegas, 10am-8pm Sun.-Thurs., 10am-9pm Fri.-Sat., adults $30, age 4-12 $20, under age 4 free) at The Venetian Hotel gives you your chance. Unlike most other museums, Madame Tussauds encourages guests to get up close and "personal" with the world leaders, sports heroes, and screen stars immortalized in wax. Photo ops and interactive activities abound. With Karaoke Revolution Presents: American Idol you can take to the stage and then hear Simon Cowell and Ryan Seacrest's thoughts on your burgeoning singing career. The crowd roars as you take it to the rack and sink the game-winner over Shaquille O'Neal's vainly outstretch arm. You'll feel right at home in the "mansion" as you don bunny ears and lounge on the circular bed with Hugh Hefner.

★ Gondola Rides

We dare you not to sigh at the grandeur of Venice in the desert as you pass beneath quaint bridges and idyllic sidewalk cafés, your gondolier serenading you with the accompaniment of the Grand Canal's gurgling wavelets. The half-mile **indoor gondolas** (3355 Las Vegas Blvd. S., 702/607-3982, 10am-11pm Sun.-Thurs., 10am-midnight Fri.-Sat., $21) skirt the Grand Canal Shoppes inside The Venetian Hotel under the mall's painted-sky ceiling fresco; **outdoor gondolas** (11am-10pm daily, weather permitting, $19) skim The Venetian's 31,000-square-foot lagoon for 12 minutes, giving riders a unique perspective on the Las Vegas Strip. Plying the waters at regular intervals, the realistic-looking gondolas seat four, but couples who don't want to share a boat can pay double.

★ Secret Garden and Dolphin Habitat

It's no mirage—those really are pure-white tigers lounging in their own plush resort on The Mirage casino floor. Legendary Las Vegas magicians Siegfried and Roy, who have dedicated much of their lives to preserving big cats, opened the **Secret Garden** (Mirage, 3400 Las Vegas Blvd. S., 702/791-7188, 11am-5:30pm daily, adults $22, age 4-12 $12) in 1990. In addition to the milky-furred tigers, the garden is home to blue-eyed, black-striped white tigers as well as panthers, lions, and leopards. Although caretakers don't "perform" with the animals, if your visit is well-timed, you could see the cats playing, wrestling, and even swimming in their pristine waterfall-fed pools. The cubs in the specially built nursery are sure to register high on the cuteness meter.

Visit the Atlantic bottlenoses at the **Dolphin Habitat** right next door, also in the middle of The Mirage's palm trees and jungle foliage. The aquatic mammals don't perform on cue either, but they're natural hams and often interact with their visitors, nodding their heads in response to trainer questions, turning aerial somersaults, and "walking" on their tails across the water. An underwater viewing area provides an unusual perspective into the dolphins' world. Feeding times are a hoot.

Budding naturalists (age 13 and over) won't want to miss Dolphin Habitat's Trainer for a Day program ($495 and up),

which allows them to feed, swim with, and pose for photos with some of the aquatic stars while putting them through their daily regimen.

★ High Roller

Taller than even the London Eye, the 550-foot **High Roller** (The Linq, 3545 Las Vegas Blvd. S., 702/777-2782 or 866/574-3851, noon-2am daily, $27-37) is the highest observation wheel in the world. Two thousand LED lights dance in intricate choreography among the ride's spokes and pods. The dazzling view from 50 stories up is unparalleled. Ride at night for a perfect panorama of the famous Strip skyline. Ride at dusk for inspiring glimpses of the desert sun setting over the mountains. Forty passengers fit in each of the High Roller's 28 compartments, lessening wait time for the half-hour ride circuit. During **"happy half hour"** (4pm-7pm $37; 10pm-1am $47) passengers can board special bar cars and enjoy unlimited cocktails during the ride. Book online to save $7 on admission.

Lower Strip

Showcase Mall

"Mall" is an overly ambitious moniker for the **Showcase Mall** (3785 Las Vegas Blvd. S.), a mini diversion on the Strip. The centerpiece, the original **M&M's World** (702/736-7611, 9am-midnight daily, free), underwent a 2010 expansion and now includes a printing station where customers can customize their bite-size treats with words and pictures. The 3,300-square-foot expansion on the third floor of the store, which originally opened in 1997, includes additional opportunities to stock up on all things M: Swarovski crystal candy dishes, an M&M guitar, T-shirts, and purses made from authentic M&M wrappers. The addition brings the chocoholic's paradise to more than

Top to bottom: the Mirage's Dolphin Habitat; High Roller observation wheel at The Linq; gondola rides in the Venetian's Grand Canal.

30,000 square feet, offering key chains, coffee mugs, lunch boxes, and the addicting treats in every color imaginable. Start with a viewing of the short 3-D film, *I Lost My M in Las Vegas.* A replica of Kyle Busch's M&M-sponsored No. 18 NASCAR stock car is on the fourth floor.

Everything Coca-Cola really should be named "A Few Things Coca-Cola." The small retail outlet has collectibles, free photo ops, and a soda fountain where you can taste 16 Coke products from around the world ($7), but it's a pale vestige of Coke's ambitious marketing ploy, à la M&M's World, that opened in 1997 and closed in 2000. The giant green Coke bottle facade, however, attracts pedestrians into the mall.

Bodies . . . the Exhibition and *Titanic* Artifacts

Although they are tastefully and respectfully presented, the dissected humans at ***Bodies . . . the Exhibition*** (Luxor, 3900 Las Vegas Blvd. S., 702/262-4400 or 800/557-7428, 10am-10pm daily, adults $32, over age 64 $30, age 4-12 $24, under age 4 free) still have the creepy factor. That uneasiness quickly gives way to wonder and interest as visitors examine 13 full-body specimens, carefully preserved to reveal bone structure and muscular, circulatory, respiratory, and other systems. Other system and organ displays drive home the importance of a healthy lifestyle, with structures showing the damage caused by overeating, alcohol consumption, and sedentary lifestyle. Perhaps the most sobering exhibit is the side-by-side comparisons of healthy and smoke-damaged lungs. A draped-off area contains fetal specimens, showing prenatal development and birth defects.

Luxor also hosts the 300 less surreal but just as poignant artifacts and reproductions commemorating the 1912 sinking of the ***Titanic*** (3900 Las Vegas Blvd. S., 702/262-4400 or 800/557-7428, 10am-10pm daily, adults $32, over age 64 $30, ages 4-12 $24, under age 4 free). The 15-ton rusting hunk of the ship's hull is the biggest artifact on display; it not only drives home the Titanic's scale but also helps transport visitors back to that cold April morning a century ago. A replica of the *Titanic*'s grand staircase—featured prominently in the 1997 film with Leonardo DiCaprio and Kate Winslet—testifies to the ship's opulence, but it is the passengers' personal effects (a pipe, luggage, an unopened bottle of champagne) and recreated first-class and third-class cabins that provide some of the most heartbreaking discoveries. The individual stories come to life as each patron is given the identity of one of the ship's passengers. At the end of tour they find out the passenger's fate.

Shark Reef

Just when you thought it was safe to visit Las Vegas . . . this 1.6-million-gallon habitat proves not all the sharks in town prowl the poker rooms. **Shark Reef** (Mandalay Bay, 3950 Las Vegas Blvd. S., 702/632-4555, 10am-8pm Sun.-Thurs., 10am-10pm Fri.-Sat., adults $20, ages 5-12 $14) is home to 2,000 animals—almost all predators. Transparent walkthrough tubes and a sinking-ship observation deck allow terrific views, bringing visitors nearly face-to-face with some of the most fearsome creatures in the world. In addition to 15 species of sharks, guests can view a sand tiger shark, whose mouth is so crammed with razor-sharp teeth that it doesn't fully close. You'll also find golden crocodiles, moray eels, piranhas, giant octopuses, the venomous lionfish, stingrays, jellyfish, water monitors, and the fresh-from-your-nightmares eight-foot-long Komodo dragon.

Mandalay Bay guests with dive certification can dive in the 22-foot-deep shipwreck exhibit at the reef. Commune with eight-foot nurse sharks as well as reef sharks, zebra sharks, rays, sawfish, and other denizens of the deep. **Scuba excursions** (3pm daily, age 18 and over, $650) include 3-4 hours underwater, a guided aquarium tour, a video, and admission for up to four guests. Wearing chain mail is required.

Off the Strip

★ Las Vegas Springs Preserve

The **Las Vegas Springs Preserve** (333 S. Valley View Blvd., 702/822-7700, 10am-6pm daily, adults $19, students and over age 64 $17, ages 5-17 $11, free under age 5) is where Las Vegas began, at least from a Eurocentric viewpoint. More than 100 years ago, the first nonnatives in the Las Vegas Valley—Mormon missionaries from Salt Lake City—stumbled on this clear artesian spring. Of course, the native Paiute and Pueblo people knew about the springs and exploited them millennia before the Mormons arrived. You can see examples of their tools, pottery, and houses at the site, now a 180-acre monument to environmental stewardship, historic preservation, and geographic discovery. The preserve is home to lizards, rabbits, foxes, scorpions, bats, and more. The nature-minded will love the cactus, rose, and sage gardens, and there's even an occasional cooking demonstration using the desert-friendly fruits, vegetables, and herbs grown here.

Las Vegas has become a leader in water conservation, alternative energy, and other environmentally friendly policies. The results of these efforts and tips on how everyone can reduce their carbon footprint are found in the Sustainability Gallery.

Nevada State Museum

Visitors can spend hours studying Mojave and Spring Mountains ecology, southern Nevada history, and local art at the **Nevada State Museum** (309 S. Valley View Blvd., 702/486-5205, 10am-6pm Thurs.-Mon., $19, included in admission to the Springs Preserve). Permanent exhibits on the 13,000-square-foot floor describe southern Nevada's role in warfare, mining, and atomic weaponry and include skeletons of a Columbian mammoth, which roamed the Nevada deserts 20,000 years ago, and the ichthyosaur, a whalelike remnant of the Triassic Period. The "Nevada from Dusk to Dawn" exhibit explores the nocturnal lives of the area's animal species. The Cahlan Research Library houses Clark County naturalization and Civil Defense records, among other treasures.

★ Atomic Testing Museum

Kids might not think it's da bomb, but if you were part of the "duck and cover" generation, the **Atomic Testing Museum** (755 E. Flamingo Rd., 702/794-5161, 10am-5pm Mon.-Sat., noon-5pm Sun., adults $22) provides plenty to spark your memories of the Cold War. Las Vegas embraced its position as ground zero in the development of the nation's atomic and nuclear deterrents after World War II. Business leaders welcomed defense contractors to town, and casinos hosted bomb-watching parties as nukes were detonated at the Nevada Test Site, a huge swath of desert 65 miles away. One ingenious marketer promoted the Miss Atomic Bomb beauty pageant in an era when patriotism overcame concerns about radiation.

The museum presents atomic history without bias, walking a fine line between appreciation of the work of nuclear scientists, politicians, and the military and the catastrophic consequences their activities and decisions could have wrought. The museum's best permanent feature is a short video in the Ground Zero Theatre, a multimedia simulation of an actual atomic explosion. The theater, a replica of an observation bunker, is rigged for motion, sound, and rushing air.

One gallery helps visitors put atomic energy milestones in historic perspective along with the age's impact on 1950s and 1960s pop culture. Another permanent exhibit explains the effects of radiation and how it is tracked and measured. Just as relevant today are the lectures and traveling exhibits that the museum hosts.

Computer simulators, high-speed

photographs, Geiger counters, and other testing and safety equipment along with first-person accounts add to the museum's visit-worthiness.

Your ticket includes admission to the Area 51 exhibit. Built in consultation with former workers at the top secret Groom Lake facility, the exhibit invites you to take the tour and decide for yourself whether alien autopsies, futuristic aircraft, and other *X-Files*-style activities are part of Area 51's mission.

Marjorie Barrick Museum of Natural History

The **Marjorie Barrick Museum of Natural History** and the adjacent **Donald H. Baepler Xeric Garden** (4505 S. Maryland Pkwy., 702/895-3381, 9am-5pm Mon.-Fri., noon-5pm Sat., donation), on the University of Nevada, Las Vegas (UNLV) campus, are good places to bone up on local history and renowned artists such as Llyn Foulkes, Richard Tuttle, and Stephen Antonakos, as well as artists with ties to southern Nevada.

Other displays are full of Native American baskets, kachinas, masks, weaving, pottery, and jewelry from the desert Southwest and Latin America, including Mexican dance masks and traditional Guatemalan textiles.

To find the museum and garden, drive onto the UNLV campus on Harmon Street and follow it around to the right, then turn left into the museum parking lot.

Entertainment

Headliners and Production Shows

Production shows are classic Las Vegas-style diversions, the kind that most people identify with the Entertainment Capital of the World. An American version of French burlesque, the Las Vegas production show has been gracing various stages around town since the late 1950s and usually includes magic, acrobats, jugglers, daredevils, and maybe an animal act. The Cirque du Soleil franchise keeps the tradition alive, but other variety shows have given way to more one-dimensional, specialized productions of superstar imitators, sexy song-and-dance reviews, and female impersonators. Most of these are large-budget, skillfully produced and presented extravaganzas, and they make for highly entertaining nights on the town.

As Las Vegas has grown into a sophisticated metropolis, with gourmet restaurants, trendy boutiques, and glittering nightlife, it has also attracted Broadway productions to compete with the superstar singers that helped launch the town's legendary status.

Since they're so expensive to produce, the big shows are fairly reliable, and you can count on them being around for the life of this edition. They do change on occasion; the smaller shows come and go with some frequency, but unless a show bombs and is gone in the first few weeks, it'll usually be around for at least a year. All this big-time entertainment is centered, of course, around Las Vegas's casino resorts, with the occasional concert at the Thomas & Mack Center on the UNLV campus.

Blue Man Group

Bald, blue, and silent (save for homemade PVC musical instruments), **Blue Man Group** (Luxor, 3900 Las Vegas Blvd. S., 702/262-4000 or 877/386-4658, 7pm and 9:30pm daily, $86-149) was one of the hottest things to hit the Strip when it debuted in 2000 after successful versions in New York, Boston, and Chicago. It continues to wow audiences with its thought-provoking, quirkily hilarious gags and percussion performances. It is part street performance, part slapstick, and all fun.

Carrot Top

With fresh observational humor, outrageous props, and flaming orange hair,

Scott Thompson stands alone as the only true full-time headlining stand-up comic in Las Vegas. He's also better known as **Carrot Top** (Luxor, 3900 Las Vegas Blvd. S., 702/262-4400 or 800/557-7428, 8pm Wed.-Mon., $60-71). His rapid-fire, stream-of-consciousness delivery ricochets from sex-aid props and poop jokes to current events, pop culture, and social injustice, making him the thinking person's class clown.

Chippendales

With all the jiggle-and-tease shows on the Strip, **Chippendales** (Rio, 3700 W. Flamingo Rd., 702/777-2782, 8:30pm and 10:30pm daily, $50-73) delivers a little gender equity. Tight jeans and rippled abs bumping and grinding with their female admirers may be the main attraction, but there is a fairly strict hands-off policy. The boys dance their way through sultry and playful renditions of "It's Raining Men" and other tunes with similar themes.

Donny and Marie

A little bit country, a little bit rock and roll, **Donny and Marie Osmond** (Flamingo, 3555 Las Vegas Blvd. S., 702/733-3333, 7:30pm Tues.-Sat., $117-135) manage a bit of hip-hop and soul as well, as they hurl affectionate put-downs at each other between musical numbers. The most famous members of the talented family perform their solo hits, such as Donny's "Puppy Love" and Marie's "Paper Roses" along with perfect-harmony duets while their faux sibling rivalry comes through with good-natured ribbing.

Terry Fator

America's Got Talent champion **Terry Fator** (Mirage, 3400 Las Vegas Blvd. S., 702/792-7777 or 800/963-9634, 7:30pm Mon.-Thurs., $59-149) combines two disparate skills—ventriloquism and impersonation—to channel Elvis, Garth Brooks, Lady Gaga, and others. Backed by a live band, Fator sings and trades one-liners with his foam rubber friends. The comedy is fresh, the impressions spot-on, and the ventriloquism accomplished with nary a lip quiver.

Matt Goss

A worthy heir to Dean Martin and Bobby Darin, crooner **Matt Goss** (Caesars Palace, 3570 Las Vegas Blvd. S., 800/745-3000, 9:30pm Tues. and Fri.-Sat., $75-144) is at home performing Eagles classics and his own originals, along with selections from the Great American Songbook. Backed by a swingin' nine-piece band and the requisite sexy dancers, Goss, in fedora and bow tie, brings his own style to standards like "I've Got the World on a String," "Luck Be a Lady," and other Rat Pack favorites.

Jersey Boys

The rise of Frankie Valli and the Four Seasons from street-corner doo-woppers to superstars gets the full Broadway treatment in ***Jersey Boys*** (Paris, 3655 Las Vegas Blvd. S., 877/242-6753, 7pm Tues.-Sun., $60-150). *Jersey Boys* is the true story of the falsetto-warbling Valli and his bandmates. Terrific sets and lighting create the mood, alternating from the grittiness of the Newark streets to the flash of the concert stage. Remember, it's the story of inner-city teens in the 1950s, so be prepared for more than a few F-bombs in the dialogue.

Kà

Cirque du Soleil's ***Kà*** (MGM Grand, 3799 Las Vegas Blvd. S., 702/531-3826 or 866/983-4279, 7pm and 9:30pm Sat.-Wed., $77-150) explores the yin and yang of life through the story of two twins' journey to meet their shared fate. Martial arts, acrobatics, puppetry, plenty of flashy pyrotechnics, and lavish sets and costumes bring cinematic drama to the variety-show acts. The show's title was inspired by the ancient Egyptian *Ka* belief, in which every human has a spiritual duplicate.

Legends in Concert

The best of the celebrity impersonator shows, ***Legends in Concert*** (Flamingo, 3555 Las Vegas Blvd. S., 702/777-7776 or 866/983-4279, 7:30pm and 9:30pm Mon., 9:30pm Tues., 4pm and 9:30pm Wed.-Thurs. and Sat., 7:30pm Sun., $55-98), brings out the "stars" in rapid-fire succession. Madonna barely finishes striking a pose before Sinatra starts doing it his way. You'll see Elvis and Michael Jackson, of course, and five or six other acts from Britney, Cher, Taylor Swift, and Lady Gaga to Garth, Reba, and Dolly. A Vegas fixture for 25 years, *Legends* is truly legendary.

Le Rêve

All the spectacle we've come to expect from the creative geniuses behind Cirque du Soleil is present in this stream-of-unconsciousness known as ***Le Rêve*** (Wynn, 3131 Las Vegas Blvd. S., 702/770-9966 or 888/320-7110, 7pm and 9:30pm Fri.-Tues., $114-130). The loose concept is a romantically conflicted woman's fevered dream (*rêve* in French). Some 80 perfectly sculpted specimens of human athleticism and beauty cavort, flip, swim, and show off their muscles around a huge aquatic stage. More than 2,000 guests fill the theater in the round, with seats all within 50 feet; those in the first couple of rows are in the "splash zone." Clowns and acrobats complete the package.

★ *LOVE*

For Beatles fans visiting Las Vegas, all you need is ***LOVE*** (Mirage, 3400 Las Vegas Blvd. S., 702/792-7777 or 866/983-4279, 7pm and 9:30pm Thurs.-Mon., $79-209). This Cirque du Soleil-produced trip down Penny Lane features dancers, aerial acrobats, and other performers interpreting the Fab Four's lyrics and recordings. With the breathtaking visual artistry of Cirque du Soleil and a custom soundscape using the original master tapes from Abbey Road Studios, John, Paul, George, and Ringo have never looked or sounded so good.

Million Dollar Quartet

A surprisingly strong story line augments the Sun Records catalog in ***Million Dollar Quartet*** (Harrah's, 3475 Las Vegas Blvd. S., 702/777-2782 or 855/234-7469, 5:30pm and 8pm Mon. and Thurs., 7pm Tues., Fri., and Sun., 6:30pm Wed., $71-97), a chronicle of the world's coolest jam session. The musical tells the events of December 4, 1956, when budding superstars Elvis Presley and Johnny Cash popped in to studio to say hello to Sun owner Sam Phillips. Carl Perkins happened to be recording at the time, and Phillips was augmenting the orchestration with an unknown pianist named Jerry Lee Lewis.

Mystère

At first glance, Cirque du Soleil production ***Mystère*** (TI, 3300 Las Vegas Blvd. S., 702/894-7722 or 800/392-1999, 7pm and 9:30pm Sat.-Wed., $76-149) is like a circus. But it also plays on other performance archetypes, including classical Greek theater, Kabuki, athletic prowess, and surrealism. The first Cirque show in Las Vegas, *Mystère* continues to dazzle audiences with its revelations of life's mysteries.

O

Bellagio likes to do everything bigger, better, and more extravagant, and ***O*** (Bellagio, 3600 Las Vegas Blvd. S., 702/693-7722 or 888/488-7111, 7:30pm and 10pm Wed.-Sun., $132-210) is no exception. This Vegas Cirque du Soleil incarnation involves a $90 million set, 80 artists, and a 1.5-million-gallon pool of water. The title comes from the French word for water, *eau*, pronounced like the letter *O* in English. The production involves both terrestrial and aquatic feats of human artistry, athleticism, and comedy. It truly must be seen to be believed.

Penn & Teller

The oddball comedy magicians **Penn & Teller** (Rio, 3700 W. Flamingo Rd.,

866/983-4279, 9pm Sat.-Wed., $91-104) have a way of making audiences feel special. Seemingly breaking the magicians' code, they reveal the preparation and sleight-of-hand involved in performing tricks. The hitch is that even when forewarned, observers still often can't catch on. And once they do, the verbose Penn and silent Teller add a wrinkle no one expects.

Britney Spears: *Piece of Me*

Rumors of the retirement of pop superstar **Britney Spears** (Planet Hollywood, 3667 Las Vegas Blvd. S., 866/919-7472, 9pm Wed. and Fri.-Sat., $77-344) were greatly exaggerated. In 2015 she extended her Vegas contract for two more years of her patented dance moves and choreography incorporating fly systems, fire, mirrors, and barely-there costumes. The diva's still got it, and she flaunts her toned frame while performing sexy and energetic renditions of her catchy hits and new material.

Showstoppers

Songs handpicked by Steve Wynn himself and a cast of 66 singers and dancers recreate climactic scenes from a dozen of Broadway's best in ***Showstoppers*** (Wynn, 3131 Las Vegas Blvd. S., 702/770-9966, 7:30pm Sat. and Mon.-Thurs., 8pm Fri., $100-150). Our favorite scenes are "Cell Block Tango" from *Chicago.*

Tony 'n Tina's Wedding

Feuding future in-laws, a drunken priest, a libidinous nun, and a whole flock of black sheep can't keep Tony and Tina from finding wedded bliss in ***Tony 'n Tina's Wedding*** (Bally's, 3645 Las Vegas Blvd. S., 702/777-2782 or 866/983-4279, 5:30pm Mon., Wed., and Fri.-Sat., $138-163). Or can they? You play the role of a wedding guest, sitting among the actors, where you learn where the family skeletons are hidden and the bodies are buried. Will you play the peacemaker, or stir up the jealousies and hidden agendas among the family members? Each show is

Million Dollar Quartet at Harrah's

different, based on the audience reaction. So keep your ears peeled; you just might pick up the juiciest gossip between the lasagna and the cannoli.

Tournament of Kings

Pound on the table with your goblet and let loose a hearty "huzzah!" to cheer your king to victory over the other nations' regents at the ***Tournament of Kings*** (Excalibur, 3580 Las Vegas Blvd. S., 702/597-7600 or 866/983-4279, 6pm Mon. and Fri., 6pm and 8:30pm Wed.-Thurs. and Sat.-Sun., $76). Each section of the equestrian theater rallies under separate banners as their hero participates in jousts, sword fights, riding contests, and lusty-maid flirting at this festival hosted by King Arthur and Merlin. A regal feast, served medieval style (that is, without utensils), starts with a tureen of dragon's blood (tomato soup). But just as the frivolity hits its climax, an evil lord appears to wreak havoc. Can the kings and Merlin's magic save the day? One of the best family shows in Las Vegas.

Zumanity

Cirque du Soleil seems to have succumbed to the titillation craze with the strange melding of sexuality, athleticism, and comedy that is ***Zumanity*** (New York New York, 3790 Las Vegas Blvd. S., 866/983-4279, 7pm and 9:30pm Tues.-Sat., $88-127). The cabaret-style show makes no pretense of story line, but instead takes audience members through a succession of sexual and topless fantasies—French maids, drag queens, schoolgirls, and light autoerotic S&M.

Showroom and Lounge Acts

Showrooms are another Las Vegas institution, with most hotels providing live entertainment—usually magic, comedy, or tributes to the big stars who played or are playing the big rooms and theaters under the same roofs.

The Vegas lounge act is the butt of a few jokes, but they offer some of the best entertainment values in town—a night's entertainment for the price of a few drinks and a small cover charge. Every hotel in Las Vegas worth its salt has a lounge, and the acts change often enough to make them hangouts for locals. These acts are listed in the free entertainment magazines and the *Las Vegas Review-Journal*'s helpful website, but unless you're familiar with the performers, it's the luck of the draw: They list only the entertainer's name, venue, and showtimes.

The Rat Pack Is Back

Relive the golden era when Frank, Dean, Sammy, and Joey ruled the Strip with ***The Rat Pack Is Back*** (Tuscany, 255 E. Flamingo Rd., 702/947-5981, 7:30pm Mon.-Sat., $60-66). Watch Sinatra try to make it through "Luck Be a Lady" amid the others' sophomoric antics. Frank plays right along, pretending to rule his crew with an iron fist, as the crew treats him with the mock deference the Chairman of the Board deserves.

All Shook Up: A Tribute to the King

A swivel-hipped, curled-lip journey through his career, ***All Shook Up*** (Planet Hollywood, 3667 Las Vegas Blvd. S., 866/932-1818, 6pm daily, $60-70) is the only all-Elvis impersonator show on the Strip. Both rotating impressionists bear a strong resemblance to the King, capturing not only his voice, but also his mannerisms, as they recount Elvis's hits from rock 'n' roll pioneer to movie idol. The intimate 300-seat showroom makes every seat a good one.

Mac King Comedy Magic Show

The quality of afternoon shows in Las Vegas is spotty at best, but **Mac King Comedy Magic Show** (Harrah's, 3475 Las Vegas Blvd. S., 866/983-4279, 1pm and 3pm Tues.-Sat., $32-42) fits the bill for talent and affordability. King's routine is clean both technically and content-wise. With a plaid suit, good manners, and a silly grin, he cuts a nerdy figure, but his tricks and banter are skewed enough to make even the most jaded teenager laugh.

Divas Las Vegas

Veteran female impersonator Frank Marino has been headlining on the Strip for 25 years, and he still looks good—with or without eye shadow and falsies. Marino stars as emcee Joan Rivers, leading fellow impersonators who lip-synch their way through cheeky renditions of tunes by Lady Gaga, Katy Perry, Cher, Madonna, and others in ***Divas Las Vegas*** (The Linq, 3535 Las Vegas Blvd. S., 702/777-2782 or 866/574-3851, 9:30pm Sat.-Thurs., $65-94).

Gordie Brown

A terrific song stylist in his own right, **Gordie Brown** (Golden Nugget, 129 E. Fremont St., 855/397-1191, 7:30pm Tues.-Thurs. and Sat-Sun., $38-76) is the thinking person's singing impressionist. Using his targets' peccadilloes as fodder for his song parodies, Brown pokes serious fun with a surgeon's precision. Props, mannerisms, and absurd vignettes incorporating several celebrity voices at once add to the madcap fun.

Comedy

Comedy in Las Vegas has undergone a shift in recent years. Nearly gone are the days of top-name comedians as resident headliners. Those gigs increasingly go to singers and production shows. In fact, Carrot Top, at the Luxor, is about the only long-term funnyman left. However, A-list funny females have a new stage, ***Lipshtick*** (Venetian, 3355 Las Vegas Blvd. S., 866/641-7469, 10pm Fri., 7:30pm Sat., $54-118), which hosts the likes of Lisa Lampanelli, Joy Behar, Wendy Williams, and Roseanne Barr. The other biggies—Daniel Tosh, Jay Leno, and Ron White, among others—still make regular appearances in the major showrooms on big Vegas weekends at venues such as **Aces of Comedy** (3400 Las Vegas Blvd. S., 702/791-7111, 10pm Fri., 8pm Sat., $55-100) at The Mirage. But most of the yuks nowadays come from the talented youngsters toiling in the comedy club trenches.

The journeymen and up-and-coming have half a dozen places to land gigs when they're in town. Among the best are **The Improv** (3475 Las Vegas Blvd. S., 800/214-9110, 8:30pm Sun. and Tues.-Thurs., 8:30pm and 10:30pm Fri.-Sat., $39-55) at Harrah's, **Brad Garrett's Comedy Club** (3799 Las Vegas Blvd. S., 866/740-7711, 8pm daily, $43-65, plus $20 when Garrett performs) at the MGM Grand, **L.A. Comedy Club** (Stratosphere, 2000 Las Vegas Blvd. S., 702/380-7777 or 800/998-6937, 8pm Sun.-Thurs., 8pm and 10pm Fri.-Sat., $30-50), and the **Laugh Factory** (Tropicana, 801 Las Vegas Blvd. S., 702/739-2222, 8:30pm and 10:30pm daily, $35-55).

Magic

Magic shows are nearly as ubiquitous as

comedy, with the more accomplished, such as Penn & Teller at Rio, Criss Angel at Luxor, and **David Copperfield** (MGM Grand, 3799 Las Vegas Blvd. S., 866/740-7711, 7pm and 9:30pm Sun.-Fri., 4pm, 7pm, and 9:30pm Sat., $121) playing long-term gigs in their own showrooms.

The best smaller-scale shows include ***Illusions* Starring Jan Rouven** (Tropicana, 3801 Las Vegas Blvd. S., 800/829-9034, 6pm Wed.-Mon., $76-124), with its death-defying illusions involving knives and water chambers; the kid-friendly **Nathan Burton Comedy Magic** (Planet Hollywood, 3663 Las Vegas Blvd. S., 702/866-0703 or 866/932-1818, 4pm Tues., Thurs., and Sat.-Sun., $20-60); and the budget-conscious **Laughternoon** (The D, 301 Fremont St., 702/388-2400, 4pm daily, $25), where Adam London turns his unhealthy obsession with duckies into comedy sleight-of-hand.

Live Music

With all the entertainment that casinos have to offer—and the budgets to bring in the best—there's some surprising talent lurking in the dives, meat markets, and neighborhood pubs around Las Vegas. Locals who don't want to deal with the hassles of a trip to the Strip and visitors whose musical tastes don't match the often-mainstream pop-rock-country genre of the resort lounges might find a gem or two by venturing away from the neon.

The newest, best, and most convenient venue for visitors, **Brooklyn Bowl** (The Linq Promenade, 3545 Las Vegas Blvd. S., Suite 22, 702/862-2695, 5pm-late daily) replicates its successful New York City formula with 32 lanes, comfortable couches, beer, and big-name groups sprinkled among the party band lineup. Elvis Costello, Wu-Tang Clan, Jane's Addiction, and the Psychedelic Furs are among the notables that have played the Brooklyn. Showtimes range from noon to midnight, often with several acts slated through the day.

With more than 20,000 square feet of space and a 2,500-square-foot dance floor, **Stoney's Rockin' Country** (6611 Las Vegas Blvd. S., Suite 160, 702/435-2855, 7pm-2am Tues. and Thurs.-Sat.) could almost *be* its own country. It is honky-tonk on a grand scale, with a mechanical bull and line-dancing lessons. Muddy Waters, Etta James, B. B. King, and even Mick Jagger have graced the stage at the reopened **Sand Dollar** (3355 Spring Mountain Rd., 702/485-5401), where blue-collar blues and smoky jazz rule. Bands start around 10pm weekdays, 7:30pm weekends. The people your mama warned you about hang out at the never-a-cover-charge **Double Down Saloon** (4640 Paradise Rd., 702/791-5775), drinking to excess and thrashing to the punk, ska, and psychobilly bands on stage.

The Arts

With so much plastic, neon, and reproduction statuary around town, it's easy to accuse Las Vegas of being a soulless, cultureless wasteland, and many have. But Las Vegans don't live in casino hotels and eat every meal in the buffet. We don't all make our living as dealers and cocktail waitresses. Las Vegas, like most others, is a city built of communities. So why shouldn't Las Vegas enjoy and foster the arts? As home to an urban university and many profitable businesses just itching to prove their corporate citizenry, southern Nevada's arts are as viable as any city of comparable size in the country.

The local performing arts are thriving, thanks to the 2012 construction of the **Smith Center for the Performing Arts** (361 Symphony Park Ave., 702/749-2012, www.thesmithcenter.com), a major cog in the revitalization of downtown, along with the development of 61 acres of former Union Pacific Railroad land the city has been working to turn into a pedestrian-friendly park and showplace. It is home to the Las Vegas Philharmonic, the Nevada Ballet Theatre, the Cabaret Jazz series, local and school performances and classes, and the best professional theatrical touring companies.

Classical Music

The **Las Vegas Philharmonic** (702/258-5438, http://lvphil.org) presents a full schedule of pops, masterworks, holiday, and youth performances at the Smith Center. The Phil also works with the local school district to develop music education classes.

Ballet

With a 36,000-square-foot facility, **Nevada Ballet Theatre** (702/243-2623, www.nevadaballet.org) trains hundreds of aspiring ballet, jazz, tap, hip hop and other dancers age 18 months through adults and provides practice and performance space for its professional company. The company presents classical and contemporary performances throughout the year at the Smith Center. The **Las Vegas Ballet Company** (702/240-3262, www.lasvegasballet.org) was founded by former Nevada Ballet Theatre principal dancers as a performance outlet for students at their ballet and modern dance academy.

Theater

Theater abounds in Las Vegas, with various troupes staging mainstream plays, musical comedy, and experimental productions. **Las Vegas Little Theatre** (3920 Schiff Dr., 702/362-7996, www.lvlt.org), the town's oldest community troupe, performs mostly mainstream shows in its Mainstage series and takes a few more chances on productions in its Black Box theater. **Cockroach Theatre Company** (1025 S. 1st St., 702/818-3422, www.cockroachtheare.com) stages mostly serious productions (think Camus, Albee, and Sartre) in the Art Square building in the Arts District. The bill at **Onyx Theatre** (953-16B E. Sahara Ave., 702/732-7225) is heavy on pop culture parody and satire.

The highest-quality acting and production values can be found at the **University of Nevada, Las Vegas, Performing Arts Center** (4505 S. Maryland Pkwy., 702/895-2787, http://pac.unlv.edu), comprising the Artemus Ham Concert Hall, the Judy Bayley Theater, and the Alta Ham Black Box Theater. The **Nevada Conservatory Theatre,** the university's troupe of advanced students and visiting professional actors, performs fall-spring. Shows run from the farcical to the poignant; a pair of Shakespeare comedies, *Water by the Spoonful*, and *Suburbia* highlight the 2015-2016 season.

Guests become witnesses, sleuths, and even suspects in **Marriage Can Be Murder** (The D, 301 Fremont St., 702/388-2111, 6:15pm daily, $66-99) interactive dinner theater. Soon the bodies start piling up between the one-liners and slapstick. Dig out your deerstalker and magnifying glass and help catch that killer.

Visual Art

Outside the downtown arts district and the fabulous art collections amassed and displayed by Steve Wynn and other casino magnates, the **Donna Beam Fine Art Gallery** (4505 S. Maryland Pkwy., 702/895-3893, www.unlv.edu/donnabeamgallery, 9am-5pm Mon.-Fri., noon-5pm Sat., free) at UNLV hosts exhibitions by nationally and internationally known painters, sculptors, designers, potters, and other visual artists. In addition to helping visitors enhance their critical thinking and aesthetic sensitivity, the exhibits teach UNLV students the skills needed in gallery management.

Rides and Games

Stratosphere Tower

Daredevils will delight in the vertigo-inducing thrill rides on the observation deck at the **Stratosphere Tower** (2000 Las Vegas Blvd. S., 702/383-5210, 10am-1am Sun.-Thurs., 10am-2am Fri.-Sat., $15-120). The newest ride, Sky Jump Las Vegas, invites the daring to plunge into space for a 15-second free fall. Angled guide wires keep jumpers on target and ease them to gentle landings. This skydive without a parachute costs $120. The other rides are 100-story-high variations on traditional thrill rides: The Big Shot is a sort of 15-person reverse bungee jump; X-Scream sends riders on a gentle (at first) roll off the edge, leaving them suspended over Las Vegas Boulevard; Insanity's giant arms swing over the edge, tilting to suspend riders nearly horizontally. These attractions are $25 each, including the elevator ride to the top of the tower. Multiple-ride packages and all-day passes are available but don't include the Sky Jump.

SlotZilla

For an up close and high-speed view of the Fremont Street Experience canopy and the iconic casino signs, take a zoom on **SlotZilla** (425 Fremont St., 702/678-5780 or 844/947-8342, noon-midnight Sun.-Thurs., noon-2am Fri.-Sat., $20-40), a 1,750-foot-long zip line that takes off from a the world's largest slot machine (only in Vegas, right?). Riders are launched horizontally, Superman-style, for a 40-mph slide. For the less adventurous, SlotZilla also operates a lower, slower, half-as-long version.

Adventuredome

Behind Circus Circus, the **Adventuredome Theme Park** (2880 Las Vegas Blvd. S., 702/794-3939, 10am-midnight daily summer, 10am-6pm Sun.-Thurs. and 10am-midnight Fri.-Sat. during the school year, over 48 inches tall $32, under 48 inches $18) houses two roller coasters, a 4-D motion simulator, laser tag, and vertigo-inducing amusements machines—all inside a pink plastic shell. The main teen and adult attractions are the coasters—El Loco and Canyon Blaster, the largest indoor coaster in the world with speeds up to 55 mph, which is pretty rough. The five-acre fun park can host birthday parties. The all-day passes are a definite bargain over individual ride prices, but carnival games, food vendors, and special rides and games not included in the pass give parents extra chances to spend money. It's not the Magic Kingdom, but it has rides to satisfy all ages and bravery levels. Besides, Las Vegas is supposed to be the *adult* Disneyland.

Wet 'n' Wild

With rides conjuring Las Vegas, the desert, and the Southwest, **Wet 'n' Wild** (7055 Fort Apache Rd., 702/979-1600, 10am-6pm Sun.-Thurs., 10am-10pm Fri.-Sat. May-Sept., $35, discounts for seniors, guests under 42 inches tall, and after 4pm) provides a welcome respite from the dry heat of southern Nevada. Challenge the Royal Flush Extreme, which whisks riders through a steep pipe before swirling them around a simulated porcelain commode and down the tube. The water park boasts 12 rides of varying terror levels, along with a Kiddie Cove. Guests must be over 42 inches tall to enjoy all the rides.

Cowabunga Bay

Wet 'n' Wild's competitor on the east side of town, **Cowabunga Bay** (900 Galleria Dr., Henderson, 702/850-9000, 11am-7pm daily Apr.-Sept., $37, under 48 inches $28) has nine waterslides, four pools, and the longest lazy river in the state.

Driving Experiences

Calling all gearheads! If you're ready to take the wheel of a 600-hp stock car, check out the **Richard Petty Driving Experience** (Las Vegas Motor Speedway, 7000 Las Vegas Blvd. N., 800/237-3889, days and times vary, $109-3,200). The "Rookie Experience" ($499) lets NASCAR wannabes put the stock car through its paces for eight laps around the 1.5-mile tri-oval after extensive in-car and on-track safety training. Participants also receive a lap-by-lap breakdown of their run, transportation to and from the Strip, and a tour of the Driving Experience Race Shop. Even more intense—and more expensive—experiences, with more laps and more in-depth instruction, are available. To feel the thrill without the responsibility, opt for the three-lap ride-along ($109) in a two-seat stock car with a professional driver at the wheel.

Exotics Racing (6925 Speedway Blvd., Ste. C-105, 702/405-7223, 7am-8pm Mon.-Fri., 8am-7pm Sat.-Sun., $300-500 for five laps) and **Dream Racing** (7000 Las Vegas Blvd. N., 702/605-3000, $300-4,500) offer similar pedal-to-the-metal thrills in Porsches, Ferraris, Lamborghinis, and more. Both Petty and Exotics offer add-ons such as videos of your drive, passenger rates, and ride-alongs with professional drivers.

Sports

Golf

With its climate, endless sunshine, and vacation destination status, it's no wonder that Las Vegas is home to more than 40 golf courses. Virtually all are eminently playable and fair, although the dry heat makes the greens fast and the city's valley location can make for some havoc-wreaking winds in the spring. Las Vegas courses, especially in recent years, have removed extraneous water-loving landscaping, opting for xeriscape and desert landscape, irrigating the fairways and greens with reclaimed water. Greens fees and amenities range from affordable municipal-type courses to some of the most exclusive country clubs anywhere. The following is a selective list in each budget category.

The only course open to the public on the Strip is **Bali Hai** (5160 Las Vegas Blvd. S., 888/427-6678, $150-325), next to Mandalay Bay on the south end of casino row. The South Pacific theme includes lots of lush green tropical foliage, deep azure ponds, and black volcanic outcroppings. A handful of long par-4s are fully capable of making a disaster of your scorecard even before you reach the par-3 sphincter-clenching 16th. Not only does it play to an island green, it comes with a built-in gallery where you can enjoy your discomfort while dining on Bali Hai's restaurant patio.

There's plenty of water to contend with at **Siena Golf Club** (10575 Siena Monte Ave., 702/341-9200 or 888/689-6469, $79-139). Six small lakes, deep fairway bunkers, and desert scrub provide significant challenges off the tee, but five sets of tee boxes even things out for shorter hitters. The large, flat-ish greens are fair and readable. The first Las Vegas course to adopt an ecofriendly xeriscape design, **Painted Desert** (5555 Painted Mirage Rd., 702/645-2570, $20-99) uses cacti, mesquite, and other desert plants to separate its links-style fairways. The 6,323-yard, par-72 course isn't especially challenging, especially if you're straight off the tee, making it a good choice for getting back to the fundamentals. Video tips from the 18-time major winner himself play on an in-cart screen at **Bear's Best** (11111 W. Flamingo Rd., 702/804-8500, $75-255) a collection of Nicklaus's favorite holes from courses he designed: Castle Pines, PGA West, and more.

Las Vegas Motor Speedway

Home to NASCAR's Sprint Cup and Boyd Gaming 300 Nationwide Series race, the **Las Vegas Motor Speedway** (7000 Las Vegas Blvd. N., 800/644-4444) is a racing omniplex. In addition to the superspeedway, a 1.5-mile tri-oval for NASCAR races, the site also brings in dragsters to its quarter-mile strip; modifieds, late models, bandoleros, legends, bombers, and more to its paved oval; and off-roaders to its half-mile clay oval.

NASCAR Weekend, typically in early March, hosts the **Kobalt 400 Sprint Cup** and the **Boyd Gaming 300 Xfinity Series.** The speedway underwent a multimillion-dollar renovation project between NASCAR Weekends in 2006 and 2007, resulting in an unprecedented interactive fan experience known as the Neon Garage. Located in the speedway's infield, Neon Garage has unique and gourmet concession stands, live entertainment, and the winner's circle. Fans can get up close or watch drivers and crews from bird's-eye perches.

IndyCar World Racing discontinued its relationship with LVMS following the horrific crash in 2011 that claimed the life of driver Dan Wheldon.

Boxing and Mixed Martial Arts

Despite many promoters opting for cheaper venues, Las Vegas retains the title as heavyweight boxing champion of the world. Nevada's legalized sports betting, its history, and the facilities at the MGM Grand Garden and Mandalay Bay Events Center make it a natural for the biggest matches.

Many of the casinos that once held mid-level bouts have opted for more lucrative events, meaning fewer chances to see up-and-comers working their way up the ladder for a shot at a minor alphabet-soup belt. Still, fight fans can find a card pretty much every month from March to October at either the Hard Rock, Sam's Town, Sunset Station, Palms, or other midsize arena or showroom. The fighters are hungry, the matches are entertaining, and the cost is low, with tickets priced $25-100.

For the megafights, however, expect to dole out big bucks to get inside the premier venues. The "cheap" seats at MGM and Mandalay Bay often cost a car payment and require the Hubble telescope to see any action. Ringside seats require a mortgage payment. Check the venues' websites for tickets.

Mixed martial arts continues to grow in popularity, with MGM and Mandalay Bay hosting UFC title fights about every other month. For those who prefer sanctioned bar fights, Big Knockout Boxing made its debut in Vegas in 2014. This take on the fight game takes place in a 17-foot-diameter circle; no ropes, no corners, no place to hide. Five or seven two-minute rounds leave precious little time for dancing, grabbing, and point scoring, making the haymaker punch the star of the show.

Accommodations

Choosing Accommodations

Casinos offer both the most opulent hotel accommodations in town and the widest variety of options. See the *Casinos* section for information on these rooms.

If you opt not to stay in a casino, you'll still find plenty of options. Las Vegas boasts more than 100 hotels and 200 motels, but sometimes that makes it harder, not easier, to choose. Keep in mind that most accommodations either sell out or nearly sell out every weekend of the year. Long weekends and holidays, especially New Year's Eve, Valentine's Day, Memorial Day, Fourth of July, Labor Day, and Thanksgiving, along with international holidays such as Cinco de Mayo, Mexican Independence Day, and Chinese New Year, are sold out weeks in advance. Special events such as concerts, title fights, the Super Bowl, the Final Four, NASCAR Weekend, and the National Finals Rodeo are sold out months in advance. Reservations are made for the biggest conventions (Consumer Electronics, Men's Apparel, and so on) a year ahead of time.

There are some minor quiet times, such as the three weeks before Christmas and July-August, when the mercury doesn't drop below 100°F. If you're just coming for the weekend, keep in mind that most of the major hotels don't even let you check in on a Saturday night. You can stay Friday and Saturday, but not Saturday alone. It may be easier to find a room Sunday-Thursday, when there aren't any large conventions or sporting events. Almost all the room packages and deep discounts are only available on these days.

Hotels

Center Strip

With a name like **Trump** (2000 Fashion Show Dr., 702/892-0000, $120-220), you know that no whim will go unfulfilled. Standard rooms open onto an Italian marble entryway leading to floor-to-ceiling windows with the requisite magnificent views. In-room amenities include dual sinks with Italian marble countertops, and 32-inch flat-screen TVs, and luxury appliances. Feather comforters and Italian linens make for heavenly restfulness. **DJT** (6:30am-10pm daily, $30-45) is a classy steakhouse, but the food is more style than substance. The hip **H2(EAU)** (11am-5pm daily, depending on the weather, $15-20) poolside, however, dishes up some tasty chicken Katsu sliders. **The Spa at Trump** offers unique packages such as the Las Vegas Oxygenating Facial, to give your pores a breath of fresh air.

One of the newest landmarks on the Las Vegas skyline, **Platinum** (211 E. Flamingo Rd., 702/365-5000 or 877/211-9211, $113-194) treats both guests and the environment with kid gloves. The resort uses the latest technology to reduce its carbon footprint through such measures as low-energy lighting throughout, eco-friendly room thermostats, and motion sensors to turn lights off when restrooms are unoccupied. Suites are an expansive 950 square feet of muted designer furnishings and accents, and they include all modern conveniences, such as high-speed Internet, high-fidelity sound systems, full kitchens, and oversize tubs. **Kil@watt** (6am-2pm daily, $10-15) with sleek silver decor accented with dark woods, is a feast for the eyes and the palate for breakfast and lunch.

Lower Strip

Feel like royalty at the ★ **Mandarin Oriental Las Vegas** (3752 Las Vegas Blvd. S., 702/590-8888, www.mandarinoriental.com/lasvegas, $295-399), which looks down on the bright lights of the Strip from a peaceful remove. A master control panel in each of the modern rooms sets the atmosphere to your liking, controlling the lights, temperature, window curtains, and more. Once everything is set, sink into a warm bath and watch TV on the flat screen embedded in the bath mirror. Another impressive feature is the valet closet, which allows hotel staff to deliver items to your room without entering your unit. The **Mandarin Bar** (888/881-9367, 4pm-1am Mon.-Thurs., 4pm-2am Fri.-Sat., 4pm-11pm Sun.) on the 23rd floor offers stunning views of the city skyline and several signature martinis. And it's all environmentally friendly, or at least LEED-certified.

Offering sophisticated accommodations and amenities without the hubbub of a rowdy casino, the **Renaissance** (3400 Paradise Rd., 702/784-5700, $129-179) has big, bright, airy standard guest rooms that come complete with triple-sheeted 300-thread-count Egyptian cotton beds with down comforters and duvets, walk-in showers, full tubs, 42-inch flat-panel TVs, a business center, and high-speed Internet. Upper-floor guest rooms overlook the Wynn golf course. The pool and whirlpool are outside, and the concierge can score show tickets and tee times. Onyx- and burgundy-clad **Envy Steakhouse** (6:30am-11am and 5pm-10pm Mon.-Sat., $35-60) has a few poultry and seafood entrées, but the Angus beef gets top billing.

Every guest room is a suite at the **Signature** (145 E. Harmon Ave., 702/797-6000 or 877/612-2121, $140-320) at MGM Grand. Even the junior suite is a roomy 550 square feet and includes a standard king bed, kitchenette, and spa tub. Most of the 1,728 smoke-free guest rooms in the gleaming 40-story tower include private balconies with Strip views, and guests have access to the complimentary 24-hour fitness center, three outdoor pools, a business center, and free wireless Internet throughout the hotel. A gourmet deli and acclaimed room service satisfy noshing needs, and **The Lounge** provides a quiet, intimate spot in soothing blues for discussing business or pleasure over drinks.

The condominium suites at **Desert Rose** (5051 Duke Ellington Way, 702/739-7000 or 888/732-8099, $120-280) are loaded, with new appliances and granite countertops in the kitchen as well as private balconies or patios outside. One-bedroom suites are quite large, at 650 square feet, and sleep four comfortably. Rates vary widely, but depending on your needs and travel dates, you might find a deal within walking distance of several casinos and the monorail.

Although it includes a full-service casino and is just steps from the Strip, the draw of the **Tuscany** (255 E. Flamingo Rd., 702/893-8933 or 877/887-2264, $90-180) is the relaxed atmosphere, from its restaurants and lounges to its lagoon pool. The sprawling 27-acre site with footpaths and impeccable landscaping belies its proximity to the rush-rush of the Strip one block west. Dining here is more low-key than at many of Tuscany's neighbors. Although there is a semiformal restaurant, **Tuscany Gardens** (5pm-10pm daily, $18-35), the casual **Cantina** (11am-9:30pm Mon.-Thurs., 11am-midnight Fri., 10am-midnight Sat., 10am-9:30pm Sun., $10-20) and **Marilyn's Café** (24 hours daily, $8-15) are more in keeping with the resort's métier. That's not to say Tuscany is strictly the purview of fuddy-duddies; the 50,000-square-foot casino has all the games you expect in Las Vegas, and there's entertainment Tuesday-Saturday in the **Piazza Lounge.** All suites, the Tuscany's guest rooms boast more than 650 square feet and come with galley kitchens, coffeemakers, 25-inch TVs, and mini fridges.

Motels

The Strip

Several good-value motels are located on Las Vegas Boulevard South between the Stratosphere and Riviera Boulevard; these places are also good to try for weekly rooms with kitchenettes. When the temperature isn't in the triple digits, they're also within walking distance to the SLS, Circus Circus, and the Adventuredome. None are anything special, but **El Mirador** (2310 Las Vegas Blvd. S., 702/384-6570, $50-60 d) is clean, if outdated.

Motels along the Lower Strip, from Bally's below Flamingo Avenue all the way out to the Mandalay Bay at the far south end of the Strip, are well placed to visit all the new big-brand casino resorts but have prices that match the cheaper places between the Strip and downtown. The independent motels are hit-and-miss. You're better off sticking with established brands like **Travelodge Las Vegas Center Strip** (3735 Las Vegas Blvd. S., 702/736-3443, $59-99), which gets a top rating for its reasonable prices; location near the MGM Grand, Luxor, and Mandalay Bay; and little extras like free continental breakfast, newspapers, and a heated swimming pool. The supersize **Super 8** (4250 Koval Ln., 702/794-0888, $45-119), just east of Bally's and Paris, is the chain's largest in the world. It offers a heated pool but no other resort amenities; on the other hand, it doesn't charge resort fees. There's free Internet access but not much of a budget for decor in the guest rooms or common areas. Stop at Ellis Island Casino & Brewery next door for ribs and microbrews.

Another group of motels clings to the south side of the convention center on Paradise and Desert Inn Roads as well as the west side between Paradise Road and the Strip on Convention Center Drive. If you're attending a convention and plan well in advance, you can reserve a very reasonable and livable room at any of several motels within a five-minute walk of the convention floor. Most of them have plenty of weekly rooms with kitchenettes, which can save you a bundle. It's a joy to be able to leave the convention floor and walk over to your room and back again if necessary—the shuttle buses to the far-flung hotels are very often crowded, slow, and inconvenient. Even if you're not attending a convention, this is a good part of town to stay in, off the main drag but in the middle of everything. You won't find whirlpool tubs, white-beach pools, or Egyptian cotton at **Rodeway Inn** (220 Convention Center Dr., 702/735-4151, $45-60), but you will find everything the budget traveler could ask for: hot showers, clean beds, and a refreshing pool. You'll also get extras such as a free continental breakfast and Wi-Fi. **Royal Resort** (99 Convention Center Dr., 702/735-6117 or 800/634-6118, $69-229) is part timeshare, part hotel, so its amenities are top-notch. Its outdoor pool area nestles against tropical landscaping, private cabanas, and a hot tub.

Downtown

Glitter Gulch fills Fremont Street from South Main Street to South 4th Street, but beyond that and on side streets, bargain-basement motels are numerous. Dozens of places are bunched together in three main groupings. It's not the best part of town, but it's certainly not the worst, and security is usually seen to by the management (but check with them to make sure). The motels along East Fremont Street and Las Vegas Boulevard North are the least expensive. Motels between downtown and the Strip on Las Vegas Boulevard South are slightly more expensive and in a slightly better neighborhood.

East Fremont Street has plenty of motels, sometimes one right next to another or separated by car dealerships and bars. It's a few minutes' drive to the downtown casinos and an excursion to the Strip. This is also RV country, with RV parks lining the highway past motel row and the big parking lots at the casinos. And with so many possibilities, it's a good stretch to cruise if you don't have reservations and most "No Vacancy" signs are lit.

Two reliable standards in this neighborhood, with guest rooms under $50, are **City Center Motel** (700 Fremont St., 702/382-4766, $59-89) and **Downtowner** (129 N. 8th St., 702/384-1441, $43-82).

Las Vegas Boulevard North from Fremont Street to East Bonanza Road, along with North Main Street and the north-numbered streets from 6th to 13th, are also packed with motels one after the other. Stay on the lighted streets. It might be a little unnerving to deal with the front desk person through bars, but downtown is very handy if that's where you want to spend your time, and these rooms can be amazingly reasonable if a room is not where you want to spend your money. **Sterling Gardens** (1808 Fremont St., 702/457-1929, $49-89) offers the basics with double rooms with two beds.

The motels on Las Vegas Boulevard South between downtown and the north end of the Strip at Sahara Avenue have the most convenient location if you like to float between downtown and the Strip or if you're getting married in one of the wedding chapels that line this stretch of the boulevard. It's also brighter and busier, and right on the main bus routes. Most of these motels also offer weekly room rates with or without kitchenettes. The **High Hat** (1300 Las Vegas Blvd. S., 702/382-8080, $50-100 d) has been around for several years.

Hostels

It's hard to beat these places for budget accommodations. They offer rock-bottom prices for no-frills "rack rooms," singles, and doubles. Downtown choices include **Hostel Cat** (1236 Las Vegas Blvd. S., 702/380-6902, $18-40). **Las Vegas Hostel** (1322 Fremont St., 702/385-1150 or 800/550-8958, $24-45) has a swimming pool and a hot tub. The rates include a pancake breakfast, pool and foosball, and wireless Internet connections. The hostel also arranges trips to the Strip and visits to the Grand Canyon and other outdoorsy attractions.

Reserved only for international and student travelers (ID required), the dorms at **Sin City Hostel** (1208 Las Vegas Blvd. S., 702/868-0222, $19-23) fit the starving student's budget and include breakfast. Located on the Strip, the hostel features a barbecue pit, a basketball court, and Wi-Fi.

RV Parking

Casino RV Parking

A number of casinos have attached RV parks. Other casinos allow RVs to park overnight in their parking lots but have no facilities.

RV Park at Circus Circus (500 Circus Circus Dr., 702/794-3757 or 800/444-2472, $39-51) is a prime spot for RVers, especially those with kids, who want to be right in the thick of things but also want to take advantage of very good facilities. The big park is all paved, with a few grassy islands and shade trees; the convenience store is open daily 24 hours. Ten minutes spent learning where the Industrial Road back entrance is will save hours of sitting in traffic on the Strip. The park has 399 spaces. All have full hookups with 20-, 30-, and 50-amp power, and 280 of the spaces are pull-through. Wheelchair-accessible restrooms have flush toilets and hot showers, and there's also a laundry, a game room, a fenced playground, a heated swimming pool, a children's pool, a spa, a sauna, and groceries.

Las Vegas KOA at Sam's Town (5225 Boulder Hwy., 702/454-8055 or 800/562-7270, $38-45) has 500 spaces for motor homes, all with full hookups and 20-, 30-, and 50-amp power. It's mostly a paved parking lot with spacious sites, a heated pool, and a spa; the rec hall has a pool table and a kitchen. And, of course, it's near the bowling, dining, and movie theater in the casino.

Arizona Charlie's East (4445 Boulder Hwy., 800/970-7280, $32) has 239 spaces and weekly rates.

RV Parks

The best of the RV parks are more expensive than the casino RV parks, but the amenities—especially the atmosphere, views, and landscaping—are worth the price.

The **Hitchin' Post** (3640 Las Vegas Blvd. N., 702/644-1043 or 888/433-8402, $35-42) offers a pool, 24-hour saloon, a new dog wash, free cable TV, and Wi-Fi at its 196 spaces. The northern Las Vegas location is perhaps not the most desirable, but security is never a problem at the park. It's clean, and the on-site restaurant-bar rustles up a nice steak.

Oasis RV Resort (2711 W. Windmill Ln., 800/566-4707, $46-80) is directly across I-15 from the Silverton Casino. Take exit 33 for Blue Diamond Road, 3 miles south of Russell Road, then go east to Las Vegas Boulevard South. Turn right and drive one block to West Windmill, then turn right into the park. Opened in 1996, Oasis has 936 spaces, and huge date palms usher you from the park entrance to the cavernous 24,000-square-foot clubhouse. Each space is wide enough for a car and motor home and comes with a picnic table and patio. The foliage is plentiful and flanks an 18-hole putting course along with family and adult swimming pools. The resort features a full calendar of poker tournaments, movies, karaoke, and bar and restaurant specials. Wheelchair-accessible restrooms have flush toilets and hot showers; there is also a laundry, a grocery store, an exercise room, and an arcade.

Food

Las Vegas buffets have evolved from little better than fast food to lavish spreads of worldwide cuisine complete with fresh salads, comforting soups, and decadent desserts. The exclusive resorts on the Strip have developed their buffets into gourmet presentations, often including delicacies such as crab legs, crème brûlée, and even caviar. Others, especially the locals' casinos and those downtown that cater to more down-to-earth tastes, remain low-cost belly-filling options for intense gamblers and budget-conscious families. The typical buffet breakfast presents the usual fruits, juices, croissants, steam-table scrambled eggs, sausages, potatoes, and pastries. Lunch is salads and chicken, pizza, spaghetti, tacos, and more. Dinner is salads, steam-table vegetables, and potatoes with several varieties of meat, including a carving table with prime rib, turkey, and pork.

Buffets are still a big part of the Las Vegas vacation aura, but when the town's swank and swagger came back in the 1990s, it brought sophisticated dining with it. Las Vegas has come a long way from the coffee-and-sandwich shop shoved in a casino corner so players could recharge quickly and rush back to reclaim their slot machine.

Most major hotels have 24-hour coffee shops, a steak house, and a buffet along with a couple of international restaurants. Non-casino restaurants around town are also proliferating quickly. Best of all, menu prices, like room rates, are consistently less expensive in Las Vegas than in any other major city in the country.

Upper Strip

Breakfast

It's all about hen fruit at ★ **The Egg & I** (4533 W. Sahara Ave., 702/364-9686, daily 6am-3pm, $10-20). They serve other breakfast fare as well, of course—the banana muffins and stuffed French toast are notable—but if you don't order an omelet, you're just being stubborn. It has huge portions, fair prices, and on-top-of-it service. Go!

The retro-deco gaudiness of the neon decor and bachelor pad-esque sunken fire pit may not do wonders for a Vegas-sized headache, but the tostada omelet at the **Peppermill Restaurant & Fireside Lounge** (2985 Las Vegas Blvd. S., 702/735-7635, daily 24 hours, $12-20) will give it what-for. For a little less zest, try the French toast ambrosia.

French and Continental

The pink accents at **Pamplemousse** (400 E. Sahara Ave., 702/733-2066, daily 5pm-10pm, $35-56) hint at the name's meaning (grapefruit) and set the stage for cuisine so fresh that the menu changes daily. If you eschew the prix fixe menu and order à la carte, ask about prices to avoid surprises. Specialties include leg and breast of duck in cranberry-raspberry sauce and a terrific escargot appetizer with butter, shallots, and red wine sauce. Save room for chocolate soufflé.

Italian

Wall frescoes put you on an Italian thoroughfare as you dine on authentic cuisine at **Fellini's** (Stratosphere, 2000 Las Vegas Blvd. S., 702/383-4859, 5pm-11pm Sun.-Thurs., 5pm-midnight Fri.-Sat., $25-45). Each smallish dining room has a different fresco. The food is more the American idea of classic Italian than authentic, but only food snobs will find anything to complain about.

Steak

The perfectly cooked steaks and attentive service that once attracted Frank Sinatra, Nat "King" Cole, Natalie Wood, and Elvis are still trademarks at **Golden Steer** (308 W. Sahara Ave., 702/384-4470, 4:30pm-10:30pm daily, $35-50). A gold-rush motif and 1960s swankiness still abide here, along with classics like crab cakes, big hunks of beef, and Caesar salad prepared tableside.

Vegas Views

The 360-seat, 360-degree **Top of the World** (Stratosphere, 2000 Las Vegas Blvd. S., 702/380-7711 or 800/998-6937, 11am-11pm daily, $50-80), on the 106th floor of Stratosphere Tower more than 800 feet above the Strip, makes a complete revolution once every 80 minutes, giving you the full city panorama during dinner. The view of Vegas defies description, and the food is a recommendable complement. Order the seafood fettuccine or surf-and-turf gnocchi with lobster and beef short rib. It's even money that you will witness a marriage proposal during your meal.

Center Strip

Asian

You may pay for the setting as much as for the food at **Fin** (The Mirage, 3400 Las Vegas Blvd. S., 866/339-4566, 5pm-10pm Thurs.-Mon., $30-50). But why not? Sometimes the atmosphere is worth it, especially when you're trying to make an impression on your mate or potential significant other. The metallic-ball curtains evoke a rainstorm in a Chinese garden and set just the right romantic but noncloying mood. Still, we have to agree that while the prices are not outrageous, the food is not gourmet quality either; you can probably find more yum for your yuan elsewhere.

Better value can be had at **Tao** (Venetian, 3377 Las Vegas Blvd. S., 702/388-8338, 5pm-midnight Sun.-Wed., 5pm-1am Thurs.-Sat., $30-40), where pan-Asian dishes—the roasted Thai Buddha chicken is our pick—and an extensive sake selection are served in decor that is a trip through Asian history, from the Silk Road to Eastern spiritualism, including imperial koi ponds, bathing beauties, and feng shui aesthetics.

At **Wing Lei** (Wynn, 3131 Las Vegas Blvd. S., 702/770-3388, 5:30pm-9:30pm Sun.-Thurs., 5:30pm-10pm Fri.-Sat., $40-65), French colonialism comes through in Chef Ming Yu's Shanghai style.

Breakfast

Any meal is a treat at **Tableau** (Wynn, 3131 Las Vegas Blvd. S., 702/770-3330, 7am-2:30pm daily, $17-25), but the duck hash and eggs and the brown butter apple pancakes in the garden atrium make breakfast the most important meal of the day at Wynn.

Buffets

The best buffet for under $85 in Las Vegas is, without a doubt, the **Village Seafood Buffet** (Rio, 3700 W. Flamingo Rd., 702/777-7943, 3:30pm-9:30pm daily, adults $49, age 4-10 $25). Vibrant maritime sculptures, watery blue-and-white decor, a cool sound system, and video screens put patrons in the mood, and garlic butter lobster tails are the main attraction. Other seafood preparations include grilled scallops, shrimp, mussels, and calamari with assorted vegetables and sauces, snow crab legs, oysters on the half shell, peel-and-eat shrimp, and steamed clams. There's even hand-carved prime rib, ham, chicken, and pasta for the nonfan of seafood. If you have room, the gelato bar serves 20 varieties. Service is surprisingly attentive for a buffet.

Many people also give the Rio top marks as the best "traditional" buffet near the Center Strip, but we think it has been overtaken by **The Buffet at TI** (TI, 3300 Las Vegas Blvd. S., 702/894-7355, 7am-10pm Mon.-Fri., breakfast $22, lunch $24, dinner $28, weekend brunch $27, weekend seafood dinner $32). The offerings are mostly standard—barbecue ribs, pizza, Chinese—but the ingredients are the freshest we've found on a buffet, and the few nontraditional buffet selections (especially the sushi and made-to-order pasta) make the higher-than-average price worthwhile.

French and Continental

The vanilla mousse-colored banquettes and chocolate swirl of the dark wood grain tables at **Payard Patisserie & Bistro** (Caesars Palace, 3570 Las Vegas Blvd. S., 702/731-7292 or 866/462-5982, 6:30am-2:30pm Sun.-Thurs., 24 hours Fri.-Sat, $18-30, pastry counter 7am-10pm Sun.-Thurs., 24 hours Fri.-Sat.) evoke the delightful French pastries for which François Payard is famous. Indeed, the bakery takes up most of the restaurant, tantalizing visitors with cakes, tarts, and petit fours. But the restaurant stands on its own, with the quiches and panini taking best in show.

Italian

It's no surprise that a casino named after the most romantic of Italian cities would be home to one of the best Italian restaurants around. **Canaletto** (Venetian, 3355 Las Vegas Blvd. S., 702/733-0070, 11am-11pm Sun.-Thurs., 11am-midnight Fri.-Sat., $15-25) focuses on Venetian cuisine. The kitchen staff performs around the grill and rotisserie—a demonstration kitchen—creating sumptuously authentic dishes. The spicy salsiccia picante thin-crust pizza gets our vote.

You can almost picture Old Blue Eyes himself between shows, twirling linguini and holding court at **Sinatra** (Encore, 3131 Las Vegas Blvd. S., 702/770-5320 or 888/352-3463, 5:30pm-10:30pm daily, $40-70). The Chairman's voice wafts through the speakers, and his iconic photos and awards decorate the walls while you tuck into classic Italian food tinged with Chef Theo Schoenegger's special touches.

Likewise, the "Old Vegas" vibe is thick at **Piero's** (355 Convention Center Dr., 702/369-2305, 5pm-10pm daily, $30-50). As enchanting as the exotic animal lithographs on the walls, Piero's has attracted celebrities ranging from Mick Jagger to Michael Jordan. The decor, colorful owner Freddie Glusman, and low-key sophistication give the place a vaguely speakeasy feel.

Seafood

Submerge yourself in the cool, fluid, atmosphere at **AquaKnox** (Venetian, 3355 Las Vegas Blvd. S., 702/414-3772, noon-3pm and 5:30pm-11pm Sun.-Thurs., noon-3pm and 5:30pm-10pm Fri.-Sat., $40-70). Its cobalt and cerulean tableware and design elements suggest a sea-sprayed embarcadero. The fish soup is the signature entrée, but the crab dishes are the way to go. If you can't bring yourself to order the crab-stuffed lobster, at least treat yourself to the crab cake appetizer.

Although it's named for the Brazilian beach paradise, **Búzio's** (Rio, 3700 W. Flamingo Rd., 702/777-7697, 5pm-10pm daily, $30-45) serves its fish American and South American style. Hawaiian ahi, Maine lobster, Alaskan crab, and Chilean sea bass are always fresh and presented in perfect complement with tomato reductions, soy emulsions, and butter sauces.

Shrimp Cocktail

Don't let the presentation—lettuce leaf, scoop of bay shrimp, dollop of cocktail sauce, and a lemon wedge in a plastic cup—turn you off. The shrimp cocktail served at **Haute Doggery** (The Linq, 3545 Las Vegas Blvd. S., Ste. L-30, 702/430-4435, 10am-midnight Sun.-Thurs., 10am-2am Fri.-Sat., $1) is heaven.

Vegas Views

West Coast fixture **Sushi Roku** (Caesars Palace, 3500 Las Vegas Blvd. S., 702/733-7373, 7am-2:30pm and 5:30pm-10:30pm Sun.-Thurs., 7am-2:30pm and 5:30pm-10:30pm Fri.-Sat., $30-50) has terrific views both inside and out. Within the restaurant is a veritable Zen garden, bamboo, and shadowy table alcoves. Outside are unparalleled views up and down the Strip. Linq's High Roller across the street makes sharp contrast to the Japanese fantasy feel.

More Strip views await at **VooDoo Steakhouse** (Rio, 3700 W. Flamingo Rd., 702/777-7923, 5pm-11pm daily, $40-60) along with steaks with a N'awlins creole and Cajun touch. Getting to the restaurant and the lounge requires a mini thrill ride to the top of the Rio tower in the glass elevator. The Rio contends that the restaurant is on the 51st floor and the lounge is on the 52nd floor, but they're really on the 41st and 42nd floors, respectively—Rio management dropped floors 40-49 as the number 4 has an ominous connotation in Chinese culture. Whatever floors they're on, the VooDoo double-decker provides a great view of the Strip. The food and drink are expensive and tame, but the fun is in the overlook, especially if you eat or drink outside on the decks.

Lower Strip

Asian

Lighting and decor suggesting screens and lanterns set the stage for a journey into the depths of Chinese cuisine at **Blossom** (Aria, 3735 Las Vegas Blvd. S., 877/230-2742, 5:30pm-10:30pm daily, $50-80). Much of the menu is exotic, bold, and playful, but there are plenty of selections tempered toward Western palates. Adventuresome diners receive the full benefit of Chef Chi Kwun Choi's creative mastery—go for the veal cheek or Jian Bo beef. The sweet-and-sour crisp-fried flounder is a signature dish for the more cautious. Chinese art in a Hong Kong bistro setting with fountain and lake views make **Jasmine** (Bellagio, 3600 Las Vegas Blvd. S., 5:30pm-10pm daily, $30-60) one of the most visually striking Chinese restaurants in town. The food is classic European-influenced Cantonese.

Breakfast

The **Veranda** (Four Seasons, 3960 Las Vegas Blvd. S., 702/632-5000, 6:30am-10pm Mon.-Fri., 7am-10pm Sat.-Sun., $30-45) transforms itself from a light, airy, indoor-outdoor breakfast and lunch nook into a late dinner spot oozing with Mediterranean ambience and a check total worthy of a Four Seasons restaurant. As you might expect from the name, dining on the terrace is a favorite among well-to-do locals, especially for brunch on spring and fall weekends. Tiramisu French toast? Yes, please!

Buffets

If you think "Las Vegas buffet" means a call to the trough of mediocre cheap prices and get-what-you-pay-for food quality, Bally's would like to invite you and your credit card to the **Sterling Brunch** (3645 Las Vegas Blvd. S., 702/967-7258, 9:30am-1:30pm Sun., $90). That's right, $90 for one meal, per person, and you have to fetch your own vittles. But the verdict is almost unanimous: It's worth it, especially if you load up on the grilled lobster, filet mignon, caviar, sushi, Perrier-Jouet champagne, and other high-dollar offerings. Leave the omelets and salads for IHOP; a plate of sinful tarts and praline nougatine pecan crepes (don't forget the vanilla sauce) is a must, along with just one more glass of champagne.

On the other hand, for the price of that one brunch at Bally's, you can eat for two days at the **Roundtable Buffet** (Excalibur, 3580 Las Vegas Blvd. S., 7am-10pm daily, breakfast $18, lunch $19, dinner $24-27, ages 5-11 get $7 off). The Excalibur started the trend of the all-day-long buffet, and the hotel sells all-day wristbands for $36-40. If that's not enough gluttony for you, the wristband also serves as a line pass. The **French Market Buffet** (The Orleans, 4500 W. Tropicana Ave., 702/365-7111, 8am-9pm daily, breakfast $10, lunch $12, dinner $19-26, Sun. brunch $22, age 16 and under get $5 off; children under 43 inches are free) has a similar all-day deal for $28 (Fri.-Sun. $31).

French and Continental

The steaks and seafood at ★ **Mon Ami Gabi** (Paris, 3655 Las Vegas Blvd. S., 702/944-4224, 7am-11pm Sun.-Thurs., 7am-midnight Fri.-Sat., $35-50) are comparable to those at any fine Strip establishment—at about half the price. It's a bistro, so you know the crepes and other lunch specials are terrific, but you're better off coming for dinner. Try the baked goat cheese appetizer.

Award-winning chef Andre Rochat lays claim to two top French establishments on this end of the Strip. **Andre's** (Monte Carlo, 3770 Las Vegas Blvd. S., 702/798-7151, 5:30pm-10pm Tues.-Sun., $40-65) has an up-to-date yet old-country feel, with smoky glass, silver furnishings, and teal-and-cream accents. The menu combines favorites from around the world with French sensibilities to create unique "French fusion" fare, such as lamb with eggplant or a peppercorn and cognac cream sauce for the delectable fillet of beef. The cellar is befitting one of the best French restaurants in town, and the selection of port, cognac, and other after-dinner drinks is unparalleled. Rochat's **Alizé** (The Palms, 4321 W. Flamingo Rd., 702/951-7000, 5:30pm-10pm daily, $45-70) is similar but includes a sweet Strip view from atop The Palms.

When you name your restaurant after a maestro, you're setting some pretty high standards for your food. Fortunately, **Picasso** (Bellagio, 3600 Las Vegas Blvd. S., 702/693-7223, 6pm-9:30pm Wed.-Mon., $113-123) is up to the self-inflicted challenge. With limited seating in its Picasso-canvased dining room and a small dining time window, the restaurant has a couple of prix fixe menus. It's seriously expensive, and if you include Kobe beef, lobster, wine pairings, and a cheese course, you and a mate could easily leave several pounds heavier and $500 lighter.

Gastropub

Inside the Hard Rock Casino, ★ **Culinary Dropout** (4455 Paradise Rd., 702/522-8100, www.culinarydropout.com, 11am-11pm Mon.-Thurs., 11am-midnight Fri., 10am-midnight Sat., 10am-11pm Sun., $15-30) takes comfort food seriously, with home-style favorites like fried chicken and grilled cheese sliders. The provolone fondue appetizer, accompanied by pillowy pretzel rolls, is a meal in itself.

Pizza

With lines snaking out its unmarked entrance, in a dark alleyway decorated with record covers, **Secret Pizza** (Cosmopolitan, 3708 Las Vegas Blvd. S., 3rd Fl., 11am-5am Fri.-Mon., 11am-4am Tues.-Thurs., slices $5-6) is not so secret anymore. Located next to Blue Ribbon Sushi on The Cosmopolitan's third floor, it's a great place to get a quick, greasy slice.

Seafood

Rick Moonen is to be commended for his advocacy of sustainable seafood harvesting practices, and ★ **RM Seafood** (Mandalay Bay, 3950 Las Vegas Blvd. S., 702/632-9300, 11:30am-11pm daily, $40-70) practices what he preaches. You can almost hear the tide-rigging whirr and the mahogany creak in the yacht-club restaurant setting.

Steak

Bringing the lounge vibe to the restaurant setting is ★ **N9NE** (The Palms, 4321 W. Flamingo Rd., 702/933-9900, 5:30pm-10pm Sun.-Thurs., 5:30pm-11pm Fri.-Sat., $50-80). Sleek furnishings of chrome highlighted by rich colored lighting add accompaniment, but N9NE never loses focus on its raison d'être: flawlessly prepared steak and seafood and impeccable service.

The care used by the small farms from which Tom Colicchio's **Craftsteak** (MGM Grand, 3799 Las Vegas Blvd. S., 702/891-7318, 5pm-10pm Sun.-Thurs., 5pm-10:30pm Fri.-Sat., $50-75) buys its ingredients is evident in the full flavor of the excellently seasoned steaks and chops. Spacious with red lacquer and light woodwork, Craftsteak's decor is conducive to good times with friends and family and isn't overbearing or intimidating.

The original **Gallagher's Steakhouse** (New York New York, 3790 Las Vegas Blvd. S., 702/740-6450, 4pm-11pm Sun.-Thurs., 4pm-midnight Fri.-Sat., $60-75) has been an institution in New York City since 1927. The restaurant is decorated with memorabilia from the golden age of movies and sports. You'll know why the longevity is deserved after sampling its famed dry-aged beef and notable seafood selection.

Tapas

The Cosmopolitan's reinvention of the social club takes diners' taste buds to flavor nirvana. Equal parts supper club, nightclub, and jazz club, ★ **Rose. Rabbit. Lie.** (Cosmopolitan, 3708 Las Vegas Blvd. S., 702/698-7000, 6pm-midnight Wed.-Thurs., 6pm-1am Fri.-Sat., $80-130) serves a mostly tapas-style menu. Sharing is encouraged, with about four small plates per person satisfying most appetites, especially if you splurge on the chocolate terrarium for dessert. The club is sectioned into several dining rooms with unique themes—pool room, music room, library—and cocktails. Expect varied entertainment throughout the evening (singers, dancers, magicians, acrobats), but no one will blame you for focusing on the food and cocktails.

Vegas Views

Paris's **Eiffel Tower Restaurant** (3655 Las Vegas Blvd. S., 702/948-6937, 11:30am-3pm and 4:30pm-10:30pm Mon.-Thurs., 11:30am-3pm and 4:30pm-11pm Fri., 11am-3pm and 4:30pm-11pm Sat., 11am-3pm and 4:30pm-10:30pm Sun., $35-75) hovers 100 feet above the Strip. Your first "show" greets you when the glass elevator opens onto the organized chaos of Chef Jean Joho's kitchen. Order the soufflé, have a glass of wine, and bask in the romantic piano strains as the bilingual culinary staff performs delicate French culinary feats, with Bellagio's fountains as a backdrop.

Downtown

Asian

A perfect little eatery for the budding Bohemia of East Fremont Street, ★ **Le Thai** (523 E. Fremont St., 702/778-0888, 11am-11pm Mon.-Thurs., 11am-midnight Fri.-Sat., 4pm-10pm Sun., $10-25) attracts a diverse clientele ranging from ex-yuppies to body-art lovers. Most come for the three-color curry, and you should too. There's nothing especially daring on the menu, but the *pad prik, ga pow,* and garlic fried rice are better than what's found at many Strip restaurants that charge twice as much. Choose your spice level wisely; Le Thai does not mess around.

Buffets

Assuming you're not a food snob, the **Garden Court Buffet** (Main Street Station, 200 N. Main St., 702/387-1896 or 800/713-8933, 7am-9pm Mon.-Thurs., 7am-10am Fri.-Sun., breakfast $8, lunch $9, dinner $12-14, Fri. seafood $23-26) will satisfy your taste buds and your bank account. The fare is mostly standard, with some specialties designed to appeal to the casino's Asian and Pacific Islander target market. At **The Buffet** (Golden Nugget, 129 E. Fremont St., 702/385-7111, 7am-10pm daily, breakfast $13, lunch $15, dinner $21, weekend brunch $19, Fri.-Sun. seafood dinner $27), the food leaves nothing to be desired, with extras like an omelet station, calzone, Greek salad, and a delicate fine banana cake putting it a cut above the ordinary buffet, especially for downtown. Glass and brass accents make for peaceful digestion.

French and Continental

Hugo's Cellar (Four Queens, 202 E. Fremont St., 702/385-4011, 5pm-10pm daily, $40-65) is romance from the moment each woman in your party receives her red rose until the last complimentary chocolate-covered strawberry is devoured. Probably the best gourmet room for the money, dimly lit Hugo's is located below the casino floor, shutting it off from the hubbub above. It is pricey, but the inclusion of sides, a mini dessert, and salad—prepared tableside with your choice of ingredients—helps ease the sticker shock. Sorbet is served between courses. The house appetizer is the Hot Rock, four meats sizzling on a lava slab; mix and match the meats with the dipping sauces.

Italian

Decidedly uncave-like with bright lights and an earthen-tile floor, **The Grotto** (Golden Nugget, 2300 S. Casino Dr., 702/386-8341, 11:30am-10:30pm Sun.-Thurs., 11:30am-11:30pm Fri.-Sat., $15-30) offers top-quality northern

Italian-influenced sandwiches and pizza with a view of the Golden Nugget's shark tank (ask for a window table). Portions are large, and the margaritas refreshing.

Seafood

The prime rib gets raves, but the seafood and the prices are the draw at **Second Street Grill** (Fremont, 200 Fremont St., 702/385-3232, 5pm-10pm Thurs. and Sun.-Mon., 5pm-11pm Fri.-Sat., $15-25). The grill bills itself as "American contemporary with Pacific Rim influence," and the menu reflects this Eastern inspiration with steaks and chops—but do yourself a favor and order the crab legs with lemon ginger butter. If you can't shake your inner landlubber, the nightly T-bone special ($23) should do the trick.

Steaks and seafood get equal billing on the menu at **Triple George** (201 N. 3rd St., 702/384-2761, 11am-10pm Mon.-Fri., 4pm-10pm Sat.-Sun., $25-55), but again, the charbroiled salmon and the martinis are what brings the suave crowd back for more.

Shrimp Cocktail

The Golden Gate's **Du-Par's** (1 Fremont St., 702/366-9378, 24 hours daily, $4) began serving a San Francisco-style shrimp cocktail in 1955, and more than 30 million have been served since. In fact, it's the oldest meal deal in Las Vegas—appropriate for the oldest hotel in Las Vegas. It goes great with a draft beer. Du-Par's Restaurant is also famous locally for melt-in-your-mouth pancakes.

Off the Strip

There are plenty of fine restaurants outside the resort corridor.

The congenial proprietor of ★ **Phat Phrank's** (4850 W. Sunset Rd., 702/247-6528, 7am-7pm Mon.-Fri., 10am-3pm Sat., $10-15) keeps the atmosphere light and the fish tacos crispy and delicious. Try all three of the house salsas; they're all great complements to all the offerings, especially the flavorful pork burrito and *adobada torta*.

Not only beatniks (or whatever the young whippersnappers are calling themselves these days) will dig the breakfast vibe at **The Beat** (520 E. Fremont St., 702/385-2328, 7am-7pm Mon.-Fri., 9am-10pm Sat., 9am-5pm Sun., $5-12) in the downtown arts district. The joe is from Colorado River Coffee Roasters in Boulder City, and the bread is from Bon Breads Baking in Las Vegas, so it's eat-local hipster heaven.

Thai Spice (4433 W. Flamingo Rd., 702/362-5308, 11am-10pm Mon.-Sat., $10-20) gives Le Thai a run for its baht as best Thai restaurant in town; the soups, noodle dishes, traditional curries, pad thai, and egg rolls are all well prepared. Tell your waiter how hot you want your food on a scale of 1 to 10. The big numbers peg the needle on the Scoville scale, so beware.

Shopping

Malls

The most upscale and most Strip-accessible of the traditional, non-casino-affiliated, indoor shopping complexes, **Fashion Show** (3200 Las Vegas Blvd. S., 702/784-7000, 10am-9pm Mon.-Sat., 11am-7pm Sun.), across from the Wynn, is anchored by Saks Fifth Avenue, Dillard's, Neiman Marcus, Macy's, and Nordstrom. The mall gets its name from the 80-foot retractable runway in the Great Hall, where resident retailers put on fashion shows on weekend afternoons. Must-shop stores include Papyrus, specializing in stationery, greeting cards, calendars, and gifts centering on paper arts and crafts, and The LEGO Store, where blockheads can find specialty building sets tied to it movies, video games, and television shows, along with free monthly mini model-building workshops for kids and teens. The one-restaurant food court has something for every taste. Better yet, dine alfresco at a Strip-side café, shaded by "the cloud," a 128-foot-tall canopy that doubles as a projection screen.

If your wallet houses dozens of Ben Franklins, **Crystals at City Center** (3720 Las Vegas Blvd. S., 702/590-9299, 10am-11pm Mon.-Thurs., 10am-midnight Fri.-Sat.) is your destination for impulse buys like a hand-woven Olimpia handbag from Bottega Veneta for her or a titanium timepiece from Porsche Design for him.

Parents can reward their children's patience with rides on cartoon animals, spaceships, and other kiddie favorites at two separate play areas in the **Meadows Mall** (4300 Meadows Ln., 702/878-3331, 10am-9pm Mon.-Sat., 10am-6pm Sun.). There are 140 stores and restaurants—all the usual mall denizens along with some interesting specialty shops. It's across the street from the Las Vegas Springs Preserve, so families can make a day of it. The **Boulevard Mall** (3528 S. Maryland Pkwy., 702/735-8268, 10am-9pm Mon.-Sat., noon-7pm Sun.) is similar. It's in an older and less trendy setting, but a new facade, family attractions, and better dining are driving a comeback.

A visit to **Town Square** (6605 Las Vegas Blvd. S., 702/269-5001, 10am-9:30pm Mon.-Thurs., 10am-10pm Fri.-Sat., 11am-8pm Sun.) is like a stroll through a favorite suburb. "Streets" wind between stores in Spanish, Moorish, and Mediterranean-style buildings. Mall stalwarts like Victoria's Secret and Abercrombie & Fitch are here along with some unusual treats—Tommy Bahama's includes a café. Just like a real town, the retail outlets surround a central park, 13,000 square feet of mazes, tree houses, and performance stages. Around holiday time, machine-made snowflakes drift down through the trees. Nightlife, from laid-back wine and martini bars to rousing live entertainment as well as the 18-screen Rave movie theater, round out a trip into "town."

Easterners and Westerners alike revel in the wares offered at **Chinatown Plaza** (4255 Spring Mountain Rd., 702/221-8448, 10am-10pm daily). Despite the name, Chinatown Las Vegas is a pan-Asian clearinghouse where Asians can celebrate their history and heritage while stocking up on favorite reminders of home. Meanwhile, Westerners can submerge themselves in new cultures by sampling the offerings at authentic Chinese, Thai, Vietnamese, and other Asian restaurants and strolling the plaza reading posters explaining Chinese customs. Tea sets, silk robes, Buddha statuettes, and jade carvings are of particular interest, as is the Diamond Bakery with its elaborate wedding cakes and sublime mango mousse cake.

Casino Plazas

Caesars Palace initiated the concept of Las Vegas as a shopping destination in 1992 when it unveiled the **Forum Shops** (702/893-4800 or 800/223-7277, 10am-11pm Sun.-Thurs., 10am-midnight Fri.-Sat.). Top brand luxury stores coexist with fashionable hipster boutiques amid some of the best people-watching on the Strip. A stained glass-domed pedestrian plaza greets shoppers as they enter the 175,000-square-foot expansion from the Strip. You'll find one of only two spiral escalators in the United States. When you're ready for a break, the gods come alive hourly to extract vengeance in the *Fall of Atlantis* and *Festival Fountain Show*; or check out the feeding of the fish in the big saltwater aquarium twice daily.

Part shopping center, part theater in the round, the **Miracle Mile** (Planet Hollywood, 3663 Las Vegas Blvd. S., 702/866-0703 or 888/800-8284, 10am-11pm Sun.-Thurs., 10am-midnight Fri.-Sat.) is a delightful (or vicious, depending on your point of view) circle of shops, eateries, bars, and theaters. If your budget doesn't quite stand up to the Forum Shops, Miracle Mile could be just your speed. Low-cost shows include an Elvis tribute, the campy *Evil Dead—The Musical* and *Zombie Burlesque*, and family-friendly animal acts and magicians.

Las Vegas icon Rita Rudner loves the **Grand Canal Shoppes** (Venetian, 3377 Las Vegas Blvd. S., 702/414-4500, 10am-11pm Sun.-Thurs., 10am-midnight Fri.-Sat.) because "Where else but in Vegas can you take a gondola to the Gap?" And where else can you be serenaded by opera singers while trying on shoes? (It's worth noting there's not really a Gap here.) The shops line the canal among streetlamps and cobblestones under a frescoed sky. Nature gets a digital assist in the photos for sale at Peter Lik gallery, and Michael Kors and Diane von Furstenberg compete for your shopping dollar. The "Streetmosphere" includes strolling minstrels and specialty acts, and many of these entertainers find their way to St. Mark's Square for seemingly impromptu performances.

Money attracts money, and Steve Wynn was able lure Oscar de la Renta to open his first retail store in the country at the indulgent **Esplanade** (Wynn, 3131 Las Vegas Blvd. S., 702/770-7000, 10am-11pm daily). A cursory look at the tenant stores is enough to convince you that the Esplanade caters to the wealthy, the lucky, and the reckless: Cartier, Rolex, Givenchy, Manolo Blahnik, and even Ferrari are at home under stained-glass skylights.

Perfectly situated in the flourishing urban arts district, the **Downtown Container Park** (707 E. Fremont St., 702/637-4244, 11am-9pm Mon.-Thurs., 11am-10pm Fri.-Sat., 11am-8pm Sun.) packs 50 boutiques, galleries, bars, and bistros into their own shipping containers. The business names hint at the hip, playful atmosphere: Crazy Legs (women's clothes), Teazled (LGBT-themed greeting cards and gifts), IndianSoulArt (Native American art, food, handicrafts).

Unless you're looking for a specific item or brand, or you're attracted to the atmosphere, attractions, architecture, or vibe of a particular Strip destination, you can't go wrong browsing the one in your hotel. You'll find other shops just as nice

Forum Shops, Caesars Palace

at **Le Boulevard** (Paris, 3655 Las Vegas Blvd. S., 702/946-7000, 8am-2am daily), **Grand Bazaar Shops** (Bally's, 3645 Las Vegas Blvd. S., 702/967-4366 or 888/266-5687, 10am-10pm Sun.-Thurs., 10am-11pm Fri.-Sat.), **The Linq** (3545 Las Vegas Blvd. S., 702/694-8100 or 866/328-1888, shop and restaurant hours vary), and **Mandalay Place** (Mandalay Bay, 3930 Las Vegas Blvd. S., 702/632-7777 or 877/632-7800, 10am-11pm daily).

Information and Services

Information Bureaus

The **Las Vegas Convention and Visitors Authority** (LVCVA, 3150 Paradise Rd., 702/892-0711 or 877/847-4858, www.lvcva.com, 8am-5pm daily) maintains a website of special hotel deals and other offers at www.lasvegas.com. One of LVCVA's priorities is filling hotel rooms.

You can also call the same number for convention schedules and entertainment offerings.

The **Las Vegas Chamber of Commerce** (575 Symphony Park Ave., Ste. 100, 702/641-5822, www.lvchamber.com) has a bunch of travel resources and fact sheets on its website. **Vegas.com** is a good resource for up-to-the-minute show schedules and reviews.

Visitors Guides and Magazines

Nearly a dozen free periodicals for visitors are available in various places around town—racks in motel lobbies and by the bell desks of the large hotels are the best bet. They all cover basically the same territory—showrooms, lounges, dining, dancing, buffets, gambling, sports, events, coming attractions—and most have numerous ads that will transport coupon clippers to discount heaven.

Anthony Curtis's monthly ***Las Vegas Advisor*** (www.lasvegasadvisor.com) ferrets out the best dining, entertainment, gambling, and hotel room values, shows, and restaurants, and presents them objectively. A year's subscription is only $50 ($37 for an electronic subscription) and includes exclusive coupons worth more than $3,000. Sign up online. ***What's On*** (www.whatsonlv.com), available in print and online, provides comprehensive information along with entertainer profiles, articles, calendars, phone numbers, and lots of ads. The online edition, with sample articles, is free. Annual subscriptions are $35 (12 monthly issues) and $65 (26 biweekly issues).

Vegas Live Show (www.vegasliveshow.com) gives quick rundowns of all the entertainment in town, along with several discount offers.

The articles in ***Las Vegas Magazine*** (www.lasvegasmagazine.com) are more in-depth and fan-magazine-y. Features include Q&A interviews with touring headliners, celebrity chefs, and pop culture mavens.

Las Vegas Weekly (www.lasvegasweekly.com), the town's alternative newspaper, mixes in political and social commentary as well as inside info on the soon-to-be-happenin' nightspots, restaurants, and hipster trends.

The annual publication ***Las Vegas Perspective*** (www.lvgea.org) is chockfull of area demographics as well as retail, real estate, and community statistics, updated every year.

Medical and Emergency Services

If you need the police, the fire department, or an ambulance in an emergency, **dial 911.**

The centrally located **University Medical Center** (1800 W. Charleston Blvd., at Shadow Ln., 702/383-2000) has 24-hour emergency service, with outpatient and trauma-care facilities. Hospital emergency rooms throughout the valley are open 24 hours, as are many privately run quick-care centers.

Most hotels will have lists of dentists and doctors, and the **Clark County Medical Society** (2590 E. Russell Rd., 702/739-9989, www.clarkcountymedical.org) website lists members based on specialty. You can also get a physician referral from **Desert Springs Hospital** (702/733-8800).

Getting Around

Car

Downtown Las Vegas crowds around the junction of I-15, US 95, and US 93. I-15 runs from Los Angeles (272 miles, 4-5 hours' drive) to Salt Lake City (419 miles, 6-8 hours). US 95 meanders from Yuma, Arizona, on the Mexican border, up the western side of Nevada, through Coeur D'Alene, Idaho, all the way up to British Columbia, Canada. US 93 starts in Phoenix and hits Las Vegas 285 miles later, then merges with I-15 for a while only to fork off and shoot straight up the east side of Nevada and continue due north all the way to Alberta, Canada.

Car Rental

When you call around to rent, ask what the *total* price of your car is going to be. With sales tax, use tax, airport fees, and other miscellaneous charges, you can pay as much as 60 percent over and above the quoted rate. Typical shoulder-season weekly rates run from about $170 total for economy and compact cars to $280 for vans and $500 for luxury sedans, but prices increase by one-third or more during major conventions and holiday periods. One recent holiday week saw economy car rates at about $230 across the board. Parking is free in casino surface lots and garages. Check with your insurance agent at home about coverage on rental cars; often your insurance covers rental cars (minus your deductible), and you won't need the rental company's. If you rent a car on most credit cards, you get automatic rental-car insurance coverage. Las Vegas rental car rates change as fast as hotel room rates, depending on the season, day of the week, and convention traffic.

Most of the large car-rental companies have desks at the **McCarran Rent-A-Car Center** (702/261-6001). Dedicated McCarran shuttles leave the main terminal from outside exit doors 10 and 11 about every five minutes bound for the Rent-A-Car Center. International airlines and a few domestic flights arrive at Terminal 3. Here, the shuttle picks up outside doors 51 through 58. Taxicabs are also available at the center. Companies represented at the center include **Advantage** (800/777-9377), **Alamo** (800/462-5266), **Avis** (800/331-1212), **Budget** (800/922-2899), **Dollar** (800/800-4000), **E-Z** (800/277-5171), **Enterprise** (800/736-7222), **Firefly** (888/296-9135), **Hertz** (800/654-3131), **National** (800/227-7368), **Payless** (800/729-5377), **Thrifty** (800/367-2277), and **Zipcar** (866/494-7227). Others will pick up customers at the center.

When arriving, follow the "Ground Transportation" signs to the Rental Car Shuttle staging area. A blue-and-white bus will pick you up in less than five minutes for the three-mile trip to the Rent-A-Car Center. Of course, the buses will ferry you from the rental drop-off area back to the airport when it's time to go home.

RV Rental

Travelers using Las Vegas as their base or departure point can rent virtually any type of recreational vehicle, from pickup truck-mounted coaches to 40-foot Class A rolling mansions. **El Monte RV** (13001 Las Vegas Blvd. S., Henderson, 702/269-0704 or 888/337-2214) south of town (take I-15 South, exiting at St. Rose Parkway; head east to Las Vegas Boulevard and drive south) deals primarily in Class C "cab-over" models and Class A rock-star tour bus behemoths. Base prices for the Class C cab-overs start at about $600-800 per week, but miles—bundled in 100-mile packages—and incidentals such as kitchenware, pillows, coffeemakers, and toasters can easily increase the total by 75 percent. El Monte's big dog, an EMW AF34 Slideout, goes for $1,800 per week before mileage and extras.

Cruise America (551 N. Gibson Rd., Henderson, 702/565-2224 or 888/980-8282) on the southeast side (take US 93 south to the Sunset Road exit east; turn right on Gibson Road) touts its exclusively cab-over fleet as having more ready-to-use sleep space and maneuverability. Its RVs range 19-30 feet, suitable for parties of 3-7 people. Seven-night rentals average $430 to 900. The company adds a mileage estimate (at about 35 cents per mile) at the time of rental and adjusts the charges based on actual miles driven when you return the vehicle. Common extra charges include linens, kitchen equipment, and generator use.

Road Bear's (4730 Boulder Hwy., 866/491-9853) Class C models sleep 4-7 and go for 42 cents per mile (at $60-85 per day, plus $200 initiation fee and other extras such as kitchen and linen kits).

Monorail

Since 2004, the site of the SLS Casino on the north end of the Strip and the MGM Grand near the south end have been connected via the **Las Vegas Monorail** (702/699-8200, 7am-midnight Mon., 7am-2am Tues.-Thurs., 7am-3am Fri.-Sun., $5, 24-hour pass $12), with stops at the SLS, Westgate, Convention Center, Harrah's/The Linq, Flamingo/Caesars Palace, Bally's/Paris, and MGM Grand. More than 30 major resorts are now within easy reach along the Strip without a car or taxi. Reaching speeds up to 50 mph, the monorail glides above traffic to cover the four-mile route in about 14 minutes. Nine trains with four air-conditioned cars each carry up to 152 riders along the elevated track running on the east side of the strip, stopping every few minutes at the stations. Tickets are available at vending machines at each station as well as at station properties.

Bus

Citizen Area Transit (CAT, 702/228-7433, www.rtcsouthernnevada.com), the public bus system, is managed by the Regional Transportation Commission. CAT runs 39 routes all over Las Vegas Valley. Fares are $6 for two hours, $8 for 24 hours, free under age 5 when riding with a guardian. Call or access the ride guide online. Bus service is pretty comprehensive, but even the express routes with fewer stops take a long time to get anywhere.

Taxi

Except for peak periods, taxis are numerous and quite readily available, and drivers are good sources of scuttlebutt (not always accurate) and entertainment (not always wholesome). Of course, Las Vegas operates at peak loads most of the time, so if you're not in a taxi zone right in front of one of the busiest hotels, it

Side Trip to Hoover Dam

The 1,400-mile Colorado River has been carving and gouging great canyons and valleys with red sediment-laden waters for 10 million years. For 10,000 years Native Americans, the Spanish, and Mormon settlers coexisted with the fitful river, rebuilding after spring floods and withstanding the droughts that often reduced the mighty waterway to a muddy trickle in fall. But the 1905 flood convinced the Bureau of Reclamation to "reclaim" the West, primarily by building dams and canals. The most ambitious of these was Hoover Dam: 40 million cubic yards of reinforced concrete, turbines, and transmission lines.

Hoover Dam remains an engineering marvel, attracting millions of visitors each year. It makes an interesting half-day escape from the glitter of Las Vegas, only 30 miles to the north. The one-hour **Dam Tour** (every 30 minutes, 9:30am-3:30pm daily, ages 8 and over, $30) offers a guided exploration of its power plant and walkways, along with admission to the visitors center. The two-hour **Power Plant Tour** (adults $15, seniors, children, and military $12, uniformed military and under age 4 free) focuses on the dam's construction and engineering through multimedia presentations, exhibits, docent talk, and a power plant tour.

Getting There

The bypass bridge diverts traffic away from Hoover Dam, saving time and headaches for both drivers and dam visitors. Still, the **35-mile drive** from central Las Vegas to a parking lot at the dam will take **45 minutes** or more. From the Strip, **I-15 South** connects with I-215 southeast of the airport, and **I-215 East** takes drivers to US 93 in Henderson. Remember that US 93 shares the roadway with US 95 and I-515 till well past Henderson. Going south on **US 93,** exit at **NV-172** to the dam. Note that this route is closed on the Arizona side; drivers continuing on to the **Grand Canyon** must retrace **NV-172** to **US 93** and cross the bypass bridge. A **parking garage** ($10) is convenient to the visitors center and dam tours, but free parking is available at turnouts on both sides of the dam for those willing to walk.

might be tough to get one. The 16 companies plying the streets of Las Vegas charge $3.45 for the flag drop and $2.68 per mile. Waiting time is $0.54 per minute.

Limo

Offering chauffeur-driven domestic and imported sedans, shuttle buses, and SUVs in addition to stretch and superstretch limos, **Las Vegas Limousines** (702/888-4848, www.lasvegaslimo.com) can transport up to 15 people per vehicle to and from sporting events, corporate meetings, airport connections, bachelor and bachelorette parties, sightseeing tours, and more. Rates are $60 per hour for a six-seat stretch limo, $80 and up for a 10-seat superstretch.

Presidential Limousine (702/438-5466, www.presidentiallimolv.com) charges $69 per hour for its stretch six-seater, $80 per hour for the superstretch eight-seater; both include TVs and video players, mobile phones, sparkling cider, and roses for the women. They don't include a mandatory fuel surcharge or driver gratuity. **Bell Limousine** (866/226-7206, www.belllimousine.com) has similar rates and fleets.

Tours

Several companies offer the chance to see the sights of Las Vegas by bus, helicopter, airplane, or off-road vehicle. There are plenty of tour operators offering similar services. Search the Internet to find tours tailored for your needs, the best prices, and the most competent providers.

The ubiquitous **Gray Line** (702/739-7777 or 877/333-6556, www.graylinelasvegas.com) offers air-conditioned motor coach tours of the city by night as well as tours of Hoover Dam and the Grand Canyon. City tours (7pm Thurs.-Sat., $69) visit the major Vegas free sights: the Bellagio Fountains and Conservatory, the "Welcome to Las Vegas" sign, the Fremont Street Experience, and some of the more opulent hotels. The Hoover Dam tour ($66) includes a buffet lunch and a stop at Ethel M's chocolatier for a self-guided tour and a free sample. Travelers can add a 15-minute helicopter flight over Lake Mead and the dam ($99 extra) or a riverboat cruise on the lake ($31 extra).

To book a lake cruise directly, contact **Lake Mead Cruises** (866/292-9191, www.lakemeadcruises.com, noon and 2 pm daily Apr.-Oct., days and times vary Feb.-Mar. and Nov., adults $26, ages 2-11 $13, Sun. 10am champagne brunch cruise adults $45, ages 2-11 $19.50, Sun., Tues., Thurs. dinner cruise adults $61.50, ages 2-11 $25).

Vegas Tours (866/218-6877, www.vegastours.com) has a full slate of outdoor, adventure, and other tours. Some of the more unusual ones include trail rides and full-day dude ranch tours ($120-$350) and a visit and tour of the Techatticup gold mine ($113-189). Tours of the Grand Canyon and other nearby state and national parks are available as well.

All Las Vegas Tours (702/233-1627 or 800/566-5868, www.alllasvegastours.com) has all the usual tours: zip-lining over the desert or between hotel towers (weight must be between 75 and 250 pounds, $30-159), tandem skydiving (age 18 and over, less than 240 pounds, $229) and ATV sand-duning (18 and over with valid driver's license, $185).

Pink Jeep Tours (702/895-6778 or 888/900-4480, www.pinkjeeptourslasvegas.com) takes visitors in rugged but cute and comfortable 10-passenger ATVs to such sites as Red Rock Canyon, Valley of Fire, and Hoover Dam.

For history, nature, and entertainment buffs looking for a more focused adventure, themed tours are on the rise in Las Vegas. **Haunted Vegas Tours** (702/677-6499, www.hauntedvegastours.com, 9:30pm Thurs.-Mon., $85) takes an interesting if macabre trip to the "Motel of Death," where many pseudo-celebrities have met their untimely ends. Guides dressed as undertakers take you to the Redd Foxx haunted house, a creepy old bridge and an eerie park. The same company offers the **Las Vegas Mob Tour** ($85), taking visitors to the sites of Mafia hits. Guides, dressed in black pin-striped suits and fedoras, tell tales of the 1970s, when Anthony "The Ant" Spilotro ran the city, and give the scoop on the fate of casino mogul Lefty Rosenthal. A pizza party is included in both tours.

Zion and Bryce

Great faults break the Colorado Plateau into a staircase across southern Utah, where cliffs and canyons dominate the landscape. Here you'll find two of the nation's most popular national parks.

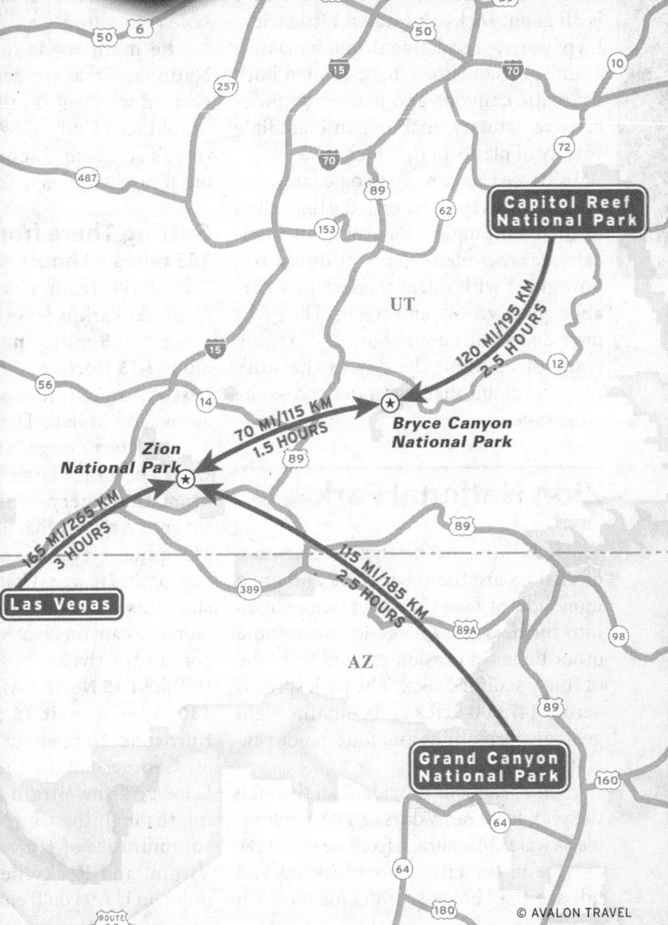

In southwestern Utah, at the meeting point of the Mojave Desert, the Great Basin, and the Colorado Plateau is a unique combination of climates and ecosystems.

The lofty cliffs of the plateau rise east of the desert country with some of the most spectacular scenery on earth. Zion is a magnificent park with stunning, soaring scenery. The geology here is all about rocks and water. Little trickles of water, percolating through massive chunks of sandstone, have created both dramatic canyons and markedly undesertlike habitats, enabling an incredible variety of plants to find niches.

In Bryce Canyon, a geologic fairyland of rock spires rises beneath the high cliffs of the Paunsaugunt Plateau. This intricate maze, eroded from soft limestone, now glows with warm shades of red, orange, pink, yellow, and cream. The rocks provide a continuous show of changing color throughout the day as the sun's rays and cloud shadows move across the landscape.

Zion National Park

The first thing that catches the attention of visitors are the sheer cliffs and great monoliths of Zion Canyon, reaching high into the heavens. Energetic streams and other forces of erosion created this land of finely sculpted rock. The park spreads across 147,000 acres and contains eight geologic formations and four major vegetation zones.

Zion's grandeur is evident all through the year. Even rainy days can be memorable as waterfalls plunge from nearly every crevice in the cliffs above. Spring and fall are the choice seasons for pleasant temperatures and the best chances of seeing wildlife and wildflowers. From about mid-October through early November, cottonwoods and other trees and plants blaze with color. Summer temperatures in the canyons can be uncomfortably hot, with highs hovering above 100°F. Summer is also the busiest season. In winter, nighttime temperatures drop to near freezing, and the weather tends to be unpredictable, with bright sunshine one day and freezing rain the next. Snow-covered slopes contrast with colorful rocks. Snow may block some of the high-country trails and the road to Lava Point, but the rest of the park is open and accessible year-round.

The main roads to and from Zion National Park are generally open all year. In winter it is mildly cold and wet in southern Utah and Zion country, and there's sometimes snow on the ground, but it rarely causes road problems.

Getting There from Las Vegas

165 miles / 3 hours

The drive from Las Vegas to Zion National Park is less than **three hours,** a mere **165 miles,** most of it zipping along **I-15 North** at 75 mph. The route passes through three states as it moves across the Mojave Desert, through the Virgin River Gorge, and into southern Utah's beautiful Dixie region. The most dramatic scenery on the drive is in the sliver of Arizona that begins just outside Mesquite, Nevada, and ends just outside of St. George, Utah. Here the interstate cuts right through the Virgin River Gorge, a canyon created and carved over eons by the river.

Take **I-15 North** out of Las Vegas for **130 miles** to **exit 16** for **UT-9 toward Hurricane/Zion,** about 10 miles beyond St. George. Follow the winding, rural UT-9 and the Virgin River east, passing through the tiny Mormon farming communities of Hurricane, La Verkin, Virgin, and Rockville. After about 30 miles on UT-9 you'll enter the green oasis

Highlights

★ **Zion Canyon Visitor Center:** At this interesting place, the highlights are the outdoor exhibits, the excellent bookstore, and a shuttle bus stop that will ferry you up the canyon (page 91).

★ **Court of the Patriarchs Viewpoint:** Hop off the shuttle bus to spend a few moments trying to fit all three mountains into your camera's viewfinder. The Patriarchs are emblematic of Zion's massive sandstone rocks (page 93).

★ **Emerald Pools Trails:** All three of these pools are indeed emerald green. The trails, of varying degrees of difficulty, are lined with wildflowers (page 98).

★ **West Rim Trail to Angels Landing:** If you want to do one vigorous day hike, this is a classic. Be prepared for spectacular views and some tenuous footing along the way—not for acrophobes or children (page 99).

★ **Hidden Canyon Trail:** After a hike that includes traversing a cliff face, you'll pop into a shady, steep-walled narrow canyon with caves, pools, a small arch, and moisture-loving plants (page 100).

★ **Sunrise and Sunset Points:** At the namesake hours, these overlooks are irresistible, especially if you have a camera in hand. Unless you are utterly jaded, don't pass these off as mere clichés (page 115).

★ **Inspiration Point:** Along the Rim Trail, see a fantastic maze of hoodoos in the "Silent City." Vertical joints in the rocks have weathered to form many rows of narrow gullies, some more than 200 feet deep (page 115).

★ **Yovimpa and Rainbow Points:** This 9,115-foot-high spot at the end of the scenic road is especially dramatic. From here you can start a day hike, a backpacking trip, or a stroll along a nature trail (page 116).

★ **Queen's Garden Trail:** The easiest hike below the rim can still leave flatlanders huffing and puffing. The trail drops through impressive features in the middle of Bryce Amphitheater to a hoodoo resembling a portly Queen Victoria (page 118).

★ **Navajo Loop Trail:** This trail leads into a narrow canyon and deep, dark Wall Street—an even narrower canyon—then returns to the rim (page 118).

Zion and Bryce Canyon National Parks

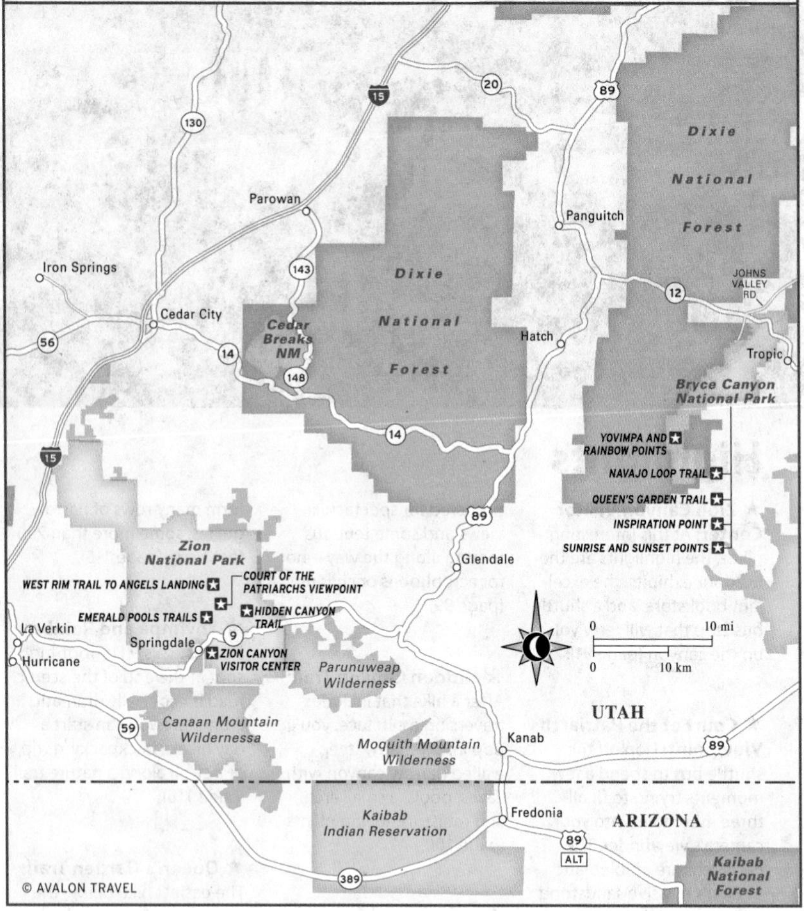

of **Springdale,** a mile outside the gates of Zion National Park.

Scenic Detour

For a scenic detour, head to **Lake Mead National Recreation Area,** about 30 miles southeast of the Strip. This **70-mile** scenic detour will add about **two hours** onto the drive, for a total drive of **200 miles** and **four hours.** From the Strip, take **I-15 South** for several miles to **I-215 East.** After about 10 miles I-215 becomes **Lake Mead Parkway/NV-564** through the town of Henderson. About 10 miles east of Henderson is the **park entrance station,** where you'll drive through and pay the entrance fee ($10 per car). Just beyond the entrance station, turn left onto **Northshore Road (NV-167)** and drive through the strange, otherworldly desert landscape, keeping eyes peeled for bighorn sheep. After 50 miles, Northshore Road leaves the park and becomes **NV-169,** which passes through the small town

Stretch Your Legs

A great painter of Western subjects with a modernist touch, Maynard Dixon (1875-1946) loved Zion country, and he and his wife, the painter Edith Hamlin (1902-1992), established a summer home and studio in 1938 at Mt. Carmel, Utah, about 15 miles east of Zion National Park. The property is now the **Maynard Dixon Living History Museum** (Bryce Canyon-Zion drive, 2200 S. State St., Mt. Carmel, Utah, 435/648-2653, www.thunderbirdfoundation.com, 10am-5pm daily, self-guided tour $10, docent-led tour $20). Managed by the Thunderbird Foundation, the museum offers tours of the home and studio that the artists lived in for many years.

of Overton before joining **I-15** in 15 miles. From there, it's about **110 miles** to Zion.

Getting There from the Grand Canyon (North Rim)

115 miles / 2.5 hours

It's only about **115 miles** from the North Rim of the Grand Canyon to Zion National Park, but count on the drive taking about **2.5 hours,** across this lonely, isolated region, on two-lane highways, passing small towns and backcountry outposts.

Take **AZ-67 North** out of Grand Canyon National Park, heading northwest through the vast highland forest of the Kaibab Plateau. Keep an eye out for elk and wild turkeys crossing the paved two-lane highway, which is typically **closed to vehicles November to March.** Continue about 35 miles, then turn left at the T-intersection to pick up **US 89A** at Jacob Lake, a town that consists of a gas station, hotel, restaurant, and campground. Follow US 89A northwest off the plateau to the flat and windswept Arizona Strip. Stay on US 89A for about 40 miles, moving through the tiny Mormon communities of Fredonia, Arizona, and Kanab, Utah. From Kanab, it's another 20 miles northwest to Mt. Carmel Junction, Utah, where you'll make a left onto **UT-9 West,** otherwise known as the **Zion-Mt. Carmel Highway.** From the US 89A/UT-9 junction it's another 15 scenic miles to the Zion National Park entrance station.

If you're driving an RV or other large vehicle (over 11 feet, 4 inches tall or 7 feet, 10 inches wide), it will cost you to enter Zion National Park along the **Zion-Mt. Carmel Highway.** The twisting, technical road from the entrance station to Canyon Junction, about five miles total, has a long, narrow tunnel that cannot easily accommodate large vehicles in its standard, two-way formation. Park rangers offer daily **traffic control** (8am-7pm daily early Mar.-early May and Sept., 8am-8pm daily early May-Aug., 8am-6pm daily Oct., 8am-4:30pm daily Nov.-early Mar. with advance arrangements), where the tunnel is converted to one-way traffic for larger vehicles, for a $15 tunnel permit fee (good for two trips through the tunnel). To avoid paying the fee, you'll need to take a detour that will add at least **one hour** (and about 40 miles) to the drive from the North Rim. From **US 89A** in Fredonia, take **AZ-389/UT-59 West** for nearly 60 miles. As you enter Hurricane, turn right (north) onto Main Street, then take the first right to pick up **UT-9.** Follow UT-9 north for about three miles. In the town of La Verkin, UT-9 turns east. Follow it for about 20 miles and enter the park from the Springdale entrance.

Stopping in Kanab

Kanab is a small town just a few miles north of the Utah-Arizona border and **80 miles** (about **1.5 hours**) from the North Rim. This canyonlands village has been a pioneer Mormon farming community and a popular location for Hollywood films, but these days it's mostly known as a useful stop for road-trippers and tourists exploring the Colorado Plateau. It's perfectly situated for visitors looking for food and comfort in this vast, isolated region.

If you get hungry on the drive to Zion, check out the **Rocking V Café** (97 W. Center St., 435/644-8001, www.rockingvcafe.com, 11:30am-10pm daily, $15-34), which serves excellent sandwiches, burgers, and Mexican dishes in a historic building crowded with art.

If you're staying overnight, the **Quail Park Lodge** (125 N. 300 W., 435/215-1447, www.quailparklodge.com, $89-189) is a cool retro-style motor lodge that has all the updated amenities you'll need to relax after a hard day of challenging the wilderness.

Getting There from Bryce Canyon National Park

70 miles / 1.5 hours

Getting from Bryce Canyon National Park to Zion National Park is a scenic drive south on **US 89,** skirting the edge of the Dixie National Forest and following the East Fork of the Virgin River, and is nearly as memorable as the parks themselves. The **70-mile** drive takes about **1.5 hours.**

Take **UT-63 North** out of the Bryce Canyon National Park for about three miles to **UT-12 West.** Stay on UT-12 for 15 miles, then turn left to get on **US 89 South.** After about 45 miles, turn right (west) onto **UT-9** at Mt. Carmel Junction. Then take UT-9, also known as the **Zion-Mt. Carmel Highway,** nearly 15 miles to the east entrance of Zion National Park.

Oversize vehicles (more than 11 feet, 4 inches tall or 7 feet, 10 inches wide) will need to pay a $15 traffic control fee to enter the park via the Zion-Mt. Carmel Highway. To avoid the fee, it's a **70-mile, 1.5-hour detour** (for a total drive of 140 miles and 3 hours). From **US 89,** turn right (west) at the intersection of US 89 and UT-14 (called **Long Valley Junction**) after about 20 miles. Then take **UT-14 West** for 40 miles until Cedar City. Turn left onto Main Street/UT-130 and get onto **I-15 South** after about two miles. Continue south for 30 miles on I-15 to **exit 27** for **UT-17 toward Toquerville/Hurricane.** After exiting the freeway, take **UT-17** through Toquerville to La Verkin for six miles, then turn left onto **UT-9 East** and continue to Zion's Springdale entrance, another 20 miles.

Best Hotels

★ **Flanigan's Inn:** Red cliffs tower over lush grounds at this refined lodge just a short walk from Zion's gates (page 107).

★ **Desert Pearl Inn:** This elegant hotel is a meticulously crafted oasis less than a mile from Zion (page 107).

★ **Cliffrose Lodge:** This stylish lodge sits on five verdant acres along the Virgin River, with cozy rooms guarded by Zion's breathtaking sandstone cliffs (page 107).

★ **Lodge at Bryce Canyon:** This 1920s lodge has a romantic Western style with few modern distractions (page 122).

★ **Bryce Canyon Inn:** In the nearby town of Tropic, this welcoming spot offers delightful, cabin-like rooms that are up-to-date but affordable (page 124).

★ **Red Brick Inn of Panguitch B&B:** This country-style bed-and-breakfast is an ideal base for visiting both Zion and Bryce Canyon (page 125).

Winter is serious business up between 8,000 and 9,000 feet in elevation, where Bryce Canyon sits. It's snowy and cold up here many months of the year. However, the roads leading out of Bryce Canyon National Park are plowed and kept open and relatively safe throughout the year.

Zion-Springdale Shuttle

During the high season, one line of the Zion Canyon **shuttle bus** (5:30am-11pm daily Apr.-Oct., runs as often as every six minutes, less frequently in early morning and late evening, no pets allowed, free) travels between Springdale and the park entrance, stopping within a short walk of every Springdale motel and near several large visitor parking lots at the edge of town.

Visiting Zion National Park

Zion National Park (435/772-3256, www.nps.gov/zion, $30 per vehicle, $25 per motorcycle, $15 per bicycle) has four main sections: Zion Canyon, a higher-elevation area east of Zion Canyon, the Kolob Terrace, and Kolob Canyons. The highlight for most visitors is Zion Canyon, which is approximately 2,400 feet deep. Zion Canyon Scenic Drive winds through the canyon along the North Fork of the Virgin River, past some of the most spectacular scenery in the park. A shuttle bus ferries visitors along this route spring-early fall. Hiking trails branch off to lofty viewpoints and narrow side canyons. Water-loving adventurers can continue past the pavement's end and hike up the Virgin River at the Narrows in upper Zion Canyon.

The spectacular Zion-Mt. Carmel Highway, with its switchbacks and tunnels, provides access to the canyons and high plateaus east of Zion Canyon. Two other roads enter the rugged Kolob section northwest of Zion Canyon. Kolob is a Mormon name meaning "the brightest star, next to the seat of God." The Kolob section includes wilderness areas rarely visited by humans.

Entrances

Zion National Park has two entrance stations, which are both accessible daily 24 hours. The main, **southern entrance** is in **Springdale, Utah.** The **eastern entrance** is about 15 miles west of Mt. Carmel, Utah, along the **Zion-Mt. Carmel Highway.**

Those with large RVs and buses and should consider entering through the Springdale entrance to avoid slow going and a $15 fee for traffic control, as the 1920s-era Zion-Mt. Carmel Highway has many switchbacks and a narrow tunnel.

Park Passes and Fees

The Zion National Park **entrance fee** is $30 per vehicle, $25 per motorcycle, and $15 per bicycle (or pedestrian). The fee is good for seven days. A **Zion Annual Pass** is $50, while an annual pass to all

Best Restaurants

★ **Deep Creek Coffee:** Get your coffee and pastries at this homey hangout in Springdale (page 108).

★ **Whiptail Grill:** An old gas station in Springdale is now a creative Mexican restaurant (page 108).

★ **Spotted Dog Café:** This sophisticated bistro surrounded by Zion's rugged grandeur offers an enticing menu (page 108).

★ **Lodge at Bryce Canyon:** The food pairs perfectly with the woodland style of one of the Southwest's great national park lodges (page 126).

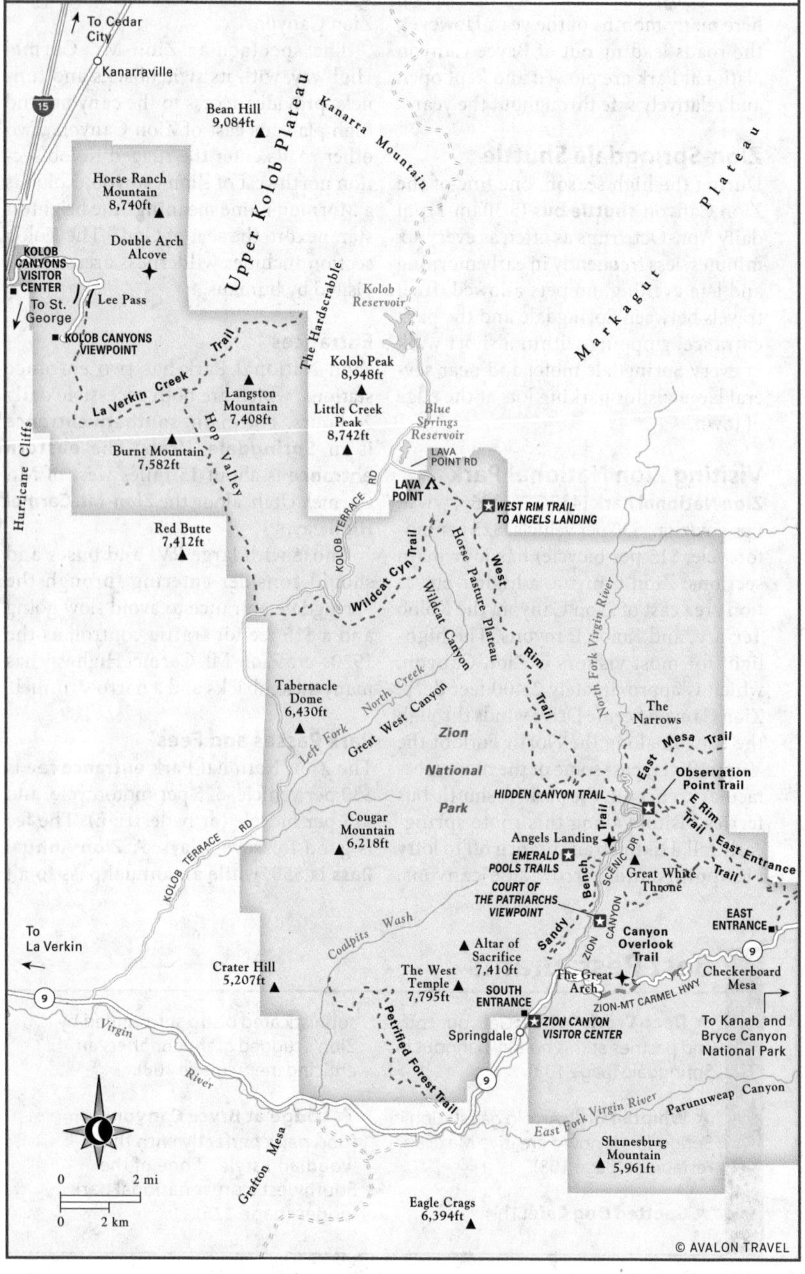

Zion National Park
To Cedar City
Kanarraville
15
Bean Hill 9,084ft
Horse Ranch Mountain 8,740ft
Double Arch Alcove
KOLOB CANYONS VISITOR CENTER
Lee Pass
To St. George
KOLOB CANYONS VIEWPOINT
Upper Kolob Plateau
Kanarra Mountain
Markagunt Plateau
The Hardscrabble
Kolob Reservoir
Kolob Peak 8,948ft
Langston Mountain 7,408ft
Little Creek Peak 8,742ft
Blue Springs Reservoir
La Verkin Creek Trail
Hop Valley
Burnt Mountain 7,582ft
LAVA POINT RD
LAVA POINT
KOLOB TERRACE RD
WEST RIM TRAIL TO ANGELS LANDING
Hurricane Cliffs
Red Butte 7,412ft
Wildcat Cyn Trail
Wildcat Canyon
Horse Pasture Plateau
West Rim Trail
North Fork Virgin River
Tabernacle Dome 6,430ft
North Creek
Left Fork
Great West Canyon
Zion National Park
The Narrows
East Mesa Trail
Observation Point Trail
HIDDEN CANYON TRAIL
E Rim Trail
East Entrance Trail
Angels Landing
EMERALD POOLS TRAILS
Cougar Mountain 6,218ft
Great White Throne
COURT OF THE PATRIARCHS VIEWPOINT
Bench Trail
Sandy
ZION CANYON SCENIC DR
EAST ENTRANCE
Coalpits Wash
To La Verkin
Altar of Sacrifice 7,410ft
Canyon Overlook Trail
Crater Hill 5,207ft
The West Temple 7,795ft
The Great Arch
Checkerboard Mesa
SOUTH ENTRANCE
ZION-MT CARMEL HWY
9
ZION CANYON VISITOR CENTER
Springdale
To Kanab and Bryce Canyon National Park
Virgin River
Petrified Forest Trail
East Fork Virgin River
Parunuweap Canyon
Shunesburg Mountain 5,961ft
Grafton Mesa
Eagle Crags 6,394ft
0 2 mi
0 2 km
© AVALON TRAVEL

of the national parks, the **Interagency Annual Pass** (also called the **America the Beautiful Pass**) will run you $80.

Visitors Centers

★ Zion Canyon Visitor Center

The park's sprawling **Zion Canyon Visitor Center** (435/772-3256, 8am-6pm daily mid-Apr.-late May and Sept.-mid-Oct., 8am-7:30pm daily late May-Aug., 8am-5pm daily mid-Oct.-mid-Apr.), between Watchman and South Campgrounds, is a hub of activity. The plaza outside the building features several interpretive plaques, including some pointing out environmentally sensitive design features of the visitors center. Inside, a large area is devoted to backcountry information; staff members can answer your questions about various trails, give you updates on the weather forecast, and help you arrange a shuttle to remote trailheads. The **backcountry desk** (435/772-0170) opens at 7am daily late April-late October, an hour earlier than the rest of the visitors center. A Backcountry Shuttle Board allows hikers to coordinate transportation between trailheads.

The busiest part of the visitors center is the bookstore, stocked with an excellent selection of books covering natural history, human history, and regional travel. Topographic and geologic maps, posters, and postcards are also sold here.

Kolob Canyons Visitor Center

Although it is small and has just a handful of exhibits, this **visitors center** (435/772-3256, 8am-5pm daily mid-Apr.-late May and Sept.-mid-Oct., 8am-6pm daily late May-Aug., 8am-4:30pm daily mid-Oct.-mid-Apr.) is a good place to stop for information on exploring the Kolob region. Hikers can learn about current trail conditions and obtain the permits required for overnight trips and Zion Narrows day trips. Books, topographic and geologic maps, posters, postcards, slides, and film are sold. The visitors center and the start of Kolob Canyons Road are just off I-15's exit 40.

Reservations

Accommodations

Zion National Park has just one in-park lodge, the **Zion Lodge** (435/772-7700 or 888/297-2757, www.zionlodge.com, $200-260), which is open year-round. To stay inside the park, especially during the **summer high season** (June-Aug.), you must make a reservation about one year in advance.

For more accommodations options, try the communities outside Zion:

- **Springdale** (UT-9): One mile from the Springdale/south entrance

- **Rockville** (UT-9): Five miles from the Springdale/south entrance

Campgrounds

The park has two large campgrounds, only one of which takes reservations. **Watchman Campground** (877/444-6777, www.recreation.gov, $16) has 181 sites, which can be reserved up to six months in advance. The **South Campground** ($16) has 126 sites, all of which are first-come, first-served.

Information and Services

Park Newsletter

The Zion National Park official ***Map and Guide,*** which is handed out to at the entrance stations and the visitors center, has all kinds of information on the park, including a list of trails and ranger-led programs.

Banking, Gas, and Groceries

Zion is a relatively small national park with **very few services.** There's only one dining option within the park, at Zion Lodge. It's best to get your **groceries, water, gas,** and **cash** before you enter the park. Springdale is the nearest and best town for stocking up on the essentials. There are no gas stations, laundry

Zion in One Day

Morning

Park your car at **Zion Canyon Visitor Center** (page 91). Enjoy the exhibits, then jump on the **free park shuttle** (page 93) for a stroll on the **Riverside Walk** (page 101) or **Weeping Rock** (page 99), which is only 0.5 mile round-trip.

Afternoon

Jump off the shuttle at Zion Lodge for lunch at the **Red Rock Grill** (page 108). Then take a longer hike: **Hidden Canyon** (page 100) is lots of fun and won't utterly deplete experienced hikers. If you don't hike much, the trails to the **Emerald Pools** (page 98) are easier.

Evening

Springdale is just a short walk or shuttle bus ride from the park entrance, and it has several very good restaurants, shops, and galleries.

Extending Your Stay

Zion country is deep enough for years of study. If you're just looking at the incredible scenery, one day in Zion will introduce you to its wonders. If you're a hiker, spend at least two days here, and three or more for a back-country adventure in the slot canyons. Consider checking out the wild and undeveloped **Kolob Canyons** (page 96) section of the park. It's about 45 miles north of Springdale along I-15.

A second day in Zion should include the classic 5.4-mile hike from the **West Rim Trail to Angels Landing** (page 99). On summer evenings, park rangers offer a variety of talks and **tours** (page 92). Use the park newspaper to find programs going on at the Zion Lodge Amphitheater, the South Campground Amphitheater, and the Watchman Campground Amphitheater.

facilities, or showers within the park. There is one **ATM,** located at the Zion Lodge.

Emergency and Medical Services

In an emergency, call 911 or the Zion National Park **emergency line** (435/772-3322). The **Zion Canyon Medical Clinic** (435/772-3226) is near the south entrance in Springdale. There are hospitals in Kanab (30 miles), St. George (40 miles), and Cedar City (60 miles).

Expect spotty cell-phone service within the park.

Tours

With the exception of ranger-led hikes, Zion Canyon Field Institute classes, horseback rides from Zion Lodge, and the running commentary from the more loquacious shuttle-bus drivers, Zion is a do-it-yourself park. Outfitters are not permitted to lead trips within the park. If you'd like a guided tour outside park boundaries, there are several outfitters in Springdale that lead biking, canyoneering, and climbing trips.

The best way to get a feel for Zion's impressive geology and variety of habitats is to take a hike with a park ranger. Many nature programs and hikes are offered late March-November; check the posted schedule at the Zion Canyon Visitor Center. Children's programs, including the popular Junior Ranger program, are held Memorial Day-Labor Day at Zion Nature Center near South Campground; ask at the visitors center for details.

The **Zion Canyon Field Institute** (435/772-3265, www.zionpark.org) is authorized to run educational programs in the park, which include animal tracking, photography, and archaeology; fees vary.

Getting Around

Car

Zion Lodge guests may obtain a pass authorizing them to drive to the lodge, but in general, private vehicles are not allowed to drive up Zion Canyon Road. It's fine to drive to the campgrounds; in fact, the road between the park entrance and the Zion-Mt. Carmel Highway junction is open to all vehicles. In the off-season, November-March, private vehicles are allowed on all roads.

Zion Canyon Shuttle

The road through Zion Canyon is narrow with few pullouts, so to keep the road from becoming a parking lot for enormous RVs, an April-October **shuttle bus** provides regular free service through the canyon. The bus line starts just inside the park entrance, at the visitors center, and runs the length of Zion Canyon Road, stopping at scenic overlooks, trailheads, and Zion Lodge.

Buses run frequently, so there's rarely much of a wait, and most of the bus drivers are friendly and well-informed, offering an engaging commentary on the sights that they pass (even pointing out rock climbers on the canyon walls).

Riding the bus is free; its operating costs are included in the park admission fee. Buses run as often as every six minutes 5:30am-11pm daily, less frequently early in the morning and in the evening. No pets are allowed on the buses. In the off-season, November-March, private vehicles are allowed on all roads, and the buses are out of service.

Sights

Zion Nature Center

At the northern end of South Campground, the **Zion Nature Center** (noon-5pm daily summer) houses programs for kids, including Junior Ranger activities for ages 6-12. Although there's no shuttle stop for the Nature Center, it's an easy walk along the Pa'rus Trail from the Zion Canyon Visitor Center or the Human History Museum. Check the park newsletter for kids' programs and family hikes. Programs focus on natural history topics such as insects and bats in the park. Many Junior Ranger activities can be done on your own—pick up a booklet ($1) at the visitors center bookstore.

Zion Human History Museum

The old park visitors center has been retooled as the **Zion Human History Museum** (10am-5pm daily early Mar.-Nov., entry included in park admission fee), covering southern Utah's cultural history with a film introducing the park and fairly bare-bones exhibits focusing on Native American and Mormon history. It's at the first shuttle stop after the visitors center. This is a good place to visit when you're too tired to hike any farther or if the weather forces you to seek shelter. The museum's back patio is a good place to watch the sun rise over the tall peaks of the West Temple and Altar of Sacrifice (so named because of the red streaks of iron on its face).

Zion Canyon

During the busy seasons, April-October, the six-mile Zion Canyon Scenic Drive is closed to private cars, and you must travel up and down Zion Canyon in a **shuttle bus** (90 minutes round-trip, free). Most visitors find the shuttle an easy and enjoyable way to visit Zion Canyon sites. The road follows the North Fork of the Virgin River upstream, passing impressive natural formations along the way, including the Three Patriarchs, Mountain of the Sun, Lady Mountain, Great White Throne, Angels Landing, and Weeping Rock. The bus stops at eight points of interest along the way; you can get on and off the bus as often as you want at these stops. The road ends at Temple of Sinawava and the beginning of the Riverside Walk Trail.

★ Court of the Patriarchs Viewpoint

A short trail from the parking area leads to the **Court of the Patriarchs Viewpoint.** The Patriarchs, a trio of peaks to the west, overlook Birch Creek; they are, from left to right, Abraham, Isaac, and Jacob. Mount Moroni, the reddish peak

Navajo Sandstone

Take a look anywhere along Zion Canyon and you'll see 1,600- to 2,200-foot cliffs of Navajo sandstone. The big walls of Zion were formed from sand dunes deposited during a hot dry period about 200 million years ago. Shifting winds blew the sand from one direction, then another—a careful inspection of the sandstone layer reveals the diagonal lines resulting from this "cross-bedding." Studies by researchers at the University of Nebraska-Lincoln conclude that the vast dunes of southern Utah were formed when the landmass on which they sit was about 15 degrees north of the equator, at about the same location as Honduras is today. The shift patterns apparent in the sandstone—the slanting striations easily seen in cliff faces—were caused in part by intense monsoon rains, which served to compact and move the dunes each rainy season.

Eventually, a shallow sea washed over the dunes. Lapping waves left shells behind, and as the shells dissolved, their lime seeped down into the sand and cemented it into sandstone. After the Colorado Plateau lifted, rivers cut deeply through the sandstone layer. The formation's lower layers are stained red from iron oxides.

on the far right, partially blocks the view of Jacob. Although the official viewpoint is a beautiful place to relax and enjoy the view, you'll get an even better view if you cross the road and head about 0.5 mile up Sand Bench Trail.

Zion Lodge

Rustic **Zion Lodge** (435/772-7700, www.zionlodge.com), with its big front lawn, spacious lobby, snack bar, restaurant, and restrooms, is a natural stop for most park visitors. You don't need to be a guest at the lodge to enjoy the ambience of its public areas, and the snack bar is not a bad place to grab lunch.

Cross the road from the lodge to catch the Emerald Pools Trails, or walk 0.5 mile north from the Zion Lodge shuttle stop to reach The Grotto.

The Grotto

The Grotto is a popular place for a picnic. From here, a trail leads back to the lodge, and across the road, the Kayenta Trail links up with the Emerald Pools Trails and the West Rim Trail leads to Angels Landing and to the Kolob Terrace section of the park.

Visible from several points along Zion Canyon Drive is the **Great White Throne.** Topping out at 6,744 feet, this bulky chunk of Navajo sandstone has become, along with the Three Patriarchs, emblematic of the park. Ride the shuttle in the evening to watch the rock change color in the light of the setting sun.

Weeping Rock

Several trails, including the short and easy Weeping Rock Trail, start here. **Weeping Rock** is home to hanging gardens and many moisture-loving plants, including the striking Zion shooting star. The rock "weeps" because this is a boundary between porous Navajo sandstone and denser Kayenta shale. Water trickles down through the sandstone, and when it can't penetrate the shale, it moves laterally to the face of the cliff.

While you're at Weeping Rock, scan the cliffs for the remains of cables and rigging that were used to lower timber from the top of the rim down to the canyon floor. During the early 1900s, this wood was used to build pioneer settlements in the area.

Big Bend

Look up: **Big Bend** is where you're likely to see rock climbers on the towering walls or hikers on Angels Landing. Because outfitters aren't allowed to bring groups into the park, these climbers presumably are quite experienced and know what they're doing.

Temple of Sinawava

The last shuttle stop is at this canyon, the **Temple of Sinawava,** where 2,000-foot-tall rock walls reach up from the sides of the Virgin River. There's not really enough room for the road to continue farther up the canyon, but it's spacious enough for a fine paved wheelchair-accessible walking path. Plants sprout from hanging gardens on the cliffs, and birds nest in some of the holes in the cliff walls. The Riverside Walk heads one mile upstream to the Virgin Narrows, a place where the canyon becomes too narrow even for a sidewalk to squeeze through. You may see people hiking up the Narrows (in the river) from the end of the Riverside Walk. Don't join them unless you're properly outfitted.

East of Zion Canyon

The east section of the park is a land of sandstone slickrock, hoodoos, and narrow canyons. You can see much of the dramatic scenery along the Zion-Mt. Carmel Highway (Hwy. 9) between the east entrance station and Zion Canyon. If you want to pull off the road and explore, try hiking a canyon or heading up a slickrock slope (the pass between Crazy Quilt and Checkerboard Mesas is one possibility). Highlights on the plateau include views of the **White Cliffs** and **Checkerboard Mesa,** both near the east entrance station, and a hike on the **Canyon Overlook Trail,** which begins just east of the long tunnel. Checkerboard Mesa's distinctive pattern is caused by a combination of vertical fractures and horizontal bedding planes, both accentuated by weathering.

The highway's spectacular descent into Zion Canyon goes first through a 530-foot tunnel, then a 1.1-mile tunnel, followed by a series of six switchbacks to the canyon floor. Because the longer tunnel, completed in 1930, is narrow, any vehicle more than 7 feet, 10 inches wide, 11 feet, 4 inches high, or 40 feet long (50 feet with trailer) must be escorted through in one-way traffic; a $15 fee, good for two passages, is charged at the tunnel to do this. Bicycles must be carried through the long tunnel on a car or truck; it's too dangerous to ride.

Kolob Terrace

The Kolob Terrace section of the park is a high plateau roughly parallel to and west of Zion Canyon. From the town of Virgin (15 miles west of the south entrance station on Hwy. 9), the steep (but now paved) **Kolob Terrace Road** runs north through ranch land and up a narrow tongue of land with drop-offs on either side, and then onto a high plateau where the land widens out. The Hurricane Cliffs rise from the gorge to the west, and the back sides of Zion Canyon's big walls are to the east. The road passes in and out of the park and terminates at Kolob Reservoir, a popular boating and fishing destination outside the park. This section of the park is much higher than Zion Canyon, so it is a good place to explore when the canyon swelters in the summertime. It's also much less crowded than the busy canyon. Snow usually blocks the way in winter.

Lava Point

The panorama from **Lava Point** (elevation 7,890 feet) takes in the Cedar Breaks area to the north, the Pink Cliffs to the northeast, Zion Canyon Narrows and tributaries to the east, the Sentinel and other monoliths of Zion Canyon to the southeast, and Mount Trumbull on the Arizona Strip to the south. Signs help identify features. Lava Point, which sits atop a lava flow, is a good place to cool off in summer—temperatures are about 20 degrees cooler than in Zion Canyon. Aspen, ponderosa pine, Gambel oak, and white fir grow here. A small primitive campground near the point offers sites during warmer months (free), but there is no water. From Virgin, take the Kolob

Terrace Road about 21 miles north to the Lava Point turnoff; the viewpoint is 1.8 miles farther on a well-marked but unpaved spur road. (Vehicles longer than 19 feet are prohibited on the Lava Point road.) Expect the trip from Virgin to Lava Point to take about an hour.

Kolob Reservoir

Kolob Reservoir is a high-country lake north of Lava Point that has good fishing for rainbow trout. An unpaved boat ramp is at the south end near the dam. People sometimes camp along the shore, although there are no facilities. Most of the surrounding land is private. To reach the reservoir, continue north 3.5 miles on Kolob Terrace Road from the Lava Point turnoff. The fair-weather road can also be followed past the reservoir to the Cedar City area. Blue Springs Reservoir, near the turnoff for Lava Point, is closed to the public.

Kolob Canyons

North and west of Zion Canyon is the remote backcountry of the Kolob. This area became a second Zion National Monument in 1937, and then was added to Zion National Park in 1956. The paved five-mile Kolob Canyons Road begins at the Kolob Canyons Visitor Center just off I-15 and ends at the Timber Creek Overlook Trail; it's open year-round.

Kolob Canyons Road

A five-mile scenic drive, **Kolob Canyons Road** winds past the dramatic Finger Canyons of the Kolob to Timber Creek Overlook Trail. The road is paved and has many pullouts where you can stop to admire the scenery. The first part of the drive follows the 200-mile-long Hurricane Fault, which forms the west edge of the Markagunt Plateau. Look for the tilted rock layers deformed by friction as the plateau rose nearly one mile. **Taylor Creek Trail,** which begins two miles past the visitors center, provides a close look at the canyons.

Lee Pass, four miles beyond the visitors center, was named after John D. Lee, who was the only person ever convicted of a crime in the infamous Mountain Meadows Massacre; he's believed to have lived nearby for a short time after the 1857 incident, in which a California-bound wagon train was attacked by an alliance of Mormons and local Native Americans. About 120 people in the wagon train were killed. Only small children too young to tell the story were spared. The close-knit Mormon community tried to cover up the incident and hindered federal attempts to apprehend the killers. Only Lee, who was in charge of Indian affairs in southern Utah at the time, was ever brought to justice; he was later executed.

La Verkin Creek Trail begins at the Lee Pass trailhead and offers trips to Kolob Arch and beyond. Signs at the end of the road identify the points, buttes, mesas, and mountains. The salmon-colored Navajo sandstone cliffs glow a deep red at sunset. **Timber Creek Overlook Trail** begins from the picnic area at road's end and climbs 0.5 mile to the overlook (elevation 6,369 feet); views encompass the Pine Valley Mountains, Zion Canyon, and distant Mount Trumbull.

Recreation

Zion's hiking trails are tailored to all abilities, making it easy to explore. Both the Pa'rus Trail and Riverside Walk are wheelchair accessible. Casual hikers can spend several days riding the shuttle bus up Zion Canyon and hopping off for day hikes. These hikes, past lush hanging gardens or up to vertiginous viewpoints, may whet your appetite for extended backpacking trips or an in-water hike up the Virgin River Narrows.

Experienced hikers can do countless off-trail routes in the canyons and plateaus surrounding Zion Canyon; rangers can suggest areas. Rappelling and other climbing skills may be needed to negotiate drops in some of the more remote canyons. Groups cannot exceed 12 hikers per trail or drainage. Overnight hikers must obtain backcountry permits from the Zion Canyon or Kolob Canyons Visitor Centers or online (http://zionpermits.nps.gov). The permit fees are based on group size: $10 for 1-2 people, $15 for 3-7, and $20 for 8-12, plus an additional $5 for online purchases. Some areas of the park—mainly those near roads and major trails—are closed to overnight use. Ask about shuttles to backcountry trailheads outside Zion Canyon at the visitors center's **backcountry desk** (435/772-0170). Shuttles are also available from **Zion Rock and Mountain Guides** (1458 Zion Park Blvd., 435/772-3303, www.zionrockguides.com) and the **Zion Adventure Company** (36 Lion Blvd., 435/772-1001, www.zionadventures.com) in Springdale.

Hiking in Zion Canyon

The trails in Zion Canyon provide perspectives of the park that are not available from the roads. Many of the hiking trails require long ascents but aren't too difficult at a leisurely pace. Carry water on all but the shortest walks. Descriptions of the following trails are given in order from the mouth of Zion Canyon to the Virgin River Narrows.

Pa'rus Trail

Distance: 3.5 miles round-trip
Duration: 2 hours
Elevation change: 50 feet
Effort: easy
Trailheads: South Campground and Canyon Junction
Shuttle stops: Zion Canyon Visitor Center and Canyon Junction

This paved, wheelchair-accessible trail runs from South Campground to the Canyon Junction shuttle-bus stop. For most of its distance, it skirts the Virgin River, and it makes for a nice early-morning or evening stroll. Listen for the trilling song of the canyon wren (easy to hear!), then try to spot the small bird in the bushes (not so easy to see). The Pa'rus Trail is the only trail in the park open to bicycles and pets.

Watchman Trail

Distance: 2.7 miles round-trip
Duration: 2 hours
Elevation change: 370 feet
Effort: easy-moderate
Trailhead: just north of Watchman Campground
Shuttle stop: Zion Canyon Visitor Center

No, this hike doesn't go to the top of 6,555-foot Watchman Peak, but it does lead to a mesa southeast of the visitors center with a good view of this prominent mountain. The hike starts off fairly unspectacularly, but it gets more interesting as it gains elevation. Be sure to look back over your shoulder for views of Zion Canyon's high walls.

At the top of the mesa, the Watchman pops into view. The short mesa-top loop trail is worth taking for its views of Springdale and its nice assortment of wildflowers, including barrel cacti.

During the middle of the day, this trail can bake in the sun. Try to hike it on a cool day or early or late in the day. In fact, it's a good shakedown hike to do on the evening you arrive at Zion. As soon as the sun drops behind the canyon walls, set out—on long summer evenings, you'll have plenty of time to complete it before dark.

Sand Bench Trail

Distance: 1.7 miles round-trip
Duration: 3 hours
Elevation change: 500 feet
Effort: easy
Trailhead: Zion Lodge
Shuttle stops: Court of the Patriarchs or Zion Lodge

This loop trail has good views of the Three Patriarchs, the Streaked Wall, and other monuments of lower Zion Canyon. During the main season, outfitters across the road from Zion Lodge organize three-hour horseback rides on the trail. The horses churn up dust and leave an uneven surface (among other things), so hikers usually prefer to go elsewhere

during those times. The trail soon leaves the riparian forest along Birch Creek and climbs onto the dry benchland. Piñon pine, juniper, sand sage, yucca, prickly pear cactus, and other high-desert plants and animals live here. Hikers can get off the shuttle at the Court of the Patriarchs Viewpoint, walk across the scenic drive, and then follow a service road to the footbridge and trailhead. A 1.2-mile trail along the river connects the trailhead with Zion Lodge. In warmer months, try to hike in the early morning or late afternoon.

★ Emerald Pools Trails

Distance: 0.6 mile one-way to Lower Emerald Pool; 1 mile to Middle Emerald Pool; 1.4 miles to Upper Emerald Pool
Duration: 1-3 hours
Elevation change: 70 feet to Lower Emerald Pool; 150 feet to Middle Emerald Pool; 350 feet to Upper Emerald Pool
Effort: easy-moderate
Trailhead: across the footbridge from Zion Lodge
Shuttle stop: Zion Lodge

Spring-fed pools, small waterfalls, and views of Zion Canyon make this hike a favorite. You have a choice of two trails. The easiest is the paved trail to the Lower Pool; cross the footbridge near Zion Lodge and turn right. The Middle Pool can be reached by continuing 350 yards on this trail.

Another trail begins at the Grotto Picnic Area, crosses a footbridge, and turns left before continuing for 0.7 mile; the trail forks left to the Lower Pool and right to the Middle Pool. A steep 0.4-mile trail leads from the Middle Pool to Upper Emerald Pool. This magical spot has a white sand beach and towering cliffs rising above. Don't expect to find solitude; these relatively easy trails are quite popular.

Although these trails are relatively

Top to bottom: hikers on the final stretch to Angels Landing; Emerald Pools, Zion; Hidden Canyon Trail.

easy, they do get icy and slippery. More people have died from falls on the Emerald Pools Trails than on the hike to Angels Landing, so do hike with attention and care.

★ West Rim Trail to Angels Landing

Distance: 5.4 miles round-trip
Duration: 4 hours
Elevation change: 1,488 feet
Effort: strenuous
Trailhead: Grotto Picnic Area
Shuttle stop: The Grotto

This strenuous trail leads to some of the best views of Zion Canyon. Start from Grotto Picnic Area (elevation 4,300 feet) and cross the footbridge, then turn right along the river. The trail, which was blasted out of the cliff side by Civilian Conservation Corps members during the 1930s, climbs the slopes and enters the cool and shady depths of Refrigerator Canyon. Walter's Wiggles, a series of 21 closely spaced switchbacks, wind up to Scout Lookout and a trail junction—it's four miles round-trip and a 1,050-foot elevation gain if you decide to turn around here. Scout Lookout has fine views of Zion Canyon. Turn right at the junction and continue 0.5 mile to the summit of Angels Landing.

Angels Landing rises as a sheer-walled monolith 1,500 feet above the North Fork of the Virgin River. Although the trail to the summit is rough, chains provide security in the more exposed places. Hike this final approach to Angels Landing with great caution and only in good weather; don't go if the trail is covered with snow or ice or if thunderstorms threaten. Children must be closely supervised, and people who are afraid of heights should skip this trail. Once on top, the panorama makes all the effort worthwhile. Not surprisingly, it's most pleasant to do this steep hike during the cooler morning hours.

Energetic hikers can continue 4.8 miles on the main trail from Scout Lookout to **West Rim Viewpoint,** which overlooks the Right Fork of North Creek. This strenuous 12.8-mile round-trip hike from Grotto Picnic Area includes 3,070 feet of elevation gain. West Rim Trail continues through Zion's backcountry to Lava Point (elevation 7,890 feet), where there's a primitive campground. A car shuttle and one or more days are needed to hike the 13.3 miles (one-way) from Grotto Picnic Area. You'll have an easier hike if you start at Lava Point and hike down to the picnic area; even so, be prepared for a long day hike. The trail has little or no water in some seasons.

Weeping Rock Trail

Distance: 0.5 mile round-trip
Duration: 30 minutes
Elevation change: 100 feet
Effort: easy
Trailhead: Weeping Rock parking area
Shuttle stop: Weeping Rock

A favorite with visitors, this easy trail winds past lush vegetation and wildflowers to a series of cliff-side springs above an overhang. Thousands of water droplets glisten in the afternoon sun. The springs emerge where water seeping through more than 2,000 feet of Navajo sandstone meets a layer of impervious shale. Signs along the way identify some of the trees and plants.

Observation Point Trail

Distance: 8 miles round-trip
Duration: 5 hours
Elevation change: 2,148 feet
Effort: strenuous
Trailhead: Weeping Rock parking area
Shuttle stop: Weeping Rock

This strenuous trail climbs to Observation Point (elevation 6,507 feet) on the edge of Zion Canyon. Trails branch off along the way to Hidden Canyon, upper Echo Canyon, the east entrance, East Mesa, and other destinations. The first of many switchbacks along the East Rim Trail begins a short way up from the trailhead at Weeping Rock parking area. You'll reach the junction for Hidden Canyon Trail after 0.8 mile. Several switchbacks later, the trail enters sinuous Echo Canyon. This incredibly narrow chasm can be explored for short distances upstream and downstream to deep pools and pour-offs. **Echo Canyon Trail** branches to the right at about the halfway point; this rough trail continues farther up the canyon and connects with trails to Cable Mountain, Deertrap Mountain, and the east entrance station (on Zion-Mt. Carmel Highway). The East Rim Trail then climbs slickrock slopes above Echo Canyon with many fine views. Parts of the trail are cut right into the cliffs; this work was done in the 1930s by the Civilian Conservation Corps. You'll reach the rim at last after three miles of steady climbing, and then it's an easy 0.6 mile hike through a forest of piñon pine, juniper, Gambel oak, manzanita, sage, and some ponderosa pine to Observation Point. Impressive views take in Zion Canyon below and mountains and mesas all around. The **East Mesa Trail** turns right about 0.3 mile before Observation Point and follows the plateau northeast to a dirt road outside the park.

★ Hidden Canyon Trail

Distance: 3 miles round-trip
Duration: 2.5-3 hours
Elevation change: 850 feet
Effort: strenuous
Trailhead: Weeping Rock parking area
Shuttle stop: Weeping Rock

See if you can spot the entrance to Hidden Canyon from below. Inside the narrow canyon are small sandstone caves, a little natural arch, and diverse plantlife. The high walls, rarely more than 65 feet apart, block sunlight except for a short time at midday. From the trailhead at the Weeping Rock parking area, follow the East Rim Trail 0.8 mile up the cliff face, then turn right and go 0.7 mile on Hidden Canyon Trail to the canyon entrance. Footing can be a bit difficult in places, but chains provide handholds

Riverside Walk

on the exposed sections. Steps chopped into the rock just inside Hidden Canyon help bypass some deep pools. After heavy rains and spring runoff, the creek forms a small waterfall at the canyon entrance. The canyon itself is about one mile long and mostly easy walking, although the trail fades away. Look for the arch on the right about 0.5 mile up the canyon.

Riverside Walk

Distance: 2.2 miles round-trip
Duration: 1.5-2 hours
Elevation change: 57 feet
Effort: easy
Trailhead: Temple of Sinawava parking area
Shuttle stop: Temple of Sinawava

This is one of the most popular hikes in the park, and except for the Pa'rus, it's the easiest. The nearly level paved trail begins at the end of Zion Canyon Scenic Drive and heads upstream along the Virgin River to the Narrows. Allow about two hours to fully take in the scenery—it's a good place to get a close-up view of Zion's lovely hanging gardens. Countless springs and seeps on the canyon walls support luxuriant plant growth and swamps. Most of the springs occur at the boundary between the porous Navajo sandstone and the less permeable Kayenta Formation below. The water and vegetation attract abundant wildlife; keep an eye out for birds and animals and their tracks. Late morning is the best time for photography. In autumn, cottonwoods and maples display bright splashes of color. At trail's end, the canyon is wide enough only for the river. Hikers continuing upstream on the Narrows hike must wade and sometimes even swim.

Hiking East of Zion Canyon

You can't take the park shuttle bus to trailheads east of Zion Canyon, so you'll want to drive if you plan on hiking in this area.

Canyon Overlook Trail

Distance: 1 mile round-trip
Duration: 1 hour
Elevation change: 163 feet
Effort: easy
Trailhead: parking area just east of the long (westernmost) tunnel on the Zion-Mt. Carmel Highway

This fun hike starts on the road east of Zion Canyon and features great views from the heights without the stiff climbs found on most other Zion trails. The trail winds in and out along the ledges of Pine Creek Canyon, which opens into a great valley. Panoramas at trail's end take in lower Zion Canyon in the distance. A sign at the viewpoint identifies Bridge Mountain, Streaked Wall, East Temple, and other features. The Great Arch of Zion—termed a "blind arch" because it's open only on one side—is below; the arch is 580 feet high, 720 feet long, and 90 feet deep.

Hiking from Kolob Terrace Road

From the town of Virgin, Kolob Terrace Road runs north and passes several trailheads, including a couple of great trails at Lava Point. These trails are far less traveled than those in Zion Canyon, and at about 7,000 feet, they stay fairly cool in summer.

Snow blocks the access road to Lava Point for much of the year; the usual season is May or June-early November. Check road conditions with the Zion Canyon or Kolob Canyons Visitor Centers. From the south entrance station in Zion Canyon, drive west 15 miles on Highway 9 to Virgin, travel north 21 miles on Kolob Terrace Road (signed for "Kolob Reservoir"), then turn right and continue 1.8 miles to Lava Point.

Northgate Peaks Trail

Distance: 4 miles round-trip
Duration: 2 hours
Elevation change: 50 feet
Effort: easy
Trailhead: Wildcat Canyon trailhead (southern end), 16 miles north of Virgin off Kolob Terrace Road

Most of the trails in this remote area of the park are long and challenging. Northgate Peaks is the exception: an easy family hike along a sandy trail. Hike out from the southern Wildcat Canyon trailhead and pass the turnoff to the Hop Valley Trail; about 200 yards farther, turn right (south) onto the Northgate Peaks Trail. The trail passes through a pine-strewn meadow to a trail's end overlook of the Great West Canyon, surrounded by highly textured sandstone domes. Wildflowers, including the strikingly pretty shooting stars, are abundant near the end of the trail. This is also a good place to look for raptors.

Wildcat Canyon Trail

Distance: 10 miles round-trip
Duration: 5 hours
Elevation change: 450 feet
Effort: moderate
Trailhead: Lava Point trailhead

The Wildcat Canyon Trail heads southwest from Lava Point to a trailhead on Kolob Terrace Road (16 miles north of Virgin), so if it's possible to arrange a shuttle, you can do this as a one-way hike in about three hours. The trail, which travels across slickrock, through forest, and past cliffs, has views of the Left Fork North Creek drainage, but it lacks a reliable water source. You can continue north and west toward Kolob Arch by taking the four-mile Connector Trail to the Hop Valley Trail.

You can also reach the Lava Point trailhead by hiking the one-mile **Barney's Trail** from Site 2 in Lava Point Campground.

Hiking in Kolob Canyons

There are two good day hikes in the Kolob Canyons: the short but steep Timber Creek Overlook Trail provides panoramic views, and the Taylor Creek Trail puts you right down into a canyon. Access these hikes from Kolob Canyons Road, which begins at I-15 south of Cedar City.

Taylor Creek Trail

Distance: 5 miles round-trip
Duration: 4 hours
Elevation change: 450 feet
Effort: easy-moderate
Trailhead: 2 miles east of Kolob Canyons Visitor Center, left side of the road

This excellent day hike from Kolob Canyons Road heads upstream into the canyon of the Middle Fork of Taylor Creek. Double Arch Alcove is 2.7 miles from the trailhead; a dry fall 350 yards farther blocks the way (water flows over it during spring runoff and after rains). A giant rockfall occurred here in 1990. From this trail you can also explore the North Fork of Taylor Creek. A separate trail along the South Fork of Taylor Creek leaves the road at a bend 3.1 miles from the visitors center, then goes 1.2 miles upstream beneath steep canyon walls.

Timber Creek Overlook Trail

Distance: 1 mile round-trip
Duration: 30 minutes

Elevation change: 100 feet
Effort: easy-moderate
Trailhead: at the end of Kolob Canyons Road, five miles from the visitors center

It's a short but relatively steep jaunt from the parking lot at the road's end to the Timber Creek Overlook. Along the way, you'll have good views of the Kolob's Finger Canyons, and on a clear day, the North Rim of the Grand Canyon is visible from the overlook.

Biking

One of the fringe benefits of the Zion Canyon shuttle bus is the great bicycling that's resulted from the lack of automobile traffic. It used to be way too scary to bike along the narrow, traffic-choked **Zion Canyon Scenic Drive,** but now it's a joy.

On the stretch of road where cars are permitted—between the Zion Canyon Visitor Center and Canyon Junction (where the Zion-Mt. Carmel Highway meets Zion Canyon Scenic Drive)—the two-mile paved **Pa'rus Trail** is open to cyclists as well as pedestrians and makes for easy, stress-free pedaling. Bicycles are allowed on the park road, but they must pull over to allow shuttle buses to pass.

If you decide you've had enough cycling, every shuttle bus has a rack that can hold two bicycles. Bike parking is plentiful at the visitors center, Zion Lodge, and most trailheads.

Outside the Zion Canyon area, **Kolob Terrace Road** is a good place to stretch your legs; it's 22 miles to Kolob Reservoir.

There's no place to mountain bike off-road within the park, but there are good mountain-biking spots, including places to practice slickrock riding, just outside the park boundaries. It's best to stop by one of the local bike shops for advice and a map of your chosen destination.

Bike rentals and maps are available in Springdale at **Zion Outfitter** (95 Zion Park Blvd., 435/772-5090, http://zionoutfitter.com) and at **Zion Cycles** (868 Zion Park Blvd., 435/772-0400, www.zioncycles.com), behind Zion Pizza and Noodle.

Horseback Riding

Trail rides on horses and mules leave from the corral near **Zion Lodge** (435/679-8665, www.canyonrides.com, mid-Mar.-Oct.) and head down the Virgin River. A one-hour trip ($40) goes to the Court of the Patriarchs, and a half-day ride ($80) follows the Sand Bench Trail. Riders must be at least age 7 for the short ride and age 10 for the half-day ride, and riders can weigh no more than 220 pounds.

Climbing

Rock climbers come to scale the high Navajo sandstone cliffs; after Yosemite, Zion is the nation's most popular big-wall climbing area. However, Zion's sandstone is far more fragile than Yosemite's granite, and it has a tendency to crumble and flake, especially when wet. Beginners should avoid these walls—experience with crack climbing is a must.

For route descriptions, pick up a copy of *Desert Rock* by Eric Bjørnstad or *Rock Climbing Utah* by Stewart M. Green. Both books are sold at the Zion Canyon Visitor Center bookstore. The backcountry desk in the visitors center also has a notebook full of route descriptions supplied by past climbers. Check here to make sure your climbing area is open—some are closed to protect nesting peregrine falcons—and remember to bring a pair of binoculars to scout climbing routes from the canyon floor.

If you aren't prepared to tackle the 2,000-foot-high canyon walls, you may want to check out a couple of **bouldering sites,** both quite close to the south entrance of the park. One huge boulder is 40 yards west of the park entrance; the other is a large slab with a crack, located 0.5 mile north of the entrance.

During the summer, it can be intensely hot on unshaded walls. The best months for climbing are March-May and September-early November.

If watching the climbers at Zion gives you a hankering to scale a wall, the **Zion Adventure Company** (36 Lion Blvd., Springdale, 435/772-1001, www.zionadventures.com) runs half-day and day-long climbing clinics for beginning and experienced climbers. Similar offerings are provided by **Zion Rock and Mountain Guides** (1458 Zion Park Blvd., Springdale, 435/772-3303, www.zionrockguides.com), **Red Desert Adventure** (435/668-2888, www.reddesertadventure.com), and **Zion Mountain School** (868 Zion Park Blvd., Springdale, 435/663-1783, www.guidesinzion.com), which specializes in private tours. All of these outfitters also guide clients on canyoneering expeditions. Outfitters are not permitted to lead climbs inside the park, so these activities are held outside of the park's boundaries.

Outfitters

Several good outfitters have shops in Springdale, just outside the park. Here you can buy all manner of gear and outdoor clothing. You can also pick up canyoneering skills, take a guided mountain-bike ride (outside the park), or learn to climb big sandstone walls.

Campers who left that crucial piece of equipment at home should visit **Zion Outdoor** (868 Zion Park Blvd., Springdale, 435/772-0630, www.zionoutdoor.com), as should anybody who needs to spruce up their wardrobe with some stylish outdoor clothing.

Zion Cycles (868 Zion Park Blvd., Springdale, 435/772-0400, www.zioncycles.com) offers rentals of all sorts of bikes, from kids bikes ($12 half-day) to road bikes ($28 half-day) to full-suspension mountain bikes ($40 half-day).

Canyoneering supplies, including gear to hike the Narrows or the Subway, are available from **Zion Adventure Company** (36 Lion Blvd., Springdale, 435/772-1001, www.zionadventures.com) and **Zion Rock and Mountain Guides** (1458 Zion Park Blvd., Springdale, 435/772-3303, www.zionrockguides.com).

Accommodations

Within the park, lodging is limited to Zion Lodge and three park campgrounds. Look to Springdale or the east entrance of the park for more options.

The quality of lodgings in the area just outside Zion National Park is quite high. Springdale offers a wide range of lodging. Rockville has several B&Bs, and Hurricane, the next town west of the park, has all the standard chain motels and the least expensive rooms in the area. During the off-season (late fall-early spring), rates drop substantially.

Inside the Park

The rustic **Zion Lodge** (435/772-7700, www.zionlodge.com, $200-260) is in the heart of Zion Canyon, three miles up Zion Canyon Scenic Drive. Zion Lodge provides the only accommodations and food options within the park. It's open year-round; reservations for guest rooms can be made up to 13 months in advance. During high season, all rooms are fully booked months in advance. Accommodations in motel rooms near the main lodge or cute cabins (gas fireplaces but no TV) run around $200; lodge rooms are $260. The lodge also has evening programs, a gift shop, and Wi-Fi in the lobby.

Zion Canyon Campgrounds

Campgrounds in the park often fill up on Easter and other major holidays. During summer, they're often full by early afternoon, so it's best to arrive early in the day. The **South Campground** and **Watchman Campground** (information 435/772-3256, $16), both just inside the south entrance, have sites with water but no showers. Watchman (164 sites) has some sites with electrical hookups ($18) along with prime riverside spots ($20). Reservations can be made in advance for some sites at Watchman Campground (877/444-6777, www.recreation.gov, $10 reservation fee) but not at South Campground. One of the campgrounds stays open year-round. During April and May of some years, the park campgrounds may have an influx of western tent caterpillars, which defoliate trees; populations vary greatly from year to year.

South Campground (126 sites) is a bit smaller than Watchman, with a few choice walk-in sites and easy access to the Pa'rus Trail, but tenters shouldn't eschew Watchman; loops C and D are for tents, and these sites are more spacious than those at South. Some of the fruit trees planted in the campgrounds by early pioneers are still producing; you can pick your own.

It should be noted that camping in Zion's two big campgrounds is pretty easy; indeed, except for the lack of showers, it can be luxurious. Campers have easy access, via the park's free shuttles, to good restaurants in Springdale. It's simple enough to find showers in Springdale; just outside the park, Zion Outfitter charges $5.

Private campgrounds are just outside the park in Springdale and just east of the park's east entrance. Camping supplies, sack lunches, and groceries are available just outside the park entrance at **Canyon Market** (Springdale shuttle stop, 95 Zion Park Blvd., 435/772-0336, 7am-10pm daily).

Kolob Campgrounds

Up the Kolob Terrace Road are six first-come, first-served sites at **Lava Point Campground** (no water, free), a small primitive campground open during warmer months. The **Red Ledge Campground** (435/586-9150, Apr.-Nov., $25) in Kanarraville is the closest commercial campground to the Kolob

Top to bottom: Pa'rus Trail, Zion Canyon; Zion Lodge; Watchman Campground.

Canyons area, and there's no other campground in this part of the park; go two miles north on I-15, take exit 42, and continue 4.5 miles into downtown Kanarraville. The campground has tent and RV sites, cabins, a store, showers, and a laundry room. The tiny agricultural community of Kanarraville was named after a local Paiute chief. A low ridge south of town marks the southern limit of prehistoric Lake Bonneville. Hikers can explore trails in Spring and Kanarra Canyons within the Spring Canyon Wilderness Study Area just east of town.

Outside the Park: Rockville

The hosts at the **Bunkhouse at Zion B&B** (149 E. Main St., Rockville, 435/772-3393, www.bunkhouseatzion.com, $60-90) are dedicated to living sustainably, and they bring this ethic into their two-room B&B. The views are remarkable from this quiet spot in Rockville.

Outside the Park: Springdale

$50-100

The least expensive lodgings in Springdale are the motel rooms at **Zion Park Motel** (865 Zion Park Blvd., 435/772-3251, www.zionparkmotel.com, $89-159), an older, well-kept motel with a small pool about one mile from the park entrance.

$100-150

Under the Eaves B&B (980 Zion Park Blvd., 435/772-3457, www.undertheeaves.com, $95-185) features six homey guest rooms, plus a spacious suite, all in a vintage home and a garden cottage. Children over age eight are welcome, and all guests get free breakfast at nearby Oscar's Café.

The **Canyon Ranch Motel** (668 Zion Park Blvd., Springdale, 435/772-3357 or 866/946-6276, www.canyonranchmotel.com, $99-119) is another good value, with small units—some with kitchenettes—scattered around a grassy shaded lawn.

Even the budget motels in Springdale are nice.

For a place with a bit of personality, or perhaps more accurately, with multiple personalities, try the **Novel House Inn at Zion** (73 Paradise Rd., 435/772-3650 or 800/711-8400, www.novelhouse.com, $139-159), a B&B with 10 guest rooms, each decorated with a literary theme and named after an author, including Mark Twain, Rudyard Kipling, and Louis L'Amour. All guest rooms have private baths and great views, and the B&B is tucked off the main drag.

The renovated **Driftwood Lodge** (1515 Zion Park Blvd., 435/772-3262 or 800/801-8811, www.driftwoodlodge.net, $139-215) is a six-building complex with a pool and spa on its spacious grounds and pet-friendly guest rooms with refrigerators and microwaves. It's a big step up from the area's budget motels.

Over $150

★ **Flanigan's Inn** (428 Zion Park Blvd., 435/772-3244 or 800/765-7787, www.flanigans.com, $129-299) is a quiet and convenient place to stay. Guest rooms are set back off the main drag and face onto a pretty courtyard. Up on the hill behind the inn, a labyrinth provides an opportunity to take a meditative walk in a stunning setting. An excellent restaurant (the Spotted Dog Café), a pool, and spa services make this an inviting place to spend several days. Two villas, essentially full-size houses, are also available.

An attractive motel for good value is **Best Western Zion Park Inn** (1215 Zion Park Blvd., 435/772-3200 or 800/934-7275, www.zionparkinn.com, $155-160), part of a complex with a restaurant, a swimming pool, a gift shop, and some of the nicest guest rooms in Springdale. In addition to regular guest rooms, there are also various suites and kitchen units available.

Probably the most elegant place to stay is the ★ **Desert Pearl Inn** (707 Zion Park Blvd., 435/772-8888 or 888/828-0898, www.desertpearl.com, $178-328), a very handsome lodge-like hotel perched above the Virgin River. Some guest rooms have views of the river; others face the pool. Much of the wood used for the beams and the finish moldings was salvaged from a railroad trestle made of century-old Oregon fir and redwood that once spanned the north end of the Great Salt Lake. The guest rooms are all large and beautifully furnished, with a modern look.

Just outside the south gates to Zion, the ★ **Cliffrose Lodge** (281 Zion Park Blvd., 435/772-3234 or 800/243-8824, www.cliffroselodge.com, $179-299) sits on five acres of lovely well-landscaped gardens with riverfront access. The guest rooms are equally nice, especially the riverside rooms, and there's a pool and a laundry room. The Cliffrose is favored by many longtime Zion fans.

The closest lodging to the park is at **Cable Mountain Lodge** (147 Zion Park Blvd., 435/772-3366 or 877/712-3366, www.cablemountainlodge.com,

$169-259), in the same complex as the big-screen theater. Along with being extremely convenient, it's very nicely fitted out, with a pool, guest rooms with microwaves and fridges or small kitchens, and appealing architecture and decor to go along with the spectacular views.

Red Rock Inn (998 Zion Park Blvd., 435/772-3139, www.redrockinn.com, $169-209) offers accommodations in individual cabins and a cottage suite, all with canyon views. Full-breakfast baskets are delivered to your door.

Campgrounds

If you aren't able to camp in the park, the **Zion Canyon Campground** (479 Zion Park Blvd., 435/772-3237, www.zioncamp.com) is a short walk from the park entrance. Along with tent sites (no dogs allowed, $30) and RV sites ($39), there are motel rooms ($120-160). The sites are crammed pretty close together, but a few are situated right on the bank of the Virgin River. Facilities include a store, a pizza parlor, a game room, a laundry room, and showers.

Food

Inside the Park

The **Red Rock Grill** (435/772-7760, www.zionlodge.com, dinner reservations required, 6:30am-10:30am, 11:30am-3pm, 5pm-10pm daily, dinner entrées $15-32), the restaurant at Zion Lodge, offers a Southwestern and Mexican-influenced menu for breakfast, lunch, and dinner daily. Also at the lodge, a snack bar, the **Castle Dome Café** (breakfast, lunch, and dinner daily spring-fall) serves fast food; a cart on the patio sells beer.

Outside the Park: Springdale

★ **Deep Creek Coffee** (932 Zion Park Blvd., 435/767-0272, deepcreekcoffee.com, 6:30am-2pm daily) is the hip place to hang out in the morning. Besides excellent coffee drinks and made-from-scratch chai, they serve tasty homemade scones and other pastries. For a more substantial meal, head across the way to **Oscar's Café** (948 Zion Park Blvd., 435/772-3232, www.cafeoscars.com, 8am-2 hours after sunset daily, $8-25), where you can get a good burger or a Mexican-influenced breakfast or lunch. The patio, set back off the main road, is especially pleasant.

An old gas station has become the ★ **Whiptail Grill** (445 Zion Park Blvd., 435/772-0283, noon-10pm daily mid-Feb.-Nov., $8-15), a casual spot serving innovative homemade food, such as incredibly good spaghetti squash enchiladas or fish tacos jazzed up with grape salsa. There's very little seating inside, so plan to eat at the outdoor tables (warmed and lit by gas torches during the evening) or take your meal to go.

The ★ **Spotted Dog Café** (Flanigan's Inn, 428 Zion Park Blvd., 435/772-3244, www.flanigans.com, breakfast buffet 7am-11am daily spring-fall, dinner 5pm-9:30pm daily spring-fall, 5pm-9:30pm Tues.-Sun. winter, dinner $14-32) is one of Springdale's top restaurants; it has a good wine list and a full bar and uses high-quality ingredients for its American bistro cuisine, including pepita-crusted grilled trout and game meat loaf (made with bacon, elk, buffalo, and beef). Be sure to order a salad with (or for) your dinner—the house salad is superb. If you want to eat outside, try to get a table on the back patio, which is quieter and more intimate than the dining area out front.

A short walk from the park entrance, **Cafe Soleil** (205 Zion Park Blvd., 435/772-0505, www.cafesoleilzionpark.com, 7am-7pm daily) is a bright, friendly place for breakfast or a lunchtime sandwich ($8-12).

Immediately outside the park entrance, **Zion Canyon Brew Pub** (95 Zion Park Blvd., 435/772-0336, www.zioncanyonbrewpub.com, noon-10pm daily, $10-16) is a handy place for a casual dinner. The beer is brewed in town (though not on-site), and the patio out back is delightful on a warm evening. (Inside seating doesn't have nearly the ambience.) The food is just a notch above standard brewpub fare, but quite tasty after a day of hiking.

A good, reasonably priced place to bring a family with picky eaters is **Zion Pizza and Noodle** (868 Zion Park Blvd., 435/772-3815, www.zionpizzanoodle.com, 4pm-close daily, $11-16), housed in an old church and serving a good selection of microbrews. The menu at this busy restaurant is wide-ranging, with lots of pasta dishes, calzones, and salads in addition to the pizza.

Another very popular place for dinner in Springdale is the **Bit & Spur Restaurant** (1212 Zion Park Blvd., 435/772-3498, www.bitandspur.com, reservations recommended during busy season, 5pm-close daily, $12-26), a lively Mexican-influenced place with a menu that goes far beyond the usual south-of-the-border concoctions. The sweet-potato tamales keep us coming back year after year. The restaurant also offers full liquor service.

The town's only full-fledged supermarket, **Sol Foods** (995 Zion Park Blvd., 435/772-3100, www.solfoods.com, 7am-11pm daily) stocks groceries, deli items, hardware, and camping supplies.

Bryce Canyon National Park

Looking at the rock formations in Bryce Canyon is like looking at puffy clouds in the sky; it's easy to find images in the shapes of the rocks. Some see the natural rock sculptures as Gothic castles, others as Egyptian temples, subterranean worlds inhabited by dragons, or vast armies of a lost empire. The Paiute tale of the Legend People relates how various animals and birds once lived in a beautiful city built for them by Coyote; when the Legend People began behaving badly toward Coyote, he transformed them all into stone.

Bryce Canyon isn't a canyon at all, but rather the largest of a series of massive amphitheaters cut into the Pink Cliffs. In Bryce Canyon National Park, you can gaze into the depths from viewpoints and trails on the plateau rim or hike down moderately steep trails and wind your way among the spires. A 17-mile scenic drive traces the length of the park and passes many overlooks and trailheads. Away from the road, the nearly 36,000 acres of Bryce Canyon National Park offer many opportunities to explore spectacular rock features, dense forests, and expansive meadows.

The park's elevation ranges 6,600-9,100 feet, so it's usually much cooler here than at Utah's other national parks. Expect pleasantly warms days in summer, frosty nights in spring and fall, and snow at almost any time of year. The visitors center, the scenic drive, and a campground stay open throughout the year.

Getting There from Zion National Park

70 miles / 1.5 hours

Bryce Canyon National Park is just **70 miles** from Zion; it's an easy, exceedingly scenic drive of about **1.5 hours** on **US 89 North,** part of it along the East Fork of the Virgin River.

Leaving Zion National Park through the east exit, take **UT-9,** also known as the **Zion-Mt. Carmel Highway,** 15 miles east to Mt. Carmel, Utah. From there, head north (a left turn) on **US 89** for about 45 miles, then turn right onto **UT-12.** Rising high into the evergreen forests and pink hoodoos of the Dixie National Forest, the 15-mile drive on UT-12—one of the most beautiful drives on the Colorado Plateau—brings you to **UT-63,** the only road into Bryce Canyon National Park. Turn south (right) toward the park, passing the complex of Ruby's Inn (a sprawling hotel, restaurant, gas station, and general store), then drive another several miles to the park entrance station.

Winter is cold and snowy in Bryce Canyon, at about 9,000 feet above sea level. The weather doesn't usually close down the park road, as it is plowed after big storms.

Getting There from Capitol Reef National Park

120 miles / 2.5 hours

The drive from Capitol Reef to Bryce Canyon sticks mostly to **UT-12,** passing between Grand Staircase-Escalante National Monument to the southeast and the Dixie National Forest to the northwest. The **120-mile** trip takes about **2.5 hours.**

After exiting Capitol Reef National Park via **UT-24** toward Torrey, turn south (left) onto **UT-12** after several miles. The winding two-lane highway descends through the forest while passing the small towns of Boulder, Escalante, Henriville, and Tropic. After 110 miles, turn south (left) on **UT-63,** the only route into Bryce Canyon National Park. Drive another two miles to the entrance station.

Though it's cold and sometimes slightly snowy here, the roads around Capitol Reef generally stay open and safe during the winter.

Stopping in Escalante

The tiny town of Escalante, Utah, is an ideal jumping-off point for exploring the nearby **Dixie National Forest** and **Grand Staircase-Escalante National Monument,** two essential destinations for hard-core hikers, canyoneers, rock-hoppers, and red-rock rats. The town stretches out along UT-12 about an hour (60 miles) northeast of Bryce Canyon National Park.

Pop into the **Escalante Interagency Visitor Center** (755 W. Main St., 435/826-5499, 8am-4:30pm daily mid-Mar.-mid-Nov., 8am-4:30pm Mon.-Fri. mid-Nov.-mid-Mar.) on your way into town, where helpful folks pass out trail guides, information, and advice on visiting and exploring the surrounding backcountry.

Stop for a bite at the **Circle D Eatery** (475 W. Main St., 435/826-4125, www.escalantecircledeatery.com, 7:30am-9:30pm Wed.-Mon., $8-19), a sleek and sophisticated bistro way in the middle of the wilderness. At **Nemo's Drive Thru** (40 E. Main St., 435/826-4500, 11am-8pm daily, $7-12), a popular place with the motorcycle riders that haunt this highway, they serve classic road food: burgers, dogs, and fries.

If you're staying overnight, the **Circle D Motel** (475 W. Main St., 801/362-2770. www.escalantecircledmotel.com, $74-99), right next to the Circle D Eatery, caters to hikers, bikers, and explorers with comfortable, clean rooms.

Visiting Bryce Canyon National Park

Bryce Canyon National Park (435/834-5322, www.nps.gov/brca, $30 per vehicle, $25 per motorcycle, $15 per bicycle/pedestrian, admission good for 7 days and unlimited shuttle use) is just south of the incredibly scenic Highway 12, between Bryce Junction and Tropic.

Special hazards you should be aware of include crumbling ledges and lightning strikes. People who wandered off trails or got too close to the drop-offs have had to be pulled out by rope. Avoid cliffs and other exposed areas during electrical storms, which are most common in late summer.

Entrances

The only entrance to Bryce Canyon National Park is along **UT-63,** about three miles from its junction with UT-12.

Park Passes and Fees

It costs $30 per vehicle, $25 per motorcycle, and $15 per bike or pedestrian to enter Bryce Canyon National Park. The fee is good for seven days. A **Bryce Canyon National Park Annual Pass** is $35,

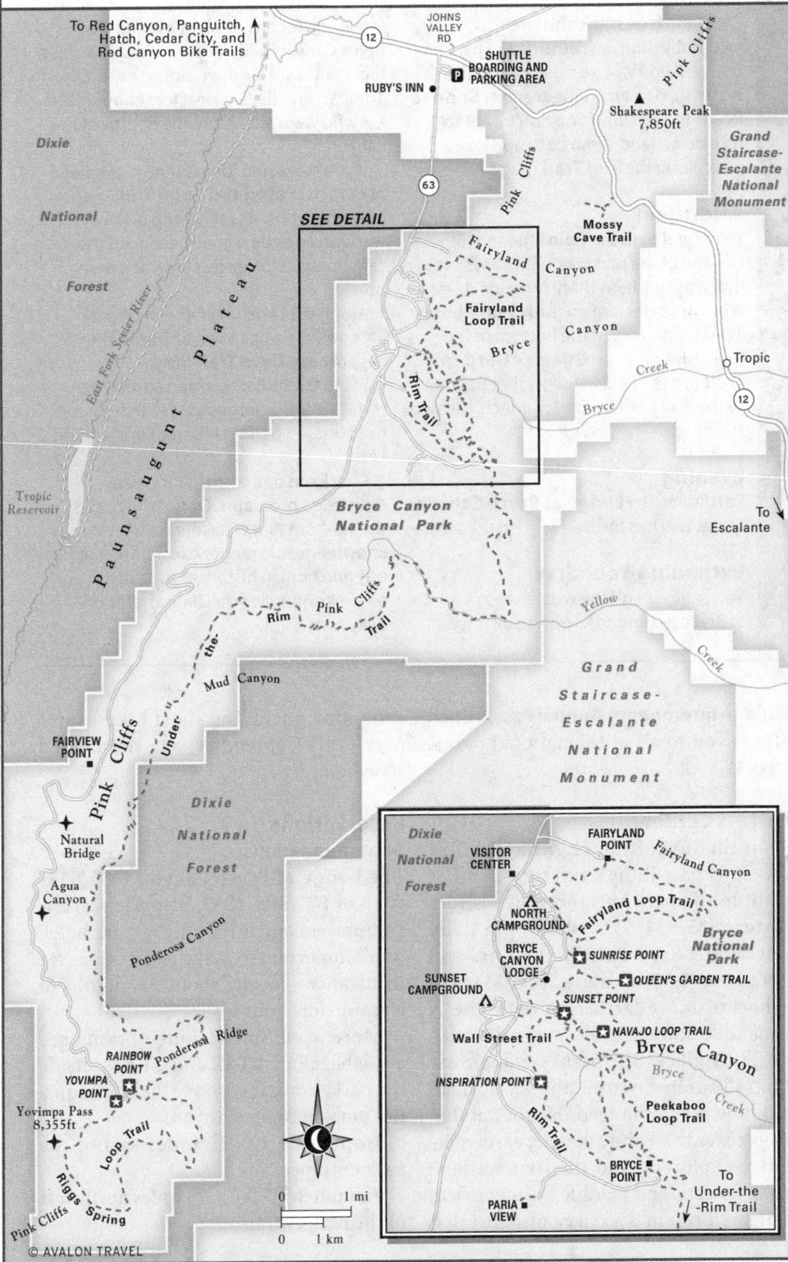
Bryce Canyon National Park
To Red Canyon, Panguitch, Hatch, Cedar City, and Red Canyon Bike Trails
JOHNS VALLEY RD
12
SHUTTLE BOARDING AND PARKING AREA
RUBY'S INN
Pink Cliffs
Shakespeare Peak 7,850ft
Grand Staircase-Escalante National Monument
Dixie National Forest
63
Pink Cliffs
Mossy Cave Trail
SEE DETAIL
Fairyland Canyon
Fairyland Loop Trail
Bryce Canyon
East Fork Sevier River
Paunsaugunt Plateau
Tropic
Creek
Bryce
12
Rim Trail
Tropic Reservoir
Bryce Canyon National Park
To Escalante
Yellow Creek
Under-the-Rim Trail
Pink Cliffs
Mud Canyon
Grand Staircase-Escalante National Monument
FAIRVIEW POINT
Pink Cliffs
Dixie National Forest
Natural Bridge
Agua Canyon
Ponderosa Canyon
Ponderosa Ridge
RAINBOW POINT
YOVIMPA POINT
Yovimpa Pass 8,355ft
Loop Trail
Riggs Spring
Pink Cliffs
0 1 mi
0 1 km
Dixie National Forest
VISITOR CENTER
FAIRYLAND POINT
Fairyland Canyon
NORTH CAMPGROUND
Fairyland Loop Trail
Bryce National Park
BRYCE CANYON LODGE
SUNRISE POINT
SUNSET CAMPGROUND
QUEEN'S GARDEN TRAIL
SUNSET POINT
NAVAJO LOOP TRAIL
Wall Street Trail
Bryce Canyon
Bryce Creek
INSPIRATION POINT
Rim Trail
Peekaboo Loop Trail
BRYCE POINT
To Under-the-Rim Trail
PARIA VIEW

Bryce in One Day

Morning

Catch the **free park shuttle** (page 114) near Ruby's Inn, just outside the park entrance. If you woke up early enough (it's worth it), don't miss the scene at **Sunrise Point** (page 115). If you don't want to hike down (and climb back up), take a walk along the **Rim Trail** (page 117).

Afternoon

Picnic at **Rainbow Point** (page 116), the end of the parkway, with views over much of southern Utah. After lunch, descend from the rim on the **Navajo Loop Trail** (page 118). At the bottom of the loop, turn onto the **Queen's Garden Trail** (page 118) and follow that back up to the rim. The Rim Trail connects the two trailheads.

Evening

For dinner, the **Lodge at Bryce Canyon** (page 122) has the best food in the area.

Extending Your Stay

You could spend the whole season at Bryce getting to know the distinct personality of each hoodoo. Two days is enough for an excellent overview of Bryce Canyon, allowing time for a few hikes and a scenic drive along the rim. Three to four days is ideal for serious hikers who want to explore the depths of the canyon.

If you're staying longer than a day, head over to the **Fairyland Loop Trail** (page 118), an eight-mile round-trip hike through an aptly named section of the canyon that is often less crowded than others.

Along UT-12 between the main park area and the small town of Tropic, the easy **Mossy Cave Trail** (page 120) leads to the titular cave and a small waterfall. This is a gorgeous area that's easy to access—a perfect hike for families with kids.

Check out one of the park's many ranger-led programs. One of the best is the 1.5-hour Rim Walk, during which a knowledgeable ranger explains the geology and human history of the canyon on an easy one-mile stroll (late afternoon daily June-Sept.).

while an **Interagency Annual Pass,** which admits you to all of the national parks, costs $80.

Visitors Center

From the turnoff on Highway 12, follow signs past Ruby's Inn for 4.5 miles south to the park entrance; the **visitors center** (435/834-5322, 8am-8pm daily May-Sept., 8am-6pm daily Apr. and Oct., 8am-4:30pm daily Nov.-Mar.) is a short distance farther on the right. A brief slide show, shown every 30 minutes, introduces the park. Geologic exhibits illustrate how the land was formed and how it has changed. Historical displays cover the Paiute people, early non-native explorers, and the first settlers; trees, flowers, and wildlife are identified. Rangers present a variety of naturalist programs, including short hikes, mid-May-early September; see the posted schedule.

Reservations

Accommodations

The **Lodge at Bryce Canyon** (435/834-8700 or 877/386-4383, http://brycecanyonforever.com) is the only in-park hotel, so it's important to make reservations far in advance—ideally about six months to a year before your visit.

More accommodations options are available along **UT-12** and **UT-63** outside the park. You can also try the communities outside Bryce Canyon:

Tropic (UT-12): 10 miles east of the park entrance

Panguitch (UT-12): 25 miles northwest of the park entrance

Hoodoos

Although many visitors assume that wind shaped Bryce Canyon's hoodoos, they were, in fact, formed by water, ice, and gravity, and the way those elements and forces have interacted over the years on rocks of varying hardness.

When the Colorado Plateau uplifted, vertical breaks—called joints—formed in the plateau. Joints allowed water to flow into the rock. As water flowed through these joints, erosion widened them into rivulets, gullies, and eventually deep slot canyons. Even more powerful than water, the action of ice freezing, melting, then freezing again, as it does about 200 days a year at Bryce, causes ice wedges to form within the rock joints, eventually breaking the rock.

Bryce Canyon is composed of layers of limestone, siltstone, dolomite, and mudstone. Each rock type erodes at a different rate, carving the strange shapes of the hoodoos. The word *hoodoo* derives from the same sources as *voodoo;* both words are sometimes used to describe folk beliefs and practices. Early Spanish explorers transferred the mystical sense of the word to the towering, vaguely humanoid rock formations that rise above Southwestern landscapes. The Spaniards believed that Native Americans worshipped these statue-like "enchanted rocks." In fact, while early indigenous people considered many hoodoo areas sacred, there is no evidence that they worshipped the stones themselves.

Campgrounds

There are two campgrounds within the park. **Sunset Campground** (877/444-6777, www.recreation.gov, May-Sept., $30 RV site, $20 tent site) is open during the high season. Of the 102 sites, only 20 tent sites are reservable, up to six months in advance. The rest of the sites are first-come, first served.

During high season (May-Sept.), 13 RV sites at **North Campground** (877/444-6777, www.recreation.gov, year-round, $30) are reservable, up to six months in advance. The rest of the 86 tent and RV sites are first-come, first-served. About half the sites are unavailable during the winter.

Information and Services

Park Newsletter

Make sure to pick up Bryce Canyon National Park's in-house newspaper, ***The Hoodoo,*** which is handed out at the entrance station and the visitor center. This excellent publication has maps, trail guides, shuttle schedules, and information on ranger programs.

Banking, Gas, and Groceries

The closest **groceries, ATM,** and **gas** are at **Ruby's Inn** (26 S. Main St.), a few miles outside of the park entrance on UT-63. You'll find the local **post office** there as well. Ruby's has the widest selection of supplies in the area.

The park's **General Store** (435/834-8700, http://brycecanyonforever.com, 8am-8pm daily Apr.-Oct.), located near Sunset Point at The Lodge at Bryce Canyon, has a small selection of groceries and camping supplies, but it's a good idea to get your essentials outside of the park. The general store also offers coin-operated laundry machines and showers.

Emergency Services

In the event of an emergency, call 911 or the **Garfield County Sheriff's Office** (435/676-2411). The closest emergency medical care is about 25 miles from Bryce Canyon, at **Garfield Memorial Hospital** (200 N. 400 E St., Panguitch, 435/676-8811, http:/intermountainhealthcare.org) in Panguitch, Utah.

Cell service in Bryce Canyon National Park is fairly spotty and should not be counted on.

Tours

The most basic tour of the park, which comes with the price of admission, is a ride on the park shuttle bus. Shuttle buses run every 12 minutes or so during the peak part of the day, and the trip from Ruby's Inn to Bryce Point takes 50 minutes. Of course, the beauty of the shuttle is that you can get off at any stop, hike for a while, and then catch another bus. However, if you're not really planning to hike, consider joining one of the free, twice-daily **shuttle bus tours** (435/834-5290, 9am and 1:30pm, reservations required and available at Ruby's Inn, Ruby's Campground, or the shuttle parking area) of the park. These tours go all the way to Rainbow Point. Shuttle season is early May-mid-October and, unlike at Zion, shuttle use is voluntary.

Ruby's Inn (26 S. Main St., 866/866-6616, www.rubysinn.com), a hotel, restaurant, and recreation complex at the park entrance, is a good place to take measure of the opportunities for organized recreation and sightseeing excursions around Bryce Canyon. The lobby is filled with outfitters who are anxious to take you out on the trail; you'll find lots of recreational outfitters, along with vendors who organize hayrides, barn dances, and chuckwagon dinners. During the summer, Ruby's also sponsors a **rodeo** (7pm Wed.-Sat., $10 adults, $7 ages 3-12) across from the inn.

Parkgoers have long explored Bryce Canyon's hoodoos on horseback, and it's still an option offered at Ruby's and at the park lodge. You can also explore the area around Bryce Canyon on a noisier steed. Guided all-terrain vehicle (ATV) tours of Red Canyon are offered by **Ruby's ATV Tours** (435/834-5232, 1-hour trip $45 driver, $15 passenger).

If you'd like to get a look at Bryce and the surrounding area from the air, take a scenic flightseeing tour with **Bryce Canyon Airlines** (Ruby's Inn, 435/834-8060), which offers both plane and helicopter tours. There's quite a range of options, but a 35-minute airplane tour ($159 pp, 2-person minimum) provides a good look at the surroundings.

Getting Around

Car

You can drive your own vehicle into Bryce Canyon National Park. However, if you do drive into the park, don't plan to pull a trailer all the way to Rainbow Point. Trailers aren't allowed past Sunset Campground. Trailer parking is available at the visitors center.

Bryce Canyon Shuttle

During the summer, Bryce hosts an enormous number of visitors. In order to keep the one main road along the rim from turning into a parking lot, the National Park Service runs the **Bryce Canyon Shuttle** (mid-May-mid-Oct., 8am-8pm, shorter hours early and late in season, every 15-20 minutes, free). Buses run during the peak summer season from the shuttle parking and boarding area at the intersection of Highways 12 and 63 to the visitors center, with stops at Ruby's Inn and Ruby's Campground. From the visitors center, the shuttle travels to the park's developed areas, including all the main amphitheater viewpoints, Sunset Campground, and the Bryce Canyon Lodge. Passengers can take as long as they like at any viewpoint, then catch a later bus. The shuttle bus service also makes it easier for hikers, who don't need to worry about car shuttles between trailheads.

Scenic Drive

From elevations of about 8,000 feet near the visitors center, the park's scenic drive gradually winds 1,100 feet higher to Rainbow Point. About midway you'll notice a change in the trees from largely ponderosa pine to spruce, fir, and aspen. On a clear day, you can enjoy vistas of more than 100 miles from many of the viewpoints. Because of parking shortages on the drive, trailers must be left at the visitors center or your campsite. Visitors wishing to see all of the viewpoints should take a walk on the Rim Trail.

Note that even though the viewpoints are described here in north-to-south order, when the park is bustling, it's better to drive all the way to the southern end of the road and visit the viewpoints from south to north, thus avoiding left turns across traffic. Of course, if you're just heading to one viewpoint or trailhead, it's fine to drive directly to it.

Fairyland Point

The turnoff for **Fairyland Point** is just inside the park boundary, but before you get to the booth where payment is required; go north 0.8 mile from the visitors center, then east one mile. Whimsical forms line Fairyland Canyon a short distance below. You can descend into the fairyland on the **Fairyland Loop Trail** or follow the **Rim Trail** for other panoramas.

★ Sunrise and Sunset Points

The **Sunrise Point** and **Sunset Point** overlooks are off to the left about one mile south of the visitors center; they're connected by a 0.5-mile paved section of the **Rim Trail.** Panoramas from each point take in large areas of Bryce Amphitheater and beyond. The lofty Aquarius and Table Cliff Plateaus rise along the skyline to the northeast; you can see the same colorful Claron Formation in cliffs that faulting has raised about 2,000 feet higher. A short walk down either the **Queen's Garden Trail** or the **Navajo Loop Trail** from Sunset Point will bring you close to Bryce's hoodoos and provide a totally different experience from what you get atop the rim.

★ Inspiration Point

It's well worth the 0.75-mile walk south along the **Rim Trail** from Sunset Point to see a fantastic maze of hoodoos in the "Silent City" at **Inspiration Point.** It's also accessible by car, from a spur road near the Bryce Point turnoff. Weathering along vertical joints has cut many rows of narrow gullies, some more than 200 feet deep. It's a short but steep 0.2-mile walk up to Upper Inspiration Point.

Bryce Point

The **Bryce Point** overlook at the south end of Bryce Amphitheater has expansive views to the north and east. It's also the start for the **Rim, Peekaboo Loop,** and **Under-the-Rim Trails.** From the turnoff two miles south of the visitors center, follow signs 2.1 miles in.

Paria View

At **Paria View,** cliffs drop precipitously into the headwaters of Yellow Creek, a tributary of the Paria River. You can see a section of the Under-the-Rim Trail winding up a hillside near the mouth of the amphitheater below. Distant views take in the Paria River Canyon, White Cliffs (of Navajo sandstone), and Navajo Mountain. The plateau rim in the park forms a drainage divide. Precipitation falling west of the rim flows gently into the East Fork of the Sevier River and the Great Basin; precipitation landing east of the rim rushes through deep canyons in the Pink Cliffs to the Paria River and on to the Colorado River and the Grand Canyon. Take the turnoff for Bryce Point, and then keep right at the fork.

Farview Point

The sweeping **Farview Point** panorama takes in a lot of geology. You'll see levels of the Grand Staircase that include the Aquarius and Table Cliff Plateaus to the northeast, Kaiparowits Plateau to the east, and White Cliffs to the southeast. Look beyond the White Cliffs to see a section of the Kaibab Plateau that forms the North Rim of the Grand Canyon in Arizona. The overlook is on the left, nine miles south of the visitors center.

Natural Bridge

The large **Natural Bridge** lies just off the road to the east, 1.7 miles past Farview Point. The span is 54 feet wide and 95 feet high. Despite its name, this is an arch formed by weathering from rain and freezing, not by stream erosion, as with a true natural bridge. Once the opening reached ground level, runoff began to enlarge the hole and to dig a gully through it.

Agua and Ponderosa Canyons

You can admire sheer cliffs and hoodoos from the **Agua Canyon** overlook to the east, 1.4 miles past Natural Bridge. With a little imagination, you may be able to pick out the Hunter and the Rabbit below. The **Ponderosa Canyon** overlook, 1.8 miles farther east, offers a panorama similar to that at Farview Point.

★ Yovimpa and Rainbow Points

The land drops away in rugged canyons and fine views at the end of the scenic drive, 17 miles south of the visitors center. At an elevation of 9,115 feet, this is the highest area of the park. **Yovimpa and Rainbow Points** are only a short walk apart yet offer different vistas. The **Bristlecone Loop Trail** is an easy one-mile loop from Rainbow Point to ancient bristlecone pines along the rim. The **Riggs Spring Loop Trail** makes a good day hike; you can begin from either Yovimpa Point or Rainbow Point and descend into canyons in the southern area of the park. The **Under-the-Rim Trail** starts from Rainbow Point and winds 23 miles to Bryce Point; day hikers can make a 7.5-mile trip by using the Agua Canyon Connecting Trail and a car shuttle.

Recreation

Although it's possible to have an entirely pleasant visit to Bryce by just riding the shuttle and hopping off to snap pictures

As the appointed hour nears, photographers gather at Sunset Point.

at various viewpoints, a short hike or horseback ride down off the rim will give you an entirely different perspective on the hoodoos, native plants, and, perhaps, wildlife of the park.

Hiking

Hikers enjoy close-up views of the wonderfully eroded features and gain a direct appreciation of Bryce's geology. Because almost all of the trails head down off the canyon's rim, they're moderately difficult, with many ups and downs, but the paths are well graded and signed. Hikers not accustomed to the 7,000- to 9,000-foot elevation will find the going relatively strenuous and should allow extra time. Be sure to carry water and drink frequently—staying well hydrated will give you more energy.

Wear a hat and sunscreen to protect against sunburn, which can be a problem at these elevations. Don't forget rain gear, because storms can come up suddenly. Always carry water for day trips; only a few natural sources exist. Ask at the visitors center for current trail conditions and water sources; you can also pick up a free hiking map at the visitors center. Snow may block some trail sections in winter and early spring. Horses are permitted only on Peekaboo Loop. Pets must stay above the rim; they're allowed on the Rim Trail only between Sunset and Sunrise Points.

Overnight hikers can obtain the required **backcountry permit** ($5-15 depending on size of group) at the visitors center. Camping is allowed only on the Under-the-Rim and Riggs Spring Loop Trails. Backpack stoves must be used for cooking; wood fires are prohibited. Although there are several isolated springs in Bryce's backcountry, it's prudent to carry at least one gallon of water per person per day. Ask about the location and flow of springs when you register for the backcountry permit.

Don't expect much solitude during the summer on the popular Rim, Queen's Garden, Navajo, and Peekaboo Loop Trails. Fairyland Loop Trail is less used, and the backcountry trails are almost never crowded. September-October are the choice hiking months—the weather is best and the crowds smallest, although nighttime temperatures in late October can dip well below freezing.

Rim Trail

Distance: 11 miles round-trip
Duration: 5-6 hours
Elevation change: 540 feet
Effort: easy
Trailheads: Fairyland Point, Bryce Point
Shuttle Stops: Fairyland Point, Bryce Point

This easy trail follows the edge of Bryce Amphitheater. Most people walk short sections of the rim in leisurely strolls or use the trail to connect with five other trails that head down beneath the rim. The 0.5-mile stretch of trail near the lodge between Sunrise and Sunset Points is paved and nearly level; other parts are gently rolling.

Fairyland Loop Trail

Distance: 8 miles round-trip
Duration: 4-5 hours
Elevation change: 2,300 feet
Effort: strenuous
Trailheads: Fairyland Point, Sunrise Point
Shuttle Stops: Fairyland Point, Sunrise Point

This trail winds in and out of colorful rock spires in the northern part of Bryce Amphitheater, a somewhat less-visited area one mile off the main park road. Although the trail is well graded, remember the steep, unrelenting climb you'll make when you exit. You can take a loop hike of eight miles from either Fairyland Point or Sunrise Point by using a section of the **Rim Trail;** a car shuttle saves three hiking miles. The whole loop is too long for many visitors, who enjoy short trips down and back to see this "fairyland."

★ Queen's Garden Trail

Distance: 1.8 miles round-trip
Duration: 1.5 hours
Elevation change: 320 feet
Effort: easy-moderate
Trailhead: Sunrise Point
Shuttle Stop: Sunrise Point

A favorite of many people, this trail drops from Sunrise Point through impressive features in the middle of Bryce Amphitheater to a hoodoo resembling a portly Queen Victoria. This is the easiest excursion below the rim. Queen's Garden Trail also makes a good loop hike with the **Navajo Loop** and **Rim Trails;** most people who do the loop prefer to descend the steeper Navajo and climb out on Queen's Garden Trail for a 3.5-mile hike. Trails also connect with the **Peekaboo Loop Trail** and go to the town of Tropic.

★ Navajo Loop Trail

Distance: 1.3 miles round-trip
Duration: 1.5 hours
Elevation change: 520 feet

Top to bottom: Navajo Loop Trail; Bryce Canyon's famous Wall Street; hoodoos carved by ice and wind.

Bristlecone Pine

Somewhere on earth, a bristlecone pine tree may be among the planet's oldest living organisms. The trees here, while not the world's oldest, are up to 1,700 years old (there's a bristlecone in California that's nearly 4,800 years old). These twisted, gnarly trees are easy to spot in the area around **Rainbow Point** because they look their age.

What makes a bristlecone live so long? For one, its dense, resinous wood protects it from insects, bacteria, and fungi that kill many other trees. It grows in a harsh dry climate where there's not a lot of competition from other plants. During droughts that would kill most other plants, the bristlecone can slow down its metabolism until it's practically dormant, then spring back to life when conditions are less severe. Although the dry desert air poses its own set of challenges, it also keeps the tree from rotting.

Besides its ancient look, a bristlecone pine can be recognized by its distinctive needles—they're packed tightly, five to a bunch, with the bunches running along the length of a branch, making it look like a bottle brush.

Effort: moderate
Trailhead: Sunset Point
Shuttle Stop: Sunset Point

From Sunset Point, the trail drops 520 vertical feet in 0.75 mile through a narrow canyon. At the bottom, the loop leads into deep, dark **Wall Street**—an even narrower 0.5-mile-long canyon—then returns to the rim. Of all the trails in the park, this is the most prone to rockfall, so hikers should be alert to slides or sounds of falling rocks; it's not uncommon for at least part of the trail to be closed because of the danger of falling rocks. Other destinations from the bottom of Navajo Trail are **Twin Bridges, Queen's Garden Trail, Peekaboo Loop Trail,** and the town of Tropic. The 1.5-mile spur trail to Tropic isn't as scenic as the other trails, but it does provide another way to enter or leave the park; ask at the visitors center or in Tropic for directions to the trailhead.

Peekaboo Loop Trail

Distance: 5.5 miles round-trip
Duration: 4 hours
Elevation change: 1,500 feet
Effort: moderate-strenuous
Trailhead: Bryce Point
Shuttle Stop: Bryce Point

This enchanting walk is full of surprises at every turn—and there are lots of turns. The trail is in the southern part of Bryce Amphitheater, which has some of the most striking rock features. The loop segment itself is 3.5 miles long, with many ups and downs and a few tunnels. The elevation change is 500-800 feet, depending on the trailhead you choose. The loop hooks up with the Navajo and the Queen's Garden Trails and can be extended by combining these loops. Peekaboo is the only trail in the park shared by horses and hikers; remember to give horseback travelers the right of way and, if possible, to step to higher ground when you allow them to pass.

Under-the-Rim Trail

Distance: 23 miles one-way
Duration: 2 days or longer
Elevation change: 1,500 feet
Effort: strenuous
Trailheads: Bryce Point, Rainbow Point
Shuttle Stops: Bryce Point, Rainbow Point

The longest trail in the park winds 23 miles below the Pink Cliffs, between Bryce Point to the north and Rainbow Point to the south. Allow at least two days to hike the entire trail; the elevation change is about 1,500 feet, with many ups and downs. Four connecting trails from the scenic drive also make it possible to travel the Under-the-Rim Trail as a series of day hikes. Another option is to combine Under-the-Rim with **Riggs Spring Loop Trail** for a total of 31.5 miles.

The **Hat Shop,** an area of delicate spires capped by erosion-resistant rock, makes a good day hiking destination; begin at Bryce Point and follow the Under-the-Rim Trail for about two miles. Most of this section is downhill (elevation change of 900 feet); you'll have to climb it on the way out.

Swamp Canyon Loop

Distance: 4.3 miles round-trip
Duration: 2 hours
Elevation change: 800 feet
Effort: moderate
Trailhead: Swamp Canyon
Shuttle Stop: Swamp Canyon

This loop comprises three trails: the Swamp Canyon Connecting Trail, a short stretch of the Under-the-Rim Trail, and the Sheep Creek Connecting Trail. Drop below the rim on the Swamp Canyon Trail to a smaller sheltered canyon that is, by local standards, a wetland. Swamp Canyon's two tiny creeks and a spring provide enough moisture for a lush growth of grass and willows. Salamanders live here, as do a variety of birds; this is usually a good trail for bird-watching.

Bristlecone Loop Trail

Distance: 1 mile round-trip
Duration: 30 minutes
Elevation change: 195 feet
Effort: easy
Trailheads: Rainbow Point, Yovimpa Point
Shuttle Stop: Rainbow Point

This easy one-mile loop begins from either Rainbow or Yovimpa Point and goes to viewpoints and ancient bristlecone pines along the rim. These hardy trees survive fierce storms and extremes of hot and cold that no other tree can. Some of the bristlecone pines here are 1,700 years old.

Riggs Spring Loop

Distance: 8.5 miles round-trip
Duration: 5 hours
Elevation change: 1,625 feet
Effort: strenuous
Trailhead: Rainbow Point
Shuttle Stop: Rainbow Point

One of the park's more challenging day hikes or a leisurely overnighter, this trail begins from Rainbow Point and descends into canyons in the southern area of the park. Of the three backcountry campgrounds along the trail, the Riggs Spring site is most conveniently located; it's about halfway around the loop. Great views of the hoodoos, lots of aspen trees, a couple of pretty meadows, and good views off to the east are some of the highlights of this hike. Day hikers often take a shortcut that bypasses Riggs Spring and saves 0.75 mile.

Mossy Cave Trail

Distance: 1 mile round-trip
Duration: 30 minutes
Elevation change: 209 feet
Effort: easy
Trailhead: Highway 12, between mileposts 17 and 18

This easy trail is just off Highway 12, northwest of Tropic, near the east edge of the park (which means that park entrance fees aren't required). Hike up Water Canyon to a cool alcove of dripping water and moss. Sheets of ice and icicles add beauty to the scene in winter. The hike is only one mile round-trip with a small elevation change. A side trail just before the cave branches right a short distance to a little waterfall; look for several small arches in the colorful canyon walls above. Although the park lacks perennial natural streams, the stream in Water Canyon flows even during dry spells. Mormon pioneers labored for three years to channel water from the East Fork of the Sevier River through a canal and down this wash to the town of Tropic. Without this irrigation, the town might not even exist. To reach the trailhead, from the visitors center, return to Highway 12 and turn east, then travel 3.7

Bryce Canyon in Winter

Although Bryce is most popular during the summer months, it is especially beautiful and otherworldly during the winter, when the rock formations are topped with snow. Because Bryce is so high (elevation ranges 8,000-9,000 feet), winter lasts a long time, often into April.

The main park roads and most viewpoints are plowed, and the **Rim Trail** is an excellent, easy **snowshoe** or **cross-country ski route.** The roads to Paria View and Fairyland Point remain unplowed and are marked as **Paria Ski Trail** (a 5-mile loop) and **Fairyland Ski Trail** (a 2.5-mile loop) for snowshoers and cross-country skiers. Rent cross-country ski equipment just outside the park at **Best Western Ruby's Inn** (26 S. Main St., 435/834-5341 or 866/866-6616, www.rubysinn.com). Miles of **snowmobile trails** are groomed outside the park.

During the winter, most of the businesses around the park entrance shut down. The notable exception is **Best Western Ruby's Inn,** which is a wintertime hub of activity. During the winter months, rates drop precipitously. January through March, most guest rooms go for about $60.

Ruby's Inn hosts the **Bryce Canyon Winter Festival** during Presidents Day weekend in February. The three-day festival includes free cross-country skiing and snowshoeing clinics, demos, and tours. This is also the time and place to pick up tips on **ski archery** and **winter photography.**

miles toward Escalante; the parking area is on the right just after a bridge, between mileposts 17 and 18.

Horseback Riding

If you'd like to get down among the hoodoos but aren't sure you'll have the energy to hike back up to the rim, consider letting a horse help you along. **Canyon Trail Rides** (Lodge at Bryce Canyon, 435/679-8665, www.canyonrides.com, Apr.-Oct.), a park concessionaire, offers guided rides near Sunrise Point, and both two-hour ($60) and half-day ($80) trips are offered. Both rides descend to the floor of the canyon; the longer ride follows the Peekaboo Loop Trail. Riders must be at least seven years old and weigh no more than 220 pounds; the horses and wranglers are accustomed to novices.

Ruby's Horseback Adventures (435/834-5341 or 866/782-0002, www.horserides.net, Apr.-Oct.) offers horseback riding in and near Bryce Canyon. There's a choice of half-day ($85) and full-day ($135, including lunch) trips, as well as a 1.5-hour trip ($65). During the summer, Ruby's also sponsors a **rodeo** (7pm Wed.-Sat., $11 adults, $8 ages 3-12) across from the inn.

Outfitters

You guessed it: If there's a piece of gear or clothing that you need, the **General Store at Ruby's Inn** (26 S. Main St., 435/834-5484, www.rubysinn.com, 7am-10:30pm daily) is the best place to look for it. Here you'll find a large stock of groceries, camping and fishing supplies, Native American crafts, books, souvenirs, and a post office. Horseback rides, helicopter tours, and airplane rides are arranged in the lobby just outside the store. In winter, cross-country skiers can rent gear and use trails near the inn as well as in the park. Snowmobile trails are also available, but snowmobiles may not be used within the park. Western-fronted shops across from Ruby's Inn offer trail rides, chuckwagon dinners, mountain bike rentals, souvenirs, and a petting farm.

Inside the park, there's another General Store (Apr.-mid-Nov.), with groceries, camping supplies, coin-operated showers, and a laundry room. It is located between North Campground and Sunrise Point.

If you need specialized outdoor gear, you're more likely to find it 50 miles east in the town of Escalante than in the Bryce Canyon neighborhood.

Accommodations

Travelers may have a hard time finding accommodations and campsites April-October in both the park and nearby areas. Advance reservations at lodges, motels, and the park campground are a good idea; otherwise, plan to arrive by late morning if you expect to find a room without reservations. You'll also find that there's a huge variation in room prices from day to day and from season to season. Use the prices cited below, for summer high season, only as a general guide; what you may find on the Internet or by phone on a particular evening may differ markedly.

The Lodge at Bryce Canyon is the only lodge inside the park, and you'll generally need to make reservations months in advance to get a room in this historic landmark (although it doesn't hurt to ask about last-minute vacancies). Other motels are clustered near the park entrance road, but many do not offer much for the money. The quality of lodgings is somewhat better in Tropic, 11 miles east on Highway 12, and in Panguitch, 25 miles to the northwest.

Inside the Park

Set among ponderosa pines a short walk from the rim, the ★ **Lodge at Bryce Canyon** (435/834-8700 or 877/386-4383, http://brycecanyonforever.com, Apr.-Oct., rooms $186-251, cabins $213) was built in 1923 by a division of the Union Pacific Railroad; a spur line once terminated at the front entrance. The lodge has lots of charm and is listed on the National Register of Historic Places. It also has by far the best location of any Bryce-area accommodations; it's the only lodging in the park itself. Accommodations options include suites in the lodge, motel-style guest rooms, and lodgepole pine cabins; all are clean and pleasant but fairly basic in terms of amenities. The location, however, could not be better.

Activities at the lodge include horseback rides, park tours, evening entertainment, and ranger talks; a gift shop sells souvenirs, while food can be found at both a restaurant and a snack bar. Try to make reservations as far in advance as possible.

Campgrounds

The park's two campgrounds both have water and some pull-through spaces. Reservations are accepted seasonally for 13 RV sites (no hookups at either campground) at **North Campground** (year-round, $30) and 20 tent and RV sites at **Sunset Campground** (May-Sept., $30 RV site, $20 tent site). Make **reservations** (877/444-6777, www.recreation.gov, May-Sept., $10 reservation fee) at least two days in advance. Otherwise, try to arrive early for a space during the busy summer season, because both campgrounds usually fill by 1 or 2pm.

North Campground is on the left just past the visitors center. The best sites here are just a few yards downhill from the Rim Trail, with easy hiking access to other park trails. At least one loop is open year-round. Sunset Campground is about 2.5 miles farther on the right, across the road from Sunset Point. Sunset has campsites accessible to people with disabilities (Loop A).

Basic groceries, camping supplies, coin-operated showers, and a laundry room are available at the General Store (mid-Apr.-late Sept.), between North Campground and Sunrise Point. During the rest of the year, you can go outside the park to Ruby's Inn for these services.

Outside the Park: UT-12 and UT-63

$50-100

During the winter, it's easy to find inexpensive accommodations in this area;

even guest rooms at Ruby's Inn start at about $60. Several motels are clustered on Highway 12, right outside the park boundary. Many of these have seen a lot of use over the years, usually without a lot of attendant upkeep. **Foster's Motel** (1150 Hwy. 12, 435/834-5227, www.fostersmotel.com, $66-115) has pine-paneled motel rooms in what appear to be older prefab modular structures; these are best suited for budget travelers who don't want to camp and don't plan to spend a lot of time in their rooms. It's four miles west of the park entrance in a small complex with a restaurant and a supermarket.

A reasonably good value for the area can be found at the **Bryce View Lodge** (991 S. Hwy. 63, 435/834-5180 or 888/279-2304, www.bryceviewlodge.com, $87-104), which has fairly basic guest rooms set back from the road near the park entrance, across the road from Ruby's Inn (it's owned by Ruby's).

$100-150

Although "resort" may be stretching it, **Bryce Canyon Resort** (13500 E. Hwy. 12, 435/834-5351, www.brycecanyonresort.com, from $129-179) is a full-service hotel complex with an indoor pool, a restaurant, a store, and lodging options that include standard motel rooms, suites, and rustic cabins that sleep up to six.

The sprawling **Best Western Ruby's Inn** (26 S. Main St., 435/834-5341 or 866/866-6616, www.rubysinn.com, $117-139) offers many year-round services on Highway 63 just north of the park boundary; winter rates are about half high-season rates. The hotel features many separate buildings with rooms, as well as an indoor pool and a hot tub and all the bustling activity you could ever want. Kitchenettes and family rooms are also available; pets are allowed. Ruby's Inn is more than just a place to stay, however: This is one of the area's major centers for all manner of recreational outfitters, dining, entertainment, and shopping. Many tour bus groups bed down here. Although it is kind of a zoo, the quality of the guest rooms at Ruby's is generally higher than at other lodgings in the immediate area. If you want something more sumptuous and relaxing, consider staying at a B&B in nearby Tropic.

Six miles west of the park turnoff, **Bryce Canyon Pines Motel** (Hwy. 12, milepost 10, 435/834-5441 or 800/892-7923, www.brycecanyonmotel.com, $110-335) is an older motel with both motel rooms and cottages, a seasonal covered pool, horseback rides, an RV park, and a restaurant (breakfast, lunch, and dinner daily early Apr.-late Oct.).

Over $150

The newest and best-appointed hotel in the area is the **Best Western Bryce Canyon Grand Hotel** (30 N. 100 E., 435/834-5700 or 866/866-6634, www.brycecanyongrand.com, $162-189). It's across the road from Ruby's, but it's actually a bit of a walk. Rooms have microwaves and refrigerators (unlike many in the area) and the sort of higher-end comforts that are expected in hotels in this price range. An outdoor pool is open in the summer; during the winter guests can go across the highway to use the indoor pool at Ruby's. This is also where the nearest dining is found.

Public Campgrounds

The Dixie National Forest has three Forest Service campgrounds located in scenic settings among ponderosa pines. They often have room when campgrounds in the park are full. Sites can be reserved at Pine Lake, King Creek, and Red Canyon Campgrounds (877/444-6777, www.recreation.gov, $10 reservation fee). **Pine Lake Campground** (mid-May-mid-Sept., $11) is at 7,700 feet in elevation, just east of its namesake lake, in a forest of ponderosa pine, spruce, and juniper. From the highway junction north of the park, head northeast 11 miles on Highway 63 (gravel), then turn southeast and go six miles. Contact the **Escalante Ranger District Office** (435/826-5499) for information on Pine Lake.

King Creek Campground (usually May-late Sept., $12) is on the west shore of Tropic Reservoir, which has a boat ramp and fair trout fishing. Trails for hikers and OHVs begin at the campground. Sites are at 8,000 feet elevation. Go 2.8 miles west of the park turnoff on Highway 12, and then head seven miles south on the gravel East Fork Sevier River Road. **Red Canyon Campground** (late May-late Sept., $15) is just off Highway 12, four miles east of US 89. It's at 7,400 feet elevation, below brilliantly colored cliffs. Contact the **Red Canyon Visitor Center** (435/676-2676, www.fs.fed.us) for more information on King Creek and Red Canyon Campgrounds.

Private Campgrounds

Private campgrounds in the area tend to cost upwards of $25; the base price for camping at Ruby's increases when there are more than two campers. The convenient **Ruby's Inn Campground** (26 S. Main St., 435/834-5301 or 866/878-9373, www.rubysinn.com, Apr.-Oct.) has spaces for tents ($30) and RVs ($42-48); full hookups are available, and showers and a laundry room are open year-round. They've also got a few tepees (from $40) and bunkhouse-style cabins (bedding not provided, $64). All of the considerable facilities at Ruby's are available to campers, and the park shuttle stops here. **Bryce Canyon Pines Campground** (Hwy. 12, milepost 10, 435/834-5441 or 800/892-7923, www.brycecanyonmotel.com, Apr.-Oct., $20 tents, $30 RVs), four miles west of the park entrance, has an indoor pool, a game room, groceries, and shaded sites.

Outside the Park: Tropic

Travelers think of Tropic primarily for its cache of motels lining Main Street (Hwy. 12), but several pleasant B&Bs also grace the town.

$50-100

At the ★ **Bryce Canyon Inn** (21 N. Main St., 435/679-8502 or 800/592-1468, www.brycecanyoninn.com, Mar.-Oct., $75 motel rooms, $99-215 cabins), the tidy cabins are nicely furnished and are one of the more appealing options in the Bryce neighborhood. The economy motel rooms are small but clean and a good deal.

Up on a bluff on the outskirts of town, the **Buffalo Sage B&B** (980 N. Hwy. 12, 435/679-8443 or 866/232-5711, www.buffalosage.com, $80) has great views and guest rooms decorated in an upscale Southwestern style.

America's Best Value Bryce Valley Inn (199 N. Hwy. 12, 435/679-8811 or 800/442-1890, www.brycevalleyinn.com, $85-113) has conventional motel rooms in an attractive wood-fronted, Western-style motel with an adjoining restaurant. Pets are permitted, but an extra fee is charged.

$100-150

One of the most pleasant places to stay in Tropic is in the **Bryce Country Cabins** (320 N. Hwy. 12, 435/679-8643 or 888/679-8643, www.brycecountrycabins.com, $99-139). The cabins overlook a meadow, and each has a private bath.

At the other end of town, the **Bullberry Inn B&B** (412 S. Hwy. 12, 435/679-8820 or 800/249-8126, http://bullberryinn.com, Apr.-Oct., $90-125) has wraparound porches, and the guest rooms have private baths and rustic-style pine furniture.

At **Bryce Canyon Livery B&B** (660 W. 50 S., 435/679-8780 or 888/889-8910, www.brycecanyonbandb.com, $115-125), every guest room has a private bath; several have balconies with views of Bryce Canyon.

Over $150

The **Stone Canyon Inn** (1380 W. Stone Canyon Ln., 435/679-8611 or 866/489-4680, www.stonecanyoninn.com, $225-350), just west of Tropic with views of Bryce, is a strikingly handsome, modern structure with several comfortable two-bedroom guest cabins with kitchens and newly built bungalows configured as suites that can sleep up to four. Along with these accommodations, which are the region's most luxurious, the Stone Canyon also has a group campground; call if you and your pals want to book it for a bike trip or family reunion. The main lodge, which originally had several guest rooms, has been converted into a restaurant.

Campgrounds

In town, you can find tent ($15) and RV ($30) camping at **Bryce Pioneer Village Motel** (80 S. Main St., 435/679-8546 or 800/222-0381, www.brycepioneervillage.com), in addition to guest rooms and cabins ($80-120). Head east to Cannonville for **Cannonville/Bryce Valley KOA** (175 N. Red Rock Dr., Cannonville, 435/679-8988 or 888/562-4710, www.koa.com, $22 tent, $28-32 RVs, $46-58 camping cabin), or continue south from Cannonville to **Kodachrome Basin State Park** (801/322-3770 or 800/322-3770, www.reserveamerica.com, $19).

Outside the Park: Panguitch

$50-100

Panguitch is the best place in greater Bryce Canyon to find an affordable motel room—there are more than a dozen older motor court lodgings, most quite basic but nicely maintained. Of these, the **Color Country Motel** (526 N. Main St., 435/676-2386 or 800/225-6518, www.colorcountrymotel.com, $58) is one of the most attractive, with an outdoor pool and clean, well-furnished guest rooms.

The **Adobe Sands** (390 N. Main St., 435/676-8874 or 866/497-7033, www.adobesandsmotel.com, May-Oct., $35-74) is pet-friendly, and it offers clean, basic guest rooms at budget prices.

Church's Blue Pine Motel (130 N. Main St., 435/676-8197, www.bluepinemotel.com, $72) is one of the most attractive, with microwaves and refrigerators in the guest rooms.

Another good midrange pick is the **Canyon Lodge Motel** (210 N. Main St., 435/676-8292 or 800/440-8292, www.canyonlodgemotel.com, $69-89) with clean, basic guest rooms plus a three-bed suite.

Along US 89, the **New Western Motel** (180 E. Center St., 435/676-8876, http://newbrycewesterninn.com, $79) has a swimming pool and a hot tub plus laundry facilities. Some guest rooms are in an older building, but all guest rooms have been refurbished.

$100-150

Stay in one of the town's landmark red-brick homes: The tidy ★ **Red Brick Inn of Panguitch B&B** (161 N. 100 W., 435/690-1048 or 866/733-2745, www.redbrickinnutah.com, $130-250) has distinctive barnlike architecture and cozy bedrooms, including two adjoining bedrooms that share a bath—perfect for families. If you like B&Bs, this is definitely the best place in town to stay.

Over $150

Cottonwood Meadow Lodge (US 89, milepost 123, 435/676-8950, www.panguitchanglers.com, $155-295) is the exception to the modest-accommodations rule in the Panguitch area. This upscale lodge features four units, all with kitchen facilities: a bunkhouse, a log cabin dating from the 1860s, a three-bedroom farmhouse, and an attractively rehabbed barn that sleeps six. It's about 15 minutes from town and about 20 minutes from Bryce Canyon National Park. Ranch animals are available for visits, and the Sevier River runs through the property, located two miles south of Highway 12 on US 89.

Campgrounds

Hitch-N-Post Campground (420 N. Main St., 435/676-2436, www.hitchnpostrv.com, year-round) offers spaces for tents ($17) and RVs ($22-29) and has showers and a laundry room. The **Big Fish KOA Campground** (555 S. Main St., 435/676-2225, Apr.-Oct., $23 tents, $35-40 RVs, $45 cabins) on the road to Panguitch Lake includes a pool, a recreation room, laundry, and showers. The closest public campground is in **Red Canyon** (Hwy. 12, 435/676-2676, $15).

Food

Inside the Park

The dining room at the ★ **Lodge at Bryce Canyon** (435/834-8700, http://brycecanyonforever.com, 7am-10:30am, 11:30am-3pm, and 5:30pm-10pm daily Apr.-Oct., $10-30) is classy and atmospheric, with a large stone fireplace and white tablecloths, and offers food that's better than anything else you're going to find in the area. For lunch, the snack bar is a good bet in nice weather; the only seating is outside on the patio or in the hotel lobby.

A short walk from the main lodge is **Valhalla Pizzeria and Coffee Shop** (435/834-8700, http://brycecanyonforever.com, 6am-11:30am, 3pm-11pm daily mid-May-mid-Oct., $8-16). Although the pizza is described as "artisanal," don't set your hopes too high. Lasagna, manicotti, and hoagies are also served.

Outside the Park: UT-12 and UT-63

If you're up for a high-volume dining experience, Ruby's Inn **Cowboy Buffet and Steak Room** (26 S. Main St., 435/834-5341, www.rubysinn.com, 6:30am-9:30pm daily, $10-25, dinner buffet $20) is an incredibly busy place. It's also one of Bryce Canyon's better restaurants, with sandwiches, steaks, and a buffet with a salad bar. Casual lunch and dinner fare, including pizza, is served in the inn's snack bar, the **Canyon Diner** (6:30am-9:30pm daily May-Oct., $4-12). The vegetarian sandwich consists of a slice of American cheese, some lettuce, and a few cucumber slices on a hot dog bun.

Bryce Canyon Resort (13500 E. Hwy. 12, 435/834-5351 or 800/834-0043, www.

Panguitch makes the most of its Old West facades.

brycecanyonresort.com, 7am-10pm daily, $8-22), near the turnoff for the park, has an on-site restaurant that features burgers and Mexican food; they also serve Utah beers.

Two long-established restaurants west of the park entrance have a low-key, noncorporate atmosphere and pretty good food. The small family-run restaurant attached to **Bryce Canyon Pines** (Hwy. 12, milepost 10, 435/834-5441 or 800/892-7923, 7am-10pm daily, $8-17) is a homey place to stop for burgers, soup, or sandwiches. The restaurant touts its fruit pies. Two miles west of the park turnoff is **Foster's** (Hwy. 12, 435/834-5227, 7am-10pm daily, $11-26), a very popular steak house with an Old West atmosphere.

Outside the Park: Tropic

There are a few dining options in town. The best place to start your search for a meal is **Clarke's** (141 N. Main St., 435/679-8633, 7am-10pm daily, $7-22), an all-around institution that, in addition to selling groceries, serves Mexican food, pasta, pizza, ice cream, and steaks from a variety of venues within a complex that's essentially the town center.

At the Stone Canyon Inn, the **Stone Hearth Grille** (1380 W. Stone Canyon Ln., 435/679-8923, www.stonehearthgrille.com, 7am-9am and 5pm-9pm daily) has an upscale atmosphere and menu.

Outside the Park: Panguitch

The culinary high point of a visit to Panguitch will likely be the mesquite-grilled meats at **Cowboy's Smokehouse Bar-B-Q** (95 N. Main St., 435/676-8030, 11:30am-9pm Mon.-Sat. mid-Mar.-mid-Oct., $10-25), where live country music and Western atmosphere are regular features. The **Flying M Restaurant** (580 N. Main St., 435/676-8008, 7am-9pm daily, $8-18) serves hearty breakfasts and standard American comfort-food dinners, including homemade turkey potpies. Stop by **Little L's Bakery** (37 N. Main St., 435/676-8750, 7am-2pm Mon.-Sat., $3-6) for coffee, pastries (good lemon blueberry bread), and sandwiches; you'll also find a good helping of small-town friendliness at this simple café.

Capitol Reef National Park

Although Capitol Reef gets far less attention than Utah's other national parks, it is a great place to visit, with excellent hiking and splendid scenery.

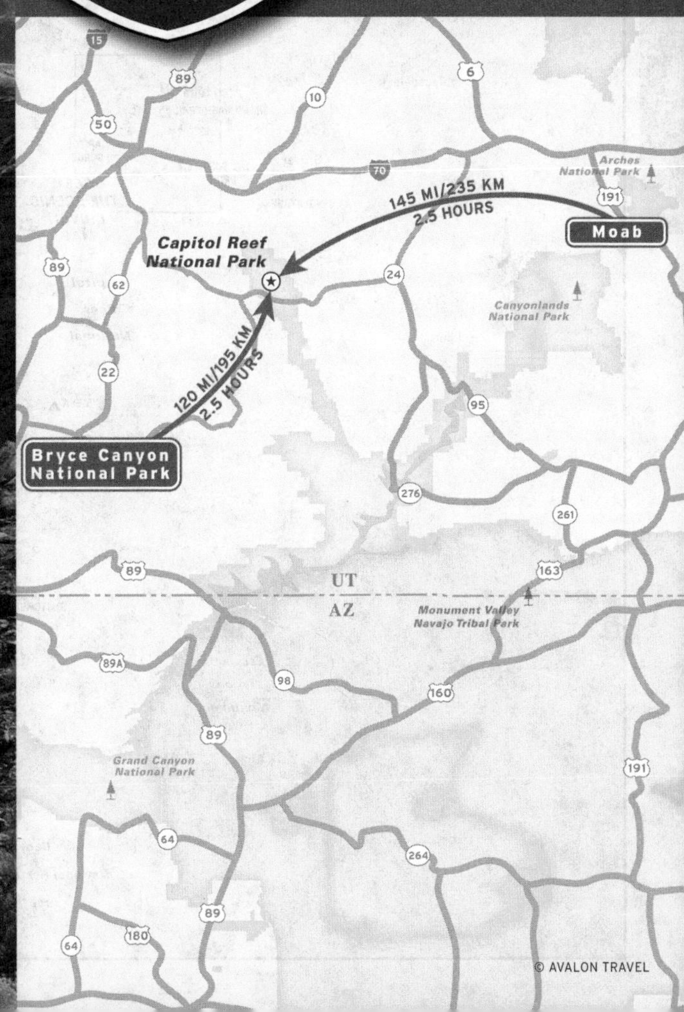

Capitol Reef National Park

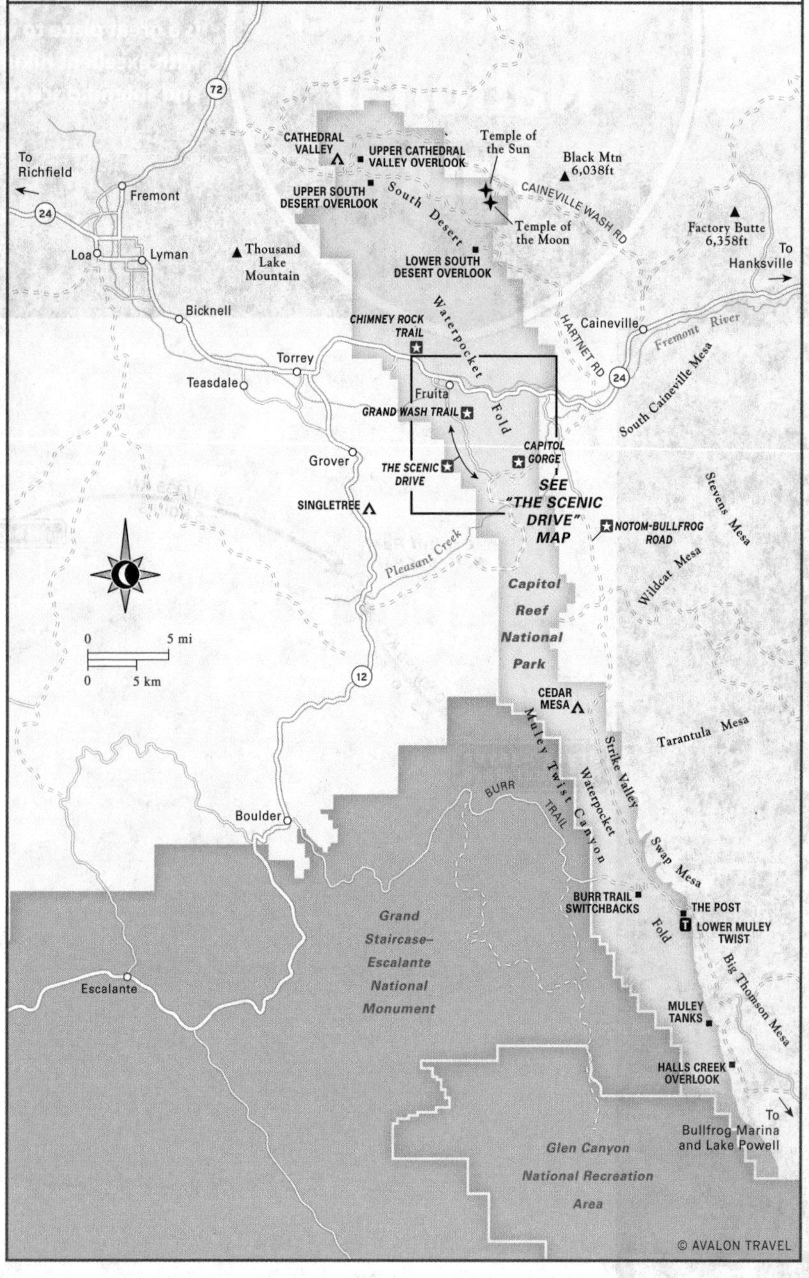

Highlights

★ **The Scenic Drive:** Capitol Reef's 21-mile roundtrip Scenic Drive encompasses not only beautiful scenery and all its attendant geology, but also human history, pioneer sites, and even free fruit in season (page 137).

★ **Notom-Bullfrog Road:** You'll pass nearly 80 miles of the Waterpocket Fold's eastern side while traveling along this road, which exposes the fold's geologic wonders. Distinctive panoramas are your reward (page 139).

★ **Chimney Rock Trail:** The trail to Chimney Rock starts right on Highway 24, and even if you weren't meaning to visit Capitol Reef, it's worth taking a couple of hours to hike to the top for panoramic views (page 143).

★ **Grand Wash Trail:** Grand Wash offers easy hiking, great scenery, and an abundance of wildflowers. Hike from the trailhead on Highway 24 into the Narrows, where the canyon walls rise to 200 feet (page 145).

★ **Capitol Gorge:** Hike past rock art left by the Fremont people and a Mormon "pioneer register" to a turnoff for a spur trail leading to natural water pockets (page 147).

Here, layers of sculpted rock in a rainbow of colors put on a fine show. Their artistry has no equal.

About 70 million years ago, gigantic forces within the earth began to uplift, squeeze, and fold more than a dozen rock formations into the central feature of the park today—the Waterpocket Fold, so named for the many small pools of water trapped by the tilted strata. Erosion has since carved spires, graceful curves, canyons, and arches. The Waterpocket Fold extends 100 miles between Thousand Lake Mountain to the north and Lake Powell to the south. The most spectacular cliffs and rock formations of the Waterpocket Fold form Capitol Reef, located north of Pleasant Creek and curving northwest across the Fremont River toward Thousand Lake Mountain. The reef was named by explorers who found the Waterpocket Fold a barrier to travel and likened it to a reef blocking passage on the ocean. One specific rounded sandstone hill reminded them of the Capitol dome in Washington DC.

Roads and hiking trails in the park provide access to the colorful rock layers and the plants and wildlife that live here. You'll also see remnants of the area's long human history—petroglyphs and storage bins of the prehistoric Fremont people, a schoolhouse and other structures built by Mormon pioneers, and several small uranium mines from the 20th century. Legends tell of Butch Cassidy and other outlaw members of the Wild Bunch who hid out in these remote canyons in the 1890s.

Even travelers short on time will enjoy a quick look at visitors center exhibits and a drive on Highway 24 through an impressive cross section of Capitol Reef cut by the Fremont River. You can see more of the park on the Scenic Drive, a narrow paved road that heads south from the visitors center. The drive passes beneath spectacular cliffs and enters Grand Wash and Capitol Gorge Canyons; allow at least 1.5 hours for the 21-mile round-trip and any side trips. The fair-weather Notom-Bullfrog Road (about half paved, with paved segments at both north and south ends) heads south along the other side of the reef for almost 70 miles, offering fine views of the Waterpocket Fold. Burr Trail Road (dirt inside the park) in the south actually climbs over the fold in a steep set of switchbacks, connecting Notom Road with Boulder. Only drivers with high-clearance vehicles can explore Cathedral Valley in the park's northern district. All of these roads provide access to viewpoints and hiking trails.

Getting to Capitol Reef National Park

From Bryce Canyon National Park

Via Johns Valley Road

120 miles / 2.5 hours

This **120-mile** route will run about **2.5 hours.** Take **UT-63 North** out of the park for about three miles (crossing UT-12) to **Johns Valley Road.** Follow Johns Valley, which becomes **UT-22** around Antimony, for about 40 miles. At the intersection with UT-62, turn right to join **UT-62 North.** After 25 miles, you'll drive through Koosharem. Another five miles on, turn right onto **UT-24 East,** heading toward Torrey. Continue to follow the highway for 40 miles until you enter the park boundaries.

Via UT-12

120 miles / 2.5 hours

This drive to Capitol Reef is also about **120 miles** and takes about **2.5 hours.** Take **UT-63 North** out of Bryce Canyon National Park and turn right on **UT-12**

Stretch Your Legs

About an hour south of Capitol Reef National Park on UT-12, the **Anasazi State Park Museum** (Bryce Canyon-Capitol Reef drive, UT-12, one mile north of Boulder, 435/335-7308, http://stateparks.utah.gov, 8am-6pm daily Mar.-Oct., 9am-5pm Mon.-Sat. Nov.-Feb., $5) preserves the Coombs Site, a small village occupied by Ancestral Puebloans from about AD 1050 to AD 1200. Archaeologists believe that, at its height, some 200 people lived in the site's 40-50 stone-and-mud dwellings. A re-creation of one of the homes is part of the self-guided tour at this excellent little museum, which also displays many fascinating artifacts discovered nearby and provides a primer on the lifeways of the ancient people that once lived in villages and cliff dwellings around the Colorado Plateau.

East for 110 miles, moving through the gorgeous high-country landscape between the Dixie National Forest to the northwest and Grand Staircase-Escalante National Monument to the southeast. UT-12 passes through the small towns of **Tropic, Escalante,** and **Boulder.** Just before reaching Torrey, UT-12 ends in a T-intersection with UT-24. Make a right to get onto **UT-24 East** and continue for just under five miles until the park entrance.

From Moab

145 miles / 2.5 hours

The shortest route from Moab to the main entrance of Capitol Reef moves briefly along **I-70**—but don't worry, you'll be back on scenic Utah two-lanes in a flash. The **145-mile** drive takes about **2.5 hours.** Take **US 191 North** out of Moab, passing the entrances to Arches and Canyonlands National Parks, and turn left to get onto **I-70 West** after 30 miles. You'll pass the town of Green River after about 15 miles, crossing over its namesake waterway. After another 15 miles, take **exit 149** for **UT-24 West.** After following UT-24 for about 45 miles, you'll pass through the small town of Hanksville, where the road comes to a T-intersection. Turn right to continue following UT-24. In about 20 miles, you'll come to another small town, Caineville. Continue for another 20 miles to the main entrance of the park.

Visiting the Park

The most accessible part of **Capitol Reef National Park** (435/425-3791, www.nps.gov/care, $10 per vehicle, $7 cyclists and pedestrians) is along Highway 24, about 11 miles east of Torrey. In fact, several trails start right off the highway, which means that it's not necessary to pay the admission fee to get a tiny taste of this park.

Entrances

The **visitors center** on UT-24, about 11 miles east of Torrey in the beautiful Fruita Historic District, serves as the main entrance to Capitol Reef National Park. There is also a fee station at the entrance to the Scenic Drive toward Capitol Gorge. You can enter the park on UT-24 from the east or west.

Park Passes and Fees

A weeklong pass to Capitol Reef National Park is a steal at $7 per individual and $10 per car. It's $30 for a **Capitol Reef Park Annual Pass.**

Especially if you're planning on visiting more than one of the national parks in this region, consider picking up the $80 **Interagency Annual Pass,** which is accepted at all of the national parks.

Visitors Center

At the **visitors center** (Hwy. 24, 8am-6pm daily June-Sept., 8am-4:30pm daily Oct.-May), start with the good 10-minute

Capitol Reef in One Day

Morning

Wake up with a walk among the pioneer-era orchards at the cliff-lined village of **Fruita** (page 137) and take in the **visitors center** (page 133). Hike the 2.5-mile round-trip **Fremont River Trail** (page 146), which starts at the Fruita Campground and climbs from the oasis-like valley up to a viewpoint that takes in the orchards, Boulder Mountain, and the reef's arched back.

Afternoon

Back in Fruita, unpack your picnic lunch at the shady picnic area of the **Gifford Farmhouse** (page 137), a renovated pioneer home in the verdant Fremont River valley. For a longer after-lunch hike, the **Capitol Gorge** (page 137) cuts a chasm through the Capitol Reef lined with petroglyphs, pioneer graffiti, and towering rock walls.

Evening

There are no dining options in the park, so you'll need to drive 11 miles west to nearby Torrey for dinner, where the **Cafe Diablo** (page 151) is famed for its excellent southwestern cuisine.

Extending Your Stay

The longer you stay in Capitol Reef, exploring its details, the better it gets. Serious hikers and backcountry motorists should take 2-3 days for a full exploration of the park.

Book a room in Torrey, settle in, and hit a few of the park's longer trails, such as the **Old Wagon Trail Loop** (page 147) and the **Chimney Rock Trail** (page 143). Both are about four miles round-trip.

Take the 70-mile scenic drive along **Notom-Bullfrog Road** (page 139), along which you'll see the eastern side of Waterpocket Fold. Don't forget to attend a ranger-guided event, especially if they're offering stargazing or moonlight walks.

slide show, shown on request, introducing Capitol Reef's natural wonders and history. Rock samples and diagrams illustrate the park's geologic formations, and photos identify local plants and birds. Prehistoric Fremont artifacts on display include petroglyph replicas, sheepskin moccasins, pottery, basketry, stone knives, spear and arrow points, and bone jewelry. Other historical exhibits outline exploration and early Mormon settlement.

Hikers can pick up a map of trails that are near the visitors center and of longer routes in the southern areas of the park; naturalists will want the checklists of plants, birds, mammals, and other wildlife, while history buffs can learn more about the area's settlement and the founding of the park. Rangers offer nature walks, campfire programs, and other special events Easter to mid-October; the bulletin board outside the visitors center lists what's going on. The visitors center is on Highway 24 at the turnoff for Fruita Campground and the Scenic Drive.

Reservations

Capitol Reef has no in-park lodge and only one campground. Though Capitol Reef is not as popular as the other Utah parks, it's a good idea to make a reservation at least a month in advance if you plan to stay in the area during the summer high season.

There are many hotels and campgrounds in the nearby towns of Torrey and Teasdale:

Torrey (UT-24): 11 miles from the park visitors center

Teasdale (off UT-24): 15 miles from the park visitors center

Campgrounds

The 71-site **Fruita Campground** (year-round, $20), surrounded by orchards alongside the Fremont River, has seven walk-in tent sites and 64 RV/tent sites, all of them first-come, first-served. During spring and fall, the campground tends to fill by early to mid-afternoon.

Information and Services

Park Newsletter

The park's ***Map and Guide,*** passed out at the visitors center, provides useful information on trails and scenic drives in the park.

Banking, Gas, and Groceries

There are really no in-park services. You must bring your own food and water, and make sure to gas up and get cash in Torrey or one of the other surrounding towns (all of them tiny, but set up for tourists) before entering the park.

Emergency and Medical Services

The rangers in the park say it all the time: "Be prepared to self-rescue." Cell phones don't work in the park, and the closest pay phone is at the visitors center. The nearest emergency room is **Wayne Community Health Center** (128 S. 300 W., Bicknell, 435/425-3744, www.waynechc.org, 8am-5pm Mon.-Fri., 9am-1pm Sat.), in Bicknell, about 20 miles west of the park on UT-24. Wayne County emergency services can be contacted by phone at 435/836-2831.

There are EMTs on staff in the park and the Wayne County Search and Rescue will help as well, but you will likely need to get to the visitors center to call via land line. Be careful, be prepared, and don't go into the backcountry if you have health issues that could flare up.

Getting Around

You really need your own vehicle to get around Capitol Reef National Park. There is no park shuttle and the best scenery is along backcountry roads, some of which are unpaved but easily passable in regular passenger cars.

To visit the more remote areas of the park, you need a four-wheel drive and expert technique. While it's usually safe and easy to drive around the park, even in the backcountry, don't enter any washes during a rainstorm.

Sights

Along Highway 24

From the west, Highway 24 drops from the broad mountain valley near Torrey onto Sulphur Creek, as dramatic rock formations soaring to the horizon. A huge amphitheater of stone rings the basin, with formations such as Twin Rocks, Chimney Rock, and the Castle glowing in deep red and yellow tones. Ahead, the canyon narrows as the Fremont River slips between the cliffs to carve its chasm through the Waterpocket Fold.

Panorama Point

Take in the incredible view from **Panorama Point,** 2.5 miles west of the visitors center on the south side of Highway 24. Follow signs south for 250 yards to Panorama Point and views of Capitol Reef, the distant Henry Mountains to the east, and looming Boulder Mountain to the west. The large black basalt boulders were swept down from Boulder Mountain to the reef as part of giant debris flows between 8,000 and 200,000 years ago.

Goosenecks Overlook

On a gravel road one mile south of Panorama Point are the Goosenecks of Sulphur Creek. A short trail leads to **Goosenecks Overlook** (elevation 6,400 feet) on the rim for dizzying views of the creek below. Canyon walls display shades of yellow, green, brown, and red. Another easy trail leads 0.3 mile to **Sunset Point** and panoramic views of the Capitol Reef cliffs and the Henry Mountains.

Fruita Schoolhouse

Remnants of the pioneer community of

Fruita stretch along the narrow Fremont River Canyon. The **Fruita Schoolhouse** is just east of the visitors center on the north side of Highway 24. Early settlers completed this one-room log structure, housing grades one through eight, in 1896. Mormon church meetings, dances, town meetings, elections, and other community gatherings took place here. A lack of students caused the school to close in 1941. Although the schoolhouse is locked, you can peer inside the windows and take photos.

Fremont Petroglyphs

Farther down the canyon, 1.2 miles east of the visitors center on the north side of Highway 24, are several panels of **Fremont petroglyphs.** Watch for the road signs and parking area. Several mountain sheep and human figures with headdresses decorate the cliff. You can see more petroglyphs by walking to the left and right along the cliff face. Stay on the trail, and do not climb the talus slope.

Behunin Cabin

Behunin Cabin is 6.2 miles east of the visitors center on the south side of Highway 24. Elijah Cutlar Behunin used blocks of sandstone to build this cabin in about 1882. For several years, Behunin, his wife, and 11 of their 13 children shared this sturdy but quite small cabin (the kids slept outside). They moved on when flooding made life too difficult. Small openings allow a look inside the dirt-floored structure, but no furnishings remain.

Fremont River Waterfall

Near the end of the narrow sandstone canyon, the small **Fremont River Waterfall,** created when the Fremont River was rerouted in 1962 to accommodate the highway, attracts photographers.

Top to bottom: Capitol Reef's Fruita Campground; Fremont petroglyphs; Gifford Farmhouse.

The river twists through a narrow artificial crack in the rock before making its final plunge into a pool below. Take the sandy path from the parking area to where you can safely view the falls from below. The pool beneath the falls used to be a popular swimming hole, but water dynamics have changed over the years; the National Park Service closed it to swimming in 2011, when three people almost drowned because of the extremely heavy flow and strong currents. Parking is 6.9 miles east of the visitors center, near milepost 86, on the north side of Highway 24. This area is closed during the warmer months and opens again when it's too cold for people to be tempted to swim.

★ The Scenic Drive

Turn south from Highway 24 at the visitors center to experience some of the reef's best scenery and to learn more about its geology. A quick tour of this 21-mile out-and-back trip requires about 1.5 hours, but several hiking trails may tempt you to extend your stay. It's worth picking up a brochure at the visitors center for descriptions of geology along the road. The Scenic Drive is paved, although side roads have gravel surfaces. Note that drivers must pay the $5 park entrance fee to travel this road.

Fruita

In the Fruita Historic District, you'll first pass orchards and several of Fruita's buildings. A **blacksmith shop** (0.7 mile from the visitors center, on the right) displays tools, harnesses, farm machinery, and Fruita's first tractor. The tractor didn't arrive until 1940, long after the rest of the country had modernized. In a recording, a rancher tells about living and working in Fruita. The nearby orchards and fields are still maintained using old-time farming techniques.

The **Gifford Farmhouse,** one mile south on the Scenic Drive, is typical of rural Utah farmhouses of the early 1900s. Cultural demonstrations are put on, and handmade baked goods and gifts are available. A picnic area is just beyond; with fruit trees and grass, this is a pretty spot for lunch. A short trail crosses orchards and the Fremont River to the **Historic Fruita School.**

Grand Wash

The Scenic Drive leaves the Fremont River valley and climbs up a desert slope, with the rock walls of the Waterpocket Fold rising to the east. Turn east to explore **Grand Wash,** a dry channel etched through the sandstone. A dirt road follows the twisting gulch one mile, with sheer rock walls rising along the sandy streambed. At the road's end, an easy hiking trail follows the wash 2.5 miles to its mouth along Highway 24.

Back on the paved Scenic Drive, continue south past Slickrock Divide to where the rock lining the reef deepens into a ruby red and forms odd columns and spires that resemble statuary. Called the **Egyptian Temple,** this is one of the most striking and colorful areas along the road.

Capitol Gorge

Capitol Gorge is at the end of the Scenic Drive, 10.7 miles from the visitors center. Capitol Gorge is a dry canyon through Capitol Reef, much like Grand Wash. Believe it or not, narrow twisting Capitol Gorge was the route of the main state highway through south-central Utah for 80 years. Mormon pioneers laboriously cleared a path so wagons could get through, a task they repeated every time flash floods rolled in a new set of boulders. Cars bounced their way down the canyon until 1962, when Highway 24 opened, but few traces of the old road remain today. Walking is easy along the gravel riverbed, but don't enter if storms threaten. An easy one-mile saunter down the gorge will take day hikers past petroglyphs and a "register" rock where pioneers carved their names.

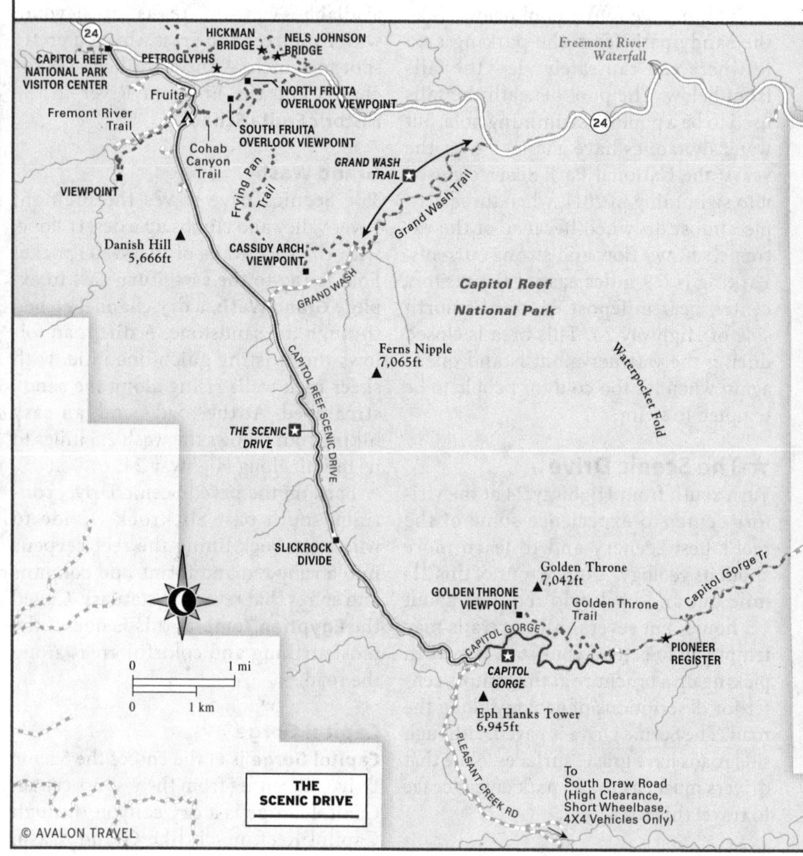

Pleasant Creek Road

The Scenic Drive curves east toward Capitol Gorge and onto **Pleasant Creek Road** (turn right 8.3 miles from the visitors center), which continues south below the face of the reef. After three miles, the sometimes rough dirt road passes Sleeping Rainbow-Floral Ranch (closed to the public) and ends at Pleasant Creek. A rugged road for 4WD vehicles—South Draw Road—continues on the other side, but it is much too rough for cars. Floral Ranch dates back to the early years of settlement at Capitol Reef. In 1939 it became the Sleeping Rainbow Guest Ranch, from the translation of the Native American name for Waterpocket Fold. Now the ranch belongs to the park and is used as a field research station by students and faculty of Utah Valley University. Pleasant Creek's perennial waters begin high on Boulder Mountain to the west and cut a scenic canyon completely through Capitol Reef. Hikers can head downstream through the three-mile-long canyon and then return the way they went in, or continue another three miles cross-country to Notom Road.

The Waterpocket Fold

About 65 million years ago, well before the Colorado Plateau uplifted, sedimentary rock layers in south-central Utah buckled, forming a steep-sided monocline, a rock fold with one very steep side in an area of otherwise nearly horizontal layers. A monocline is a "step-up" in the rock layers along an underlying fault. The rock layers on the west side of the Waterpocket Fold have been lifted more than 7,000 feet higher than the layers to the east. The 100-mile-long fold was then subjected to millions of years of erosion, which slowly removed the upper layers to reveal the warped sedimentary layers at its base. Continued erosion of the sandstone has left many basins, or "water pockets," along the fold. These seasonal water sources, often called "water tanks," are used by desert animals, and they were a water source for prehistoric people. Erosion of the tilted rock layers continues today, forming colorful cliffs, massive domes, soaring spires, stark monoliths, twisting canyons, and graceful arches. Getting a sense of the Waterpocket Fold requires some off-pavement driving. The best viewpoint is along **Burr Trail Road,** which climbs up the fold between Boulder and Notom-Bullfrog Road.

North District

Only the most adventurous travelers enter the remote canyons and desert country of the park's northern district. The few roads cannot be negotiated by 4WD vehicles, let alone ordinary cars, in wet weather. In good weather, high-clearance vehicles (good clearance is more important than four-wheel drive) can enter the region from the east, north, and west. The roads lead through the stately sandstone monoliths of Cathedral Valley, volcanic remnants, badlands country, many low mesas, and vast sand flats. Foot travel allows closer inspection of these features or lengthy excursions into the canyons of Polk, Deep, and Spring Creeks, which cut deeply into the flanks of Thousand Lake Mountain.

Mountain bikers enjoy these challenging roads as well, but they must stay on established roads. Much of the north district is good for horseback riding too.

The district's two main roads—Hartnett Road and Cathedral Road (aka Caineville Wash Rd.)—combine with a short stretch of Highway 24 to form a loop, with a campground at their junction. The five sites at **Cathedral Valley Campground** provide a place to stop for the night; rangers won't permit car camping elsewhere in the district. The campground is on the 4WD Cathedral Valley Loop road about 36 miles from the visitors center (from the park entrance, head 12 miles east on Highway 24, turn north and ford the Fremont River, and then follow Hartnett Road about 24 miles to the campground); check on road conditions at the visitors center before heading out. The **Upper Cathedral Valley Trail,** just below the campground, is an enjoyable one-mile walk offering excellent views of the Cathedrals. Backcountry hikers must have a permit and camp at least 0.5 mile from the nearest road. Guides to the area can be purchased at the visitors center.

South District

★ Notom-Bullfrog Road

Capitol Reef is only a small part of the Waterpocket Fold. By taking the **Notom-Bullfrog Road,** you'll see over 70 miles of the fold's eastern side. This route crosses some of the younger geologic layers, such as those of the Morrison Formation, which form colorful hills. In other places, eroded layers of the Waterpocket Fold jut up at 70-degree angles. The Henry Mountains to the east and the many canyons on both sides of the road add to the memorable panoramas. The northernmost 10 miles of the road have been paved, and about 25 miles are paved on the southern end near Bullfrog, a settlement on the shores of Lake Powell. The rest of the road is dirt and gravel, and it can get pretty washboarded and bumpy. Most cars should have no trouble negotiating this road in good weather. Keep an eye on the weather before setting out, though; the dirt-and-gravel surface can be dangerous for any vehicle when wet. Sandy spots and washouts may present a problem for low-clearance vehicles; contact the visitors center to check current conditions. Have a full tank of gas and carry extra water and food; no services are available between Highway 24 and Bullfrog Marina. Purchase a small guide to this area at the visitors center. Features and mileage along the drive from north to south include the following:

- **Mile 0.0:** The turnoff from Highway 24 is 9.2 miles east of the visitors center and 30.2 miles west of Hanksville (another turnoff from Highway 24 is three miles east).
- **Mile 2.2:** Pleasant Creek; the mouth of the canyon is 5-6 miles upstream, although it's only about three miles away if you head cross-country from south of Notom. Hikers can follow the canyon three miles upstream through Capitol Reef to Pleasant Creek Road (off the Scenic Drive).
- **Mile 4.1:** Notom Ranch is to the west; once a small town, Notom is now a private ranch.
- **Mile 8.1:** Burrow Wash; hikers can explore the narrow canyon upstream.
- **Mile 9.3:** Cottonwood Wash; another canyon hike just upstream.
- **Mile 10.4:** Five Mile Wash; yet another canyon hike. Pavement ends.
- **Mile 13.3:** Sheets Gulch; a scenic canyon is upstream here.
- **Mile 14.1:** Sandy Ranch Junction; high-clearance vehicles can turn east and go 16 miles to the Henry Mountains.
- **Mile 14.2:** Oak Creek Access Road; the creek cuts a two-mile-long canyon through Capitol Reef and makes a good day hike. Backpackers sometimes start upstream at Lower Bowns Reservoir (off Hwy. 12) and hike the 15 miles to Oak Creek Access Road. The clear waters of Oak Creek flow year-round but are not potable.
- **Mile 14.4:** Oak Creek crossing.
- **Mile 20.0:** Entering Capitol Reef National Park; a small box has information sheets.
- **Mile 22.3:** Cedar Mesa Campground is to the west; the small five-site campground is surrounded by junipers and has fine views of the Waterpocket Fold and the Henry Mountains. Free sites have tables and grills; there's a pit toilet but no drinking water. Red Canyon Trail (4 miles round-trip) begins here and heads west into a huge box canyon in the Waterpocket Fold.
- **Mile 26.0:** Bitter Creek Divide; streams to the north flow to the Fremont River; Halls Creek on the south side runs through Strike Valley to Lake Powell, 40 miles away.
- **Mile 34.1:** Burr Trail Road Junction; turn west up the steep switchbacks to ascend the Waterpocket Fold and continue to Boulder and Highway 12 (36 miles). Burr Trail is the only road that actually crosses the top of the fold, and it's one of the most scenic in the park. Driving conditions are similar to the Notom-Bullfrog Road—OK for cars when dry. Pavement begins at the park

boundary and continues to Boulder. Although paved, the Burr Trail still must be driven slowly because of its curves and potholes. The section of road through Long Canyon has especially pretty scenery.

- **Mile 36.0:** Surprise Canyon trailhead; a hike into this narrow, usually shaded canyon takes 1-2 hours.
- **Mile 36.6:** Post Corral; a small trading post here once served sheepherders and some cattle ranchers, but today this spot is just a reference point. Park here to hike to Headquarters Canyon. A trailhead for Lower Muley Twist Canyon via Halls Creek is at the end of a 0.5-mile-long road to the south.
- **Mile 37.5:** Leaving Capitol Reef National Park. Much of the road between here and Glen Canyon National Recreation Area has been paved.
- **Mile 45.5:** Road junction; turn right (south) to continue to Bullfrog Marina (25 miles) or go straight (east) for Starr Springs Campground (23 miles) in the Henry Mountains.
- **Mile 46.4:** The road to the right (west) goes to Halls Creek Overlook. This turnoff is poorly signed and easy to miss; look for it 0.9 mile south of the previous junction.
- **Mile 49.0:** Colorful clay hills of deep red, cream, and gray rise beside the road. This clay turns to goo when wet, providing all the traction of axle grease.
- **Mile 54.0:** Beautiful panorama of countless mesas, mountains, and canyons; Lake Powell and Navajo Mountain can be seen to the south.
- **Mile 65.3:** Junction with paved Highway 276; turn left (north) for Hanksville (59 miles) or right (south) to Bullfrog Marina (5.2 miles).
- **Mile 70.5:** End at Bullfrog Marina in Glen Canyon National Recreation Area.

Lower Muley Twist Canyon

"So winding that it would twist a mule pulling a wagon," said an early visitor. **Lower Muley Twist Canyon** has some of the best hiking in the southern district of the park. In the 1880s Mormon pioneers used the canyon as part of a wagon route between Escalante and new settlements in southeastern Utah, replacing the even more difficult Hole-in-the-Rock route.

Unlike most canyons of the Waterpocket Fold, Muley Twist runs lengthwise along the crest for about 18 miles before finally turning east and leaving the fold. Hikers starting from Burr Trail Road can easily follow the twisting bends down to Halls Creek, 12 miles away. Two trailheads and the Halls Creek route allow a variety of trips.

Start from Burr Trail Road near the top of the switchbacks (2.2 miles west of Notom-Bullfrog Rd.) and hike down the dry gravel streambed. After four miles, you have the option of returning the same way, taking the Cut Off route east 2.5 miles to the Post Corral trailhead (off Notom-Bullfrog Rd.), or continuing eight miles down Lower Muley Twist Canyon to its end at Halls Creek. On reaching Halls Creek, turn left (north) and travel five miles up the creekbed or the old jeep road beside it to the Post. This section of creek is in an open dry valley. With a car shuttle, the Post would be the end of a good two-day, 17-mile hike, or you could loop back to Lower Muley Twist Canyon via the Cut Off route and hike back to Burr Trail Road for a 23.5-mile trip. It's a good idea to check the weather beforehand and avoid the canyon if storms threaten.

Cream-colored sandstone cliffs lie atop the red Kayenta and Wingate Formations.

Impressively deep undercuts have been carved into the lower canyon. Spring and fall offer the best conditions; summer temperatures can exceed 100°F. Elevations range from 5,640 feet at Burr Trail Road to 4,540 feet at the confluence with Halls Creek to 4,894 feet at the Post.

An information sheet is available at the visitors center, and the trailheads have a small map and route details. Topographic maps of Wagon Box Mesa, Mount Pennell, and Hall Mesa as well as the 1:100,000-scale Escalante and Hite Crossing maps are sold at the visitors center. You'll also find this hike described in David Day's *Utah's Favorite Hiking Trails* and in the small spiral-bound *Explore Capitol Reef Trails* by the Capitol Reef Natural History Association, available at the visitors center. Carry all the water you'll need for the trip because natural sources are often dry or polluted.

Upper Muley Twist Canyon

Upper Muley Twist Canyon has plenty of scenery. Large and small natural arches along the way add to its beauty. Upper Muley Twist Road turns north off Burr Trail Road about one mile west from the top of a set of switchbacks. Cars can usually go in 0.5 mile to a trailhead parking area; high-clearance 4WD vehicles can head another three miles up a wash to the end of the primitive road. Look for natural arches on the left along this last section. **Strike Valley Overlook Trail** (0.75 mile round-trip) begins at the end of the road and leads to a magnificent panorama of the Waterpocket Fold and beyond. Return to the canyon, where you can hike as far as 6.5 miles to the head of Upper Muley Twist Canyon.

Two large arches are a short hike upstream; Saddle Arch, the second one, on the left, is 1.7 miles away. The **Rim Route** begins across from Saddle Arch, climbs the canyon wall, follows the rim (offering good views of Strike Valley and the Henry Mountains), and descends back into the canyon at a point just above the narrows, 4.75 miles from the end of the road. The Rim Route is most easily followed in this direction. Proceed upcanyon to see several more arches. A narrow section of canyon beginning about four miles from the end of the road must be bypassed to continue; look for rock cairns showing the way around to the right. Continuing up the canyon past the Rim Route sign will take you to several small drainages marking the upper end of Muley Twist Canyon. Climb a high tree-covered point on the west rim for great views; experienced hikers with a map can follow the rim back to Upper Muley Twist Road. There is no trail and no markers on this route. Bring all the water you'll need; there are no reliable sources in Upper Muley Twist Canyon.

Recreation

Fifteen trails for day hikes begin within a short drive of the visitors center. Of these, only Grand Wash, Capitol Gorge, and the short paths to Sunset Point and Goosenecks are easy. The others involve moderately strenuous climbs over irregular slickrock. Signs and rock cairns mark the way, but it's all too easy to wander off if you don't pay attention to the route.

Although most hiking trails can easily be done in a day, backpackers and hikers might want to try longer trips in Chimney Rock-Spring Canyons to the north or Muley Twist Canyon and Halls Creek to the south. Obtain the required backcountry permit (free) from a ranger and camp at least 0.5 mile from the nearest maintained road or trail. (Cairned routes like Chimney Rock Canyon, Muley Twist Canyon, and Halls Creek don't count as trails but are backcountry routes.) Bring a stove for cooking; backcountry users are not permitted to build fires. Avoid camping or parking in washes at any time—torrents of mud and boulders can carry away everything.

Hiking from Highway 24

Stop by the visitors center to pick up a map showing hiking trails and trail descriptions. These trailheads are located along the main highway through the park and along the Fremont River. Note that the Grand Wash Trail cuts west through the reef to the Scenic Drive.

★ Chimney Rock Trail

Distance: 3.5 miles round-trip
Duration: 2.5 hours
Elevation change: 800 feet
Effort: moderate-strenuous
Trailhead: 3 miles west of the visitors center, on the north side of Highway 24

Towering 660 feet above the highway, Chimney Rock (elevation 6,100 feet) is a fluted spire of dark red rock (Moenkopi Formation) capped by a block of hard sandstone (Shinarump Member of the Chinle Formation). The trail leads pretty much straight uphill from the parking lot to a ridge overlooking Chimney Rock, and then levels off a bit. Panoramic views take in the face of Capitol Reef. Petrified wood along the trail has been eroded from the Chinle Formation (the same rock layer found in Petrified Forest National Park in Arizona). It is illegal to take any petrified wood.

Spring Canyon Route

Distance: 10 miles one-way
Duration: 6 hours
Elevation change: 540 feet
Effort: moderate
Trailhead: Chimney Rock parking lot

Except for its length, this hike through the deep and narrow Spring Canyon is not particularly difficult. It begins at the top of the Chimney Rock Trail and runs to the Fremont River and Highway 24; since it begins and ends on the highway, a car shuttle can eliminate the need to hike out and back. The wonderfully eroded forms of Navajo sandstone present a continually changing exhibition. The riverbed is normally dry. (Some maps show all or part of this as "Chimney Rock Canyon.") Check with rangers for the weather forecast before setting off, because flash floods can be dangerous, and the Fremont River (which you must wade across) can rise quite high. Normally, the river runs less than knee-deep to Highway 24 (3.7 miles east of the visitors center). With luck, you'll have a car waiting for you. Summer hikers can beat the often-intense heat with a crack-of-dawn departure. Carry water, as this section of canyon lacks a reliable source.

From the Chimney Rock parking area, hike Chimney Rock Trail to the top of the ridge and follow the signs for Chimney Rock Canyon. Enter the unnamed lead-in canyon and follow it downstream. A sign marks Chimney Rock Canyon, which is 2.5 miles from the start. From this point, it's an additional 6.5 miles downstream to reach the Fremont River. A section of narrows requires some rock-scrambling (bring a cord to lower backpacks), or the area can be bypassed on a narrow trail to the left above the narrows. Farther down, a natural arch high on the left marks the halfway point.

Upper Chimney Rock Canyon could be explored on an overnight trip (permit required). A spring (purify the water before drinking it) is located in an alcove on the right side, about one mile up Chimney Rock Canyon from the lead-in canyon. Wildlife uses this water source, so camp at least 0.25 mile away. Chimney Rock Canyon, the longest in the park, begins high on the slopes of Thousand Lake Mountain and descends nearly 15 miles southeast to join the Fremont River.

Sulphur Creek Route

Distance: 5 miles one-way
Duration: 3-5 hours
Elevation change: 540 feet
Effort: moderate-strenuous
Trailhead: across Highway 24 from Chimney Rock parking lot

This moderately difficult hike begins by following a wash across the highway

Datura: A Plant with a Past

As dusk approaches, the huge white flowers of the datura open, and their sweet smell attracts moths, beetles, and wasps. As intoxicating as the datura's fragrance may be, it doesn't hold a candle to the plant itself, which is a potent hallucinogen. It also contains toxic alkaloids, including nerve toxins capable of killing humans and animals.

Datura, also known as jimsonweed, has a rich history of folk use. Many indigenous peoples in the Americas, including the Zuni, the Chumash, and even the Aztecs, were familiar with its uses; some regarded it as sacred. It has been used as a shamanic ritual drug as well as a topical analgesic. Accounts from Jamestown, Virginia, one of the earliest British settlements in North America, report a group of soldiers going insane after eating datura in 1676.

Up until 1968 datura was a component of some over-the-counter asthma medicines; it was banned when it gained popularity among American youth, who began using these medications recreationally. Atropine, an anticholinergic substance often used by ophthalmologists to dilate pupils, is datura's main psychoactive component. It's a central nervous system depressant that mostly causes users to feel drowsy—some report vivid dreams—and also increases the heart rate, sometimes to dangerous levels.

from the Chimney Rock parking area, then descends to Sulphur Creek and heads down the narrow canyon to the visitors center; it's five miles if you've arranged a car or bike shuttle, and double that if you have to hike back to your starting point. It's best to hike Sulphur Creek during warm weather, because you'll be wading in the normally shallow creek passing through a slot canyon. Wear sneakers or other shoes that you don't mind getting wet. Before starting out, check to make sure the water level isn't too high for hiking (you can do this by examining the route's endpoint behind the visitors center; it should be ankle-deep or less for a safe and fun hike).

Three small waterfalls are along the route, but it's fairly easy to climb down rock ledges to the side of the water; two falls are just below the Goosenecks and the third is about 0.5 mile before the visitors center. Carry water with you.

Hickman Natural Bridge

Distance: 2 miles round-trip
Duration: 1.5 hours
Elevation change: 380 feet
Effort: easy-moderate
Trailhead: 2 miles east of the visitors center, on the north side of Highway 24

The graceful Hickman Natural Bridge spans 133 feet across a small streambed. Numbered stops along the self-guided trail correspond to descriptions in a pamphlet available at the trailhead or visitors center. Starting from the parking area (elevation 5,320 feet), the trail follows the Fremont River's green banks a short distance before climbing to the bridge. The last section of trail follows a dry wash shaded by cottonwoods, junipers, and piñon pines. You'll pass under the bridge (eroded from the Kayenta Formation) at trail's end. Capitol Dome and other sculptured sandstone features surround the site. Joseph Hickman, for whom the bridge was named, served as principal of Wayne County High School and later in the state legislature; he and another local, Ephraim Pectol, led efforts to promote Capitol Reef.

Rim Overlook Trail

Distance: 4.5 miles round-trip
Duration: 3-5 hours
Elevation change: 540 feet
Effort: moderate-strenuous

Trailhead: Hickman Natural Bridge trailhead

A splendid overlook 1,000 feet above Fruita beckons hikers up the Rim Overlook Trail. Take the Hickman Natural Bridge Trail from the parking area, turn right at the signed fork, and hike for about two miles. Allow 3.5 hours from the fork for this hike. Panoramic views take in the Fremont River valley below, the great cliffs of Capitol Reef above, the Henry Mountains to the southeast, and Boulder Mountain to the southwest.

Continue another 2.2 miles from the Rim Overlook to reach **Navajo Knobs.** Rock cairns lead the way over slickrock along the rim of the Waterpocket Fold. A magnificent view at trail's end takes in much of southeastern Utah.

★ Grand Wash Trail

Distance: 4.5 miles round-trip
Duration: 2-3 hours
Elevation change: negligible
Effort: easy
Trailhead: 4.7 miles east of the visitors center, on the south side of Highway 24

One of only five canyons cutting completely through the reef, Grand Wash offers easy hiking, great scenery, and an abundance of wildflowers. There's no trail—just follow the dry riverbed. (Flash floods can occur during storms.) Only a short distance from Highway 24, canyon walls rise 800 feet above the floor and narrow to as little as 20 feet in width; this stretch of trail is known as the Narrows. After the Narrows, the wash widens, and wildflowers grow everywhere. The Cassidy Arch trailhead is two miles from Highway 24.

The hike can also be started from a trailhead at the end of Grand Wash Road, off the Scenic Drive. A car or bike shuttle can make it a one-way hike of about 2.5 miles.

Hiking the Scenic Drive

These hikes begin from trailheads along the Scenic Drive. Drivers must pay the national park admission fee to travel this road.

Fremont Gorge Overlook Trail

Distance: 4.5 miles round-trip
Duration: 2-3 hours
Elevation change: 1,000 feet
Effort: moderate-strenuous
Trailhead: Fruita blacksmith shop

From the start at the Fruita blacksmith shop, the trail climbs a short distance, then crosses Johnson Mesa and climbs steeply to the overlook about 1,000 feet above the Fremont River. The overlook is not a place for the acrophobic—even people who aren't ordinarily afraid of heights might find it a little daunting.

Cohab Canyon Trail

Distance: 3.5 miles round-trip
Duration: 2.5 hours
Elevation change: 400 feet
Effort: moderate-strenuous
Trailheads: across the road from Fruita Campground (one mile south of the visitors center) and across Highway 24 from the Hickman Natural Bridge trailhead

Cohab is a pretty little canyon overlooking the campground. Mormon polygamists ("cohabitationists") supposedly used the canyon to escape federal marshals during the 1880s. It's possible to hike this trail from either trailhead. Starting from the campground, the trail first follows steep switchbacks before continuing along more gentle grades to the top of the reef, 400 feet higher and one mile from the campground. You can take a short trail to viewpoints or continue 0.75 mile down the other side of the ridge to Highway 24.

Another option is to turn right at the top on Frying Pan Trail and head to Cassidy Arch (3.5 miles one-way) and Grand Wash (4 miles one-way). The trail from Cassidy Arch to Grand Wash is steep. All of these interconnecting trails offer many hiking possibilities, especially if you can arrange a car shuttle. For example, you could start up Cohab Canyon

Trail from Highway 24, cross over the reef on Frying Pan Trail, make a side trip to Cassidy Arch, descend Cassidy Arch Trail to Grand Wash, walk down Grand Wash to Highway 24, then walk (or car shuttle) 2.7 miles along the highway back to the start, for 10.5 miles total.

Hiking the Frying Pan Trail involves an additional 600 feet of climbing from either Cohab Canyon or Cassidy Arch Trail. Once atop Capitol Reef, the trail follows the gently rolling slickrock terrain.

Fremont River Trail

Distance: 2.5 miles round-trip
Duration: 2 hours
Elevation change: 770 feet
Effort: moderate-strenuous
Trailhead: Fruita Campground amphitheater

The trail starts out quite easy, passing orchards along the Fremont River (elevation 5,350 feet). This part of the trail is wheelchair accessible. After 0.5 mile, it begins a climb up sloping rock to a Miners Mountain viewpoint overlooking Fruita, Boulder Mountain, and Capitol Reef. Bring $0.50 for a trail brochure describing traditional agricultural practices in the valley and the geological formations visible at the top of the trail.

Cassidy Arch

Distance: 3.5 miles round-trip
Duration: 3 hours
Elevation change: 670 feet
Effort: moderate-strenuous
Trailhead: end of drivable section of Grand Wash Road
Directions: Turn left off the Scenic Drive, 3.6 miles from the visitors center, and follow Grand Wash Road to the trailhead.

Cassidy Arch Trail begins near the end of Grand Wash Road, ascends the north wall of Grand Wash, and then winds across slickrock to a vantage point close to the arch. Energetic hikers will enjoy good views of Grand Wash, the great domes of Navajo sandstone, and the arch itself. The notorious outlaw Butch Cassidy may have traveled through Capitol Reef and seen

Just a short scramble above Capitol Gorge is a series of natural water tanks, or water pockets.

this arch. Frying Pan Trail branches off Cassidy Arch Trail at the one-mile mark, and then wends its way across three miles of slickrock to Cohab Canyon.

Old Wagon Trail Loop

Distance: 3.5 miles round-trip
Duration: 3 hours
Elevation change: 1,000 feet
Effort: moderate-strenuous
Trailhead: on the Scenic Drive, 6 miles south of the visitors center, between Grand Wash and Capitol Gorge

Wagon drivers once used this route as a shortcut between Grover and Capitol Gorge. The old trail crosses a wash to the west, and then ascends steadily through piñon and juniper woodland on Miners Mountain. After 1.5 miles, the trail leaves the wagon road and continues north for 0.5 mile to a high knoll and the best views of the Capitol Reef area.

★ Capitol Gorge

Distance: 2 miles round-trip
Duration: 1-2 hours

Elevation change: 100 feet
Effort: easy-moderate
Trailhead: Capitol Gorge parking area

Follow the well-maintained dirt road to the parking area in Capitol Gorge to begin this hike. The first mile downstream is the most scenic: Fremont petroglyphs (in poor condition) appear on the left after 0.1 mile; narrows of Capitol Gorge close in at 0.3 mile; a "pioneer register" on the left soon after consists of names and dates of early travelers and ranchers scratched in the canyon wall. If you're able to, scramble up some rocks and follow a cairn-marked trail across the slickrock, then head up out of the wash at the trail marker to see natural water tanks, about 0.8 mile from the trail. These depressions in the rock collect water and give the Waterpocket Fold its name. Back in the wash, listen for canyon wrens—their song starts on a high note and then trills down the scale. From the turnoff to the water tanks, hikers can continue another three miles downstream to Notom Road.

Golden Throne Trail

Distance: 4 miles round-trip
Duration: 3 hours
Elevation change: 1,100 feet
Effort: strenuous
Trailhead: Capitol Gorge parking area

The Golden Throne Trail begins at the trailhead at the end of the drivable part of Capitol Gorge. Instead of heading down Capitol Gorge from the parking area, turn left up this trail for a steady climb to dramatic views of the reef and surrounding area. The Golden Throne is a massive monolith of yellow-hued sandstone capped by a thin layer of red rock. This is a good hike to take around sunset, when the rocks take on a burnished glow.

Mountain Biking

Ditch the car and really get to know this country with a big loop tour. For a strenuous ride with steep grades, take the **Boulder Mountain Loop.** Start from

Highway 24 near Capitol Reef, take the Notom-Bullfrog Road to Burr Trail Road, and then take Highway 12 over Boulder Mountain to Highway 24 and back to Capitol Reef. This is definitely the sort of trip that requires some touring experience and a decent level of training (Boulder Mountain is quite a haul). This route can run 80-125 miles over several days. (A car shuttle for the Highway 24 portion can shorten the ride.)

In the remote northern section of the park, cyclists can ride the challenging **Cathedral Valley Loop.** The complete loop is more than 60 miles long. Little water is available along the route, so it's best ridden in spring or fall, when temperatures are low. Access the loop on either Hartnett Road (11.7 miles east of the visitors center) or Caineville Wash Road (18.6 miles east of the visitors center). A small campground is located about 36 miles into the loop.

Although the Scenic Drive doesn't have much of a shoulder, it's not a bad bicycling road, especially early in the morning before car traffic has picked up. Dirt spur roads off the Scenic Drive lead up Grand Wash, into Capitol Gorge, and up South Draw to Pleasant Creek.

Contact the visitors center for more information on these and other routes.

Climbing

Rock climbing is allowed in the park. Climbers should check with rangers to learn about restricted areas, but registration is voluntary. Permits are not required unless climbers plan to camp overnight. Climbers must use "clean" techniques (no pitons or bolts) and keep at least 100 feet from rock-art panels and prehistoric structures. Because of the abundance of prehistoric rock art found there, the rock wall north of Highway 24—between the Fruita School and the east end of Kreuger Orchard (mile 81.4)—is closed to climbing. Other areas closed to climbing include Hickman Natural Bridge and all other arches and bridges, Temple of the Moon and Temple of the Sun, and Chimney Rock.

The harder, fractured sandstone of the **Wingate Formation** is better suited to climbing than Entrada sandstone. The rock is given to flaking, however, so climbers should use caution. Be sure that your chalk matches the color of the rock; white chalk is prohibited.

Accommodations

Torrey (population 180) is an attractive little village with a real Western feel. Only 11 miles west of the Capitol Reef National Park visitors center, at the junction of Highways 12 and 24, it's a friendly and convenient place to stay, with several excellent lodgings and a good restaurant.

There are other little towns along the Fremont River, which drains this steep-sided valley. Teasdale is a small community just four miles west, situated in a grove of piñon pines. Bicknell, a small farm and ranch town, is eight miles west of Torrey.

Inside the Park

Campgrounds

Fruita Campground (year-round, $20), one mile south of the visitors center on the Scenic Drive, has 71 sites for tents and RVs with drinking water and heated restrooms, but no showers or hookups. Campers must get their water from the visitors center November-April. The surrounding orchards and lush grass make this an attractive spot. Sites are first-come, first-served and often fill by early afternoon in the busy May-October season. One group campground (reservations required, $3 pp, $50 minimum) and a picnic area are nearby. Submit written reservation requests for the group site to Group Campsite Reservations, Capitol Reef National Park, HC 70, Box 15, Torrey, UT 84775.

Two campgrounds offer first-come, first-served primitive sites with no water.

The five-site **Cedar Mesa Campground** (year-round, free) is in the park's southern district, just off Notom-Bullfrog Road (dirt); campers enjoy fine views of the Waterpocket Fold and the Henry Mountains. From the visitors center, go east 9.2 miles on Highway 24, then turn right and go 22 miles on Notom-Bullfrog Road (avoid this road if it's wet). **Cathedral Valley Campground** (year-round, free) serves the park's northern district; it has six sites near the Hartnett Junction, about 30 miles north of Highway 24. Take either Caineville Wash Road or Hartnett Road. Both roads are dirt and should be avoided when wet. Hartnett has a river ford.

If you're just looking for a place to park for the night, check out the public land east of the park boundary, off Highway 24. Areas on both sides of the highway (about nine miles east of the visitors center) can be used for free primitive camping.

Backcountry camping is allowed in the park; obtain a free backcountry permit at the visitors center.

Outside the Park: Torrey and Teasdale

Under $50

There are a few small bunkhouse cabins at the center of town, at the **Torrey Trading Post** (75 W. Main St., Torrey, 435/425-3716, www.torreytradingpost.com, $40). They aren't loaded with frills—the toilets and showers are in men's and women's bathhouses—but the price is right, pets are permitted, and there's a place to do laundry. A larger cabin with a bathroom goes for $130.

$50-100

The **Capitol Reef Inn and Cafe** (360 W. Main St., Torrey, 435/425-3271, www.capitolreefinn.com, spring-fall, $59) has homey motel rooms and a good café serving breakfast, lunch, and dinner. In the front yard, the motel's owner and his brother have built a kiva resembling those used by Native Americans. It's obviously a labor of love, and a pretty cool place to explore.

At the east end of Torrey, the **Rim Rock Inn** (2523 E. Hwy. 24, Torrey, 435/425-3388 or 888/447-4676, www.therimrock.net, Mar.-Dec., $64-74) does indeed perch on a rim of red rock; it's just about as close as you can get to the park. The motel and its two restaurants are part of a 120-acre ranch, so the views are expansive.

In a grove of trees immediately behind downtown Torrey's old trading post and country store is **Austin's Chuck Wagon Lodge** (12 W. Main St., Torrey, 435/425-3335 or 800/863-3288, www.austinschuckwagonmotel.com, Mar.-Dec., rooms $61-162, cabins $147), with guest rooms in an older motel ($61), a newer lodge-like building, or newer two-bedroom cabins. There's also a pool and a hot tub.

In a pretty setting three miles east of Torrey, **Cowboy Homestead Cabins** (intersection of Hwy. 12 and Hwy. 24, Torrey, 435/425-3414 or 888/854-5871, www.cowboyhomesteadcabins.com, $89) has attractive one- and two-bedroom cabins with private baths, kitchenettes, and outdoor gas barbecue grills.

Head five miles down the Notom-Bullfrog Road to find accommodations at the **Notom Ranch Bed & Breakfast** (Notom Rd., Torrey, 435/456-9153, www.notomranchbandb.com, $75), a working ranch on the edge of the park with Western-themed guest rooms and expansive views.

$100-150

If you're looking for comfortable motel rooms with perks like an in-room coffeemaker and ironing board and an outdoor pool, a good choice is the **Capitol Reef Resort** (2600 E. Hwy. 24, Torrey, 435/425-3761, http://capitolreefresort.com, $140-160), northeast of Torrey.

The lovely **SkyRidge Inn Bed and Breakfast** (950 W. Hwy. 24, Torrey, 435/425-3222 or 877/824-1508, www.skyridgeinn.com, $119-169) is one mile east of downtown Torrey. The modern inn has been decorated with high-quality

The Orchards of Capitol Reef

Capitol Reef was one of the last places in the West to be found by settlers. The first reports came in 1866 from a detachment of Mormon militia pursuing insurgent Utes. In 1872, Professor Almon H. Thompson of the Powell Expedition led the first scientific exploration in the fold country and named several park features along the group's Pleasant Creek route. Mormons, expanding their network of settlements, arrived in the upper Fremont Valley in the late 1870s and spread downriver to Hanksville. Junction (renamed Fruita in 1902) and nearby Pleasant Creek (Sleeping Rainbow-Floral Ranch) were settled about 1880. Floods, isolation, and transportation difficulties forced many families to move on, especially downstream from Capitol Reef. Irrigation and hard work paid off with prosperous fruit orchards and the sobriquet "The Eden of Wayne County." The aptly named Fruita averaged about 10 families, who grew alfalfa, sorghum (for syrup), vegetables, and a wide variety of fruit. Getting the produce to market required long and difficult journeys by wagon. The region remained one of the most isolated in Utah until after World War II.

Although Fruita's citizens have departed, the National Park Service still maintains the old orchards. They are lovely in late April, when the trees are in bloom beneath the towering canyon walls. Visitors are welcome to pick and carry away the cherries, apricots, peaches, pears, and apples during harvest seasons. Harvest begins in late June-early July and ends in October. You'll be charged about the same as in commercial pick-your-own orchards. You can also wander through any orchard and eat all you want on the spot for free before and during the designated picking season.

Southwestern art and artifacts; all six guest rooms have private baths. SkyRidge sits on a bluff amid 75 acres, and guests are invited to explore the land on foot or bike.

In Teasdale, four miles west of Torrey, **Pine Shadows** (125 S. 200 W., Teasdale, 435/425-3939 or 800/708-1223, www.pineshadowcabins.net, $110) offers spacious, modern cabins, equipped with two queen beds plus full baths and kitchens, in a piñon forest.

Muley Twist Inn (off 125 S., outside Teasdale, 435/425-3640 or 800/530-1038, www.muleytwistinn.com, $99-150), an elegantly decorated five-bedroom B&B, is on a 30-acre parcel with great views. One guest room is fully accessible to wheelchair users. It's another really wonderful place to come home to at the end of a day of driving or hiking.

Stay in a renovated 1914 schoolhouse: The **Torrey Schoolhouse Bed and Breakfast** (150 N. Center St., Torrey, 435/633-4643, Apr.-Sept., $125-155) has been renovated but retains many period touches and an old-fashioned atmosphere. Modern amenities include a shiatsu massage chair in every room, memory foam mattress toppers, flat-screen TVs, and a wheelchair-accessible suite.

Over $150

The ★ **Lodge at Red River Ranch** (2900 W. Hwy. 24, Teasdale, 435/425-3322 or 800/205-6343, www.redriverranch.com, $160-245, 2-night minimum) is between Bicknell and Torrey beneath towering cliffs of red sandstone on the banks of the Fremont River. This wonderful wood-beamed lodge sits on a 2,200-acre working ranch, but there's nothing rustic or unsophisticated about the accommodations. The three-story structure is newly built, although in the same grand architectural style as old-fashioned mountain lodges. The great room has a massive stone fireplace, cozy chairs and couches, and a splendid Old West atmosphere. There are 15 guest rooms, most decorated according to a theme, and all have private baths. Guests are welcome to wander ranch paths, fish for trout, or meander in the gardens and orchards. Breakfast and dinner are served in the lodge restaurant but are not included in the price of lodgings; box lunches can be ordered.

Campgrounds

Although most campers will try for a site at Capitol Reef National Park, the campgrounds there do not take reservations and fill up quickly. Torrey has a couple of private campgrounds that cater to both RV and tent campers. **Thousand Lakes RV Park** (Hwy. 24, 1 mile west of Torrey, 435/425-3500 or 800/355-8995, www.thousandlakesrvpark.com, Apr.-late Oct., $18 tents, $33 RVs with full hookups) has showers, wireless Internet, a laundry room, and a store. Thousand Lakes also has cabins, ranging from spartan (no linens, $35) to deluxe (sleeps 8, linens provided, $95). Right in town, the **SandCreek RV Park** (540 W. Hwy. 24, Torrey, 435/425-3577, www.sandcreekrv.com, Apr.-mid-Oct., $15 tents, $25-30 RVs, $35 camping cabins) has shaded tent spaces in a pleasant grassy field. Showers ($5 for nonguests) and laundry facilities ($5 to wash and dry) are available.

The U.S. Forest Service's **Sunglow Campground** (Forest Rd. 143, east of Bicknell, 435/836-2811, $8) is just east of Bicknell at an elevation of 7,200 feet. The seven first-come, first-served sites are open and have water mid-May-late October. The surrounding red cliffs really light up at sunset, hence the name. Several other Forest Service campgrounds are on the slopes of Boulder Mountain along Highway 12 between Torrey and Boulder. These places are all above 8,600 feet and usually don't open until late May-early June.

Food

Outside the Park: Torrey

Torrey's restaurant of note is ★ **Cafe Diablo** (599 W. Main St., Torrey, 435/425-3070, www.cafediablo.net, 11:30am-10pm daily Apr.-Oct., $22-32). The specialty is zesty Southwestern cuisine, with excellent dishes like fire-roasted pork tenderloin, eggplant- and poblano-stuffed tamales, and pumpkin-seed trout. This is one of the few places where you can order free-range rattlesnake meat, cooked into crab cake-like patties. Because there aren't many restaurants this good in rural Utah, this place is worth a detour, though it must be said that it's not the place for a quiet romantic dinner—it's a high-volume, fast-paced, high-energy dining experience. Lunchtime, which features a Cuban sandwich ($12), crab chalupas ($12), turkey *picadillo* ($12), and more, tends to be a bit quieter.

Another pleasant surprise in this small town is the **Capitol Reef Inn and Cafe** (360 W. Main St., Torrey, 435/425-3271, www.capitolreefinn.com, 7am-9pm daily, $10-15), where there's an emphasis on healthy and, when possible, locally grown food. It's easy to eat your veggies here—the 10-vegetable salad will make up for some of the less nutritious meals you've had on the road.

For something a little less elevated, try the burgers and milk shakes at **Slacker's Burger Joint** (165 E. Main St., Torrey, 435/425-3710, noon-8pm Mon.-Thurs., noon-9pm Fri.-Sat., noon-5pm Sun., $6-12), in the center of town. The pastrami burger is rightfully famous, and an afternoon milk shake hits the spot after a day of hiking.

Outside the Park: Caineville

About 12 miles east of Capitol Reef, stop by the tiny ★ **Mesa Market** (Hwy. 24, Caineville, 435/487-9711, www.mesafarmmarket.com, 7am-7pm daily late Mar.-Oct., $3-17) for artisanal cheese and yogurt, sourdough bread baked in a wood-fired oven, and whatever produce is growing in the back 40. You won't find better picnic makings anywhere in southeastern Utah, and if he has a minute to spare, the owner will explain the sustainable nature of his farm and dairy.

Arches and Canyonlands

The Colorado River and its tributaries have carved the Colorado Plateau's vivid red and orange sandstone into extraordinary shapes.

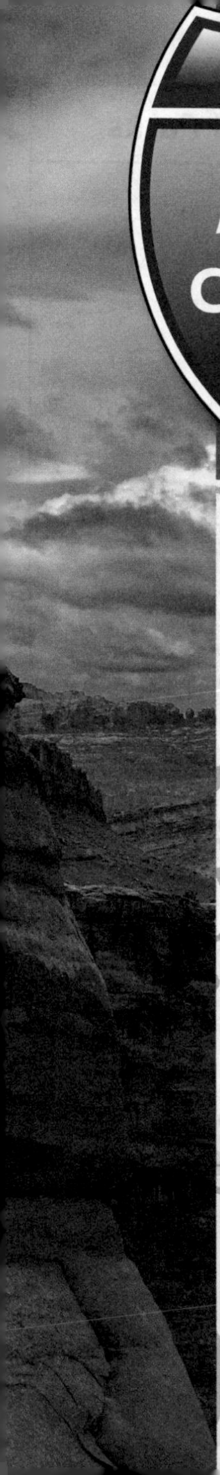

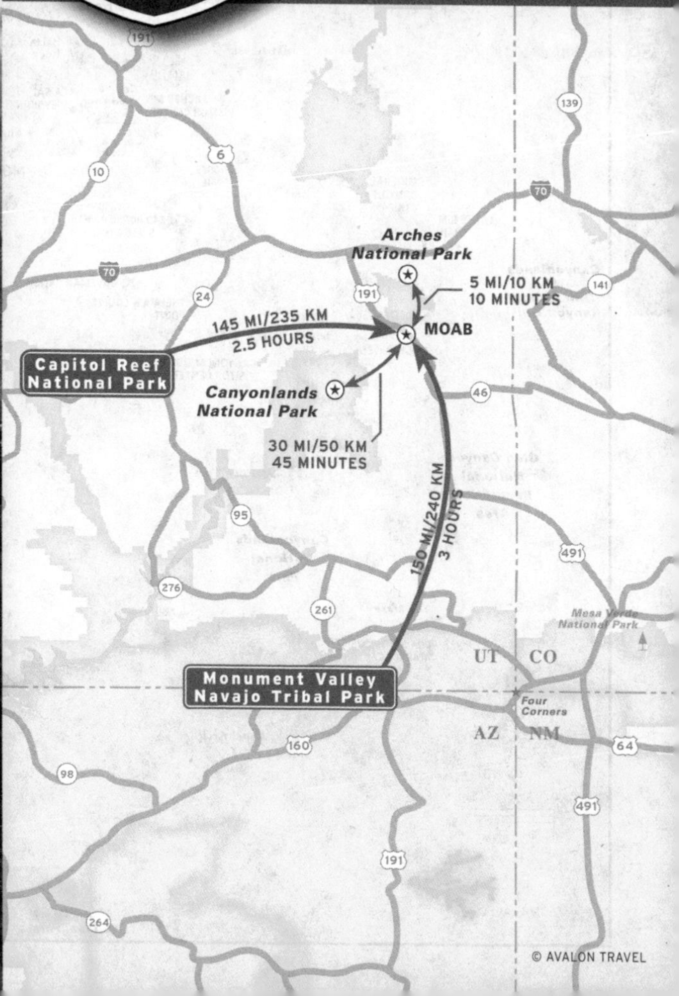

Arches National Park
5 MI/10 KM
10 MINUTES
MOAB
145 MI/235 KM
2.5 HOURS
Capitol Reef National Park
Canyonlands National Park
30 MI/50 KM
45 MINUTES
150 MI/240 KM
3 HOURS
Monument Valley Navajo Tribal Park
Mesa Verde National Park
UT
CO
AZ
NM
Four Corners
191
139
6
10
70
24
141
46
95
491
276
261
160
64
98
264
© AVALON TRAVEL

Arches and Canyonlands National Parks

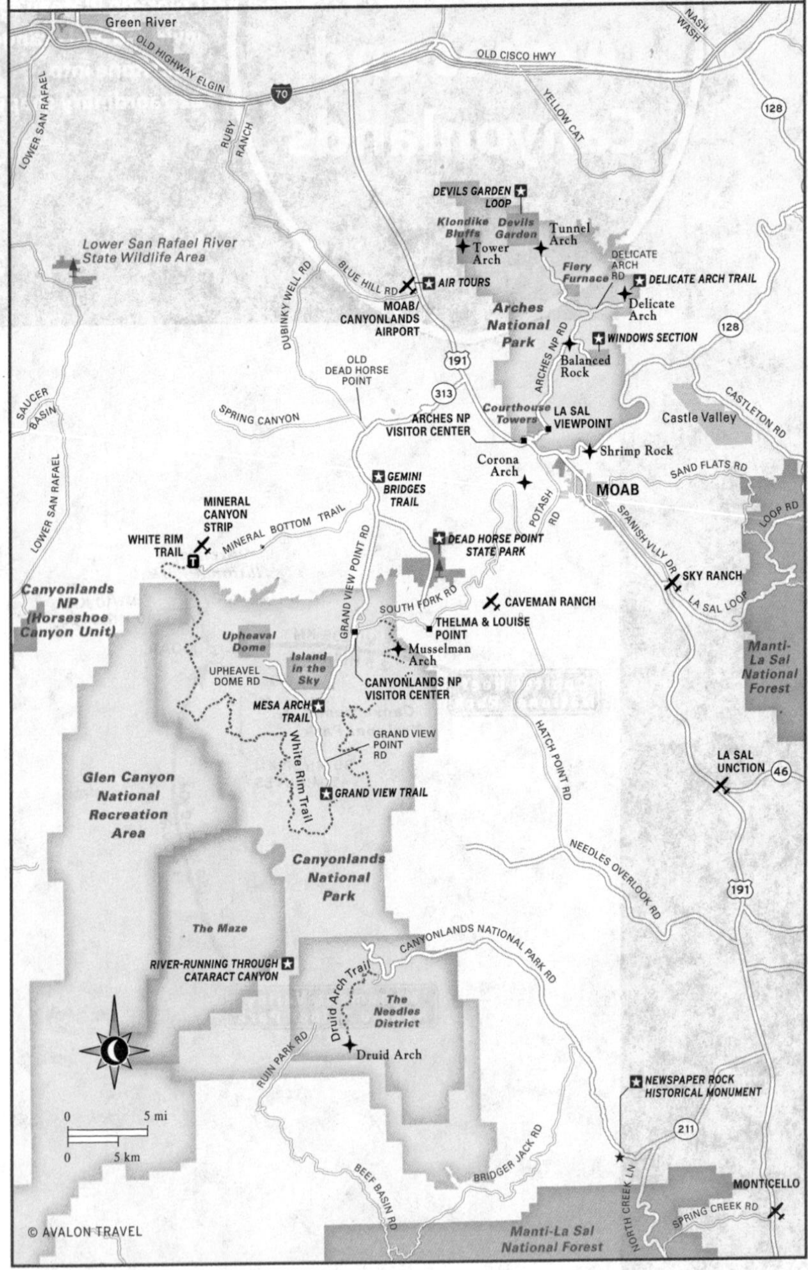

Highlights

★ **Dead Horse Point State Park:** This peninsula of land perched 2,000 feet above the Colorado River has spectacular viewpoints, great camping, and mountain bike trails for the whole family (page 162).

★ **Gemini Bridges Trail:** Have some fun biking this mostly downhill ride. Most cyclists do this 14-mile one-way ride with a shuttle vehicle (page 173).

★ **Air Tours:** Flightseeing trips showcase this amazing landscape from the viewpoint of an eagle (page 179).

★ **Windows Section:** Some of the area's largest arches are here—so are some of its largest crowds. Past the first arch, the crowds thin out (page 193).

★ **Delicate Arch Trail:** Delicate Arch is mystical when viewed close up, after a tough 1.5-mile hike to its base (page 197).

★ **Devils Garden Loop:** This 7.2-mile loop trail leads through a landscape of bizarre rock fins and offers the park's best day hiking (page 198).

★ **Mesa Arch Trail:** The sun rising through Mesa Arch is a sight to behold—if you have time and energy for just one hike in Canyonlands, this should be it (page 211).

★ **Grand View Trail:** This short hike along slickrock cliffs captures the essence of the Island in the Sky. In the distance, the odd promontories of the Needles District punctuate the skyline (page 211).

★ **Newspaper Rock Historical Monument:** One of Utah's foremost prehistoric rock-art sites is also one of the most easily accessible. The distinctive petroglyphs span 2,000 years of human history (page 214).

★ **River-Running Through Cataract Canyon:** Especially in spring, the 26 or more rapids here give a wild ride on the Colorado River (page 229).

Intricate mazes of canyons, delicate arches, and massive rock monoliths make this region seem primordial at times and lunar at others.

It has a beauty and scenic drama that's unique, and first-time visitors often need a while to appreciate this strange land before they're won over by the infinite colors and variety of the sculptured rock. Two national parks—Arches and Canyonlands—preserve some of the most astounding of these landscapes, while numerous state parks, national monuments, and recreation areas protect other sights of great interest and beauty. At every turn, the landscape invites exploration, offering solitude, ruins of prehistoric villages, wildlife, and dramatic records of geologic history.

Besides the drama of the landscape, outdoor recreation is now what brings people to this corner of Utah: There are so many recreational options available here that plain old hiking almost seems passé. Moab is central for slickrock mountain biking, which brings people in from around the world to ride the area's red-rock cliffs and canyons. Another "sport" drawing legions of fans to the area is "off-roading," or exploration of the canyon backcountry on four-wheel-drive and all-terrain vehicles (ATVs). The huge surge of popularity for off-roading has the Bureau of Land Management (BLM), which governs much of the nonpark land in the area, considering restrictions on the number of people able to drive the backcountry, as the off-road vehicles are tearing up fragile ecosystems and causing other environmental damage.

Moab

By far the largest town in southeastern Utah, Moab (population 5,150) makes an excellent base for exploring Arches and Canyonlands National Parks and the surrounding canyon country. Moab is near the Colorado River in a green valley enclosed by high red sandstone cliffs. Moab's existence on the fringe of Mormon culture and the sizable young non-Mormon population give the town a unique character.

As Moab's popularity has grown, so have concerns that the town and the

Best Accommodations

★ **Kokopelli Lodge:** Affordable and centrally located in Moab, this midcentury motor court has personality to spare (page 183).

★ **Best Western Canyonlands Inn:** A civilized hotel in the heart of Moab, this inn offers upscale comfort in a contemporary Southwest style (page 184).

★ **Gonzo Inn:** Stay at this central Moab spot to experience a colorful, unique vision of Southwestern decor, along with large, comfortable rooms and an enticing pool and spa (page 184).

★ **Sunflower Hill Luxury Inn:** Just a few blocks off Moab's main drag, this is a convenient hideaway with charming rooms, private balconies, and lush gardens (page 184).

★ **Sorrel River Ranch:** Fall asleep in a posh cabin-style room on the banks of the Colorado River at this luxurious resort on a 240-acre ranch outside of Moab (page 184).

★ **Up the Creek:** Pitch your tent in this small campground, a green and peaceful spot that's just two blocks from Main Street in Moab (page 185).

surrounding countryside are simply getting loved to death. On a busy day, hundreds of mountain bikers form queues to negotiate the trickier sections of the famed Slickrock Trail, and more than 20,000 people crowd into town on busy weekends to bike, hike, float, and party. As noted in an article in *Details* magazine, "Moab is pretty much the Fort Lauderdale of the intermountain West."

While many people come to Moab because of what it's near, there's certainly enough to do in the town to justify adding an extra day to a park-focused itinerary just for exploring Moab and environs. Moab is the most hospitable town in this part of Utah, so take time to stop and enjoy its quirky charms. The adrenaline reaches a fever pitch during spring break, so don't plan a quiet weekend in Moab anytime around Easter.

Getting There from Capitol Reef National Park

145 miles / 2.5 hours

The fastest route from Capitol Reef National Park to Moab and Arches and Canyonlands National Parks, a **2.5-hour** drive of some **145 miles,** includes a brief sprint on I-70.

Take **UT-24 East** from Capitol Reef National Park for about 35 miles to the crossroads at Hanksville. Then continue north (turn left) on UT-24 for 45 miles through the wonderfully strange desert landscape along the eastern edges of San Rafael Reef and Goblin Valley State Park to **I-70 East.** Drive east for about 10 miles, where you'll pass over the Green River and through the town of the same name. After another 20 miles, leave the interstate at **US 191 South toward Crescent Junction (exit 182).** Take **US 191** for 30 miles to Moab, passing the entrances to both Canyonlands and Arches along the way.

A longer route, but one that passes several interesting and scenic spots, is **240 miles** and takes **4.5 hours.** Use this route if you want to visit Canyonlands National Park's remote **Needles District.** At the Hanksville crossroads (35 miles on UT-24), head south on **UT-95,** on which you'll pass the turnoff for Natural Bridges National Monument. After 120 miles, it's time to go north (turn left) on **US 191.** From there it's about 80 miles to Moab. Along the way you'll pass the turnoff to the Needles District, which also leads to Newspaper Rock, an incredible petroglyph site that should not be missed, and Hole 'n the Rock, a fun, touristy stop along the highway that is exactly what its name suggests.

Stopping in Hanksville

A small town about 30 miles east of Capitol Reef National Park, where

Best Restaurants

★ **Love Muffin:** The perfect place to pick up an early-morning breakfast burrito—there are at least eight kinds to choose from (page 186).

★ **EklectiCafe:** Vegetarians flock to this small café on Moab's main drag, where the ingredients are organic, the coffee is fair trade, and the food is fantastic (page 186).

★ **Milt's Stop & Eat:** This old-school American diner in Moab serves some of the best burgers and shakes anywhere (page 186).

★ **Eddie McStiff's:** A classic bar and grill, this popular pub has excellent food, a fun bar scene, and live bands (page 187).

★ **Desert Bistro:** Make a reservation if you want to try this regional favorite in central Moab, a sophisticated gem with the best patio dining in town (page 187).

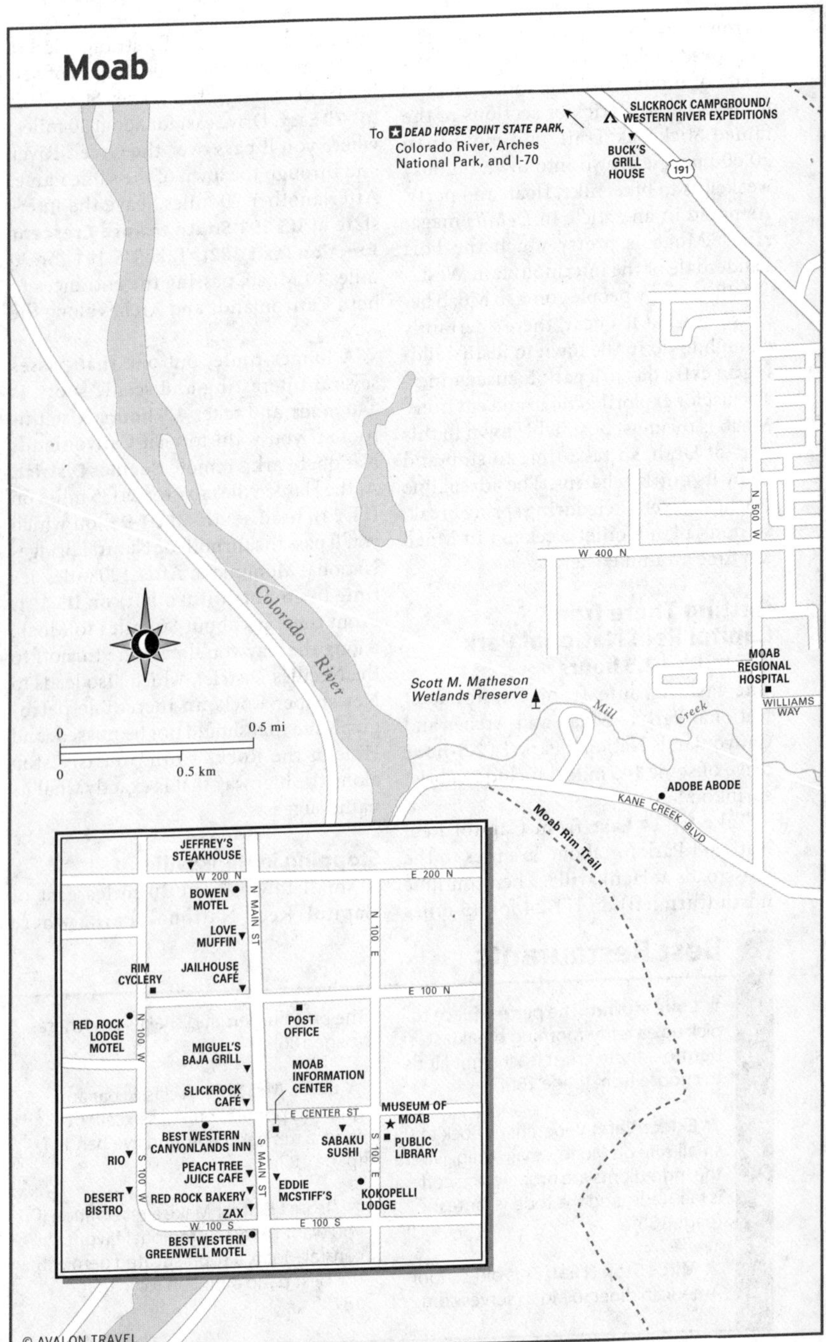
Moab
To DEAD HORSE POINT STATE PARK, Colorado River, Arches National Park, and I-70
SLICKROCK CAMPGROUND/ WESTERN RIVER EXPEDITIONS
BUCK'S GRILL HOUSE
191
N 500 W
W 400 N
Colorado River
MOAB REGIONAL HOSPITAL
WILLIAMS WAY
Scott M. Matheson Wetlands Preserve
Mill Creek
0
0.5 mi
0
0.5 km
ADOBE ABODE
KANE CREEK BLVD
Moab Rim Trail
JEFFREY'S STEAKHOUSE
W 200 N
E 200 N
BOWEN MOTEL
N MAIN ST
N 100 E
LOVE MUFFIN
RIM CYCLERY
JAILHOUSE CAFÉ
E 100 N
POST OFFICE
RED ROCK LODGE MOTEL
N 100 W
MIGUEL'S BAJA GRILL
MOAB INFORMATION CENTER
SLICKROCK CAFÉ
E CENTER ST
MUSEUM OF MOAB
BEST WESTERN CANYONLANDS INN
SABAKU SUSHI
PUBLIC LIBRARY
S MAIN ST
S 100 E
RIO
S 100 W
PEACH TREE JUICE CAFE
DESERT BISTRO
RED ROCK BAKERY
EDDIE MCSTIFF'S
KOKOPELLI LODGE
ZAX
W 100 S
E 100 S
BEST WESTERN GREENWELL MOTEL
© AVALON TRAVEL

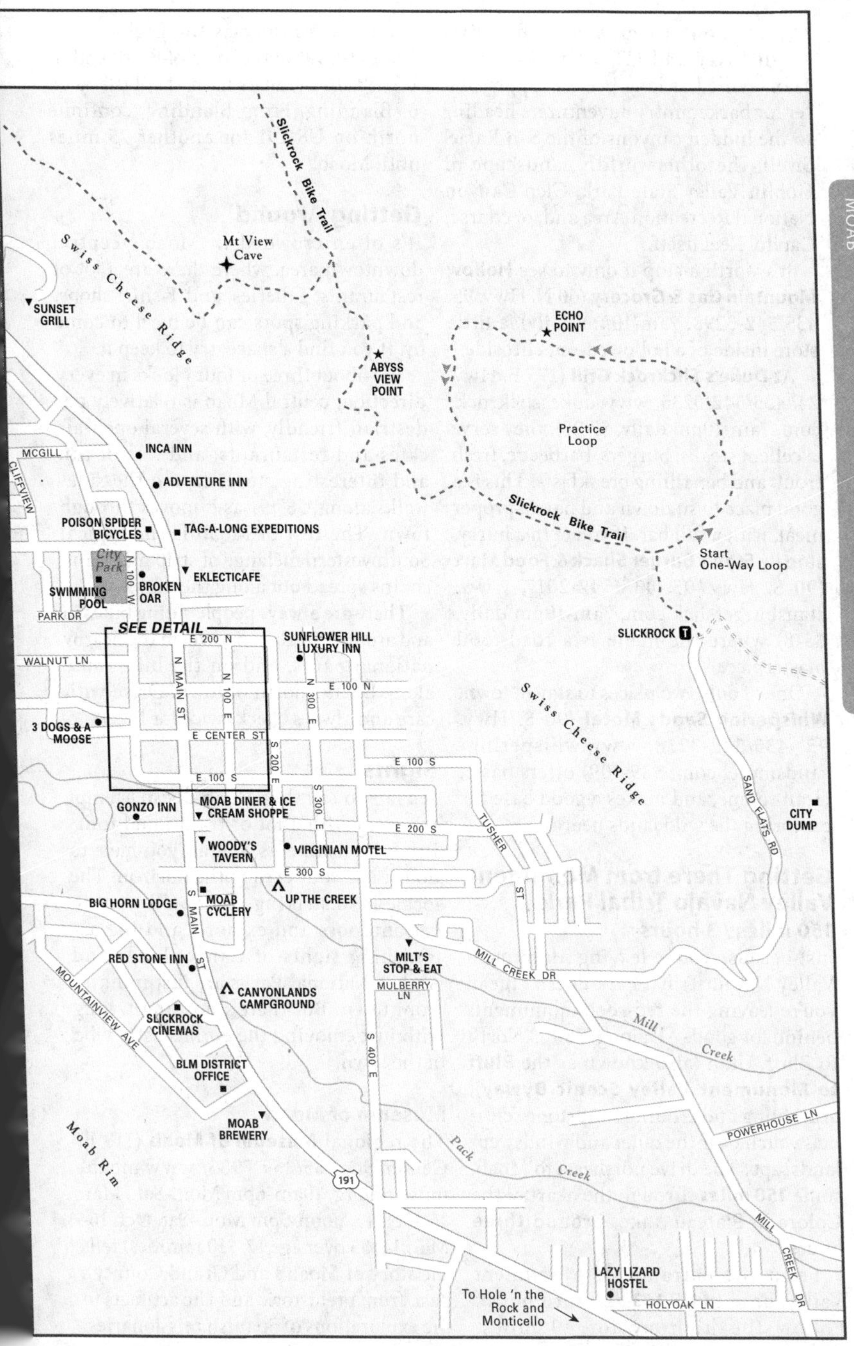

Slickrock Bike Trail
Swiss Cheese Ridge
Mt View Cave
SUNSET GRILL
ECHO POINT
ABYSS VIEW POINT
Practice Loop
Slickrock Bike Trail
Start One-Way Loop
SLICKROCK
MCGILL
CLIFFVIEW
INCA INN
ADVENTURE INN
POISON SPIDER BICYCLES
TAG-A-LONG EXPEDITIONS
City Park
N 100 W
EKLECTICAFE
SWIMMING POOL
BROKEN OAR
PARK DR
SEE DETAIL
E 200 N
SUNFLOWER HILL LUXURY INN
WALNUT LN
N MAIN ST
N 100 E
N 300 E
E 100 N
Swiss Cheese Ridge
3 DOGS & A MOOSE
E CENTER ST
S 200 E
E 100 S
E 100 S
SAND FLATS RD
CITY DUMP
GONZO INN
MOAB DINER & ICE CREAM SHOPPE
S 300 E
E 200 S
TUSHER ST
WOODY'S TAVERN
VIRGINIAN MOTEL
E 300 S
UP THE CREEK
BIG HORN LODGE
MOAB CYCLERY
S MAIN ST
MILT'S STOP & EAT
MILL CREEK DR
RED STONE INN
MOUNTAINVIEW AVE
CANYONLANDS CAMPGROUND
MULBERRY LN
SLICKROCK CINEMAS
Mill Creek
S 400 E
BLM DISTRICT OFFICE
POWERHOUSE LN
MOAB BREWERY
Moab Rim
Pack Creek
191
MILL CREEK DR
LAZY LIZARD HOSTEL
To Hole 'n the Rock and Monticello
HOLYOAK LN

the Fremont River meets the Dirty Devil River and UT-24 meets UT-95, Hanksville has long been a supply center for backcountry adventurers heading to the hidden canyons of the San Rafael Swell, the otherworldly landscape of Goblin Valley State Park, Glen Canyon National Recreation Area and, of course, Capitol Reef itself.

It's worth a stop if only to see **Hollow Mountain Gas & Grocery** (60 N. Hwy. 95, 435/542-3298, 7am-10pm daily), a little store inside of a hollowed-out cliff side.

At **Duke's Slickrock Grill** (275 E. Hwy. 24, 435/542-3235, www.dukesslickrock.com, 7am-10pm daily, $7-28), they serve excellent steaks, burgers, barbecue, fresh trout, and big, filling breakfasts. This is a good place to sit down and have a proper meal, with a full bar. If you're in a hurry, stop by **Stan's Burger Shack & Food Mart** (90 S. Hwy. 95, 435/542-2017, www.stansburgershck.com, 7am-10pm daily, $5-8) where the menu is a road-food masterpiece.

One of only two places to stay in town, **Whispering Sands Motel** (90 S. Hwy. 95, 435/542-3238, www.whisperingsandsmotel.com, $89-109) offers basic, clean rooms, and makes a good base for exploring the wild lands nearby.

Getting There from Monument Valley Navajo Tribal Park

150 miles / 3 hours

Just because you're leaving Monument Valley Navajo Tribal Park doesn't mean you're leaving the red-rock monuments behind for good. All along US 163 North to Bluff, Utah (also known as the **Bluff to Monument Valley Scenic Byway**), crumbling and eroding sandstone sentinels watch over the quiet and windswept landscape. The drive northeast to Moab, some **150 miles** through the heart of the Colorado Plateau, takes around **three hours.**

From the entrance of Monument Valley, head to **US 163** and turn north. Follow the highway for 40 miles. Continue straight as the highway becomes **US 191** at the town of Bluff. Follow US 191 for 30 miles more until the town of Blanding. From Blanding, continue north on US 191 for another 75 miles until Moab.

Getting Around

It's often crowded in Moab's central downtown area, where there are a lot of restaurants, galleries, and T-shirt shops, and parking spots can be hard to come by. If you find a space, try to keep it.

For about three or four blocks in every direction, central Moab is relatively pedestrian-friendly, with several open-air cafés and restaurants, and lots of fun and interesting stores facing the sidewalks along US 191 as it moves through town. The rest of Moab is the typical Southwestern mélange of strip malls and chains spread out along the highway.

There are always people riding bikes in and around Moab—in town, in the nearby national parks, and on the bike route along US 191 north of town. Drive with care and always check twice for bikers.

Sights

It's fair to say that Moab doesn't tempt travelers with a lot of traditional tourism establishments, but all you have to do is raise your eyes to the horizon. The locale is so striking that you'll want to get outdoors and explore, and the astonishing sights of Canyonlands and Arches National Parks are just minutes from town. But there's nothing wrong with just enjoying the enthusiastic vibe of the town.

Museum of Moab

The regional **Museum of Moab** (118 E. Center St., 435/259-7985, www.moabmuseum.org, 10am-6pm Mon.-Sat., Mar. 15-Oct. 15, noon-5pm Mon.-Sat. Oct. 16-Mar. 14, $5 over age 17, $10 families) tells the story of Moab's and Grand County's past, from prehistoric and Ute artifacts to the explorations of Spanish missionaries.

Stretch Your Legs

Utah's first national monument, **Natural Bridges National Monument** (Capitol Reef to Moab drive, UT-275, 35 miles west of Blanding, UT, 435/692-1234, www.nps.gov/nabr, visitors center 8am-5pm daily Apr. and early Oct.-mid-Oct., 8am-6pm daily May-Sept., 9am-5pm daily mid-Oct.-Mar., $5-10) is a good excuse to get out of the car on the drive from Capitol Reef to Moab. Here, you can gaze upon three different natural bridges in the awe-inspiring Utah landscape. If you're planning on visiting both Arches and Canyonlands, you can save some money on admission to Natural Bridges by purchasing the Southeast Utah Parks Annual Pass ($50).

The Ancestral Puebloan ruins and artifacts at **Edge of the Cedars State Park Museum** (Monument Valley to Moab drive, 600 W. 400 N., off of US 191, 435/678-2238, http://stateparks.utah.gov, 9am-5pm Mon.-Sat., 10am-4pm Sun., $5) in Blanding, Utah, are worth a stop and a stroll. About halfway between Moab and Monument Valley (1.5 hours, 75 miles), the park protects an impressive collection of Ancestral Puebloan pottery as well as the remains of a far-flung Chacoan great house, a ruin that was once part of a trade and cultural network that ruled the Four Corners region circa AD 800-1100.

Photos and tools show pioneer Moab life, much of which centered on ranching or mining. You'll also find displays of rocks and minerals as well as the bones of huge dinosaurs, including the backbone of a sauropod found by a rancher just outside town.

Hole 'n the Rock

Fifteen miles south of Moab, Albert Christensen worked 12 years to excavate his dream home within a sandstone monolith south of town. When he died in 1957, his wife, Gladys, worked another eight years to complete the 5,000-square-foot house, called **Hole 'n the Rock** (11037 S. US 191, 435/686-2250, www.theholeintherock.com, 9am-5pm daily, $6 adults, $3.50 ages 5-10). It's now a full-on roadside attraction. The interior has notable touches like a 65-foot chimney drilled through the rock ceiling, paintings, taxidermy exhibits, and a lapidary room. The 14-room home is open for 12-minute-long guided tours and offers a gift shop, petting zoo, exotic animals, picnic area, and snack bar.

Mill Canyon Dinosaur Trail

The 0.5-mile **Mill Canyon Dinosaur Trail,** with numbered stops, identifies the bones of dinosaurs that lived in the wet climate that existed here 150 million years ago. You'll see fossilized wood and dinosaur footprints too. Pick up the brochure from the **Moab Information Center** (25 E. Center St., at Main St., 435/259-8825 or 800/635-6622, www.discovermoab.com) or at the trailhead.

To reach the dinosaur site, drive 15 miles north of Moab on US 191, then turn left (west) at an intersection just north of milepost 141. Cross the railroad tracks and continue two miles on a rough dirt road (impassable when wet) to the trailhead.

You'll find many other points of interest nearby. A copper mill and tailings dating from the late 1800s are across the canyon. The ruins of Halfway Stage Station, where travelers once stopped on the Thompson-Moab run, are a short distance down the other road fork. Jeepers and mountain bikers can do a 13- to 14-mile loop to Monitor and Merrimac Buttes; a sign just off US 191 has a map and details.

Copper Ridge Dinosaur Trackways

Apatosaurus, aka brontosaurus, and theropod tracks crisscross an ancient riverbed at the **Copper Ridge Dinosaur**

Trackways site. It's easy to make out the two-foot-wide hind footprints of the brontosaurus, but its small front feet didn't leave much of a dent in the sand. Three-toed tracks of the carnivorous theropods, possibly allosaurus, are 8-15 inches long, and some show an irregular gait—perhaps indicating a limp.

The Copper Ridge tracks are 23 miles north of Moab on US 191; turn right (east) 0.75 mile north of milepost 148. Cross the railroad tracks and turn south, following signs two miles to the tracks.

★ Dead Horse Point State Park

Just east of Canyonlands National Park's Island in the Sky District and a short drive northwest of Moab is one of Utah's most spectacular state parks. At **Dead Horse Point State Park** (435/259-2614, www.stateparks.utah.gov, day-use $10 per vehicle), the land drops away in sheer cliffs, and 2,000 feet below, the Colorado River twists through a gooseneck on its long journey to the sea. The river and its tributaries have carved canyons that reveal a geologic layer cake of colorful rock formations. Even in a region with impressive views around nearly every corner, Dead Horse Point stands out for its exceptionally breathtaking panorama. You'll also see below you, along the Colorado River, the result of powerful underground forces: Salt, under pressure, has pushed up overlying rock layers into an anticline. This formation, the Shafer Dome, contains potash that is being processed by the Moab Salt Plant. You can see the mine buildings, processing plant, and evaporation ponds, which are tinted blue to hasten evaporation.

A narrow neck of land only 30 yards wide connects the point with the rest of the plateau. Cowboys once herded wild horses onto the point, then placed a fence across the neck to make a 40-acre corral. They chose the desirable animals from the herd and let the rest go. According to one tale, a group of horses left behind after such a roundup became confused by

Dead Horse Point State Park is full of outstanding views.

the geography of the point. They couldn't find their way off and circled repeatedly until they died of thirst within sight of the river below. You may also hear other stories of how the point got its name.

Besides the awe-inspiring views, the park also has a **visitors center** (8am-6pm daily mid-Mar.-mid-Oct., 9am-5pm daily mid-Oct.-mid-Mar.), a very popular campground, a picnic area, a group area, a nature trail, hiking trails, and great mountain biking on the **Intrepid Trail System.** Spectacularly scenic hiking trails run along the east and west rims of the peninsula-like park; hikers are also allowed to use the Intrepid trails. Rangers lead hikes during the busy spring season and on some evenings during the summer, including monthly full-moon hikes. Whether you're visiting for the day or camping at Dead Horse Point, it's best to bring plenty of water. Although water is available here, it is trucked in.

Dead Horse Point is easily reached by paved road, either as a destination itself or as a side trip on the way to the Island in the Sky District of Canyonlands National Park. From Moab, head northwest 10 miles on US 191, then turn left and travel 22 miles on Highway 313. The drive along Highway 313 climbs through a scenic canyon and tops out on a ridge with panoramas of distant mesas, buttes, mountains, and canyons. There are several rest areas along the road.

Scenic Drives

Each of the following routes is at least partly accessible to standard low-clearance highway vehicles. If you have a 4WD vehicle, you have the option of additional off-road exploring.

You'll find detailed travel information on these and other places in Charles Wells's *Guide to Moab, UT Backroads & 4-Wheel Drive Trails,* which, along with a good selection of maps, is available at the **Moab Information Center** (25 E. Center St., at Main St., 435/259-8825 or 800/635-6622, www.discovermoab.com). Staff members at the info center usually know current road and trail conditions.

Utah Scenic Byway 279

Highway 279 goes downstream along the west side of the Colorado River Canyon on the other side of the river from Moab. Pavement extends 16 miles past fine views, prehistoric rock art, arches, and hiking trails. A potash plant marks the end of the highway; a rough dirt road continues to Canyonlands National Park. From Moab, head north 3.5 miles on US 191, then turn left onto Highway 279. The highway enters the canyon at the "portal," 2.7 miles from the turnoff. Towering sandstone cliffs rise on the right, and the Colorado River drifts along just below on the left.

Stop at a signed pullout on the left, 0.6 mile past the canyon entrance, to see **Indian Ruins Viewpoint,** a small prehistoric Native American ruin tucked under a ledge across the river. The stone structure was probably used for food storage.

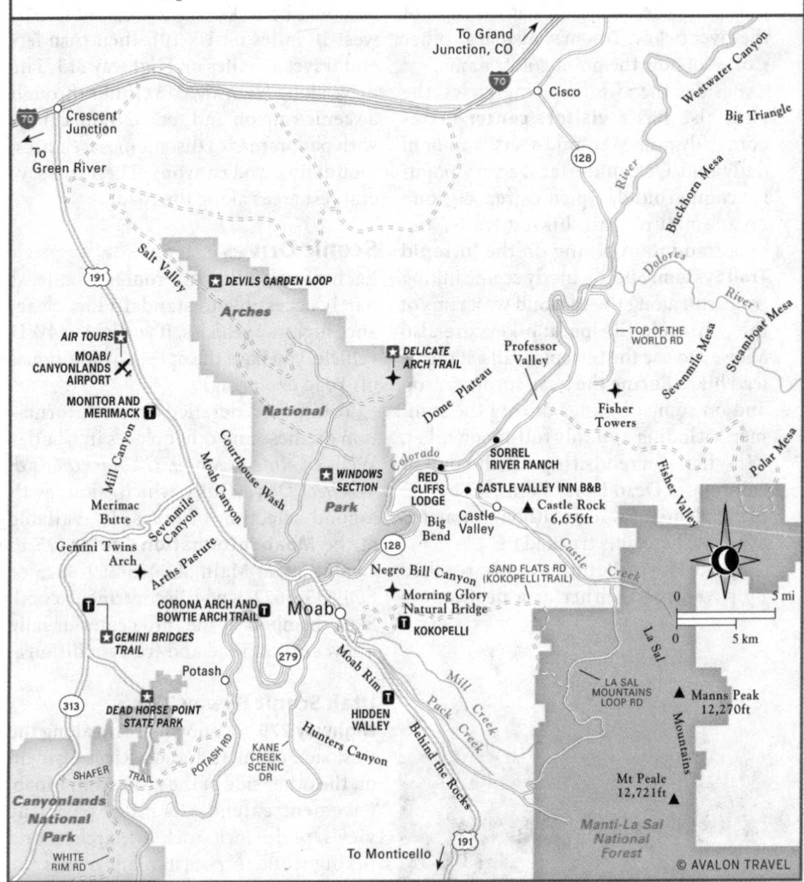

Groups of **petroglyphs** cover cliffs along the highway 5.2 miles from US 191, which is 0.7 mile beyond milepost 11. Look across the river to see the Fickle Finger of Fate among the sandstone fins of Behind the Rocks. A petroglyph of a bear is 0.2 mile farther down the highway. Archaeologists think that the Fremont people and the later Utes did most of the artwork in this area.

A signed pullout on the right, 6.2 miles from US 191, points out **dinosaur tracks** and petroglyphs visible on rocks above. Sighting tubes help locate the features. It's possible to hike up the steep hillside for a closer look.

Ten miles west of the highway turnoff is the trailhead for the **Corona Arch Trail** (3 miles round-trip).

The aptly named **Jug Handle Arch,** with an opening 46 feet high and 3 feet wide, is close to the road on the right, 13.6 miles from US 191. Ahead the canyon opens up where underground pressure from salt and potash has folded the rock layers into an anticline.

At the **Moab Salt Plant,** mining operations inject water underground to dissolve potash and other chemicals, then pump the solution to evaporation ponds. The ponds are dyed blue to hasten evaporation, which takes about a year. You can see these colorful ponds from Dead Horse Point and Anticline Overlook on the canyon rims.

High-clearance vehicles can continue on the unpaved road beyond the plant. The road passes through varied canyon country, with views overlooking the Colorado River. At a road junction in Canyonlands National Park's Island in the Sky District, you have a choice of turning left for the 100-mile White Rim Trail (4WD vehicles only past Musselman Arch), continuing up the steep switchbacks of the Shafer Trail Road (4WD recommended) to the paved park road, or returning the way you came.

Utah Scenic Byway 128

Highway 128 turns northeast from US 191 just south of the Colorado River bridge, two miles north of Moab. This exceptionally scenic canyon route follows the Colorado for 30 miles upstream before crossing at Dewey Bridge and turning north to I-70. The entire highway is paved. The Lions Park picnic area at the turnoff from US 191 is a pleasant stopping place. Big Bend Recreation Site is another good spot 7.5 miles up Highway 128.

The rugged scenery along this stretch of the Colorado River has been featured in many films—mostly Westerns, but also *Thelma and Louise*—and commercials. If you're intrigued, stop by the free **Film Museum** at Red Cliffs Ranch, a resort near milepost 14.

The paved and scenic **La Sal Mountains Loop Road,** with viewpoints overlooking Castle Valley, Arches and Canyonlands National Parks, Moab Rim, and other scenic features, has its northern terminus at Castle Valley, climbs high into the La Sals, and then loops back to Moab. Vegetation along the drive runs the whole range from the cottonwoods, sage, and rabbitbrush of the desert to forests of aspen, fir, and spruce. The 62-mile loop road can easily take a full day with stops for scenic overlooks, a picnic, and a bit of hiking or fishing. Because of the high elevations, the loop's season usually lasts May-October. Before venturing off the Loop Road, it's a good idea to check current back-road conditions with the **Moab Information Center** (25 E. Center St., at Main St., 435/259-8825 or 800/635-6622, www.discovermoab.com). You can also ask for a road log of sights and side roads. The turnoff from Highway 128 is 15.5 miles up from US 191.

A graded county road, **Onion Creek Road,** turns southeast off Highway 128 about 20 miles from US 191 and heads up Onion Creek, crossing it many times. Avoid this route if storms threaten. The unpleasant-smelling creek contains poisonous arsenic and selenium. Colorful rock formations of dark red sandstone line the creek. After about eight miles, the road climbs steeply out of Onion Creek to upper Fisher Valley and a junction with Kokopelli's Trail, which follows a jeep road over this part of its route.

Some of the area's most striking sights are the gothic spires of **Fisher Towers,** which soar as high as 900 feet above Professor Valley. Supposedly, the name Fisher is not that of a pioneer but a corruption of the geologic term *fissure* (a narrow crack). In 1962, three climbers from Colorado made the first ascent of Titan Tower, the tallest of the three towers. The almost vertical rock faces, overhanging bulges, and sections of rotten rock made for an exhausting 3.5 days of climbing; the party descended to the base for two of the nights. Their final descent from the summit took only six hours. In 2008 a slackliner walked a rope strung between the two tallest towers, and visitors to the towers can frequently see climbers and occasionally slackline walkers. The BLM has a small campground and picnic area nearby, and a hiking trail skirts the base of the

Rock Art Around Moab

The fertile valley around Moab has been home to humans for thousands of years. Prehistoric Fremont and Ancestral Puebloan people once lived and farmed in the bottoms of the canyons around Moab. Their rock art, granaries, and dwellings can still be seen here. Nomadic Utes had replaced the earlier groups by the time the first European settlers arrived. They left fewer signs of settlement but added their artistry to the area's rock-art panels. You don't need to travel far to see excellent examples of native pictographs and petroglyphs.

Sego Canyon: If you approach Moab along I-70, consider a side trip to one of the premier rock-art galleries in Utah. Sego Canyon is about five miles north of I-70; take exit 185, the Thompson Springs exit. Drive through the slumbering little town and continue up the canyon behind it (BLM signs also point the way). A side road leads to a parking area where the canyon walls close in. Sego Canyon is a showcase of prehistoric rock drawings and images that are thousands of years old. The Barrier Canyon Style drawings may be 8,000 years old; the Fremont Style images were created in the last 1,000 years. Compared to these ancient pictures, the Ute etchings are relatively recent: Experts speculate that they may have been drawn in the 1800s, when Ute villages still lined Sego Canyon. The newer petroglyphs and pictographs are more representational than the older ones. The ancient Barrier Canyon figures are typically horned ghostlike beings. The Fremont Style images depict stylized human figures made from geometric shapes; the crudest figures are the most recent. The Ute images are of bison and hunters on horseback.

Potash Road (Hwy. 279): From US 191 just north of the Colorado River bridge, take Highway 279 west along the river 5.2 miles to these easily accessed petroglyphs. There's even a sign ("Indian Writing") to guide you to them.

Golf Course Rock Art: Take US 191 south to the Moab Golf Course, which is about four miles from the corner of Main and Center Streets in downtown Moab. Turn left and proceed to Spanish Trail Road. Approximately one mile past the fire station, turn right onto Westwater Drive. Proceed 0.5 mile to a small pullout on the left side of the road. An area approximately 30 by 90 feet is covered with human and animal figures, including "Moab Man" and what is popularly referred to as the "reindeer and sled."

Kane Creek Boulevard: Kane Creek Boulevard (south of downtown Moab; watch for the McDonald's) follows the Colorado River and leads to a number of excellent rock-art sites. From the junction with US 191, turn west and proceed 0.8 mile to the intersection of Kane Creek Drive and 500 West. Keep left and continue along Kane Creek Drive approximately 2.3 miles to the mouth of Moon Flower Canyon. Along the rock cliff just beyond the canyon, you will see a rock-art panel behind a chain-link fence. Continue another 1.2 miles to a huge rock surface streaked with desert varnish is covered with images of bighorn sheep, snakes, and human forms. For a unique rock-art image, continue on Kane Creek Boulevard past the cattle guard, where the road turns from pavement to graded gravel road. After traveling 1.7 miles from the previous site (a total of 5.3 miles from the intersection of Kane Creek Drive and 500 West), watch for two pullouts. Down the slope from the road is a large boulder with rock art on all four sides. The most amazing image is of a woman giving birth.

Courthouse Wash: Although this site is located within Arches National Park, it is accessed from a parking lot off US 191 just north of the Colorado River bridge, one mile north of Moab. A 0.5-mile hike leads to the panel, which is almost 19 feet high and 52 feet long. It has both pictographs and petroglyphs, with figures resembling ghostly humans, bighorn sheep, scorpions, and a large beaked bird.

A *Rock Art Auto Tour* brochure is available at the **Moab Information Center** (25 E. Center St., at Main St., 435/259-8825 or 800/635-6622, www.discovermoab.com, 8am-7pm Mon.-Sat., 9am-6pm Sun. early Mar.-Nov.).

three main towers. An unpaved road turns southeast off Highway 128 near milepost 21, which is 21 miles from US 191, and continues two miles to the picnic area.

The existing **Dewey Bridge,** 30 miles up the highway, replaced a picturesque wood-and-steel suspension bridge built in 1916, which burned in 2008. Here, the BLM has built the Dewey Bridge Recreation Site, with a picnic area, a trailhead, a boat launch, and a small campground.

Upstream from Dewey Bridge are the wild rapids of **Westwater Canyon.** The Colorado River cut this narrow gorge into dark metamorphic rock. You can raft or kayak down the river in one day or a more leisurely two days; many local outfitters offer trips. Camping is limited to a single night. Unlike most desert rivers, this section of the Colorado River also offers good river-running at low water levels in late summer and autumn. Westwater Canyon's inner gorge, where boaters face their greatest challenge, is only about 3.5 miles long; however, you can enjoy scenic sandstone canyons both upstream and downstream.

The rough 4WD **Top-of-the-World Road** climbs to an overlook with outstanding views of Fisher Towers, Fisher Valley, Onion Creek, and beyond. Pick up a map at the **Moab Information Center** (25 E. Center St., at Main St., 435/259-8825 or 800/635-6622, www.discovermoab.com) to guide you to the rim. The elevation here is 6,800 feet, nearly 3,000 feet higher than the Colorado River.

Kane Creek Scenic Drive

Kane Creek Road heads downstream along the Colorado River on the same side as Moab. The four miles through the Colorado River Canyon are paved, followed by six miles of good dirt road through Kane Springs Canyon. This route also leads to several hiking trails and campgrounds. People with high-clearance vehicles or mountain bikes can continue across Kane Springs Creek to Hurrah Pass and an extensive network of 4WD trails. From Moab, drive south on Main Street (US 191) for one mile, then turn right onto Kane Creek Boulevard, which becomes Kane Creek Road.

Recreation

Moab is at the center of some of the most picturesque landscapes in North America. Even the least outdoorsy visitor will want to explore the river canyons, natural arches, and mesas. Mountain biking and river tours are the recreational activities that get the most attention in the Moab area, although hikers, climbers, and horseback riders also find plenty to do. If you're less physically adventurous, you can explore the landscape on scenic flights or follow old mining roads in a jeep to remote backcountry destinations.

It's easy to find outfitters and sporting goods rental operations in Moab; it's the largest business segment in town. And there's a remarkable cohesion to the town's operations: It seems that everyone markets everyone else's excursions and services, so just ask the closest outfitter for whatever service you need, and chances are excellent you'll get hooked up with what you want.

Make the **Moab Information Center** (25 E. Center St., at Main St., 435/259-8825 or 800/635-6622, www.discovermoab.com, 8am-7pm Mon.-Sat., 9am-6pm Sun. early Mar.-Nov.) your first stop in town. It's an excellent source for information about the area's recreational options. The center is staffed by representatives of the National Park Service, the BLM, the U.S. Forest Service, and the Canyonlands Field Institute; they can direct you to the adventure of your liking. The center also has literature, books, and maps for sale. BLM officials can point you to the developed and undeveloped designated campsites near the Moab Slickrock Bike Trail, Kane Creek, and along the Colorado River; you must use the designated sites in these areas.

To reach most of Moab's prime hiking trails requires a short drive to trailheads. For more options, head to nearby Arches and Canyonlands National Parks. **Canyonlands Field Institute** (435/259-7750 or 800/860-5262, http://cfimoab.org) leads day hikes (Sat.-Sun. mid-Apr.-mid-Oct., $65-100 for day hiking trips, includes transportation and park admission) at various locations near Moab; join one to really learn about the area's natural history. The institute also offers rafting trips down the Colorado and multiday trips with an archaeological and natural history focus.

Hiking Kane Creek Scenic Drive and US 191 South

The high cliffs just southwest of town provide fine views of the Moab Valley, the highlands of Arches National Park, and the La Sal Mountains.

Moab Rim Trail

Distance: 6 miles round-trip
Duration: 4 hours
Elevation change: 940 feet
Effort: moderate
Trailhead: Kane Creek Boulevard, 2.6 miles northwest of its intersection with US 191 in Moab

If you're hiking, expect to share this route with mountain bikers and 4WD enthusiasts. The trail climbs northeast 1.5 miles along tilted rock strata of the Kayenta Formation to the top of the plateau west of Moab, with the first of several great views over town and the Spanish Valley. Once on top, hikers can follow jeep roads southeast to Hidden Valley Trail, which descends to US 191 south of Moab—a 5.5-mile trip one-way. Experienced hikers can also head south from the rim to Behind the Rocks, a fantastic maze of sandstone fins.

Hidden Valley Trail

Distance: 2.3 miles round-trip to Behind the Rocks overlook
Duration: 3 hours
Elevation change: 680 feet
Effort: moderate
Trailhead: 3 miles south of Moab on US 191 and right onto Angel Rock Road. After two blocks, turn right onto Rimrock Road and drive to the parking area.

You'll see not only a hidden valley from this trail, but also panoramas of the Moab area and the Behind the Rocks area. The trail ascends a series of steep switchbacks to a broad shelf below the Moab Rim, then follows the shelf (hidden valley) to the northwest. It then crosses a low pass and follows a second shelf in the same direction. Near the end of the second shelf, the trail turns left to a divide, where you can see a portion of the remarkable fins of Behind the Rocks. The trail continues 0.3 mile from the divide down to the end of the Moab Rim Trail, with the possibility of hiking on loop trails. Instead of turning left to the divide, you can make a short side trip (no trail) to the right for views of Moab.

Hunters Canyon

Distance: 4 miles round-trip
Duration: 4 hours
Elevation change: 240 feet
Effort: moderate
Trailhead: on Kane Creek Scenic Drive, 7.5 miles west of its intersection with US 191. Hunters Canyon is on the left, 1 mile beyond the switchbacks.
Directions: To reach the trailhead from Moab, drive eight miles on Kane Creek Boulevard along the Colorado River and up Kane Creek Canyon. The road is asphalted where it fords Hunters Creek, but the asphalt is usually covered with dirt washed over it by the creek.

A rock arch and other rock formations in the canyon walls and the lush vegetation along the creek are highlights of a Hunters Canyon hike. Off-road vehicles have made tracks a short way up; you'll be walking, mostly along the creekbed. Short sections of trail lead around thickets of tamarisk and other water-loving

Odd Formations Behind the Rocks

A look at a topographic map will show that something strange is going on in the area called **Behind the Rocks.** Massive fins of Navajo sandstone, 100-500 feet high, 50-200 feet thick, and up to 0.5 mile long cover a large area. Narrow vertical cracks, sometimes only a few feet wide, separate the fins. The concentration of arches in the area is similar to that in Arches National Park, with more than 20 major named arches. Where canyon drainages penetrate the sandstone, pour-offs form into 400- to 1,000-foot-deep sheer-walled canyons, often exposing perennial springs at the bottom. Behind the Rocks was inhabited extensively by the Ancestral Puebloan and Fremont peoples, the two cultures apparently overlapping here. Petroglyph panels, habitation caves, stone ruins, and middens abound throughout the area.

No maintained trails exist, and some routes require technical climbing skills. The maze offers endless routes for exploration. If you get lost, which is very easy to do, remember that the fins are oriented east-west; the rim of the Colorado River Canyon is reached by going west, and Spanish Valley is reached by going east. Bring plenty of water, a topographic map (Moab 7.5-minute), and a compass. Access routes are **Moab Rim** and **Hidden Valley Trails** (from the north and east) and **Pritchett Canyon** (from the west and south). Although it is only a couple of miles from Moab, Behind the Rocks seems a world away.

plants. Look for Hunters Arch on the right, about 0.5 mile up. Most of the water in Hunters Canyon comes from a deep pool surrounded by hanging gardens of maidenhair ferns. A dry fall and a small natural bridge are above the pool. This pretty spot marks the hike's three-mile point and an elevation gain of 240 feet. At this point, the hike becomes very brushy.

You can make a longer hike by going up Hunters Canyon and descending on Pritchett Canyon Road. The road crosses the normally dry creekbed just upstream from the deep pool. To bypass the dry fall above the pool, backtrack 300 feet down the canyon and rock-scramble up a short, steep slope on the right heading upstream. At a junction just east of here, a jeep road along the north rim of Hunters Canyon meets Pritchett Canyon Road. Walk northeast 0.5 mile on Pritchett Canyon Road to a spur trail (on the left) leading to Pritchett Arch. Then continue 4.5 miles on Pritchett Canyon Road to Kane Creek Boulevard. This country is more open and desertlike than Hunters Canyon. A 3.2-mile car shuttle or hike is required for the return to the Hunters Canyon trailhead.

Hiking Highway 279

Portal Overlook Trail

Distance: 4 miles round-trip
Duration: 3 hours
Elevation change: 980 feet
Effort: moderate
Trailhead: JayCee Park Recreation Site, Highway 279, 4.2 miles west of the Highway 279-US 191 junction

The Portal Overlook Trail switchbacks up a slope, then follows a sloping sandstone ledge of the Kayenta Formation for two miles to an overlook. A panorama (the "portal") takes in the Colorado River, Moab Valley, Arches National Park, and the La Sal Mountains. This trail is a twin of the Moab Rim Trail across the river. Expect to share it with mountain bikers.

Corona Arch and Bowtie Arch Trail

Distance: 3 miles round-trip
Duration: 2 hours
Elevation change: 200 feet
Effort: moderate
Trailhead: Highway 279, 10 miles west of the Highway 279-US 191 junction

If you have time for only one hike in the Moab area, this one is especially recommended. The trail leads across slickrock country to two impressive arches. You can't see them from the road, although a third arch—Pinto—is visible. The trail climbs 1.5 miles up from the parking area, crosses railroad tracks, and follows a jeep road and a small wash to an ancient gravel bar. Pinto Arch, also called Gold Bar Arch, stands to the left, but there's no trail to it. Follow rock cairns to Corona and Bowtie Arches. Handrails and a ladder help in the few steep spots.

Despite being only a few hundred yards apart, each arch has a completely different character and history. Bowtie formed when a pothole in the cliffs above met a cave underneath. It used to be called Paul Bunyan's Potty before that name was appropriated for an arch in Canyonlands National Park. The hole is about 30 feet in diameter. Corona Arch, reminiscent of the larger Rainbow Bridge, eroded out of a sandstone fin. The graceful span is 140 feet long and 105 feet high. Both arches are composed of Navajo sandstone.

Hiking Highway 128

Negro Bill Canyon

Distance: 4 miles round-trip

Duration: 3-4 hours

Elevation change: 330 feet

Effort: easy-moderate

Trailhead: Highway 128, 3 miles east of the Highway 128-US 191 junction

One of the most popular hiking destinations in the Moab area, the Negro Bill Canyon trail follows a lively stream dammed by beavers and surrounded by abundant greenery and sheer cliffs. The high point of the hike is **Morning Glory Natural Bridge,** the sixth-longest natural rock span in the country at 243 feet.

William Granstaff was the first African American to live in the area, about 1877-1881; modern sensibilities have changed his nickname to "Negro Bill." The trailhead and a large parking area are on the right just after crossing a concrete bridge three miles from US 191. The Granstaff Campground, run by the BLM, is on the banks of the Colorado River just across the road from the trailhead.

The trail follows the creek up the canyon, with numerous stream crossings. Although the crossings are not difficult, hikers must be comfortable with stepping from rock to rock.

To see Morning Glory Natural Bridge, head two miles up the main canyon to the second side canyon on the right, then follow a good but fairly steep side trail for 0.5 mile up to the long, slender bridge. The spring and small pool underneath keep the air cool even in summer; ferns, columbines, and abundant poison ivy grow here.

Experienced hikers can continue up the main canyon about eight miles and rock-scramble (there's no trail) up the right side, then drop into Rill Creek, which leads to the North Fork of Mill Creek and into Moab. The total distance is about 16 miles one-way; you'll have to find your own way between canyons. The upper Negro Bill and Rill Canyons can also be reached from Sand Flats Road. The Moab and Castle Valley 15-minute and Moab 1:100,000 topographic maps cover the route. This makes a good overnight trip, although fast hikers have done it in a day. Expect to do some wading and rock-scrambling. Water from the creeks and springs is available in both canyon systems, but be sure to purify it first.

A car shuttle is necessary between the Negro Bill and Mill Creek trailheads. You can reach Mill Creek from the end of Powerhouse Lane on the east edge of Moab, but don't park here: Vehicle break-ins are a serious problem. Have someone meet you or drop you off here or park closer to town near houses. A hike up the North Fork offers very pretty scenery. A deep pool and waterfall are 0.75 mile upstream; follow Mill Creek upstream and take the left (north) fork. Negro Bill and

Mill Creek Canyons are BLM wilderness study areas.

Fisher Towers

Distance: 4.4 miles round-trip
Duration: 4 hours
Elevation change: 670 feet
Effort: moderate
Trailhead: off Highway 128; 21 miles east of the Highway 128-US 191 junction, turn right and go 2.2 miles on an improved dirt road to a parking lot

These spires of dark red sandstone rise 900 feet above Professor Valley. You can hike around the base of these needle rocks on a trail accessed by a short flight of stairs from the BLM picnic area. The trail follows a small slickrock-covered ridge leading away from the main cliffs; when the ridge narrows, go left into the ravine through a small cut in the ridge. From the bottom of the ravine, the trail heads steeply up and then begins to wind directly beneath the Fisher Towers. After skirting around the largest tower, the Titan, the trail ascends and ends after 2.2 miles on a ridge with a panoramic view. The Fisher Towers attract many very good rock climbers, and hikers may find that they linger along the trail to watch some spectacular climbing exploits. Carry water, as much of the trail is exposed and is frequently quite hot.

Biking

The first mountain bikes came to Moab in 1982, when they were used to herd cattle. That didn't work out so well, but within a decade or so, Moab had become the West's most noted mountain bike destination. In addition to riding the famed and challenging slickrock trails (slickrock is the exposed sandstone that composes much of the land's surface here, and despite its name, bike tires grab it quite nicely) that wind through astonishing desert landscapes, cyclists can pedal through alpine

Top to bottom: hiking the Hidden Valley Trail; the Fisher Towers; Morning Glory Natural Bridge, a highlight of the hike up Negro Bill Canyon.

meadows in the La Sal Mountains or take nearly abandoned 4WD tracks into the surrounding backcountry. Beware: The most famous trails—like the Slickrock Bike Trail—are not for beginners. Other trails are better matched to the skills of novices. A good online resource for trails and advice is the **Moab Bike Patrol** (www.moabbikepatrol.com).

It's a good idea to read up on Moab-area trails before planning a trip; heaps of books and pamphlets are available. You can also hire an outfitter to teach you about the special skills needed to mountain bike in slickrock country, or join a guided tour. The **Moab Information Center's website** (www.discovermoab.com) also has good information about bike trails.

Most people come to Moab to mountain bike mid-March-late May, and then again in the fall mid-September-end of October. Unless you are an early riser, summer is simply too hot for extended bike touring in these desert canyons. Be prepared for crowds, especially in mid-March during spring break. The Slickrock Trail alone has been known to attract more than 150,000 riders per year.

If you've never biked on slickrock or in the desert, here are a few basic guidelines. Take care if venturing off a trail—it's a long way down some of the sheer cliff faces. A trail's steep slopes and sharp turns can be tricky, so a helmet is a must. Knee pads and riding gloves also protect from scrapes and bruises. Fat bald tires work best on the rock; partially deflated knobby tires do almost as well. Carry plenty of water—one gallon in summer, half a gallon in cooler months. Tiny plant associations, which live in fragile cryptobiotic soil, don't want you tearing through their homes; stay on the rock and avoid sandy areas.

Dozens of trails thread through the Moab area; one good place for beginners to start is on the **Intrepid Trail System** at Dead Horse Point State Park. Descriptions of several local trails follow.

MOAB Brand Trails

The interconnected loops and spur trails here form the **MOAB Brand Trails** system (named for cattle brands that spell out M-O-A-B) with several options that are especially good for beginners or riders who are new to slickrock.

The seven-mile **Bar-M** loop is easy and makes a good family ride, although you might share the packed-dirt trail with motor vehicles; try **Circle O** (no motor vehicles) for a good three-mile initiation to slickrock riding.

More experienced slickrock cyclists can find some challenges on the **Deadman's Ridge, Long Branch,** and **Killer-B** routes at the southern end of the trail system.

To reach the trailhead for all these rides, head about eight miles north of town on US 191 to the Bar M Chuckwagon, and park at the south end of their private lot.

Slickrock Bike Trail

Undulating slickrock in the Sand Flats Recreation Area just east of Moab challenges even the best mountain bike riders; this is not an area in which to learn riding skills. Originally, motorcyclists laid out the **Slickrock Bike Trail,** although now most riders rely on leg and lung power. The 1.7-mile practice loop near the trail's beginning allows first-time visitors a chance to get a feel for the slickrock. The "trail" consists only of painted white lines. Riders following it have less chance of getting lost or finding themselves in hazardous areas. Plan on about five hours to do the 10.5-mile main loop, and expect to do some walking.

Side trails lead to viewpoints overlooking Moab, the Colorado River, and the arms of Negro Bill Canyon. Panoramas of the surrounding canyon country and the La Sal Mountains add to the pleasure of biking.

To reach the trailhead from Main Street in Moab, turn east and go 0.4 mile on 300 South, turn right and go 0.1 mile

Mountain Bike Etiquette

When mountain biking in the Moab area, don't expect an instant wilderness experience. Because of the popularity of the routes, the fragile desert environment is under quite a bit of stress, and you'll need to be considerate of the thousands of other people who share the trails. By keeping these rules in mind, you'll help keep Moab from being loved to death.

- **Ride only on open roads and trails.** Much of the desert consists of extremely fragile plant and animal ecosystems, and riding recklessly through cryptobiotic soils can destroy desert life and lead to erosion. If you pioneer a trail, chances are someone else will follow the tracks, leading to ever more destruction.
- **Protect and conserve scarce water sources.** Don't wash, swim, walk, or bike through potholes, and camp well away from isolated streams and water holes. The addition of your insect repellent, body oils, suntan lotion, or bike lubrication can destroy the thriving life of a pothole. Camping right next to a remote stream can deprive shy desert wildlife of life-giving water access.
- **Leave all Native American sites and artifacts as you find them.** First, it's against the law to disturb antiquities; second, it's stupid. Enjoy looking at rock art, but don't touch the images—body oils hasten their deterioration. Don't even think about taking potsherds, arrowheads, or artifacts from where you find them. Leave them for others to enjoy or for archaeologists to interpret.
- **Dispose of solid human waste thoughtfully.** The desert can't easily absorb human fecal matter. Desert soils have few microorganisms to break down organic material, and, simply put, mummified turds can last for years. Be sure to bury solid waste at least 6-12 inches deep in sand and at least 200 feet away from streams and water sources. Pack out toilet paper in plastic bags.

on 400 East, turn left (east) and go 0.5 mile on Mill Creek Drive, then turn left and go 2.5 miles on Sand Flats Road. The Sand Flats Recreation Area, where the trail is located, charges $5 for an automobile day pass, $2 for a bicycle or motorcycle. Camping ($10) is available, but there is no water.

Farther up Sand Flats Road, the quite challenging, often rock-strewn **Porcupine Rim Trail** draws motorcyclists, jeeps, and mountain bikers; after about 11 miles, the trail becomes single-track, and four-wheelers drop out. The whole trail is about 15 miles long.

★ Gemini Bridges Trail

The 14-mile one-way **Gemini Bridges Trail** passes tremendous twin rock arches (the bridges) and the slickrock fins of the Wingate Formation, making this one of the most scenic of the trails in the Moab area; it's also one of the more moderate trails in terms of necessary skill and fitness. The trail begins 12.5 miles up Highway 313, just before the turnoff to Dead Horse Point State Park. It's a stiff 21-mile uphill ride from Moab to reach the trailhead, so you may want to consider a shuttle. Several companies, including **Coyote Shuttle** (435/260-2097, www.coyoteshuttle.com, $20), provide this service, enabling cyclist to concentrate on the fun, mostly downhill ride back toward Moab. The Gemini Bridges Trail, which is shared with motorcycles and 4WD vehicles, ends on US 191 just north of town.

Intrepid Trail System

Mountain bikers, including novices, should bring their rides to Dead Horse

Point, where the **Intrepid Trail System** offers about 15 miles of slickrock and sand single-track trails in three loops that range from a one-mile beginner's loop to a more challenging nine-mile loop. All routes start at the visitors center and have great views into the canyon country. To reach **Dead Horse Point State Park** (435/259-2614, www.stateparks.utah.gov, $10) from Moab, take US 191 nine miles north, then turn west onto Highway 313 and follow it 23 miles to the park entrance.

Monitor and Merrimac Trail

A good introduction to the varied terrains of the Moab area, the 13.2-mile **Monitor and Merrimac Trail** also includes a trip to a dinosaur fossil bed. The trail climbs through open desert and up Usher Canyon, then explores red sandstone towers and buttes across slickrock before dropping down Mill Canyon. At the base of the canyon, you can leave your bike and hike the Mill Canyon Dinosaur Trail before completing the loop to the parking area. Reach the trailhead by traveling 15 miles north of Moab on US 191 and turning west (left) onto Mill Canyon Road, just past milepost 141.

Sovereign Single-Track Trail

Not every bike trail here is over slickrock; the challenging **Sovereign Single-Track Trail** is good to ride in hot weather. The trail, which contains rocky technical sections, a bit of slickrock, and more flowing single-track, is shared with motorcycles. Several trailheads access this trail; a popular one is from Willow Springs Road. From Moab, travel 11 miles north on US 191 and turn right onto Willow Springs Road, following this sandy road 2.5 miles to the trailhead. To best see the options, pick up a map at a local bike store.

Kokopelli's Trail

Mountain bikers have linked a 142-mile series of back roads, paved roads, and bike trails through the magical canyons of eastern Utah and western Colorado, called **Kokopelli's Trail.** The trail is usually ridden from east to west, starting in Loma, Colorado, and passing Rabbit Valley, Cisco Boat Landing, Dewey Bridge, Fisher Valley, and Castle Valley before landing on Sand Flats Road in Moab. Lots of optional routes, access points, and campsites allow for many possibilities. This multiday trip requires a significant amount of advance planning; **Bikerpelli Sports** (www.bikerpelli.com) is a good place to start this process.

Road Biking

Although the Moab area is great for biking, riding along busy US 191 is no fun. The **Moab Canyon Pathway** starts at the Colorado River bridge at the north end of town and closely parallels the highway north to Arches National Park. From the entrance to the park, the path, which is separated from the road, continues north, climbing to the junction of US 191 and Highway 313, the road to Dead Horse Point State Park and Canyonlands' Island in the Sky District. From this intersection, the bike path is on a relatively wide shoulder; it's a 35-mile ride to Canyonlands' Grand View Point, or a mere 24-mile uphill chug to Dead Horse Point.

The paved route provides easy cycling access to the MOAB Brand mountain bike trails just off US 191 and a more challenging ride to the Intrepid trails in Dead Horse Point State Park and the Gemini Bridges Trail, which starts just outside the park.

Bike Tours

Most of the bicycle rental shops in Moab offer daylong mountain bike excursions, while outfitters offer multiday tours that vary in price depending on the difficulty of the trail and the degree of comfort involved. The charge for these trips is usually around $200-250 per day, including food and shuttles. Be sure to inquire whether rates include bike rental.

Rim Tours (1233 S. US 191, 435/259-5223 or 800/626-7335, www.rimtours.com) is a well-established local company offering several half-day (around $90 pp for 2-3 cyclists), full-day (around $125 pp for 2-3 cyclists), and multiday trips. **Magpie Cycling** (800/546-4245, magpieadventures.com) is a small local business that runs day trips, which cover instruction on mountain biking techniques, and overnight rides, mostly in Canyonlands, including a four-day tour of the White Rim Trail ($955).

Western Spirit Cycling (478 Mill Creek Dr., 435/259-8732 or 800/845-2453, www.westernspirit.com) offers mountain and road bike tours in the western United States, with about one-third of them in Utah. Moab-area trips include the White Rim, the Maze, and Kokopelli's Trail (5 days, $1,200). Another Moab-based company with tours all over the West is **Escape Adventures** (Moab Cyclery, 391 S. Main St., 435/259-7423 or 800/596-2953, www.escapeadventures.com), which leads multiday mountain bike trips, including one into the remote Maze section of Canyonlands National Park (5 days, $1,295); some of the tours combine cycling with rafting, climbing, and hiking.

Rentals and Repairs

Rim Cyclery (94 W. 100 N., 435/259-5333 or 888/304-8219, www.rimcyclery.com, 9am-6pm daily) is Moab's oldest bike and outdoor gear store, offering both road and mountain bike sales, rentals, and service. Mountain bike rentals are also available at **Poison Spider Bicycles** (497 N. Main St., 435/259-7882 or 800/635-1792, www.poisonspiderbicycles.com, 8am-7pm daily spring and fall, 9am-6pm daily winter and summer) and **Chile Pepper** (702 S. Main St., 435/259-4688 or 888/677-4688, www.chilebikes.com, 8am-6pm daily Mar.-Nov., 9am-5pm daily Dec.-Feb.). **Moab Cyclery** (391 S. Main St., 435/259-7423 or 800/559-1978, www.moabcyclery.com, 8am-6pm daily) offers rentals, tours, shuttles, and gear. Expect to pay about $45-80 per day to rent a mountain bike, a little less for a road bike.

Shuttle Services

Several of the Moab area's best mountain bike trails are essentially one-way, and unless you want to cycle back the way you came, you'll need to arrange a shuttle service to pick you up and bring you back to Moab or your vehicle. Also, if you don't have a vehicle or a bike rack, you will need to use a shuttle service to get to more distant trailheads. **Coyote Shuttle** (435/260-2097, www.coyoteshuttle.com) and **Roadrunner Shuttle** (435/260-2724, www.roadrunnershuttle.com) both operate shuttle services; depending on distance, the usual fare is $20-30 per person. Both companies also shuttle hikers to trailheads and pick up rafters.

Rafting and Boating

Even a visitor with a tight schedule can get out and enjoy the canyon country on rafts and other watercraft. Outfitters offer both laid-back and exhilarating day trips, which usually require little advance planning. Longer multiday trips include gentle canoe paddles along the placid Green River and thrilling expeditions down the Colorado River.

You'll need to reserve well in advance for most of the longer trips because the BLM and the National Park Service limit trips through the backcountry, and space, especially in high season, is at a premium. Experienced rafters can also plan their own unguided trips, although you'll need a permit for all areas except for the daylong Fisher Towers float upstream from Moab.

The rafting season runs April-September, and jet-boat tours run February-November. Most do-it-yourself river-runners obtain their permits by applying in January-February for a March drawing; the **Moab Information Center's BLM ranger** (25 E. Center St., at Main St., 435/259-8825 or 800/635-6622) can advise on this process and provide the latest information about available cancellations.

Rafting and Kayaking Trips

For most of the following trips, full-day rates include lunch and beverages, while part-day trips include just lemonade and soft drinks. On overnight trips, you'll sleep in tents in backcountry campgrounds.

The **Colorado River** offers several exciting options. The most popular day run near Moab starts upstream near Fisher Towers and bounces through several moderate rapids on the way back to town. Full-day raft trips (about $65 pp adults) run from Fisher Towers to near Moab. Half-day trips ($45-50 pp adults) run over much the same stretch of river but don't include lunch.

For a more adventurous rafting trip, the Colorado's rugged **Westwater Canyon** offers lots of white water and several Class III-IV rapids near the Utah-Colorado border. These long day trips are more expensive, typically around $170-180 per day. The Westwater Canyon is also often offered as part of multiday adventure packages.

The **Cataract Canyon** section of the Colorado River, which begins south of the river's confluence with the Green River and extends to the backwater of Lake Powell, usually requires four days of rafting to complete. However, if you're in a hurry, some outfitters offer time-saving trips that motor rather than float through placid water and slow down only to shoot rapids, enabling these trips to conclude in as little as one day. This is the wildest white water in the Moab area, with big boiling Class III-IV rapids. Costs range $425-1,500, depending on what kind of craft, the number of days, and whether you fly, hike, or drive out at the end of the trip.

The **Green River** also offers Class II-III rafting and canoeing opportunities, although they are milder than those on the Colorado. Trips on the Green make good family outings. Most trips require five days, leaving from the town of Green River and taking out at Mineral Bottom, just before Canyonlands National Park. Highlights of the Green River include Labyrinth Canyon and Bowknot Bend. Costs range $695-950 for a five-day rafting trip.

Rafting and Kayaking on Your Own

The Class II-III **Fisher Towers** section of the Colorado River is gentle enough for amateur rafters to negotiate on their own. A popular one-day raft trip with mild rapids begins from the **Hittle Bottom Recreation Site** (Hwy. 128, 23.5 miles north of Moab, near Fisher Towers) and ends 14 river miles downstream at **Take-out Beach** (Hwy. 128, 10.3 miles north of US 191). You can rent rafts and the mandatory life jackets in Moab, but you won't need a permit on this section of river.

Experienced white-water rafters can obtain permits from the **BLM's Westwater Ranger Station** (82 E. Dogwood Ave., 435/259-7012, www.blm.gov, 8am-noon Mon.-Fri.) up to two months prior to launch date. Don't show up at the office expecting to get a same-day or next-day permit; it's important to plan well in advance. The usual put-in is at the Westwater Ranger Station nine miles south of I-70's exit 227; another option is the Loma boat launch in Colorado. A start at Loma adds a day or two to the trip along with the sights of Horsethief and Ruby Canyons. Normal take-out is at Cisco, although it's possible to continue 16 miles on slow-moving water through open country to Dewey Bridge.

Canyon Voyages (211 N. Main St., 435/259-6007 or 800/733-6007, www.canyonvoyages.com) and **Navtec Expeditions** (321 N. Main St., 435/259-7983 or 800/833-1278, www.navtec.com) are two local rafting companies that rent rafts (from $80 per day) and kayaks (about $35 per day) for those who would rather organize their own river adventures.

Rafting Outfitters

Moab is full of river-trip companies, and most offer a variety of day and multiday trips; in addition, many will combine raft trips with biking, horseback riding, hiking, or 4WD excursions. Check out the many websites at www.discovermoab.com/tour.htm. The following list includes major outfitters offering a variety of rafting options. Most lead trips to the main river destinations on the Colorado and Green Rivers as well as other rivers in Utah and the West. Red River Adventures runs trips in smaller self-paddled rafts and inflatable kayaks. Inquire about natural history or petroglyph tours if these specialty trips interest you.

- **Adrift Adventures** (378 N. Main St., 435/259-8594 or 800/874-4483, www.adrift.net)
- **Canyon Voyages** (211 N. Main St., 435/259-6007 or 800/733-6007, www.canyonvoyages.com)
- **Navtec Expeditions** (321 N. Main St., 435/259-7983 or 800/833-1278, www.navtec.com)
- **Red River Adventures** (1140 S. Main St., 435/259-4046 or 877/259-4046, www.redriveradventures.com)
- **Sheri Griffith Expeditions** (503/259-8229 or 800/332-2439, www.griffithexp.com)
- **Tag-A-Long Expeditions** (452 N. Main St., 435/259-8946 or 800/453-3292, www.tagalong.com)
- **Western River Expeditions** (225 S. Main St., 435/259-7019 or 866/904-1163, www.westernriver.com)

Canoeing

Canoeists can also sample the calm waters of the Green River on multiday excursions with **Moab Rafting and Canoe Company** (805 N. Main St., 435/259-7722, www.moab-rafting.com), which runs scheduled guided trips (from about $125 pp per day minimum of 4, to custom trips for 2-3 people for $325 pp) to four sections of the Green and to calmer stretches of the Colorado River. They also rent canoes (around $30-45 per day), including the necessary equipment.

Another good source for DIY canoe and kayak trips on the Green is **Tex's Riverways** (435/259-5101 or 877/662-2839, www.texsriverways.com), which specializes in rentals, shuttles, and support for self-guided trips.

Jet Boats and Motorboats

Guided jet-boat excursions through Canyonlands National Park range from $50-150 for a half-day trip. **Tag-A-Long Expeditions** (452 N. Main St., 435/259-8946 or 800/453-3292, www.tagalong.com) and **Adrift Adventures** (378 N. Main St., 435/259-8594 or 800/874-4483, www.adrift.net) both offer half-day trips and full-day combination jet boat-jeep excursions.

Canyonlands by Night & Day (435/259-5261 or 800/394-9978, www.canyonlandsbynight.com, Apr.-mid-Oct., $69 adults, $59 ages 4-12, includes dinner) tours leave at sunset in an open tour boat and go several miles upstream on the Colorado River; a guide points out canyon features. The sound and light show begins on the way back; music and historical narration accompany the play of lights on the canyon walls. Reservations are a good idea because the boat fills up fast. Daytime jet-boat tours ($89 adults, $79 children) are longer—about four hours—and go a little farther. Trips depart from the Spanish mission-style office just north of Moab, across the Colorado River.

4WD Exploration

Road tours offer visitors a special opportunity to view unique canyon-country arches and spires, indigenous rock art, and wildlife. An interpretive brochure at the **Moab Information Center** (25 E. Center St., at Main St., 435/259-8825 or 800/635-6622, www.discovermoab.com) outlines the Moab Area Rock Art Auto Tour, which routes motorists to petroglyphs tucked away behind golf courses and ranches. You might also pick up a map of Moab-area 4WD trails: four rugged 15- to 54-mile loop routes through the desert that take 2.5-4 hours to drive. Those who left their trusty four-by-fours and off-road-driving skills at home can take an off-road jeep tour with a private operator. Most Moab outfitters offer jeep or Hummer tours, often in combination with rafting or hiking options.

The **Moab Adventure Center** (255 S. Main St., 435/259-7019 or 866/904-1163, www.moabadventurecenter.com) runs two-hour ($81 adults, $49 youths) and half-day ($169 adults, $122 youths) guided Hummer safaris. The Adventure Center, which can book you on any number of trips, can also arrange jeep rentals (from $175-195 per day).

Jeep and other 4WD-vehicle rentals are available at a multitude of Moab outfits, including **Farabee Jeep Rentals** (35 Grand Ave., 435/259-74944 or 877/970-5337, www.moabjeeprentals.com), **Canyonlands Jeep Adventures** (225 S. Main St., 435/259-4412, www.canyonlandsjeep.com), and **Cliffhanger Jeep Rentals** (40 W. Center St., 435/259-0889, www.cliffhangerjeeprental.com). Expect to pay around $180 per day.

ATVs and Dirt Bikes

As an alternative to four-by-four touring in the backcountry, there's all-terrain vehicle (ATV) and motorcycle "dirt biking," typically but not exclusively geared toward youngsters and families. Although youths ages 8-15 may operate an ATV, provided they possess an

Exploring the slickrock with all-terrain vehicles is a popular activity near Moab.

Education Certificate issued by Utah State Parks and Recreation or an equivalent certificate from their home state, parents should research ATV safety before agreeing to such an outing. Much of the public land surrounding Moab is open to ATV exploration, with many miles of unpaved roads and existing trails on which ATVs can travel. However, ATV and dirt bike riding is not allowed within either Arches or Canyonlands National Parks.

One particularly popular area for ATVs is **White Wash Sand Dunes,** with many miles of dirt roads in a strikingly scenic location. It is 48 miles northwest of Moab, reached by driving 13 miles south from I-70's exit 175, just east of Green River. The dunes are interspersed with large cottonwood trees and bordered by red sandstone cliffs. In addition to the dunes, White Wash is a popular route around three sides of the dunes.

ATVs and dirt bikes are available from a number of Moab-area outfitters, including **High Point Hummer** (281 N. Main St., 435/259-2972 or 877/486-6833, www.highpointhummer.com) and **Moab Tour Company** (543 N. Main St., 435/259-4080 or 877/725-7317, www.moabtourcompany.us). A half-day dirt bike or ATV rental starts at around $150.

★ Air Tours

You'll have a bird's-eye view of southeastern Utah's incredible landscape from Moab's Canyonlands Field with **Redtail Aviation** (435/259-7421 or 800/842-9251, www.redtailaviation.com). Flights (minimum 2 people, $125-235 pp) include Canyonlands National Park's Needles, Island in the Sky, and Maze Districts. Longer tours are also available, and flights operate year-round.

Skydiving

If you think the Arches and Canyonlands area looks dramatic from an airplane, imagine the excitement of parachuting into the desert landscape. **Skydive Moab** (Canyonlands Fields Airport, US 191, 16 miles north of Moab, 435/259-5867, www.skydivemoab.com) offers jumps for both first-time and experienced skydivers. First-timers receive 30 minutes of ground schooling, followed by a half-hour flight before a tandem parachute jump with an instructor from 10,000 feet. Tandem skydives, including instruction and equipment, start at $225. For experienced skydivers with their own equipment, jumps start at $18; equipment and parachutes are available for rent.

Climbing

Just outside town, the cliffs along Highway 279 and Fisher Towers attract rock climbers. For world-class crack climbing, head south to Indian Creek, near the Needles District of Canyonlands National Park.

Moab has a couple of stores with rock climbing gear and informative staff: **Gearheads** (471 S. Main St., 435/259-4327) and **Pagan Mountaineering** (59

S. Main St., 435/259-1117, www.paganclimber.com). The friendly folks at Pagan also offer a climbing guide service to the local rock. **Moab Desert Adventures** (415 N. Main St., 804/814-3872, www.moabdesertadventures.com) offers rock climbing and canyoneering lessons, both for beginners and experienced climbers; families are welcome. A half day of climbing instruction is $165 pp; rates are lower for groups of 2-3 students.

Horseback Riding

Head up the Colorado River to **Red Cliffs Lodge** (Hwy. 128, milepost 14, 435/259-2002 or 866/812-2002, www.redcliffslodge.com) for guided trail rides amid the dramatic scenery of Castle Valley. Half-day rides are $95 per person; children must be at least eight years old, and an adult must accompany children. Riders must weigh less than 220 pounds. Several tour operators, including **Adrift Adventures** (378 N. Main St., 435/259-8594 or 800/874-4483, www.adrift.net) and the **Moab Adventure Center** (225 S. Main St., 435/259-7019 or 866/904-1163, www.moabadventurecenter.com), offer horseback rides in conjunction with rafting, hiking, and jeep exploration.

Golf

The **Moab Golf Club** (2705 SE Bench Rd., 435/259-6488, www.moabcountryclub.com, $47) is an 18-hole par-72 public course in a well-watered oasis amid stunning red-rock formations. To get here from Moab, go south five miles on US 191, turn left onto Spanish Trail Road and follow it two miles, then go right on Murphy Lane and follow it to Bench Road and the golf course.

Local Parks

The **city park** (181 W. 400 N.) has shaded picnic tables and a playground. It's also home to the **Moab Recreation and Aquatic Center** (374 Park Ave., 435/259-8226), a new community center with indoor and outdoor swimming pools, a weight room, and group exercise classes.

Two miles north of town, **Lions Park** (US 191 and Hwy. 128) offers picnicking along the Colorado River, although ongoing bridge construction makes it less than peaceful. **Rotary Park** (Mill Creek Dr.) is family-oriented and has lots of activities for kids.

Entertainment and Events

For a town of its size, Moab puts on a pretty good nightlife show, with lots of young hikers, bikers, and rafters reliving their daily conquests in bars and brewpubs. There are also notable seasonal music events, ranging from folk to classical.

Nightlife

A lot of Moab's nightlife focuses on the well-loved **Eddie McStiff's** (57 S. Main St., 435/259-2337, www.eddiemcstiffs.com, 11:30am-close daily), right downtown, with 12 handcrafted beers on draft, two outdoor seating areas, and live music on a regular basis.

Woody's Tavern (221 S. Main St., 435/259-9323) has live bands on the weekend—you might hear bluegrass, roots rock, reggae, or jam bands. **Club Rio** (2 S. 100 W., 435/259-2654) is a sports bar with frequent live music and entertainment.

Come for some barbecue and stay for the blues (or vice versa; both are good) at **Blu Pig** (811 S. Main St., 435/259-3333). Another restaurant with a lively bar scene is **Buck's Grill House** (1393 US 191, 435/259-5201); they bring in bands a couple of times a week.

For a more family-friendly evening out, consider the **Bar M Chuckwagon's Live Western Show and Cowboy Supper** (7000 N. US 191, 435/259-2276, http://barmchuckwagon.com, hours vary), a kind of Western-themed dinner theater that includes mock gunfights, live country music, and other Old West entertainment in addition to a chuckwagon buffet dinner.

Another longtime tradition for evening entertainment is **Canyonlands by Night** (435/259-5261, www.canyonlandsbynight.com), a cruise on the Colorado River that ends with a sound-and-light presentation along the sandstone cliffs. Dinner packages are available; children under age four are not permitted, per Coast Guard regulations.

For a selection of movies, head for **Slickrock Cinemas** (580 Kane Creek Blvd., 435/259-4441).

Events

To find out about local happenings, contact the **Moab Information Center** (25 E. Center St., at Main St., 435/259-8825 or 800/635-6622, www.discovermoab.com) or browse ***Moab Happenings,*** available free around town or online (www.moabhappenings.com).

Unsurprisingly, Moab offers quite a few annual biking events. The **Moab Skinny Tire Festival,** held the first week of March, and the **Moab Century Tour,** held in September, are both supported road bike events that benefit the fight against cancer. For information on both, visit www.skinnytirefestival.com or call 435/259-3193. The mountain bike endurance race event **24 Hours of Moab** (www.grannygear.com/races), held in early October, pits four-person relay teams against the rugged terrain of the Behind the Rocks area. This is one of North America's major events for mountain bikers, bringing more than 500 teams and 5,000 spectators to Moab.

Other major annual athletic events include the **Canyonlands Half Marathon and Five Mile Run** (www.moabhalfmarathon.org), held the third Saturday in March. A women's half marathon held in early June, the **Thelma and Louise Half Marathon,** is organized by the same group.

Moab's most popular annual event, more popular than anything celebrating two wheels, is the **Easter Jeep Safari** (www.rr4w.com), which is the Sturgis or Daytona Beach of recreational four-wheeling. Upward of 2,000 4WD vehicles (it's not exclusively for jeeps, although ATVs are not allowed) converge on Moab for a week's worth of organized back-country trail rides. "Big Saturday" (the day before Easter) is the climax of the event, when all participating vehicles parade through Moab. Plan well ahead for lodging if you are thinking about visiting Moab during this event, as hotel rooms are often booked a year in advance.

Memorial Day weekend brings artists, musicians, and art cars to the city park for the **Moab Arts Festival** (435/259-2742, www.moabartsfestival.org).

The dust is kicked up at the **Spanish Trail Arena** (3641 S. US 191, just south of Moab) with the professional **Canyonlands PRCA Rodeo** (www.moabcanyonlandsrodeo.com), held the last weekend in May or first weekend in June, with a rodeo, a parade, a dance, horse racing, and a 4-H gymkhana.

The **Moab Music Festival** (435/259-7003, www.moabmusicfest.org) is first and foremost a classical chamber music festival, but every year a few jazz, bluegrass, or folk artists are included in the lineup. More than 30 artists are currently involved in the festival, held in late August and early September. Many of the concerts are held in dramatic outdoor settings. The **Moab Folk Festival** (www.moabfolkfestival.com) is the town's other big annual musical event, attracting top-notch acoustic performers to Moab the first weekend of November.

Shopping

Main Street, between 200 North and 200 South, has nearly a dozen galleries and gift shops with T-shirts, outdoor apparel, Native American art, and other gifts. **Back of Beyond Books** (83 N. Main St., 435/259-5154) features an excellent selection of regional books and maps. Pick up those missing camping items at **Gearheads** (471 S. Main St., 435/259-4327, 8am-10pm daily spring-fall, shorter hours winter), an amazingly well-stocked outdoor store. If you're heading out to camp or hike in the desert, Gearheads is a good place to fill your water jugs with free filtered water.

Moab's largest grocery store, **City Market** (425 S. Main St., 435/259-5181, 6am-11pm daily), is a good place to pick up supplies; it has a pharmacy and a gas station.

Stop by the **Moonflower Market** (39 E. 100 N., 435/259-5712, 9am-8pm daily) for natural-food groceries; it's a well-stocked store.

Accommodations

Moab has been a tourism destination for generations and offers a wide variety of lodging choices, ranging from older motels to new upscale resorts. US 191 is lined with all the usual chain motels, but we tend to go for the smaller local operations that are within walking distance of downtown restaurants and shopping, and that's mostly what you'll find listed here. Check with hotel booking sites for chain motel rooms farther out.

Moab/Canyonlands Central Reservations (435/259-5125 or 800/505-5343, www.moabutahlodging.com) can make bookings at area vacation homes, which include some relatively inexpensive apartments. Another handy tool is www.moab-utah.com, which has a complete listing of lodging websites for the Moab area.

The only time Moab isn't busy is in the dead of winter, November-February. At all other times, be sure to make reservations well in advance. Summer room rates are listed here; in winter rates typically drop 40 percent.

Under $50

The **Lazy Lizard Hostel** (1213 S. US 191, 435/259-6057, www.lazylizardhostel.com) costs just $10 for simple dorm-style accommodations. To stay at this casual

Moab's downtown is pedestrian-friendly and has many shops and restaurants.

classic Moab lodging, you won't need a hostel membership, and all guests share access to a hot tub, a kitchen, a barbecue, a coin-operated laundry, and a common room with cable TV. Showers for non-guests ($3) and private guest rooms ($32) are also offered. Log cabins can sleep two ($36-38) to six ($40-54) people. The Lazy Lizard is one mile south of town, behind A-1 Storage; the turnoff is about 200 yards south of Moab Lanes.

$50-100

A reasonably priced motel that's simple, friendly, and noncorporate is the ★ **Kokopelli Lodge** (72 S. 100 E., 435/259-7615 or 888/530-3134, www.kokopellilodge.com, $79-84), offering small but colorful pet-friendly guest rooms and a convenient location one block off the main drag. Kokopelli also offers a number of condos on its website if you're looking for a relatively inexpensive option with multiple beds and full kitchens.

There's nothing fancy about the **Red Rock Lodge Motel** (51 N. 100 W., 435/259-5431 or 877/253-5431, www.red-rocklodge.com, $89-109), but it has a great location, pet-friendly guest rooms with fridges and coffeemakers, a hot tub, and a locked bicycle storage facility.

A simple but quite adequate place is the **Bowen Motel** (169 N. Main St., 435/259-7132 or 800/874-5439, www.bowenmotel.com, $82-92), a homey motel with an outdoor pool. The Bowen offers a variety of room types, including three-bedroom family suites and a 1,800-square-foot three-bedroom house with full kitchen. A couple of older but well-cared-for motels just north of downtown have guest rooms starting at about $90: the **Adventure Inn** (512 N. Main St., 435/662-2466 or 866/662-2466, www.adventureinnmoab.com) and the **Inca Inn** (570 N. Main St., 435/259-7261 or 866/462-2466, www.incainn.com), with a pool.

$100-150

A few blocks south of downtown, the **Red Stone Inn** (535 S. Main St., 435/259-3500 or 800/772-1972, www.moabredstone.com, $104-109) is a one-story, knotty-pine-sided motel; all guest rooms have efficiency kitchens. Other amenities include a bicycle maintenance area, a covered patio with a gas barbecue grill, a hot tub, and guest laundry. Motel guests have free access to the hotel pool next door at the Red Stone's sister property, the sprawling **Big Horn Lodge** (550 S. Main St., 435/259-6171 or 800/325-6171, www.moabbighorn.com, $100-119), which has similar knotty-pine guest rooms equipped with microwaves and fridges as well as a pool and a steak restaurant. Package deals for a guest room plus jeep tours, raft trips, and other activities are offered.

At the heart of downtown Moab, **Best Western Greenwell Motel** (105 S. Main St., 435/259-6151 or 800/528-1234, www.bestwesternmoab.com, $149-162) has a pool, fitness facilities, an on-premises restaurant, and some kitchenettes.

Eight very long blocks from downtown, on a quiet property that backs on Mill Creek and The Nature Conservancy holdings, is **Adobe Abode** (778 Kane Creek Blvd., 435/259-7716, www.adobeabodemoab.com, $139-149), a B&B-style inn with large guest rooms done up in handsome Southwestern style. The inn also offers a pool table and evening refreshments, a large and tasty breakfast, and a hot tub.

If you want seclusion in a quiet community 18 miles east of Moab, stay at the **Castle Valley Inn B&B** (424 Amber Ln., Castle Valley, 435/259-6012, www.castlevalleyinn.com, $105-220). The inn adjoins a wildlife refuge in a stunning landscape of red-rock mesas and needle-pointed buttes. You can stay in one of the main house's five guest rooms or in one of the three bungalows with kitchens. Facilities include a hot tub. To reach Castle Valley Inn, follow Highway 128 east from Moab for 16 miles, turn south, and continue 2.3 miles toward Castle Valley.

Over $150

The newly revamped ★ **Best Western Canyonlands Inn** (16 S. Main St., 435/259-2300 or 800/649-5191, www.canyonlandsinn.com, $175-299) is at the heart of Moab, with suites, a pool, a fitness room and spa, a restaurant, and a bike storage area. This property recently went through a major remodel and is the best address in the downtown area if you're looking for upscale amenities.

One of the most interesting accommodations options in Moab is the ★ **Gonzo Inn** (100 W. 200 S., 435/259-2515 or 800/791-4044, www.gonzoinn.com, $169-215). With a look somewhere between an adobe inn and a postmodern warehouse, the Gonzo doesn't try to appear anything but hip. Expect large guest rooms with vibrant colors and modern decor, a pool, and a friendly welcome.

Set in a lovely and quiet residential area, the ★ **Sunflower Hill Luxury Inn** (185 N. 300 E., 435/259-2974 or 800/662-2786, www.sunflowerhill.com, $165-235) offers high-quality accommodations. Choose from a guest room in one of Moab's original farmhouses, a historic ranch house, or a garden cottage. All 12 guest rooms have private baths, air-conditioning, and queen beds; there are also two suites. Guests share access to an outdoor swimming pool and a hot tub, bike storage, patios, and large gardens. Children over age seven are welcome, and the place is open year-round.

Families or groups might want to rent a condo at **Moab Springs Ranch** (1266 N. US 191, 435/259-7891 or 888/259-5759, www.moabspringsranch.com, $142-252 d, check website for full range of options) on the north end of town on the site of Moab's oldest ranch. The townhomes have a park-like setting with a swimming pool and a hot tub, and they sleep up to 10.

A cluster of four charming and pet-friendly cottages dubbed **3 Dogs & a Moose** (171 and 173 W. Center St., 435/260-1692, www.3dogsandamoosecottages.com) is just off the main drag. The two smaller cottages ($125-175) are perfect for couples, and the larger cottages ($275-285) sleep up to six.

Guest Ranches

A short drive from Moab along the Colorado River's red-rock canyon is the region's premium luxury guest ranch, the ★ **Sorrel River Ranch** (Hwy. 128, 17 miles northeast of Moab, 435/259-4642 or 877/317-8244, www.sorrelriver.com, $429-579). The ranch sits on 240 acres in one of the most dramatic landscapes in the Moab area—just across the river from Arches National Park and beneath the soaring mesas of Castle Valley. Accommodations are in a series of beautifully furnished wooden lodges, all tastefully fitted with Old West-style furniture. All units have kitchenettes and a patio with a porch swing or back deck overlooking the river; some guest rooms have both. Horseback rides are offered into the arroyos behind the ranch, and kayaks and bicycles are available for rent. The ranch's restaurant, the **River Grill** (435/259-4642, 7am-2pm and 6pm-9pm daily Apr.-Oct., 7am-10am and 6pm-9pm daily Nov.-Mar., $28-38), has some of the best views in Utah and an adventurous menu offering everything from blue corn-dusted halibut to grilled elk chops.

Sharing a similar view of the Colorado River and Castle Valley but three miles closer to Moab is the sprawling **Red Cliffs Lodge** (Hwy. 128, milepost 14, 435/259-2002 or 866/812-2002, www.redcliffslodge.com, $239), which houses guests in "mini suites" in the main lodge building and in a number of riverside cabins that can sleep up to six ($339). The lodge offers the Cowboy Grill bar and restaurant, horseback rides, and mountain bike rentals and will arrange river raft trips. The lodge is also the headquarters for Castle Creek Winery and the site of the free Moab Museum of Film & Western Heritage, which displays a collection of movie memorabilia from Westerns filmed in the area.

Campgrounds

Moab Campgrounds

It's really easy and comfy to camp at ★ **Up the Creek** (210 E. 300 S., 435/260-1888, www.moabupthecreek.com, mid-Mar.-early Nov., $25 for 1 person, $32 for 2, $40 for 3, $5 dogs), a walk-in, tents-only campground tucked into a residential neighborhood near downtown Moab. The shady campground, with a bathhouse and showers, picnic tables, and a few propane grills (campfires are prohibited), is right alongside a bike path.

RV parks cluster at the north and south ends of town. **Moab Valley RV Resort** (1773 N. US 191, at Hwy. 128, 2 miles north of Moab, 435/259-4469, www.moabvalleyrv.com, $25 tents, from $40 RVs) is open year-round; it has showers, a pool, a playground, and free wireless Internet access. There's also a selection of cabins (bedding provided, $53-90) available—some are simple sleeping rooms, others have baths and fridges. Pets are allowed only in RVs. Although this place is convenient, it is pretty close to a large ongoing environmental cleanup project involving removal of radioactive mine tailings. **Moab KOA** (3225 S. US 191, 435/259-6682 or 800/562-0372, http://moabkoa.com, Mar.-Nov., $25 tents, from $79 RVs with hookups, $64-170 cabins), just off the highway four miles south of town, has showers, a laundry room, a store, miniature golf, and a pool.

More convenient to downtown, **Canyonlands RV Resort and Campground** (555 S. Main St., 435/259-6848 or 800/522-6848, www.canyonlandsrv.com, $27-34 tents, $41-51 RVs, $60-70 cabins) is open year-round; it has showers, a laundry room, a store, a pool, and two-person air-conditioned cabins—bring your own bedding. One mile north of Moab, **Slickrock Campground** (1301½ N. US 191, 435/259-7660 or 800/448-8873, http://slickrockcampground.com, $26 tents or RVs without hookups, $34-39 with hookups, $54 cabins with air-conditioning and heat but no bath or kitchen) remains open year-round; it has nice sites with some shade as well as showers, a store, an outdoor café, and a pool.

You'll also find campgrounds farther out at Arches and Canyonlands National Parks, Dead Horse Point State Park, Canyon Rims Recreation Area, and east of town in the cool La Sal Mountains.

BLM Campgrounds

There are 26 **BLM campgrounds** (most $8-12) in the Moab area. Although these spots can't be reserved, sites are abundant enough that campers are rarely unable to find a spot. The campgrounds are concentrated on the banks of the Colorado River—along Highway 128 toward Castle Valley, along Highway 279 toward the potash factory, and along Kane Creek Road—and at the Sand Flats Recreation Area near the Slickrock Trail. Only a few of these campgrounds can handle large

RVs, none have hookups, and few have piped water. For a full list of BLM campground and facilities, go online (www.discovermoab.com/campgrounds_blm.htm).

Dead Horse Point State Park Campground

Soak in Dead Horse Point's spectacular scenery at the park's **Kayenta Campground** (reservations 800/322-3770, www.reserveamerica.com, $20 camping, $9 reservations fee), just past the visitors center, which offers sites with water and electric hookups but no showers. The campground nearly always fills up during the main season, so it's almost essential to reserve well in advance. Winter visitors may camp on the point; no hookups are available, but the restrooms have water.

If you aren't able to secure a spot inside the park, try the BLM's **Horsethief Campground** (no drinking water, $12) on Highway 313 a few miles east of the state park entrance. It has nearly 60 sites, all first-come, first-served, so it's usually possible to find a spot.

Food

Moab has the largest concentration of good restaurants in southern Utah; no matter what else the recreational craze has produced, it has certainly improved the food. Several Moab-area restaurants are closed for vacation in February, so call ahead if you're visiting in winter.

Breakfast and Light Meals

Food isn't limited to muffins at ★ **Love Muffin** (139 N. Main St., 435/259-6833, www.lovemuffincafe.com, 7am-1pm daily, $6-8), but if you decide to skip the breakfast burritos or insanely tasty red quinoa, the Burple Nurple muffin may be just what you need. While you're eating breakfast, order a muffaletta or barbecued tofu sandwich to pack along for lunch.

Another good option for a tasty but healthy breakfast or lunch is ★ **EklectiCafe** (352 N. Main St., 435/259-6896, 7am-2:30pm Mon.-Sat., 7:30am-1:30pm Sun., $6-9), a charming and busy little café serving delicious organic and vegetarian dishes. For a more traditional breakfast, try the **Jailhouse Café** (101 N. Main St., 435/259-3900, 7am-noon Wed.-Mon., $7-11), a Moab classic.

Dense, chewy bagels and good sandwiches make the **Red Rock Bakery** (74 S. Main St., 435/259-5941, 7am-2pm daily) worth a visit.

Peace Tree Juice Café (20 S. Main St., 435/259-0101, 7am-10pm daily, $8-22) is a great place for breakfast omelets and scrambles, and has a big menu of smoothies. At lunch and dinner you'll find sandwiches, salads, wraps, and burgers. The Peace Tree is right in the heart of Moab and has a lovely deck for alfresco dining.

Two Moab diners have an old-fashioned ambience and really good food. At the **Moab Diner & Ice Cream Shoppe** (189 S. Main St., 435/259-4006, http://moabdiner.com, 6am-9pm Mon.-Sat., $5-12), the breakfasts are large, with a Southwestern green chile edge to much of the food. The house-made ice cream is delicious. Another spot with great burgers and shakes is ★ **Milt's Stop & Eat** (356 Millcreek Dr., 435/259-7424, www.miltsstopandeat.com, 11am-8pm Tues.-Sun., $4-7)—it's a local classic, and just the place to stop after a day of biking or hiking.

Casual Dining

Unless otherwise noted, each of the following establishments has a full liquor license.

Zax (96 S. Main St., 435/259-6555, www.zaxmoab.com, 6:30am-close daily, $7-13) is a high-volume all-things-to-all-people restaurant in the heart of downtown. If you're with kids, this might be the ticket for sandwiches, steaks, pasta, pizza, or salad.

Check out **Miguel's Baja Grill** (51 N. Main St., 435/259-6546, www.miguelsbajagrill.com, 5pm-9pm daily, $10-20)

Moab Wineries

Southern Utah is not exactly the first place you think of when you envision fine wine, but for a handful of wine pioneers, the Moab area is the *terroir* of choice. Actually, conditions around Moab are similar to parts of Spain and the eastern Mediterranean, where wine grapes have flourished for millennia. The area's first wine grapes were planted in the 1970s through the efforts of the University of Arizona and the Four Corners Regional Economic Development Commission. The results were positive, as the hot days, cool nights, and deep sandy soil produced grapes of exceptional quality and flavor. A fruit-growing cooperative was formed in Moab to grow wine grapes, and by the 1980s the co-op was producing wine under the Arches Winery label. As teetotal Utah's first winery, Arches Winery was more than a novelty—its wines were good enough to accumulate nearly 40 prizes at national wine exhibitions.

Arches Winery was a true pioneer, and now two wineries produce wine in the Moab area, both open for wine-tasting. In addition, many of Moab's fine restaurants offer wine from these local wineries.

Castle Creek Winery (Red Cliffs Lodge, Hwy. 128, 14 miles east of Moab, 435/259-3332, http://redcliffslodge.com/winery, noon-5:30pm Mon.-Sat.), formerly Arches Winery, produces pinot noir, merlot, cabernet sauvignon, chenin blanc, chardonnay, and late-harvest gewürztraminer.

Spanish Valley Vineyards and Winery (4710 Zimmerman Ln., 6 miles south of Moab, 435/259-8134, www.moab-utah.com/spanishvalleywinery, noon-7pm Mon.-Sat. Mar.-Oct., noon-5pm Mon.-Sat. Feb. and Nov.) produces riesling, gewürztraminer, cabernet sauvignon, and syrah.

for well-prepared Baja-style seafood, including good fish tacos. It's a busy place, so make a reservation or be prepared to wait.

Get away from high-volume assembly-line restaurants at **Sabaku Sushi** (90 E. Center St., 435/259-4455, www.sabakusushi.com, 5pm-10pm Tues.-Sun., rolls $4-15), which offers surprisingly good sushi in a friendly atmosphere. Arrive at 5pm for the sushi happy hour.

The **Broken Oar** (53 W. 400 N., 435/259-3127, 5pm-10pm Mon.-Sat., $11-25) is just north of downtown in a classy log building that looks like a ski lodge. In addition to burgers, pasta, and steaks, the restaurant offers a selection of meats from their smoker. The beer and wine menu veers toward local producers.

Brewpubs

After a hot day out on the trail, who can blame you for thinking about a cold brew and a hearty meal? Luckily, Moab has two excellent pubs to fill the bill. ★ **Eddie McStiff's** (57 S. Main St., 435/259-2337, www.eddiemcstiffs.com, 11:30am-close daily, $9-19) is an extremely popular place to sip a cool beer or a mojito, eat standard pub food (the pizza is a good bet), and meet other travelers; in good weather there's seating in a nice courtyard. You'd have to try hard not to have fun here.

There's more good beer and perhaps better food at the **Moab Brewery** (686 S. Main St., 435/259-6333, www.themoabbrewery.com, 11:30am-10pm Sun.-Thurs., 11:30am-11pm Fri.-Sat., $8-21), although it doesn't attract the kind of scene you'll find at Eddie McStiff's. The atmosphere is light and airy, and the food is good—steaks, sandwiches, burgers, and a wide selection of salads. Try the spinach salad with smoked salmon ($9) or prime rib ($19). There's deck seating when weather permits.

Fine Dining

The ★ **Desert Bistro** (36 S. 100 W.,

435/259-0756, www.desertbistro.com, reservations recommended, dinner from 5:30pm Tues.-Sun. Mar.-Nov., $22-50), a longtime favorite for regional fine dining, has moved to a new location in downtown Moab. Its seasonal, sophisticated Southwest-meets-continental cuisine features local meats and game plus fresh fish and seafood. The patio dining is some of the nicest in Moab, and the indoor dining rooms are pretty and peaceful.

Buck's Grill House (1393 N. US 191, 435/259-5201, www.bucksgrillhouse.com, 5pm-close daily, $9-33) is a steak house with an easygoing Western atmosphere and imaginative refinements on standard steak house fare. Dishes like duck tamales, elk stew with root vegetables, and a vegetarian meatless loaf are excellent.

Jeffrey's Steakhouse (218 N. 100 W., 435/259-3588, www.jeffreyssteakhouse.com, 5pm-close daily, $22-40), tucked off the main drag in an elegantly renovated small house with an upstairs bar, is about as classy and upscale as you'll find in Moab, with a small menu of steaks, chicken, lamb, and salmon.

The **River Grill** (Sorrel River Ranch, Hwy. 128, 17 miles northeast of Moab, 435/259-4642, www.sorrelriver.com, 7am-2pm and 6pm-9pm daily Apr.-Oct., 7am-10am and 6pm-9pm daily Nov.-Mar., $28-38) has a lovely dining room that overlooks spires of red rock and the dramatic cliffs of the Colorado River. The scenery is hard to top, and the food is good, with a focus on prime beef and continental specialties. Dinner reservations are strongly recommended.

The **Sunset Grill** (900 N. US 191, 435/259-7146, www.moab-utah.com/sunsetgrill, 5pm-close Mon.-Sat., $14-24) is located in uranium king Charlie Steen's mansion, situated high above Moab, with million-dollar sweeping views of the valley. Choose from steaks, fresh seafood, and a selection of pasta dishes—what you'll remember is the road up here and the view.

Information and Services

Moab is a small town, and people are generally friendly. Between the excellent Moab Information Center and the county library—and the friendly advice of people in the street—you'll find it easy to assemble all the information you need to have a fine stay.

Visitor Information

The **Moab Information Center** (25 E. Center St., at Main St., 435/259-8825 or 800/635-6622, www.discovermoab.com, 8am-7pm Mon.-Sat., 9am-6pm Sun. early Mar.-Nov.) is the place to start for nearly all local and area information. The National Park Service, the BLM, the U.S. Forest Service, the Grand County Travel Council, and the Canyonlands Natural History Association are all represented here. Visitors who need help from any of these agencies should start at the information center rather than at the agency offices. Free literature is available, the selection of books and maps for sale is large, and the staff is knowledgeable. The center's website is also well organized and packed with information.

The **BLM district office** (82 E. Dogwood Ave., 435/259-2100, 7:45am-4:30pm Mon.-Fri.) is on the south side of town behind Comfort Suites. Some land-use maps are sold here, and this is the place to pick up river-running permits.

Services

The **Grand County Public Library** (257 E. Center St., 435/259-1111, 9am-8pm Mon.-Fri., 9am-5pm Sat.) is a good place for local history and general reading. The **post office** (50 E. 100 N., 435/259-7427) is downtown.

Moab Regional Hospital (450 W. Williams Way, 435/719-3500) provides medical care. For ambulance, sheriff, police, or fire emergencies, dial **911.**

Arches National Park

A concentration of rock arches of marvelous variety has formed within the maze of sandstone finds at Arches National Park, one of the most popular national parks in the United States. Balanced rocks and tall spires add to the splendor. Paved roads and short hiking trails provide easy access to some of the more than 1,500 arches in the park. The park comprises 76,519 acres—small enough to be appreciated in one day, yet large enough to warrant extensive exploration.

If you're short on time, a drive through the Windows Sections (23.5 miles round-trip) affords a look at some of the largest and most spectacular arches. To visit all the stops and hike a few short trails takes a full day.

Getting There from Moab

5 miles / 10 minutes

Arches National Park is an easy **five-mile, 10-minute** drive north from central Moab on **US 191.** The entrance is marked by a large sign on the east side of the highway, where visitors often pull over to take pictures. There's often a relatively long line through the entrance stations, especially during the spring and summer high season.

Getting There from Canyonlands National Park

25 miles / 40 minutes

It's both possible and popular to visit both Canyonlands and Arches in one day, stopping at the best viewpoints and maybe taking a short hike or two. Many visitors, basing themselves out of Moab, stop at Arches first.

Arches is about **25 miles (40 minutes)** from Canyonlands. From the Island in the Sky Visitor Center, drive north out of the park on **Grand View Point Road.** After seven miles, the road becomes **UT-313 East.** Continue for 15 miles to **US 191,** where you'll turn right to go south. The entrance to Arches is about seven miles farther, on the left.

Visiting Arches National Park

Entrances

The sole entrance to **Arches National Park** (435/719-2299, www.nps.gov/arch, $25 per vehicle, $15 per motorcycle, $10 bicyclists and pedestrians) is five miles north of downtown Moab on US 191.

Park Passes and Fees

It costs $25 for a seven-day pass to Arches National Park for those coming in by car or RV. For individuals entering the park with no car, admission is $10 for a seven-day pass.

If your plans include visiting Canyonlands National Park plus Hovenweep and Natural Bridges National Monuments, consider the **Southeast Utah Parks Annual Pass** (also called the Local Passport, $50), which buys annual entry to all of these federal preserves. Purchase the pass at any of the park or national monument entrances.

Visitors Center

Just past the park entrance booth, the expansive **visitors center** (7:30am-6pm daily mid-June-Aug., 8am-6pm daily Sept.-Oct., 8am-4:30pm daily Nov.-Mar.) provides a good introduction to what you can expect ahead. Exhibits identify the rock layers, describe the geologic and human history, and illustrate some of the wildlife and plants of the park. A large outdoor plaza is a good place to troll for information when the visitors center is closed.

A short slide program runs regularly, and staff members are available to answer your questions, issue back-country permits, and check you in for a ranger-led tour in the Fiery Furnace area of the park. Look for the posted list of special activities; rangers host campfire programs and lead a wide variety of guided walks April-September. You'll also find checklists, pamphlets, books,

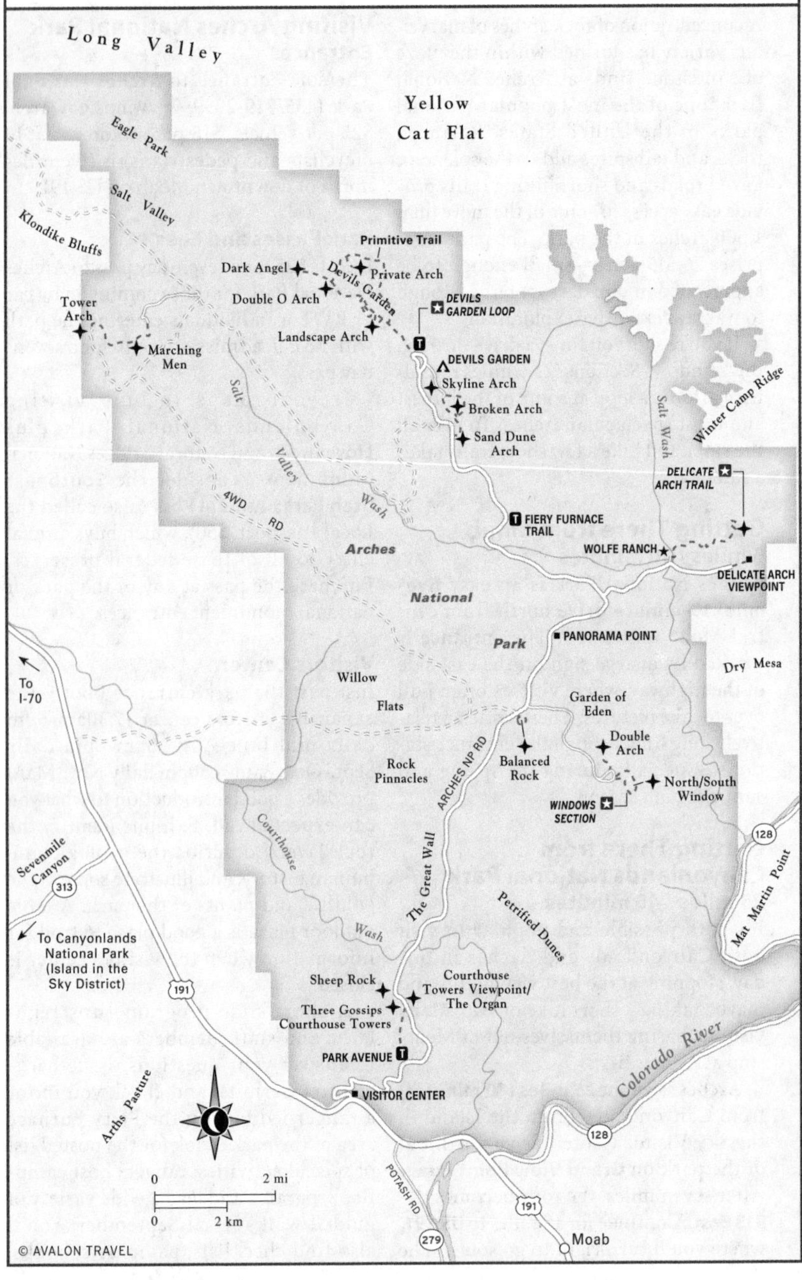

Arches National Park
Long Valley
Yellow Cat Flat
Eagle Park
Salt Valley
Klondike Bluffs
Primitive Trail
Dark Angel
Private Arch
Devils Garden
Double O Arch
DEVILS GARDEN LOOP
Tower Arch
Landscape Arch
Marching Men
DEVILS GARDEN
Skyline Arch
Broken Arch
Sand Dune Arch
Salt Valley Wash
4WD RD
Salt Wash
Winter Camp Ridge
DELICATE ARCH TRAIL
FIERY FURNACE TRAIL
WOLFE RANCH
DELICATE ARCH VIEWPOINT
Arches National Park
PANORAMA POINT
To I-70
Willow Flats
Dry Mesa
Garden of Eden
Double Arch
Balanced Rock
Rock Pinnacles
ARCHES NP RD
North/South Window
WINDOWS SECTION
Courthouse Wash
The Great Wall
Sevenmile Canyon
313
128
Mat Martin Point
Petrified Dunes
To Canyonlands National Park (Island in the Sky District)
191
Sheep Rock
Courthouse Towers Viewpoint/ The Organ
Three Gossips
Courthouse Towers
Colorado River
PARK AVENUE
VISITOR CENTER
Arths Pasture
128
0
2 mi
0
2 km
POTASH RD
191
279
Moab
© AVALON TRAVEL

Arches in One Day

Morning

Stop at the **visitors center** (page 189) to learn about the natural and human history of the park, then take the adjacent Desert Nature Trail to identify plants that make Arches home. From the visitors center, drive 11 miles to **The Windows trailhead** (page 196), where a number of easy trails lead to four arches carved into a fin of rock. Continue to the **Delicate Arch trailhead** (page 197), and hike up to the iconic arch before the day gets too hot.

Afternoon

Enjoy a picnic lunch and views from the picnic area at **Devils Garden trailhead** (page 195), seven miles north of the Windows. Then explore a bit of the trail: Tunnel and Pine Tree Arches are less than a mile in from the trailhead. If you still have some time, stop on the way back out of the park and take a stroll on the **Park Avenue Trail** (page 196).

Evening

There are no dining facilities in the park, so enjoy a refined meal at the **Desert Bistro** (page 187) in Moab, five miles south of the park entrance.

Extending Your Stay

One extra day in Arches will suffice for all but the most serious hikers, who may want to spend an additional 2-3 days here.

Go off-trail with a park ranger through the remote and labrynthine **Fiery Furnace section** (page 195). Offered only in spring and fall, this daily, three-hour guided hike is popular and limited to 25 people, so make a reservation before your visit.

Drive the rough road to **Klondike Bluffs and Tower Arch** (page 195) to catch a glimpse of the Marching Men.

maps, posters, postcards, and film for purchase. See the rangers for advice and the free backcountry permit required for overnight trips. The easy 0.2-mile **Desert Nature Trail** begins near the visitors center and identifies some of the native plants. Picnic areas are outside the visitors center and at Balanced Rock and Devils Garden.

Desert bighorn sheep frequent the area around the visitors center and can sometimes be seen from US 191 just south of the park entrance. A sheep crossing about three miles north of the visitors center is also a good place to scan the steep talus slopes for these nimble animals.

A road guide to Arches National Park, available at the visitors center, has detailed descriptions that correspond to place names along the main road. Be sure to stop only in parking lots and designated pullouts. Watch out for others who are sightseeing in this popular park. With less than 30 miles of paved road in the entire park, the traffic can be surprisingly heavy in the summer high season.

Reservations

Arches has no in-park lodging and just one campground. Lodging options abound in Moab, five miles down the road. **Devils Garden** (877/444-6777, www.recreation.gov, $20) offers 50 sites on the red and dusty-green land about 18 miles inside the park. It fills up fast from March through the end of October, when reservations are required at least four days in advance. To secure a spot, start planning at least six months out.

Information and Services

Park Newsletter

Pick up the ***Arches Visitors Guide,*** the park's newsletter, at the entrance station or the visitors center. The guide has a useful map and trail descriptions. Its main lesson is that there are no services in Arches National Park.

Banking, Gas, and Groceries

Bring your own water, food, and other supplies, and gas up in Moab before you enter the park.

Emergency and Medical Services

There's **cell service** in parts of the park, but it may be spotty in some of the outer rings.

If you can get cell service, dial **911** in an emergency to reach the **Grand County Sheriff's Office.** If you don't have service, find a ranger, many of whom are trained EMTs. Otherwise, get to the visitors center as fast as possible and dial 911 from a pay phone there (no coins needed). In town, **Moab Regional Hospital** (450 W. Williams Way, 435/719-3500) provides medical care.

Getting Around

You must have your own vehicle to visit the viewpoints and trailheads of Arches. The developed stops are relatively far apart along the twisting, narrow road through the park.

During the summer high season it's often difficult to find a parking space at some of the stops, but parking anywhere else along the road is strictly forbidden. Watch out for tour buses, RVs, and bicyclists, giving each ample room and the right-of-way.

Sights

Moab Fault

The park road begins a long but well-graded climb from the visitors center up the cliffs to the northeast. A pullout on the right after 1.1 miles offers a good view of Moab Canyon and its geology. The rock layers on this side of the canyon have slipped down more than 2,600 feet in relation to the other side. This movement took place about six million years ago along the **Moab Fault,** which follows the canyon floor. Rock layers at the top of the far cliffs are nearly the same age as those at the bottom on this side.

Park Avenue

If you could stack the rocks of this side on top of rocks on the other side, you'd have a complete stratigraphic column of the Moab area—more than 150 million years' worth.

Park Avenue

The **South Park Avenue overlook** and trailhead are on the left 2.1 miles from the visitors center. Great sandstone slabs form a skyline on each side of this dry wash. A trail goes north one mile down the wash to the North Park Avenue trailhead (1.3 miles ahead by road). Arrange to be picked up there, or backtrack to your starting point. The large rock monoliths of Courthouse Towers rise north of Park Avenue. Only a few small arches exist now, although major arches may have formed there in the past.

Balanced Rock

Gravity-defying **Balanced Rock** is on the right, 8.5 miles from the visitors center. A boulder more than 55 feet high rests precariously atop a 73-foot pedestal. Chip Off the Old Block, a much smaller version of Balanced Rock, stood nearby until it collapsed in the winter of 1975-1976. For a closer look at Balanced Rock, take the 0.3-mile trail encircling it. There's a picnic area across the road. Author Edward Abbey lived in a trailer near Balanced Rock for a season as a park ranger in the 1950s; his journal became the basis for the classic *Desert Solitaire.*

★ Windows Section

The **Windows Section** of Arches is 2.5 miles past Balanced Rock, on a paved road to the right. Short trails (0.25-1 mile one-way) lead from the road's end to some massive arches. The Windows trailhead is the start for North Window (an opening 51 feet high and 93 feet wide), South Window (66 feet high and 105 feet wide), and Turret Arch (64 feet high and 39 feet wide). Double Arch, a short walk from a second trailhead, is an unusual pair of arches; the larger opening—105 feet high and 163 feet wide—is best appreciated by walking inside. The smaller opening is 61 feet high and 60 feet wide. Together, the two arches frame a large opening overhead.

Garden of Eden Viewpoint, on the way back to the main road, promises a good panorama of Salt Valley to the north. Under the valley floor, the massive body of salt and gypsum that's responsible for the arches comes close to the surface. Faroff Delicate Arch can be seen across the valley on a sandstone ridge. Early visitors to the Garden of Eden saw rock formations resembling Adam (with an apple) and Eve. Two other viewpoints of the Salt Valley area lie farther north on the main road.

Wolfe Ranch and Delicate Arch

A bit of pioneer history survives at **Wolfe Ranch,** 2.5 miles north on the main road from the Windows junction (turn right and drive 1.8 miles to the parking area). John Wesley Wolfe came to this spot in

Why Are There Arches?

The park's distinctive arches are formed by an unusual combination of geologic forces. About 300 million years ago, evaporation of inland seas left behind a salt layer more than 3,000 feet thick in the Paradox Basin of this region. Sediments, including those that later became the arches, then covered the salt. Unequal pressures caused the salt to gradually flow upward in places, bending the overlying sediments as well. These upfolds, or anticlines, later collapsed when groundwater dissolved the underlying salt.

The faults and joints caused by the uplift and collapse opened the way for erosion to carve hundreds of freestanding fins. Alternate freezing and thawing action and exfoliation (flaking caused by expansion when water or frost penetrates the rock) continued to peel away more rock until holes formed in some of the fins. Rockfalls within the holes helped enlarge the arches. Nearly all arches in the park eroded out of Entrada sandstone.

Eventually all the present arches will collapse, as Wall Arch did in 2008, but there should be plenty of new ones by the time that happens. The fins' uniform strength and hard upper surfaces have proved ideal for arch formation. Not every hole in the rock is considered an arch. To qualify, the opening must be at least three feet in one direction, and light must be able to pass through. Although the term *windows* often refers to openings in large walls of rock, windows and arches are really the same.

Water seeping through the sandstone from above has created a second type of arch—the pothole arch. You may also come across a few natural bridges cut from the rock by perennial water runoff.

A succession of rock layers is on display at Arches. The rocks on top of the salt beds—the rocks you actually see at Arches—are mostly Entrada sandstone, which is a pretty general category of rock. Within this Entrada Formation are three distinct types of sandstone. The formation's dark red base layer is known as the Dewey Bridge member. It's softer than the formation's other sandstones and erodes easily. Dewey Bridge rocks are topped by the pinkish-orange Slick Rock member, the park's most visible rocks. The Slick Rock layer is much harder than the Dewey Bridge, and the combination of the two layers—softer rocks overlaid by harder—is responsible for the differential erosion that forms hoodoos and precariously balanced rocks. The thin top layer of Entrada sandstone, a white rock similar to Navajo sandstone, is called the Moab Tongue.

1888, hoping the desert climate would provide relief for health problems related to a Civil War injury. He found a good spring high in the rocks, grass for cattle, and water in Salt Wash to irrigate a garden. The ranch that he built provided a home for him and some of his family for more than 20 years, and cattlemen later used it as a line ranch. Then sheepherders brought in their animals, which so overgrazed the range that the grass has yet to recover. A trail guide available at the entrance tells about the Wolfe family and the features of their ranch. The weather-beaten cabin built in 1906 still survives. A short trail leads to petroglyphs above Wolfe Ranch; figures of horses indicate that Ute people, rather than earlier inhabitants, did the artwork. Park staff can give directions to other rock-art sites; great care should be taken not to touch the fragile artwork.

Delicate Arch stands in a magnificent setting atop gracefully curving slickrock. Distant canyons and the La Sal Mountains lie beyond. The span is 45 feet high and 33 feet wide. A moderately strenuous three-mile round-trip hike leads to the arch. Another perspective on Delicate Arch can be obtained by driving 1.2 miles beyond Wolfe Ranch. Look for the small arch high above. A short, steep trail (0.5 mile round-trip) climbs a hill for the best view.

Fiery Furnace

The **Fiery Furnace Viewpoint** and trailhead are three miles from the Wolfe Ranch junction, on the right side of the main road. The Fiery Furnace gets its name from sandstone fins that turn flaming red on occasions when thin cloud cover at the horizon reflects the warm light of sunrise or sunset. The shady recesses beneath the fins provide a cool respite from the hot summer sun.

Closely packed sandstone fins form a maze of deep slots, with many arches and at least one natural bridge inside. Both for safety reasons and to reduce human impact on this sensitive area, which harbors several species of rare plants, hikers are encouraged to join a ranger-led hike. The hike is moderately strenuous and involves steep ledges, squeezing through narrow cracks, a couple of jumps, and hoisting yourself up off the ground. There is no turning back once the hike starts, so make sure you're physically prepared and properly equipped.

Rangers lead three-hour hikes (Mar.-Oct., $10 adults, $5 ages 5-12 and Interagency Senior Pass and Access Pass holders) into the Fiery Furnace twice each day. Unlike most ranger-led activities, a fee is charged for these hikes. Group size is limited to about 25 people, and children under age five are not allowed. Walks often fill weeks in advance. Make reservations online at www.recreation.gov or in person at the visitors center up to seven days in advance. To visit the Fiery Furnace without a ranger, visitors must obtain a permit at the visitors center ($4 adults, $2 ages 5-12 and Interagency Senior Pass and Access Pass holders). A couple of Moab outfitters also lead hikes into the Fiery Furnace; these cost considerably more, but there's usually space available.

Skyline Arch

Skyline Arch is on the right, one mile past the Sand Dune/Broken Arch trailhead. In desert climates, erosion can proceed imperceptibly for centuries until a cataclysmic event happens. In 1940 a giant boulder fell from the opening of Skyline Arch, doubling the size of the arch in seconds. The hole is now 45 feet high and 69 feet wide. A short trail leads to the base of the arch.

Devils Garden

The Devils Garden trailhead, picnic area, and campground are all near the end of the main park road. **Devils Garden** offers fine scenery and more arches than any other section of the park. The hiking trail leads past large sandstone fins to Landscape and six other named arches. Carry water if the weather is hot or if you might want to continue past the one-mile point at Landscape Arch. Adventurous hikers could spend days exploring the maze of canyons among the fins.

Klondike Bluffs and Tower Arch

Relatively few visitors come to the spires, high bluffs, and fine arch in this northwestern section of the park. A fair-weather dirt road turns off the main drive 1.3 miles before Devils Garden trailhead, winds down into Salt Valley, and heads northwest. After 7.5 miles, turn left on the road to **Klondike Bluffs** and proceed one mile to the Tower Arch trailhead. These roads may have washboards, but they are usually passable by cars in dry weather; don't drive on them if storms threaten. The trail to **Tower Arch** winds past the **Marching Men** and other rock formations (three miles round-trip). Alexander Ringhoffer, who discovered the arch in 1922, carved an inscription on the south column. The area can also be fun to explore off-trail with a map and compass or a GPS receiver. Those with 4WD vehicles can drive close to the arch on a separate jeep road. Tower Arch has an opening 34 feet high by 92 feet wide. A tall monolith nearby gave the arch its name.

4WD Road

A rough road near Tower Arch in the

Klondike Bluffs turns southeast past **Eye of the Whale Arch** in Herdina Park to Balanced Rock on the main park road, 10.8 miles away. The road isn't particularly difficult for 4WD enthusiasts, although normal backcountry precautions should be taken. A steep sand hill north of Eye of the Whale Arch is difficult to climb for vehicles coming from Balanced Rock; it's better to drive from the Tower Arch area instead.

Recreation

Because of its great popularity and proximity to Moab, Arches sees a lot of visitors. Most are content, however, to drive the parkways and perhaps saunter to undemanding viewpoints. You can quickly leave the crowds behind by planning a hike to more outlying destinations. Arches' outback offers magnificent rewards for hikers willing to leave the pavement behind and get dusty on a backcountry trail.

Hiking

Established hiking trails lead to many fine arches and overlooks that can't be seen from the road. You're free to wander cross-country too, but stay on rock or in washes to avoid damaging the fragile cryptobiotic soils. Wear good walking shoes with rubber soles for travel across slickrock. The summer sun can be especially harsh on the unprepared hiker—don't forget water, a hat, and sunscreen. The desert rule is to carry at least one gallon of water per person for an all-day hike. Take a map and compass or a map and GPS unit for off-trail hiking. Be cautious on the slickrock, as the soft sandstone can crumble easily. Also, remember that it's easier to go up a steep slickrock slope than it is to come back down.

You can reach almost any spot in the park on a day hike, although you'll also find some good overnight camping possibilities. Areas for longer trips include Courthouse Wash in the southern part of the park and Salt Wash in the eastern part. All backpacking is done off-trail. A backcountry permit must be obtained from a ranger before camping in the backcountry.

Backcountry regulations prohibit fires and pets, and they allow camping only out of sight of any road (at least one mile away), or trail (at least 0.5 mile away), and at least 300 feet from a recognizable archaeological site or nonflowing water source.

Park Avenue

Distance: 1 mile one-way
Duration: 1 hour round-trip
Elevation change: 320 feet
Effort: easy-moderate
Trailheads: Park Avenue or North Park Avenue trailhead

Get an eyeful of massive stone formations and a feel for the natural history of the park on the easy-moderate Park Avenue Trail. The Park Avenue trailhead, just past the crest of the switchbacks that climb up into the park, is the best place to start. The vistas from here are especially dramatic: Courthouse Towers, the Three Gossips, and other fanciful rock formations loom above a natural amphitheater. The trail drops into a narrow wash before traversing the park highway at the North Park Avenue trailhead. Hikers can be dropped off at one trailhead and picked up 30 minutes later at the other.

The Windows

Distance: 1 mile round-trip
Duration: 1 hour
Elevation change: 140 feet
Effort: easy
Trailhead: end of Windows Road

Ten miles into the park, just past the impossible-to-miss Balanced Rock, follow signs and a paved road to the Windows Section. A one-mile round-trip loop along a sandy trail leads to the Windows—a cluster of enormous arches that are impossible to see from the road. Highlights include the **North** and **South Windows** and **Turret Arch.** Unmarked trails lead to vistas and scrambles along the stone faces that make up the ridge. If this easy loop leaves you eager for more exploration in the area, a second trail starts from just past the Windows parking area and goes to **Double Arch.** This 0.5-mile trail leads to two giant spans that are joined at one end. These easy trails are good for family groups because younger or more ambitious hikers can scramble to their hearts' content along rocky outcrops.

Delicate Arch Viewpoint

Distance: 0.5 mile round-trip
Duration: 15-30 minutes
Elevation change: 100 feet
Effort: easy-moderate
Trailhead: 1.2 miles past Wolfe Ranch, at the end of Wolfe Ranch Road

If you don't have the time or the endurance for the relatively strenuous hike to Delicate Arch, you can view the astonishing arch from a distance at the Delicate Arch Viewpoint. From the viewing area, hikers can scramble up a steep trail to a rim with views across Cache Valley. Even though this is a short hike, it's a good place to wander around the slickrock for a while. It's especially nice to linger around sunset, when the arch captures the light and begins to glow. If you'd rather not scramble around on the slickrock, a short path leads about 100 yards from the parking area to a decent view of the arch.

★ Delicate Arch Trail

Distance: 3 miles round-trip
Duration: 2 hours
Elevation change: 500 feet
Effort: moderate-strenuous
Trailhead: Wolfe Ranch

For those who are able, the hike to the base of Delicate Arch is one of the park's highlights. Shortly after the trail's start

Top to bottom: The Windows; Delicate Arch; park rangers leading hikers into the Fiery Furnace.

Tower Arch is actually both an arch and a tower, and there's no mistaking the tower for just another big sandstone rock.

Because of the dirt-road access to this hike, it's best to skip it if there's been recent rain or if rain is threatening.

Biking

Cyclists are required to keep to established roads in the park; there is no single-track or trail riding allowed. You'll also have to contend with heavy traffic on the narrow paved roads and dusty washboard surfaces on the dirt roads. Beware of deep sand on the 4WD roads, traffic on the main park road, and summertime heat wherever you ride.

One good, not-too-hard ride is along the Willow Springs Road. Allow 2-3 hours for an out-and-back, starting from the Balanced Rock parking area and heading west.

Perhaps the best bet for relatively fit mountain bikers is the 24-mile ride to Tower Arch and back. From the Devils Garden parking area, ride out the **Salt Valley Road,** which can be rough. After about 7.5 miles, turn left onto a jeep road that leads to the "back door" to Tower Arch.

Nearby, Bureau of Land Management and Canyonlands National Park areas offer world-class mountain biking.

Climbing

Rock climbers don't need a permit in Arches, although you should first discuss your plans with a ranger. All features named on U.S. Geological Survey maps are closed to climbing: That means any of the arches and many of the most distinctive towers are off-limits. Slacklining is also prohibited in the park. There are still plenty of long-standing routes for advanced climbers to enjoy, although the rock in Arches is sandier and softer than in other areas around Moab.

Several additional climbing restrictions are in place. No new permanent climbing hardware may be installed in any fixed location. If an existing bolt or other hardware item is unsafe, it may be replaced. This effectively limits all technical climbing to existing routes or new routes not requiring placement of fixed anchors. Other restrictions are detailed on the park's website.

The most commonly climbed areas are along the sheer stone faces of **Park Avenue.** Another popular destination is **Owl Rock,** the small, owl-shaped tower located in the Windows Section of the park. For more information on climbing in Arches, consult the bible of Moab-area climbing, *Desert Rock* by Eric Bjørnstad, or ask for advice at **Pagan Mountaineering** (59 S. Main St., Moab, 435/259-1117, www.paganclimber.com), a climbing and outdoor-gear store that also offers a climbing guide service.

Camping

Devils Garden Campground (elevation 5,355 feet, with water, year-round, $20) is near the end of the 18-mile scenic drive. It's an excellent place to camp, with some sites tucked under rock formations and others offering great views, but it's extremely popular. The well-organized traveler must plan accordingly and reserve a site in advance for March-October. Reservations (www.recreation.gov, $9 booking fee plus $20 camping fee) must be made no less than 4 days and no more than 240 days in advance. All campsites can be reserved, so during the busy spring, summer, and fall seasons, campers without reservations are pretty much out of luck. In winter, sites 1-24 are available as first-come, first-served. A camp host is on-site, and firewood is available ($5), but there are no other services or amenities.

If you aren't able to score a coveted Arches campsite, all is not lost. There are many Bureau of Land Management campsites within an easy drive of the park. Try the primitive BLM campgrounds on Highway 313, just west of US 191 and on the way to Canyonlands

National Park's Island in the Sky District. Another cluster of BLM campgrounds is along the Colorado River on Highway 128, which runs northeast from US 191 at the north end of Moab.

Canyonlands National Park

The canyon country puts on its supreme performance in this vast park, which spreads across 527 square miles. The deeply entrenched Colorado and Green Rivers meet in its heart, and then continue south, as the mighty Colorado, through tumultuous Cataract Canyon Rapids.

The park is divided into four districts and a separate noncontiguous unit. The Colorado and Green Rivers form the River District and divide the park into three other regions. Island in the Sky is north, between the rivers; the Maze is to the west; and Needles is to the east. The Horseshoe Canyon Unit is farther to the west. Each district has its own distinct character. No bridges or roads directly connect the three land districts and the Horseshoe Canyon Unit, so most visitors have to leave the park to go from one region to another.

The huge park can be seen in many ways and on many levels. Paved roads reach a few areas, 4WD roads go to more places, and hiking trails reach still more, but much of the land shows no trace of human passage. To get the big picture, you can fly over this incredible complex of canyons on an air tour; however, only a river trip or a hike lets you experience the solitude and detail of the land.

The park can be visited in any season of the year, with spring and autumn the best choices. Summer temperatures can climb over 100°F; carrying and drinking lots of water becomes critical then (bring at least one gallon per person per day). Winter days tend to be bright at sunny, although nighttime temperatures can dip into the teens or even below zero Fahrenheit. Winter visitors should inquire about travel conditions, as snow and ice occasionally close roads and trails at higher elevations.

Getting There from Moab

30 miles / 45 minutes

The most accessible and busy section of Canyonlands is the **Island in the Sky District**, a **30-mile, 45-minute** drive from Moab. Take **US 191 north** for 10 miles, then turn left to join **UT-313.** Follow UT-313 for about 15 miles, at which point the highway becomes **Grand View Point Road.** About seven miles along Grand View Point Road you'll find the Island in the Sky Visitor Center.

The **Needles District** to the south of Moab is a bit more remote but still easy to reach. It's a **75-mile, 1.5-hour** drive. Take **US 191 south** from Moab for about 40 miles. At the junction with UT-211, turn right. The Needles entrance is about 35 miles along UT-211.

Getting There from Arches National Park

25 miles / 40 minutes

It's only a **25-mile, 40-minute** drive from Arches National Park to Canyonlands National Park's **Island in the Sky District.** Take **US 191 north** from Arches for about seven miles. Turn left to join **UT-313,** then continue on UT-313 for just over 20 miles to the Island in the Sky Visitor Center.

To reach the **Needles District** from Arches, drive **south** on **US 191** for about 45 miles to **UT-211 West.** From there, it's about 35 miles to the Needles Visitor Center.

Visiting Canyonlands National Park

There are four districts and a noncontiguous unit in **Canyonlands National Park** (www.nps.gov/cany, $25 per vehicle, $15 per motorcycle, $10 bicyclists and pedestrians, good for one week in all districts, no fee to enter Maze or Horseshoe

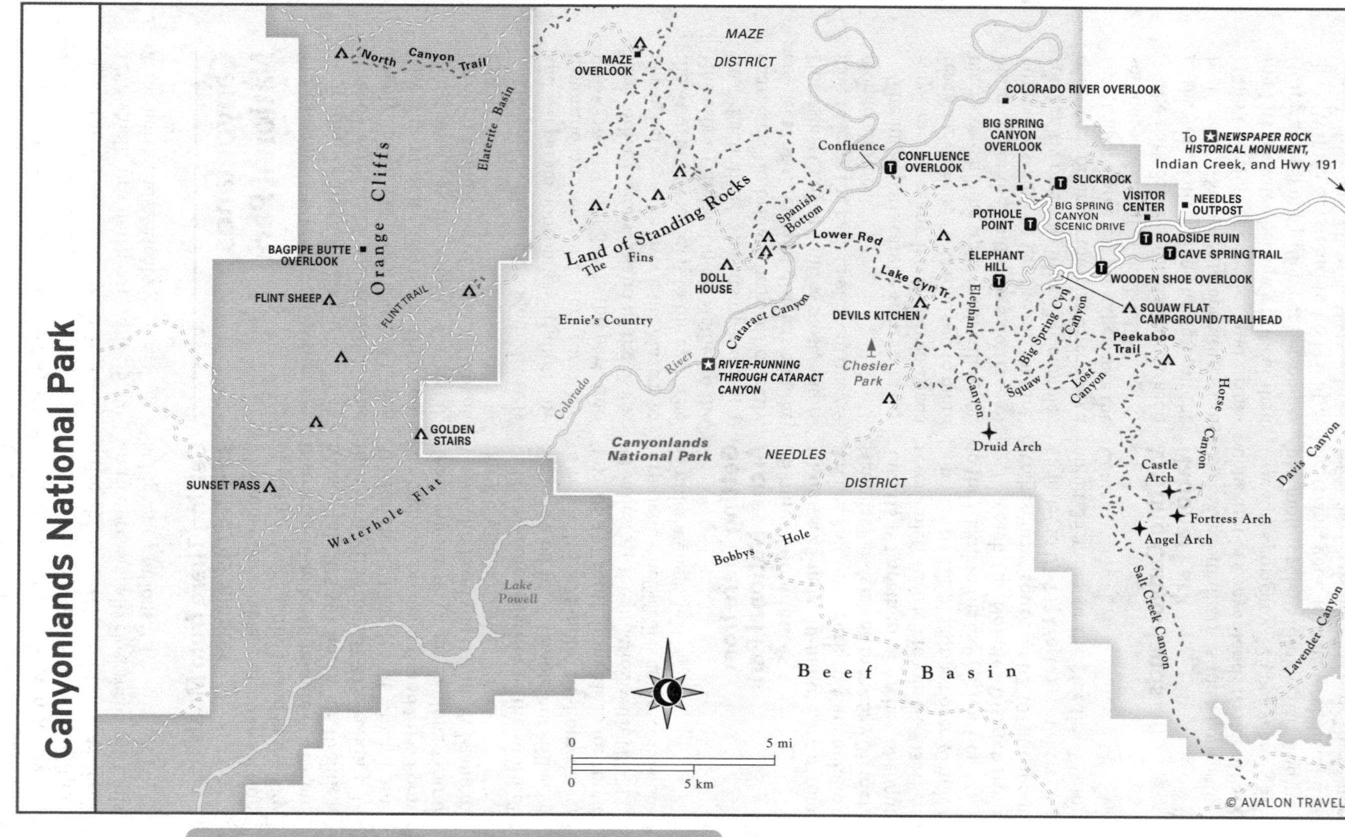

Canyonlands National Park
North Canyon Trail
MAZE OVERLOOK
MAZE DISTRICT
Elaterite Basin
Orange Cliffs
BAGPIPE BUTTE OVERLOOK
FLINT SHEEP
FLINT TRAIL
Land of Standing Rocks
The Fins
DOLL HOUSE
Spanish Bottom
Lower Red Lake Cyn Tr
Confluence
CONFLUENCE OVERLOOK
COLORADO RIVER OVERLOOK
BIG SPRING CANYON OVERLOOK
SLICKROCK
POTHOLE POINT
BIG SPRING CANYON SCENIC DRIVE
VISITOR CENTER
NEEDLES OUTPOST
To NEWSPAPER ROCK HISTORICAL MONUMENT, Indian Creek, and Hwy 191
ROADSIDE RUIN
CAVE SPRING TRAIL
ELEPHANT HILL
WOODEN SHOE OVERLOOK
SQUAW FLAT CAMPGROUND/TRAILHEAD
Ernie's Country
Cataract Canyon
DEVILS KITCHEN
Elephant Canyon
Big Spring Cyn
Canyon
Peekaboo Trail
Colorado River
RIVER-RUNNING THROUGH CATARACT CANYON
Chesler Park
Squaw
Lost Canyon
Horse Canyon
GOLDEN STAIRS
Canyonlands National Park
NEEDLES DISTRICT
Druid Arch
SUNSET PASS
Waterhole Flat
Castle Arch
Fortress Arch
Angel Arch
Davis Canyon
Bobbys Hole
Lake Powell
Salt Creek Canyon
Lavender Canyon
Beef Basin
0 5 mi
0 5 km
© AVALON TRAVEL

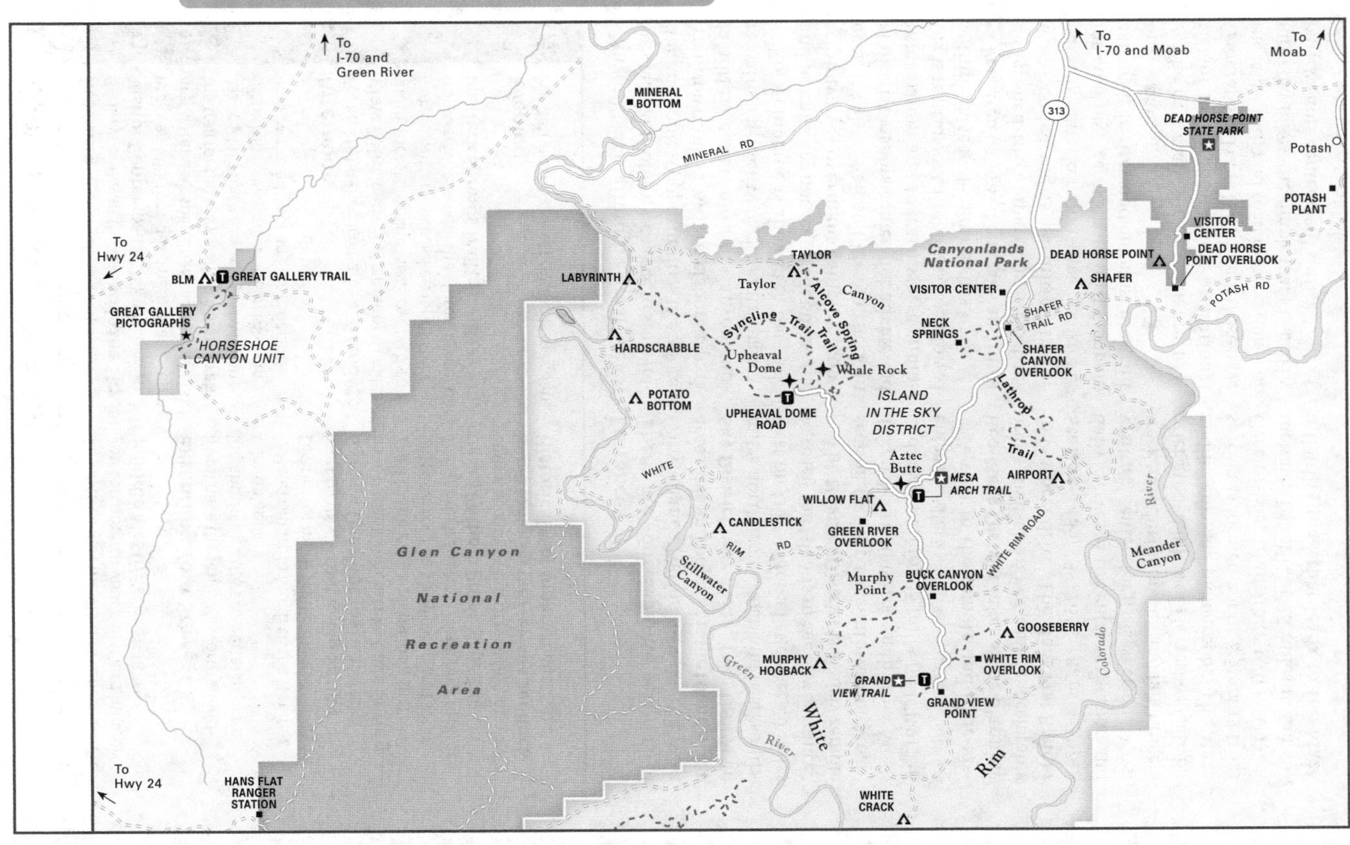

To I-70 and Green River
MINERAL BOTTOM
MINERAL RD
To I-70 and Moab
To Moab
313
DEAD HORSE POINT STATE PARK
Potash
POTASH PLANT
VISITOR CENTER
DEAD HORSE POINT
DEAD HORSE POINT OVERLOOK
POTASH RD
SHAFER
To Hwy 24
BLM
GREAT GALLERY TRAIL
GREAT GALLERY PICTOGRAPHS
HORSESHOE CANYON UNIT
LABYRINTH
TAYLOR
Taylor
Canyon
Alcove Spring Trail
Canyonlands National Park
VISITOR CENTER
NECK SPRINGS
SHAFER TRAIL RD
SHAFER CANYON OVERLOOK
Syncline Trail
HARDSCRABBLE
Upheaval Dome
Whale Rock
POTATO BOTTOM
UPHEAVAL DOME ROAD
ISLAND IN THE SKY DISTRICT
Lathrop Trail
WHITE
Aztec Butte
MESA ARCH TRAIL
AIRPORT
WILLOW FLAT
CANDLESTICK
GREEN RIVER OVERLOOK
RIM RD
WHITE RIM ROAD
River
Meander Canyon
Glen Canyon National Recreation Area
Stillwater Canyon
Murphy Point
BUCK CANYON OVERLOOK
GOOSEBERRY
MURPHY HOGBACK
WHITE RIM OVERLOOK
Colorado
Green
GRAND VIEW TRAIL
GRAND VIEW POINT
White
River
Rim
To Hwy 24
HANS FLAT RANGER STATION
WHITE CRACK

Canyonlands in One Day

Morning

Begin your day at the **Island in the Sky Visitor Center** (page 205), which overlooks an 800-foot-deep natural amphitheater. After a six-mile drive south, you'll find the trail for the easy walk to **Mesa Arch** (page 211), which rewards you with one of the most dramatic vistas in Utah: an arch on the edge of an 800-foot cliff.

Afternoon

For lunch, hit the picnic area at **Grand View Point** (page 209), another six miles south, for astonishing views over red-rock canyons. After lunch, take a longer hike from a trailhead near the visitors center on the **Neck Springs Trail** (page 211).

Evening

For dinner, the closest dining is in Moab, 32 miles east of the visitors center, where you can quench your thirst and hunger at **Eddie McStiff's** (page 187).

Extending Your Stay

If you have the time, it's worth spending another 1-2 days to better explore Canyonlands.

Head out from Moab to the Needles District for more scenic drives and hikes. Start by driving out to **Big Spring Canyon Overlook** (page 216) and have a picnic lunch. Hike **Cave Spring Trail** (page 216), an easy loop that passes an old cowboy camp and some ancient rock art. Next, walk on a slickrock trail to **Pothole Point** (page 216). On your way into or out of Needles, don't forget to stop at the **Newspaper Rock Historical Monument** (page 214).

Canyon), each affording great views, spectacular geology, a chance to see wildlife, and endless opportunities to explore. You won't find crowds or elaborate park facilities because most of Canyonlands remains a primitive backcountry park.

Rock climbing is allowed in the park, and permits are not required, unless the trip involves overnight camping; however, it's always a good idea to check in at district visitors centers for advice and information and to learn where climbing is restricted. Climbing is not allowed within 300 feet of cultural sites.

Pets aren't allowed on trails and must be leashed in campgrounds. No firewood collecting is permitted in the park; backpackers must use gas stoves for cooking. Vehicle and boat campers can bring in firewood but must use grills or fire pans.

The best maps for the park are a series of topographic maps by National Geographic/Trails Illustrated; these have the latest trail and road information. For most day hikes, the simple maps issued by park visitors centers will suffice.

Entrances

There are four separate sections of Canyonlands National Park. The most accessible and popular is the **Island in the Sky District** near Moab. Take US 191 10 miles north from Moab and head southwest on UT-313 for a little over 20 miles to reach the Islands in the Sky entrance.

The **Needles District** is a fairly remote section of the park southwest of Moab. Take US 191 40 miles south from Moab and head west for 35 miles on UT-211 to enter Needles.

A visit to the remote and little-visited **Maze District** takes some planning and a high-clearance vehicle, preferably four-wheel drive. The **Hans Flat Ranger Station** (435/259-2652, 8am-4:30pm daily) serves as the entrance station and visitors center for this section. Most weekends during spring and fall, rangers offer guided hikes of Horseshoe Canyon and its amazing pictographs. The Maze section is located about 2.5 hours from Green River, Utah. Take I-70 to UT-24, then head south for 25 miles to the 45-mile dirt road that leads to the Maze (turn left just after the entrance to Goblin Valley State Park).

The **Rivers District** includes the Colorado and Green Rivers, and can be accessed at various points along these rivers. It's best to book a guided river trip to access these remote areas.

Park Passes and Fees

It costs $25 per vehicle, $15 per motorcycle, and $10 for bicyclists or pedestrians to enter the park for seven days.

The **Southeast Utah Parks Annual Pass** ($50) provides access to Canyonlands and Arches for a year, as well as Hovenweep and Natural Bridges National Monuments. The National Park Service's **Interagency Annual Pass/America the Beautiful Pass** ($80) gets you into every national park for a year.

Visitors Centers

Since Canyonlands covers so much far-flung territory, separate visitors centers serve each district. One website (www.nps.gov/cany) serves the whole park and is a good source for current information and permit applications. There are visitors centers at the entrances to the **Island in the Sky District** (435/259-4712, 8am-6pm daily Mar.-late Dec.) and the **Needles District** (435/259-4711, 8am-6pm daily). The **Hans Flat Ranger Station** (435/259-2652, 8am-4:30pm daily) is on a remote plateau above the even more isolated canyons of the Maze District and the Horseshoe Canyon Unit. The River District is administered out of the **National Park Service Office** (2282 SW Resource Blvd., Moab, 435/719-2313, 8am-4pm Mon.-Fri.). This office can generally handle inquiries for all districts of the park. For backcountry information, or to make backcountry reservations, call 435/259-4351. Handouts from the ranger offices describe natural history, travel, and other aspects of the park.

If you are in Moab, it is most convenient to stop at the **Moab Information Center** (25 E. Center St., at Main St., 435/259-8825 or 800/635-6622, 8am-7pm Mon.-Sat., 9am-6pm Sun. early Mar.-Nov.), where a national park ranger is often on duty. All visitors centers have brochures, maps, and books, as well as someone to answer your questions.

Reservations

There are no accommodations within the park. Canyonlands has two campgrounds. In the Island in the Sky District, the **Willow Flat Campground** (www.nps.gov/cany, first-come, first-served, $15 per night) has 12 sites. The Needles District has the 26-site **Squaw Flat Campground** (www.nps.gov/cany, $20 per night), which is also first-come, first-served. Both campgrounds typically fill each day March-June and early September-mid-October, so plan on arriving early to nab a spot if you're visiting during these periods.

Information and Services

Park Newsletter

The ***Canyonlands Visitor Guide,*** which is passed out free at the entrance stations and visitors centers, has useful maps and trail guides for both Island in the Sky and Needles Districts.

Banking, Gas, and Groceries

There are **no services** in any of the park's sections. Make sure to stock up on water, food, gas, and other supplies before you enter the park. Moab is the best place to purchase supplies in the region.

Emergency and Medical Services

Cell phone reception is spotty inside the park, and the closest emergency services are in Moab.

In an emergency, if cell phone service is available, call **911.** Otherwise, find a ranger, many of whom are trained EMTs, or get to the nearest visitors center and dial 911 from one of the pay phones (free). In town, **Moab Regional Hospital** (450 W. Williams Way, 435/719-3500) provides medical care.

Orientation

Unless you have a great deal of time, you can't really do the entire park in one trip. It's best to pick one section and concentrate on it.

Island in the Sky District

The mesa-top Island in the Sky District has paved roads to impressive belvederes such as Grand View Point and the strange Upheaval Dome. If you're short on time or don't want to make a rigorous backcountry trip, you'll find this district the best choice. It is easily visited as a day trip from Moab. The "Island," which is actually a large mesa, is much like nearby Dead Horse Point on a giant scale; a narrow neck of land connects the north side with the "mainland."

If you're really on a tight schedule, it's possible to spend a few hours exploring Arches National Park, then head to Island in the Sky for a drive to the scenic Grand View overlook and a brief hike to Mesa Arch or the Upheaval Dome viewpoint. A one-day visit should include these elements, plus a hike along the Neck Springs Trail. For a longer visit, hikers, mountain bikers, and those with suitable high-clearance 4WD vehicles can drop off the Island in the Sky and descend about 1,300 feet to White Rim Road, which follows the cliffs of the White Rim around most of the island. Plan to spend at least 2-3 days exploring this 100-mile-long road.

Needles District

Colorful rock spires prompted the name of the Needles District, which is easily accessed from Highway 211 and US 191 south of Moab. Splendid canyons contain many arches, strange rock formations, and archaeological sites. Overlooks and short nature trails can be enjoyed from the paved scenic drive in the park; if you are only here for a day, hike the Cave Spring and Pothole Point Trails. On a longer visit, make a loop of the Big Spring and Squaw Canyon Trails, and hike to Chesler Park. A 10-mile round-trip hike will take you to the Confluence Overlook, a great view of the junction of the Green and Colorado Rivers.

Drivers with 4WD vehicles have their own challenging roads through canyons and other highly scenic areas.

Maze District

Few visitors make it over to the Maze District, which is some of the wildest country in the United States. Only the rivers and a handful of 4WD roads and hiking trails provide access. Experienced hikers can explore the maze of canyons on unmarked routes. Plan to spend at least 2-3 days in this area; even if you're only taking day hikes, it can take a long time to get to any destination here. That said, a hike from the Maze Overlook to the Harvest Scene pictographs is a good bet if you don't have a lot of time. If you have more than one day, head to the Land of Standing Rocks area and hike north to the Chocolate Drops.

Horseshoe Canyon Unit

Horseshoe Canyon Unit, a detached section of the park northwest of the Maze District, is equally remote. It protects the Great Gallery, a group of pictographs left by prehistoric Native Americans. This ancient artwork is reached at the end of a series of long unpaved roads and down a canyon on a moderately challenging hiking trail. Plan to spend a full day exploring this area.

River District

The River District includes long stretches of the Green and the Colorado Rivers. River-running is one of the best ways to experience the inner depths of the park. Boaters can obtain helpful literature and advice from park rangers. Groups planning their own trip through Cataract Canyon need a river-running permit. Flat-water permits are also required. River outfitters based in Moab offer trips ranging from half a day to several days in length.

Getting Around

Canyonlands National Park does not have a visitor shuttle. Neither is the park designed for pedestrians, as the major viewpoints and trailheads are spread out. You really need your own vehicle to visit the park.

The Island in the Sky District, the most popular section, has paved roads and plenty of parking at the viewpoints and trailheads. More remote areas of the park require a four-wheel-drive vehicle. Traffic can be somewhat heavy in the Island area during the summer high season. Look out for bicyclists, RVs, tour buses, and motorcycles.

Tours

Rangers lead interpretive programs in the **Island in the Sky and Needles Districts** (Mar.-Oct.), and they guide hikers into **Horseshoe Canyon** (Sat.-Sun. spring and fall), weather permitting. Call the **Hans Flat Ranger Station** (435/259-2652) for details.

Outfitters

Outfitters must be authorized by the National Park Service to operate in Canyonlands. Most guides concentrate on river trips, but some can take you on mountain bike trips, including vehicle-supported tours of the White Rim 4WD Trail. Most of the guides operating in Canyonlands are based in Moab. For a complete list of authorized outfitters, visit the park website (www.nps.gov/cany).

Biking

- **Escape Adventures** (at Moab Cyclery, 391 S. Main St., Moab, 435/259-7423 or 800/596-2953, www.escapeadventures.com)
- **Rim Tours** (1233 S. US 191, Moab, 435/259-5223 or 800/626-7335, www.rimtours.com)
- **Western Spirit Cycling** (478 Mill Creek Dr., Moab, 435/259-8732 or 800/845-2453, www.westernspirit.com)

Rafting

- **Adrift Adventures** (378 N. Main St., Moab, 435/259-8594 or 800/874-4483, www.adrift.net)
- **Sheri Griffith Expeditions** (503/259-8229 or 800/332-2439, www.griffithexp.com)
- **Tag-A-Long Expeditions** (452 N. Main St., Moab, 435/259-8946 or 800/453-3292, www.tagalong.com)
- **Western River Expeditions** (225 S. Main St., Moab, 435/259-7019 or 866/904-1163, www.westernriver.com)

Backcountry Exploration

A complex system of fees is charged for backcountry camping, 4WD exploration, and river rafting. Except for the main campgrounds at Willow Flat (Island in the Sky) and Squaw Flat (Needles), you'll need a **backcountry camping permit** (http://canypermits.nps.gov). There is a $30 fee for a backpacking permit and, in the Needles District, a $10 day-use fee for a 4WD vehicle. Each of the three major districts has a different policy for backcountry vehicle camping, so it's a good idea to make sure that you understand the details. Backcountry permits are also needed for any trips with horses or stock; check with a ranger for details.

It's possible to reserve a backcountry permit in advance; for spring and fall travel to popular areas like Island in the Sky's White Rim Trail or the Needles backcountry, this is an extremely good idea. Find application forms on the Canyonlands website (www.nps.gov/cany). Forms should be completed and returned at least two weeks in advance of your planned trip. Telephone reservations are not accepted.

Back-road travel is a popular method

of exploring the park. Canyonlands National Park offers hundreds of miles of exceptionally scenic jeep roads, favorites both with mountain bikers and 4WD enthusiasts. Park regulations require all motorized vehicles to have proper registration and licensing for highway use, and all-terrain vehicles are prohibited in the park; drivers must also be licensed. Normally you must have a vehicle with both 4WD and high clearance. It's essential for both motor vehicles and bicycles to stay on existing roads to prevent damage to the delicate desert vegetation. Carry tools, extra fuel, water, and food in case you break down in a remote area.

Before making a trip, drivers and cyclists should talk with a ranger to register and to check on current road conditions, which can change drastically from one day to the next. The rangers can also tell you where to seek help if you get stuck. Primitive campgrounds are provided on most of the roads, but you'll need a backcountry permit from a ranger. Books on backcountry exploration include Charles Wells's *Guide to Moab, UT Backroads & 4-Wheel Drive Trails,* which includes Canyonlands, and Damian Fagan and David Williams's *A Naturalist's Guide to the White Rim Trail.*

One more thing about backcountry travel in Canyonlands: You may need to pack your poop out of the backcountry. Because of the abundance of slickrock and the desert conditions, it's not always possible to dig a hole, and you can't just leave your waste on a rock until it decomposes (decomposition is a very slow process in these conditions). Check with the ranger when you pick up your backcountry permit for more information.

Island in the Sky District

The main part of this district sits on a mesa high above the Colorado and Green Rivers. It is connected to points north by a narrow land bridge just wide enough for the road, known as "the neck," which forms the only vehicle access to the 40-square-mile Island in the Sky. Panoramic views from the "Island" can be enjoyed from any point along the rim; you'll see much of the park and southeastern Utah.

Short hiking trails lead to overlooks and to Mesa Arch, Aztec Butte, Whale Rock, Upheaval Dome, and other features. Longer trails make steep, strenuous descents from the Island to the White Rim Road below. Elevations on the Island average about 6,000 feet.

Although the massive cliffs in the area look to be perfect for rock climbing, in fact much of the rock is not suitable for climbing, and the remoteness of the area means that few routes have been explored. One exception is Taylor Canyon, in the extreme northwest corner of the park, which is reached by lengthy and rugged 4WD roads.

Bring water for all hiking, camping, and travel in Island in the Sky. Except for the bottled water sold at the visitors center, there is no water available in this district of the park.

Getting to Island in the Sky District

From Moab, drive 10 miles north on US 191 and turn left (west) onto Highway 313. If you are coming in from I-70, drive 20 miles south on US 191 from exit 182 to reach the junction. Continue on this paved road for 22 miles west then south to reach the park entrance. These aren't fast roads: From Moab, allow 45 minutes to reach the park.

Sights

Visitors Center

Stop here for information about Island in the Sky and to see exhibits on geology and history; books and maps are available for purchase. The **visitors center** (435/259-4712, 8am-6pm daily Mar.-late Dec.) is located just before the neck crosses to Island in the Sky. From Moab, go northwest 10 miles on US 191, then turn left and drive 15 miles on Highway 313 to the junction for Dead Horse Point

State Park. From here, continue straight for seven miles.

Shafer Canyon Overlook

Half a mile past the visitors center is the **Shafer Canyon Overlook** (on the left, just before crossing the neck). The overlook has good views east down the canyon and onto the incredibly twisting **Shafer Trail Road.** Ranchers Frank and John Schafer built the trail in the early 1900s to move stock to additional pastures (the *c* in their name was later dropped by mapmakers). Uranium prospectors upgraded the trail to a 4WD road during the 1950s so that they could reach their claims at the base of the cliffs. Today, Shafer Trail Road connects the mesa top with White Rim Road and Potash Road, four miles and 1,200 vertical feet below. High-clearance vehicles should be used on the Shafer. It's also fun to ride this road on a mountain bike. Road conditions can vary considerably, so contact a ranger before starting. Shafer Trail Viewpoint, across the neck, provides another perspective 0.5 mile farther.

Back on top of the Island, the paved park road leads south from the neck six miles across Gray's Pasture to a junction. The Grand View Point Overlook road continues south while the road to Upheaval Dome turns west.

Buck Canyon Overlook

As the park road continues south, a series of incredible vistas over the canyons of the Green and Colorado Rivers peek into view. The first viewpoint is **Buck Canyon Overlook,** which looks east over the Colorado River Canyon. Two miles farther is the **Grand View Picnic Area,** a handy lunch stop.

Grand View Point

At the end of the main road, one mile past the Grand View Picnic Area, is **Grand View Point,** perhaps the most spectacular panorama from Island in the Sky. Monument Basin lies directly below, and countless canyons, the Colorado River, the Needles, and mountain ranges are in the distance. The easy one-mile **Grand View Trail** continues past the end of the road for other vistas from the point.

Return to the main road to explore more overlooks and geological curiosities in the western portion of Island in the Sky.

Green River Overlook

The **Green River Overlook** is just west of the main junction on a paved road. From the overlook, Soda Springs Basin and a section of the Green River (deeply entrenched in Stillwater Canyon) can be seen below. Small Willow Flat Campground is on the way to the overlook.

Upheaval Dome Road

At the end of the road, 5.3 miles northwest of the junction, is **Upheaval Dome.** This geologic oddity is a fantastically deformed pile of rock sprawled across a crater about three miles wide and 1,200 feet deep. For many years, Upheaval Dome has kept geologists busy trying to figure out its origins. They once assumed that salt of the Paradox Formation pushed the rock layers upward to form the dome. Now, however, strong evidence suggests that a meteorite impact created the structure. The surrounding ring depression, caused by collapse, and the convergence of rock layers upward toward the center correspond precisely to known impact structures. Shatter cones and microscopic analysis also indicate an impact origin. When the meteorite struck, sometime in the last 150 million years, it formed a crater up to five miles across. Erosion removed some of the overlying rock—perhaps as much as a vertical mile. The underlying salt may have played a role in uplifting the central section.

The easy **Crater View Trail** leads to overlooks on the rim of Upheaval Dome; the first viewpoint is 0.5 mile round-trip, and the second is one mile round-trip. There's also a small **picnic area** here.

Four-Wheeling in Canyonlands

For people who think that just as a dog needs to run free every once in a while, sport-utility vehicles need to occasionally escape the home-to-work loop, Canyonlands is a tonic.

Each of the park's three main districts has a focal point for 4WD travel. In the Island in the Sky, it's the 100-mile-long **White Rim Road.** Four-wheelers in the Needles head to **Elephant Rock** for the challenging climb to a network of roads. The Maze's **Flint Trail** traverses clay slopes that are extremely slippery when wet. Though all of the park's 4WD roads are rugged, those in the Maze are especially challenging, and this area is by far the most remote.

Drivers should note that ATVs are not permitted in national parks. All vehicles must be street-legal. The most commonly used vehicles are jeeps. Four-wheel drivers should be prepared to make basic road or vehicle repairs and should carry the following items:

- at least one full-size spare tire
- extra gas
- extra water
- a shovel
- a high-lift jack
- chains for all four tires, especially October-April

Also note that towing from any backcountry area of Canyonlands is very expensive: It's not uncommon for bills to top $1,000.

Permits are required for overnight trips; camping is only in designated sites.

White Rim Road

This driving adventure along **White Rim Road** follows the White Rim below the sheer cliffs of Island in the Sky. A close look at the light-colored surface reveals ripple marks and cross beds laid down near an ancient coastline. The plateau's east side is about 800 feet above the Colorado River. On the west side, the plateau meets the bank of the Green River.

Travel along the winding road presents a constantly changing panorama of rock, canyons, river, and sky. Keep an eye out for desert bighorn sheep. You'll see all three levels of Island in the Sky District, from the high plateaus to the White Rim to the rivers.

Only 4WD vehicles with high clearance can make the trip. With the proper vehicle, driving is mostly easy but slow and winding; a few steep or rough sections have to be negotiated. The 100-mile trip takes 2-3 days. Allow an extra day to travel all the road spurs.

Mountain bikers find this a great trip too; most cyclists arrange an accompanying 4WD vehicle to carry water and camping gear. Primitive campgrounds along the way provide convenient stopping places. Both cyclists and 4WD drivers must obtain reservations and a **backcountry permit** (http://canypermits.nps.gov, $30) for the White Rim campsites from the Island in the Sky visitors center. Find application forms on the Canyonlands website (www.nps.gov/cany); return the completed application at least two weeks in advance of your planned trip. Questions can be fielded via telephone (435/259-4351, 8am-12:30pm Mon.-Fri.), but no telephone reservations are accepted. Demand exceeds supply during the popular spring and autumn seasons, when you should make reservations as far in advance as possible. No services or developed water sources exist anywhere on the drive, so be sure to have plenty of fuel and water with some to spare. Access points are Shafer Trail Road (from near Island in the Sky) and Potash Road (Hwy. 279 from Moab) on the east and Mineral Bottom Road on the west. White Rim sandstone forms the distinctive plateau crossed on the drive.

Hiking

Neck Springs Trail

Distance: 5.8-mile loop
Duration: 3-4 hours
Elevation change: 300 feet
Effort: moderate
Trailhead: Shafer Canyon Overlook

The trail begins near the Shafer Canyon Overlook and loops down Taylor Canyon to Neck and Cabin Springs, formerly used by ranchers (look for the remains of the old cowboy cabin near Cabin Springs), then climbs back to Island in the Sky Road at a second trailhead 0.5 mile south of the start. A brochure should be available at the trailhead. Water at the springs supports maidenhair fern and other plants. Also watch for birds and wildlife attracted to this spot. Bring water with you, as the springs are not potable.

★ Mesa Arch Trail

Distance: 0.25 mile one-way
Duration: 30 minutes
Elevation change: 80 feet
Effort: easy
Trailhead: on the left, 5.5 miles from the neck

This easy trail leads to a spectacular arch on the rim of the mesa. On the way, the road crosses the grasslands and scattered juniper trees of Gray's Pasture. A trail brochure available at the start describes the ecology of the mesa. The sandstone arch frames views of rock formations below and the La Sal Mountains in the distance. Photographers come here to catch the sun rising through the arch.

White Rim Overlook Trail

Distance: 0.75 mile one-way
Duration: 1 hour
Elevation change: 25 feet
Effort: easy
Trailhead: Grand View Picnic Area

Hike east along a peninsula to an overlook of Monument Basin and beyond. There are also good views of White Rim Road and potholes.

Gooseberry Trail

Distance: 2.5 miles one-way
Duration: 5 hours
Elevation change: 1,400 feet
Effort: strenuous
Trailhead: Grand View Picnic Area

Gooseberry Trail drops off the mesa and makes an extremely steep descent to White Rim Road, just north of Gooseberry Campground. The La Sal Mountains are visible from the trail.

★ Grand View Trail

Distance: 1 mile one-way
Duration: 2 hours
Elevation change: 50 feet
Effort: easy
Trailhead: Grand View Point Overlook

At the overlook, Grand View Trail continues past the end of the road for other vistas from the point, which is the southernmost tip of Island in the Sky. This short hike across the slickrock will really give you a feel for the entire Canyonlands National Park. From the mesa-top trail, you'll see the gorges of the Colorado and Green Rivers come together; across the chasm is the Needles District. Look down to spot vehicles traveling along the White Rim Trail at the base of the mesa.

Aztec Butte Trail

Distance: 1 mile one-way
Duration: 1.5 hours
Elevation change: 200 feet
Effort: moderate
Trailhead: Aztec Butte parking area, 1 mile northwest of road junction on Upheaval Dome Road

It's a bit of a haul up the slickrock to the top of this sandstone butte, but once you get here, you'll be rewarded with a good view of the Island and Taylor Canyon. Atop the butte a loop trail passes several Ancestral Puebloan granaries. Aztec Butte is one of the few areas in Island in the Sky with Native American ruins; the shortage of water in this area prevented permanent settlement.

Whale Rock Trail

Distance: 0.5 mile one-way
Duration: 1 hour
Elevation change: 100 feet
Effort: easy-moderate
Trailhead: Upheaval Dome Road, on the right, 4.4 miles northwest of the road junction

A relatively easy trail climbs Whale Rock, a sandstone hump near the outer rim of Upheaval Dome. In a couple of places you'll have to do some scrambling up the slickrock, which is made easier and a bit less scary thanks to handrails. From the top of the rock, there are good views of the dome.

Upheaval Dome Viewpoint Trail

Distance: 1 mile one-way
Duration: 1.5 hours
Elevation change: 150 feet
Effort: easy
Trailhead: Upheaval Dome parking area

The trail leads to Upheaval Dome overviews; it's about 0.5 mile to the first overlook and a mile to the second. The shorter trail leads to the rim with a view about 1,000 feet down into the jumble of rocks in the craterlike center of Upheaval Dome. The longer trail descends the slickrock and offers even better views. Energetic hikers can explore this formation in depth by circling it on the Syncline Loop Trail or from White Rim Road below.

Syncline Loop Trail

Distance: 8-mile loop
Duration: 5-7 hours
Elevation change: 1,200 feet
Effort: strenuous
Trailhead: Upheaval Dome parking area

Syncline Loop Trail makes a circuit completely around Upheaval Dome. The trail crosses Upheaval Dome Canyon about halfway around from the overlook; walk east 1.5 miles up the canyon to enter the crater itself. This is the only nontechnical

A short hike leads to the clifftop Mesa Arch.

route into the center of the dome. A hike around Upheaval Dome with a side trip to the crater totals 11 miles, and it is best done as an overnight trip. Carry plenty of water for the entire trip; this dry country can be very hot in summer. The Green River is the only reliable source of water. An alternate approach is to start near Upheaval Campsite on White Rim Road; hike four miles southeast on through Upheaval Canyon to a junction with the Syncline Loop Trail, then another 1.5 miles into the crater. The elevation gain is about 600 feet.

Alcove Spring Trail

Distance: 10 miles one-way
Duration: overnight
Elevation change: 1,500 feet
Effort: strenuous
Trailhead: 1.5 miles southeast of the Upheaval Dome parking area

Alcove Spring Trail connects with White Rim Road in Taylor Canyon. Five miles of the 10-mile distance is on the steep trail down through Trail Canyon and five miles is on a jeep road in Taylor Canyon. One downside of this trail is the 4WD traffic, which can be pretty heavy during the spring and fall. From the Taylor Canyon end of the trail, it is not far to the Upheaval Trail, which heads southeast to its junction with the Syncline Trail, which in turn leads to the Upheaval Dome parking area. Allow at least one overnight if you plan to hike this full loop. Day hikers should plan to turn around after the first five-mile section; this is still a very full day of hiking. Carry plenty of water—the trail is hot and dry.

Campgrounds

There is only one developed campground in the Island in the Sky District. **Willow Flat Campground** on Murphy Point Road has only 12 sites ($10), available on a first-come, first-served basis; sites tend to fill up in all seasons except winter. No water or services are available.

Camping is available just outside the park at **Dead Horse Point State Park** (reservations 800/322-3770, www.reserveamerica.com, $25 plus $9 reservation fee), which is also very popular, so don't plan on getting a spot without reserving way ahead. There are also primitive Bureau of Land Management campsites along Highway 313.

Needles District

The Needles District, named for the area's distinctive sandstone spires, showcases some of the finest rock sculptures in Canyonlands National Park. Spires, arches, and monoliths appear in almost every direction. Prehistoric ruins and rock art exist in greater variety and quantity here than elsewhere in the park. Perennial springs and streams bring greenery to the desert.

While a scenic paved road leads to the district, this area of the park has only about a dozen miles of paved roads. Needles doesn't have a lot to offer travelers who are unwilling to get out of their vehicles and hike; however, it's the best section of the park for a wide variety of day hikes. Even a short hike opens up the landscape and leads to remarkable vistas and prehistoric sites.

Getting to the Needles District

To reach the Needles District, go 40 miles south from Moab (or 14 miles north of Monticello) on US 191, turn west onto Highway 211, and continue for 38 miles.

Sights

Visitors Center

Stop at the **visitors center** (west end of Hwy. 211, 435/259-4711, 8am-6pm daily, with extended hours during spring and fall) for information on hiking, back roads, and other aspects of travel in the Needles, as well as backcountry permits, required for all overnight stays in the backcountry, and maps, brochures, and books. Take a moment to look at the little computer-animated slide show on the region's geology—its graphics make it all become clear. When the office isn't open, you'll find information posted outside on the bulletin board.

★ Newspaper Rock Historical Monument

Although not in the park itself, **Newspaper Rock** lies just 150 feet off Highway 211 on Bureau of Land Management land on the way to the Needles District. At Newspaper Rock, a profusion of petroglyphs depict human figures, animals, birds, and abstract designs. These represent 2,000 years of human history during which prehistoric people and Ancestral Puebloan, Fremont, Paiute, Navajo, and Anglo travelers passed through Indian Creek Canyon. The patterns on the smooth sandstone rock face stand out clearly, thanks to a coating of dark desert varnish. A short nature trail introduces you to the area's desert and riparian vegetation.

The cracks in the rock walls around **Indian Creek** offer world-class rock climbing; climbers should track down a copy of *Indian Creek: A Climbing Guide,* by David Bloom, for details and lots of pictures. **Moab Desert Adventures** (415 N. Main St., Moab, 804/814-3872, www.moabdesertadventures.com) offers guided climbing at Indian Creek.

From US 191 between Moab and Monticello, turn west onto Highway 211 and travel 12 miles to Newspaper Rock. Indian Creek's climbing walls start about three miles west of Newspaper Rock.

Needles and Anticline Overlooks

Although outside the park, these viewpoints atop the high mesa east of Canyonlands National Park offer magnificent panoramas of the surrounding area. Part of the BLM's **Canyon Rims Recreation Area** (www.blm.gov), these easily accessed overlooks provide the kind of awe-inspiring vistas over the Needles District that would otherwise require a hike in the park. The turnoff for both overlooks is at milepost 93 on US 191, which is 32 miles south of Moab and 7 miles north of Highway 211. There are also two campgrounds along the access road.

For the **Needles Overlook,** follow the paved road 22 miles west to its end (turn left at the junction 15 miles in). The BLM maintains a picnic area and interpretive exhibits here. A fence protects visitors from the sheer cliffs that drop off more than 1,000 feet. You can see much of Canyonlands National Park and southeastern Utah. Look south for the Sixshooter Peaks and the high country of the Abajo Mountains; southwest for the Needles (thousands of spires reaching for the sky); west for the confluence area of the Green and Colorado Rivers, the Maze District, the Orange Cliffs, and the Henry Mountains; northwest for the lazy bends of the Colorado River Canyon and the sheer-walled mesas of Island in the Sky and Dead Horse Point; north for the Book Cliffs; and northeast for the La Sal Mountains. The changing shadows and colors of the canyon country make for a continuous show throughout the day.

For the **Anticline Overlook,** continue straight north at the junction with the Needles road and drive 17 miles on a good gravel road to the fenced overlook at road's end. You'll be standing 1,600 feet above the Colorado River. The sweeping panorama over the canyons, the river, and the twisted rocks of the Kane Creek Anticline is nearly as spectacular as that from Dead Horse Point, only 5.5 miles west as the crow flies. Salt and other minerals of the Paradox Formation pushed up overlying rocks into the dome visible below. Down-cutting by the Colorado River has revealed the twisted rock layers. Look carefully at the northeast horizon to see an arch in the Windows Section of Arches National Park, 16 miles away.

The BLM operates two campgrounds in the Canyon Rims Recreation Area. **Hatch Point Campground** (10 sites, water May-mid-Oct., $12) has a scenic mesa-top setting just off the road to the Anticline Overlook, about nine miles north of the road junction. Closer to the highway is **Windwhistle Campground** (water May-mid-Oct., $12); it's six miles west of US 191 on the Needles Overlook road.

Needles Outpost

Needles Outpost, a general store just outside the park boundary offers a **campground** (435/979-4007, www.canyonlandsneedlesoutpost.com, mid-Mar.-late Oct., $20 tent or RV, no hookups), groceries, ice, gas, propane, a café, showers ($3 campers, $7 noncampers), and pretty much any camping supply you might have left at home. The campground is a great alternative to the park; sites have a fair amount of privacy and great views onto the park's spires. The turnoff from Highway 211 is one mile before the Needles Visitors Center.

Top to bottom: Newspaper Rock; barrel cactus flowers along Pothole Point Nature Trail; hiking Big Spring Canyon Trail.

Big Spring Canyon Overlook Scenic Drive

The main paved park road continues 6.5 miles past the visitors center to **Big Spring Canyon Overlook.** On the way, you can stop at several nature trails or turn onto 4WD roads. The overlook takes in a view of slickrock-edged canyons dropping away toward the Colorado River.

Hiking

The Needles District includes about 60 miles of backcountry trails. Many interconnect to provide all sorts of day hike and overnight opportunities. Cairns mark the trails, and signs point the way at junctions. You can normally find water in upper Elephant Canyon and canyons to the east in spring and early summer, although whatever remains is often stagnant by midsummer. Always ask the rangers about sources of water, and don't depend on its availability. Treat water from all sources, including springs, before drinking it. Chesler Park and other areas west of Elephant Canyon are very dry; you'll need to bring all your water. Mosquitoes, gnats, and deerflies can be pesky late spring-midsummer, especially in the wetter places, so be sure to bring insect repellent. To plan your trip, obtain the small hiking map available from the visitors center, the National Geographic/Trails Illustrated's Needles District map, or USGS topographic maps. Overnight backcountry hiking requires a permit ($30 per group). Permits can be hard to get at the last minute during the busy spring hiking season, but you can apply for your permit any time after mid-July for the following spring. Find permit applications on the Canyonlands website (www.nps.gov/cany). Note that campers at sites in Chesler Park, Elephant Canyon, and at Peekaboo will be required to pack out their human waste.

Roadside Ruin Trail

Distance: 0.3 mile round-trip
Duration: 20 minutes
Elevation change: 20 feet
Effort: easy
Trailhead: on the left, 0.4 mile past the visitors center

This is one of two easy hikes near the visitors center. It passes near a well-preserved Ancestral Puebloan granary. A trail guide available at the start tells about the Ancestral Puebloans and the local plants.

Cave Spring Trail

Distance: 0.6 mile round-trip
Duration: 45 minutes
Elevation change: 50 feet
Effort: easy
Trailhead: Cave Spring
Directions: Turn left 0.7 mile past the visitors center and follow signs about 1 mile to the trailhead.

Don't miss the Cave Spring Trail, which introduces the geology and ecology of the park and leads to an old cowboy line camp. Pick up the brochure at the beginning. The loop goes clockwise, crossing some slickrock; two ladders assist hikers on the steep sections. Native Americans first used these rock overhangs for shelter, and faint pictographs still decorate the rock walls. Much later—from the late 1800s until the park was established in 1964—cowboys used these open caves as a line camp. The National Park Service has re-created the line camp, just 50 yards in from the trailhead, with period furnishings and equipment. If you're not up for the full hike, or would rather not climb ladders, the cowboy camp and the pictographs are just a five-minute walk from the trailhead.

This trail is a good introduction to hiking on slickrock and using rock cairns to find your way. Signs identify plants along the route.

Pothole Point Nature Trail

Distance: 0.6 mile round-trip
Duration: 40 minutes
Elevation change: 20 feet
Effort: easy
Trailhead: parking area on the left side of Big Spring Canyon Overlook Scenic Drive, five miles past the visitors center

Pothole Ecosystems

At Canyonlands it's easy to be in awe of the deep canyons and big desert rivers. But the little details of Canyonlands geology and ecology are pretty wonderful too. Consider the potholes: shallow depressions dusted with windblown dirt. These holes, which range from less than an inch to several feet deep, fill after rainstorms and bring entire little ecosystems to life.

Pothole dwellers must be able to survive long periods of dryness, then pack as much living as possible into the short wet periods. Some creatures, like the tadpole shrimp, live only for a couple of weeks. Others, like the spadefoot toad, hatch from drought-resistant eggs when water is present, quickly pass through the critical tadpole stage, then move onto dry land, returning to mate and lay eggs in potholes.

Although pothole dwellers are tough enough to survive in a dormant form during the long dry spells, most are very sensitive to sudden water-chemistry changes, temperature changes, sediment input, being stepped on, and being splashed out onto dry land. Humans should never use pothole water for swimming, bathing, or drinking, as this can drastically change the salinity or pH of a pool. Organisms are unable to adapt to these human-generated changes, which occur suddenly, unlike slow, natural changes. While the desert pothole ecosystems may seem unimportant, they act as an indicator of the health of the larger ecosystems in which they occur.

Highlights of this hike across the slickrock are the many potholes dissolved in the Cedar Mesa sandstone. A brochure illustrates the fairy shrimp, tadpole shrimp, horsehair worms, snails, and other creatures that spring to life when rain fills the potholes. Desert varnish rims the potholes; it forms when water evaporates, leaving mineral residues on the surface of the rocks. In addition to the potholes, you'll enjoy fine views of distant buttes from the trail.

Slickrock Trail

Distance: 2.4 miles round-trip
Duration: 2 hours
Elevation change: 150 feet
Effort: easy-moderate
Trailhead: parking area on the right side of Big Spring Canyon Overlook Scenic Drive, 6.2 miles past the visitors center

The Slickrock Trail leads north to a series of four viewpoints, including a panoramic view over much of southeastern Utah, and overlooks of Big Spring and Little Spring Canyons. As its name indicates, much of the trail is across slickrock, but there are enough pockets of soil to support a good springtime display of wildflowers. The trailhead is almost at the end of the paved road, where **Big Spring Canyon Overlook,** 6.5 miles past the visitors center, marks the end of the scenic drive but not the scenery.

Confluence Overlook Trail

Distance: 5.5 miles one-way
Duration: 5 hours
Elevation change: 1,250 feet
Effort: moderate-strenuous
Trailhead: Big Spring Canyon Overlook

The Confluence Overlook Trail begins at the end of the paved road and winds west to an overlook of the Green and Colorado Rivers 1,000 feet below; there's no trail down to the rivers. The trail starts with some ups and downs, crossing Big Spring and Elephant Canyons, and follows a jeep road for a short distance. Much of the trail is through open country, so it can get quite hot. Higher points have good views of the Needles to the south. You might see rafts in the water or bighorn sheep on the cliffs. Except for a few short steep sections, this trail is level and fairly easy; it's the length of this 11-mile round-trip to the confluence as well as the hot sun that make it challenging. A very early start is recommended in summer because there's little shade. Carry water even if you don't plan to go all the way. This enchanting country has lured many a hiker beyond his or her original goal.

Peekaboo Trail

Distance: 5 miles one-way
Duration: 5-6 hours
Elevation change: 550 feet
Effort: strenuous
Trailhead: Squaw Flat trailhead
Directions: A road to Squaw Flat Campground and Elephant Hill turns left 2.7 miles past the visitors center. The Squaw Flat trailhead sits a short distance south of the campground and is reached by a separate signed road. You can also begin from a trailhead in the campground itself.

Peekaboo Trail winds southeast over rugged up-and-down terrain, including some steep sections of slickrock (best avoided when wet, icy, or covered with snow) and a couple of ladders. There's little shade, so carry water. The trail follows Squaw Canyon, climbs over a pass to Lost Canyon, then crosses more slickrock before descending to Peekaboo Campground on Salt Creek Road (accessible by 4WD vehicles). Look for Ancestral Puebloan ruins on the way and rock art at the campground. A rockslide took out Peekaboo Spring, which is still shown on some maps. Options on this trail include a turnoff south through Squaw or Lost Canyon to make a loop of 8.75 miles or more.

Squaw Canyon Trail

Distance: 3.75 miles one-way
Duration: 4 hours
Elevation change: 700 feet
Effort: moderate
Trailhead: Squaw Flat trailhead
Directions: A road to Squaw Flat Campground and Elephant Hill turns left 2.7 miles past the visitors center. The Squaw Flat trailhead is a short distance south of the campground and is reached by a separate signed road. You can also begin from a trailhead in the campground itself.

Squaw Canyon Trail follows the canyon south. Intermittent water can often be found until late spring. You can take a connecting trail (Peekaboo, Lost Canyon, or Big Spring Canyon) or cross a slickrock pass to Elephant Canyon.

Lost Canyon Trail

Distance: 3.25 miles one-way
Duration: 4-5 hours
Elevation change: 360 feet
Effort: moderate-strenuous
Trailhead: Squaw Flat trailhead
Directions: A road to Squaw Flat Campground and Elephant Hill turns left 2.7 miles past the visitors center. The Squaw Flat trailhead sits a short distance south of the campground and is reached by a separate signed road. You can also begin from a trailhead in the campground itself.

Lost Canyon Trail is reached via Peekaboo or Squaw Canyon Trails and makes a loop with them. Lost Canyon is surprisingly lush, and you may be forced to wade through water. Most of the trail is in the wash bottom, except for a section of slickrock to Squaw Canyon.

Big Spring Canyon Trail

Distance: 3.75 miles one-way
Duration: 4 hours
Elevation change: 370 feet
Effort: moderate-strenuous
Trailhead: Squaw Flat trailhead
Directions: A road to Squaw Flat Campground and Elephant Hill turns left 2.7 miles past the visitors center. The Squaw Flat trailhead is a short distance south of the campground and is reached by a separate signed road. You can also begin from a trailhead in the campground itself.

Big Spring Canyon Trail crosses an outcrop of slickrock from the trailhead, then follows the canyon bottom to the head of the canyon. It's a lovely springtime hike with lots of flowers, including the fragrant cliffrose. Except in summer, you can usually find intermittent water along the way. At canyon's end, a steep slickrock climb leads to Squaw Canyon Trail and back to the trailhead for a 7.5-mile loop. Another possibility is to turn southwest to the head of Squaw Canyon, then hike over a saddle to Elephant Canyon, for a 10.5-mile loop.

Chesler Park

Distance: 3 miles one-way
Duration: 3-4 hours
Elevation change: 920 feet
Effort: moderate
Trailhead: Elephant Hill parking area or Squaw Flat trailhead—increases the round-trip distance by 2 miles
Directions: Drive west 3 miles past the Squaw Flat Campground turnoff (on passable dirt roads) to the Elephant Hill picnic area and trailhead at the base of Elephant Hill.

The Elephant Hill parking area doesn't always inspire confidence: Sounds of racing engines and burning rubber can often be heard from above as vehicles attempt the difficult 4WD road that begins just past the picnic area. However, the noise quickly fades as you hit the trail. Chesler Park is a favorite hiking destination. A lovely desert meadow contrasts with the red and white spires that give the Needles District its name. An old cowboy line camp is on the west side of the rock island in the center of the park. The trail winds through sand and slickrock before ascending a small pass through the Needles to Chesler Park. Once inside, you can take the **Chesler Park Loop Trail** (5 miles) completely around the park. The loop includes the unusual 0.5-mile **Joint Trail,** which follows the bottom of a very narrow crack. Camping in Chesler Park is restricted to certain areas; check with a ranger.

Druid Arch

Distance: 5.5 miles one-way
Duration: 5-7 hours
Elevation change: 1,000 feet
Effort: strenuous
Trailhead: Elephant Hill parking area or Squaw Flat trailhead—increases the round-trip distance by 2 miles
Directions: Drive west 3 miles past the Squaw Flat Campground turnoff (on passable dirt roads) to the Elephant Hill picnic area and trailhead at the base of Elephant Hill.

Druid Arch reminds many people of the massive slabs at Stonehenge in England, which are popularly associated with the druids. Follow the Chesler Park Trail two miles to Elephant Canyon, turn up the canyon for 3.5 miles, and then make a steep 0.25-mile climb, which includes a ladder and some scrambling, to the arch. Upper Elephant Canyon has seasonal water but is closed to camping.

Lower Red Lake Canyon Trail

Distance: 9.5 miles one-way
Duration: 2 days
Elevation change: 1,000 feet
Effort: strenuous
Trailhead: Elephant Hill parking area or Squaw Flat trailhead (increases the round-trip distance by 2 miles)
Directions: Drive west 3 miles past the Squaw Flat campground turnoff (on passable dirt roads) to the Elephant Hill picnic area and trailhead at the base of Elephant Hill.

Lower Red Lake Canyon Trail provides access to the Colorado River's Cataract Canyon. This long, strenuous trip is best suited for experienced hikers and ideally completed in two days. Distance from the Elephant Hill trailhead is 19 miles round-trip; you'll be walking on 4WD roads and trails. If you can drive Elephant Hill 4WD Road to the trail junction in Cyclone Canyon, the hike is only eight miles round-trip. The most difficult trail section is a steep talus slope that drops 700 feet in 0.5 mile into the lower canyon. The canyon has little shade and lacks any water source above the river. Summer heat can make the trip grueling; temperatures tend to be 5-10°F hotter than on other Needles trails. The river level drops between midsummer and autumn, allowing hikers to go along the shore both downstream to see the rapids and upstream to the confluence. Undertows and strong currents make the river dangerous to cross.

Mountain Biking and 4WD Exploration

Visitors with bicycles or 4WD vehicles can explore the many backcountry roads that lead to the outback. More than 50 miles of challenging roads link primitive campsites, remote trailheads, and sites with ancient cultural remnants. Some roads in the Needles District are rugged and require previous experience in handling 4WD vehicles on steep inclines and in deep sand. Be aware that towing charges from this area commonly run over $1,000.

The best route for mountain bikers is the seven-mile-long Colorado Overlook Road, which starts near the visitors center. Although very steep for the first stretch and busy with 4WD vehicles spinning their wheels on the hill, Elephant Hill Road is another good bet, with just a few sandy parts. Start here and do a combination ride and hike to the Confluence Overlook. It's about eight miles from the Elephant Hill parking area to the confluence; the final 0.5 mile is on a trail, so you'll have to lock up your bike and walk this last bit. Horse Canyon and Lavender Canyon are too sandy for pleasant biking.

All motor vehicles and bicycles must purchase a $10 day-use permit and remain on designated roads. Overnight backcountry trips with bicycles or motor vehicles require a permit ($30 per group).

Salt Creek Canyon 4WD Road

The rugged **Salt Creek Canyon 4WD Road** begins near Cave Spring Trail, crosses sage flats for the next 2.5 miles, and then terminates at Peekaboo Campground. Hikers can continue south into a spectacular canyon on Upper Salt Creek Trail.

Horse Canyon 4WD Road turns off to the left shortly before the mouth of Salt Canyon. The round-trip distance, including a side trip to Tower Ruin, is about 13 miles; other attractions include Paul Bunyan's Potty, Castle Arch, Fortress Arch, and side canyon hiking. Salt and Horse Canyons can easily be driven in 4WD vehicles. Salt Canyon is usually closed in summer because of quicksand after flash floods and in winter due to shelf ice.

Davis and Lavender Canyons

Both **Davis and Lavender Canyons** are accessed via Davis Canyon Road off Highway 211; contain great scenery, arches, and Native American historic sites; and are easily visited with high-clearance vehicles. Davis is about 20 miles round-trip, while sandy Lavender Canyon is about 26 miles round-trip. Try to allow plenty of time in either canyon, because there is much to see and many inviting side canyons to hike. You can camp on BLM land just outside the park boundaries, but not in the park itself.

Colorado Overlook 4WD Road

The popular **Colorado Overlook 4WD Road** begins beside the visitors center and follows Salt Creek to Lower Jump Overlook. It then bounces across slickrock to a view of the Colorado River, upstream from the confluence. Driving, for the most part, is easy-moderate, although it's very rough for the last 1.5 miles. Round-trip distance is 14 miles. This is also a good mountain bike ride.

Elephant Hill 4WD Loop Road

The rugged backcountry **Elephant Hill 4WD Loop Road** begins three miles past the Squaw Flat Campground turnoff. Only experienced drivers with stout vehicles should attempt the extremely rough and steep climb up Elephant Hill (coming up the back of Elephant Hill is even worse). The loop is about 10 miles round-trip. Connecting roads go to the Confluence Overlook trailhead (the viewpoint is one mile round-trip on foot), the Joint trailhead (Chesler Park is two miles round-trip on foot), and several canyons. Some road sections on the loop are one-way. In addition to Elephant Hill, a few other difficult spots must be negotiated. The parallel canyons in this area are grabens caused by faulting, where a layer of salt has shifted deep underground.

This area can also be reached by a long route south of the park using Cottonwood Canyon and Beef Basin Road from Highway 211, about 60 miles one-way. You'll enjoy spectacular vistas from the Abajo Highlands. Two very steep descents from Pappys Pasture into Bobbys Hole effectively make this section one-way; travel from Elephant Hill up Bobbys Hole is possible but much more difficult than going the other way, and it may require hours of road-building. The Bobbys Hole route may be impassable at times; ask about conditions at the BLM office in Monticello or at the Needles Visitors Center.

Campgrounds

The **Squaw Flat Campground** (year-round, no reservations, $20) about six miles from the visitors center, has water and 26 sites, many snuggled under the slickrock. RVs must be less than 28 feet long. Rangers present evening programs at the campfire circle on Loop A spring through autumn.

If you can't find a space at Squaw Flat, a common occurrence in spring and fall, the private campground at **Needles Outpost** (435/979-4007, www.canyonlandsneedlesoutpost.com, mid-Mar.-late Oct., $20 tents or RVs, no hookups, showers $3), just outside the park entrance, is a good alternative.

Nearby BLM land also offers a number of places to camp. A string of campsites along **Lockhart Basin Road** are convenient and inexpensive. Lockhart Basin Road heads north from Highway 211 about five miles east of the entrance to the Needles District. **Hamburger Rock Campground** (no water, $6) is about one mile up the road. North of Hamburger Rock, camping is dispersed, with many small (no water, free) campsites at turnoffs from the road. Not surprisingly, the road gets rougher the farther north you travel; beyond Indian Creek Falls, it's best to have 4WD. These campsites are very popular with climbers who are here to scale the walls at Indian Creek.

There are two first-come, first-served campgrounds ($12) in the **Canyon Rims Special Recreation Management Area** (www.blm.gov). **Windwhistle Campground,** backed by cliffs to the south, has fine views to the north and a nature trail; follow the main road from US 191 for six miles and turn left. At **Hatch Point Campground,** in a piñon-juniper woodland, you can enjoy views to the north. Go 24 miles in on the paved and gravel roads toward Anticline Overlook, then turn right and continue for one mile. Both campgrounds have water May-mid-October, tables, grills, and outhouses.

The Maze District

Only adventurous and experienced travelers will want to visit this rugged land west of the Green and Colorado Rivers. Vehicle access wasn't even possible until 1957, when mineral-exploration roads first entered what later became Canyonlands National Park. Today, you'll need a high-clearance 4WD vehicle, a horse, or your own two feet to get around, and most visitors spend at least three days in the district. The National Park Service plans to keep this district in its remote and primitive condition. An airplane flight, which is recommended if you can't come overland, provides the only easy way to see the scenic features.

The names of erosional forms describe the landscape—Orange Cliffs, Golden Stairs, the Fins, Land of Standing Rocks, Lizard Rock, the Doll House, Chocolate Drops, the Maze, and Jasper Canyon. The many-fingered canyons of the Maze gave the district its name; although it is not a true maze, the canyons give that impression. It is extremely important to have a good map before entering this part of Canyonlands. National Geographic/

Trails Illustrated makes a good one, called *Canyonlands National Park Maze District, NE Glen Canyon NRA*.

Getting to the Maze District

Dirt roads to the **Hans Flat Ranger Station** (435/259-2652, 8am-4:30pm daily) and Maze District branch off from Highway 24 (across from the Goblin Valley State Park turnoff) and Highway 95 (take the usually unmarked Hite-Orange Cliffs Road between the Dirty Devil and Hite Bridges at Lake Powell). The easiest way in is the graded 46-mile road from Highway 24; it's fast, although sometimes badly corrugated. The 4WD Hite Road (also called Orange Cliffs Rd.) is longer, bumpier, and, for some drivers, tedious; it's 54 miles from the turnoff at Highway 95 to the Hans Flat Ranger Station via the Flint Trail. All roads to the Maze District cross Glen Canyon National Recreation Area. From Highway 24, two-wheel-drive vehicles with good clearance can travel to Hans Flat Ranger Station and other areas near, but not actually in, the Maze District. From the ranger station it takes at least three hours of skillful four-wheeling to drive into the canyons of the Maze.

One other way of getting to the Maze District is by river. **Tex's Riverways** (435/259-5101 or 877/662-2839, www.texsriverways.com, about $115 pp) can arrange a jet-boat shuttle on the Colorado River from Moab to the Spanish Bottom. After the two-hour boat ride, it's 1,260 vertical feet uphill in a little over one mile to the Doll House via the Spanish Bottom Trail.

Planning an Expedition

Maze District explorers need a **backcountry permit** (http://canypermits.nps.gov, $30) for overnight trips. Note that a backcountry permit in this district is not a reservation. You may have to share a site, especially in the popular spring months. As in the rest of the park, only designated sites can be used for

camping in style at Needles Outpost

vehicle camping. You don't need a permit to camp in the adjacent Glen Canyon National Recreation Area (NRA) or on BLM land.

There are no developed sources of water in the Maze District. Hikers can obtain water from springs in some canyons (check with a ranger to find out which are flowing) or from the rivers; purify all water before drinking. The Maze District has 21 campsites scattered around its remote backcountry, a few of which take up to six hours of hard, technical four-wheeling to reach. Most of the sites have a nine-person, three-vehicle limit. The campsite at Flint Seep takes up to 16 people and five vehicles. There are no bathrooms, water, or picnic tables, and you have to obtain a backcountry permit to use the sites.

The National Geographic/Trails Illustrated topographic map of the Maze District describes and shows the few roads and trails here; some routes and springs are marked on it too. Agile hikers experienced in desert and canyon travel may want to take off on cross-country routes, which are either unmarked or lightly cairned.

Extra care and preparation must be undertaken for travel in both Glen Canyon NRA and the Maze. Always ask rangers beforehand for current conditions. Be sure to leave an itinerary with someone reliable who can contact the rangers if you're overdue returning. Unless the rangers know where to look for you in case of breakdown or accident, a rescue could take weeks.

Sights

Land of Standing Rocks

Here in the heart of the Maze District, strangely shaped rock spires stand guard over myriad canyons. Six camping areas offer scenic places to stay (permit required). Hikers have a choice of many ridge and canyon routes from the 4WD road, a trail to a confluence overlook, and a trail that descends to the Colorado River near Cataract Canyon.

Getting to the **Land of Standing Rocks** takes some careful driving, especially on a three-mile stretch above Teapot Canyon. The many washes and small canyon crossings here make for slow going. Short-wheelbase vehicles have the easiest time, of course. The turnoff for Land of Standing Rocks Road is 6.6 miles from the junction at the bottom of the Flint Trail via a wash shortcut (add about three miles if driving via the four-way intersection). The lower end of the Golden Stairs foot trail is 7.8 miles in; the western end of the Ernies Country route trailhead is 8.6 miles in; the Wall is 12.7 miles in; Chimney Rock is 15.7 miles in; and the Doll House is 19 miles in, at the end of the road. If you drive from the south on Hite-Orange Cliffs Road, stop at the self-registration stand at the four-way intersection, about 31 miles in from Highway 95; you can write your own permit for overnights in the park.

Tall, rounded rock spires near the end

of the road reminded early visitors of dolls, hence the name Doll House. The Doll House is a great place to explore, or you can head out on nearby routes and trails.

North Point

Hans Flat Ranger Station and this peninsula, which reaches out to the east and north, are at an elevation of about 6,400 feet. Panoramas from **North Point** take in the vastness of Canyonlands, including the Maze, Needles, and Island in the Sky Districts. From **Millard Canyon Overlook,** just 0.9 mile past the ranger station, you can see arches, Cleopatra's Chair, and features as distant as the La Sal Mountains and Book Cliffs. For the best views, drive out to Panorama Point, about 10.5 miles one-way from the ranger station. A spur road to the left goes two miles to Cleopatra's Chair, a massive sandstone monolith and area landmark.

Hiking

Maze Overlook Trail

Distance: 3 miles one-way (to Harvest Scene)
Duration: 3-4 hours
Elevation change: 550 feet
Effort: strenuous
Trailhead: at the end of the road in the Maze District

Here, at the edge of the sinuous canyons of the Maze, the Maze Overlook Trail drops one mile into the South Fork of Horse Canyon; bring a 25-foot-long rope to help lower backpacks through one difficult section. Once in the canyon, you can walk around to the Harvest Scene, a group of prehistoric pictographs, or do a variety of day hikes or backpacking trips. These canyons have water in some places; check with the ranger when you get your permit. At least four routes connect with the 4WD road in Land of Standing Rocks, shown on the Trails Illustrated map. Hikers can also climb Petes Mesa from the canyons or head downstream to explore Horse Canyon, but a dry fall blocks access to the Green River. You can stay at primitive camping areas (backcountry permit required) and enjoy the views.

The Golden Stairs

Distance: 2 miles one-way
Duration: 3 hours
Elevation change: 800 feet
Effort: moderate
Trailhead: bottom of Flint Trail, at Golden Stairs camping area
Directions: Drive the challenging Flint Trail, a 4WD route, to its bottom. The top of the Golden Stairs is 2 miles east of the road junction at the bottom of the Flint Trail.

Hikers can descend this steep foot trail to the Land of Standing Rocks Road in a fraction of the time it takes for drivers to follow the roads. The trail offers good views of Ernies Country, the vast southern area of the Maze District, but it lacks shade or water. The eponymous stairs are not actual steps carved into the rock, but a series of natural ledges.

Chocolate Drops Trail

Distance: 4.5 miles one-way
Duration: 5 hours
Elevation change: 550 feet
Effort: strenuous
Trailhead: Chocolate Drops
Directions: The Land of Standing Rocks turnoff is 6.6 miles from the junction at the bottom of the Flint Trail. The trailhead is just east of the Wall camping area.

The well-named Chocolate Drops can be reached by a trail from the Wall near the beginning of the Land of Standing Rocks. A good day hike makes a loop from Chimney Rock to the Harvest Scene pictographs; take the ridge route (toward Petes Mesa) in one direction and the canyon fork northwest of Chimney Rock in the other. Follow your topographic map through the canyons, and the cairns between the canyons and ridge. Other routes from Chimney Rock lead to lower Jasper Canyon (no river access) or into Shot and Water Canyons and on to the Green River.

Spanish Bottom Trail

Distance: 1.2 miles one-way
Duration: 3 hours
Elevation change: 1,260 feet
Effort: strenuous
Trailhead: Doll House, near Camp 1, just before the end of the Land of Standing Rocks Road

This trail drops steeply to Spanish Bottom beside the Colorado River; a thin trail leads downstream into Cataract Canyon and the first of a long series of rapids. **Surprise Valley Overlook Trail** branches to the right off the Spanish Bottom Trail after about 300 feet and winds south past some dolls to a T junction (turn right for views of Surprise Valley, Cataract Canyon, and beyond); the trail ends at some well-preserved granaries, after 1.5 miles one-way. From the same trailhead, the **Colorado-Green River Overlook Trail** heads north five miles one-way from the Doll House to a viewpoint of the confluence. See the area's Trails Illustrated map for routes, trails, and roads.

4WD Exploration

Flint Trail 4WD Road

This narrow, rough 4WD road connects the Hans Flat area with the Maze Overlook, Doll House, and other areas below. The road, driver, and vehicle should all be in good condition before attempting this route. Winter snow and mud close the road late December-March, as can rainstorms anytime. Check on conditions with a ranger before you go. If you're starting from the top, stop at the signed overlook just before the descent to scout for vehicles headed up (the Flint Trail has very few places to pass). The top of the Flint Trail is 14 miles south of Hans Flat Ranger Station; at the bottom, 2.8 nervous miles later, you can turn left and go two miles to the Golden Stairs trailhead or 12.7 miles to the Maze Overlook; keep straight 28 miles to the Doll House or 39 miles to Highway 95.

Horseshoe Canyon Unit

This canyon contains exceptional prehistoric rock art in a separate section of Canyonlands National Park. Ghostly life-size pictographs in the Great Gallery provide an intriguing look into the past. Archaeologists think that the images had religious importance, although the meaning of the figures remains unknown. The Barrier Canyon Style of these drawings has been credited to an archaic culture beginning at least 8,000 years ago and lasting until about AD 450. Horseshoe Canyon also contains rock art left by the subsequent Fremont and Ancestral Puebloan people. The relationship between the earlier and later prehistoric groups hasn't been determined.

Call the **Hans Flat Ranger Station** (435/259-2652) to inquire about ranger-led hikes to the Great Gallery (Sat.-Sun. spring); when staff members are available, additional walks may be scheduled. In-shape hikers will have no trouble making the hike on their own, however.

Getting to the Horseshoe Canyon Unit

Horseshoe Canyon is a noncontiguous unit of Canyonlands, and requires quite a bit of driving to reach. The access road turns east from Highway 24 between Hanksville (14 miles south) and I-70 exit 149 (19 miles north). The access road is signed, but it's also handy to note that the turn is across the road from the entrance to Goblin Valley State Park. Once on this graded dirt road, travel 30 miles east to Horseshoe Canyon, keeping left at the Hans Flat Ranger Station and Horseshoe Canyon turnoff 25 miles in. In good weather, the road is passable to most passenger cars, though the road has many washboard sections and blowing sand can be a hazard. If you have questions, call **Hans Flat Ranger Station** (435/259-2652) or another of the park's visitors centers. Allow an hour to make the journey in from Highway 24 to the canyon and the Great Gallery trailhead.

Hiking

Great Gallery Trail

Distance: 3.5 miles one-way
Duration: 4-6 hours
Elevation change: 800 feet
Effort: moderate-strenuous
Trailhead: parking area on the canyon's west rim

Horseshoe Canyon is northwest of the Maze District. From the rim and parking area, the trail descends 800 feet in one mile on an old jeep road, which is now closed to vehicles. At the canyon bottom, turn right and go two miles upstream to the Great Gallery. The sandy canyon floor is mostly level; trees provide shade in some areas.

Look for other rock art along the canyon walls on the way to the Great Gallery. Take care not to touch any of the drawings, because they're fragile and irreplaceable. The oil from your hands will remove the paints. Horseshoe Canyon also offers pleasant scenery and spring wildflowers. Carry plenty of water. Neither camping nor pets are allowed in the canyon, although horses are OK, but you can camp on the rim. Contact the **Hans Flat Ranger Station** (435/259-2652) or the **Moab Information Center** (435/259-8825 or 800/635-6622) for road and trail conditions.

Horseshoe Canyon can also be reached via primitive roads from the east. A 4WD road runs north 21 miles from Hans Flat Ranger Station and drops steeply into the canyon from the east side. The descent on this road is so rough that most people prefer to park on the rim and hike the last mile of road. A vehicle barricade prevents driving right up to the rock-art panel, but the 1.5-mile walk is easy.

The River District

The River District is the name of the administrative unit of the park that oversees conservation and recreation for the Green and Colorado Rivers.

The Green River cuts through the Canyonlands.

Generally speaking, there are two boating experiences on offer in the park's River District. First are the relatively gentle paddling and rafting experiences on the Colorado and Green Rivers above their confluence. After these rivers meet, deep in the park, the resulting Colorado River then tumbles into Cataract Canyon, a white-water destination par excellence with abundant Class III-V rapids.

While rafting and canoeing enthusiasts can plan their own trips to any section of these rivers, by far the vast majority of people sign on with outfitters, often located in Moab, and let them do the planning and work. Do-it-yourselfers must start with the knowledge that permits are required for most trips but are not always easily procured; because these rivers flow through rugged and remote canyons, most trips require multiple days and can be challenging to plan.

No matter how you execute a trip through the River District, there are several issues to think about beforehand. There are no designated campsites along the rivers in Canyonlands. During periods of high water, camps can be difficult to find, especially for large groups. During late summer and fall, sandbars are usually plentiful and make ideal camps. There is no access to potable water along the river, so river-runners either need to bring along their own water or be prepared to purify river water.

While it's possible to fish in the Green and Colorado Rivers, these desert rivers don't offer much in the way of species that most people consider edible. You'll need to bring along all your foodstuffs.

The park requires all river-runners to pack out their solid human waste. Specially designed portable toilets that fit into rafts and canoes can be rented from most outfitters in Moab.

River-Running Above the Confluence

The Green and Colorado Rivers flow smoothly through their canyons above the confluence of the two rivers. Almost any shallow-draft boat can navigate these waters: Canoes, kayaks, rafts, and powerboats are commonly used. Any travel requires advance planning because of the remoteness of the canyons and the scarcity of river access points. No campgrounds, supplies, or other facilities exist past Moab on the Colorado River or the town of Green River on the Green River. All river-runners must follow park regulations, which include carrying life jackets, using a fire pan for fires, and packing out all garbage and solid human waste. The river flow on both the Colorado and the Green Rivers averages a gentle 2-4 mph (7-10 mph at high water). Boaters typically do 20 miles per day in canoes and 15 miles per day on rafts.

The Colorado has one modest rapid, called the Slide (1.5 miles above the

Endangered Fish of the Colorado River Basin

Colorado pikeminnow (*Ptychocheilus lucius*): Native only to the Colorado and its tributaries, this species is the largest minnow in North America. It has been reported to weigh up to 100 pounds and measure six feet long. Loss of habitat caused by dam construction has greatly curtailed its size and range. Fishers often confuse the smaller, more common roundtail chub (*Gila robusta*) with the Colorado pikeminnow; the chub is distinguished by a smaller mouth extending back only to the front of the eye.

Humpback chub (*Gila cypha*): Scientists first described this fish only in 1946 and know little about its life. This small fish usually weighs less than two pounds and measures less than 13 inches. Today the humpback chub hangs on the verge of extinction; it has retreated to a few small areas of the Colorado River where the water still runs warm, muddy, and swift. The bonytail chub (*Gila elegans*) has a similar size and shape, but without a hump; its numbers are also rapidly declining.

Humpback or razorback sucker (*Xyrauchen texanus*): This large sucker grows to weights of 10-16 pounds and lengths of about three feet. Its numbers have been slowly decreasing, especially above the Grand Canyon. It requires warm, fast-flowing water to reproduce. Mating is a bizarre ritual in the spring: When the female has selected a suitable spawning site, two male fish press against the sides of her body. The female begins to shake her body until the eggs and spermatozoa are expelled simultaneously. One female can spawn three times, but she uses a different pair of males each time.

confluence), where rocks constrict the river to one-third of its normal width; the rapid is roughest during high water levels in May-June. This is the only difficulty on the 64 river miles from Moab. Inexperienced canoeists and rafters may wish to portage around it. The most popular launch points on the Colorado are the **Moab Dock** (just upstream from the US 191 bridge near town) and the **Potash Dock** (17 miles downriver on Potash Rd./Hwy. 279).

On the Green River, boaters at low water need to watch for rocky areas at the mouth of Millard Canyon (33.5 miles above the confluence, where a rock bar extends across the river) and at the mouth of Horse Canyon (14.5 miles above the confluence, where a rock and gravel bar on the right leaves only a narrow channel on the left side). The trip from the town of Green River through Labyrinth and Stillwater Canyons is 120 miles. Launch points include **Green River State Park** (off I-70, town of Green River) and **Mineral Canyon** (52 miles above the confluence and reached on a fair-weather road from Hwy. 313). Boaters who launch at Green River State Park pass through Labyrinth Canyon; a free interagency permit is required for travel along this stretch of the river. Permits are available from the **BLM office** (82 Dogwood Ave., Moab, 435/259-2100, 7:45am-noon Mon.-Fri.), the **Canyonlands National Park headquarters** (2282 SW Resource Blvd., Moab, 435/719-2313, 8am-4pm Mon.-Fri.), **Green River State Park** in Green River, or the **John Wesley Powell River History Museum** (1765 E. Main St., Green River, 435/564-3427, 8am-7pm daily). A permit can also be downloaded from the **BLM website** (www.blm.gov).

No roads go to the confluence. The easiest return to civilization for nonmotorized craft is a pickup by jet boat from Moab by **Tex's Riverways** (435/259-5101 or 877/662-2839, www.texsriverways.com) or **Tag-A-Long Tours** (800/453-3292, www.tagalong.com). A far more difficult way out is hiking either of two trails just above the Cataract Canyon Rapids to 4WD roads on the rim. Don't plan to attempt this unless you're a very strong hiker and have a packable watercraft.

National park rangers require that boaters above the confluence obtain a **backcountry permit** (http://canypermits.nps.gov, $30) either in person from the **Moab National Park Service office** (2282 SW Resource Blvd., 435/719-2313, 8am-4pm Mon.-Fri.), via the Internet (http://canypermits.nps.gov), or by mail (National Park Service Reservation Office, 2282 SW Resource Blvd., Moab, UT 84532-3298) or fax (435/259-4285) at least two weeks in advance.

Notes on boating the Green and Colorado Rivers are available on request from the National Park Service's **Moab office** (435/259-3911). Bill and Buzz Belknap's *Canyonlands River Guide* has river logs and maps pointing out items of interest on the Green River below the town of Green River and all of the Colorado River from the upper end of Westwater Canyon to Lake Powell.

★ River-Running Through Cataract Canyon

The Colorado River enters Cataract Canyon at the confluence and picks up speed. The rapids begin four miles downstream and extend for the next 14 miles to Lake Powell. Especially in spring, the 26 or more rapids give a wild ride equal to the best in the Grand Canyon. The current zips along at up to 16 mph and forms waves more than seven feet high. When the excitement dies down, boaters have a 34-mile trip across Lake Powell to Hite Marina; most people either carry a motor or arrange for a powerboat to pick them up. Depending on water levels, which can vary wildly from year to year, the dynamics of this trip and the optimal take-out point can change. Depending on how much motoring is done, the trip through Cataract Canyon takes 2-5 days.

Because of the real hazards of running the rapids, the National Park Service requires boaters to have proper equipment and a permit ($30). Many people go on commercial trips with Moab outfitters on which everything has been taken care of. Private groups must contact the **Canyonlands River Unit of the National Park Service** (435/259-3911, www.nps.gov/cany) far in advance for permit details.

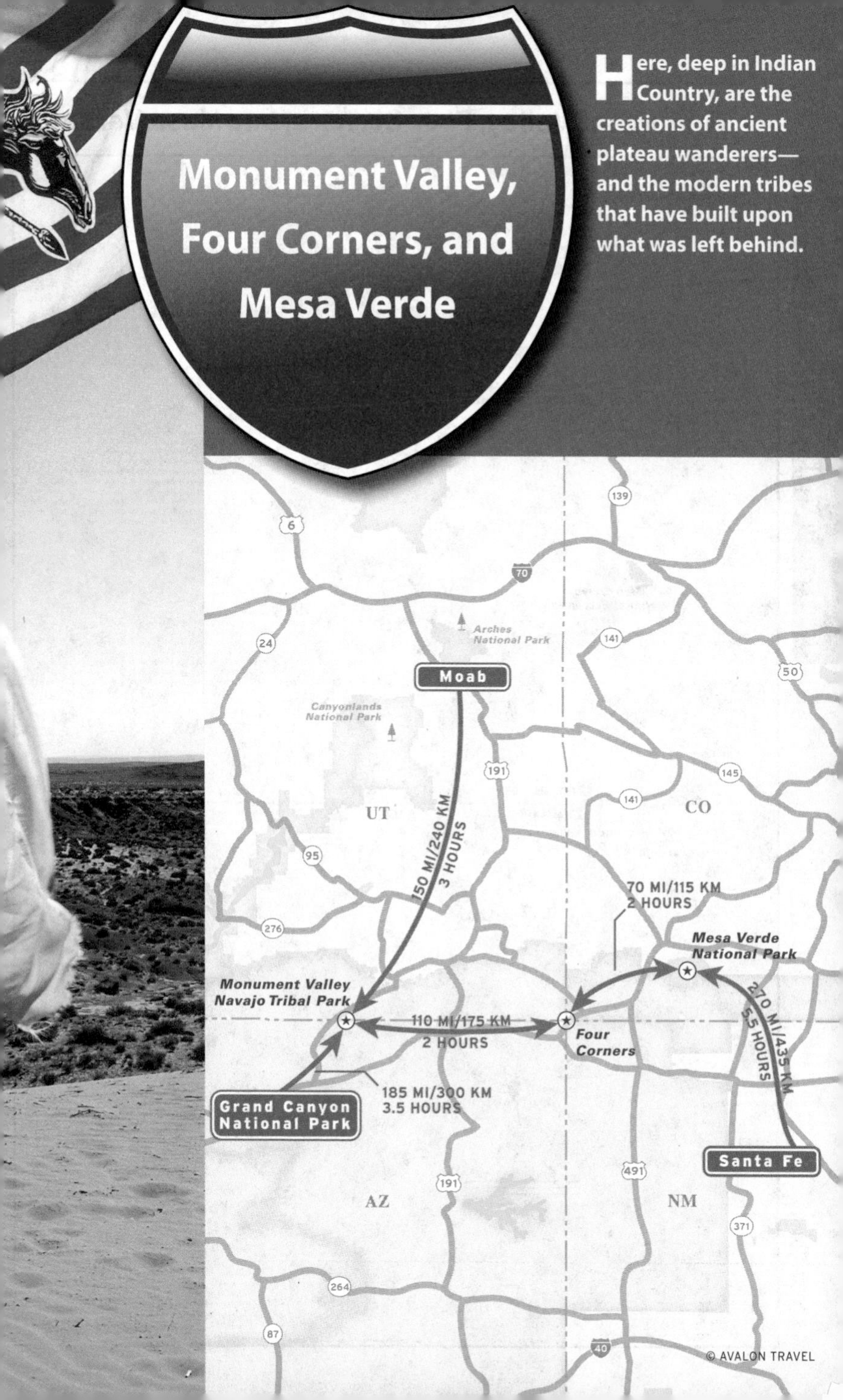
Monument Valley, Four Corners, and Mesa Verde
Here, deep in Indian Country, are the creations of ancient plateau wanderers—and the modern tribes that have built upon what was left behind.
Arches National Park
Moab
Canyonlands National Park
UT
CO
150 MI/240 KM 3 HOURS
70 MI/115 KM 2 HOURS
Mesa Verde National Park
Monument Valley Navajo Tribal Park
110 MI/175 KM 2 HOURS
Four Corners
270 MI/435 KM 5.5 HOURS
Grand Canyon National Park
185 MI/300 KM 3.5 HOURS
Santa Fe
AZ
NM
© AVALON TRAVEL

Monument Valley, Four Corners, and Mesa Verde

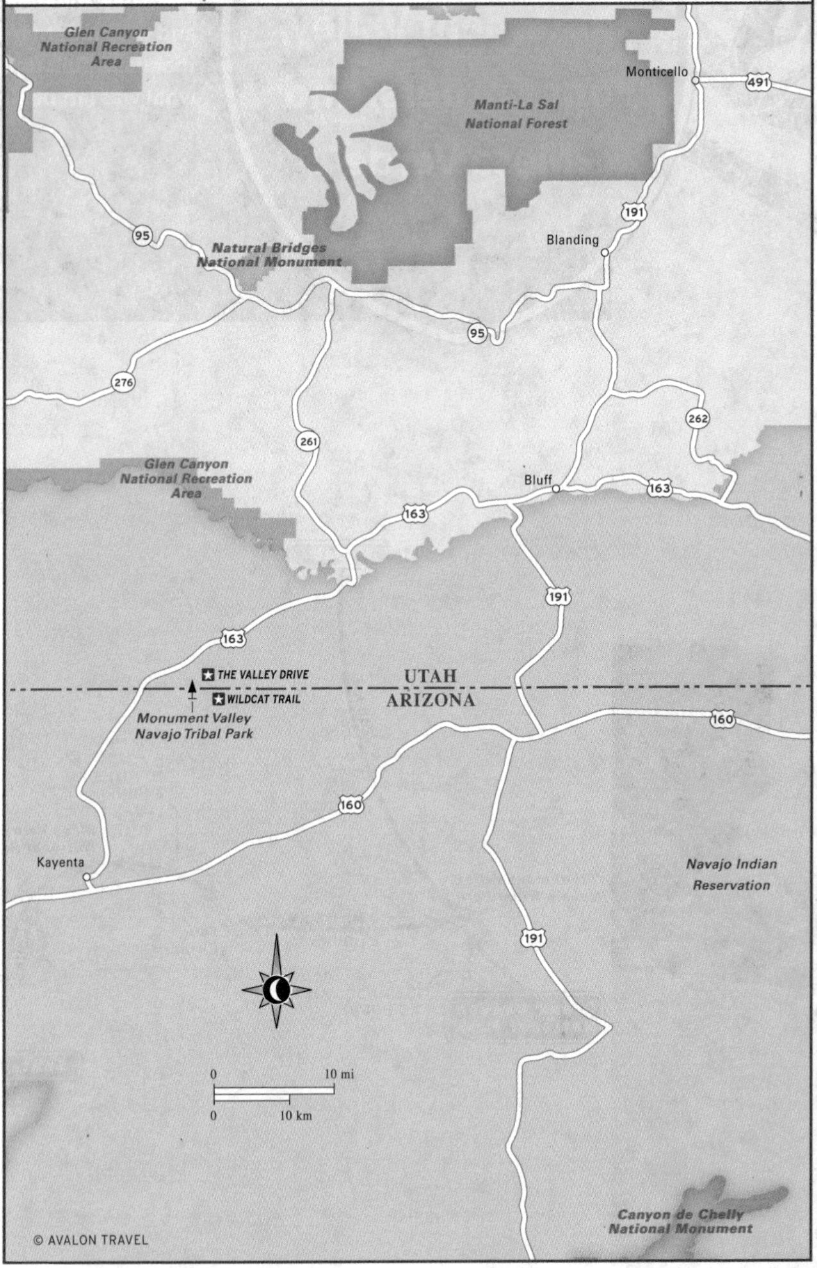

Glen Canyon National Recreation Area
Monticello
491
Manti-La Sal National Forest
191
95
Blanding
Natural Bridges National Monument
95
276
262
261
Glen Canyon National Recreation Area
Bluff
163
163
191
163
THE VALLEY DRIVE
UTAH
ARIZONA
WILDCAT TRAIL
Monument Valley Navajo Tribal Park
160
160
Kayenta
Navajo Indian Reservation
191
0
10 mi
0
10 km
Canyon de Chelly National Monument
© AVALON TRAVEL

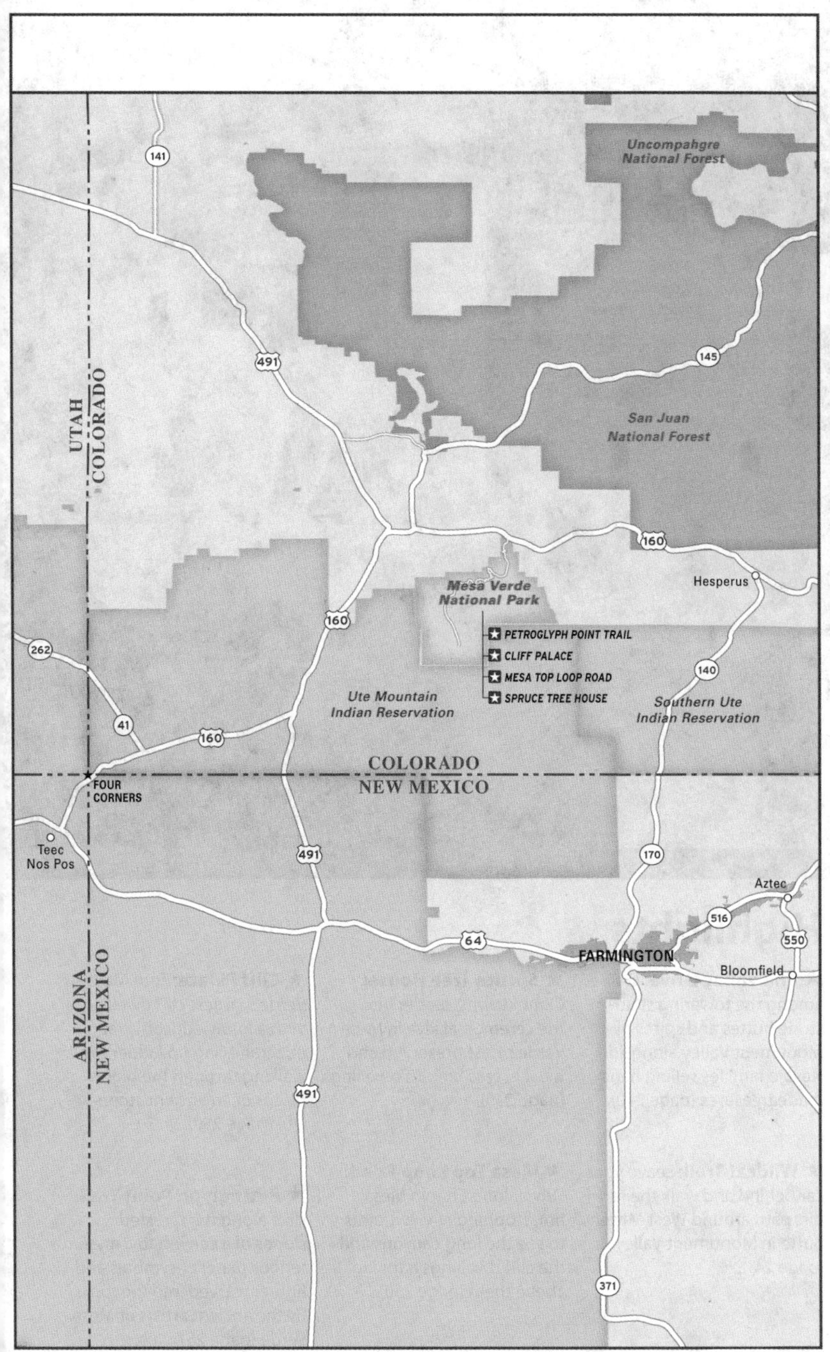

141
Uncompahgre
National Forest
491
UTAH
COLORADO
145
San Juan
National Forest
160
Hesperus
Mesa Verde
National Park
PETROGLYPH POINT TRAIL
CLIFF PALACE
MESA TOP LOOP ROAD
SPRUCE TREE HOUSE
262
140
Ute Mountain
Indian Reservation
Southern Ute
Indian Reservation
41
COLORADO
NEW MEXICO
FOUR
CORNERS
Teec
Nos Pos
170
Aztec
516
550
64
FARMINGTON
Bloomfield
ARIZONA
NEW MEXICO
371

Highlights

★ **The Valley Drive:** Cruise among the towering sandstone buttes and spires of Monument Valley alongside Navajo families selling handmade treasures (page 240).

★ **Spruce Tree House:** Climb down a ladder into the ceremonial kiva in Mesa Verde's best preserved and most accessible cliff dwelling (page 249).

★ **Cliff Palace:** Tour Mesa Verde's largest cliff dwelling with a knowledgeable ranger, scrambling up ladders and walking through the high plazas of an ancient stone city (page 250).

★ **Wildcat Trail:** Leave your car behind and walk the red-dirt path around West Mitten Butte in Monument Valley (page 241).

★ **Mesa Top Loop Road:** Drive along Chapin Mesa's rim, stopping at viewpoints to see the long canyons and the cliff dwellings hanging above them (page 250).

★ **Petroglyph Point Trail:** Hike along the forested slopes of a canyon to a mysterious panel of symbols and figures, carved into the rocks by the ancient artists of Mesa Verde (page 251).

To visit Monument Valley and the Four Corners and climb Mesa Verde to its cliff dwellings are to encounter a different version of beauty, history, and time.

While Monument Valley, with its red sandstone buttes, spires, and castles, worn and sculpted by wind and rain, is vast and improbable, on Mesa Verde the focus shifts to the awe-inspiring stone cliff dwellings, built nearly 1,000 years ago with stone tools and an intimate knowledge of nature's gifts and sorrows.

In this region, you'll drive narrow two-lane highways through reservation land and small river valleys populated by ranchers and farmers. But you'll also come across a well-oiled tourist trade that hearkens back to the early 1900s. Here you always seem to be far away from everything, overwhelmed by strange beauty, and lost in a romantic past.

Monument Valley Navajo Tribal Park

The drive north from Kayenta or south from Mexican Hat along US 163 to Monument Valley Navajo Tribal Park is almost as dramatically scenic as the destination itself. About a third of the way along the paved northern route, you'll see the aptly named **Owl Rock** to the west, and the hulking, jagged **Agathla Peak** to the east (also known as El Capitan), which tribal lore says marks the center of the world.

If there was any question that this is one of the most celebrated and enticing landscapes in the world, listen to the conversations around you as you visit Monument Valley—and you must visit Monument Valley, if only to prove that all the images you've seen are real. It sounds like "It's a Small World" out on this arid, dusty valley. Italian, German, British, and various Eastern European visitors gather at every lookout, seeking something distinctly Western, or American, in the iconic jutting red rocks.

It was director John Ford who brought this strange, remote place to the world and made it a stand-in for the West's dueling freedom and danger, most memorably in *The Searchers.* Now, to drive around the park is to enter a thousand car commercials, magazine layouts, road films, and Westerns, a landscape that's comfortably, beautifully familiar even if you're seeing it for the first time.

The Navajo have thankfully not overdeveloped this sacred place—some would argue it's underdeveloped for its potential—so the only way to see the park without a Navajo guide is to drive the 17-mile unpaved **loop road** (6am-8:30pm daily May-Sept., 8am-4:30pm daily Oct.-Apr.), which has 11 pullout scenic views of the rock spires and lonely buttes. Upon entering the park, you'll get a map of the drive with the names of each "Monument"—names like Wetherill Mesa, John Ford's Point, and The Thumb. If you can, it's worth arriving about an hour or so before sundown to see sunset over the valley—you'll wonder how you got here, and you'll stay until the lights go out. Be warned, though, that with the constant stream of cars driving the dry, dirt road, the air tends to get dusty.

You're allowed to take photographs here, but only of the natural wonders. Remember to ask permission before taking pictures of any Navajos or their private property, and don't be surprised if they charge you a few bucks.

Getting to Monument Valley Navajo Tribal Park

The Navajo Nation stretches over some 27,000 square miles of the Four Corners region, most of it lightly populated, save for a few scattered towns. When you pass

Stretch Your Legs

Close by the sombrero formation outside of Mexican Hat, you'll pass the entrance to **Goosenecks State Park** (Moab to Monument Valley drive, 435/678-2238, http://stateparks.utah.gov, 24 hours daily) and **Valley of the Gods** (Moab to Monument Valley drive, 435/587-1500, 24 hours daily) both of which make good stops to combine with a visit to Monument Valley.

To reach Goosenecks State Park, head one mile northwest from the junction of US 163 and UT-261 on UT-261, about four miles northwest of Mexican Hat. Turn left on UT-316. The small park is at the end of the road and offers an amazing view of a bend in the San Juan River far below.

About seven miles east of Mexican Hat on US 163, and 10 miles northeast of Mexican Hat on UT-261, at San Juan County Road 242, Valley of the Gods is a lesser, quieter Monument Valley with a 17-mile gravel and dirt road that loops around several strangely eroded monuments and buttes. The drive takes 1-2 hours.

through a sizable settlement, always stop for gas and other supplies, as it is likely a long way to the next one.

From Moab

150 miles / 3 hours

The **150-mile** drive to Monument Valley from Moab will take about **three hours** and is almost entirely on US 191. Drive **south** on **US 191.** After about 105 miles, a few miles past the town of Bluff, continue straight at the US 191/US 163 junction to join **US 163.** About 20 miles later, look for the precariously balanced rock formation that looks like a sombrero, from which Mexican Hat gets its name.

It's a good idea to stop at one of the few gas stations in Mexican Hat to fill up before entering the reservation and Monument Valley. After you fill up, get back on **US 163** and continue for 20 miles, then turn left onto **Monument Valley Road.** It's a little over five miles to the park entrance.

Expect a bit of traffic during the summer high season; it's busy but manageable and not likely to cause delays.

From the Grand Canyon South Rim

185 miles / 3.5 hours

To get to the park from the South Rim, it's a **3.5-hour** drive of about **185 miles.** From Grand Canyon Village, take **Center Road** to **US 180 East** and follow it for two miles until the junction with **AZ-64.** Continue on what's also referred to as the **Desert View Drive** for a little more than 50 miles to the junction with **US 89.** Head **north** (a left turn) on US 89 and you'll soon pass through Cameron, where there's an excellent trading post, restaurant, and hotel. After about 15 miles, turn right to pick up **US 160 East.** This part of the drive cuts through the Navajo Nation. It's about 10 miles on US 160 to reach Tuba City, the capital of this section of the Navajo Nation.

You'll pass the entrance to Navajo National Monument about 50 miles northeast of Tuba City. Continue for 20 miles, then turn left to get onto **US 163 North.** In a few miles, the highway leads to Kayenta, the reservation town closest to Monument Valley Tribal Park and a good place to base yourself (though some people prefer the off-reservation town of Mexican Hat, Utah, about 45 miles north of Kayenta on US 163). After 25 miles on this fantastically scenic stretch of US 163, turn right onto **Monument Valley Road.** The park is just over five miles down the road.

Stopping in Tuba City

About 85 miles (1.5 hours) from the South Rim via US 89 and US 160, Tuba City is the capital of the western reservation and a good place to stop if you're headed across the reservation to Monument Valley and other points east.

For an interesting primer on Navajo culture, check out the **Explore Navajo Interactive Museum** (Main St. and Moenave Rd., 928/640-0684, www.explorenavajo.com, 8am-6pm Mon.-Sat., noon-6pm Sun., $9 adults, $6 children 7-12), then head over to the **Historic Tuba City Trading Post** (Main St. and Moenave Rd., 928/283-5441, 8am-6pm daily), where they sell some amazing Navajo arts and crafts.

The Quality Inn Navajo Nation (Main St. and Moenave Rd., 928/283-4545, www.qualityinntubacity, $92-127) is the best place in Tuba City to stay overnight. The **Hogan Restaurant** (inside the Quality Inn, 928/283-5260, 6am-10pm daily, $5-15) has excellent Navajo tacos, Mexican food, and American staples like burgers and sandwiches.

From the Four Corners Monument

110 miles / 2 hours

Both routes to Monument Valley from Four Corners are the same length and take the same time to drive. Choose your approach based on whether you want to stay in **Kayenta,** on Navajo lands, or **Mexican Hat,** north of the valley. Of the two, Kayenta has more hotel options, as there are several large chains there.

To approach Monument Valley from the south, it's an approximately **110-mile, two-hour** drive that follows US 160 for most of the time. From Four Corners, join **US 160 West.** After about six miles, the highway comes to a T-intersection in Teec Nos Pos. Turn right to continue on US 160 West. After 70 miles, turn right onto **US 163 North.** From there, it's just over a mile to **Kayenta.** Continue north on US 163 for another 20 miles, then turn right onto **Monument Valley Road.** The park entrance is a little over five miles down the road.

To approach Monument Valley from the north, it's also a **110-mile, two-hour** drive. From Four Corners, take **US 160 West,** turning right at the T-intersection in Teec Nos Pos. Continue for 30 miles to **US 191.** Turn right to go north on US 191, and follow the highway for 40 miles until the intersection with **US 163.** Turn left to go west to **Mexican Hat,** about 20 miles farther on. From there, continue west on US 163 for another 20 miles, then turn left onto **Monument Valley Road.** Drive about five miles down the road to reach the park entrance.

Visiting the Park

Monument Valley Navajo Tribal Park (435/727-5874 or 435/727-5870, http://navajonationparks.org, 6am-8pm daily May-Sept., 8am-5pm daily Oct.-Apr., $20) is a busy scene during the summer high season, roughly May-September. With high temperatures in the 80s and 90s and a huge blue sky contrasting perfectly with the red dirt and sandstone in the valley, the park draws visitors from all over the world to see the mythic landscape for themselves. Fortunately, that landscape is big enough to engulf them all, so it never seems too crowded here, and the polyglot atmosphere at the stops along the Valley Drive only adds to the experience. From November to March, Monument Valley goes a bit quiet and peaceful, and, at more than 5,000 feet above sea level, there's sometimes a thin layer of snow covering the red land. High temperatures range from the 40s to the upper 50s during the low season.

While the tribal park comprises some 92,000 acres, very little of that is open to visitors without a Navajo guide. The Valley Drive, a scenic drive through the heart of the valley, and the Wildcat Trail, an easy stroll around one of the valley's most iconic buttes, are all you can do on your own—but they are enough to build an unforgettable visit.

Guides for **jeep and horseback tours** of the backcountry are readily available at the park for those who want to see more and are willing to pay for it. Guides are available for hire through the **Monument Valley Navajo Tribal Park Visitor Center** and Goulding's Lodge. The **Navajo Parks**

and Recreation Department has a list of reputable guides on its website (www.navajonationparks.org).

Entrances

There is only one entrance to Monument Valley. Look for the turnoff to Monument Valley Road from US 163, about 20 miles from Mexican Hat to the north and about 25 miles from Kayenta on the south.

During the high season, on weekends especially, the line to get in may require sitting in an idling car for 5-10 minutes. A map of Valley Drive is available at the entrance station.

Fees

Entering the park costs $20 per vehicle with up to four people. Kids younger than seven get in free. You'll spend considerably more if you hire a guide, which you must do if you want to do anything other than drive the Valley Drive or hike the Wildcat Trail. This is not a national park or monument, so federal passes don't work here.

Visitors Center

Perched on a promontory overlooking the valley and the dirt road that snakes through it and around the eroded-sandstone sculptures, the **Monument Valley Navajo Tribal Park Visitor Center** (6am-8pm daily May-Sept., 8am-5pm daily Oct.-Apr.) near the entrance station is an obvious place to start your visit. There's a small museum with displays on Navajo culture and history, as well as the history of Hollywood's use of this iconic landscape, and a wall or two showing contemporary Navajo art. Staff here can set you up with a guide if you want to go deeper into the valley and learn about the tribe's religious, cultural, and economic ties to the valley. There's a small patio outside the visitors center, which is right next to the View Hotel, restaurant, and trading post-gift shop, where you can sit and contemplate the natural art before you.

Information and Services

It's a good idea to bring your own food

Monument Valley

and water, and make sure to gas up in Kayenta, Arizona (30 miles south of the park), or Mexican Hat, Utah (25 miles north of the park), before visiting. Cell phone service is not likely. Visitors with respiratory problems should bring a mask; it can get dusty out here.

Upon entering the park, you'll get an informative map. The friendly folks at the visitors center and gift shop can answer your questions.

The visitors center has snacks and a restaurant that's open during the high season (May-Sept.) serving Navajo and American dishes.

Just off Monument Valley Road on your way into the park there are a few blue buildings where Navajo vendors sell handicrafts and food. Bring some cash, as the vendors likely won't accept credit cards. Credit cards are accepted at the restaurant, hotel, and gift shop.

There are no **emergency services** within the park; however, the visitors center, hotel, and restaurant are close to the Valley Drive and there are always people around. The closest emergency room is in Kayenta at the **Kayenta Health Center** (US 163, 928/697-4000, www.ihs.gov/navajo).

Getting Around

Unless you book a tour with a Navajo guide to explore the park in a jeep or on horseback, the only way to see anything is with your own vehicle. The Valley Drive is a dirt road, but it can be negotiated with most regular passenger cars.

Tours

As impressive as the buttes and jutting rock castles along the main road around the valley are, they are but a small sampling; many more hulking, crumbling buttes, as well as wondrous arches, delicate spires, petroglyphs, and traditional Navajo homesteads are scattered throughout this vast, remote land, accessible only with a hired guide at your side.

There is no shortage of Navajo guides, and you can easily hire one inside the park at the visitors center. The **Navajo Parks and Recreation Department** (www.navajonationparks.org) has a list of reputable, Navajo-owned guide companies on its website. Prices vary slightly between companies, but you can generally expect to pay about $65 for a 1.5-hour ride in an open jeep around the main road and $115-165 for an all-day backcountry immersion tour. You have to book a 2.5-hour or longer tour (around $75 per person) to go anywhere beyond the Wildcat Trail or the Valley Drive.

Call ahead and book in advance for an all-day tour, as these are usually subject to group minimums. If you really want to go deep into the traditional Navajo world, guide Roy Black of **Black's Jeep** (928/429-0637, www.blacksmonumentvalleytours.com) will take you on a three-hour horseback ride that includes an overnight stay in a Navajo hogan ($140 per person; call far in advance), a mud-and-log dwelling.

Black also offers jeep and other horseback tours.

Serious photographers should consider booking a guide. Guide Tom J. Phillips of **Keya-Hozhoni Tours** (928/674-1960, www.monumentvalley.com) charges $30 an hour to show photographers the best shots outside the mainstream. The tour starts before the sun rises, lasts for four or five hours in the morning, and picks up again for four or five hours in the later afternoon. The company also offers regular jeep and horseback tours.

★ The Valley Drive

The best way to see the valley and its monuments up close and on your own time is to head out into the hazy red lands via the 17-mile, self-guided **Valley Drive.** The route, which is all dirt and a bit rough in some spots, has 11 pullouts for longer views of some of the more famous mesas, buttes, and spires. At many of these numbered stops, which otherwise have no services, you'll find Navajo families selling jewelry and souvenirs. Plan to spend at least two hours exploring the valley. If dust bothers you, so too will the Valley Drive, but try not to let that stop you: This is one of the most scenic, inspirational, and absolutely essential drives in the Southwest. Take water and food along, and check your tires before you head out. The roughest part of the drive is at the start, going down a steep hill into the valley, but the rest is easy and flat. Don't follow too close behind other cars; you'll be buried in red dust if you do. The tribe does not allow motorcycles or RVs on the Valley Drive.

The road into the valley starts just past the visitors center parking lot and has two lanes until Camel Butte, where it becomes a one-way loop around **Rain God Mesa.** The first stop, just as you enter the valley, provides a classic, much-photographed

---

Top to bottom: Three Sisters, on the Valley Drive; horses in Monument Valley; Navajoland scenery.

view of the "mittens," **West Mitten Butte** and **East Mitten Butte,** named so because of the spires that rise from the side of each butte to form what looks like a hand in a mitten. Just a short scoot up the road is **Merrick Butte,** named, according Richard Klinck in his classic history of the valley, *Land of Room Enough and Time Enough,* for James Merrick, a soldier turned prospector who was killed near the butte for trespassing on a Navajo silver mine. The huge mesa opposite Merrick Butte is called **Mitchell Mesa,** for it is said that at its base died Ernest Mitchell, Merrick's partner in trespass and violent death.

The second stop on the drive, **Elephant Butte,** is supposed to look like the titular pachyderm. The third and fourth numbered stops, **The Three Sisters** and **John Ford's Point,** are two of the best. The sisters are side-by-side spires on the edge of Mitchell Mesa, and the point is named for the famous director who revealed this valley to the world through his Westerns. The fifth stop is **Camel Butte,** named for the stone-frozen ungulate that to many it resembles. Just a bit up the road from the fifth stop, a ramshackle hut and corral provides **horseback tours of the backcountry** (30-minute to 6-hour tours, $45-165, credit cards accepted). You can also stop here and take pictures of the horses, but make sure to ask first, and be prepared to pay $5.

The sixth numbered stop on the drive provides a view of the formation called **The Hub,** which looks somewhat like the hub of a wagon wheel, and of huge **Rain God Mesa,** marking the center of the valley. Here the road turns to loop around Rain God Mesa, with pull-offs at **Thunderbird Mesa** and the edge of **Spearhead Mesa.** Here you'll see red sand dunes and, far off in the valley beyond the road, the impossibly delicate spire called the **Totem Pole,** which rises next to a gathering of thicker spires the Navajo call **Yei Bi Chei**—"dancers emerging from a hogan." The ninth stop is at the far tip of Spearhead Mesa, where there's a short, easy trail out to **Artist Point Overlook.** The view here is spectacular, and it's easy to see how the promontory got its name. Continuing on around the other side of Rain God Mesa, you'll see **Cly Butte,** at the base of which is buried "Old Cly," a beloved Navajo medicine man who died in 1934. Cly Butte is the last numbered stop, seen from a short side road up to the penultimate stop, the **North Window Overlook,** which provides a breathtaking view of the valley's northern section. The loop ends at Camel Butte, behind which rises a spire called **The Thumb.** Then it's back to the visitors center along the two-lane route from Camel Butte. You'll pass the same monuments on the way back, obviously, and feel free to stop at them again.

★ Wildcat Trail

The only hiking you can do in the absence of a hired Navajo guide is along this 3.2-mile loop trail around **West Mitten Butte.** It's an easy, quiet walk along a red-dirt path among gray-green scrub and sagebrush, with the spires and buttes looming close and lizards whipping over red rocks. The trail starts 0.4 miles north of the visitors center. It's easy enough for kids, but there's no shade, and it can get windy out there. Take water with you, and plan on being out for two hours or more.

Accommodations and Food

For all its fame, Monument Valley is still a considerably remote place, and there aren't a lot of services out here. Don't come hungry; eat in Kayenta or Mexican Hat before you head out, or bring your own food with you. That's not to say that there's nothing to eat at all.

The **View Restaurant** (435/727-3468, www.monumentvalleyview.com, 7am-2pm and 5pm-8pm daily, $5-25) inside the park has decent Navajo, Mexican, and American food for breakfast, lunch, and dinner. In between meals there are only packaged sandwiches, fruit, and snacks available. At the junction of Highway 163 and the park entrance road, there's a small shopping center where you can get snacks and fry bread, and there are a few gift shops selling local crafts and curios.

When the tribe developed **The View Hotel** (435/727-5555, www.monumentvalleyview.com, $390 and above), the only in-park, noncamping accommodations available at Monument Valley, they probably could have thrown up a few trailers and a kiddy pool and charged $100 per night. The location alone is the attraction; everything else just gets in the way. But they didn't do that, thankfully. The View is instead a complement to the landscape, a low and tucked-away line of rooms near the Mitten Buttes, with patios facing east over the valley where the sun comes alive in the morning. The color of the hotel fairly merges with that of the buttes, monuments, and vast red dunes, making it appear inevitable. The rooms are just a few years old, very comfortable, and decorated in a generic Southwestern style. It's the view that you're paying for, obviously, and you will pay a lot, if you can get a reservation. There are no cheap rooms, especially during the spring and summer high season.

Camping

Campsites are available at the **Mitten View Campground** ($10 per night up to 6 people, $20 up to 13, half price Oct.-Apr.) year-round, first-come, first-served. Each site has a table, grill, ramada, and trash can, and there are restrooms and coin-operated showers. No hookups are available, but a dump station is open during the summer. Check in at the visitors center to get a campsite.

Goulding's Lodge

This compound just outside the park features a hotel with luxury amenities, a campground, a museum, and a trading post selling Navajo crafts. It keeps the name of the first trader to settle in the valley, Harry Goulding, who opened a trading post here in 1928, exchanging staples for Navajo jewelry and rugs. The story goes that in the late 1930s Goulding himself went to Hollywood to convince Ford to come to Monument Valley to film *Stagecoach.*

★ **Goulding's Lodge** (435/727-3231, www.gouldings.com, $175-247 summer, $73-95 winter) has 62 rooms and 8 family-friendly, multiroom suites with cable TV and DVD players. There's an indoor swimming pool and exercise room, and you can even rent one of the many classic Westerns available and watch it in your room. The **Stagecoach Dining Room** serves American and Navajo food (such as lamb stew, Navajo tacos, and fry bread) for breakfast, lunch, and dinner. The well-equipped **Goulding's Campground** offers tent sites for $28 per night and full hookup sites for $48 per night. A camping cabin with a TV, kitchen, and bathroom is available for $124 per night. There's also a convenience store, gas station, coin laundry, car wash, and indoor pool at the campground.

Goulding's offers **tours** of the monument with Navajo guides for $53 (must be over 8 years old) for 2.5 hours, $66 for 3.5 hours, and $119 per person for an all-day excursion, which includes a cookout lunch.

Outside the Park: Mexican Hat

The few accommodations in Mexican Hat are generally less expensive than the chain hotels in Kayenta and are much less expensive than the View Hotel in Monument Valley. Moreover, a few restaurants here serve alcohol, which is prohibited on the reservation.

The **San Juan Inn and Trading Post** (Hwy. 163 and the San Juan River, 800/447-2022, www.sanjuaninn.net, summer $94-114, winter $65-78) is right on the banks of the beautiful San Juan River and next to the bridge that spans it, offering basic rooms that are comfortable and clean, with air-conditioning, TV, and spotty Wi-Fi. Perhaps the best thing about this place, which is the top place to stay and eat in Mexican Hat, is the **Old Bridge Bar & Grill** (7am-9pm daily, $5-20). This rustic little place in middle of nowhere serves a big, filling breakfast, tasty Mexican food, and Navajo tacos, plus burgers and all the other grill-style mainstays. It also has a full bar and pool tables and strikes one as a place where a lot of backcountry adventurers hang out when they are not running rivers or scaling mesas.

The unique **Mexican Hat Lodge** (Hwy. 163 across from the Shell gas station, 435/683-2222, $84-279) has basic rooms with TVs and phones, offering a fun, laid-back, and friendly vibe that is more akin to a bed-and-breakfast than a regular motel. The restaurant here is called **The Swinging Steak** ($13-40), and it has a pleasant patio where you can watch your steak being cooked over a swinging grill. They serve wine and beer, but it's the low-alcohol Utah variety.

Outside the Park: Kayenta

Because it is so close to Monument Valley, there are several nice chain hotels in Kayenta, most of them along Highway 160 as you enter town. The **Hampton Inn Kayenta** (US 160, near intersection with US 163, 928/697-3170, http://hamptoninn3.hilton.com, $100-150) is very comfortable and offers free wireless Internet, a pool, a gift shop, a restaurant, and free continental breakfast. The **Best Western Wetherill Inn** (US 163, 928/697-3231, www.gouldings.com, $83-143) has a pool, wireless Internet, a gift shop, and a complimentary breakfast.

One of the best restaurants on Navajoland, the ★ **Blue Coffee Pot Café** (0.25 mile east of US 160 and US 163 junction, 928/697-3396, $4-12) in Kayenta serves outstanding home-style Navajo, American, and Mexican food in a hogan-shaped building just off Highway 160. The Navajo taco here is simply fantastic, as are the beef ribs. The staff is friendly, if a bit harried in this busy place, and you might find yourself sitting at a table next to a 90-something Navajo woman dressed like it's the 19th century.

The ★ **Amigo Café** (US 163, 928/697-8448, $5-10) just north of the junction serves Mexican, Navajo, and American food and is popular with the locals. The **Burger King** (928/697-3534) on Highway 160 (near the Hampton Inn) has the usual, with the added feature of a Navajo Code Talkers exhibit, which you can view as you chow down on your french fries.

Four Corners Monument

A concrete slab marks the only spot in the United States where you can put your finger on four states at once. More than 2,000 people a day are said to stop at the marker in the summer season.

Getting to the Four Corners Monument

From Monument Valley Navajo Tribal Park

110 miles / 2 hours

To get to Four Corners from Monument Valley, it's a **110-mile, two-hour** drive. Take **Monument Valley Road** out of the park (west) for about six miles. Turn left to get on **US 163 West** and follow the highway for just over 20 miles until you reach Kayenta, a small reservation town. Just a few miles farther on US 163, turn left at the junction with **US 160 East** and drive for a little more than 70 miles. At the town of Teec Nos Pos, turn left to continue on US 160 for about six miles until the intersection with **NM-597,** where you'll turn left. The monument is a half-mile down the road.

From Mesa Verde National Park

70 miles / 2 hours

To get to Four Corners from the Mesa Verde National Park Visitor Center, it's a **70-mile, two-hour** drive, including the 20 winding miles (40 minutes) down

Mesa Verde to the park entrance. Pick up **US 160 West/US 491 South** and drive for 30 miles until the highways diverge. Turn right to continue on US 160 West, continuing 20 miles until the **NM-597 junction.** Turn right, following the signs for the monument, which is about half a mile down the road.

Four Corners Monument

About 70 miles east on Highway 160 from Kayenta is the **Four Corners Monument** (928/871-6647, 8am-7pm daily Apr.-late May, 8am-8pm daily late May-mid-Sept., 8am-6pm daily mid-Sept.-Oct., 8am-5pm daily Nov.-Mar., $5, children 6 and under free, cash only), the only place in the United States where, if you do a little bit of Twister-style contorting, you can exist briefly in four states at once—Arizona, Colorado, New Mexico, and Utah. You're not likely to stay long after you take the obligatory picture.

In the summer months there are usually Navajo artisans and others selling crafts. Note that admission can be paid only in cash. The nearest ATM is in Teec Nos Pos, Arizona, about five miles from the monument.

Mesa Verde National Park

The Hopi, the Zuni, the Acoma, and the Laguna, the ancestors of today's Pueblo people, lived in the canyons and along the rims of the vast Mesa Verde (Green Table), in what is now southwestern Colorado, for some 700 years—from about AD 600 to AD 1300. For a long time they lived in small villages on the mesa top, collecting nuts from the piñon-juniper forest and growing corn, beans, and squash in the good soil. They made baskets, sandals, and rope from the yucca that grows in the forest, hunted deer and wild turkeys, and found berries and wild onions in the canyons below. Relatively late in their time here, in the latter 1100s, they began to build the mesa's famous cliff dwellings. The dwellings are large, multistoried stone apartments tucked away in natural sandstone alcoves high above the canyon floors, some of them with hundreds of rooms, towers, plazas, and ceremonial kivas, and each with a small hole in the floor, called a *sipapu*, which they believed to be a door to another world. They didn't have metal tools or the wheel. And yet, their masterworks still stand today.

A long regional drought and its attendant social pressures convinced the builders of the cliff dwellings, generally referred to as Ancestral Puebloans, to move out of the mesa country around AD 1300, leaving their great stone cities. When the largest of the cliff dwellings was rediscovered in 1888 by local ranchers Richard Wetherill and Charlie Mason, who were acting on intelligence from Utes, the ruins were still intact to an amazing degree. To preserve Cliff Palace and the more than 600 smaller dwellings hanging from the eroded cliffs of the Mesa Verde, Teddy Roosevelt created Mesa Verde National Park in 1906. Today it is one of the great highlights of a journey to the Colorado Plateau and should not be missed.

Getting to Mesa Verde National Park

From the Four Corners Monument

70 miles / 2 hours

To get to Mesa Verde National Park Visitor Center at the base of the mesa from Four Corners, it's a **70-mile, two-hour** drive. From the monument, join **US 160 East** and follow it for 20 miles until the junction with **US 491.** Continue on **US 160 East/US 491 North** by turning left (north). Continue on for another 20 miles until the two highways diverge, staying on US 160 by veering right. After 10 miles, take the exit for Mesa Verde National Park, then turn right onto **Mesa Top Ruins Road.** Take the first left and follow the road to reach the

Mesa Verde in One Day

Morning

Start your day by booking a ranger-guided tour of **Cliff Palace** (page 250). Before or after the one-hour tour, head over to **Chapin Mesa Archeological Museum** (page 249) and check out the dioramas and other displays on the Ancestral Puebloans, then walk down the short, paved trail for a self-guided tour of **Spruce Tree House** (page 249).

Afternoon

Have a Navajo taco at **Spruce Tree Terrace** (page 253), then hike the 2.8-mile **Petroglyph Point Trail** (page 251), which loops back up to the top of the mesa. After the hike, take a leisurely drive along the **Mesa Top Loop Road** (page 250), stopping for views of the cliff dwellings.

Evening

Have dinner and cocktails at the elegant **Metate Room** (page 252) near Far View Lodge, watching twilight descend over the green landscape.

Extending Your Stay

By staying another day, you can explore several more cliff dwellings, like **Balcony House** (page 250) on Chapin Mesa and Long House on **Wetherill Mesa** (page 250), which waits at the end of a twisty scenic drive.

visitors center. To reach the park sights on Chapin Mesa, it's another 20 miles up a winding road, about a 45-minute drive.

From Santa Fe

Via US 84

270 miles / 5.5 hours

The most scenic route to Mesa Verde National Park from Santa Fe, a **270-mile, 5.5-hour** drive, heads northwest on US 84 through the Chama River Valley. From Santa Fe, join **US 285 North/US 84 West.** After 25 miles, in Española, follow signs for US 285/US 84 and turn left. After almost 10 miles, US 285 diverges east; continue straight on US 84 West. Continue for about 70 miles, passing through the towns of Abiquiu and Los Ojos. At the junction with NM-17, turn left to follow **US 64 West/US 84 West.** Continue driving, following US 84 and crossing the **Colorado border.** After about 45 miles, turn left onto **US 160 West** in the town of Pagosa Springs.

After 60 miles, you'll pass through the town of Durango. At the junction with US 550, turn left to continue on **US 160,** which you'll follow for another 35 miles before taking the exit for Mesa Verde National Park. Turn left onto **Mesa Top Ruins Road.** Follow the signs for the visitors center, or continue for 20 more miles (40 minutes) on Mesa Top Ruins Road to reach Chapin Mesa and the park's sights.

Stopping in Chama

A tiny town on the Rio Chama near the New Mexico-Colorado border, Chama is about two hours (110 miles) northwest of Santa Fe on US 84. It's a good place to stop for lunch or dinner, and historic railroad fans may want to take a ride on the **Cumbres & Toltec Scenic Railroad** (500 Terrace Ave., 575/756-2125, www.cumbrestoltec.com, $79 adults, $39 kids), a narrow-gauge steamer that still chugs around this high green country. Short trips are offered during the summer (10am-noon Wed.-Thurs. and Sun. July 5-Aug. 9). The trip includes a ride on the train from Chama to Cumbres, returning to Chama via motor coach. Full-day trips with a stop for lunch are offered late May through mid-October.

Try the red chile at **Fina's Diner** (2298 Hwy. 17, 575/756-9195, 6:30am-2pm daily, $5-10), where they also serve excellent diner fare in a friendly, homey atmosphere. The **High Country Restaurant and Saloon** (2299 Hwy. 17, 575/756-2384,

11am-10pm daily, $10-20) is a bit more upscale. It has good food and is a popular stop for wanderers and tourists.

If you're staying overnight, try the **Chama River Bend** (2625 Hwy. 64, 575/756-2264, www.chamariverbend-lodge.com, $79-109), which offers nice, clean rooms in a peaceful streamside setting.

Via US 550

270 miles / 4.5 hours

Another route from Santa Fe, which is about **270 miles** and **4.5 hours,** travels west on US 550 for most of the drive. From Santa Fe, get on **I-25 South,** drive for 40 miles, then take **exit 242** for **US 550 North.** Continue on US 550 North for 150 miles until you reach the town of Bloomfield. Follow signs for US 550 by turning right onto **Broadway Avenue,** then left onto **1st Street.** In about 10 miles, you'll reach the town of Aztec. Turn left (west) onto **Chaco Street,** then left onto **Aztec Boulevard** after a half-mile. After another half-mile, **turn right (north)** onto **NM-574/Old State Highway 173** and continue driving for 15 miles. At the junction, **turn right** to get onto **NM-170.**

In five miles, you'll cross the **Colorado border,** at which point the highway becomes **CO-140 North.** In 25 miles, past the town of Hesperus, turn left to join **US 160 West.** After another 25 miles, take the exit for Mesa Verde National Park, then turn left onto **Mesa Top Ruins Road.** Follow signs for the visitors center, or continue for 20 more miles down Mesa Top Ruins Road to reach Chapin Mesa.

Stopping in Aztec

About three hours from Santa Fe along US 550, the town of Aztec is home to **Aztec Ruins National Monument** (84

Top to bottom: Four Corners Monument; cliff dwellings, Mesa Verde National Park; Chapin Mesa Archeological Museum at Mesa Verde National Park.

County Rd. 2900, 505/334-6174, www.nps.gov/azru, 8am-6pm daily summer, 8am-5pm daily winter, $5), a small park that preserves the ruins of a 400-room, 900-year-old Pueblo Great House, one of the largest outside of nearby Chaco Canyon. A highlight of the half-mile, self-guided tour is the amazing reconstruction of a ceremonial kiva.

The small town of about 7,000 people also has a few good places to eat and relax. **The Bistro** (122 N. Main Ave., 505/334-0109, www.aztecbistro.com, 7am-2:30pm Mon.-Fri., 8am-noon Sat., $5-12) has a coffeehouse atmosphere with a wide selection of well-made dishes for breakfast and lunch (including very good green chile stew). It's located in downtown Aztec in a refurbished 1950s gas station. If you're too tired to keep driving, the **Enchantment Lodge** (1800 W. Aztec Blvd., 505/334-6143, $65d) is a clean and friendly place with basic but comfortable rooms.

Visiting the Park

Though very busy during the high season (May-September), with elevations between 7,000 and 8,500 feet, **Mesa Verde National Park** (US 160, 970/529-4465, www.nps.gov/meve, daily year-round, $10-15 per vehicle, $5-8 per motorcycle, bicyclist, or pedestrian) grows cold, often snowy, and quiet during the winter. During the spring and summer, the weather on Chapin Mesa, the main section of the park, is just about perfect: warm days and cool nights, with intermittent rainstorms July through September. The lodge and campground are closed from late October to mid-April. The road to Wetherill Mesa is closed late October to early May.

If you're just visiting for the day, stick to Chapin Mesa. Even then, you're likely to drive more than 50 miles, so make sure your vehicle is gassed up and road-ready. Aside from the gorgeous natural setting, Mesa Verde is mostly about the ruins and their builders. There are opportunities all over the park to learn about the Ancestral Puebloans who constructed these amazing structures. The best way to learn about and to explore the cliff dwellings is a ranger-guided tour of Cliff Palace, the largest cliff dwelling in North America.

Entrances

Mesa Top Ruins Road is the only road in and out of Mesa Verde National Park. The **entrance station** is just a mile or so down the road from the junction with US 160, after the turn off to the visitors center. From the visitors center at the bottom of the mesa to the end of Chapin Mesa it's a winding 20 miles, which takes at least 40 minutes to drive.

Park Passes and Fees

During the summer high season (late May-early Sept.), it costs $15 per car and $8 for motorcycles, bicyclists, and pedestrians to enter Mesa Verde National Park. In winter, when many of the sights and services in the park are closed, the entrance fee goes down to $10 per car and $5 for motorcycles, bikes, and pedestrians. Admission is good for seven days. The park offers an **annual pass** for $30. An annual pass to all of the national parks, known as the **Interagency Annual Pass/America the Beautiful Pass,** is $80.

Only two of cliff dwellings are self-guided. Cliff Palace, Balcony House, and Long House require a **ranger-guided tour** (multiple tours per day May-Sept., $4 per person). Purchase your tickets at the Visitor and Research Center before heading up the mesa. Tickets are also sold at the Chapin Mesa Museum and at the Morefield Ranger Station near the campground.

Visitors Centers

Make sure to stop at the **Mesa Verde Visitor and Research Center** (8am-5pm daily early Apr.-late May and early Sept-early Nov., 7:30am-7pm daily late May-early Sept., 8:30am-4:30pm daily early Nov.-early Apr.) at the bottom of the mesa before you hit the winding, 21-mile road to the top. It has a bookstore, ATM, bathrooms, displays on the history and culture of the mesa's former inhabitants, and rangers who will help you plan your visit.

About 20 miles along the road on Chapin Mesa, the **Chapin Mesa Archeological Museum** (9am-4:30pm daily Jan.-early Mar., 9am-5pm daily early Mar.-early Apr. and early Nov.-late Dec., 8am-6:30pm daily early Apr.-mid-Oct., 8am-5pm daily mid-Oct.-early Nov.) also has helpful rangers, along with a bookstore and fascinating displays about the ruins and those who built them.

On Wetherill Mesa, the **Wetherill Mesa Information Kiosk** (9am-6:30pm daily late May-early Sept.) offers advice on seeing the park's more far-flung sights, and there's a small snack bar as well.

The **Morefield Campground Ranger Station** (5pm-8:30pm daily late May-late Aug.) is another option for buying tour tickets. There are also rangers on hand to offer advice.

Reservations

Because so much of the park is closed during the winter months, and also because the summers are just about perfect up on the Mesa Verde, it's always busy during the high season (May-Sept.), especially on weekends. Reservations are a must, and the farther out you make them the better.

Accommodations

The only in-park place to stay is **Far View Lodge** (970/529-4422 or 800/449-2288, www.visitmesaverde.com), which has 150 rooms and is only open from mid-April to late October. If you want to stay in the park and save yourself a daily drive of at least 30 miles to and from Cortez or Mancos (nearly an hour on the slow road into and out of the park), start planning at least six months out.

For more accommodations options, try the communities outside the park:

- **Cortez** (US 160): 10 miles west of the visitors center
- **Mancos** (US 160): Eight miles east of the visitors center

Camping

The 267-space **Morefield Campground** (800/449-2288, www.visitmesaverde.com), about four miles up the mesa from the park entrance, is very popular during the high season , so reservations there also need to be made far in advance. The campground offers only primitive camping in winter. Both are managed by **Aramark** (970/529-4422 or 800/449-2288, www.visitmesaverde.com), the park concessionaire.

Information and Services

Perhaps the most important thing to remember about visiting Mesa Verde National Park is that, way up on the mesa, you're cut off from the nearest towns by an hour-long drive, most of it going slow down a twisting, narrow road. During the high season from May to September, this is less of a concern than it is during the lonely winter months.

The park has two cafeteria-style restaurants, and there's a well-stocked store and a **gas station** at Morefield Campground, about four miles up the road from the park entrance. Still, no matter when you visit, it's a good idea to gas up in one of the towns below the mesa (as you're likely to drive about 50 miles a day in the park) and to bring your own food and water.

Don't count on your **cell phone** working in the park. **Wi-Fi** is available at the Far View Lodge, the Morefield Campground store, and both restaurants.

There's an **ATM** at the visitors center at the bottom of the mesa and a **post office** near park headquarters on Chapin Mesa.

In case of an emergency, **call 911** from a phone at one the park facilities or find a ranger. For **first aid,** head over to the

Chief Ranger's Office (970/529-4672, 8am-5pm daily late May-Oct.), near the Chapin Mesa Archeological Museum.

Getting Around

You must have your own vehicle to get around Mesa Verde National Park. There is no shuttle service here.

From mid-April to late October, Aramark, the park concessionaire, offers the four-hour **700 Years Tour** (800/449-2288, http://visitmesaverde.com, 8am and 1:30 pm daily, adults $41-48, children 5-11 $26-35, children 4 and under free), which takes you to the park's major sights in a big comfy bus. It's a good idea to book a tour before your visit, but you can also purchase tickets at the Far View Lodge, the visitors center, Morefield Campground, and Far View Terrace. The tours are fairly expensive, and they don't go to any areas that you can't get to on your own.

The steep and twisting road to Wetherill Mesa, which leads to the park's more out-of-the-way sights, is limited to vehicles less than 25 feet long, closed to bicycles, and shuts down altogether from late October to early May.

Sights

Chapin Mesa

Split in places by water-carved canyons, Mesa Verde is divided into two main areas, **Chapin Mesa** and Wetherill Mesa. Open year-round, Chapin Mesa has the most impressive ruins and the best hiking trails, and is the center of most of the park's action. If you only have one day in the park, stick to the evergreen piñon-and-juniper forest on Chapin Mesa.

One ruin here, the amazing Spruce Tree House, is open for self-guided tours during the high season, while the park's largest ruin, Cliff Palace, and the more humble but fascinating Balcony House, are accessible only via ranger-guided tours ($4). There are two six-mile scenic loop drives on Chapin Mesa with unforgettable views of the canyons and ruins.

Chapin Mesa gets busy in the summer with an international crowd of explorers, tourists, and road-trippers, requiring some patience and good will.

Chapin Mesa Archeological Museum

Housed in a wood-and-stone building on the edge of the canyon that holds Spruce Tree House, the **Chapin Mesa Archeological Museum** (Chapin Mesa, 21 miles from park entrance, 9am-4:30pm daily Jan.-early Mar., 9am-5pm daily early Mar.-early Apr. and early Nov.-late Dec., 8am-6:30pm daily early Apr.-mid-Oct., 8am-5pm daily mid-Oct.-early Nov.) should make your list if only for its preservation of the lost art of dioramas. There are several intricate masterpieces of the genre on display here, presenting in miniature a detailed interpretation of daily life during the rise and fall of the cliff dwellings. Here you'll also encounter artifacts discovered throughout the park, and displays on Ancestral Puebloan culture and lifeways. There's also a 25-minute film about the park here, and the building itself is a classic from the rustic golden age of National Park Service architecture and design. There are of course also helpful rangers on hand, as well as an excellent bookstore. The museum offers free ranger-guided tours of Spruce Tree House three times a day during the high season. For a self-guided tour, pick up the $1 booklet at the museum, which also sells a guide to the nearby Petroglyph Trail for 50 cents.

★ Spruce Tree House

If you don't want to pay $4 extra for a ranger-guided tour of Cliff Palace, then a self-guided or free ranger-guided tour of **Spruce Tree House** is the only way to explore one of the park's amazing ancient stone apartment buildings up close. The third largest and "best preserved" of the park's cliff dwellings, Spruce Tree House thrived AD 1200-1280. At its height, probably about 60-90 people lived in its expertly constructed stone rooms.

A highlight of this 216-foot long, 89-foot deep sandstone alcove is a climb down a wooden ladder into the kiva, a ceremonial space. The kiva's roof was reconstructed by the park service in 1908 after the original collapsed sometime during the hundreds of years that the ruin sat silent and forgotten.

Tucked away in a forested, spring-fed canyon, Spruce Tree House requires its visitors to walk a short but steep, paved trail into the canyon from a trailhead outside the Chapin Mesa Archeological Museum. From early November to early March, you can only tour the ruin with a ranger, but the tour is free. Self-guided tours are permitted from early March to early November. During this time, free ranger-guided tours are offered three times a day from the museum.

★ Mesa Top Loop Road

There are two scenic loop drives on Chapin Mesa with many pull-offs and views of the cliff dwellings and dramatic canyons. The best is the six-mile **Mesa Top Loop Road** (24 hours daily) which moves past several gorgeous canyon views and pit-house sites to a view of a cliff dwelling called **Square Tower House,** then on to the **Sun Point View overlook** and the self-guided ruin **Sun Temple,** both of which offer amazing views of Cliff Palace.

The **Cliff Palace Loop Road,** also six miles, leads to views of Soda Canyon and **Balcony House,** and is the location of the Cliff Palace trailhead.

★ Cliff Palace

If you only take one ranger-guided tour during your visit to Mesa Verde, make it the one-hour tour of the queen of the cliff dwellings, **Cliff Palace** (tours every half hour 9am-6pm late May-mid-Sept., call ahead for tour times mid-Sept.-Oct., $4). The largest known ruin in North America, Cliff Palace dates from about AD 1200, less than a century before its builders abandoned it. At its height it might have had as many as 150 rooms, including 21 kivas. One park naturalist has speculated that this sprawling stone complex, with its many towers and plazas, was once "a busy, happy city of about 400 people." It's one of those places that must be seen in person to get its full effect. No photograph can replicate the feeling of standing high up in Cliff Palace.

To reach this special place, you have to follow a ranger up four different ladders. It's not as difficult as it sounds, but it's not for everyone. Unless you're deathly afraid of heights, the climb is pretty easy, fun, and definitely worth it.

Balcony House

Balcony House (tours every half-hour 9am-5pm daily late May-late Aug., every hour 9am-5pm daily late Aug.-mid-Oct.) may be a bit underwhelming if you've just been at Cliff Palace, but it's worth the one-hour tour for those who can't get enough of the cliff dwellings. With about 40 rooms and two kivas, Balcony House is believed to have been built quite late in the occupation of Mesa Verde, perhaps in the 1270s. The tour includes climbing one 32-foot ladder and two 10-foot ladders, crawling through an 18-inch-wide, 12-foot-long tunnel, and scrambling up stone steps hewn into the rock. It's a lot of fun and an expedition you won't soon forget.

Wetherill Mesa

Wetherill Mesa is a relatively remote section of the park that is open from early May to late October. The slow 12-mile drive along a steep and twisting road to reach the sights here takes about half an hour from the turnoff near Far View, which is about 15 miles from the park entrance. Far less crowded than Chapin Mesa and still showing the effects of a wildfire in 2000, Wetherill Mesa offers a quieter experience for those who take the time to reach it. The only visitors center in this section is a small information kiosk staffed by a ranger. The road to Wetherill Mesa is closed to bicycles and vehicles over 25 feet long.

Step House, a small cliff dwelling started around AD 1226 in the very shadow of a pit-house occupied for at least 600 years before, is the only cliff dwelling on Wetherill Mesa open to self-guided tours. The easy but fairly steep 0.75-mile trail past the ruin is open between Memorial Day and Labor Day.

A ranger-guided tour of **Long House** (9:30am, 10:30am, 2pm, and 4pm daily late May-early Sept., $4) is for die-hard fans of cliff dwellings. The ruin is the second largest in the park, with some 150 rooms in a long spring-fed alcove high above a canyon. The cliff dwelling was likely occupied for less than 80 years. The tour takes two hours, and requires a 2.25-mile hike and climbing up a 15-foot ladder—and that's after the long drive to Wetherill Mesa. However, if you put in the time and effort, you won't be sorry.

Recreation

Hiking

Soda Canyon Overlook Trail

Distance: 1.2 miles round-trip
Duration: 1 hour
Elevation change: negligible
Effort: easy
Trailhead: Cliff Palace Loop Road, 0.5 miles north of Balcony House parking lot

This is an easy stroll through the rim-top piñon-juniper forest to a point that provides excellent views of Soda Canyon, Balcony House, and other, smaller sights hanging above the canyon. This is a good hike for families who want to experience walking in the forest without a lot of effort.

★ Petroglyph Point Trail

Distance: 2.8 miles round-trip
Duration: 2 hours
Elevation change: 300 feet
Effort: moderate-difficult
Trailhead: outside the Chapin Mesa Archeological Museum

One of the highlights of the park, the Petroglyph Point Trail runs high up the slopes of Spruce Canyon to a well-preserved and mysterious panel of Ancestral Puebloan petroglyphs etched into the desert varnish on the rocks along the trail. It begins just outside the Chapin Mesa Archeological Museum and passes the Spruce Tree House ruin. From the trail, which is relatively difficult, rocky, and narrow, there are long and amazing views of the canyons that cut through Mesa Verde. After passing the petroglyphs, the trail winds up to the top of the mesa and moves easily through the quiet and open piñon-juniper forest back to Chapin Mesa Archeological Museum. This trail is even better with a detailed guide to its flora and fauna, which is available for 50 cents in the museum.

Spruce Canyon Trail

Distance: 2.4 miles round-trip
Duration: 2-3 hours
Elevation change: 600 feet
Effort: moderate
Trailhead: outside the Chapin Mesa Archeological Museum

This trail descends into Spruce Canyon from the Chapin Mesa Archeological Museum, passes Spruce Tree House, and runs through the peaceful bottomlands of the canyon. It rises back up to the rim country after making a loop through the canyon—a tough but rewarding climb.

Badger House Community Trail

Distance: 2.25 miles round-trip
Duration: 2 hours
Elevation change: negligible
Effort: easy
Trailhead: Wetherill Mesa information kiosk

An easy walk along a sometimes gravel, sometimes paved route on Wetherill Mesa, this trail provides access to numerous pit-house ruins and other older, mesa-top sights that sometimes get forgotten in the rush to see the more dramatic cliff dwellings.

Nordebskiold Site No. 16 Trail

Distance: 2 miles round-trip
Duration: 1.5-2 hours
Elevation change: 100 feet
Effort: easy
Trailhead: Wetherill Mesa information kiosk

Named for the young Swedish archaeologist who excavated many of the ruins at Mesa Verde in the 1890s, this easy trail through a fire-scarred landscape on Wetherill Mesa leads to a wonderful view of the eponymous ruin, tucked into a sandstone alcove in the canyon far below.

Accommodations

Aramark (970/529-4422 or 800/449-2288, www.visitmesaverde.com) is the park concessionaire, operating the lodge, the campground, and all of the in-park restaurants.

There are all kinds of accommodations down in Mancos Valley below Mesa Verde, in the small towns of Cortez to the west and Mancos to the east. In Cortez, the largest town near the park, various chain hotels line US 160/Main Street through town. It takes at least an hour to reach the park's main sights on Chapin Mesa from either Cortez or Mancos.

Inside the Park

Mesa Verde's only hotel, the 150-room ★ **Far View Lodge** (970/529-4422 or 800/449-2288, www.visitmesaverde.com, mid-Apr.-late Oct., $100-200), located about 15 miles up the mesa from the park entrance, is ideal for road-trippers. You can park your rig right outside your room, and there are doors between many of the rooms that come in handy for families. While the rooms themselves are fairly basic, the views can't be beat. Don't be surprised if you see wildlife, especially deer, milling around outside. The lodge is a short walk from the Far View Terrace Café and the Metate Room. It's about six miles down the main road from the Spruce Tree House trailhead and the museum.

The only other in-park option for a sleepover is **Morefield Campground** (early Apr.-Oct., $27-37). About 4 miles from the park entrance and 17 miles from Spruce Tree House and the museum, the 267-site campground has 15 full-hookup sites, a store, café, gas station, showers, and laundry. Both of these options require reservations about six months out.

Outside the Park: Cortez and Mancos

There are quite a few hotels in Cortez, most of them chains spread out along Main Street/US 160 through town. About eight miles east of the visitors center on US 160, Mancos is much smaller than Cortez.

The independently owned motels in the Mancos Valley below Mesa Verde tend to be lower-end, budget accommodations. The **Tomahawk Lodge** (728 S. Broadway, Cortez, 970/565-8521, $69) is clean and affordable, offering basic rooms and a relatively quiet spot to lay your head. The **Retro Inn** (2040 E. Main Street, Cortez, 970/670-7638, $72-118) has a bit more personality.

The **Enchanted Mesa Motel** (862 W. Grand Ave., Mancos, 970/533-7729, $81) in Mancos has been welcoming visitors since the 1950s, with basic, clean rooms, in-room refrigerators, free Wi-Fi, and old-fashioned friendliness.

Food

Inside the Park

A breed apart from the plastic trays and self-service of the other in-park eateries, the upscale ★ **Metate Room** (5pm-9:30pm daily mid-Apr.-late Oct., $6-32), near the Far View Lodge about 15 miles from the park entrance, serves regionally inspired and sourced dishes in an elegant atmosphere with long, beautiful views and excellent cocktails. It's a bit pricey but generally worth it. Make a reservation within 24 hours of your visit.

Aramark (970/529-4422 or 800/449-2288, www.visitmesaverde.com), the park concessionaire, operates all of the in-park restaurants. **Spruce Tree Terrace** (11am-3:30pm daily Jan.-early Mar., 11am-4:30pm daily early Mar.-mid-Apr., 10am-5pm daily mid-Apr.-late May, 9am-6:30pm daily late May-late Aug., 10am-5pm daily late Aug.-late Oct., 11am-3:30pm daily late Oct.-Dec., $5-10) is a smaller café with counter service. There's a relatively wide-ranging menu of Navajo and American food and a pleasant patio that gets really busy in summer.

At Far View, about 15 miles from the park entrance, the **Far View Terrace Café** (7am-10am, 11am-3pm, and 5pm-8pm daily May-Oct., $5-10) is a food court-style cafeteria, offering all manner of dishes, including pizza, Navajo tacos, Mexican food, burgers, and made-to-order omelets. Expect a line here during the high season.

Outside the Park: Cortez and Mancos

There are myriad restaurants in Cortez, most of them spread out along Main Street/US 160 through town. About eight miles east of the visitors center on US 160, Mancos is smaller than Cortez but has a few good places to eat.

An excellent lunch spot, **The Farm Bistro** (34 W. Main St., Cortez, 970/565-3834, www.thefarmbistrocortez.com, 11am-3pm Mon.-Fri., $4-11) in Cortez serves fantastic burgers, pita sandwiches, soups, salads, and other lunchtime classics using a variety of local and regional ingredients.

At ★ **Pepperhead** (44 W. Main St., Cortez, 970/566-3303, www.pepperheadcortez.com, 11am-8:30pm Tues.-Sat., $5-14) in Cortez, they make some of the best huevos rancheros, pork chile, and *rellenos* anywhere, and they also offer many vegetarian dishes. **El Burro Pancho** (125 E. Main St., Cortez, 970/565-4633, 11am-9pm daily, $5-17) in Cortez offers hot and heaping plates of expertly prepared Mexican food in a friendly atmosphere.

A popular place in Mancos, **Absolute Bakery & Cafe** (110 S. Main St., Mancos, 970/533-1200, www.absolutebakery.com, 7am-2pm Mon.-Sat., 7am-noon Sun., $5-10) has a small but enticing menu and is a great place for a decadent breakfast.

Try the microbrews created at the **Mancos Brewing Company** (550 Railroad Ave., Mancos, 970/533-9761, www.mancosbrewingcompany.com, 4pm-9pm Wed.-Sun., $5-15), where you're likely to meet a few locals enjoying their drinks with pub-style food.

Santa Fe and Taos

These small clusters of mud-colored buildings in the mountains of northern New Mexico seem to subsist on dreams and creativity alone.

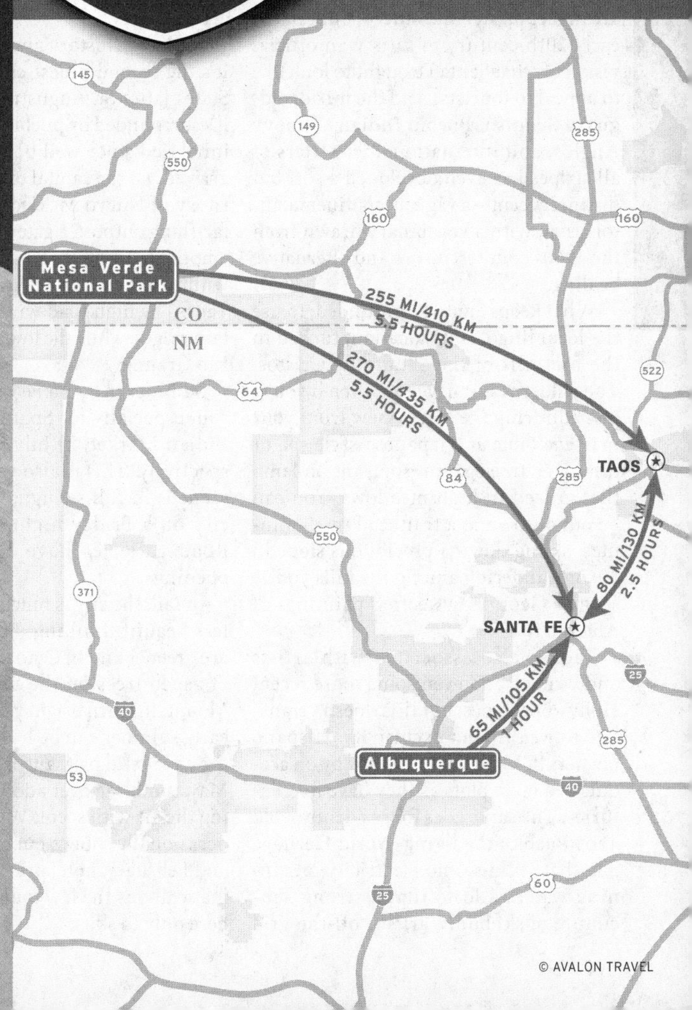

One of Santa Fe's several monikers is "Fanta Se," a play on the name that suggests the city's disconnection from reality, while Taos has a rougher, muddier feel.

Santa Fe's fabric is a by-product of this creativity—many of the "adobe" buildings in the distinctive downtown area are in fact plaster and stucco, built in the early 20th century to satisfy an official vision of what Santa Fe ought to look like to appeal to tourists. And the mix of old-guard Spanish, Pueblo Indians, groovy Anglos, and international jet-setters of all stripes has even developed a soft but distinct accent—a vaguely continental intonation, with a vocabulary drawn from the 1960s counterculture and alternative healing.

What keeps Santa Fe grounded, to use the local lingo, is its location, tucked in the foothills of the Sangre de Cristos. The wilderness is never far, even if you're just admiring the forest view from your massage table at a Japanese-style spa or dining at an elegant restaurant on lamb that grazed in high meadows. You can be out of town at a trailhead in 15 minutes, skiing down a precipitous slope in 30, or wandering among the hills you've seen in Georgia O'Keeffe's paintings of Abiquiu in 60.

Taos is also associated with artists and writers, and even some more recent Hollywood types, but this doesn't translate to wealth and exclusivity. Hispano farmers in Valle Valdez scrape by on acequia-fed farm plots as they have for centuries. The same goes for residents of old Taos Pueblo, the living World Heritage Site that still uses no electricity or running water. Add to that a strong subculture of ski bums, artists, off-the-grid eco-homesteaders, and spiritual seekers, and you have a community that, while not typically prosperous, is more loyal and dedicated to preserving its unique way of life than perhaps any other small town in the western United States.

Santa Fe

In Santa Fe's Yellow Pages, "Art galleries" take up five pages, and "Artists" have their own heading. In all, nearly half the city is employed in the larger arts industry.

Santa Fe's history gives it strong roots. It's the second-oldest city in the United States (after St. Augustine, Florida), and it's surrounded by pueblos that have been inhabited since well before the Spanish arrived. As the capital of the Spanish territory of Nuevo México, Santa Fe was a far-flung outpost, a gateway to the wilder, emptier lands to the north. And it still is, with two scenic routes running north to Taos: The high road winds along mountain ridges, while the low road follows the Rio Grande.

Summer in Santa Fe is ultra-high season, especially for Spanish Market and Indian Market, in July and August respectively. This is also when the gallery scene is in full swing; plan to be in the city on a Friday night, when Canyon Road galleries have their convivial openings.

In fall, the city is much calmer and offers beautiful hiking, because the hills are greener and in October, dense groves of aspen trees on the Sangre de Cristo Mountains turn bright yellow. Spring and early summer can be hot and windy, but the city is still pleasant, as lilacs bloom in May, tumbling over adobe walls and filling the air with scent. Winter is cold and occasionally snowy, but clear. In January and February, hotel prices can drop dramatically, as the few tourists in town are here only to ski.

Highlights

★ **La Fonda:** The Santa Fe Trail trade route ended on the doorstep of this hotel, which has harbored the city's assorted characters for centuries (page 266).

★ **Canyon Road Galleries:** This winding street is the heart of Santa Fe's art scene and its social life (page 267).

★ **Museum of International Folk Art:** In the main exhibition hall of this Santa Fe museum, all the world's crafts, from Appalachian quilts to Zulu masks, are jumbled together in an inspiring display of human creativity (page 270).

★ **Santuario de Chimayó:** Faith is palpable in this village church north of Santa Fe, known as "the Lourdes of America," thanks to the healing powers attributed to the holy dirt found here (page 297).

★ **Taos Art Museum at Fechin House:** In the early 1930s, Russian artist Nicolai Fechin designed his Taos home in a fantastical fusion of Tartar, Spanish, and American Indian styles (page 307).

★ **Mabel Dodge Luhan House:** See where America's counterculture thrived in the mid-20th century, as encouraged by the arts doyenne who made Taos her home (page 308).

★ **San Francisco de Asis Church:** With its massive adobe buttresses and earthy glow, this 350-year-old Franciscan mission is one of the most recognizable in the world (page 310).

★ **Taos Pueblo:** The stepped adobe buildings at New Mexico's most remarkable pueblo seem to rise organically from the earth. Don't miss the ceremonial dances here, about eight times a year (page 310).

★ **Rio Grande Gorge:** "New Mexico's Grand Canyon" is an 800-foot-deep channel cut through the rock to the west of Taos (page 312).

★ **Hiking Around Taos:** The mountains and mesas in this region are some of the most stunning places in the state to get some fresh air—you can even climb the state's highest peak (page 319).

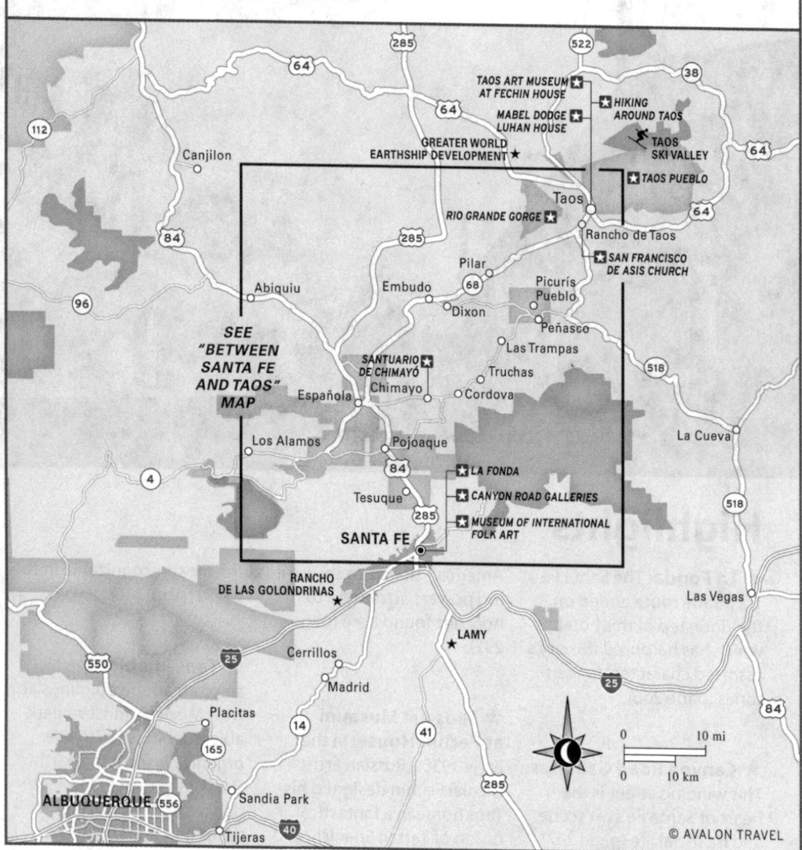

Getting There from Mesa Verde National Park

270 miles / 5.5 hours

From Mesa Verde, it's a **5.5-hour, 270-mile** drive to Santa Fe. After winding down the Mesa Verde to the park entrance (20 miles, 40 minutes), join **US 160 East** and drive to the town of Durango, which is just **35 miles** east of the park. At the junction with US 550, veer right to continue following US 160 East. In 60 miles, the highway leads to the town of Pagosa Springs. Where US 160 turns northward, turn right to join **US 84 East.** After about 30 miles, you'll cross into New Mexico. Continue for another 100 miles on US 84, passing through Abiquiu. In the town of Española, follow the highway as it goes over the Rio Grande. Continue on **US 285 South/US 84 East** for 25 miles, after which, use the left lane to exit toward Downtown Plaza/Museum. Follow **North Guadalupe Street** for just under a mile then turn left onto **West San Francisco Street** and continue for a half-mile until you reach the Santa Fe Plaza.

Stopping in Pagosa Springs

Deep in the evergreen forest, about 115 miles and 2.5 hours from Mesa Verde

National Park, the deepest hot spring in the world bubbles and steams in the small resort town of Pagosa Springs. The geothermal "mother spring" here is at least 1,000 feet deep, gushing out at 144°F.

Your bones will thank you if you stop for a few hours to soak in the 18 pools available to the public at the **The Springs Resort** (165 Hot Springs Blvd., 800/255-0934. www.pagosahotsprings.com, 7am-midnight daily late May-early Sept., 7am-11pm daily early Sept.-late May, day passes adults $26-53, children under 13 $14-29). The developed pools outside the posh Bath House look out on the San Juan River. Pool temperatures range from 83°F to the 114°F Lobster Pot. Spending time soaking in the pools and watching the river roll by may cause lethargy. If this happens to you, the resort has comfortable, stylish rooms ($189-305), and a very friendly, helpful staff.

The town itself has many excellent restaurants and other, less expensive, non-spring places to stay. The **Riff Raff Brewing Company** (274 Pagosa St./US 160, 970/264-4677, http://riffraffbrewing.com, 11am-10pm daily, $8-20) offers a creative and flavorful take on pub food and brews some of the best craft beers in the region.

Right across the river from the hot springs, **Tequila's** (439 Pagosa St./US 160, 970/264-9989, 11am-10pm Sun.-Thurs, 11am-11pm Fri.-Sat., $5-20) is popular with tourists, serving good Mexican food in a gorgeous patio setting.

Getting There from Albuquerque (Route 66)

65 miles / 1 hour

From Albuquerque to Santa Fe, it's a straight shot north on **I-25** for **65 miles.** You'll reach Santa Fe in just **over an hour.** From I-25, take exit 284 for **NM-466/Old Pecos Trail.** Turn left onto Old Pecos Trail and follow the road for about three miles. Old Pecos becomes **Old Santa Fe Trail,** which leads to downtown Santa Fe in another mile.

Getting There from Taos

80 miles / 2.5 hours

The most direct route from Taos to Santa Fe is the Low Road along the Rio Grande. The **70-mile** drive takes about **1.5 hours.** Leave Taos via **NM-68 South,** continuing for 45 miles to Española. From there, stay left to follow **US 285 South/US 84 East** to Santa Fe.

Best Accommodations

★ **Silver Saddle Motel:** This small motel in Santa Fe offers a bit of Southwestern ambience for an affordable price (page 280).

★ **Santa Fe Sage Inn:** A short walk to downtown Santa Fe and free breakfast make this clean little highway motel ideal for budget travelers (page 280).

★ **La Fonda:** This historic, central place to stay has all the old Santa Fe touches (page 281).

★ **Inn at the Delta:** The rooms in this elegant adobe inn in the small town of Española are decorated with locally made furniture (page 292).

★ **Rancho Jacona:** On the road to Los Alamos, this farm rents casitas in an unforgettable setting (page 292).

★ **Mabel Dodge Luhan House:** This enchanting bed-and-breakfast has a style all its own (page 322).

★ **El Pueblo Lodge:** Just a short walk from Taos's central plaza, you'll find clean and stylish rooms for a fair price (page 323).

A longer, even more scenic route, the famed High Road, is an approximately **80-mile** winding climb into the Sangre de Cristo Mountains, passing a series of historic, Spanish-era villages. Count on this route taking **2.5 hours** at the very least, much longer with stops to stroll around and take pictures. From Taos, get on **NM-68 South,** drive for 3.5 miles, then turn left onto **NM-518.** After 15 winding miles, turn right to get on **NM-75 West.** Continue for less than 10 miles until the junction with NM-76. Turn left to join **NM-76 South.** Continue for about 20 miles, passing through the town of Truchas, until the junction with **Juan Medina Road/County Road 98.** Turn left onto CR-98 and drive for just under five miles until the intersection with **NM-503.** Turn right and follow NM-503 for just under 10 miles to Pojoaque. Then turn left onto **US 285 South/US 84 East** and drive for 15 miles, then follow signs for downtown Santa Fe.

By Train

The **Rail Runner** (866/795-7245, www.riometro.org) goes from Albuquerque to downtown Santa Fe—the final stop is at the rail yard in the **Guadalupe district** (410 S. Guadalupe St.). The ride takes a little over 90 minutes and costs $9, or $10 for a day pass (only $9 if you buy it online), and the last train back to Albuquerque leaves at 9pm weekdays, 10:07pm Saturdays, and 8:12pm Sundays.

Sights

Orientation

Santa Fe is a small town. Most of the major sights are within walking distance from the central plaza; generally, you'll find yourself within the oval formed by **Paseo de Peralta,** a road that almost completely circles the central district. On its southwest side it connects with **Cerrillos Road,** a main avenue lined with motel courts, shopping plazas, and chain restaurants. Compared with the central

Best Restaurants

★ **Tia Sophia's:** This authentic old favorite in Santa Fe claims to have invented the breakfast burrito (page 282).

★ **Café Pasqual's:** This small, popular bistro in central Santa Fe serves creative cuisine using fresh and organic ingredients (page 282).

★ **Santa Fe Bite:** It's the place in Santa Fe to get your burger fix (page 283).

★ **Horseman's Haven:** Try the green chile here if you dare; it's possibly the hottest and best in Santa Fe (page 287).

★ **Zuly's:** This friendly, memorable place to stop for delicious New Mexican food is in Dixon, on the Low Road from Santa Fe to Taos (page 295).

★ **Rancho de Chimayó:** This charming spot in the village of Chimayó, along the High Road to Taos, serves authentic New Mexican dishes from a cozy adobe house (page 299).

★ **Sugar Nymphs Bistro:** This popular restaurant in Peñasco, a village on the High Road to Taos, creates unique dishes inspired by the local history and landscape (page 301).

★ **Gutiz:** This spot in Taos serves a flavorful mixture of Latin and French flavors in a patio setting (page 326).

★ **El Meze:** This Taos restaurant reaches back to New Mexico's ties with Spain and the Middle East to build its own inspired and creative cuisine (page 327).

historic district, it's unsightly, but there are some great local places to eat along this way, as well as the few inexpensive hotels in town.

Downtown

Santa Fe Plaza

When Santa Fe was established in 1610, its layout was based on Spanish laws governing town planning in the colonies—hence the central plaza fronted by the Casas Reales (Palace of the Governors) on its north side. The **Santa Fe Plaza** is still the city's social hub, and the blocks surrounding it are rich with history. In the center of the plaza is the **Soldiers' Monument,** dedicated in 1867 to those who died in "battles with...Indians in the territory of New Mexico." The word "savage" has been neatly excised, following a policy applied to historic markers throughout the state.

New Mexico History Museum and Palace of the Governors

Opened in 2009, the **New Mexico History Museum** (113 Lincoln Ave., 505/476-5200, www.nmhistorymuseum.org, 10am-5pm daily June-Sept., 10am-5pm Tues.-Sun. Oct.-May, $9) was intended to give a little breathing room for a collection that had been in storage for decades. Oddly, though, it feels like very few actual objects are on display. The exhibits give a good basic overview, though if you're already familiar with the state's storied past, you might not find much new here.

The museum incorporates the **Palace of the Governors,** the former seat of Santa Fe's government. Built 1610-1612, it's one of the oldest government buildings in the United States, giving it plenty of time to accumulate stories. De Vargas fought the Indian rebels here room by room when he retook the city in 1693, ill-fated Mexican governor Albino Pérez was beheaded in his office in 1837, and Governor Lew Wallace penned *Ben Hur* here in the late 1870s. The exhibits here showcase some of the most beautiful items in the state's collection: trinkets and photos from the 19th century, as well as the beautiful 18th-century Segesser hide paintings, two wall-size panels of buffalo skin. These works, along with the room they're in (trimmed with 1909 murals of the Puyé cliffs) are worth the price of admission. In a couple of the restored furnished rooms, you can compare the living conditions of the Mexican leadership circa 1845 to the relative comfort the U.S. governor enjoyed in 1893.

Walking tours depart from the blue gate on the Lincoln Avenue side of the New Mexico History Museum at 10:15am (Mon.-Sat. mid-Apr.-mid-Oct., $10), covering all the plaza-area highlights in about two hours.

New Mexico Museum of Art

Famed as much for its building as for the art it contains, the **New Mexico Museum of Art** (107 W. Palace Ave., 505/476-5072, www.nmartmuseum.org, 10am-5pm daily May-Oct., 10am-5pm Tues.-Sun. Nov.-Apr., $9) is dedicated to work by New Mexican artists. Built in 1917, it is a beautiful example of Pueblo Revival architecture, originally designed as the New Mexico pavilion for a world expo in San Diego two years prior. The curvaceous stucco-clad building combines elements from the most iconic pueblo mission churches—the bell towers, for instance, mimic those found at San Felipe. Inside, the collection starts with Gerald Cassidy's oil painting *Cui Bono?* on display since the museum's opening in 1917 and still relevant, as it questions the benefits of pueblo tourism. Look out for an excellent collection of Awa Tsireh's meticulous watercolors of ceremonial dances at San Ildefonso Pueblo, alongside works by other local American Indian artists.

On your way out, don't miss the adjacent St. Francis Auditorium, where three artists adorned the walls with art nouveau murals depicting the life of Santa Fe's patron saint. It's rare to see a secular style usually reserved for languorous

Downtown Santa Fe

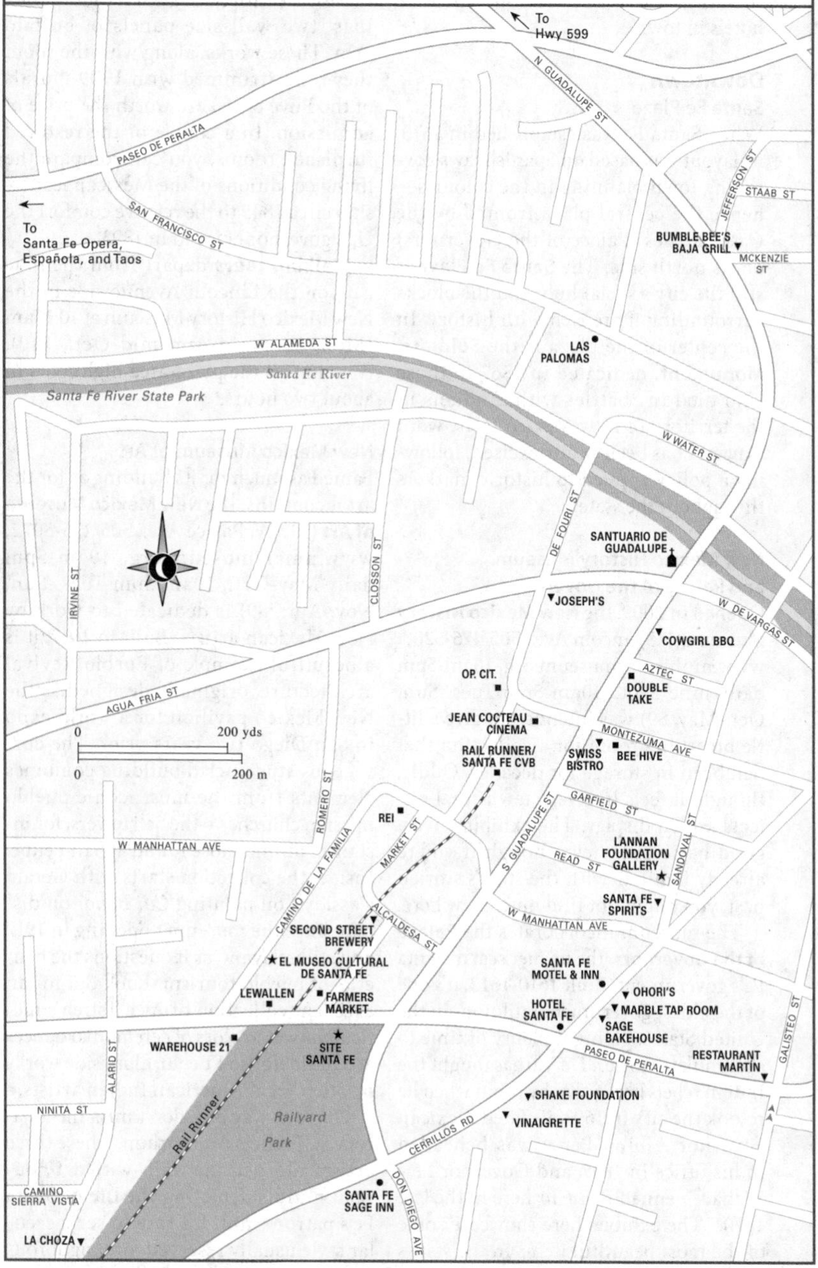

To Hwy 599
N GUADALUPE ST
PASEO DE PERALTA
JEFFERSON ST
STAAB ST
To Santa Fe Opera, Española, and Taos
SAN FRANCISCO ST
BUMBLE BEE'S BAJA GRILL
MCKENZIE ST
W ALAMEDA ST
LAS PALOMAS
Santa Fe River
Santa Fe River State Park
W WATER ST
DE FOURI ST
SANTUARIO DE GUADALUPE
IRVINE ST
CLOSSON ST
JOSEPH'S
W DE VARGAS ST
COWGIRL BBQ
AZTEC ST
OP. CIT.
DOUBLE TAKE
AGUA FRIA ST
JEAN COCTEAU CINEMA
0 200 yds
0 200 m
MONTEZUMA AVE
RAIL RUNNER/ SANTA FE CVB
SWISS BISTRO
BEE HIVE
GARFIELD ST
REI
ROMERO ST
MARKET ST
S GUADALUPE ST
SANDOVAL ST
W MANHATTAN AVE
CAMINO DE LA FAMILIA
LANNAN FOUNDATION GALLERY
READ ST
SANTA FE SPIRITS
ALCALDESA ST
W MANHATTAN AVE
SECOND STREET BREWERY
EL MUSEO CULTURAL DE SANTA FE
SANTA FE MOTEL & INN
OHORI'S
LEWALLEN
FARMERS MARKET
HOTEL SANTA FE
MARBLE TAP ROOM
SAGE BAKEHOUSE
GALISTEO ST
WAREHOUSE 21
SITE SANTA FE
PASEO DE PERALTA
RESTAURANT MARTÍN
ALARID ST
NINITA ST
SHAKE FOUNDATION
VINAIGRETTE
Railyard Park
Rail Runner
CERRILLOS RD
DON DIEGO AVE
SANTA FE SAGE INN
CAMINO SIERRA VISTA
LA CHOZA

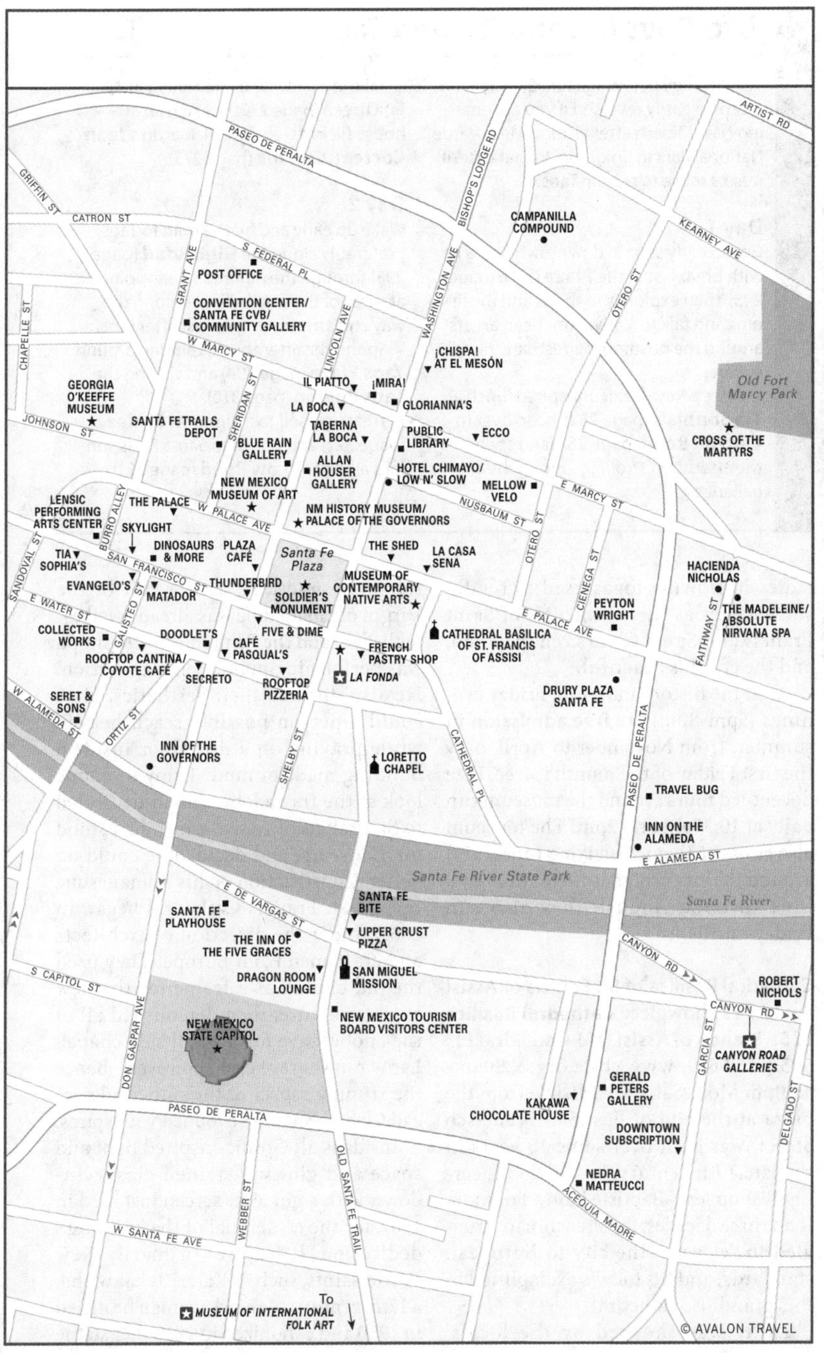
ARTIST RD
PASEO DE PERALTA
BISHOP'S LODGE RD
GRIFFIN ST
CATRON ST
CAMPANILLA COMPOUND
KEARNEY AVE
S FEDERAL PL
GRANT AVE
POST OFFICE
WASHINGTON AVE
OTERO ST
CONVENTION CENTER/ SANTA FE CVB/ COMMUNITY GALLERY
LINCOLN AVE
CHAPELLE ST
W MARCY ST
¡CHISPA! AT EL MESÓN
Old Fort Marcy Park
GEORGIA O'KEEFFE MUSEUM
SHERIDAN ST
IL PIATTO
¡MIRA!
LA BOCA
GLORIANNA'S
JOHNSON ST
SANTA FE TRAILS DEPOT
TABERNA LA BOCA
PUBLIC LIBRARY
ECCO
CROSS OF THE MARTYRS
BLUE RAIN GALLERY
ALLAN HOUSER GALLERY
HOTEL CHIMAYO/ LOW N' SLOW
MELLOW VELO
E MARCY ST
NEW MEXICO MUSEUM OF ART
LENSIC PERFORMING ARTS CENTER
BURRO ALLEY
THE PALACE
W PALACE AVE
NUSBAUM ST
NM HISTORY MUSEUM/ PALACE OF THE GOVERNORS
SKYLIGHT
DINOSAURS & MORE
PLAZA CAFÉ
Santa Fe Plaza
THE SHED
LA CASA SENA
CIENEGA ST
TIA SOPHIA'S
SAN FRANCISCO ST
HACIENDA NICHOLAS
SANDOVAL ST
EVANGELO'S
MATADOR
THUNDERBIRD
SOLDIER'S MONUMENT
MUSEUM OF CONTEMPORARY NATIVE ARTS
PEYTON WRIGHT
FAITHWAY ST
THE MADELEINE/ ABSOLUTE NIRVANA SPA
E WATER ST
GALISTEO ST
FIVE & DIME
E PALACE AVE
CATHEDRAL BASILICA OF ST. FRANCIS OF ASSISI
COLLECTED WORKS
DOODLET'S
CAFÉ PASQUAL'S
FRENCH PASTRY SHOP
ROOFTOP CANTINA/ COYOTE CAFÉ
LA FONDA
SECRETO
ROOFTOP PIZZERIA
DRURY PLAZA SANTA FE
SERET & SONS
W ALAMEDA ST
ORTIZ ST
PASEO DE PERALTA
INN OF THE GOVERNORS
SHELBY ST
LORETTO CHAPEL
CATHEDRAL PL
TRAVEL BUG
INN ON THE ALAMEDA
E ALAMEDA ST
Santa Fe River State Park
Santa Fe River
E DE VARGAS ST
SANTA FE BITE
SANTA FE PLAYHOUSE
UPPER CRUST PIZZA
THE INN OF THE FIVE GRACES
CANYON RD
S CAPITOL ST
DRAGON ROOM LOUNGE
SAN MIGUEL MISSION
ROBERT NICHOLS
CANYON RD
NEW MEXICO TOURISM BOARD VISITORS CENTER
NEW MEXICO STATE CAPITOL
GARCIA ST
CANYON ROAD GALLERIES
DON GASPAR AVE
GERALD PETERS GALLERY
DELGADO ST
KAKAWA CHOCOLATE HOUSE
PASEO DE PERALTA
DOWNTOWN SUBSCRIPTION
OLD SANTA FE TRAIL
NEDRA MATTEUCCI
WEBBER ST
ACEQUIA MADRE
W SANTA FE AVE
MUSEUM OF INTERNATIONAL FOLK ART
To
© AVALON TRAVEL

Two Days in Santa Fe and Taos

The strategy below starts in Santa Fe, but it can be easily reversed if you are entering New Mexico after visiting Mesa Verde National Park in Colorado. In that case, it makes sense to start in Taos.

Day 1

Get an early start in downtown Santa Fe with breakfast at the **Plaza Café** (page 283), then explore the shops and museums and talk to Native American artists around the bustling, pedestrian-friendly square.

After a New Mexico-inspired lunch at **Tia Sophia's** (page 282), head over to **Canyon Road** (page 267) and spend the afternoon strolling among the art galleries.

Take in a show at the famous **Santa Fe Opera** (page 272) or catch an art-house flick at George R. R. Martin's **Jean Cocteau Cinema** (page 273).

Day 2

Wake up early and hit the road to Taos, preferably along the **High Road** (page 295) through the mountains, stopping at a few of the small villages along the way and arriving in Taos just after lunch.

Spend the afternoon exploring around **Taos Plaza** (page 304) and visiting the **Taos Pueblo** (page 310).

Treat yourself to a dinner at **El Meze** (page 327) and return to Santa Fe as sun falls along the **Low Road** (page 291).

ladies in flowing togas used to render such scenes as the apotheosis of Saint Francis and Santa Clara's renunciation, and the effect is beautiful.

As at the history museum, Friday evenings (5pm-8pm) are **free admission** in summer; from November to April, only the first Friday of the month is free. Free docent-led **tours** around the museum run daily at 10:30am and 2pm. The museum also runs art-themed **walking tours** ($10) around the city center at 10am Mondays; June through August, they also run Fridays at 10am.

Cathedral Basilica of St. Francis of Assisi

Santa Fe's showpiece **Cathedral Basilica of St. Francis of Assisi** (131 Cathedral Pl., 505/982-5619, www.cbsfa.org, 9:30am-4:30pm Mon.-Sat., free), visible from the plaza at the end of East San Francisco Street, was built over some 15 years in the late 19th century, by the domineering Bishop Jean-Baptiste Lamy. For more than three decades, the Frenchman struggled to "elevate" the city to European standards, and his folly is exemplified in this grandiose cathedral.

Lamy was shocked by the locals' religious practices, as the cult of the Virgin of Guadalupe was already well established, and the Penitente brotherhood was performing public self-flagellation. He also disliked their aesthetics. How could a person possibly reach heaven while praying on a dirt floor inside a building made of mud? Lamy took one look at the tiny adobe church dedicated to St. Francis of Assisi, which had stood for 170 years, and decided he could do better. Construction on his Romanesque revival St. Francis Cathedral began in 1869, under the direction of architects and craftsmen from Europe. They used the old church as a frame for the new stone structure, then demolished all of the adobe, save for a small side chapel. Lamy ran short of cash, however—hence the stumpy aspect of the cathedral's facade, which should be topped with spires.

Inside is all Gothic-inspired light and space and glowing stained-glass windows, with a gilt altar screen installed in 1987, for the centennial of the building's dedication. It features primarily New World saints, such as Kateri Tekakwitha, a 17th-century Mohawk woman beatified in 1980 and canonized in 2012 (her statue

New Mexico Culture Pass

A **museum pass** ($25) good for 12 months grants onetime access to all of the state-run museums and historic sites. This includes four Santa Fe institutions—the New Mexico Museum of Art, the New Mexico History Museum, the Museum of Indian Arts & Culture, and the Museum of International Folk Art—as well as two in Albuquerque (the National Hispanic Cultural Center and the natural history museum), and the Coronado and Jemez historic sites. It also covers attractions farther afield, in Las Cruces, Alamogordo, and more—great if you're a state resident or you're already planning a longer return visit within the year.

also stands outside the cathedral). She is depicted with a turtle, representing her membership in the Turtle Clan.

The salvaged adobe chapel remains off to the left of the altar. It is dedicated to the figure of La Conquistadora, a statue brought to Santa Fe from Mexico in 1625, carried away by the retreating Spanish during the Pueblo Revolt, then proudly reinstated in 1693 and honored ever since. She glows in her shimmering robes, under a heavy viga ceiling—all of which probably makes Lamy shudder in his crypt in front of the main altar (he died in 1888).

On your way out, check the great cast-bronze doors—they're usually propped open, so you'll have to peer behind to see the images depicting the history of Catholicism in New Mexico. One plaque shows the Italian stoneworkers constructing the cathedral, and another shows families fleeing from attack in 1680—a rare depiction of the Pueblo Revolt that's sympathetic to the Spanish.

Loretto Chapel

Step inside the small **Loretto Chapel** (207 Old Santa Fe Tr., 505/982-0092, 9am-5pm Mon.-Sat., 10:30am-5pm Sun., $3) and you leave the Southwest behind. Initiated by Bishop Lamy in 1873, the building was the first Gothic structure erected west of the Mississippi. The decorative elements reflect his fondness for all things European: the stations of the cross rendered by Italian masons, the harmonium and stained-glass windows imported from France. Even the stone from which it was built was hauled at great expense from quarries 200 miles south.

What really draws the eye is the elegant spiral staircase leading to the choir loft. Made entirely of wood, it makes two complete turns without a central support pole. It was built in 1878 by a mysterious carpenter who appeared seemingly at the spiritual behest of the resident Sisters of Loretto. These nuns—whom Lamy had summoned from Missouri in 1853 to run a school—had resorted to prayer because Lamy's funding hadn't been quite enough. The carpenter toiled in silence for six months, the story goes, then disappeared, without taking any payment. He was never heard from again—though some historians claim to have tracked him down to Las Cruces, where he met his end in a bar fight. The Sisters of Loretto went broke in 1968; the chapel was desanctified when it sold in 1971.

Georgia O'Keeffe Museum

Opened in 1997, the **Georgia O'Keeffe Museum** (217 Johnson St., 505/946-1000, www.okeeffemuseum.org, 9am-5pm Sat.-Thurs., 9am-7pm Fri. June-Oct.; 10am-5pm Sat.-Thurs., 10am-7pm Fri. Nov.-May, $12), northwest of the plaza, honors the artist whose name is inextricably bound with New Mexico. The contrary member of the New York avant-garde ("Nothing is less real than realism," she famously said) started making regular visits to the state in the 1920s, then moved to Abiquiu full-time in 1949, a few

It's Not *All* Adobe

Santa Fe's distinctive look is the product of the stringent Historic Styles Ordinance, which dictates even the shade of brown stucco finish required for buildings around the plaza. But look closely, and you'll see some variations. **Colonial** is the term applied to adobe (or adobe-look) buildings, usually one story, with their typical rounded edges and flat roofs supported by vigas, the long crossbeams made of single tree trunks. The style was developed by the Spanish colonists in the 16th, 17th, and 18th centuries, based on their previous experience with adobe architecture and forms they saw in the pueblos.

In the 19th century, when New Mexico became a U.S. territory, timber-frame houses came into fashion. These so-called **territorial** buildings were often two stories tall, with balconies, and trimmed with brick cornices and Greek revival details, such as fluted wood columns and pediments above windows. The Catron Building, on the northeast corner of the plaza, is a fine example.

But the tide turned again in the early part of the 20th century, when the **Pueblo Revival** style brought the Spanish colonial look back in vogue. Architects like John Gaw Meem and Isaac Rapp admired the mission churches and pueblos for their clean-lined minimalism. Because they used frame construction, Pueblo Revival buildings could be taller: Rapp's New Mexico Museum of Art towers on the northwest corner of the plaza, and Meem's additions to La Fonda make it five stories. The trend coincided with an aggressive tourism campaign and the development of a comprehensive look for the city, and in the process many territorial houses were simply covered over in a thick layer of faux-adobe plaster. The result is not precisely historic, but the city planners achieved their goal: Santa Fe looks like no other city in the United States.

years after the death of her husband, photographer Alfred Stieglitz.

Many of O'Keeffe's finest works—her signature sensuous, near-abstract flower blossoms, for instance—have already been ensconced in other famous museums, so the collection here can seem a little thin. To get the most out of a visit, join a docent **tour** (10:30am or 2pm daily). Exhibits draw on the work that she kept, plus ephemera and other work her foundation has amassed since her death in 1986. Often the space is given over to exhibitions on her contemporaries or those whose work she influenced or admired.

Museum of Contemporary Native Arts

Set in the city's former post office, the **Museum of Contemporary Native Arts** (108 Cathedral Pl., 505/983-8900, www.iaia.edu, 10am-5pm Mon. and Wed.-Sat., noon-5pm Sun., $10) is the showcase for students, professors, and alumni of the prestigious Institute of American Indian Arts. The space is relatively small, and the shows can be hit or miss, which makes it a bit pricey. If your time is limited, the Museum of Indian Arts & Culture is a better bet. But the gift shop stocks items with a good blend of modern and traditional styles that are quite well priced.

★ La Fonda

La Fonda (100 E. San Francisco St., 505/982-5511), on the corner of San Francisco Street and Old Santa Fe Trail, has been offering respite to travelers in some form or another since 1607. "The Inn at the End of the Trail" boomed in the early years of the trade route across the West, and also in the later gold-digging era, with a casino and saloon. It hosted the victory ball following General Kearny's takeover of New Mexico in the Mexican-American War. During the Civil War it housed Confederate general H. H. Sibley. Lynchings and shootings took place in the lobby. In the 1920s, it got a bit safer for the average tourist, as it joined the chain of Harvey Houses along the country's railways, and the architect Mary Jane Colter (best known for designing the hotels at the Grand Canyon) redesigned the interior. Since the 1960s, it has been a family-owned hotel.

The stacked Pueblo Revival place you see today dates from 1920, and it hums with history—something about the waxed tile floors, painted glass, and heavy furniture conveys the pleasant clamor of conversation and hotel busyness the way more modern lobbies do not. Guests pick up their keys at an old wood reception desk, drop their letters in an Indian-drum-turned-mailbox, and chat with the concierge below a poster for Harvey's Indian Detour car trips. Also look around—including up on the mezzanine level—at the great art collection. La Plazuela restaurant, in the sunny center courtyard, is a beautiful place to rest (with good posole), and the bar is timeless, with live country music many nights.

New Mexico State Capitol

A round building with an entrance at each of the cardinal points, the 1966 **New Mexico State Capitol** (491 Old Santa Fe Tr., 505/986-4589, 8am-5:30pm Mon.-Fri.) mimics the Zia sun symbol used on the state flag. Inside, the Roundhouse, as it's commonly known, houses the excellent **Capitol Art Collection** (505/986-4614, www.nmcapitolart.org, 8am-5pm Mon.-Fri., free), with works by the state's best-known creative types, all accessible for free. You'll find paintings and photographs in the halls on the senate side, in the upstairs balcony area, and in the fourth-floor Governor's Gallery. In the floor of the rotunda is a mosaic rendition of the state seal: the Mexican brown eagle, grasping a snake and shielded by the American bald eagle. And don't forget to look up at the stained-glass skylight, with its intricate Indian basket-weave pattern.

When the legislature is in session—late January through February in even-numbered years, late January through March in odd—visitors are welcome to sit in the galleries and watch the proceedings.

★ Canyon Road Galleries

The intersection of Paseo de Peralta and **Canyon Road** is ground zero for the city's **art market.** This is the beginning of a half-mile strip that contains more than 80 galleries, and in the summer, Canyon Road is a solid mass of strolling art lovers, aficionados and amateurs alike. It's especially thronged on summer Fridays, when most galleries have an open house or an exhibition opening, from around 5pm until 7pm or 8pm.

It's hard to believe, but the street wasn't always chockablock with thousand-dollar canvases. Starting in the 1920s, transplant artists settled on this muddy dirt road, the area gradually came to be associated with creative exploits, and eventually the art market really boomed in the 1980s. Before that, it was farmland, irrigated by the "Mother Ditch," Acequia Madre, which still runs parallel one block to the south—take a walk up here to get a sense of what the neighborhood used to be like.

There's a city parking lot at the east (upper) end of the road. Public restrooms (9:30am-5:30pm daily) are near the west end, in the complex at 225 Canyon Road, behind Expressions gallery.

Old Santa Fe Trail

From the plaza, the historic **Old Santa Fe Trail** trade route, now paved and looking like any other city street, runs off to the east. Just past Paseo de Peralta and the small Santa Fe River, it passes through Barrio de Analco, one of Santa Fe's oldest residential neighborhoods, established by the Tlaxcala Indians who came from Mexico as servants of the first Spanish settlers. The road then runs past the state capitol and to a junction with Old Pecos Trail, the main route to I-25.

San Miguel Mission

The **San Miguel Mission** (401 Old Santa Fe Tr., 505/983-3974, 9am-5pm Mon.-Sat. 10am-4pm Sun., $1), a sturdy adobe building where Mass is still said in Latin at noon on Sunday, is the oldest church structure in the United States. It was built starting in 1610, then partially reconstructed a century later, after it was set aflame in the Pueblo Revolt. Its stone buttresses are the product of a desperate attempt to shore up the sagging walls in the late 19th century. The interior is snug and whitewashed, with painted buffalo hides on the walls and an altar screen that was restored in 1955 after having been covered over in house paint for decades. The late-18th-century work is attributed to the anonymous Laguna Santero, a Mexican artist who earned his name from the intricately carved and painted screen at the Laguna Pueblo church, near Albuquerque.

Guadalupe and the Railyard

This neighborhood southwest of the plaza developed around the depot for the rail spur from the main line at Lamy. Now it's the terminus for the Rail Runner from Albuquerque. The clutch of cafés and shops here are more casual and local, and generally feel different from the plaza, as **Guadalupe** is just outside beyond the reach of the most stringent adobe-look building codes.

South of the train depot is the **Railyard** (www.railyardsantafe.com), a mixed-use district where former warehouses and workshops have been adapted to new business, including a permanent indoor home for the city farmers market. The south side of this area is the green space of **Railyard Park,** nicely landscaped with local grasses and fruit trees.

Santuario de Guadalupe

Built 1776-1796, the **Santuario de Guadalupe** (417 Agua Fria St., 505/983-8868, www.ologsf.com, 9am-noon and 1pm-4pm Mon.-Sat., free) is the oldest shrine to the Virgin of Guadalupe in the

the Railyard shopping area

United States. The interior is spare, just folding chairs set up on the wood floor, in front of a Mexican baroque oil-on-canvas altar painting from 1783. Mass is still said regularly, and musical groups, particularly the Santa Fe Desert Chorale, make use of the space's excellent acoustics. A museum in the small anteroom displays relics from earlier incarnations of the building, such as Greek-style columns carved in wood. The chapel is closed on Saturdays during the winter.

SITE Santa Fe

This boxy, modern exhibition space is dedicated to all things new in the art world, mounting high-concept one-off shows that often transform the interior (and sometimes exterior). **SITE Santa Fe** (1606 Paseo de Peralta, 505/989-1199, www.sitesantafe.org, 10am-5pm Thurs. and Sat., 10am-7pm Fri., noon-5pm Sun., $10) hosts the Santa Fe Biennial in even-numbered years. It's also open Wednesdays in July and August, and entrance is free on Fridays and on Saturday till noon, when the farmers market is on, kitty-corner across the train tracks.

Museum Hill

These museums, on the southeast side, are worth leaving the plaza area. The new Santa Fe Botanical Garden is also up here, opposite the folk art museum. At press time, it was still in its earliest phases—check to see how it's growing.

Museum of Spanish Colonial Art

The museum of the **Spanish Colonial Arts Society** (750 Camino Lejo, 505/982-2226, www.spanishcolonial.org, 10am-5pm daily June-Aug., 10am-5pm Tues.-Sun. Sept.-May, $5) exhibits a strong collection of folk art and historical objects dating from the earliest Spanish contact. One-of-a-kind treasures—such as the only signed *retablo* by the 19th-century *santero* Rafael Aragón—are shown alongside more utilitarian items from the colonial past, such as silk mantas, wool rugs, and decorative tin. New work by contemporary artisans is also on display—don't miss Luis Tapia's meta-*bulto, The Folk-Art Collectors.*

Museum of Indian Arts & Culture

The excellent **Museum of Indian Arts & Culture** (710 Camino Lejo, 505/476-1250, www.miaclab.org, 10am-5pm daily May-Oct., 10am-5pm Tues.-Sun. Nov.-April, $9) is devoted to Native American culture from across the country, with the cornerstone exhibit *Here, Now and Always,* which traces the New Mexican Indians from their ancestors on the mesas and plains up to their present-day efforts at preserving their culture. It displays inventive spaces (looking into a HUD-house kitchen on the rez, or sitting at desks in a public schoolroom), sound clips, and stories. Another wing is devoted to contemporary art, while the halls of craft work display gorgeous beaded moccasins, elaborate headdresses, and more. The gift shop has beautiful jewelry and other tidbits from local artisans.

★ Museum of International Folk Art

A marvelous hodgepodge, the **Museum of International Folk Art** (708 Camino Lejo, 505/476-1200, www.internationalfolkart.org, 10am-5pm daily May-Oct., 10am-5pm Tues.-Sun. Nov.-Apr., $9) is one of Santa Fe's biggest treats—if you can handle visual overload. In the main exhibition space, some 10,000 folk-art pieces from more than 100 countries are on permanent display, hung on walls, set in cases, even dangling from the ceiling, juxtaposed to show off similar themes, colors, and materials. The approach initially seems jumbled but in fact underscores the universality of certain concepts and preoccupations.

A separate wing is dedicated to northern New Mexican Hispano crafts (a good complement to the Museum of Spanish Colonial Art) and a lab area where you can see how pieces are preserved. Temporary exhibits take up the rest of the space, usually with colorful interactive shows. Don't skip the gift shop, which stocks some smaller versions of the items in the galleries.

Wheelwright Museum of the American Indian

In the early 1920s, Mary Cabot Wheelwright, an adventurous East Coast heiress, made her way to New Mexico, where she met a Navajo medicine man named Hastiin Klah. Together they devised the **Wheelwright Museum of the American Indian** (704 Camino Lejo, 505/982-4636, www.wheelwright.org, 10am-5pm daily, $5), which opened in 1937 as the House of Navajo Religion. The mission has since incorporated all Native American cultures, with exhibits of new work by individual artists rotating every few months. The building is modeled after the Navajo hogan, with huge viga timbers supporting the eight-sided structure. The basement gift shop is a re-creation of a 19th-century trading post, which would feel like a tourist trap if it weren't for the authentically creaky wood floors and the beautiful antique jewelry on display. In June 2015, the museum opened a new wing, housing displays of southwestern jewelry.

Santa Fe Metro Area

Rancho de las Golondrinas

About a 15-minutes' drive southeast, **Rancho de las Golondrinas** (334 Los Pinos Rd., 505/471-2261, www.golondrinas.org, 10am-4pm Wed.-Sun. June-Sept., $6), the "Ranch of the Swallows," is a 200-acre museum built around a restored Spanish colonial *paraje,* a way station on the Camino Real. Museum staff members in period costumes demonstrate crafts and other aspects of early New Mexican history in the blacksmith shop, the schoolhouse, the mills, and even a rebuilt Penitente *morada* (the docent who works here is a Penitente himself and may sing some of the group's hymns). The ranch hosts big to-dos—a sheepshearing fair in early June and a frontier-themed horse show in August, among other things. It's a good idea to pack your own picnic; there's a basic café at the ranch, but it's open only on weekends. Allow a few hours to see the whole place. In April, May, and October, the museum is open on weekdays for guided tours by appointment; call 505/473-4169 to make arrangements. In these shoulder months, the ranch is also occasionally open for special theme weekends.

Lamy

Probably worth the drive only if you're a rail fan, this village is little more than a depot, though it is a mighty fine place to step off Amtrak's *Southwest Chief.* Across the road, the **Lamy Railroad & History Museum** (151 Old Lamy Tr., 505/466-1650, www.lamymuseum.org, noon-4pm Sat.) is a sprawling Old West saloon and dining room that doubles as

Open-Air Bars

Get to the **Bell Tower Bar** (100 E. San Francisco St., 505/982-5511, 11am-sunset Apr.-Oct.) early if you can, as this spot on the rooftop at La Fonda fills up fast. It's usually packed with tourists, but the view—from the fifth floor, the highest in the center of town—is inspiring.

If there's no room at Bell Tower, the next best spot is **Thunderbird** (50 Lincoln Ave., 505/490-6550, 11:30am-midnight daily), which has a second-floor porch with views onto the plaza. At happy hour, margaritas are $5; it starts early (4pm-6pm), but kicks in again after 10pm.

Hidden away inside a block near the plaza, **Taberna La Boca** (125 Lincoln Ave., 505/988-7102, 11:30am-2pm and 5pm-11pm daily) has a nice patio with a chummy scene starting at happy hour (5pm-7pm). At that time, wine or sherry can be had from $3 a glass, and traditional tapas start at $2.

Over on Canyon Road, **El Farol** (808 Canyon Rd., 505/983-9912, 11am-11pm Sun.-Thurs., 11am-midnight Fri.-Sat.) is a perennial favorite. A bar since 1835, it's the gallery owners' clubhouse, and exuberant dancing occasionally breaks out on the tiny dance floor. There's a long front deck, and a nice back patio too. Happy hour is 3pm-6pm.

The mellow patio scene at **Cowgirl BBQ** (319 S. Guadalupe St., 505/982-2565, 11:30am-midnight Mon.-Thurs., 11am-1am Fri.-Sat., 11am-11:30pm Sun.) gets started early, with happy hour kicking off at 3pm and lasting till 6pm, with two-for-one apps and $4 margaritas. It's good later, too, with live music many nights.

a treasure trove of old railroading days; there's even a model train set. The place has a spotty record of opening, so call ahead if you plan to make the trip. (On the other hand, it may also be operating as a full restaurant.)

Take Old Las Vegas Highway (or I-25) southeast out of Santa Fe; six miles out of town, turn south on US 285. After six miles, turn left for the last bumpy mile to Lamy.

Entertainment and Events

Nightlife

With balmy summer evenings and a populace that always seems to be able to knock off work a little early, Santa Fe typically favors happy hour over late-night carousing.

The lobby watering hole at La Fonda hotel, **La Fiesta Lounge** (100 E. San Francisco St., 505/982-5511, 11am-11pm Sun.-Thurs., 11am-11:30pm Fri.-Sat.), has likely been the setting for thousands of local legends, true or not. Nowadays, it's a bit tamer, but it still has a fine, old-fashioned feel, with portraits of rodeo queens on the wall and live local country acts on the small corner stage.

A longtime city haunt, the **Dragon Room Lounge** (406 Old Santa Fe Tr., 505/983-7712, 4pm-midnight Tues.-Sun.) is so dim you might not notice at first the huge tree growing up from the left side of the bar. Guys in cowboy hats chat with mountain bikers and dressed-up cocktail drinkers. There's live music Tuesday, Thursday, and Saturday.

Stalwart **Maria's** (555 W. Cordova Rd., 505/983-7929, 11am-10pm daily) may have cut back on the tequila in the margaritas, but considering how staggeringly strong they were before, that might be a good thing. The drinks are still impeccably balanced, made with fresh lime, and available with nearly any brand of tequila you can imagine.

The bar in the Hotel Chimayó, **Low n' Slow** (125 Washington Ave., 505/988-4900, 2pm-10pm Mon.-Thurs., noon-11pm Fri.-Sun.), is worth a mention for its theme alone: As a tribute to cool car culture, it's decked out with cool upholstery and hubcap chandeliers. The lowrider theme continues in cocktails named after car details. Tuesday is trivia night.

¡Chispa! at El Mesón (213 Washington St., 505/983-6756, 5pm-11pm Tues.-Sat.) has live music five nights a week, with a particularly devoted crew of regulars on Tuesday, for tango night. You can order traditional tapas or bigger dishes from El Mesón's excellent dinner menu at the bar, or just join in the dancing on the small wood floor.

Performing Arts

The 2,128-seat **Santa Fe Opera** (US 84/285, 505/986-5900, www.santafeopera.org) is the city's premier arts venue. The elegant open-air amphitheater seven miles north of Santa Fe acts as "summer camp" for the country's best singers to perform a mix of repertory and modern works during July and August. If you think opera is all about tuxes, plush seats, and too-long arias, give the SFO a chance. Half the fun is arriving early to "tailgate" in the parking lot, which involves gourmet goodies, lots of champagne, and time to mill around and check out other attendees' bolo ties. In addition to your picnic dinner, pack blankets to ward off the chill after the sun sets. If you have kids to entertain, time your visit for bargain-priced "family nights" or a special dress rehearsal with extra info to introduce young ones to the art form.

Set in a 1931 Moorish curlicue palace, the **Lensic Performing Arts Center** (211 W. San Francisco St., 505/988-1234, www.lensic.com) is Santa Fe's best stage after the opera house, with 820 seats and an eclectic schedule. The six-week-long **Santa Fe Chamber Music Festival** (www.sfcmf.org) schedules events here, as well as at the St. Francis Cathedral, with performances nearly every day in July and August. The chamber orchestra **Santa Fe Pro Musica** (505/988-4640, www.santafepromusica.com) also performs at the Lensic, fall through spring, as well as in Loretto Chapel and other intimate venues.

Festivals and Events

Santa Fe's summer is packed. In mid-July, the **International Folk Art Market** (505/992-7600, www.folkartalliance.org) showcases traditional crafts from all over the globe, often from the artists in person. It's set up on Museum Hill, so the center of the city is not disrupted. On Sunday, tickets are cheaper and vendors are ready to make deals.

In late July, **Spanish Market** (505/982-2226, www.spanishcolonial.org) takes over the plaza with traditional New Mexican woodwork (especially *santos*), weaving, and furniture.

The city's biggest annual event is in late August, when 100,000 visitors come for **Santa Fe Indian Market** (505/983-5220, www.swaia.org). Like Spanish Market, it's centered on the plaza, with some 1,200 Native American artisans selling jewelry, pottery, weaving, and more. Alongside, the **Indigenous Fine Art Market** (www.indigefam.org), based at Railyard Park, emphasizes more contemporary work. It's all a bit of a frenzy, but festive, due to free music and dance performances in the week leading up to the market itself.

After all the frenetic summer tourism, locals celebrate the arrival of fall with the weeklong **Fiesta de Santa Fe** (505/204-1598, www.santafefiesta.org), which has been celebrated in some form since 1712. It begins with a reenactment of De Vargas's *entrada* into the city, then a whole slew of balls and parades, including the Historical/Hysterical Parade and a children's pet parade—eccentric Santa Fe at its finest. The kickoff event is usually the **Burning of Zozobra** (855/ZOZ-OBRA, www.burnzozobra.com), a neo-pagan bonfire; the schedule has fluctuated a bit, but most recently, it was on the Friday before Labor Day. Some downtown businesses close for some Fiestas, particularly on Zozobra day.

In late September, foodies flock to the city for the **Santa Fe Wine and Chile Festival** (505/438-8060, www.

The Burning of Zozobra

Every fall a raucous chant fills the air in Santa Fe's Fort Marcy Park: "Burn him! Burn him! Burn him!" It's not a witch hunt, but the ritual torching of Zozobra, a 50-foot-tall marionette with long, grasping arms, glowering eyes, and a moaning voice. Old Man Gloom, as he's also known, represents the accumulated sorrows of the populace, as in the weeks before the event, he's stuffed with divorce papers, pictures of ex-girlfriends, hospital gowns, and other anxiety-inducing scraps. Setting this aflame purges these troubles and allows for a fresh start.

This Santa Fe tradition sounds like a medieval rite, but it dates only from the 1920s, when artist Will Shuster—a bit of a local legend who's also credited with inventing piñon-juniper incense and starting the tradition of citywide bonfires on Christmas Eve—wanted to lighten up the heavily Catholic Fiesta de Santa Fe. Shuster, who had moved to Santa Fe in 1920 to treat his tuberculosis, was inspired by the Mummers Parade from his native Philadelphia, as well as the Yaqui Indians in Tucson, Arizona, who burn Judas in effigy in the week before Easter. A 1926 *Santa Fe New Mexican* article describes the spectacle Shuster developed, with the help of the Kiwanis Club:

> Zozobra ... stood in ghastly silence illuminated by weird green fires. While the band played a funeral march, a group of Kiwanians in black robes and hoods stole around the figure.... [Then] red fires blazed at the foot ... and leaped into a column of many colored flames.... And throwing off their black robes the spectators emerged in gala costume, joining an invading army of bright-hued harlequins with torches in a dance around the fires as the band struck up "La Cucaracha."

Shuster oversaw Zozobra nearly every year until 1964. In the late 1930s, Errol Flynn, in town with Olivia de Havilland and Ronald Reagan to film *The Santa Fe Trail,* set Zozobra aflame. A few years later, during World War II, the puppet was dubbed Hirohitlomus. In 1950, Zozobra appeared on the New Mexico state float in the Rose Bowl parade and won the national trophy.

Although Zozobra (aka O.M.G.) has a Twitter account these days and accepts worries-to-burn online, the spectacle is roughly unchanged, with dozens of white-clad children playing "glooms," followed by a "fire dancer" who taunts Zozo until he bursts into flame; fireworks cap it off. It's a fine sight, and a great cross section of Santa Feans attend. But anyone leery of crowds may prefer to watch from outside the perimeter of the ball field.

santafewineandchile.org), five days of tastings and special dinners at various venues around town.

Cinema

The delightful little **Jean Cocteau Cinema** (418 Montezuma Ave., 505/466-5528, www.jeancocteaucinema.com, $10) was shuttered for several years before resident author George R. R. Martin (now known to the TV-watching world as the man behind *Game of Thrones*) bought the place in 2013 and revamped it. Now the 120-seat theater is back to showing the eclectic art-house offerings to an enthusiastic local audience. On weekends, there's usually a retro late show at 11pm.

Shopping

Even people who clutch their purse strings tightly may be a little undone by the treasures for sale in Santa Fe. The rational approach would be to consider the most expensive shops more as free museums. (The cheapest, on the other hand, are stocked with made-in-China junk and eternally on the brink of "going out of business" and should be avoided.) Downtown around the plaza are souvenir shops and a few influential galleries. On Canyon Road cluster art dealers of all stripes. South Guadalupe Street and surrounding blocks have more funky and fun boutiques. If you buy too much to carry, **Pak Mail** (369 Montezuma Ave., 505/989-7380) can ship your treasures home safely; it even offers free pickup from hotels.

Art Galleries

With seemingly every other storefront downtown occupied by a gallery, Santa Fe's art scene can be overwhelming. The densest concentration of work is on Canyon Road, though it can seem a bit crowded with Southwestern kitsch. Summer hours are given here; in the winter, most galleries are closed at least Monday and Tuesday.

Definitely in the museum-quality category is **Peyton Wright** (237 E. Palace Ave., 505/989-9888, 9:30am-5pm Mon.-Sat.), a large house where one-off shows deal in modern American masters (need a Marsden Hartley for your foyer?) as well as old-world treasures that look as if they've been culled from a czar's forgotten vault. For quite the opposite feel, lighten up at **Chuck Jones Studio Gallery** (135 W. Palace Ave., 505/983-5999), where you can see original cels and sketches from early Disney films as well as more recent animated hits such as *SpongeBob SquarePants* and *The Simpsons*. Or you can just chill out and watch the good stuff on TV.

Local Artists

At the top end of Canyon Road, **Red Dot Gallery** (826 Canyon Rd., 505/820-7338, 10am-5pm Thurs.-Sun.) is the exhibition space for Santa Fe Community College students and alumni, a nice antidote to the high-toned vibe on the rest of the street. In the convention center, the **Community Gallery** (201 W. Marcy St., 505/955-6705, 10am-5pm Tues.-Fri., 9:30am-4pm Sat.) is run by the Santa Fe Arts Commission and always has a wide mix of work on display.

Contemporary

Santa Fe's contemporary scene has cooled a bit since its boom in the 2000s. But granddaddy **LewAllen** (1613 Paseo de Peralta, 505/988-3250, 10am-6pm Mon.-Fri., 10am-5pm Sat.) has survived and is one of the anchors in the Railyard, with a vast industrial space, fittingly across the street from the SITE Santa Fe museum.

Off Canyon Road, **Eight Modern** (231 Delgado St., 505/995-0231, 9:30am-5:30pm Mon.-Sat., 11am-4pm Sun.) focuses on colorful, abstract, and pop art. Nearby, **Nüart Gallery** (670 Canyon Rd., 505/988-3888, 10am-5pm Sat., daily) showcases Latin American magical realism.

Native American and Southwestern

Near Canyon Road, **Gerald Peters Gallery** (1011 Paseo de Peralta, 505/954-5700, 10am-5pm Mon.-Sat.) and **Nedra Matteucci Galleries** (1075 Paseo de Peralta, 505/982-4631, 9am-5pm Mon.-Sat.) are the biggies when it comes to Taos Society of Artists and other Western art, though both have contemporary artists too. Even if nothing inside hits the spot, the one-acre sculpture garden and ponds in back of Nedra Matteucci are a treat. Smaller **Robert Nichols Gallery** (419 Canyon Rd., 505/982-2145, 10am-5pm Mon.-Sat., 11am-5pm Sun.) specializes in Native American pottery, including some with often funny, boundary-pushing sensibilities.

Near the plaza, **Blue Rain Gallery** (130 Lincoln Ave., 505/954-9902, 10am-6pm Mon.-Sat.) showcases work from many pueblo residents, such as Tammy Garcia's modern takes on traditional Santa Clara pottery forms—she sometimes renders bowls in blown glass or applies the geometric decoration to jewelry. Across the street, **Allan Houser Gallery** (125 Lincoln Ave., 505/982-4705, 10am-5pm Mon.-Sat.) displays the work of the Southwest's best-known Native American sculptor; it also maintains a sculpture garden outside the city, with visits by appointment.

Sculpture

North of Santa Fe in the village of Tesuque, the bronze foundry **Shidoni** (1508 Bishops Lodge Rd., 505/988-8001, 9am-5pm Mon.-Sat.) has two large gardens full of metalwork sculpture, open from sunrise to sunset every day. If you want to see the foundry, show up at noon on a weekday ($3, for a self-guided tour) or any time between noon and 5pm on Saturday ($5, to see the bronze pouring). Immediately adjacent, **Tesuque Glassworks** (1510 Bishops Lodge Rd., 505/988-2165, 9am-5pm daily) functions as a co-op with a whole range of glass artists using the furnace and displaying their work. To get to Tesuque, head north out of Santa Fe on Washington Avenue, which becomes Bishops Lodge Road; Shidoni will be on the left side.

Clothing and Jewelry

¡Mira! (101 W. Marcy St., 505/988-3585, 10:30am-5:30pm Mon.-Sat., noon-5pm Sun.) has a hip mix of clothes and housewares, with T-shirts by local designers ("Fanta Se" in the old Santa Fe Railroad logo, say) as well as cool imports from places like Ghana. Just down the block, **Glorianna's** (55 W. Marcy St., 505/982-0353, 10am-4:30pm Mon.-Tues. and Thurs.-Sat., often closed for lunch 1pm-2pm) is a treasure trove of beads, packed to bursting with veritable eggs of raw turquoise, trays of glittering Czech glass, and ropes of African trade beads.

The city's best consignment shop is **Double Take** (321 S. Guadalupe St., 505/989-8886, 10am-6pm Mon.-Sat.), a sprawling two-story space with an excellent selection of boots, as well as cool clothing, rodeo-themed 1950s sofas, Fiestaware, and plenty more.

Another good secondhand outlet is **Ooh La La!** (518 Old Santa Fe Tr.,

Top to bottom: the annual International Folk Art Market; blown glass sculptures at Shidoni in Tesuque; procession in front of Cathedral Basilica of St. Francis of Assisi.

505/820-6433, 10:30am-5:30pm Mon.-Sat., noon-4pm Sun.), where the city's clotheshorses offload their impulse-buy Armani and Chloé. The shop is a little cramped, but racks are well organized by size and color.

Anyone who wears glasses should stop at **Ojo Optique** (125 Lincoln Ave., 505/988-4444, 10am-7pm Mon.-Sat., noon-5pm Sun.), which specializes in frames from boutique eyewear designers, working independent of the giant conglomerates that control most of the industry.

Gift and Home

The owner of **Seret & Sons** (224 Galisteo St., 505/988-9151, 9am-5:30pm Mon.-Fri., 9am-6pm Sat., 9:30am-5pm Sun.) is a Santa Fe icon who deals in finely woven rugs, antique doors, and life-size wooden elephants from his cavernous warehouse just south of the plaza.

For funky folk art that won't break the bank, head for the equally gigantic **Jackalope** (2820 Cerrillos Rd., 505/471-8539, 9am-6pm Mon.-Sat., 10am-6pm Sun.), where seemingly acres are given over to mosaic-topped tables, wooden chickens, Mexican pottery vases, and inexpensive souvenirs. Sharing the space is a community of prairie dogs—good distraction for children while adults cruise the breakables.

Open-Air Markets

One of the most familiar sights of Santa Fe is the portal of the **Palace of the Governors,** where American Indian vendors from all over New Mexico spread out their wares as they've been doing since the 1930s. More than 500 vendors are licensed to sell here after going through a strict application process that evaluates their technical skills. Every morning the 69 spots, each 12 bricks wide, are doled out by lottery. Expect anything from silver bracelets to pottery to *heishi* (shell bead) necklaces to freshly harvested piñon nuts. It's a great opportunity to buy direct from a skilled artisan and learn about the work that went into a piece.

As much a quirky fashion show and social scene as a shopping event, the **Santa Fe Flea** (505/982-2671, www.santafetraditionalflea.com) convenes vintage aficionados, fine artists, crafty folks, and "tailgate traders" of miscellaneous oddities. From late May through mid-October, it takes place at the **Santa Fe Downs** (27475 West Frontage Rd., just off Hwy. 599, north of I-25, 8am-3pm Fri.-Sun.). In winter, many of the vendors move indoors to **El Museo Cultural** (555 Camino de la Familia, 8am-3pm Sat.-Sun. late Nov.-Apr.) at the Railyard complex.

The **Pueblo of Tesuque Flea Market** (15 Flea Market Rd., 505/670-2599, www.tesuquefleamarket.com, 9am-4pm Fri.-Sun., Mar.-Dec.) mixes local artists with traders from Africa, Guatemala, and elsewhere, and there are usually some good snacks (if not always amazing bargains) to be had. Take exit 171 (Flea Market Rd.) off US 84/285, just north of the Santa Fe Opera.

In the Santa Fe Farmers Market Pavilion, the **Railyard Artisan Market** (1607 Paseo de Peralta, www.artmarketsantafe.com, 10am-4pm) runs every Sunday. The selection is better in the shoulder seasons, when fewer competing craft fairs siphon off vendors.

Sweet Treats

Todos Santos (125 E. Palace Ave., 505/982-3855, 10am-5pm Mon.-Sat.) adds the sweet smell of chocolate to the air in Sena Plaza. The closet-size shop has the perfect (if short-lived) Santa Fe souvenir: *milagros,* the traditional Mexican Catholic prayer charms shaped like body parts, rendered in Valrhona chocolate and covered in a delicate layer of gold or silver leaf. If you prefer nuts and chews, head to longtime candy vendor **Señor Murphy** (100 E. San Francisco St., 505/982-0461, 10am-5:30pm daily) for some "caramales" (chewy balls of caramel

Santa Fe for Kids

In addition to the **Santa Fe Children's Museum** (1050 Old Pecos Tr., 505/989-8359, 10am-6pm Tues.-Wed., Fri.-Sat., 10am-6:30pm Thurs., noon-5pm Sun., www.santafechildrensmuseum.org, $7.50), the following are fun options, all open 10am-5pm Monday-Saturday, except where noted.

- **Bee Hive** (328 Montezuma Ave., 505/780-8051, also open noon-4pm Sun.) A lovingly curated kids' bookstore, often with story time on Saturdays.
- **Dinosaurs & More** (137 W. San Francisco St., 505/988-3299, also open Sun.) The owner can tell a story about nearly every meteorite, fossil, and geode in the place.
- **Doodlet's** (120 Don Gaspar St., 505/983-3771) Open since 1955, this corner shop is filled with bits and bobs for kids and adults, from toy accordions to kitchen tchotchkes.
- **Harrell House of Natural Oddities** (DeVargas Center, 177-B Paseo de Peralta, 505/695-8569, 10am-7pm Mon.-Fri., 10am-6pm Sat., noon-5pm Sun., $5) An amazing live collection of spiders, snakes, lizards, and more. Kids can pet giant millipedes and fuzzy tarantulas.
- **Moon Rabbit Toys** (112 W. San Francisco St., 505/982-9373, also open noon-4pm Sun.) Worth seeking out inside the Plaza Mercado, for its house-designed strategy games.
- **Toyopolis** (150 Washington Ave., 505/988-5422) The closest toy store to the plaza, for emergency distraction.
- **Warehouse 21** (1614 Paseo de Peralta, 505/989-4423, www.warehouse21.org) This teen arts center hosts a range of workshops, performances, and more.

and piñon nuts wrapped up in little corn husks) and other New Mexico-inspired sweets.

Sports and Recreation

It's no accident *Outside* magazine has its offices here. After work and on weekends, Santa Feans leave the town to the tourists and scatter into the surrounding mountains on foot or bike. You'll find something to do all four seasons, though hikes above the foothills shouldn't be attempted till mid-May at least (and not until you're acclimated to the altitude). If you're in town in the fall, don't miss the leaves turning on the aspens, usually in mid-October (for a great, low-effort view, ride the lift at the ski basin). The access route for activities in the Sangre de Cristos is Highway 475—it starts out from the north side of Santa Fe as Artists Road, then the name changes to Hyde Park Road, and farther north it's Ski Basin Road.

Information and Guides

Just off Highway 14, immediately south of I-25, the **Public Lands Information Center** (301 Dinosaur Tr., 505/954-2002, www.publiclands.org, 8am-4:30pm Mon.-Sat.) is the best starting point for any planning. The staff will also know the latest status on areas affected by wildfires or floods. **Outspire!** (505/660-0394, www.outspire.com) runs guided full- and half-day outings—hiking in summer, snowshoeing in winter. For gear, check **REI** (500 Market St., 505/982-3557) in the Railyard district.

Biking

Mountain bikers have fantastic outlets very close to Santa Fe, while those who prefer the open road will love the challenges in the winding highways through the mountains north of the city. **Rob & Charlie's** (1632 St. Michaels Dr., 505/471-9119, 9:30am-6pm Mon.-Sat., noon-5pm Sun. in summer) is a reliable shop.

To rent a bike, see **Mellow Velo** (132 E. Marcy St., 505/995-8356, 9am-6pm Mon.-Fri., 9am-5pm Sat., 9am-3pm Sun., from $20/day), just off the plaza.

Mountain Biking

The **Dale Ball Trails** are 22 miles of single-track routes for both hikers and mountain bikers, winding through stands of piñon and juniper in the foothills. Two trailheads give access to the North, Central, and South Sections of the trail. From the northern trailhead, on Sierra del Norte (immediately off Highway 475 after mile marker 3), the North Section trails vary a bit in elevation, but the Central Section (south from the parking area) is more fun because it's a longer chunk of trails. The southern trailhead, on Cerro Gordo just north of its intersection with Canyon Road, gives access to the Central Section and the South Section, which is for advanced riders only. Note that the trail that starts at the southern trailhead lot, part of the Santa Fe Canyon Preserve, is for foot traffic only—ride your bike one-tenth of a mile down Cerro Gordo to the start of the Dale Ball system.

A local classic, the **Santa Fe Rail Trail** is a paved path starting in Railyard Park, then turns to dirt outside the city limits. Revamped and smoothed out a bit in 2012, the trail is a pleasant, relatively easy route along the railroad tracks to Lamy. The trail is about 12.5 miles one-way; except for a grade near I-25, it's fairly level.

Road Biking

Make sure you're acclimated to the altitude before you set out on any lengthy trip—the best tour, along the High Road to Taos, will take you through some of the area's highest elevations. Starting in Chimayó shaves some not-so-scenic miles off the ride and gives you a reasonable 45-mile jaunt to Taos. The annual **Santa Fe Century** (www.santafecentury.com) takes place every May, running a 104-mile loop south down the Turquoise Trail and back north via the old farm towns in the Galisteo Basin, southeast of Santa Fe.

Hiking

Hikers can enjoy these dedicated trails, in addition to the multiuse trails for bicyclists.

Santa Fe Canyon Preserve

For an easy saunter in town, head for the 190-acre patch of the foothills known as **Santa Fe Canyon Preserve,** which is managed by the **Nature Conservancy** (505/988-3867). The area is open only to people on foot—no mountain bikes and no pets. The preserve covers the canyon formed by the now-diverted Santa Fe River. An easy interpretive loop trail leads around the area for 1.5 miles, passing the remnants of the dam and winding through dense stands of cottonwoods and willows. The trailhead is on Cerro Gordo Road just north of its intersection with Upper Canyon Road.

Atalaya Mountain

One of the easiest-to-reach trails in the Santa Fe area (you can take the M city bus to the trailhead on the campus of St. John's College) is also one of the more challenging. The hike heads up to the 9,121-foot peak of **Atalaya Mountain,** starting out as a gentle stroll along the city's edge, then becoming increasingly steep, for a round-trip of approximately seven miles. Allow about four hours for the full up-and-back.

Aspen Vista

The most popular trail in the Sangre de Cristos is probably **Aspen Vista.** But don't be put off by the prospect of crowds, as the promised views of golden aspen groves are indeed spectacular—in the densest spots, when the sun is shining through the leaves, the air itself feels yellow. Even though it's at a high elevation, it's an easy hike, on a service road with a gradual slope. The full length is 11.5 miles, but it's the first 2.5 miles that are the most aspen-intense. A little under 4 miles in, you get a great view of Santa Fe below; this makes a good turnaround point for a two-hour hike. Look for the parking area on the right of Ski Basin Road (Hwy. 475), just under 13 miles up the road from town.

Spas

Ten Thousand Waves (3451 Hyde Park Rd., 505/982-9304, www.tenthousandwaves.com, 9am-10:30pm Wed.-Mon., noon-10:30pm Tues. July-Oct.) is such a Santa Fe institution that it could just as well be listed under the city's major attractions. This traditional Japanese-style bathhouse just outside of town has two big communal pools and seven smaller private ones tucked among the trees so as to optimize the views of the mountains all around; many have adjoining cold plunges and saunas. The place also offers full day-spa services, with intense massages and luxe facials and body scrubs. Prices are relatively reasonable, starting at $24 for unlimited time in the public baths and $112 for one-hour massages. In the winter (Nov.-June), the baths open at 10:30am (at 2pm Tues.) and close earlier on weeknights.

In town, **Absolute Nirvana Spa** (106 Faithway St., 505/983-7942, www.absolutenirvana.com, 10am-6pm Sun.-Thurs., 10am-8pm Fri.-Sat.) offers Balinese treatments and massages. Afterward, you can relax in the gardens with a cup of tea and some organic sweets from the adjacent tearoom.

A bit farther from the center, but very highly rated by locals, **Body of Santa Fe** (333 W. Cordova Rd., 505/986-0362, www.bodyofsantafe.com, 9am-9pm daily) is praised for its affordable treatments (massages from $80/hour) and relaxed atmosphere. There's a nice café on-site too.

Winter Sports

Sixteen miles northeast of town in the Santa Fe National Forest, **Ski Santa Fe** (Hwy. 475, 505/982-4429, www.skisantafe.com, $70 full-day lift ticket) is a well-used day area with 77 fairly challenging trails. A major selling point: virtually no lift lines.

For cross-country skiers, the groomed **Norski Trail** starts about a quarter of a mile before the Ski Santa Fe parking lot, off the west side of the road. The standard route is about 2.5 miles, winding through the trees and along a ridgeline, and you can shorten or lengthen the tour by taking various loops and shortcuts, as long as you follow the directional arrows counterclockwise.

Just seven miles out of town along the road to the ski area, **Hyde Memorial State Park** (Hwy. 475, 505/983-7175, www.nmparks.com) has an ice rink, a couple of nicely maintained sledding runs, and some shorter cross-country ski routes.

For gear, **Cottam's Ski Shop** (740 Hwy. 475, 505/982-0495) is the biggest rental operation in the area, handily located on the way to Aspen Vista.

Accommodations

Santa Fe offers some great places to stay, but none are cheap. Prices quoted for the bigger hotels are standard rack rates; chances are, you'll find substantially lower ones by calling or booking online, at least at the higher-end properties. Prices spike in July and August, often up to holiday rates. If you're coming for Indian Market or Christmas, try to book at least eight months in advance. On the other hand, despite ski season, rates are often quite low in early December, January, and February.

$50-100

Wedged in among the chain hotels on Cerrillos, the self-described "kitschy"

★ **Silver Saddle Motel** (2810 Cerrillos Rd., 505/471-7663, www.santafesilversaddlemotel.com, $62 s, $67 d) plays up the retro charm. Cozy rooms may be pretty basic and have cinder-block walls, but they're decked out with Western accoutrements and kept clean—and the price, which includes breakfast, can't be beat. A handful of later-built rooms have some extra square footage.

As hostels go, **Santa Fe International Hostel** (1412 Cerrillos Rd., 505/988-1153, www.hostelsantafe.com) is not the worst, but neither is it one of the more inspiring—unless you clamp on your rose-colored glasses and view it as an old-school hippie project (it *is* run as a nonprofit). The dorms ($20 pp) and private rooms ($25 s, $35 d) are dim, and cleanliness can be spotty, as you're relying on the previous guests' efforts, as part of the required daily chores. The kitchen has free food, but you have to pay for Internet access ($2/day), and everything is cash only.

For camping, the closest tent sites to the center are at **Hyde Memorial State Park** (Hwy. 475, 505/983-7175, www.nmparks.com), about four miles northwest of the city, with both primitive ($8) and developed sites with electricity ($14). The commercial **Rancheros de Santa Fe** (736 Old Las Vegas Hwy., 505/466-3482, www.rancheros.com, Mar.-Oct.), a 20-minute drive east of the plaza, is an option, but it's geared mainly to RVs; the tent sites ($25) are packed together and not very shady. A little farther along, the **KOA** (934 Old Las Vegas Hwy., 505/466-1419, www.santafekoa.com) has some shadier tent sites ($25), good laundry facilities, and a game room.

Possibly the best lodging deal in Santa Fe, the **Quaker Meeting House** (630 Canyon Rd., 505/983-7241, www.santa-fe.quaker.org, $45 s, $55 d) rents a guest casita with a kitchenette. It's a small space, and it's a three-night minimum, but the location on Canyon Road can't be beat. Payment is cash only.

$100-150

The bones of ★ **Santa Fe Sage Inn** (725 Cerrillos Rd., 505/982-5952, www.santafesageinn.com, $115 d) are a standard highway motel, but the super-clean rooms are done in sharp, modern red and black, with Southwestern rugs hung on the walls. Little touches such as free Wi-Fi, plush beds, and an above-average breakfast (fresh bagels, fruit, yogurt, and more) make this an excellent deal. The place even has a swimming pool. It's walking distance to the center, and it's right across the street from the Railyard Park and the farmers market.

Despite its location on uncharming Cerrillos Road, about two miles from the plaza, **El Rey Inn** (1862 Cerrillos Rd., 505/982-1931, www.elreyinnsantafe.com, $105 s, $140 d) counts as one of the more charming hotels in Santa Fe. Built in 1935, it has been meticulously kept up and adjusted for modern standards of comfort, with beautiful gardens, a hot tub, a big swimming pool, and a fireside open-air Jacuzzi. The 86 rooms, spread over 4.5 acres, vary considerably in style (and in price), from the oldest section with snug adobe walls and heavy viga ceilings to airier rooms with balconies. Rooms at the back of the property, away from traffic noise, are preferable.

Santa Fe Motel & Inn (510 Cerrillos Rd., 505/982-1039, www.santafemotel.com, $149 d) is an excellent budget option close to the center, with rooms done up in simple, bright decor that avoids motel sameness despite the generic motor-court layout. A few kitchenettes are available, along with some more private casitas with fireplaces. Lots of nice touches—such as bread from the Sage Bakehouse across the street along with the full breakfast—give the place a homey feel without the tight quarters of a typical bed-and-breakfast.

$150-200

In a handy location west of the plaza, **Las Palomas** (460 W. San Francisco St.,

505/982-5560, www.laspalomas.com, $153 d) is good to know about for last-minute booking. A cluster of four separate complexes, it usually has room when smaller B&Bs are full, and online booking discounts can be generous. But room layouts vary significantly, and some casitas have bedrooms facing parking lots, which feels no better than a motel. Call to book, if you can.

East of the plaza, twin bed-and-breakfasts under the same ownership offer two kinds of style: The rooms at **Hacienda Nicholas** (320 E. Marcy St., 505/986-1431, www.haciendanicholas.com, $165 d) have a tasteful Southwest flavor, decorated with a few cowboy trappings and Gustave Baumann prints; most rooms have fireplaces. Across the street, **The Madeleine** (106 Faithway St., 505/982-3465, www.madeleineinn.com, $165 d) is set in a wood Victorian, but the lace curtains are offset with rich Balinese fabrics. In both places, breakfast is a continental spread, but that doesn't mean you'll go away hungry—the banana bread is fantastic.

Hotel Chimayó (125 Washington Ave., 505/988-4900, www.hotelchimayo.com, $169 d) offers good value very close to the plaza, though not everyone will like its folky style, done up with wooden crosses and striped rugs from its namesake village. Upstairs rooms have private balconies, and some suites have fireplaces.

Majority-owned by Picurís Pueblo, **Hotel Santa Fe** (1501 Paseo de Peralta, 800/825-9876, www.hotelsantafe.com, $169 d) is both a successful business experiment and a very nice hotel, with one of the few large outdoor pools in town, set against the neo-pueblo hotel walls. The standard rooms are a bit small—the real value is in the luxe Hacienda wing, where the huge rooms with fireplaces and butler service can be as low as $199 online—a steal compared with other high-end places in town.

The 100-room **Inn of the Governors** (101 W. Alameda St., 505/982-4333, www.innofthegovernors.com, $189 d) doesn't look like much on the outside, but inside it has a personable only-in-Santa-Fe feel, starting with the afternoon "tea and sherry hour," when guests are plied with free drinks and *bizcochitos*. Its unique profit-sharing system may account for the exceptionally nice staff. Other perks: Breakfast is generous, parking is free (unheard-of elsewhere downtown), and there's even a tiny pool. Rooms in the Governors Wing are quietest.

$200-250

The iconic, family-owned ★ **La Fonda** (100 E. San Francisco St., 505/982-5511, www.lafondasantafe.com, $229 s, $249 d) underwent a major renovation in 2013, which lightened up its guest rooms considerably. They feel slightly more generic and modern as a result, though many do have original folk art, and a few have *latilla* ceilings and kiva fireplaces—along with all the necessary luxuries, such as pillow-top beds. You can soak up most of the place's atmosphere in the public areas, of course, but the location couldn't be better. It helps to have flexible dates—in periods of high demand, the rates can spike to exorbitant levels.

Opened in 2014, **Drury Plaza Santa Fe** (228 E. Palace Ave., 505/424-2175, www.druryplazasantafe.com, $210 d) has a somewhat corporate feel, but it occupies a big historic hospital complex behind the St. Francis Cathedral—a very convenient location, at a pretty good price for amenities like a rooftop pool, full breakfast, and free drinks in the afternoon. Rooms are a little small but very comfortably furnished.

Inn on the Alameda (303 E. Alameda St., 505/984-2121, www.innonthealameda.com, $229 d) is a good option for people who want adobe style *and* space, and its location near Canyon Road is handy for gallery-hoppers. The big rooms have triple-sheeted beds, wireless Internet access, and overstuffed armchairs that are only lightly dusted with Southwestern flair; most also have a patio or balcony.

Gas fireplaces are usually an additional $20. The continental breakfast spread is generous, and there's a wine-and-cheese hour every afternoon.

A rental condo is a great option if you have a family or group, and those at **Campanilla Compound** (334 Otero St., 800/828-9700, www.campanillacompound.com, $235) are especially nice, with whitewashed walls, fireplaces, and Mexican-tiled kitchens. Each unit has plenty of space inside and out, with a private patio or porch, and, thanks to the location on a hill, some have excellent views of the city and the sunset. There's a two-night minimum.

A wonderfully restful spot is **Houses of the Moon** (3451 Hyde Park Rd., 505/992-5003, www.tenthousandwaves.com, $239 d), the guest cottages at Ten Thousand Waves spa. Some have more of a local feel, with viga ceilings and kiva fireplaces, while others are straight from Japan, both samurai era and contemporary anime. Some larger suites have kitchens. Rates include a suitably organic granola breakfast as well as free access to the communal and women's tubs.

Over $250

Special occasion? The Relais & Chateaux property **The Inn of the Five Graces** (150 E. De Vargas St., 505/992-0957, www.fivegraces.com, $450 per suite) can transport you to exotic lands—for at least slightly less than a plane ticket. Outside, it looks like a typical historic Southwestern lodge, a collection of interconnected adobe casitas on Santa Fe's oldest street. But inside, the 24 sumptuous suites are done in the style of an opium dream: antique Turkish kilims, heavy wood doors, and mosaics—all courtesy of the boho-style dealers Seret & Sons. Rates include full breakfast, delivered to your room if you like.

Food

Dining is one of Santa Fe's great pleasures. For a relatively tiny population, it offers a dazzling range of restaurants. Sure, you can get a cheese-smothered, crazy-hot plate of green-chile-and-chicken enchiladas, but most locals eat more globally than that. "Santa Fe cuisine" cheerfully incorporates Asian, Southwestern, and Mediterranean flavors, with an emphasis on organic and holistic.

Downtown

The ring formed by Alameda Street and Paseo de Peralta contains some classic Santa Fe spots, plus a few hidden treats. On the plaza itself, the carnitas cart and the fajitas cart are classics too—and the Chicago hot dog stand, when it's set up, gets strong votes for authenticity.

New Mexican

★ **Tia Sophia's** (210 W. San Francisco St., 505/983-9880, 7am-2pm Mon.-Sat., 8am-1pm Sun., $8) is one of the last places in the plaza area that feels untouched by time and tourists, serving old-time New Mexican plates to a slew of regulars without a touch of fusion—so authentic, in fact, the kitchen claims to have invented the breakfast burrito decades back.

The Shed (113½ E. Palace Ave., 505/982-9030, 11am-2:30pm and 5:30pm-9pm daily, $17) has been serving up platters of enchiladas since 1953—bizarrely, with a side of garlic bread. But that's just part of the tradition at this colorful, comfortable, marginally fancy place that's as popular with tourists as it is with die-hard residents. There are perfectly decent distractions like lemon-garlic shrimp and fish tacos on the menu, but it's the red chile you should focus on.

Fresh and Local

Open since the late 1970s, ★ **Café Pasqual's** (121 Don Gaspar St., 505/983-9340, 8am-3pm and 5:30pm-9:30pm daily, $28) has defined its own culinary category, relying almost entirely on organic ingredients. Its breakfasts are legendary, but the food is delicious any time of day. Just brace yourself for the inevitable line, as the brightly painted dining room seats only 50 people, and loyal fans number in the thousands. Expect nearly anything on the menu: smoked-trout hash or Yucatán-style *huevos motuleños* for breakfast; for dinner, mole enchiladas or Vietnamese squid salad.

Classic American

Longtime burger connoisseurs may remember Bobcat Bite, just outside of the city. It closed in 2013, and ★ **Santa Fe Bite** (311 Old Santa Fe Tr., 505/982-0544, 11am-9pm Tues.-Fri., 8am-9pm Sat., 8am-8pm Sun., $12) is the new and even better incarnation, close to the plaza, in much more comfortable digs. The same 10-ounce burgers, from beef ground fresh every day, on a home-baked bun, are the stars. But there's plenty more, including tacos, big salads, and, on Fridays, fish-and-chips. Wash it down with a cold Mexican Coke.

Cafés

Plaza Café (54 Lincoln Ave., 505/982-1664, 7am-9pm daily, $11) may look shiny and new, but it's a city institution where residents roll in to read the paper and load up on coffee and great renditions of New Mexican and American diner favorites. This is no greasy spoon, though—the granola is house-made, the posole is perfectly toothsome, and the piñon blue-corn pancakes are fluffy and fresh.

Ecco (105 E. Marcy St., 505/986-9778, 7am-9pm Mon.-Thurs., 7am-10pm Fri., 8am-10pm Sat., 8am-7pm Sun.) is packed with coffee junkies and Wi-Fi fanatics in the mornings; later, people come in for panini (at the counter next door) and gelato.

The **French Pastry Shop** (100 E. San Francisco St., 505/983-6697, 6:30am-5pm daily, $7) has been doling out sweet crepes, buttery pastries, *croques monsieurs,* and chewy baguette sandwiches for more than 40 years. Early mornings attract a fascinating crew of Santa Fe regulars.

For a very casual lunch, stop in at the **Five & Dime General Store** (58 E. San Francisco St., 505/992-1800, 8:30am-10pm Mon.-Sat., 9am-9pm Sun., $5), on the south side of the plaza. In this former Woolworth's where, allegedly, the Frito pie was invented (Frito-Lay historians beg to differ), the knickknack shop has maintained its lunch counter and still serves the deadly combo of corn chips, homemade red chile, onions, and shredded cheese, all composed directly in the Fritos bag. Eat in, or, better, lounge on the plaza grass—and don't forget the napkins.

Italian

Rooftop Pizzeria (60 E. San Francisco St., 505/984-0008, 11am-10pm Sun.-Thurs., 11am-11pm Fri.-Sat., $15) is a good place to enjoy a view along with your meal, on a long balcony overlooking Water Street (enter on the plaza side of the shopping complex and head upstairs). You have the option of a crust with a hint of blue-corn meal, and toppings range from plain old onions to duck and crab, and they come in combinations like the BLT (the lettuce is added after the pie comes out of the oven, luckily). It also has a good selection of wines by the glass. Winter closing time is an hour earlier.

Off the plaza, next to Mission San Miguel, **Upper Crust Pizza** (329 Old Santa Fe Tr., 505/982-0000, 11am-10pm daily, $12) has a pleasantly rustic atmosphere, with a nice creaky front porch, often with a live country crooner. It does regular, whole-wheat, or gluten-free crust. Hot deli sandwiches and big superfresh salads round out the menu.

Locals head to amber-lit **Il Piatto** (95 W. Marcy St., 505/984-1091, 11:30am-10:30pm Mon.-Sat., 4:30pm-10:30pm Sun., $22) for casual Italian and a neighborly welcome from the staff, who seem to be on a first-name basis with everyone in the place. Hearty pastas like pappardelle with duck are served in generous portions—a half order will more than satisfy lighter eaters. This is a great place to take a breather from enchiladas and burritos, without breaking the bank. Its bar offers a pleasant later happy hour, 9pm-10:30pm every night.

Mexican

The specialty at **Bumble Bee's Baja Grill** (301 Jefferson St., 505/820-2862, 11am-8:30pm Sun.-Thurs., 11am-9pm Fri.-Sat., $5) is Baja-style shrimp tacos, garnished with shredded cabbage and a creamy sauce, plus a spritz of lime and your choice of house-made salsas. Lamb tacos are also delicious, as are the fried-fresh tortilla chips and that Tijuana classic, Caesar salad.

Spanish

Cozy creative-tapas joint **La Boca** (72 W. Marcy St., 505/982-3433, 11:30am-10pm daily, little plates $7-14) starts from Spain, then pulls in other Mediterranean influences: a salad spiked with apricots and figs, Moroccan *merguez*, and more. The little plates can add up fast, unless you're there 3pm-5pm weekdays, when there's a selection for half price. Reserve, ideally, and go early if you're sensitive to noise.

If you prefer a more traditional approach to Spanish food, head for the offshoot **Taberna La Boca** (125 Lincoln Ave., 505/988-7102, 11:30am-2pm and 5pm-11pm daily, $12), around the corner, tucked in the middle of the block. The atmosphere is a bit more casual here, with music in the evenings, and paella is a deal on Tuesdays, when a three-course meal is $20, as are select bottles of wine.

Guadalupe and the Railyard

An easy walk from the plaza, these few square blocks hold some of the better, quirkier dining options in town.

produce at the Santa Fe Farmers Market

New Mexican

The under-the-radar cousin of The Shed, **La Choza** (905 Alarid St., 505/982-0909, 11am-2:30pm and 5pm-9pm Mon.-Sat., $16) has a similar creative New Mexican menu but can be more of a local hangout—though it has become better known now that the rail yard has been developed around it. This also makes it a handy destination if you're coming to Santa Fe on the train—just walk back down the tracks a few minutes.

Fresh and Local

If you're on green-chile-and-cheese overload, head to **Vinaigrette** (709 Don Cubero Alley, 505/820-9205, 11am-9pm Mon.-Sat., $14) and dig into a big pile of fresh greens. The so-called salad bistro uses largely organic ingredients from its farm in Nambé, in imaginative combos, like a highbrow taco salad with chorizo and honey-lime dressing. The setting is pure homey Santa Fe, with tea towels for napkins, iced tea served in canning jars, and local art on the whitewashed walls. There's a pretty patio too. Heading north on Cerrillos Road, turn off just after La Unica Cleaners.

Just outside the Paseo de Peralta loop, the **Tune-Up Café** (1115 Hickox St., 505/983-7060, 7am-10pm Mon.-Fri., 8am-10pm Sat.-Sun., $9) is a homey one-room joint that locals love, whether for fish tacos or a suitably Santa Fe-ish brown-rice-and-nut burger. The Salvadoran *pupusas* are tasty.

Swiss Bistro & Bakery (401 S. Guadalupe St., 505/988-1111, 7am-3pm Mon.-Wed., 7am-9pm Thurs.-Sun., $11) has a delectable selection of pastries, and, thanks to the owner's interest in vegetable gardening, beautiful heirloom varieties of tomatoes and other rare produce make their way into typical Euro delights like quiche, crepes, and schnitzel.

The popular **Santa Fe Farmers Market** (1607 Paseo de Peralta, 505/983-4098, www.santafefarmersmarket.com, 8am-1pm Tues., 7am-noon Sat., Sat. only Dec.-Apr.) is a great place to pick up fresh treats as well as souvenir chile *ristras*. It's in a market hall in the Railyard complex, off Paseo de Peralta near Guadalupe Street.

Classic American

All things Texan are the specialty at **Cowgirl BBQ** (319 S. Guadalupe St., 505/982-2565, 11:30am-10:30pm Sun.-Wed., 11:30am-4pm Thurs., 11:30am-11pm Fri., 11am-11pm Sat., $15)—but it has been a Santa Fe fixture for so long that it doesn't seem like "foreign" food. It's a kitsch-filled spot that's as friendly to kids as it is to margarita-guzzling, barbecue-rib-gnawing adults. Non-meat-eaters won't feel left out: An ooey-gooey butternut squash casserole comes with a salad on the side. Both carnivores and veggies can agree on the pineapple upside-down cake and the ice-cream "baked potato."

Beloved local chef Chris Knox, formerly of the great restaurant Aqua Santa,

Santa Fe's Finest Dining

In Santa Fe, there is a certain category of restaurant that one reader of this guide dubbed "Vegas-style"—that is, a place where the blingier your bolo tie or cowboy boots, the better. They're not totally superficial—in fact, **Coyote Café** (132 W. Water St., 505/983-1615, 5:30pm-9pm Sun.-Thurs., 5:30pm-10pm Fri.-Sat., $40) at least deserves a spot in the history books for having pioneered haute Southwestern cuisine in the late 1980s, under Chef Mark Miller. Today that restaurant is owned by the same team as **Geronimo** (724 Canyon Rd., 505/982-1500, 5:45pm-9pm daily, $42), and both have opted for more generic fine dining with the occasional local nod—chile-rubbed pork chops, haute green-chile mac-and-cheese, etc. **La Casa Sena** (125 E. Palace Ave., 505/988-9232, 11am-9pm Mon.-Wed., 11am-10pm Thurs.-Sat., $30) and **The Compound** (653 Canyon Rd., 505/982-4353, 11:30am-2:30pm and 5pm-9pm Mon.-Sat. and 5:30pm-9pm Sun., $38) run in the same vein, though both have notably beautiful settings.

They're all acceptable in terms of food, but certainly not great value, and you'll be dining, for the most part, alongside other visitors, not locals. The best way to see the scene without emptying your wallet is at their bars. The Coyote Café has its lively **Rooftop Cantina** (505/983-1615, 11:30am-11pm daily Apr.-Oct.), and the snug bar at Geronimo is a good place to put your feet up after a Canyon Road cruise. La Casa Sena is set in a truly dreamy garden courtyard. Order a cocktail and an appetizer, or perhaps lunch, and enjoy the eye candy.

went casual with **Shake Foundation** (631 Cerrillos Rd., 505/988-8992, 11am-6pm daily, $6), a casual outdoor burger joint that's so good people flock to it even in winter. The dainty burgers (you might want a double) are good, vouched-for beef or lamb, served on lavishly buttered buns, and piñon nuts are an optional topping for the Taos Cow ice cream. Even the Caesar salad is ingenious: a veritable bouquet of whole romaine leaves, to dip and dunk in a creamy dressing.

Cafés

Make room in your morning for an almond croissant from **Sage Bakehouse** (535 Cerrillos Rd., 505/820-7243, 7:30am-2:30pm Mon.-Sat., $4). Washed down with a mug of coffee, these butter-soaked pastries will have you set for hours. Before you leave, pick up some sandwiches for later—classic combos like smoked turkey and cheddar on the bakery's excellent crust. And maybe a pecan-raisin wreath. And a cookie too.

A few steps away is **Ohori's Coffee, Tea & Chocolate** (505 Cerrillos Rd., 505/988-9692, 7:30am-6pm Mon.-Fri., 8am-6pm Sat., 9am-2pm Sun.), Santa Fe's small-batch coffee epicures. Its dark-as-night brew makes Starbucks seem weak. There's a second shop just out of the center at 1098 South St. Francis Drive.

Fine Dining

Whether you want hearty bar food or an ethereal creation that will take your taste buds in new directions, Chef Joseph Wrede, formerly of the great Joseph's Table in Taos, delivers. His lovely, candlelit space, **Joseph's** (428 Agua Fria St., 505/982-1272, www.josephsofsantafe.com, 4:30pm-10pm Sun.-Thurs., 4:30pm-11pm Fri.-Sat., $28), is this author's favorite restaurant in Santa Fe. Wrede worships fresh produce, and his best dishes are vegetable-centric, though not necessarily vegetarian. But he's also into local meats, so carnivores will find hearty elk steaks and a seemingly simple lamb patty that may be the state's best green-chile cheeseburger. Book ahead if you can, or try for a seat at the bar. And whatever happens, don't miss the duck-fat ice cream.

Restaurant Martín (526 Galisteo St., 505/820-0919, 11:30am-2pm and 5:30pm-10pm Tues.-Fri. and Sun., 5:30pm-10pm Sat., $34) is run by longtime local hero Chef Martín Rios. His "progressive American" food can be more style than substance, especially for full-price dinners, but it's a good place for a grown-up lunch—smooth service and a mix of full plates as well as a big burger on a cornmeal bun ($14).

Canyon Road

Gallery hopping can make you hungry—but there are only a handful of places to eat on Canyon Road, and most are more dedicated to getting caffeine into your system.

Cafés

For morning brew, jog off the strip to **Downtown Subscription** (376 Garcia St., 505/983-3085, 7am-6pm daily), an airy coffee shop that stocks perhaps a million magazines. Chocolate freaks should go a little farther to **Kakawa Chocolate House** (1050 E. Paseo de Peralta, 505/982-0388, 10am-6pm Mon.-Sat., noon-6pm Sun., $4), opposite the Gerald Peters Gallery. It specializes in historically accurate hot chocolate, based on Mesoamerican and medieval European recipes, and you can also get regular coffee drinks, truffles, and pastries here. It's in a tiny adobe house—after one drink, you'll be bouncing off the walls.

For a mellower high, head to the top end of Canyon Road and **The Teahouse** (821 Canyon Rd., 505/992-0972, 9am-9pm daily, $12), where some 13 pages of the menu are devoted to teas, plus organic vittles such as kale salad with sunflower-seed dressing, and a deliciously hearty bowl of oats, rice, and wheat berries for breakfast. The service could be euphemistically described as "very Santa Fe" (i.e., spacey), but the food is good, and it's a great place to put your feet up after a long art crawl.

Spanish

The lively evening spot is stalwart **El Farol** (808 Canyon Rd., 505/983-9912, 11am-10pm Sun.-Thurs., 11am-11pm Fri.-Sat., $8). It's very popular as a bar, but its outside seating, under a creaky wooden portal and on a back patio, is an appealing place for a big stuffed sandwich (tuna and egg with arugula, say) or garlicky Spanish snacks.

Cerrillos Road

This commercial strip isn't Santa Fe's most scenic zone, but you'll find some great culinary gems out this way.

New Mexican

Green chile has been getting milder over the years—but not at ★ **Horseman's Haven** (4354 Cerrillos Rd., 505/471-5420, 8am-8pm Mon.-Sat., 8:30am-2pm Sun., $8), which claims to serve the hottest green chile in Santa Fe. It picks and mixes chile varieties to offer a couple of consistent grades. Like all good chile purveyors, it's in an unassuming box of a building next to a gas station, and it takes cash only.

Long notorious for its dazzling list of margaritas, **Maria's** (555 W. Cordova Rd., 505/983-7929, 11am-10pm daily, $10) is well worth settling into for a meal of hearty New Mexican classics, starting with a genuinely hot table salsa and chips. Both red and green are solid here, and the tamales are exceptionally rich and creamy (even the vegetarian ones!).

African

Just next to the Hobby Lobby in a strip mall, **Jambo** (2010 Cerrillos Rd., 505/473-1269, 11am-9pm Mon.-Sat., $11) has a menu of spicy, earthy food that's well priced and almost always satisfying. The menu features primarily Indian-inflected dishes from East Africa—lentil stew spiked with chile and softened with coconut, for instance—as well as Caribbean and Moroccan stews.

Asian

A little oasis of Asian-inflected organic food in a chain-restaurant part of town, **Mu Du Noodles** (1494 Cerrillos Rd., 505/983-1411, 5:30pm-9pm Tues.-Sat., $18) cuts the strip-mall glare with warm-hued walls and bamboo screens. The menu ranges from Central Asia to Japan, offering lamb pot stickers, coconutty and spicy Malaysian *laksa,* and Indian yellow curry along the way. Reviving citrus-ade with ginger is delicious hot or cold, or you can order beer or wine. It's open Mondays in summer.

Cafés

Community activists need caffeine too—and they head to the **Santa Fe Baking Co.** (504 W. Cordova Rd., 505/988-4292, 6am-8pm Mon.-Sat., 6am-6pm Sun., $9) to get it. The scene is talkative (local radio station KSFR broadcasts a live show from here weekday mornings), and vegetarians will find a lot to eat—but so will fans of gut-busters such as chile dogs. Breakfast is served all day.

Counter Culture (930 Baca St., 505/995-1105, 8am-3pm Sun.-Mon., 8am-9pm Tues.-Sat., $12) is generally a locals-only scene, well liked for its range of food (green chile, Vietnamese sandwiches, cinnamon buns), its casual-industrial vibe, and its outdoor space where kids can run around.

Mexican

Great things come out of the modest truck called **El Chile Toreado** (W. Cordova Rd., 505/800-0033, 8:15am-3pm Mon.-Fri., 8:15am-2pm Sat., $7), parked on Cordova Road, just east of Cerrillos. Its green salsa is a near-mystical cilantro experience, and its carnitas may be the best in town. It also serves excellent breakfast burritos—get one with Mexican chorizo.

Santa Fe Metro Area

Fresh and Local

At exit 290 off I-25, **Café Fina** (624 Old Las Vegas Hwy., 505/466-3886, 7am-3pm Mon.-Fri., 8am-3pm Sat.-Sun., $9) is a casual order-at-the-counter place, with a short but flavor-packed menu (ricotta pancakes, Reuben sandwiches) from mostly organic ingredients. The view from the hill here is lovely.

On the grounds of the Plants of the Southwest nursery, **The Kitchen** (3095 Agua Fria St., 505/438-8888, 11am-2pm daily May-Nov., $9) is the ultimate grass-roots café: one woman cooking a single vegetarian lunch each day. Wholesome home cooking, with a European bent.

The all-vegetarian **Tree House** (163 Paseo de Peralta, 505/474-5543, 9am-6pm Mon., 8am-6pm Tues.-Sat., $10) is somewhat incongruously set in the DeVargas Center mall, but its food, from the nut-and-rice-stuffed "birdhouse burger" to cherry pie, conjures a wholesome, hippie-ish A-frame in the woods. (Gluten-free baked goods are available too.)

American

Out on Old Las Vegas Highway, the frontage road for I-25, **Harry's Roadhouse** (96 Old Las Vegas Hwy., 505/989-4629, 7am-9:30pm daily, $11) is a good destination, or an easy place to pop off the freeway (at the Old Santa Fe Trail exit). The patio has a great view across the flatlands, there's a full bar, and the diner-style menu includes cold meat-loaf sandwiches, catfish po'boys, lamb stew, and an awe-inspiring breakfast burrito. Oh, and pie: Chocolate mousse, lemon meringue, and coconut cream pies could be crowding the pastry case at any given time.

Asian

The restaurant at Ten Thousand Waves, **Izanami** (3451 Hyde Park Rd., 505/428-6390, 11am-10pm daily, small plates $5-14), melds old Japan and new, without feeling like a theme restaurant. On the menu, there's pickled burdock root and sticky sweet potatoes, as well as wagyu-beef burgers and tempura-fried artichokes, served in small plates to share.

The dining room has a rustic mountain-lodge feel, with an optional shoes-off tatami-mat seating area. Throw in a vast sake menu and surprisingly reasonable prices, and it's one of Santa Fe's coolest places to eat, whether you make the drive up for dinner or just wander over after your bath.

Mexican

In a strip mall off St. Michaels Drive, **Felipe's Tacos** (1711-A Llano St., 505/473-9397, 9am-5:30pm Mon.-Fri., 9am-3pm Sat., $6) makes soft tacos just like you get south of the border: steaming corn tortillas wrapped around grilled chicken or steak, or the chile-soaked pork *al pastor,* and then topped with radish slices, salsa, and lime. Bigger appetites will want a hefty burrito. There are lots of vegetarian combos as well, plus fresh limeade to drink.

Information and Services

Tourist Information

The **Santa Fe Convention and Visitors Bureau** (800/777-2489, www.santafe.org) hands out its visitors guide and other brochures from offices at the **convention center** (201 W. Marcy St., 8am-5pm Mon.-Fri.) and at the **Rail Runner depot** (401 S. Guadalupe St., 9am-5pm Mon.-Sat., 10am-2pm Sun.); the depot office is closed on Sundays November-April.

The New Mexico Tourism Department runs a **visitors center** (491 Old Santa Fe Tr., 505/827-7336, www.newmexico.org, 8am-5pm Mon.-Fri.) near San Miguel Mission.

For info on the outdoors, head to the Bureau of Land Management's comprehensive **Public Information Access Center** (301 Dinosaur Tr., 505/954-2000, www.publiclands.org, 8am-4:30pm Mon.-Fri.), just off Highway 14 (follow Cerrillos Road until it passes under I-25). You can pick up detailed route descriptions for area day hikes, as well as guidebooks, topo maps, and hunting and fishing licenses.

Books and Maps

Santa Fe has several particularly good bookshops in the center of town. **Travel Bug** (839 Paseo de Peralta, 505/992-0418, 7:30am-5:30pm Mon.-Sat., 11am-4pm Sun.) specializes in maps, travel guides, gear, and free advice. For more general books, **Collected Works** (202 Galisteo St., 505/988-4226, 8am-8pm Mon.-Sat., 8am-6pm Sun.) is the place to go for a trove of local-interest titles. Finally, the eclectic new and secondhand stock at **op.cit.** (500 Montezuma Ave., 505/428-0321, 8am-7pm Mon.-Sat., 8am-6pm Sun.), in Sanbusco Center, is endlessly browsable.

Local Media

The ***Santa Fe New Mexican*** is Santa Fe's daily paper. On Fridays, it publishes events listings and gallery news in its ***Pasatiempo*** insert. For left-of-center news and commentary, the ***Santa Fe Reporter*** is the free weekly rag, available in most coffee shops and cafés.

Banks

First National Santa Fe (62 Lincoln Ave., 505/992-2000, 8am-5pm Mon.-Fri.) is on the west side of the plaza.

Post Office

Santa Fe's **main post office** (120 S. Federal Pl., 505/988-2239, 8am-5:30pm Mon.-Fri., 9am-4pm Sat.) is conveniently just north of the plaza, near the district courthouse.

Laundry

Most self-service laundries are on or near Cerrillos Road. One of the largest and nicest is **St. Michael's Laundry** (1605 St. Michaels Dr., 505/989-9375, 6am-9pm daily), a couple of blocks east of Cerrillos Road. It also has drop-off service.

Getting Around

Bus and Shuttle

Santa Fe Pick-Up (505/231-2573, www.santafenm.gov, free) is a shuttle designed for passengers arriving on the Rail Runner—though any tourist can use it. Its route starts and ends in front of Jean Cocteau Cinema, on Montezuma Avenue just north of the depot, and it stops at the capitol, the St. Francis Cathedral, four points on Canyon Road, Museum Hill, and a few other tourist-friendly spots around town. It runs every 20 minutes or so, 6:30am-6:30pm Monday to Friday and 7:30am-4:30pm Saturday.

The reasonably useful city bus system, **Santa Fe Trails** (505/955-2001, www.santafenm.gov), can take you to all of the major sights from the handy central depot on Sheridan Street northwest of the plaza. The M route goes to Museum Hill; Route 2 runs along Cerrillos Road. Buses on all routes run only every 30 to 60 minutes. The Museum Hill and Cerrillos Road buses run on Sundays. Fare is $1, or you can buy a day pass for $2, payable on board with exact change.

Car

The area around the plaza is a maze of one-way streets, and parking is limited and expensive. **Hertz, Budget, Avis,** and **Thrifty** all have branches on Cerrillos Road.

Between Santa Fe and Taos

The drive from Santa Fe to Taos, no matter which route you choose, is an important and memorable part of a visit to northern New Mexico. The main options are the Low Road along the Rio Grande or the High Road through the mountains. You can also take a more roundabout route through Ojo Caliente, a village built around hot springs.

The Low Road leads through a lush river valley, passing small farming and ranching communities, while the High Road takes you deep into the mountains to a series of small Spanish-era towns that have not entirely bowed to modernity. The evocative vision of the artist Georgia O'Keeffe brings many visitors to this part of the world, and a more circuitous route north and west from Santa Fe to Taos moves past the artist's former home at Abiquiu, then backtracks slightly to pick up the road to the relaxing hot springs at Ojo Caliente.

Tesuque and Pojoaque

Just north of Santa Fe, the highway overpasses are decorated with the original Tewa names of pueblos. Tesuque (Te Tesugeh Owingeh, "village of the cottonwood trees") is marked by **Camel Rock,** a piece of sandstone on the west side of the highway that has eroded to resemble a creature that looks right at home in this rocky desert.

Farther north, Pojoaque manages the **Poeh Museum** (78 Cities of Gold Rd., 505/455-5041, 10am-4pm Mon.-Sat., www.poehcenter.org, free), in a striking old-style adobe building just off the highway. It shows (and sells) local artwork, as well as a permanent installation relating the Pojoaque people's path (*poeh*) through history.

Just north of the Cities of Gold Casino is a tasting room for New Mexico's largest craft distillery, **Don Quixote Distillery** (18057 US 84/285, www.dqdistillery.com, noon-6pm daily). You can sample the husband-and-wife team's blue-corn-based vodka and gin flavored with locally foraged juniper berries and other botanicals. They also make intense vanilla extract, bitters, and port wine based on New Mexican monks' 16th-century recipe. It's on the west side of the highway, just north of the exit for Highway 502; coming from the south, you'll have to double back at the next light.

Getting There

From downtown Santa Fe, northbound Guadalupe Street turns into US 84/285,

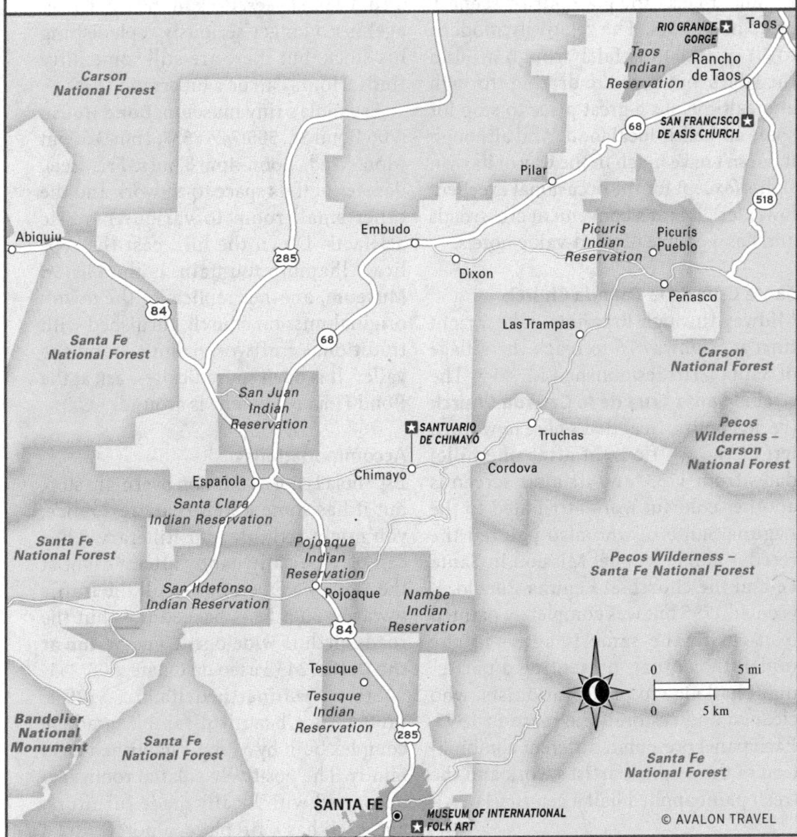

which runs north through Tesuque in 5 miles and Pojoaque in 15 miles. Though this stretch of casinos and tax-free cigarette shops isn't particularly scenic, don't be tempted to race through it—the area is a major speed trap.

Low Road to Taos

The lush farmland around the Rio Grande is the highlight of this drive north—the valley filled with apple orchards is as green as New Mexico gets. The route begins past the modern town of Española, winding into an ever-narrower canyon and finally emerging at the point where the high plains meet the mountains. This dramatic arrival makes it the better route for heading north to Taos; you can then loop back south via the High Road.

Getting There

This low-road route is more direct than the High Road to Taos, and has fewer potential diversions. Driving the 70 miles direct from downtown Santa Fe to Taos (on US 84/285 and Hwy. 68), with no stops, takes about an hour and a half. There are no gas stations between Española and Taos.

Española

Midway between Santa Fe and Taos, Española lacks the glamour or scenery of its neighbors. The relatively modern town of 10,000 is fairly rough around the edges, but if you're driving through at mealtime, it's a great place to stop for some authentic local food. And although it doesn't have much in the way of its own sights (except for the occasional excellent lowrider), it is at a convenient crossroads and has a couple of good-value hotels.

Santa Cruz de la Cañada Church

Midway through Española, take a right turn at Highway 76 to reach the village of Santa Cruz, established in 1695. The sizable **Santa Cruz de la Cañada Church** (varied hours, free) that's here now (turn left at the traffic light after one mile) dates from 1733, and its altar screen is another colorful work attributed to the Laguna Santero, who also painted the reredos at San Miguel Mission in Santa Fe and the church at Laguna Pueblo. It is dated 1795 but was completely painted over—with the same images—in the mid-19th century, presenting a particular challenge to preservationists, who cleaned and restored the piece in 1995. Each panel presents a different combination of the original artist's work and the fresh paint applied half a century later.

Other Sights

No, you haven't made a wrong turn—you're still in Española. The **Chimayó Trading Post** (110 Sandia Dr., 505/753-9414, 10am-4pm Wed.-Sat.), on the west side of the main highway, relocated here in the 1930s, after several decades at its original location in Chimayó. Now it's a listed landmark, as one of the last remaining historic trading posts, and it has everything you'd expect: creaky wood floors, dim lighting, and a jumbled stock of treasures that includes of course Chimayó rugs, as well as Nepalese silver jewelry; cut-tin candleholders, made locally; skeins of handmade wool yarn; postcards; and even free coffee. The remaining elderly owner (one of a pair of airline employees, back in the real jet-set age) is no longer seriously replenishing his stock, but there are still some nifty finds. Hours can be a bit erratic.

Española's tiny museum, **Bond House** (706 Bond St., 505/747-8535, 1pm-3:30pm Mon.-Wed., noon-4pm Thurs.-Fri., free), devotes half its space to artwork and the other small room to various historic artifacts. Down the hill, past the replica Alhambra fountain, is the **Misión Museum,** another replica, of the town's original mission church, furnished with traditional craftwork from around the valley. It is open sporadically—ask at the Bond House if no one is around.

Accommodations

Española is not a common overnight stop, but it has some hotels that are so nice, you might rethink your itinerary. They can be especially handy after a night at the Santa Fe Opera, when all the traffic toward Santa Fe is backed up—but the road north is wide open. The ★ **Inn at the Delta** (243 Paseo de Oñate, 505/753-9466, www.innatthedelta.biz, $120 s, $160 d) is a beautiful rambling adobe complex built by a long-established local family. The positively palatial rooms are decorated with locally made furniture, and each has a fireplace, a porch, and a jet tub. Rates include breakfast.

South of town, on the road to Los Alamos, ★ **Rancho Jacona** (277 County Rd. 84, 505/455-7948, www.ranchojacona.com, $170 d) is a working farm dotted with 11 casitas, each with a kitchen and space for three to eight people. You'll likely get some fresh chicken eggs for breakfast, and kids can frolic in the pool. There's a three-night minimum.

A project of the local pueblo, the **Santa Claran** (460 N. Riverside Dr., 877/505-4949, www.santaclaran.com, $85 d) also has spacious rooms, tastefully done in subdued grays and browns. Perks include fridges and laundry machines, but

Ceremonial Dances

This is an approximate schedule for dances at pueblos in the Santa Fe area. Pueblo feast days are always on the same date every year, but seasonal dances (especially Easter and other spring rituals) can vary. Confirm details and start times—usually afternoon, but sometimes following an evening or midnight Mass—with the **Indian Pueblo Cultural Center** (505/843-7270, www.indianpueblo.org) before setting out.

- **January 1** - Ohkay Owingeh (San Juan): cloud or basket dance
- **January 6** - Picurís: various dances; Nambé: buffalo, deer, and antelope dances
- **January 22** - San Ildefonso: vespers and firelight procession at 6pm
- **January 23** - San Ildefonso: Feast of San Ildefonso, with buffalo and deer dances
- **January 25** - Picurís: Feast of San Pablo
- **February 2** - Picurís: various dances for Candlemas (Día de la Candelaria)
- **Easter** - Nambé: bow dance; San Ildefonso: various dances
- **June 13** - Ohkay Owingeh (San Juan), Santa Clara, and Picurís: Feast of San Antonio
- **June 24** - Ohkay Owingeh (San Juan): Feast of San Juan Bautista
- **July 4** - Nambé: celebration at the waterfall
- **August 9-10** - Picurís: Feast of San Lorenzo
- **August 12** - Santa Clara: Feast of Santa Clara
- **September 8** - San Ildefonso: corn dance
- **October 4** - Nambé: Feast of San Francisco de Asís
- **November 12** - Tesuque: Feast of San Diego
- **December 12** - Pojoaque: Feast of Nuestra Señora de Guadalupe
- **December 24** - Picurís and Ohkay Owingeh (San Juan): torchlight procession at sundown, followed by Los Matachines; Tesuque and Nambé: various dances, beginning after midnight Mass
- **December 25** - San Ildefonso, Ohkay Owingeh (San Juan), Picurís, and Tesuque: various dances
- **December 26** - Ohkay Owingeh (San Juan): turtle dance
- **December 28** - Picurís and Santa Clara: children's dances to celebrate Holy Innocents Day

Internet is wired only in rooms; there's wireless access in the lobby.

Food

Thirsty? Look out for **Saints & Sinners** (503 S. Riverside Dr., 505/753-2757), a long-established package liquor store where you can also crack open a beer. It stocks an excellent selection of tequilas, and the neon sign should get landmark status (yes, they sell souvenir T-shirts). Cash only.

For a quick bite, stop at **El Parasol** (603 Santa Cruz Rd., 505/753-8852, 7am-9pm Mon.-Sat., $5), a takeout stand with picnic tables under cottonwood trees and a Spanglish menu ("pollo with guacamole taco"). Another option: the big Mexican-style sandwiches at **Tortas Rainbow** (745 N. Riverside Dr., 505/747-1791, 9am-8pm

Side Trip to Los Alamos

Los Alamos, home of the atomic bomb, is a product of the modern age. You may only spend a few hours here, visiting the museum and admiring the view from this high plateau, but you'll still sense a different atmosphere from anywhere else in New Mexico. Visit on a weekday, as more businesses are open.

During World War II, an elite boys' school was requisitioned by the army to become the top-secret base for development of the nuclear bomb, home for a time to science luminaries like J. Robert Oppenheimer, Richard Feynman, and Niels Bohr. The Manhattan Project and its aftermath, the Cold War arms race, led to the establishment of Los Alamos National Lab (LANL). In 1957 the base became a town; it's now home to about 18,000 people.

The town is spread over three long mesas that extend from the mountain behind. Highway 502 arrives in the middle mesa, depositing you on Central Avenue in the main downtown area. The north mesa is mostly residential, while the south mesa is occupied by the labs and two routes that run down the mountain and connect with Highway 4.

See what the area was like pre-Manhattan Project at the fascinating **Los Alamos Historical Museum** (1050 Bathtub Row, 505/662-4493, www.losalamoshistory.org, 9:30am-4:30pm Mon.-Fri., 11am-4pm Sat.-Sun., free) set in an old building of the Los Alamos Ranch School, the boys' camp that got the boot when the army moved in. The exhibits cover everything from relics of the early Tewa-speaking people up to juicy details on the social intrigue during the development of the A-bomb. In front of the museum is **Fuller Lodge Art Center** (2132 Central Ave., 505/662-1635, 10am-4pm Mon.-Sat., free), originally the Ranch School's dining room and kitchen. It usually has a community art exhibit downstairs, plus a room upstairs restored to the era when schoolteachers bunked here.

Set up by Los Alamos National Lab, the **Bradbury Science Museum** (1350 Central Ave., 505/667-4444, www.lanl.gov/museum, 10am-5pm Tues.-Sat., 1pm-5pm Sun.-Mon., free) has the feel of a science fair, with plenty of buttons to push and gadgets to play with. Most interesting are the relics of the early nuclear age: Fat Man and Little Boy casings, gadgetry from the Nevada Test Site, and the like. **Atomic City Van Tours** (505/662-3965, www.buffalotoursla.com, 1:30pm daily Mar.-Oct., $15) leave from the parking lot in front of the museum. The 1.5-hour tour is a good way to see more of the town, which is otherwise a bit difficult to navigate, and learn some of the history. Call ahead to reserve.

Los Alamos is not exactly bursting with restaurants, and many are open weekdays only. For lunch, **El Parasol** (1903 Central Ave., 505/661-0303, 7am-7pm Mon.-Fri., 8am-3pm Sat., 9am-2pm Sun., $6) is reliable and well priced.

Getting There

Los Alamos is 36 miles (45 minutes by car) from downtown Santa Fe, via US 84/285 north to Highway 502 West at Pojoaque. If you are coming from the north, from Española it's 20 miles (30 minutes) west on Highway 30 to Highway 502.

daily, $6). It's in a strip mall and can be easy to miss—look for (ironically) the Subway.

For a sit-down breakfast or lunch, diner-style **JoAnn's Ranch O Casados** (938 N. Riverside Dr., 505/753-1334, 7am-9pm Mon.-Sat., 7am-4pm Sun., $10) does all-day breakfast, plus very good and inexpensive enchiladas, fajitas, and more. The red chile is rich and mellow, and you can get half orders of many dishes.

Open for dinner as well, long-established **La Cocina** (415 S. Santa Clara Bridge Rd., 505/753-3016, 7am-8:30pm Mon.-Sat., 7am-8pm Sun., $12) does all the New Mexican classics, including burritos made with local lamb.

Getting There

Española is about a 45-minute drive from central Santa Fe via US 84/285 north. Leaving Española, take Highway 68 (also called Riverside Drive) north from here to Taos (45 miles), or cross over the Rio Grande and continue on US 84 to Abiquiu (22 miles). From an intersection in the middle of Española, Highway 76 leads east to Chimayó (8 miles), then to Truchas and the other high-road towns on the way to Taos. From the old main plaza on the west side of the Rio Grande, Highway 30 is the back road to Los Alamos (20 miles).

Embudo and Dixon

The village of Embudo is really just a bend in the river, where the Chili Line railroad from Denver used to stop (the old station is across the river). But it offers a random roadside attraction in the **Classical Gas Museum** (1819 Hwy. 68, 505/852-2995, free) a front yard filled with old service station accoutrements. If the gate is open, the owner is probably home, and you can peek inside to see a beautiful collection of neon signs and restored gas pumps. There's also a good eating option: **Sugar's** (1799 Hwy. 68, 505/852-0604, 11am-6pm Thurs.-Sun., $6), a small roadside trailer that doles out seriously big food, such as barbecue brisket burritos. It's takeout only, but there are a few plastic picnic tables where you can sit down.

If you're into wine, keep an eye out for the various wineries just north of here: **Vivác** (2075 Hwy. 68, 505/579-4441, 10am-6pm Mon.-Sat., 11am-6pm Sun.) is on the main highway and **La Chiripada** (505/579-4437, 10am-6pm Mon.-Sat., noon-6pm Sun.) is down Highway 75 a few miles in the pleasant little town of Dixon, known for its dense concentration of artists, organic farmers, and vintners. The convivial **farmers market** runs on summer and fall Wednesdays (4:30pm-7pm), and in early November, look for the long-running **Dixon Studio Tour** (www.dixonarts.org). A good year-round reason to make the turn is ★ **Zuly's** (234 Hwy. 275, 505/579-4001, 8:30am-3pm Tues.-Thurs., 8:30am-7pm Fri., 9am-7pm Sat., $8), serving strong coffee and classic New Mexican food with a bit of hippie flair; hours cut back slightly in winter.

Pilar

Beginning just south of the village of Pilar and stretching several miles north, **Orilla Verde Recreation Area** ($3/car) is public land along either side of the Rio Grande, used primarily as a put-in or haul-out for rafting, but you can camp on the riverbanks as well. Petaca and Taos Junction have the best sites ($7 per night).

Running about 1.2 miles one-way along the west edge of the river, the **Vista Verde Trail** is an easy walk with great views and a few petroglyphs to spot in a small arroyo about a third of the way out. The trailhead is located on the other side of the river, half a mile up the hill from the Taos Junction Bridge off the dirt road Highway 567 (turn left off the highway in Pilar, then follow signs into Orilla Verde). Stop first on the main highway at the **Rio Grande Gorge Visitors Center** (Hwy. 68, 575/751-4899, 8:30am-4:30pm daily June-Aug., 10am-2pm daily Sept.-May) for maps and other information.

Across the road, **Pilar Yacht Club** (Hwy. 68, 575/758-9072, 8am-6pm daily mid-May-Aug., 9am-2pm daily Apr.-mid-May and Sept.-Oct.) is the center of the action, selling tubes for lazy floats, serving food to hungry river rats, and functioning as an office for a couple of outfitters.

High Road to Taos

Chimayó, Córdova, Truchas, Las Trampas, Peñasco—these are the tiny villages strung, like beads on a necklace, along the winding highways through the mountains to Taos. This is probably the area of New Mexico where Spanish heritage has been least diluted—or at any rate relatively untouched by Anglo influence, for there has been a long history

Side Trip to Abiquiu

Abiquiu is inextricably linked with the artist Georgia O'Keeffe, who made the place her home for more than 40 years. For more information on Abiquiu, see *Moon Santa Fe, Taos & Albuquerque*, by Zora O'Neill.

The **village of Abiquiu** was established in 1754. O'Keeffe's house forms one side of the old plaza; on the other is the **Santo Tomás de Abiquiu Church,** built in the 1930s. Past O'Keeffe's house is the village *morada,* dramatically set on a hilltop. You're not welcome to poke around, however—the village maintains a privacy policy similar to those of the pueblos. So it's best to visit on a guided tour of the house.

The **Georgia O'Keeffe Home** (505/685-4539, www.okeeffemuseum.org, $12), where she lived 1949-1984, fronts the small plaza in the village center of Abiquiu. It's open for guided tours (mid-Mar.-Nov.). The rambling adobe, parts of which were built in the 18th century, is a great reflection of O'Keeffe's aesthetic, which fused the starkness of modernism with an organic sensuality.

The schedule varies by month, but there are five **tours** ($35) daily on Tuesday, Thursday, and Friday. From June through October, tours are also scheduled on Wednesdays and Saturdays ($45). Longer, special tours with Judy Lopez ($65), who worked with O'Keeffe for more than a decade, run Thursdays from June to November. A Wednesday-night "behind-the-scenes" tour ($60) includes a visit to O'Keeffe's fallout shelter, among other things. Make tour reservations at least a month in advance.

Ghost Ranch (US 84, 505/685-1000, www.ghostranch.org), a 21,000-acre retreat owned by the Presbyterian Church, is famous for several things: First, Georgia O'Keeffe owned a parcel of land and maintained a studio here. Then, in 1947, paleontologists discovered about a thousand skeletons of the dinosaur *Coelophysis,* the largest group discovered in the world. Guided **tours** (various times, $25-35) of the grounds run mid-March through November. One walking tour visits O'Keeffe's painting spot in the red Chinle hills behind the ranch. **Horseback rides** ($85) visit various spots key to O'Keeffe's painting life.

Accommodations and Food

At the **Abiquiu Inn** (21120 US 84, 505/685-4378, www.abiquiuinn.com, $160 d), lodging consists of pretty casitas with great views of the river and a cluster of motel rooms. The inn's restaurant, **Café Abiquiu** (7am-9pm daily, $13) is delectable, with fresh ingredients, a mix of traditional New Mexican and more creative food, and especially good and creative breakfasts.

You can stay at **Ghost Ranch** (US 84, 505/685-4333, www.ghostranch.org, $50-125) when it's not full for retreats. You can also camp for $19. Rates include breakfast. Day visitors can take simple meals at the **dining hall** (noon-1pm and 5pm-6pm).

Christ in the Desert Monastery (Forest Rd. 151, 801/545-8567, www.christdesert.org, $70 s, $90 d, two-night minimum) offers wonderful accommodations for a suggested donation, which includes all meals. At the 11.5-mile mark on the same road, **Rio Chama Campground** (first-come, first-served, free) is good if you want to get away from it all.

Getting There

Abiquiu is about 50 miles (one hour) from downtown Santa Fe. From Santa Fe, take US 84/285 north for 26 miles to Española. From Española, continue on US 84 north for 23 miles to Abiquiu.

of exchange between the Spanish towns and the adjacent pueblos. The local dialect is distinctive, and residents can claim ancestors who settled the towns in the 18th century. The first families learned to survive in the harsh climate with a 90-day growing season, and much of the technology that worked then continues to work now; electricity was still scarce even in the 1970s, and adobe construction is common.

To casual visitors, these communities, closed off by geography, can seem a little insular, but pop in at the galleries that have sprung up in a couple of the towns, and you'll get a warm welcome. And during the **High Road Art Tour** (www.highroadnewmexico.com), over two weekends in September, modern artists and more traditional craftspeople famed particularly for their wood-carving skills open their home studios.

The route starts on Highway 503, heading east off US 84/285 just north of Pojoaque.

Getting There

From downtown Santa Fe, the High Road to Taos is about 80 miles. Follow US 84 West/US 285 North for about 15 miles to Pojoaque. Turn right (east) on Highway 503, following signs for Nambé Pueblo. After less than 10 miles, turn left onto County Road 98 to Chimayó, then right after several miles on Highway 76.

In about 30 miles, make a hard left onto Highway 518, and in 15 miles, you'll arrive in Ranchos de Taos, just north of the church and about five miles south of the main Taos plaza. The drive straight through takes a little more than two hours; leave time to dawdle at churches and galleries, take a hike, or have lunch along the way.

Nambé Pueblo

A few miles off Highway 503, **Nambé Falls Recreation Area** (505/455-2306, $10/car) is open to the public for swimming and fishing. A rough trail leads to the falls themselves, a double cascade of water from the dam on the river here. It's a nice place to stretch your legs, but its alleged opening hours (7am-7pm daily) are not always adhered to, and you may find it closed.

Incidentally, the Nambé line of high-end housewares has nothing to do with this pueblo of 1,700 people—weaving and micaceous pottery are some of the traditional crafts here. The biggest annual event is Fourth of July, celebrated with dances and a crafts market.

Chimayó

From Nambé Pueblo, Highway 503 continues to a T junction; make a hard left onto Highway 98 to descend into the valley of Chimayó, site of the largest mass pilgrimage in the United States. During Holy Week, some 50,000 people arrive on foot, often bearing large crosses. The destination is a remarkable church.

★ Santuario de Chimayó

The pilgrimage tradition began in 1945, as a commemoration of the Bataan Death March, but the **Santuario de Chimayó** (Hwy. 98, 505/351-9961, www.holychimayo.us, 9am-6pm daily May-Sept., 9am-5pm daily Oct.-Apr.) had a reputation as a miraculous spot from its start, in 1814. It began as a small chapel, built at the place where a local farmer, Bernardo Abeyta, is said to have dug up a glowing crucifix; the carved wood figure was placed on the altar. The building later fell into disrepair, but in 1929, the architect John Gaw Meem bought it, restored it, and added its sturdy metal roof; Meem then granted it back to the archdiocese in Santa Fe.

Unlike many of the older churches farther north, which are now open very seldom, Chimayó is an active place of prayer, always busy with tourists as well as visitors seeking solace, with many side chapels and a busy gift shop. (Mass is said weekdays at 11am and on Sunday at 10:30am and noon year-round.) The approach from the parking area passes chain-link fencing into which visitors have woven twigs to form crosses, each set of sticks representing a prayer. Outdoor pews made of split tree trunks accommodate overflow crowds, and a wheelchair ramp gives easy access to the church.

But the original adobe *santuario* seems untouched by modernity. The front wall of the dim main chapel is filled with an elaborately painted altar screen from the first half of the 19th century, the work of Molleno (nicknamed "the Chile Painter" because forms, especially robes, in his paintings often resemble red and green chiles). The vibrant colors seem to shimmer in the gloom, forming a sort of stage set for Abeyta's crucifix, Nuestro Señor de las Esquípulas, as the centerpiece. Painted on the screen above the crucifix is the symbol of the Franciscans: a cross over which the arms of Christ and Saint Francis meet.

Most pilgrims make their way directly to the small, low-ceiling antechamber that holds *el pocito*, the little hole where the glowing crucifix was allegedly first dug up. From this pit they scoop up a small portion of the exposed red earth, to apply to withered limbs and arthritic joints, or to eat in hopes of curing internal ailments. (The parish refreshes the well each year with new dirt, after it has been blessed by the priests.) The adjacent sacristy displays handwritten testimonials, prayers, and abandoned crutches; the figurine of Santo Niño de Atocha is also said to have been dug out of the holy ground here as well. (Santo Niño de Atocha has a dedicated chapel just down the road—the artwork here is modern, bordering on cutesy, but the back room, filled with baby shoes, is poignant.)

Chimayó Museum

The only other official sight in the village is the tiny **Chimayó Museum** (Plaza del Cerro, 505/351-0945, www.chimayomuseum.org, 11am-3pm Wed.-Sat., free), set

Santuario de Chimayó

on the old fortified plaza. It functions as a local archive and displays a neat collection of vintage photographs. Look for it behind Ortega's weaving shop.

Shopping

Chimayó has also been a weaving center for centuries, commercially known since 1900, when Hispano weavers started selling locally crafted "Indian" blankets to tourists. The two main shops are **Ortega's** (505/351-4215, 9am-5pm Mon.-Sat.), at the intersection of County Road 98 and Highway 76, and **Centinela Traditional Arts** (505/351-2180, 9am-6pm Mon.-Sat., 10am-5pm Sun.), about one mile east on Highway 76. While both are rigorously traditional in techniques, the work at Centinela shows more creative use of color and pattern.

Accommodations

Chimayó makes a good base for exploring north of Santa Fe, as you're away from the unscenic highways south of Española

yet still at a convenient crossroads. For old Spanish style, opt for **Rancho de Chimayó** (Hwy. 76, 505/351-2222, www.ranchodechimayo.com, $79 d), an offshoot of the restaurant across the road, just north of the church. The converted hacienda building, with a central courtyard, has seven rooms, some with fireplaces and all with a rustic, low-tech (no TVs or a/c) feel. Or you can stay with a known wood-carving family, at **El Mesón de la Centinela** (Hwy. 76, 505/351-2280, www.innatchimayo.com, $85 d), which has three homey casitas with patios, all part of a big adobe ranch house. Look for the turn off Highway 76, opposite Centinela Traditional Arts.

For more modern style, **Rancho Manzana** (26 Camino de Mision, 505/351-2227, www.ranchomanzana.com, $75 s, $115 d) has a rustic-chic feel, with excellent breakfasts (the owner also runs cooking classes). En route to Española, **Casa Escondida** (64 County Rd. 100, 505/351-4805, www.casaescondida.com, $115 s, $145 d) is the slickest place in the area, with eight rooms, a big backyard, a hot tub, and a sunny garden.

Food

For lunch, head across the parking lot from the Santuario de Chimayó to **Leona's** (505/351-4569, 10am-5pm Fri.-Mon., $3), where you can pick up bulk chile and pistachios as well as delicious tamales and crumbly *bizcochitos*. For a more leisurely sit-down meal, ★ **Rancho de Chimayó** (County Rd. 98, 505/351-4444, www.ranchodechimayo.com, 11:30am-9pm daily May-Oct., 11:30am-9pm Tues.-Sun. Nov.-Apr., $12) offers great local food on a beautiful terrace—or inside the old adobe home by the fireplace in wintertime. Likewise, the menu offers all possible options: posole or rice, whole pintos or refried beans, smooth red sauce (from Chimayó chiles) or chunkier *chile caribe*. The place is also open for breakfast on weekends, 8:30am-10:30am.

Córdova

From Chimayó, turn right (east) on Highway 76 (west takes you to Española), to begin the climb up the Sangre de Cristo Mountains. Near the crest of the hill, about three miles along, a small sign points to Córdova, a village best known for its austere unpainted *santos* and *bultos* done by masters such as George López and José Dolores López. Another family member, **Sabinita López Ortiz** (9 County Rd. 1317, 505/351-4572, variable hours), sells her work and that of five other generations of wood-carvers. **Castillo Gallery** (County Rd. 1317, 505/351-4067, variable hours) mixes traditional woodwork with more contemporary sculpture.

Truchas

Highway 76 winds along to the little village of Truchas (Trout), founded in 1754 and still not much more than a long row of buildings set into the ridgeline. On the corner where the highway makes a hard left north, is the village *morada*, the meeting place of the local Penitente brotherhood.

Head straight down the smaller road to reach **Nuestra Señora del Rosario de las Truchas Church,** tucked into a small plaza off to the right of the main street. It's open to visitors only June-August—if you do have a chance to look inside the dim, thick-walled mission, you'll see precious examples of local wood carving. Though many of the more delicate ones have been moved to a museum for preservation, those remaining display an essential New Mexican style—the sort of "primitive" thing that Bishop Lamy of Santa Fe hated. They're preserved today because Truchas residents hid them at home during the late 19th century. Santa Lucia, with her eyeballs in her hand, graces the altar, and a finely wrought crucifix hangs to the right, clad in a skirt because the legs have broken off.

Just up the road is **The Cordovas Handweaving Workshop** (32 County Rd. 75, 505/689-1124, 8am-5pm Mon.-Sat.), an unassuming wooden house that echoes with the soft click-clack of a broadloom, as this Hispano family turns out subtly striped rugs in flawless traditional style, as it has done for generations. Prices are quite reasonable.

Las Trampas

Farther north on Highway 76, the village of Las Trampas was settled in 1751, and its showpiece, **San José de Gracia Church** (10am-4pm Sat.-Sun. June-Aug.), was built nine years later. It remains one of the finest examples of New Mexican village church architecture. Its thick adobe walls are balanced by vertical bell towers; inside, the clerestory at the front of the church—a very typical design—lets light in to shine down on the altar, which was carved and painted in the late 1700s. Other paradigmatic elements include the *atrio,* or small plaza between the low adobe boundary wall and the church itself, utilized as a cemetery, and the dark narthex where you enter, confined by the choir loft above, but serving only to emphasize the sense of light and space created in the rest of the church by the clerestory and the small windows near the viga ceiling.

As you leave the town heading north, look to the right—you'll see a centuries-old acequia that has been channeled through a log flume to cross a small arroyo. Less than a mile north of the village, you pass the turn for El Valle and Forest Road 207, which leads to the **Trampas Lakes** trailhead. This 6.1-mile hike goes through gorgeous alpine scenery—steep rock walls jutting from dense forest, myriad wildflowers, and the two lakes themselves, which are clear and frigid. A spur trail at the last junction leads to **Hidden Lake** (2 miles round-trip). This route makes a very pleasant overnight trek, giving you time to fish and relax at the end, but with an early start, you could also do the trail as an intense all-day outing.

Picurís Pueblo

The smallest pueblo in New Mexico, Picurís has only about 300 members. It is also one of the few Rio Grande pueblos that has not built a casino; instead, it capitalizes on its beautiful natural setting, a lush valley where bison roam and aspen leaves rustle. You can picnic here and fish in small but well-stocked Tu-Tah Lake. The **San Lorenzo de Picurís Church** looks old, but it was in fact rebuilt by hand in 1989, following exactly the form of the original 1776 design—the process took eight years. As at Nambé, local traditions have melded with those of the surrounding villages; the Hispano-Indian Matachines dances are well attended on Christmas Eve. Start at the **visitors center** (575/587-1099 or 575/587-1071, 9am-5pm Mon.-Sat.) to pick up maps. The pueblo is a short detour from the High Road proper: At the junction with Highway 75, turn west, then follow signs off the main road.

Peñasco

Peñasco is best known to tourists as the home of ★ **Sugar Nymphs Bistro** (15046 Hwy. 75, 575/587-0311, 11:30am-2:30pm Mon.-Wed.., 11:30am-3pm and 5:30pm-8pm Thurs.-Sat., 11am-2:30pm Sun., $12), a place with "country atmosphere and city cuisine," where you can get treats like grilled lamb, fresh-pressed cider, piñon couscous, and staggering wedges of layer cake. An adjoining **Peñasco Theatre** (www.penascotheatre.org) hosts quirky music and theatrical performances June to September. In winter, restaurant hours are more limited, so call ahead.

This is also the northern gateway to the **Pecos Wilderness Area**—turn on Forest Road 116 to reach Santa Barbara Campground and the Santa Barbara Trail to Truchas Peak, a 23-mile round-trip that requires advance planning. Contact the Española ranger district office (1710 N. Riverside Dr., 505/753-7331, 8am-4:30pm Mon.-Fri.) or the one in the town of Pecos for conditions before you hike.

Taos

Adobe buildings cluster around a plaza. Steep mountain beckon. Art galleries, organic bakeries, and yoga studios proliferate. But the town of Taos is not just a miniature Santa Fe. It's more isolated, reached by two-lane roads along either the winding mountain-ridge route or the fertile Rio Grande Valley, and it has a rougher, muddier feel. The glory of the landscape, from looming Taos Mountain to the blue mesas dissolving into the flat western horizon, can be breathtaking.

The mysticism surrounding Taos Pueblo is intense, as is the often wild creativity of the artists who have lived here. No wonder people flock here on pilgrimages: to the ranch where D. H. Lawrence lived, to the hip-deep powder at Taos Ski Valley, to the San Francisco de Asis Church that Georgia O'Keeffe painted.

Taos's busiest tourist season is summer, when a day's entertainment can consist of some strolling and museum-going, then settling in to watch the afternoon thunderheads gather and churn, followed by the sun setting under lurid red streaks across the broad western mesas. Wintertime also gets busy with skiers between November and April, but as they're all up on the mountain during the day, museums scale back their hours, and residents reclaim the town center, curling up with books at the many coffee shops. Taos Pueblo closes to visitors to up to 10 weeks in February and March. By May, the peaks are relatively clear of snow, and you can hike to high meadows filled with wildflowers. Fall is dominated by the smell of wood smoke and the beat of drums, as the pueblo and the rest of the town turn out for the Feast of San Geronimo at the end of September.

From Santa Fe, it's possible to visit Taos as a day trip—as plenty of people do in the summertime—but you'll of course get a better sense of the place if you stay overnight.

Getting There from Santa Fe

80 miles / 2.5 hours

From Santa Fe, the drive to Taos takes about **1.5 hours (70 miles)** along the direct **Low Road** through the river valley. Start by getting on **US 285 North/US 84 West,** then drive for 25 miles. Just before the town of Española, keep right to join **NM-68 North.** Continue for 45 miles before reaching Taos.

If taking the **High Road,** plan on at least **2.5 hours** for the **80-mile** drive. The start of the drive is the same as the Low Road: Take **US 285 North/US 84 West** for 15 miles until the town of Pojoaque. From there, instead of continuing on US 285/US 84, turn right to join **NM-503.** Follow NM-503 for about 10 miles, then turn left onto **Juan Medina Road/County Road 98,** following signs for **High Road to Taos Scenic Byway.** Continue for about five miles. At the intersection with NM-76, turn right to join **NM-76 North** and follow it for 20 miles. At the NM-76/NM-75 junction, turn right to pick up **NM-75 East.** After nearly 10 miles, turn left onto **NM-518 North,** driving for 15 miles until you arrive in Taos.

Getting There from Mesa Verde National Park

255 miles / 5.5 hours

From Mesa Verde National Park, it's a **5.5-hour, 255-mile** drive to Taos. It's a **20-mile, 40-minute** drive to the park entrance. From there, take **US 160 East** for 35 miles to Durango. Another 60 miles through the beautiful pine forest and you're in Pagosa Springs, where US 160 meets US 84. Keep right, following signs for Chama, to join **US 84 East.** Continue for 60 more miles, crossing into New Mexico along the way, until the junction with US 64. Turn left to follow **US 64 East** and drive for 80 miles until you reach Taos.

Getting There by Bus or Shuttle

For pickup at the Albuquerque airport, **Twin Hearts Express** (575/751-1201, $50 one-way) runs a shuttle four times a day (11:30am, 1:30pm, 3:30pm, and 5:30pm), with drop-offs at most hotels in Taos. Allow at least 2.5 hours for travel time.

From Santa Fe, there's great weekend service from city-sponsored **Taos Express** (575/751-4459, www.taosexpress.com, $10 round-trip), which runs from Taos and back once on Friday afternoon, and again on Saturday and Sunday, completing a loop in the morning and another in the afternoon. The one-way trip takes 1 hour and 50 minutes, and you must reserve a seat in advance.

Between Santa Fe and Taos (and communities around and in between, including the pueblos), the **North Central Regional Transit District** (866/206-0754, www.ncrtd.org) offers commuter bus service. It's not very frequent, but it covers a lot, making it an option for the hard-core car-free traveler.

In Santa Fe, the bus picks up passengers near the Rail Runner main depot (Montezuma at Guadalupe) and at the South Capitol station. In Taos, it drops off at the Loretto parking lot, one block west of the plaza; going back south, it also picks up passengers at the Sagebrush Inn (1508 Paseo del Pueblo Sur). The schedule syncs with the Rail Runner's arrival in Santa Fe (and it can carry bicycles), making it a potentially seamless three-hour trip all the way from Albuquerque. It can also stop at the Santa Fe airport.

Getting Around

Car

In Taos, you will need a car to get to outlying sights, but will also have to bear the daily traffic jam on Paseo del Pueblo. There are paid parking lots close to the plaza, and a free one less than a quarter mile down Kit Carson Road. For rental cars, **Enterprise** (1350 Paseo del Pueblo Sur, 575/758-5333, www.enterprise.com, 8am-5pm Mon.-Fri., 9am-noon Sat.) has a convenient office.

Taos: Fact and Fiction

Just as San Francisco de Asis Church has inspired countless painters and photographers, the people of Taos have found their way into novels and short stories.

One of Taos's more revered figures is **Padre Antonio Martinez,** a popular priest in the mid-1800s who clashed with **Bishop Jean-Baptiste Lamy** in Santa Fe. So some Taos residents aren't fond of Willa Cather's *Death Comes for the Archbishop* (New York: Vintage, 1990), even if it is a classic. The 1927 novel is based on the mission of Lamy, with sympathy for his efforts to straighten out "rogue" Mexican priests like Martinez. The padre gets more balanced coverage in *Lamy of Santa Fe* (Middletown, CT: Wesleyan University Press, 2003), a Pulitzer Prize-winning biography by Paul Horgan.

Famous Western novelist Frank Waters, a Taos resident for almost 50 years, fictionalized **Edith Warner,** a woman who ran a small café frequented by the Los Alamos scientists while they developed the nuclear bomb. *The Woman at Otowi Crossing* (Athens, OH: Swallow Press, 1987) is his portrait of a woman who seeks isolation in the New Mexico wilderness but is drawn back into the world through the largest event of her time. The novel is fairly true to life, but a biography, *The House at Otowi Bridge: The Story of Edith Warner and Los Alamos* (Albuquerque: University of New Mexico Press, 1973), is stricter with the facts. It's by Peggy Pond Church, who lived at Los Alamos for 20 years before the area was taken over by the military.

Another Taos writer, **John Nichols,** earned acclaim for his 1974 comic novel *The Milagro Beanfield War* (New York: Owl Books, 2000), later made into a film by Robert Redford. The war of the title is an escalating squabble in a tiny village over the acequia, the type of irrigation ditch that's still used in Valle Valdez and other agricultural communities in the area. But if you think it takes comic melodrama and a star such as Redford to make irrigation interesting, look into the beautiful and fascinating *Mayordomo: Chronicle of an Acequia in Northern New Mexico* (Albuquerque: University of New Mexico Press, 1993), **Stanley Crawford**'s memoir about his term as "ditch boss" in the valley where he runs his garlic farm.

Bus and Shuttle

Within Taos, the **Chile Line bus** runs north-south from the Ranchos de Taos post office to the Taos Pueblo, approximately every 40 minutes 7:30am-5:30pm Monday-Friday. The fare (exact change only) is $0.50. Mid-December-April, a **ski shuttle** ($1) runs to Taos Ski Valley, with five buses daily making stops at key motels en route to the mountain; not all buses stop at all hotels. Contact the **city** (575/751-4459, www.taosgov.com) for maps and schedules.

Sights

Orientation

The area referred to as Taos encompasses a few nearby communities as well. Arriving via the Low Road, on Highway 68, you pass first through **Ranchos de Taos;** it's connected to Taos Plaza by Paseo del Pueblo Sur, a stretch of chain stores and cheap motels. The intersection with Kit Carson Road (US 64) is the center of town proper (**Taos Plaza** is just west); for **parking,** there's a pay lot at the light, or a free lot a few blocks farther east on Kit Carson.

Heading north past Kit Carson, the road becomes Paseo del Pueblo Norte. It curves west after half a mile, and a smaller road continues north about two miles to **Taos Pueblo.** Paseo del Pueblo Norte carries on through what is technically the separate village of El Prado, then to a four-way intersection that will forever be called "the old blinking light," even though the flashing yellow signal was replaced with a newfangled three-color traffic light in the 1990s. Here US

Taos Plaza

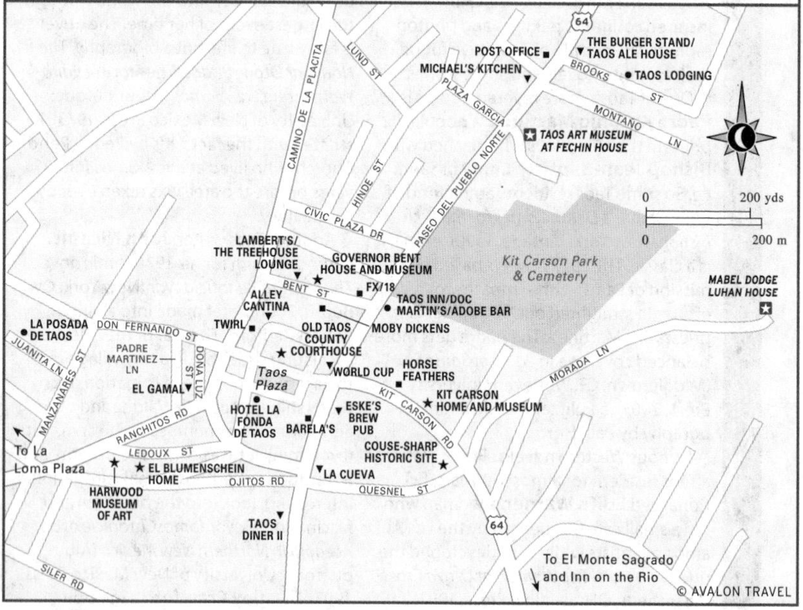

64 shoots **west to the Rio Grande,** and Highway 522 leads northwest to the outlying village of **Arroyo Hondo,** then to Questa and the Enchanted Circle. Highway 150 goes north to **Arroyo Seco,** and eventually to **Taos Ski Valley,** at the base of the slopes.

Taos Plaza

The central **Taos Plaza,** enclosed by adobe buildings with deep portals, is easy to miss if you just cruise through on the main road—it's just west of the intersection with Kit Carson Road. Once an informal area at the center of a cluster of settlers' homes, the plaza was established around 1615 but destroyed in the Pueblo Revolt of 1680. New homes were built starting in 1710, as defense against Comanche and Jicarilla raiders. But fires repeatedly gutted the block-style buildings, so the structures that edge the plaza all date from around 1930—and unfortunately virtually all are now filled with rather cheesy souvenir shops.

On the plaza's north side, the **old Taos County courthouse** contains a series of WPA-sponsored murals painted in 1934 and 1935 by Emil Bisttram and a team of other Taos artists. The door is usually open when the farmers market is on, but not reliably at other times. Still, it's worth a try: Enter on the ground floor through the North Plaza Art Center and go upstairs, toward the back of the building. On the south side, the **Hotel La Fonda de Taos** harbors a small collection of D. H. Lawrence's "erotic" paintings (2pm, 4pm, and 6pm daily, $6 admission, free to guests). The paintings are tame by today's standards, but they flesh out (no pun intended) the story of the writer's time in Taos, some of which is described in his book *Mornings in Mexico.*

In the center is a **monument** to New Mexicans killed in the Bataan Death March of World War II. The U.S. flag

Taos Museum Passes

The **Museum Association of Taos** (www.taosmuseums.org) manages five museums in town and offers a nontransferable **Super Ticket** ($25), valid for one year—a good deal if you plan to visit three or more exhibits. You can buy it at any of the participating museums: the Taos Art Museum at Fechin House, the Millicent Rogers Museum, the Harwood Museum of Art, the E. L. Blumenschein Home, and Hacienda de los Martinez.

Alternatively, if you plan to visit just **Hacienda de los Martinez** and the **E. L. Blumenschein Home,** ask about discounted admission to both places for $12 (as opposed to $8 each).

flies day and night, a tradition carried on after an incident during the Civil War when Kit Carson and a crew of his men nailed the flag to a pole and guarded it to keep Confederate sympathizers from taking it down.

In front of the historic La Fonda hotel, a large bronze **statue of Padre Antonio Martinez** gestures like a visionary. This local hero produced the area's first newspaper, *El Crepúsculo de la Libertad* (The Dawn of Freedom), which later became the *Taos News*; he also established a coed school, a seminary, and a law school. Bishop Lamy in Santa Fe criticized his liberal views, especially after Martinez defied Lamy's call for mandatory tithing, and Lamy later excommunicated him. Martinez continued to minister to locals at a chapel in his house until his death in 1867. The statue's enormous hands suggest his vast talent and influence in the town.

Harwood Museum of Art

The **Harwood Museum of Art** (238 Ledoux St., 575/758-9826, 10am-5pm Mon.-Sat., noon-5pm Sun., closed Mon. Nov.-Mar., $10), set in the sprawling Pueblo Revival-style home of the Harwood patrons, tells the story of Taos's rise as an art colony, beginning with Ernest Blumenschein's fateful wagon accident, which left him and his colleague Bert Phillips stranded in the tiny town in 1898.

Modern Taos painters are represented as well in the temporary exhibit spaces upstairs, and it's interesting to see the same material—the mountain, the pueblo, the river, local residents—depicted in different styles over the decades. Also upstairs is a small but very good assortment of Hispano crafts, including some beautiful 19th-century tinwork and a couple of *santos* by Patrocino Barela, the Taos wood-carver who modernized the art in the 1930s. A separate back wing is dedicated to seven ethereal abstractions by painter Agnes Martin.

E. L. Blumenschein Home

Ernest Blumenschein, one of the founding fathers of the Taos Society of Artists, moved into what is now the **E. L. Blumenschein Home** (222 Ledoux St., 575/758-0505, www.taoshistoricmuseums.org, 10am-5pm Mon.-Sat., noon-5pm Sun. Apr.-Oct., 10am-4pm Mon., Tues., and Thurs.-Sat. Nov.-Mar., $8) in 1919 with his wife, Mary Shepherd Greene Blumenschein, also an accomplished artist. The house's decoration largely reflects her taste, from the sturdy wood furnishings in the dining room to the light-filled studio and the cozy wood-paneled library.

Throughout, the walls are hung with sketches and paintings by their contemporaries. Some of the finest are in the back "Green Room," including a beautiful monotype of Taos Mountain by Oscar E. Berninghaus. The main bedroom, entered through a steep arch, is decorated with Mary's lush illustrations for *The Arabian Nights*. Throughout, you can admire the variety of ceiling styles, from rough-hewn split cedar (*rajas*) to tidy golden aspen boughs (*latillas*).

La Loma Plaza

To see what Taos Plaza looked like before the souvenir-shop economy, stroll down Lower Ranchitos Road and turn on Valdez Road to reach **La Loma Plaza.** The center of a smaller farm settlement in the 1780s, the ring of adobe homes around a central open space is dusty and little changed through the centuries. Exit the plaza by continuing uphill and bearing right—this takes you past La Loma's tiny old chapel and onto paved San Antonio Street, which leads downhill and back to Lower Ranchitos.

Governor Bent House and Museum

This dusty little backroom exhibit space is odd, but well worth a visit if it happens to be open (the posted hours aren't always maintained). The **Governor Bent House and Museum** (117 Bent St., 10am-5pm daily, $3) is the former residence of Charles Bent who, following the onset of the Mexican-American War, was appointed the first governor of the territory of New Mexico in 1846, based on his extensive experience as a Western trader (he and his brother had built Bent's Fort, an important trading center in southern Colorado). But Bent died in 1847, at the hands of an angry mob dissatisfied by the new U.S. government.

Amid the slightly creepy clutter, which includes a malevolent-looking ceremonial buffalo head, Inuit knives, and photos of Penitente rituals from an old *Harper's* magazine, is the very hole in the very wall that Bent's family quickly dug to escape while Bent tried to reason with the murderous crowd. The back room only gets stranger, with taxidermy, sinister doctor's instruments, and lots of old guns. The place may feel like an antiques store where nothing's for sale, but it still gives a surprisingly good overview of the period.

Nicolai Fechin's hand-built house is home to the Taos Art Museum.

★ Taos Art Museum at Fechin House

This sunny space, the former home of artist and wood-carver Nicolai Fechin, is a showcase not only for a great collection of paintings, but also for Fechin's lovely woodwork. When the Russian native moved to Taos in 1927, hoping to cure his tuberculosis, he purchased seven acres of land, including the small, two-story **Taos Art Museum** (227 Paseo del Pueblo Norte, 575/758-2690, 10am-5pm Tues.-Sun. May-Oct., till 4pm Nov.-Apr., $8). He proceeded to hand-carve the lintels, staircases, bedsteads, and more, in a combination of Russian Tartar and local styles. His blending of traditions is flawless and natural—a small altar, also in the dining room, is set with Orthodox icons but could just as easily hold local *santos*.

The collection of paintings shown here is eclectic: Victor Higgins's 1936 *Indian Nude* recalls Gauguin, while Dorothy Brett's *Rainbow and Indians* from 1942 is more enamored of the powerful landscape. One room is dedicated to Fechin's own portrait work, characterized by broad, dynamic brushstrokes and a canny eye for distinctive facial features. One work is an etching of the same set of haggard, mustachioed twins who are rendered in oil by Ernest Hennings on a canvas hanging at the Harwood Museum. After all the work Fechin did on the house, he stayed in Taos only six years, when his wife divorced him. He moved on to Los Angeles with his daughter, Eya (her sunny study, on the ground floor, contains the child-scale furniture that her father made for her). After her father died in 1955, Eya, by then practicing psychodrama and dance therapy, returned to live in the studio (the back building that also houses the gift shop) and helped establish the main house as a museum.

Kit Carson Park and Cemetery

A shady sprawl of gravestones in a corner of **Kit Carson Park** (on Paseo del Pueblo Norte north of the Taos Inn), Taos's oldest cemetery was established in 1847 to bury the dead from the Taos Rebellion, a melee incited by wealthy Spanish landowners and Catholic priests anxious about their loss of influence under the Americans. Mobs killed New Mexico's first American governor, Charles Bent, as well as scores of other Anglo landowners in the area. The cemetery earned its current name when the bodies of Carson and his wife were moved here in 1869, according to his will.

Many of Taos's oldest families are buried here. Mabel Dodge Luhan had been a very close friend of the trader Ralph Meyers, and they often joked about being buried together. When Mabel died in 1962, a few years after Ralph, writer Frank Waters recalled their wishes and suggested that Meyers's grave be scooted over to make room for Mabel. She was the last person to be buried in the cemetery, in 1962, and her grave is squeezed into the far southwest corner. Other local luminaries at rest here include Padre Antonio Martinez, who

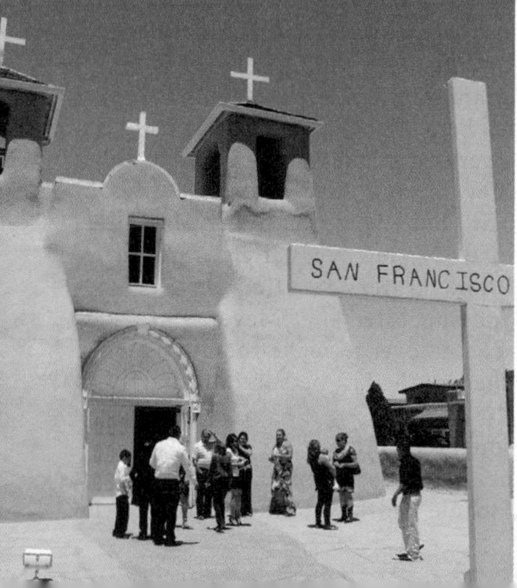

stood up to Catholic bishop Lamy, and an Englishman named Arthur Manby, whose grave actually stands outside of the cemetery proper, due to his lifetime of shady business deals, land grabs, and outright swindles perpetrated in town.

★ Mabel Dodge Luhan House

Now used as a conference center and B&B, arts patroness **Mabel Dodge Luhan's House** (240 Morada Ln., 575/751-9686, www.mabeldodgeluhan.com, 9am-7pm daily, free) is open to curious visitors as well as overnight guests. Knock at the main building first; the caretaker will give you information for a self-guided tour around the public areas of the house.

Mabel Dodge, who had fostered art salons in New York City and Florence, decamped to Taos in 1916, following her third husband. Her name became inextricably linked with Taos's 20th-century history, thanks to all the budding artists and writers she encouraged to visit. D. H. Lawrence dubbed Taos "Mabeltown," and figures as grand and varied as Greta Garbo, Willa Cather, Ansel Adams, Georgia O'Keeffe, Robinson Jeffers, and Carl Jung made the long trek to her home.

Bordering the Taos Pueblo, the house was built starting in 1918. Unsurprisingly, given Dodge's artistic taste, she exercised a firm hand in its design. Alongside a small original structure—a low row of adobe rooms that were already a century old at that point—she added a three-story main building, topped with a huge sunroom open on three sides. This, and the similarly glass-enclosed bathroom on the second floor, scandalized her neighbors, the pueblo residents.

One of them, however, didn't seem to mind: Tony Luhan, the foreman of the construction project, became her next husband. But Mabel's custom love nest brought out some latent prurience even in D. H. Lawrence, who objected to the

Top to bottom: Taos Inn; Hacienda de los Martinez; San Francisco de Asis Church.

curtainless bathroom windows; to soothe his sensibilities, he painted colorful swirls directly on the glass.

Couse-Sharp Historic Site

Tours of the **Couse-Sharp Historic Site** (146 Kit Carson Rd., 575/751-0369, www.couse-sharp.org, May-Oct., donation) are by appointment only, but it is well worth arranging to see the interior of the painter Eanger Irving Couse's home and studio. Couse, a friend of E. L. Blumenschein's, came to Taos in 1902 with his wife, Virginia, and spent the summers here, working as a figurative painter, until he died in 1936.

Not only has the Couse home and garden been meticulously kept up (as has adjacent property owned by friend and fellow painter Joseph Henry Sharp), but the tours are led by Couse's granddaughter and her husband, who have a wealth of stories to share. And not only artists will be intrigued; Couse's son, a mechanical engineer who developed mobile repair vehicles, built a vast machine shop here.

Kit Carson Home and Museum

Old photographs, memorabilia, and assorted trinkets from the frontier era conjure the spirit of the legendary scout at the **Kit Carson Home and Museum** (113 Kit Carson Rd., 575/758-4945, www.kitcarsonhomeandmuseum.com, 10am-5:30pm daily in summer, 11am-4pm daily in winter, $5), where he lived with his third wife, Josefa Jaramillo, from 1843 until they both died in 1868.

The definitive mountain man, Carson was one of many solitary scouts, trackers, and trappers who explored the American West. He was an intrepid adventurer who, after a childhood on the barely settled edge of Missouri, joined a wagon train headed down the Santa Fe Trail; he arrived in Taos in 1826. His talent for tracking, hunting, and translating from Spanish and various Indian languages soon put him in high demand. Whether he was scouting for John C. Frémont west to Los Angeles or serving as an officer in the Civil War, or forcing the Navajos on the Long Walk to Fort Sumner, he called Taos home.

Taos Inn

Distinguished by its large glowing thunderbird sign, the oldest neon sign in town, the **Taos Inn** (125 Paseo del Pueblo Norte, 575/758-2233, www.taosinn.com) was as central to previous generations of Taoseños as it is now. Granted, today it's the hotel bar that everyone goes to, but starting in the 1890s, it was the home of Dr. T. P. Martin, Taos's first and only county doctor, who had a good reputation for accepting chickens or venison from his poorer patients in lieu of cash. His home looked out on a small plaza and a well—which has since been covered over and made into the hotel lobby.

Hacienda de los Martinez

The word *hacienda* conjures a sprawling complex and fields, but the reality in 19th-century Taos was quite different, as the carefully restored **Hacienda de los Martinez** (708 Hacienda Rd., off Lower Ranchitos Rd., 575/758-1000, www.taoshistoricmuseums.org, 10am-5pm Mon.-Sat., noon-5pm Sun. Apr.-Oct., 10am-4pm Mon., Tues., and Thurs.-Sat. Nov.-Mar., $8) from 1804 shows. Its builder and owner, Severino Martinez, was a prominent merchant who hosted the Taos trade fairs at the hacienda and eventually became the mayor of Taos in the 1820s. His oldest son was Padre Antonio Martinez, the valley leader who clashed with the French bishop Jean-Baptiste Lamy.

Despite the family's high social standing, life was fairly rugged, cramped, and cold: 21 simple rooms arranged around two courtyards allowed space for sleeping, cooking, and, in the single room with a wood floor, dancing. Some of the spaces have been furnished to reflect their original use; others are dedicated to exhibits, such as a very interesting display on slavery in the area, and an especially creepy wood carving of Doña Sebastiana, Lady Death, with her glittering mica eyes, in the collection of Penitente paraphernalia. During the summer, local craftspeople are on hand to demonstrate weaving, blacksmithing, and the like in the house's workshops; in the fall, the trade fair is reenacted.

★ San Francisco de Asis Church

Just as photographs of the Great Pyramid of Cheops seldom show the sprawl of modern Cairo crowding up to its base, **San Francisco de Asis Church** (east side of US 68 in Ranchos de Taos, 575/758-2754, 9am-4pm daily, Mass 7am, 9:30am, and 11:30am Sun., donation) is depicted in, say, Georgia O'Keeffe's paintings and Ansel Adams's photographs, as a shadow-draped fortress isolated on a hilltop. In fact, the iconic church, completed in the early 19th century as a Franciscan mission, is at the center of a plaza, ringed with buildings.

It's easy to see what has fascinated so many artists: the clean lines, the shadows created by the hulking buttresses, the rich glow of the adobe in the sun. The church is living architecture, as much a part of the earth as something raised above it. As with every traditional adobe structure, it must be refinished every year with a mix of clay, sand, and straw; it is then coated with a fine layer of water and sand, and buffed with sheepskin. This happens over two weeks in June, during which the church is open only at lunchtime and on Sunday.

Inside, the whitewashed walls are covered with *bultos* and *retablos*. In the **parish hall** (9am-3:30pm daily, $3) is the 1896 painting *The Shadow of the Cross,* an eight-foot-high canvas in which the figure of Christ can be seen to luminesce—allegedly miraculously.

★ Taos Pueblo

Even if you've been in New Mexico for a while and think you're inured to adobe, **Taos Pueblo** (575/758-1028, www.taospueblo.com, 8am-4:30pm Mon.-Sat., 8:30am-4:30pm Sun., 8:30am-4pm daily in winter, closed for 10 weeks Feb.-Mar., $16) is an amazing sight. Two clusters of multistory mud-brick buildings make up the core of this village, which claims, along with Acoma Pueblo, to be the oldest continually inhabited community in the United States. The current buildings, annually repaired and recoated with mud, are from the 1200s, though it's possible that all their constituent parts have been fully replaced several times since then.

About 150 people (out of the 1,200 or so total Taos Pueblo residents) live here year-round. These people, along with the town's designation as a UNESCO World Heritage Site, have kept the place remarkably as it was in the pre-Columbian era, save for the use of adobe bricks (as opposed to clay and stone), which were introduced by the Spanish, as the main structural material. The apartment-like homes, stacked up at various levels and reached by wood ladders, have no electricity or running water, though some use propane gas for heat and light.

As you explore, be careful not to intrude on private space: Enter only buildings that are clearly marked as shops, and stay clear of the ceremonial kiva areas on the east side of each complex. These round structures form the ritual heart of the pueblo, a secret space within an already private culture.

San Geronimo Church

The path from the Taos Pueblo admission gate leads directly to the central plaza, a broad expanse between Red Willow Creek (source of the community's drinking water, flowing from sacred Blue Lake higher in the mountains) and **San Geronimo Church.** The latter, built in 1850, is perhaps the newest structure in the village, a replacement for the first mission the Spanish built, in 1619, using forced Indian labor. The Virgin

Dennis Hopper in Taos

In 1968, a Taos Pueblo elder told Dennis Hopper, "The mountain is smiling on you!" No wonder the *Easy Rider* actor and real-life renegade claimed the town as what he called his "heart home." His early years here were wild: He's notorious for having ridden his motorcycle across the roof of the Mabel Dodge Luhan House, which he bought in 1969. Over the decades, he mellowed just a bit, and Taos locals came to think of him as one of their own. In 2009, as part of a 40th-anniversary celebration of the Summer of Love, the Harwood Museum mounted an exhibit of his photography and paintings, along with works by some of his compatriots from that era.

Hopper died not long after, in 2010. His funeral was held at the San Francisco de Asis Church, and attended by fellow 1960s veterans Peter Fonda and Jack Nicholson. Following Pueblo tradition, Hopper was buried in a pine box under a dirt mound, in the nearby **Jesus Nazareno Cemetery.** Fans can pay their respects there. To find it, take Highway 518 south; about a quarter mile along, turn left (east) on Espinoza Road. The cemetery is a short way along, off the left side of the road. From the main gate Hopper's grave is near the back, on the right-hand side.

Mary presides over the room roofed with heavy wood beams; her clothes change with every season, a nod to her dual role as the Earth Mother. (Taking photos is strictly forbidden inside the church at all times and, as at all pueblos, at dances as well.)

The older church, to the north behind the houses, is now a cemetery—fitting, given its tragic destruction. It was first torn down during the Pueblo Revolt of 1680; the Spanish rebuilt it about 20 years later. In 1847 it was again attacked, this time by U.S. troops sent in to quell the rebellion against the new government, in retaliation for the murder of Governor Charles Bent. The counterattack brutally outweighed what had sparked it. More than 100 pueblo residents, including women and children, had taken refuge inside the church when the soldiers bombarded and set fire to it, killing everyone inside and gutting the building. Since then, the bell tower has been restored, but the graves have simply intermingled with the ruined walls and piles of dissolved adobe mud. All of the crosses—from old carved wood to new finished stone—face sacred Taos Mountain.

Pueblo Crafts

You're welcome to wander around and enter any of the craft shops and galleries that are open—a good opportunity to see inside the mud structures and to buy some of the distinctive Taos pottery, which is only very lightly decorated but glimmers with mica from the clay of this area. These pots are also renowned for cooking especially tender beans. On your way out of the pueblo, you may want to stop in at the **Oo-oonah Art Center** (575/779-3486, 1pm-5pm daily Oct.-Apr.), where the gallery displays the work of pueblo children and adults enrolled in its craft classes.

Millicent Rogers Museum

A dashing, thrice-married New York City socialite and designer, Millicent Rogers moved to Taos in 1947. She brought Southwestern style to national attention as she modeled Navajo-style velvet broomstick skirts, concha belts, and pounds of silver-and-turquoise jewelry for photo spreads in *Vogue* and *Harper's Bazaar.* Though she died just six years after she moved to Taos, at the age of 51, she managed to accumulate a fantastic amount of stuff. The **Millicent Rogers**

Museum (1504 Millicent Rogers Rd., 575/758-2462, www.millicentrogers.org, 10am-5pm daily Apr.-Oct., 10am-5pm Tues.-Sun. Nov.-Mar., $10) was established by her son, Paul Peralta-Ramos, and is set in the warren of adobe rooms that make up her former home.

The collection reflects her discerning taste, with flawless pieces of pottery, rugs, and jewelry—both local works and her own designs. Peralta-Ramos also contributed his own collection, including beautiful pieces of Hispano devotional art. Aside from the works' individual beauty, they make an excellent broad introduction to the crafts of the area, from ancient times to modern. But it's not all rooted in local culture: Rogers's goofy illustrations of a fairy tale for her children fill the last room. The gift shop here is particularly thorough and includes beautiful vintage jewelry and very old rugs.

West on US 64

★ Rio Grande Gorge

Heading west on US 64 from the "old blinking light," you pass the Taos airstrip on the left; then, after a few more miles, the ground simply drops away. This is the **Rio Grande Gorge** (also called the Taos Gorge), plunging at its most alarming point 800 feet down into malevolent-looking basalt. The river courses below, but it's not just millions of years of rushing water that have carved out the canyon—seismic activity also caused a rift in the earth's surface. The crack extends north to just beyond the Colorado state line and south almost to Española.

The elegant, unnervingly delicate-looking bridge that spans it was built in 1965 to supplement entrepreneur John Dunn's rickety old toll crossing eight miles north. Critics mocked the newer structure as "the bridge to nowhere" because the highway on the western bank had yet to be built, but the American Institute of Steel Construction granted it the Most Beautiful Steel Bridge award in 1966. At 650 feet above the river, the cantilever truss was a stunning engineering feat; it is still the sixth-highest bridge in the United States. On either side of the bridge is the stretch of white water called the Taos Box, two words that inspire wild tales in any seasoned river-runner. The Class III and IV rapids are considered the best place for rafting in New Mexico.

On the west side of the gorge is a rest area, and the start of the **West Rim Trail,** running south from the parking lot and yielding great views of the bridge to the north.

Greater World Earthship Development

If you brave the slender gorge bridge and continue a mile or so west on US 64, you soon see some whimsically curved and creatively stuccoed houses along the right side of the road. These are Earthships: modular, low-priced homes that function entirely on collected rainwater and wind and solar power. Although they look like fanciful Hobbit homes or Mars colony pods, Earthships are made of rather common stuff: The walls, built into hillsides for efficient heating and cooling, are stacks of used tires packed with rammed earth, while bottles stacked with cement and crushed aluminum cans form front walls and colorful peepholes.

Greater World is the largest of three local all-Earthship subdivisions, and headquarters of the architecture office that developed the design. The **Greater World Earthship Development visitors center** (575/613-4409, www.earthship.com, 9am-6pm daily in summer, 10am-4pm daily in winter, $7) is the most unconventional model home and sales office you'll ever visit. You can take the self-guided tour of a basic Earthship and watch a video about the building process and the rationale behind the design. If you're hooked, you can of course get details on buying a lot in the development or purchasing the plans to build your own place elsewhere. Or try before you buy: You can stay the night in an Earthship here, starting at $130. Look for

New Mexico's Communes

Something about New Mexico's vast empty spaces inspires utopian thinking, as if the landscape were a blank slate, a way to start from scratch and do things right. Spanish settlers felt it in the 16th century. Gold miners banked on it in the 1800s. And in the 1960s, freethinkers, free-lovers, and back-to-the-landers fled crowded cities and boring suburbs to start communities such as the Hog Farm and the New Buffalo commune, both near Taos. For a while, New Mexico was the place to be: Dennis Hopper immortalized New Buffalo in his film *Easy Rider,* Janis Joplin chilled out in Truchas, and Ken Kesey drove his bus, *Further,* through the state. At the end of the decade, some 25 communes had been established.

In most of the rest of the United States, these experimental communities and their ideals were just a brief moment of zaniness—their legacy appears to be Hog Farm leader Wavy Gravy's consecration on a Ben & Jerry's label. But in New Mexico, many of the ideals set down by naked organic gardeners and tripping visionaries took root and sprouted in unexpected ways. Yogi Bhajan, a Sikh who taught mass kundalini yoga sessions in New Mexico in 1969, later became a major contributor to the state economy through all the businesses he established. Buddhist stupas dot the Rio Grande Valley, the product of Anglo spiritual seekers working with Tibetan refugees brought to New Mexico by Project Tibet, cofounded by John Allen, who also ran the commune Synergia Ranch near Santa Fe. Allen was also instrumental in building Biosphere 2, the experimental glass dome in the Arizona desert—probably the most utopian vision yet to have sprouted in New Mexico.

the green building on the right 1.8 miles past the bridge.

Taos Ski Valley

Highway 150 winds relentlessly up through Hondo Canyon, the steep mountain slopes crowded with tall, dense pines that in winter disappear into a wreath of clouds. The road dead-ends at the village of **Taos Ski Valley.** When you get out of the car and take in the vertiginous view up to Kachina Peak (elevation 12,481 feet and often white-capped even in July), you'll see why it inspires legions of reverential skiers every winter, when an average of 305 inches of snow falls on the mountain—almost 10 times the amount they get down in town.

For decades, it was *only* skiers here. Snowboarders were banned, allegedly because the slopes were too steep—more than half the trails are rated expert level, and many of them are left ungroomed. But the mountain was finally opened to all in 2008. It was a major adjustment for TSV's loyal customers, and it leaves just three resorts in the country that don't allow snowboarding (Utah's Deer Valley and Alta, and Mad River Glen in Vermont).

In the summer, there's free music at the resort center on Saturday afternoons, and Hondo Canyon's many trails make for very good hiking or picnicking. The road is dotted on either side with picnic areas and campgrounds—Cuchilla del Medio is a particularly nice area for a picnic. The **visitors center** (575/776-1413, www.taosskivalley.com) in the ski area parking lot stocks trail descriptions and maps.

Entertainment and Events

Taos is a small town: no glitzy dance clubs, no bars where you're expected to dress up. Nighttime fun is concentrated in a handful of places where, even after a couple of visits, you'll get to know the regulars quickly. The various townwide celebrations—including music and dancing on the plaza on summer Thursdays—draw a good cross section of the population.

Nightlife

Bars and Clubs

Starting around 5pm, the **Adobe Bar** (125 Paseo del Pueblo Norte, 575/758-2233), in the lobby of the Taos Inn (look for the neon thunderbird sign), is where you'll run into everyone you've seen over the course of the day, sipping a Cowboy Buddha ($12) or some other specialty margarita—the best in town. Mellow jazz or acoustic guitar sets the mood from 7pm. To give hotel residents a break, the bar closes at 10pm.

The dance floor at the **Sagebrush Inn** (1508 Paseo del Pueblo Sur, 575/758-2254) gets packed with cowboy-booted couples stepping lively to country cover bands whose members always seem to resemble Kenny Rogers. The scene encompasses all of Taos, from artists to pueblo residents to mountain men with grizzled beards. Booze is a bargain, and the fireplace is big.

Wood-paneled **Eske's Brew Pub** (106 Des Georges Ln., 575/758-1517) is across from the plaza, tucked back from the southeast corner of the intersection of Paseo del Pueblo Sur and Kit Carson Road. With live music on Fridays and Saturdays, it serves its house-made beer to a chummy après-ski crowd. You're in New Mexico—you should at least *try* the green-chile ale.

Everyone's default late-night spot is **The Alley Cantina** (121 Teresina Ln., 575/758-2121) for another hour or so. This warren of interconnected rooms (one of which is supposedly the oldest in Taos . . . but don't they all say that?) can be potentially baffling after a few drinks. There's shuffleboard for entertainment if you're not into the ensemble onstage—its name usually ends in "Blues Band"; a cover of $5-7 applies on weekends. The kitchen is open until 11pm.

Cocktail Lounges

A more upscale member of Taos's bar scene is **The Treehouse Lounge** (123 Bent St., 575/758-1009, 5pm-10pm daily), the upper floor of an adobe house downtown. With a full bar and the creative minds running it, the range of cocktails ($10) is highly stimulating. Happy hour is 2:30pm-5:30pm.

Live Music

Is your drinking unsustainable? Fix that at the **KTAOS Bar** (9 Hwy. 150, 575/758-5826, ext. 206, www.ktao.com, 4pm-9pm Sun.-Thurs., 4pm-11pm Fri.-Sat.), the social wing of the local radio station, which happens to be entirely solar-powered. You can peek into the radio studios or dance on the lawn out back, in front of the large stage that hosts major shows. Happy hour (4pm-6pm) sees drinks as low as $2, and kids are usually welcome, with plenty of room to play.

If your style is cramped by old adobes, head out to **Taos Mesa Brewing** (20 ABC Mesa Rd., 575/758-1900, www.taosmesa-brewing.com, noon-late daily), on US 64 opposite the airport, where there's plenty of room to groove. The metal Quonset hut looms like a far-flung Burning Man camp, and the entertainment roster is eclectic, from theremin masters to major global artists performing outside (cover from $5 some nights). The crowd is all of Taos's younger hippies, plus hops aficionados of all stripes. The food ($10) is veg- and beer-friendly.

Finally, check the schedule at **Old Martina's Hall** (4140 Hwy. 68, 575/758-3003, www.oldmartinashall.com) for special events in this renovated old adobe theater. It may not get as wild as back in the days when Dennis Hopper owned the joint, but the new wood dance floor is a treat.

The Arts

Given the high concentration of artists of all stripes, it's no surprise that Taos's theater scene is so rich for such a small town. Check at the **Taos Center for the Arts** (133 Paseo del Pueblo Norte, 575/758-2052, www.tcataos.org) to find out what shows may be on; the group also organizes

What to Expect at Pueblo Dances

Visiting a pueblo for a ceremonial dance or feast-day celebration is one of the most memorable parts of a trip to New Mexico. But it's important to remember that a pueblo dance is not at all for the benefit of tourists. It is a ceremony and a religious ritual, not a performance—you are a guest, not an audience.

Keep this in mind as a guide to your own behavior. Applause is not appropriate, nor is conversation during the dance. Queries about the meaning of the dances are generally not appreciated. Never walk in the dance area, and try not to block the view of pueblo residents. The kivas, as holy spaces, are always off-limits to outsiders. During feast days, some pueblo residents may open their doors to visitors, perhaps for a snack or drink—but be considerate of others who may also want to visit, and don't stay too long. Photography is strictly forbidden at dances (sometimes with the exception of Los Matachines, which is not a religious ritual). Don't even think about trying to sneak a shot with your camera phone, as tribal police will be more than happy to confiscate it.

On a practical level, be prepared for a lot of waiting around. Start times are always approximate, and everything depends on when the dancers are done with their kiva rituals. There will usually be a main, seasonal dance—such as the corn dance at the summer solstice—followed by several others. If you go in the winter, dress very warmly, but in layers. Ceremonies often start inside the close-packed, overheated church, and then dances often proceed outside in the cold.

chamber music performances and film screenings.

SMU in Taos (6580 Hwy. 518, 575/758-8322, www.smu.edu/taos) organizes a summer lecture series at its Fort Burgwin campus about seven miles east of Ranchos de Taos. The Tuesday-night gatherings (from 7:30pm, free), from late May through mid-August, bring noted historians, anthropologists, authors, and others with an interest in the Southwest.

The Storyteller (110 Old Talpa Canyon Rd., 575/751-4245, www.storyteller7.com) shows first-run films on seven screens, with an occasional arty option.

Festivals and Events

July is chockablock: the loopy creativity of the **Arroyo Seco Fourth of July parade,** then, in the second week, the **Taos Pueblo Powwow** (www.taospueblo.com), a major get-together of Pueblo Indians and tribal members from around the country. Try to be there for the Grand Entry, the massive opening procession. The event takes place at the powwow grounds in El Prado near the Overland Sheepskin store. The next weekend, the town turns out for the **Fiestas de Taos** (www.fiestasdetaos.com), a three-day celebration of Santiago de Compostela and Santa Ana, with a parade, food and crafts booths on the plaza, and the crowning of the Fiestas Queen.

For years, v radio station hosted the multiday **Taos Solar Music Festival** (www.solarmusicfest.com) in July as well. The solar-powered event, which drew thousands of happy campers and some excellent performers, went on hiatus for a bit, but, as of press time for this book, was supposed to restart in 2015.

Taos galleries put out their finest at the **Taos Fall Arts Festival** (www.taosfallarts.com), a two-week-long exhibition in late September and early October that shows the works of more than 150 Taos County artists.

Taos's biggest annual festivity (for which many local businesses close) is the **Feast of San Geronimo,** the patron saint assigned to Taos Pueblo by the Spanish when they built their first mission there in 1619. The holiday starts the evening of September 29 with vespers in the pueblo church and continues the next day with

Ceremonial Dances at Taos Pueblo

In addition to the Feast of San Geronimo, ceremonial dances are open to visitors. This is only an approximate schedule. Dates can vary from year to year, as can the particular dances. Contact the **pueblo** (505/758-1028, www.taospueblo.com) for times, or check the listings in the *Tempo* section of the paper for that week.

Every night May through October, there are demonstration dances at the **Kachina Lodge** (413 Paseo del Pueblo Norte)—a little touristy, but nice if your trip doesn't coincide with a dance at the pueblo itself.

- **January 1** - Turtle dance
- **January 6** - Deer or buffalo dance
- **May 3** - Feast of Santa Cruz: corn dance
- **June 13** - Feast of San Antonio: corn dance
- **June 24** - Feast of San Juan: corn dance
- **July 25-26** - Feast of Santiago and Santa Ana: corn dances and footraces
- **September 29-30** - Feast of San Geronimo
- **December 24** - Sundown procession and children's dance
- **December 25** - Various dances

footraces and a pole-climbing contest. Hacienda de los Martinez usually reenacts a 19th-century Taos trade fair, with mountain men, music, and artisans' demonstrations.

On the first weekend in October, the **Taos Wool Festival** (www.taoswoolfestival.org) has drawn textile artists as well as breeders since 1983. Admire the traditional Churro sheep or an Angora goat and then pick up a scarf made from its wool.

In winter, the glow of *farolitos* and torchlight on snow produces a magical effect. On the first weekend in December, the **tree-lighting ceremony** on the plaza draws the whole town, and the rest of the season sees numerous celebrations, such as the reenactments of the Virgin's search for shelter, called Las Posadas, which take place at Our Lady of Guadalupe Church west of the plaza on the third weekend in December. At the pueblo, vespers is said at San Geronimo Church on Christmas Eve, typically followed by a children's dance. On Christmas Day, the pueblo hosts either a deer dance or the Spanish Matachines dance.

Shopping

Arts and Crafts

In the Overland Ranch complex, **Magpie** (1405 Paseo del Pueblo Norte, 781/248-0166, 11am-5pm Tues.-Sat.) promises "wonderful things for your nest." The owner, a Taos native returned from living on the East Coast, has selected a colorful array of handcrafted furniture, pottery, handmade jewelry and more, nearly all produced by Taos residents.

Daniel Barela, great-grandson of legendary wood-carver Patrocino Barela (whose work is on view in the Harwood Museum), can often be found working in **Barela's Traditional Fine Art** (124-A Paseo del Pueblo Sur, 575/779-5720, noon-3pm daily). The raw, casual gallery space houses his and his relatives' hand-carved saint figures, as well as work by several Salazars, another noted woodworking family.

Taos Drums (3956 Hwy. 68, 800/424-3786, 10am-5pm Mon.-Fri., 11:30am-5pm Sun.) is a giant shop and factory dedicated to making Taos Pueblo-style percussion instruments, from thin hand drums to great booming ones out of hollow logs. Trying out the wares is encouraged. The shop is on the west side of the highway five miles south of the plaza.

Taos has long nurtured a strong community of fiber artists—weavers, knitters, spinners of yarn. In the John Dunn Shops just north of the plaza, visit **Mooncat Fiber** (120-B Bent St., 575/758-9341, 10am-6pm daily) for hand-spun yarns and some finished pieces, and **Common Thread** (124-E Bent St., 575/758-8987, 10am-5:30pm daily), which deals in beautiful imported fabrics from India, Guatemala, and more, both in one-off pieces and by the yard.

Up in Arroyo Seco, **Weaving Southwest** (487 Hwy. 150, 575/758-0433, 10am-5:30pm Mon.-Sat., 11am-5pm Sun.) stocks raw wool, yarns, and gorgeous finished clothing and rugs as well.

Clothing and Jewelry

Gussy yourself up in Western trappings from **Horse Feathers** (109-B Kit Carson Rd., 575/758-7457, 10:30am-5:30pm daily), where you can pick up a full cowpoke getup, from ten-gallon hat to jingling spurs. The big money is in the vintage cowboy boots, but you can find less expensive, eclectic gift items, such as giant belt buckles or campfire cookbooks from 1900.

Gift and Home

FX/18 (103-C Bent St., 575/758-8590, 11am-6pm Mon.-Sat., noon-5pm Sun.) has a great selection of goodies: groovy housewares, lively kids' stuff, nifty stationery. And the selection of contemporary Southwest-style jewelry is particularly good.

Up Highway 150, **Arroyo Seco Mercantile** (488 Hwy. 150, 575/776-8806, 10am-5:30pm Mon.-Sat., 11am-5pm Sun.) is the town's former general store, now a highly evolved junk shop that has maintained the beautiful old wood-and-glass display cases. Its stock ranges from the practical (books on passive-solar engineering and raising llamas) to the frivolous, with lots of the beautiful, like antique wool blankets.

Toys

Taos is also home to an exceptionally magical toy store, **Twirl** (225 Camino de la Placita, 575/751-1402, www.twirlhouse.com, 10am-6pm daily). Tucked in a series of low-ceiling adobe rooms, it's crammed with everything from science experiments to wooden trains to fairy costumes. Even the kiva fireplace gets a fantastical 1,001 Nights treatment, and there's a big roster of activities in the huge play space out back.

Sports and Recreation

The wild setting presses in all around Taos, and the mountains loom up behind every town view. Downhill skiing is the main draw in the winter, but you can also try more solitary snowshoeing and Nordic skiing. In summer, peak-baggers will want to strike out for Wheeler, the state's highest, while rafters, rock climbers, and mountain bikers can head the other direction, to the dramatic basalt cliffs of the Rio Grande Gorge. In the water, river-runners challenge the churning rapids of the legendary Taos Box (late May and early June make up the best season for this).

Practicalities

Stop in at the **Carson National Forest Supervisor's Office** (208 Cruz Alta Rd., 575/758-6200, 8:30am-4:30pm Mon.-Fri.) for booklets on recommended trails and maps. Just down the street, the **Bureau of Land Management Taos Field Office** (226 Cruz Alta Rd., 575/758-8851, 8am-4:30pm Mon.-Fri.) can help with prep for rafting or longer camping trips, with plenty of maps and brochures.

The **Taos Youth and Family Center** (407 Paseo del Cañon, 575/758-4160, 9am-8pm Mon.-Thurs., 9am-7pm Fri.-Sun.) has a big indoor pool, as well as an ice-skating rink. Hours are more limited in fall and winter.

Sudden thunderstorms are common in summer months, as are flash floods and even freak blizzards. Well into May, snow can blanket some of the higher passes, so wherever you go, always carry more warm clothing than you think you'll need. And don't skimp on the sunscreen, even when it's below freezing.

Biking

Taos has several great trails for mountain biking. A popular ride close to town is **West Rim Trail** along the Rio Grande Gorge, either from the gorge bridge up to John Dunn Bridge, about 15 miles round-trip, or from the gorge bridge south to the Taos Junction Bridge near Pilar, about 18 miles out and back. Either way, you'll have great views and fairly level but rugged terrain. For some downhill action, **Taos Ski Valley** offers mountain biking in summer; the 3.6-mile Berminator route is good for intermediate cyclists.

For road touring, you can make a pleasant 25-mile loop from Taos through Arroyo Hondo and Arroyo Seco. With no steep grades, it's a good way to get adjusted to the altitude. Head north up Paseo del Pueblo Norte, straight through the intersection with Highway 150, then, in Arroyo Hondo, turn right onto County Road B-143. Cross Highway 230, and you arrive in Arroyo Seco behind The Snowmansion. Turn right on Highway 150 to loop back to Taos.

For a longer road challenge, take on the 84-mile Enchanted Circle. Each September, more than a thousand riders participate in the **Enchanted Circle Century Tour** (800/348-6444, www.redriverenchantedcirclecenturytour.com), sponsored by the Red River Chamber of Commerce. A mountain-biking race takes place the day after.

Gearing Up (129 Paseo del Pueblo Sur, 575/751-0365) rents mountain and hybrid bicycles for $50 per day. If you're bringing your bicycle with you, consider having it shipped here, and they'll reassemble it and have it waiting when you arrive.

El Salto Falls

★ Hiking

With Taos Mountain and Wheeler Peak in the backyard, you can ramble along winding rivers or haul up 2,000 feet in less than four miles. Be prepared for a cold snap or storm at any time, and don't plan on anything before May—it takes that long for the snow to thaw, though even in high summer, you can still hit some of the white stuff in the alpine meadows. If you prefer some animal companionship (and something to carry your pack) while hiking, contact **Wild Earth Llama Adventures** (800/758-5262, www.llamaadventures.com), which runs day hikes with lunch ($99), as well as multiday treks (from $375). These are just a few suggestions for spots to hike.

Taos Ski Valley

Varied trails lead off Highway 150 en route to Taos Ski Valley. Just before the parking lot for the ski area, **Gavilan Trail** (no. 60) leads off the north side of the road. It's plenty steep but leads to a high mountain meadow. The route is five miles round-trip, or you can connect with other trails once you're up on the rim.

Purists will want to head for **Wheeler Peak Summit Trail** (no. 67), which scales New Mexico's highest mountain in about four miles (one-way). The first two miles of the route are on the relatively easy and popular **Williams Lake Trail** (no. 62), which starts near the end of Twining Road, a narrow dirt road that leads out of the top of the Taos Ski Valley parking lot. (Before starting up Twining Road, stop first at the visitors center in the parking lot, for trail descriptions.) Williams Lake is a nice destination and, after you get past the early rocky stretch, the trail is pleasant hiking. In summer, on the Saturday closest to the full moon, there's a free guided **moonlight hike** to Williams Lake, starting at 7:30pm; check the schedule at www.taosskivalley.com.

If all that sounds too strenuous, you can take the **chairlift** (10am-4:30pm Thurs.-Mon. June-Aug., $15) up to the top of the mountain, then wander down any of several wide, well-marked trails, all with stunning views.

El Salto Falls

Some theorize that the mysterious "Taos Hum"—the faint, low drone that many in the area claim to hear—emanates from the caves at **El Salto Falls** (575/776-2371, $4), a scenic spot on a patch of private land in Arroyo Seco. Whether or not you solve this sonic mystery, the falls are a great Taos natural landmark, and an easy hike or a challenging one, depending on just how much you'd like to see. Save this hike for dry weather, unless you have a four-wheel drive—the road is rough when muddy or snowy.

In Arroyo Seco, take El Salto Road east (go straight where Highway 150 makes a hard right); after about a mile is a sign on the left asking visitors to pay. Leave cash in the honor box on the porch of the house just off the road, and fill out a waiver and a permit to place on your dashboard. Continue driving another 0.7 mile and bear left; from here, it's 0.9 mile up to a green gate and small parking area. Walk in, following the road as it curves left, then bearing right. This leads in just a few minutes to the lowest, largest cave and the first waterfall—though most of the year, it is often just a trickle. Intrepid hikers can climb up to the right of the cave, to ever smaller falls and notches in the cliff face.

Hot Springs

Two spots along the Rio Grande have natural pools of warm water, by-products of the seismic upsets that formed the gorge. They're popular with locals, and clothing is optional. Don't crowd in if several people are already in the spring, and never leave trash behind.

The easier spot to reach is **Blackrock Springs,** accessible by a 0.25-mile hike. From the intersection with US 64, head north on Highway 522 about six miles to where the road dips; immediately after the bridge, turn left on County Road B-005, which runs along the north side of the small Rio Hondo and past the New Buffalo commune. The road crosses the water, then climbs a hill and descends again, toward the Rio Grande. Cross the old John Dunn Bridge to reach the west side, then turn left and park at the first switchback. Hike down the rocks and downstream to the springs.

Also called Stagecoach Springs, **Manby Springs** are at the edge of the river where the stage road used to meet a bridge and cross to the west side of the gorge. The hike down is on the old road, now quite rocky, and takes about 20 minutes. (In the late afternoon, keep an eye out for bighorn sheep near the trail.) To find the parking area, take US 64 four miles west, just past the airport, and turn right on Tune Drive; follow this to the end, approximately another four miles. The old road is off the southwest side of the parking area.

Hunting and Fishing

Taos's mountain streams and lakes teem with fish. The feisty cutthroat trout is indigenous to Valle Vidal, north of Questa, or you can hook plenty of browns in the wild waters of the Rio Grande. Eagle Nest Lake and Cabresto Lake (northeast of Questa) are both stocked every year. If you'd like a guide to show you around, **Cutthroat Fly Fishing** (575/776-5703, www.cutthroatflyfishing.com) and **The Solitary Angler** (866/502-1700, www.thesolitaryangler.com) are two good operators. Stop into the shop at the **Tailwater Gallery** (204-B Paseo del Pueblo Norte) for tackle and info on flows and other conditions.

Elk are the primary target in hunters' rifle scopes, but you can also bag mule deer, bear, and antelope; **High Mountain Outfitters** (575/751-7000, www.huntingnm.com) is one of the most experienced expedition leaders, and it has access to private land for hunting exotics. Visit the website of the **New Mexico Department of Game and Fish** (www.wildlife.state.nm.us) for details on seasons, permits, and licenses.

Rafting and Tubing

The **Taos Box,** the 16-mile stretch of the Rio Grande between the John Dunn Bridge and Pilar, provides perhaps the best rafting in New Mexico, with Class III rapids with ominous names like Boat Reamer and Screaming Left-Hand Turn. The river mellows out a bit south of the Taos Box, then leads into a shorter Class III section called the Racecourse—the most popular run, usually done as a half-day trip. Beyond this, in the Orilla Verde Recreation Area around Pilar, the water is wide and flat, a place for a relaxing float with kids or other water newbies; you can flop in an inner tube if you really want to chill out. North of the John Dunn Bridge, there's another intermediate run called La Junta that's a half-day trip.

Los Rios River Runners (800/544-1181, www.losriosriverrunners.com) leads trips to all these spots as half-day outings ($54), day trips (from $105), and overnight trips. Another outfitter, **Far-Flung Adventures** (575/758-2628, www.farflung.com), can add on rock climbing and horseback riding. With both organizations, you can choose whether you want a paddleboat—where you're actively (and sometimes strenuously) paddling—or an oar boat, where guides row, and you can sit back. The best season is late May and early June, when the water is high from mountain runoff.

Rock Climbing

From popular sport-climbing spots such as the basalt Dead Cholla Wall in the Rio Grande Gorge to the more traditional routes at Tres Piedras, Taos is a climber's dream. One of the most impressive pitches is at **Questa Dome,** north of Taos on Highway 378, where the flawless granite on the Questa Direct route is graded 5.10 and 5.11. And you're not limited to the summer, as winter sees some terrific ice climbs at higher elevations.

Taos Mountain Outfitters (113 N. Plaza, 575/758-9292, 9am-6pm Mon.-Tues., 10am-8pm Wed.-Fri., 8am-8pm Sat., 10am-6pm Sun.) can provide maps, ropes, and more details. For climbing lessons or guided tours, contact **Mountain Skills** (575/776-2222, www.climbtaos.com) in Arroyo Seco.

Spectator Sports

The local baseball team, the **Taos Blizzard** (www.taosblizzard.com), faces off against eight other teams in the exceedingly minor **Pecos League** (www.pecosleague.com) from around New Mexico, Arizona, west Texas, and Colorado. Games in season (mid-May through July) are at 7pm at the Taos High School ball field (134 Cervantes St.).

Winter Sports

Taos Ski Valley (866/968-7386, www.skitaos.org, $82 full-day lift ticket) is a mecca for downhill skiing. The resort is open from late November through the first weekend in April, with 110 trails served by 15 lifts and snowmaking capacity on all beginner and intermediate areas in dry spells. The highly regarded Ernie Blake Snowsports School is one of the best places to learn the basics or polish your skills. Novice "yellowbirds" can take one ($115) or two ($180) days of intensive instruction specially geared to new skiers.

For cross-country skiing and snowshoeing, **Enchanted Forest** (575/754-6112, www.enchantedforestxc.com, $18 full-day pass), between Elizabethtown and Red River on the Enchanted Circle loop, offers miles of groomed trails. There are also easy ski access points in the Carson National Forest—at Capulin Campground on US 64, for instance, five miles east of Taos and along **Manzanita Trail** in the Hondo Canyon on the road to the ski valley.

Don't have your own gear? **Cottam's Ski & Outdoor** (207-A Paseo del Pueblo Sur, 575/758-2822, 7am-7pm Mon.-Fri., 7am-8pm Sat.-Sun.) has the biggest stock of rental skis, snowboards, and snowshoes. The shop also sells everything else you'll need to get out and enjoy the snow; there's another location at the **ski valley** (575/776-8719) and one at **Angel Fire** (575/377-3700).

Accommodations

Taos hotels can be a bit overpriced, especially at the lower end, where there are few reliable bargains. But because Taos is awash in centuries-old houses, bed-and-breakfasts have thrived. For those skeptical of B&Bs, don't despair: The majority of them have private bathrooms, separate entrances, and not too much country-cute decor. Certainly, just as in Santa Fe, the Southwestern gewgaws can be applied with a heavy hand, but wood-burning fireplaces, well-stocked libraries, hot tubs, and big gardens can make up for that.

For better deals, consider staying

outside of Taos proper. **Arroyo Seco** is about a half-hour drive from the plaza, as is the **Earthship** subdivision, and rates here and in **Ranchos de Taos** can be a little lower. In the summer, the lodges near the ski valley cut their prices by almost half—a great deal if you want to spend some time hiking in the canyon and don't mind driving to town for food and entertainment. If you're in town without a car, Taos's Chile Line bus serves a few good budget choices; the line caters to skiers in the winter, with pickups from down on the southern end of town all the way up to the ski valley.

Central Taos

$50-100

Not a hotel at all, but simply a clutch of well-maintained one- and two-bedroom private casitas, **Taos Lodging** (109 Brooks St., 575/751-1771, www.taoslodging.com, $75 studio) is in a quiet, convenient block about a 10-minute walk north from the plaza. Here, eight cottages, arranged around a central courtyard, have assorted floor plans, but all have porches, full kitchens, and living rooms, as well as access to a shared outdoor hot tub. The smallest, a 350-square-foot studio, sleeps two comfortably; the largest ($130 for two) sleep up to six. Plus, the same group manages two additional properties nearby, for those who want a larger condo.

Of the various motels on the south side, none are excellent, but **Sun God Lodge** (919 Paseo del Pueblo Sur, 575/758-3162, www.sungodlodge.com, $69 d) is better than most. Maintenance can be spotty, but rooms are set around a big grassy, tree-shaded courtyard and, in back, a small hot tub; there's also a laundry. But note that this can foster a somewhat rowdy atmosphere, especially in ski season or after big summer events.

$100-150

In addition to being a tourist attraction, the ★ **Mabel Dodge Luhan House** (240

El Pueblo Lodge

Morada Ln., 575/751-9686, www.mabeldodgeluhan.com, $105 d) also functions as a homey bed-and-breakfast. Even the least expensive rooms, in a 1970s outbuilding, feel authentically old and cozy, with wood floors and antique furniture. In the main house, Mabel's original bedroom ($200) is the grandest (you can even sleep in her bed). But for those who don't mind waking at the crack of dawn, the upstairs solarium ($130) is gloriously sunny, with gorgeous views of the mountain. Either way, you'll feel a little like you're bunking in a museum (which means those who want modern amenities like air-conditioning should look elsewhere). Breakfast is a cut above standard B&B fare.

Walking distance from the plaza, ★ **El Pueblo Lodge** (412 Paseo del Pueblo Norte, 575/758-8700, www.elpueblolodge.com, $120 d) is a budget operation with nice perks such as free laundry. Rooms vary from a snug nook in the oldest adobe section to new, slick motel rooms complete with gas fireplaces. Those in the 1960s motel strip are a good combo of atmosphere and amenities. The grounds are pleasant, with a heated outdoor pool, a hot tub, and hammocks slung between the big cottonwoods in the summertime.

$150-200

Inn on the Rio (910 E. Kit Carson Rd., 575/758-7199, www.innontherio.com, $150 d) might be more accurately called Motel on the Creek. But what a motel: Each of the 12 thick-walled rooms has been decorated with rich colors and retro Western details. The vintage wall heaters, still cranking from the old motorcourt days, keep the rooms as toasty as a fireplace would. A hot tub between the two wings, plus luxe sheets and locally made bath gels, are nice upgrades. Pair this with longtime resident owners and a great morning meal, and you have all the benefits of a bed-and-breakfast without the feeling that you have to tiptoe in late at night. Rates are lower on weekdays in summer.

La Posada de Taos (309 Juanita Ln., 575/758-8164, www.laposadadetaos.com, $169 d) hits the sweet spot between luxury comforts and casual charm. All the amenities are here, such as wood fireplaces (in five of the six rooms) and whirlpool tubs (in three), but the overall atmosphere is homey and informal, and the decor is distinctly Taos without being heavy-handed, with sparing country touches. The price is right too, coming in on the lower end compared to other places with the same perks. El Solecito, in the older adobe section with its own back terrace, is a particularly nice room.

Of the two landmark hotels in town, **Hotel La Fonda de Taos** (108 S. Plaza, 575/758-2211, www.lafondataos.com, $179 d) has a few more modern perks, such as gas fireplaces and mostly reliable Internet. Plus, you can feel quite grand opening your balcony doors over the plaza (though you may also be subjected to predawn street-cleaning noise). But the **Historic Taos Inn** (125 Paseo del Pueblo Norte, 575/758-2233, www.taosinn.com, $185 d), established in 1936 in the former home of the town doctor, has a cozier feeling, even if it is slightly overpriced. Rooms in the main building are more historic feeling and cheaper (about $120 in high season); in the courtyard section or other outbuildings, you may get a kiva fireplace.

Everything at **Hacienda del Sol** (109 Mabel Dodge Ln., 575/758-0287, www.taoshaciendadelsol.com, $180 d) is built in relation to Taos Mountain, which looms up in the backyard with no other buildings cluttering the view. With this view, even the smallest of the 11 rooms in the adobe complex feels expansive. The style is cozy without being too oppressively Southwestern, and perks like robes, bathtubs, and mini fridges approximate hotel service. The innkeepers are former cruise-ship employees, and they keep this place shipshape as well.

Decorated with an artist's eye, the five guest cottages at **Casa Gallina** (613 Callejon, 575/758-2306, www.casagallina.net, $195 d) showcase beautiful handicrafts from Taos and around the globe. Kitchens can be stocked with occasional goodies from the garden and eggs from resident hens (they're also pressed into service for the fresh and delicious breakfasts). And it doesn't hurt that the meticulous owner also happens to be a massage therapist.

$200-250

The most lavish hotel in town, **El Monte Sagrado** (317 Kit Carson Rd., 575/758-3502, www.elmontesagrado.com, $219) is unfortunately not as well run as it could be, and repeat guests have mentioned maintenance issues. That said, the style of the place is cool, especially in the eclectic Global Suites, and it has a good sustainable infrastructure, with water-reuse systems, solar panels, and more. The least-expensive rooms, the Taos Mountain rooms, are a little generic, with their white-linens-and-dark-wood look, but they carry a reasonable price for entry into the swank grounds, which include a lovely spa.

Over $250

Fully renovated in 2013 (it used to be the Casa de las Chimeneas), **Palacio de Marquesa** (405 Cordoba Rd., 575/758-4777, www.marquesataos.com, $275 d) is run by the excellent Heritage Hotels group. The rooms have an air of what might be called Pueblo Minimalism: heavy beamed ceilings, with white walls, white leather chairs, and marble baths. What might feel too austere is warmed up with kiva fireplaces and radiant floor heating. Spa services and the option of breakfast delivered to your room add to the cocoon-like feel.

Arroyo Seco

$50-100

The best lodging bargain in the area is **The Snowmansion** (Hwy. 150, Arroyo Seco, 575/776-8298, www.snowmansion.com). Conveniently set midway to the Taos Ski Valley in bustling "downtown" Arroyo Seco, this cheerful place offers bunks in dorm rooms ($25) and private rooms (from $50). In the summer, you can also camp (from $20) or sleep in a tepee ($55), and nosh on veggies from the hostel garden. But as the name suggests, winter sports fanatics are the main clientele, and if you don't want to be woken by skiers racing for the Chile Line bus outside, opt for an individual cabin with shared bath ($45).

Ranchos de Taos

$100-150

At the south edge of Ranchos de Taos, **Adobe & Pines Inn** (4107 Hwy. 68, 575/751-0947, www.adobepines.com) is built around an 1830s hacienda, shaded by old trees and overlooking a lush garden. Of the eight rooms, six are quite large (from $179), with especially lavish bathrooms. But even the two smallest rooms ($109 and $119) have fireplaces—and everyone gets the exceptionally good breakfasts, with fresh eggs from the on-site chickens.

Rio Grande Gorge

$100-150

For an only-in-Taos experience, stay the night in an **Earthship** (US 64, 575/751-0462, www.earthship.com, $130 d). Four of the curvy, off-the-grid homes are available, with room for up to six people in the largest one. Not only does an Earthship feel like a Hobbit house with banana trees (in the south-facing greenhouse areas), but you're out in the larger, all-Earthship subdivision, with great views of the mountain. And yes, you'll have running water, a refrigerator, and all the other comforts. It's a bit of a drive from town (west of the Rio Grande), but it's a unique experience.

Food

For a town of its size, Taos has a broad selection of restaurants. But most close relatively early, and many smaller places don't take plastic—so load up on cash and get seated by 8pm at the latest. You'll need reservations only during the holidays, and the whole dining scene is relatively casual. At one of the New Mexican places, be sure to try some posole—it's more common here than in Albuquerque or Santa Fe, often substituted for rice as a side dish alongside pinto beans. Also, the breakfast burrito—a combo of scrambled eggs, green chile, hash browns, and bacon or sausage in a flour tortilla—is commonly wrapped up in foil and served to go, perfect if you want an early start hiking or skiing.

Central Taos

New Mexican

A small, festively painted place on the north side of town, the family-run **Orlando's** (1114 Don Juan Valdez Ln., 575/751-1450, 10:30am-9pm daily, $10) is invariably the first restaurant named by anyone, local or visitor, when the question of best chile comes up. That said, there are occasional whisperings about inconsistency (heresy!). But Orlando's still generally serves very satisfying, freshly made New Mexican standards, such as green-chile chicken enchiladas. The posole is quite good too—perfectly firm, earthy, and flecked with oregano. It's always busy, but a fire pit outdoors makes the wait more pleasant on cold nights.

On the road to Taos Pueblo, **Tiwa Kitchen** (328 Veterans Hwy., 575/751-1020, 11am-4pm Wed.-Mon., $13) is a friendly, super-family-run place (your "waitress" might be not much taller than your table) that specializes in Pueblo food. That means all the usual chile-laced goods, plus nice hyper-local touches like fry bread stuffed with buffalo meat or, for dessert, topped with chokecherry syrup from homegrown fruit.

A drive-through never offered something so good: **Mante's Chow Cart** (402 Paseo del Pueblo Sur, 575/758-3632, 7am-9pm Mon.-Thurs. and Sat., 7am-10pm Fri., $7) specializes in breakfast burritos, as well as genius inventions like the Susie, a whole *chile relleno* wrapped up in a flour tortilla with salsa and guacamole. Perfect road food.

Road-food aficionados will appreciate the old-school atmosphere of **El Taoseño** (819 Paseo del Pueblo Sur, 575/758-4142, 6am-9pm Mon.-Thurs., 6am-10pm Fri.-Sat., 6am-2pm Sun., $8), which has been open since 1983 and looks it. It's not Taos's tastiest New Mexican food, but it is cheap and fast and kid-friendly.

Fresh and Local

The Love Apple (803 Paseo del Pueblo Norte, 575/751-0050, 5pm-9pm Tues.-Sun., $20) wears its local, organic credentials on its sleeve, and the food delivers in simple but powerful flavor combinations, such as a quesadilla made sweet with apple and squash, and posole enriched with local lamb and caramelized onions. The atmosphere is like early-days Chez Panisse filtered through a northern New Mexican lens: a thick-walled adobe chapel, with candles glimmering against wine bottles along the walls. In summer, the restaurant is open seven nights a week (plus brunch 10am-2pm Sun.), but it can get hot inside, so go early to snag a patio table.

Café

The location of **World Cup** (102-A Paseo del Pueblo Norte, 575/737-5299, 7am-7pm daily, $3) on the corner of the plaza makes it a popular pit stop for both tourists and locals—the latter typically of the drumming, dreadlocked variety, lounging on the stoop.

Breakfast and Lunch

Euro-Latino might be the best catchall term for the menu at ★ **Gutiz** (812-B Paseo del Pueblo Norte, 575/758-1226, 8am-3pm Tues.-Sun., $10), which borrows from France and Spain and adds a dash of green chile. Start your day with a chocolate croissant or an impressive tower of scrambled eggs and spinach. Lunch sees traditional croques monsieurs or cumin-spiced chicken sandwiches.

Michael's Kitchen (304-C Paseo del Pueblo Norte, 575/758-4178, 7am-2:30pm Mon.-Thurs., 7am-8pm Fri.-Sun., $8) is famous for New Mexican breakfast items like huevos rancheros and blue-corn pancakes with pine nuts, served all day, but everyone will find something they like on the extensive menu at this down-home, wood-paneled family restaurant filled with chatter and the clatter of dishes. "Health Food," for instance, is a double order of chile cheese fries. The front room is devoted to gooey doughnuts, cinnamon rolls, and pie.

Taos Diner (908 Paseo del Pueblo Norte, 575/758-2374, 7am-2:30pm daily, $10) is as straight-ahead as its name. The pleasant surprise: Much of the enchiladas, egg plates, pancakes, and other typical diner fare is prepared with organic ingredients. Plus, the largely local scene provides good background theater to your meal—the servers seem to know everyone. There's a second outpost, **Taos Diner II** (216-B Paseo del Pueblo Sur, 575/751-1989, 7am-3pm daily), just south of the plaza.

Set in bucolic gardens with a view of Taos Mountain, **Farmhouse Café** (1405 Paseo del Pueblo Norte, 575/758-5683, 7am-5pm daily, $12) is a beautiful spot to revive over a hearty salad, a bison burger, or a homemade pastry, including killer gluten-free options like a chocolate-peanut-butter crispy-rice bar. In summer, the café also serves dinner, usually on weekends only. Look for it behind the Overland Sheepskin store.

Just west of the plaza, **El Gamal** (112 Doña Luz St., 575/613-0311, 9am-5pm Mon.-Wed., 9am-9pm Thurs.-Sat., 11am-3pm Sun., $7) brings the best of Israeli street snacks to Taos, with *shakshuka* (spicy scrambled eggs) and bagels for breakfast and falafel and *sabich* (eggplant and egg) sandwiches at lunch, washed down with a fizzy yogurt soda. There's also more standard hippie fare on the menu: homemade granola and the like.

In the Taos Inn, elegant **Doc Martin's** (125 Paseo del Pueblo Norte, 575/758-1977, 11am-10pm Mon.-Fri., 7:30am-2:30pm and 4pm-10pm Sat.-Sun., $10) is fine at dinner, but weekend brunch is when the kitchen really shines—especially on dishes like the Kit Carson (poached eggs on yam biscuits topped with red chile) or blue-corn pancakes with blueberries. The lunch menu is also tasty and doesn't reach the stratospheric prices of dinner.

American

The Burger Stand (401 Paseo del Pueblo Norte, 575/758-5522, 11am-11pm daily, $9) is an outpost of a Kansas restaurant—but it fits right in in Taos, in large part because it makes not one but two killer veggie burgers—we recommend the one topped with feta cheese, pickled green beans, and rich romesco sauce. (The beef and lamb burgers are great too, and decked out in similarly creative ways.) It doesn't hurt that it's set inside the Taos Ale House, where there's great beer and music—and, best of all, it's open relatively late.

Italian

Taos Pizza Out Back (712 Paseo del Pueblo Norte, 575/758-3112, 11am-10pm daily, $8) serves up the best pie in town, using mostly local and organic ingredients. A glance at the menu—with items like green chile and black beans, and the popular portobello-gorgonzola combo—often makes first-timers blanch, but after a bite or two they're converts, like everyone else in town. Soups and a good Greek salad are also available, if you want to round out your meal.

Mexican

Tiny **La Cueva** (135 Paseo del Pueblo Sur, 575/758-7001, 10am-9pm daily, $8) looks like a New Mexican restaurant at first glance, as it has all the usual green-chile-smothered dishes. But its owners are from south of the border and round out the menu with fantastically fresh and homemade-tasting dishes like chicken mole enchiladas and an omelet with housemade chorizo, as well as exceptionally savory beans. No alcohol, though.

Fine Dining

★ **El Meze** (1017 Paseo del Pueblo Norte, 575/751-3337, 5:30pm-9:30pm Mon.-Sat., $24) just might be Taos's best restaurant, thanks to both its exceptional food and tiny touches such as complimentary mineral water and plush blankets for cool evenings outside. Chef Frederick Muller shows the link between New Mexico, Spain, North Africa, and the Middle

Top to bottom: off-the-grid lodging Earthship; Farmhouse Café; The Burger Stand.

East, in dishes that are both brainy and deep-down satisfying. Delectable mountain trout is seasoned with Spanish paprika and served with a lavish herb salad, while fried green olives stuffed with blue cheese are the bar snack to beat in all of New Mexico. The setting is cozy in winter, inside a thick-walled hacienda, and expansive in summer, with a large patio with a view of Taos Mountain.

Open since 1988 but relatively new to this cozy adobe house, **Lambert's** (123 Bent St., 575/758-1009, 11:30am-2:30pm and 5:30pm-9pm Mon.-Sat., $32) is a Taos favorite, where everyone goes for prom, anniversaries, and other landmark events. Its New American menu is a bit staid, but everything is executed perfectly. Get one of the game-meat specials if you can; otherwise, the signature pepper-crusted lamb is fantastic. A full liquor license means good classic cocktails, which you can also enjoy upstairs at the **Treehouse Lounge** (2:30pm-close).

Markets

Planning a picnic? Stop at **Cid's Grocery** (623 Paseo del Pueblo Norte, 575/758-1148, 8am-8pm Mon.-Sat.) for great takeout food, as well as freshly baked bread and a whole range of organic and local goodies, from New Mexican wines to fresh elk steaks.

From mid-May through October, the **Taos Farmers Market** (www.taosfarmersmarket.org, 8am-1pm Sat.) takes place on the plaza. Vendors sell some prepared food and good gifts like local honey, so you won't be left out even if you don't have a kitchen.

Ranchos de Taos

Just off the plaza near the church, **Ranchos Plaza Grill** (6 St. Francis Plaza, 575/758-5788, 11am-3pm and 5pm-8:30pm Tues.-Sat., 11am-3pm Sun., $11) is a casual spot, known for its red *chile caribe,* made from crushed, rather than ground, chiles, for a really rustic effect.

Across the road, the chile at **Old Martina's Hall** (4140 Hwy. 68, 575/758-3003, www.oldmartinashall.com, 7am-9:30pm Wed.-Mon., $20) may be dialed down for out-of-state palates, but this somewhat upscale place has other redeeming qualities. The once-derelict adobe theater with a soaring ceiling has been lovingly redone, now hosting special events, and serves the likes of goat-cheese salads, farro risotto, and truffle fries. It's more casual for breakfast and lunch ($10 for sandwiches), and the light is lovely. Check out all the rooms and levels. The building is across the road from the turn to the church.

Arroyo Seco

Abe's Cantina y Cocina (489 Hwy. 150, 575/776-8516, 7am-5pm Mon.-Fri., 7am-1:30pm Sat., $4), a creaky old all-purpose general store/diner/saloon, has earned fans from all over for its satisfying and cheap breakfast burritos. There's a full menu of tacos and green-chile cheeseburgers, if you care to eat in, and a nice back patio. And don't miss the sweet, flaky empanadas next to the cash register in the store.

For coffee, though, you'll want to go next door to **Taos Cow** (485 Hwy. 150, 575/776-5640, 7am-7pm daily), a chilled-out coffee bar par excellence, with writers scribbling in one corner and flute players jamming in another. But it's the ice cream that has made the Taos Cow name (you'll see it distributed all around town, and elsewhere in New Mexico and Colorado). The most popular flavors are tailored to local tastes: Café Olé contains cinnamon and Mexican chocolate chunks, while Cherry Ristra is vanilla with piñon nuts, dark chocolate, and cherries. Sandwiches ($9) are an option too, if you want real sustenance.

ACEQ (480 Hwy. 150, 575/776-0900, 5pm-close daily, $15) merges green chile with Brooklynesque comfort food, all making the most of local produce and meats. Think "New Mexico poutine" (fries topped with gravy and queso; we'll let it slide that the oozy melted cheese is a Texan import), baby back ribs, and a kale Caesar salad. The brunch menu, with dishes like lamb *chilaquiles*, gets raves.

Taos Ski Valley

For nourishment by the ski area, fortify yourself with a green-chile cheeseburger or bowl of smoky-hot green-chile stew at the **Stray Dog Cantina** (105 Sutton Pl., Taos Ski Valley, 575/776-2894, 8am-9pm daily, $12), which gets busy after 3pm, when tired skiers come down from a day on the slopes. In the summer, it doesn't open till 11am on weekdays, but it's a nice destination for a drive, as you can sit on the deck and listen to the river flow by.

More adventurous drivers can head for **Bavarian Lodge** (100 Kachina Rd., 575/776-8020, 11:30am-9pm daily in ski season, $15), way up Twining Road near the southeast edge of the ski area and Kachina Lift 4. You'll need four-wheel drive in winter; in summer, the huge front deck is a lovely place to have a beer (served by actual German speakers) in the pines, though note that it's open only around the weekend (11:30am-4:30pm Thurs. and Mon., 11:30am-8:30pm Fri.-Sat.). The menu is typical Wiener schnitzel and spaetzle.

Information and Services

A few miles south of the plaza, the **Taos Visitors Center** (1139 Paseo del Pueblo Sur, 575/758-3873, www.taos.org, 9am-5pm daily) is helpful, as long as you don't show up right before closing time. Stop here for flyers and maps galore, free coffee, and the very thorough weekly news and events bulletin (also posted online), which includes gallery listings, music, and more.

Moby Dickens (124-A Bent St., No. 6 Dunn House, 575/758-3050, 10am-5pm Mon.-Wed., 10am-6pm Thurs.-Sat., noon-5pm Sun.) is Taos's best bookstore, well informed on local history and culture and stocking plenty of maps, as well as rare books, a good CD collection, and assorted gifts.

US Bank (120 W. Plaza, 575/737-3540, 9am-5pm Mon.-Fri.), just off the southwest corner of the plaza, is the most convenient bank and ATM while on foot. The drive-through service at **Centinel Bank of Taos** (512 Paseo del Pueblo Sur, 575/758-6700, 9am-5pm Mon.-Fri.) is easily accessible from the main drag.

The Taos **post office** (710 Paseo del Pueblo Sur, 575/751-1801, 9am-1pm and 2pm-4:30pm Mon.-Sat.) is on the south side; there's another on the **north side** (318 Paseo del Pueblo Norte, 575/758-2081, 8:30am-5pm Mon.-Fri.).

Wired? (705 Felicidad Ln., 575/751-9473, www.wiredcoffeeshop.com, 8am-5pm daily), behind Albertson's off La Posta Road, is a laid-back Internet café and business center with a big garden, good veggie and raw-food meals, and free wireless access for laptops; computer use is $2 for 15 minutes.

Blue Swall
MOTE
VACANCY
TV
HISTORIC
PROPERTY
INSPECTION
INVITED
TRUCK & RV
PARKING
FE·16·95

Route 66

All the wanderers came this way: the California dreamers and the Dust Bowl refugees, the soldiers and their families looking for a break, the Beat hot-rods and hippie hitch-hikers looking for kicks.

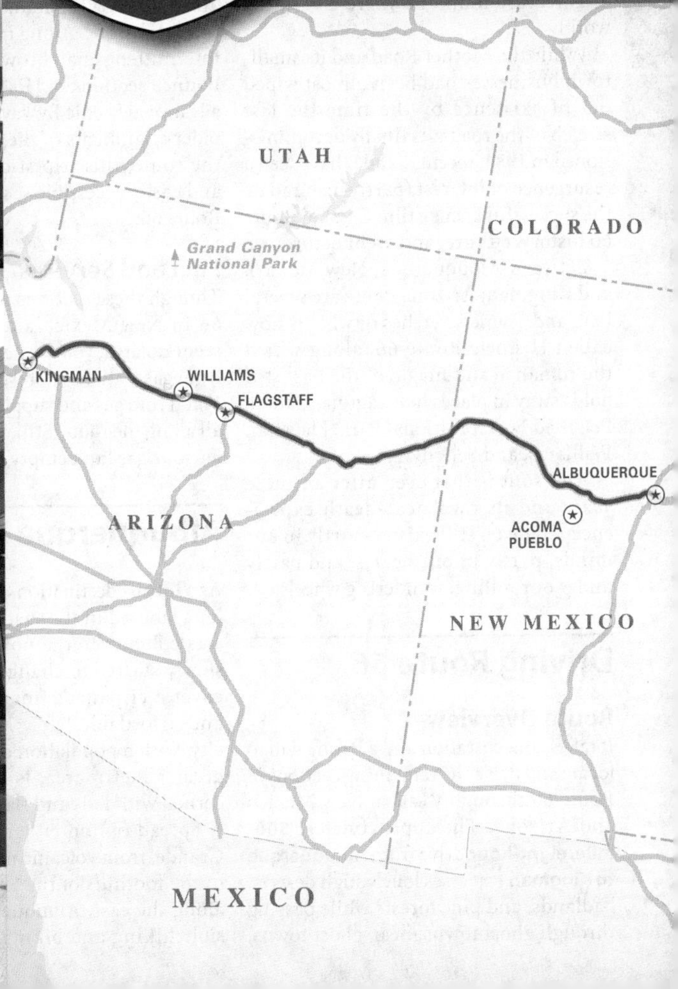

UTAH

COLORADO

Grand Canyon National Park

KINGMAN

WILLIAMS

FLAGSTAFF

ALBUQUERQUE

ACOMA PUEBLO

ARIZONA

NEW MEXICO

MEXICO

Once stretching some 2,400 miles from Chicago to Los Angeles, from the old world to the new, Route 66 reflected the confidence of a nation on the rise.

It was also the birthplace of a distinctively American car culture that still thrives today and of a species of playful architecture found nowhere else in the world.

While the Mother Road and its small-town businesses had been almost wiped out of existence by the time the last stretch of the road was finally decommissioned in 1984, recent decades have seen a resurgence of interest (partly inspired by the successful Disney film *Cars*) in Route 66 history, culture, and architecture.

Between Albuquerque, New Mexico, and Kingman, Arizona, there are several long and scenic stretches of what is now called Historic Route 66, along which the romance and magic of the past still holds sway in places like Laguna, Gallup, Petrified Forest National Park, Flagstaff, Williams, and Seligman.

And so it is that even after all these years and its own near-death experience, Route 66 still exists—partly in our minds, partly in our hearts, and partly under our rolling, wandering wheels.

Driving Route 66

Route Overview

It takes concentration and a strong will to locate and drive the remaining sections of Route 66 through western New Mexico and Arizona. The approximately **500-mile, eight-hour** drive from **Albuquerque to Kingman** traverses lonely high deserts, badlands, and pine forests while passing through ghost towns, near-ghost towns, and surviving old towns caught in a time warp.

The route, punctuated by the familiar architecture and design of mid-20th-century American road culture, involves a good bit of hopping on and off I-40, which replaced Route 66 and generally follows its later alignments. The longest unbroken section of Historic Route 66, about 165 miles, runs from Ash Fork to Topock, Arizona, a small town on the Colorado River. The route described below begins along Central Avenue, aka Route 66, in Albuquerque and ends in Kingman, about 120 miles from Ash Fork. Along much of the route intermittent small brown road signs announce sections of Historic Route 66 as a National Scenic Byway. While there are older alignments of the great road along the route, this trip sticks to the paved and easily accessible sections of Historic Route 66.

Fuel and Services

Though these sections of Historic Route 66 in New Mexico and Arizona often seem isolated, you are never very far away from gas stations, stores, and restaurants. You'll find gas and supplies in abundance all along the route. Still, you should never let your gas tank empty out.

Albuquerque

As a tourist destination, Albuquerque has long labored in the shadow of the jet-set arts colonies to the north, but that has slowly started to change as visitors discover a city that's fun, down-to-earth, and affordable. New Mexico's largest city, with a population of 900,000 in the greater metro area, is proudly unconcerned with fads and flawless facades.

Spread out on either side of the Rio Grande, from volcanic mesas on the west to the foothills of the Sandia Mountain along the east, Albuquerque has accessible hiking and biking trails that run

Highlights

★ **ABQ Trolley Co.:** The best tour in New Mexico is aboard an open-sided, faux-adobe tram-on-wheels, with the lively, knowledgeable owners sharing Albuquerque lore (page 338).

★ **Sandia Peak Tramway:** Zip up the world's longest single-cable tram to the crest of the mountain that looms over Albuquerque. At the top is a vertigo-inducing view (page 343).

★ **Petroglyph National Monument:** The city's West Mesa is covered with fine rock carvings made centuries ago by the ancestors of the local Pueblo people (page 344).

★ **Ballooning:** In the American capital for hot-air balloons, enjoy the silent city on a dawn flight. You'll get a bird's-eye view, and dip down to skim the Rio Grande (page 349).

★ **Acoma Pueblo:** This windswept village on a mesa west of Albuquerque is one of the oldest communities in the United States. Visit for the views as well as for the delicate black-on-white pottery made only here (page 358).

★ **Nuestra Señora de Guadalupe Church:** Stunning murals decorate the whitewashed walls of Zuni Pueblo's oldest adobe church. Colorful and intricately detailed, the kachinas look vividly real (page 361).

★ **Petrified Forest National Park:** Walk among the slickrock remains of a swampy forest, now a parched land strewn with reminders of the earth's unfathomable age (page 368).

★ **Museum of Northern Arizona:** Don't miss the Colorado Plateau's premier museum, where you'll learn about the plants, animals, geology, and people that make the northlands such a fascinating landscape (page 378).

★ **Sunset Crater Volcano and Wupatki National Monuments:** Explore the foothills of a silent black-rock crater and the architectural wonders of the Northern Sinagua golden age—800-year-old red-rock apartment buildings rising from the dry scrublands (page 380).

★ **Walnut Canyon National Monument:** Hike above a diversely vegetated canyon, moving from desert to forest in one short walk, past high-wall ruins built of stacked and mortared stone (page 382).

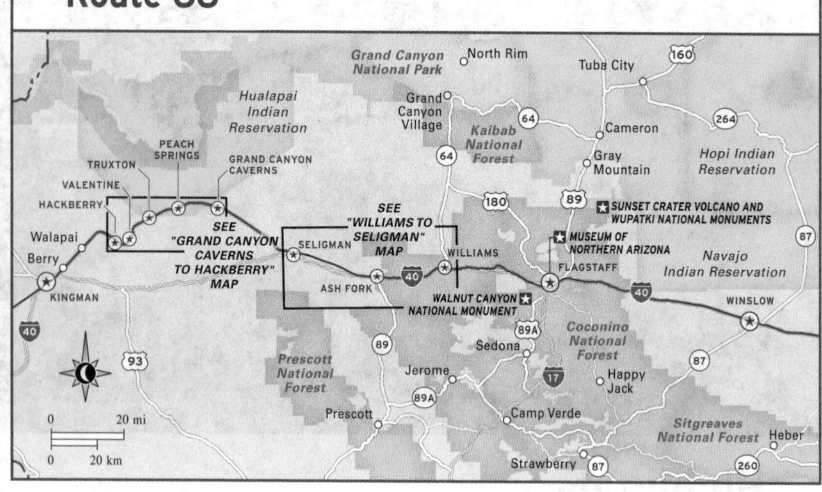

through diverse environments. In the morning, you can stroll under centuries-old cottonwood trees near the wide, muddy river; in the afternoon, you can hike along the edge of a windswept mountain range with views across the empty land beyond the city grid. And at the end of the day, you'll see Albuquerque's most remarkable feature, the dramatic light show on the Sandia Mountains—Spanish for "watermelon," for the bright pink hue they turn at sundown.

Getting There from Santa Fe

60 miles / 1 hour

Albuquerque is **60 miles (one hour)** south of Santa Fe on **I-25.** Take **exit 224A** for **Central Avenue,** which is **Old Route 66** through Albuquerque.

Getting There from Mesa Verde National Park

270 miles / 5 hours

Getting to the ABQ from Mesa Verde takes about **five hours,** a **270-mile** drive. After descending the Mesa Verde to the entrance to the park (40 minutes, 20 miles), turn right to head east on **US 160,** passing through the town of Mancos. After 25 miles on US 160, turn right and pick up **CO-140 South.**

In 25 miles you'll cross into New Mexico and the highway will become **NM-170.** After another five miles, turn left to get on **NM-574,** which will take you into the town of Aztec, New Mexico. In about 15 miles, NM-574 comes to a T-intersection with **Aztec Boulevard;** here, turn left to get on Aztec Boulevard, veer right to follow **Chaco Street,** then turn right onto **Main Avenue/US 550 South.** Continue for 150 miles on US 550 through Bloomfield, Nageezi, and Cuba, before joining **I-25 South.** After about 15 miles on I-25, take **exit 226A/226B** to merge onto **I-40 West** toward Gallup. From here, take **exit 157A,** about two miles on, for **Rio Grande Boulevard,** which will deposit you in Albuquerque's Old Town.

Stopping in Cuba

Cuba, New Mexico, a tiny town along US 550 about 185 miles (3.5 hours) from Mesa Verde and about 85 miles (1.5 hours) north of Albuquerque, has a few good restaurants and hotels.

Probably the best restaurant in this

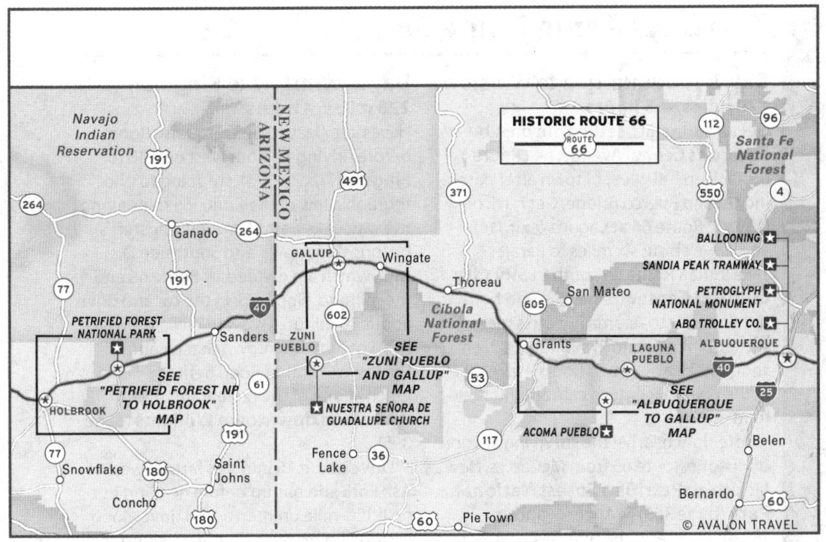

old Hispano village, which was founded in late 1700s, **El Bruno's** (6449 Main St., 575/289-9429, 11am-10pm daily, $12) has excellent chile and other New Mexican favorites. The **Frontier Motel** (6474 Main St., 575/289-3474, $60-70) is a good bargain, with clean and comfortable rooms, some with kitchenettes.

Getting There by Air

Albuquerque International Sunport (ABQ, 505/244-7700, www.cabq.gov/airport) is a pleasant single-terminal airport served by all major U.S. airlines. It's on the south side of the city, just east of I-25, about four miles from downtown. It has free wireless Internet access throughout. Near bag claim is an info desk maintained by the convention and visitors bureau.

All the major car-rental companies are in a single complex adjacent to the airport, connected by shuttle bus. Hertz's two other city locations are usually less expensive because you bypass the airport service fee; if you're renting for more than a week, the savings can offset the cab fare.

Transit from the airport includes **bus Route 50** ($1), which runs to the Alvarado Transportation Center (Central and 1st St.) downtown every half hour 7am-8pm, and on Saturdays every hour and 10 minutes 9:45am-6:50pm; there is no Sunday service. The ride takes about 25 minutes.

Less frequent, but free, the **Airport Connection shuttle** (aka city bus Route 250) runs weekdays only (9:10am, 4:01pm, 5:09pm, and 6:10pm) to the downtown Alvarado Transportation Center. The schedule is timed to meet the Rail Runner train to Santa Fe, departing about 30 minutes later. Another free weekday bus (Route 222) runs to the Bernalillo Rail Runner stop, though this is less convenient for visitors. Verify online at www.riometro.org, as the train schedule can change.

Getting There by Train

The **Rail Runner** (866/795-7245, www.riometro.org) connects downtown Santa Fe with Albuquerque. The main stop in Albuquerque is downtown, at the Alvarado Transportation Center, at Central and 1st Street. If the not-so-frequent schedule fits yours, it's fantastic service to or from Santa Fe, but within Albuquerque, the system doesn't

Two Days Along Route 66

Day 1: Albuquerque to Winslow

270 miles, 4.5 hours

Get an early start, setting out on Albuquerque's Central Avenue, aka Route 66. Pick up I-40 west of town after passing the Rio Puerco Bridge. Get back on Historic Route 66 at Laguna (exit 114) and drive about six miles to Paraje. Take Indian Route 23 south to **Sky City Cultural Center** (page 358) and book the first tour to Acoma Pueblo's mesa-top settlement (9:30am in summer), which should take about two hours. Have lunch at the cultural center's café and hit the road.

After lunch, drive the surviving sections of Historic Route 66 from McCartys, New Mexico, to **Petrified Forest National Park** (page 368) in Arizona, about 150 miles. Spend the final few hours of the day driving the main road through the national park, stopping at various viewpoints.

A final 45-minute sprint on I-40 west to Winslow and you're in the refined atmosphere of **La Posada** (page 373), a former Harvey House railroad hotel that has been restored to its former glory. Have dinner at the hotel's exceptional restaurant, **The Turquoise Room** (page 374).

Day 2: Winslow to Kingman

220 miles, 4 hours

Have breakfast at The Turquoise Room before driving an hour west on I-40 to **Flagstaff** (page 375), stopping to photograph a few of the Route 66 ruins along the way. Take a stroll around Flagstaff's historic downtown and Southside District, which are divided by Route 66 and the railroad. Hop back in the car and drive about 30 minutes west to Williams, which has a quaint downtown that celebrates the town's Mother Road heritage. Have lunch at one of the restaurants along Route 66 in **downtown Williams** (page 395).

Drive about 15 minutes farther west to Ash Fork and gas up before heading out on a 120-mile uninterrupted drive along Historic Route 66 to Kingman. Along the way, stop for a one-hour tour of **Grand Canyon Caverns** (page 401), a stroll through the gift shops in **Seligman** (page 399), and a bottle of soda pop at the **Hackberry General Store** (page 402).

Spend the night in Kingman at the Route 66-themed **El Trovatore Motel** (page 408) or the **Hill Top Motel** (page 408) and have dinner at **Mr. D'z Route 66 Diner** (page 408).

go anywhere visitors typically go. If you ride, keep your ticket—you get a free transfer from the train to any city bus.

Getting Around

Public Transportation

With the city bus system, **ABQ Ride** (505/243-7433, www.cabq.gov/transit), it's possible to reach all of the major sights along Central Avenue, but you can't get to the Sandia Peak Tramway or anywhere in the East Mountains. The most tourist-friendly bus line is Route 66 (of course), the one that runs along Central Avenue, linking Old Town, downtown, and Nob Hill; service runs until a bit past 1am on summer weekends. The double-length red **Rapid Ride** buses (Route 766) follow the same route but stop at only the most popular stops. The fare for all buses, regardless of trip length, is $1 (coins or bills, no change given); passes are available for one ($2), two ($4), and three ($6) days and can be purchased on the bus. The D-Ride bus is a free loop-route bus around downtown.

Bike

Albuquerque's **bike-route system** (www.cabq.gov/bike) is reasonably well developed, the terrain is flat, and the sun is usually shining. Rent bikes from **Routes** (404 San Felipe St. NW, 505/933-5667, www.routesrentals.com, 8am-7pm

Albuquerque

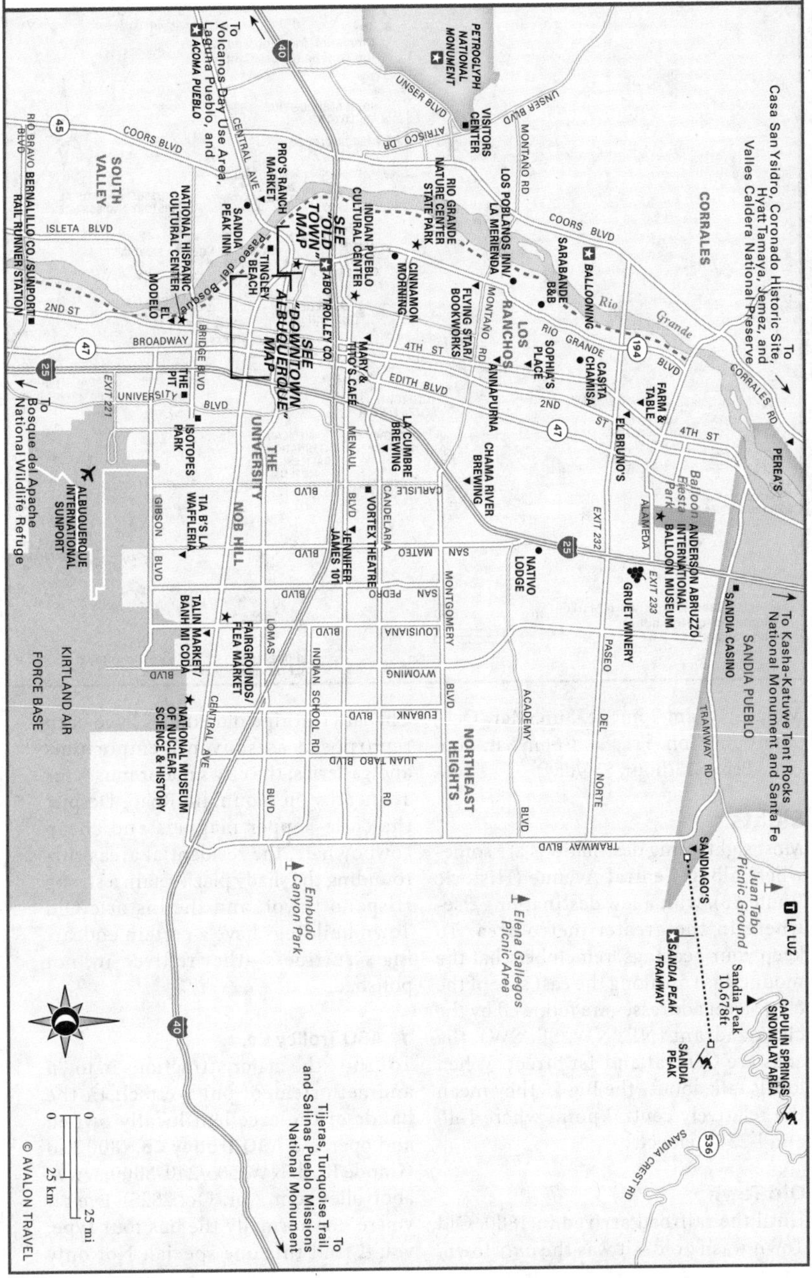

To Casa San Ysidro, Coronado Historic Site, Hyatt Tamaya, Jemez, and Valles Caldera National Preserve
CORRALES
PETROGLYPH NATIONAL MONUMENT
VISITORS CENTER
UNSER BLVD
ATRISCO DR
MONTAÑO RD
COORS BLVD
LOS POBLANOS INN/ LA MERIENDA
RIO GRANDE NATURE CENTER STATE PARK
SARABANDE B&B
BALLOONING
Rio Grande
CORRALES RD
LOS RANCHOS
RIO GRANDE BLVD
SOPHIA'S PLACE
CASITA CHAMISA
FARM & TABLE
PEREA'S
EL BRUNO'S
4TH ST
2ND ST
To Volcanos Day Use Area, Laguna Pueblo, and ACOMA PUEBLO
CENTRAL AVE
PRO'S RANCH MARKET
INDIAN PUEBLO CULTURAL CENTER
CINNAMON MORNING
FLYING STAR/ BOOKWORKS
ANNAPURNA
SEE "OLD TOWN" MAP
ABQ TROLLEY CO.
SANDIA PEAK INN
TINGLEY BEACH
Paseo del Bosque
NATIONAL HISPANIC CULTURAL CENTER
EL MODELO
SOUTH VALLEY
ISLETA BLVD
RIO BRAVO BLVD
BERNALILLO CO./SUNPORT RAIL RUNNER STATION
BROADWAY
BRIDGE BLVD
SEE "DOWNTOWN ALBUQUERQUE" MAP
MARY & TITO'S CAFE
EDITH BLVD
THE PIT
UNIVERSITY BLVD
EXIT 221
To Bosque del Apache National Wildlife Refuge
ISOTOPES PARK
THE UNIVERSITY
LA CUMBRE BREWING
CHAMA RIVER BREWING
MENAUL BLVD
CANDELARIA
CARLISLE BLVD
VORTEX THEATRE
JENNIFER JAMES 101
SAN MATEO BLVD
NATIVO LODGE
EXIT 232
ALAMEDA
Balloon Fiesta Park
ANDERSON ABRUZZO INTERNATIONAL BALLOON MUSEUM
EXIT 233
GRUET WINERY
SANDIA CASINO
SANDIA PUEBLO
To Kasha-Katuwe Tent Rocks National Monument and Santa Fe
ALBUQUERQUE INTERNATIONAL SUNPORT
TIA B'S LA WAFFLERIA
NOB HILL
GIBSON BLVD
SAN PEDRO
MONTGOMERY BLVD
LOUISIANA BLVD
FAIRGROUNDS/ FLEA MARKET
TALIN MARKET/ BANH MI CODA
LOMAS BLVD
WYOMING BLVD
INDIAN SCHOOL RD
EUBANK BLVD
ACADEMY
PASEO DEL NORTE
NORTHEAST HEIGHTS
JUAN TABO BLVD
KIRTLAND AIR FORCE BASE
NATIONAL MUSEUM OF NUCLEAR SCIENCE & HISTORY
TRAMWAY RD
TRAMWAY BLVD
SANDIAGO'S
Juan Tabo Picnic Ground
LA LUZ
Embudo Canyon Park
Elena Gallegos Picnic Area
SANDIA PEAK TRAMWAY
Sandia Peak 10,678ft
CAPULIN SPRINGS SNOWPLAY AREA
SANDIA PEAK
SANDIA CREST RD
To Tijeras, Turquoise Trail, and Salinas Pueblo Missions National Monument
0 2.5 mi
0 2.5 km

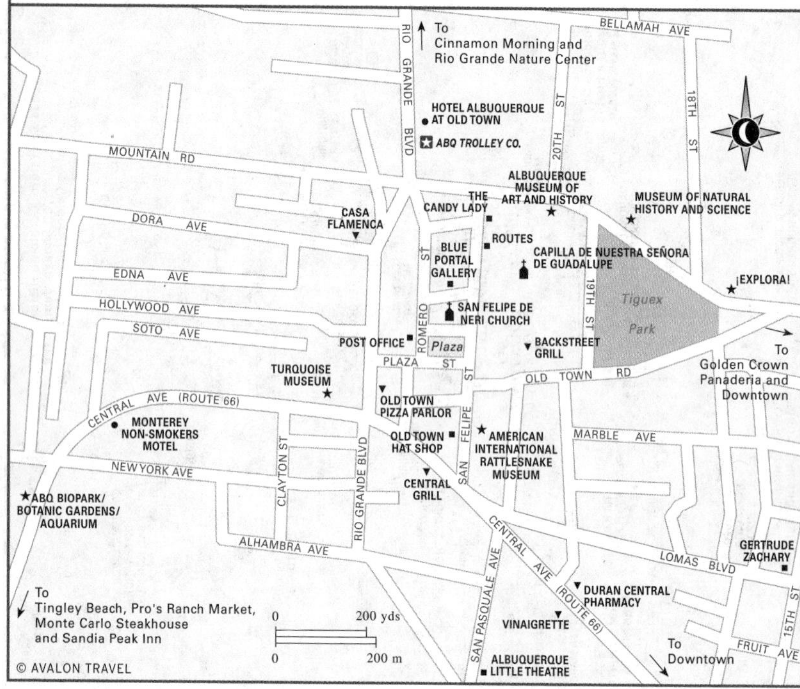

Mon.-Fri., 7am-7pm Sat.-Sun. Mar.-Oct., 9am-6pm Mon.-Fri., 8am-6pm Sat.-Sun. Nov.-Feb., $15/hour, $35/day).

Sights

Most sightseeing destinations are somewhere along Central Avenue (Historic Route 66), with a few destinations elsewhere in the greater metro area. To keep your bearings, remember that the mountains run along the east side of the city. Street addresses are followed by the city quadrant (NE, NW, SE, SW); the axes are Central and 1st Street. When locals talk about "the Big I," they mean the relatively central point where I-40 and I-25 intersect.

Old Town

Until the railroad arrived in 1880, Old Town wasn't old—it was the *only* town. The labyrinthine old adobes have been repurposed as souvenir emporiums and galleries; the city's major museums are nearby on Mountain Road. Despite the chile-pepper magnets and cheap cowboy hats, the residential areas surrounding the shady plaza retain a strong Hispano flavor, and the historic Old Town buildings have a certain endearing scruffiness—they're lived-in, not polished.

★ ABQ Trolley Co.

To cruise the major attractions in town and get oriented, put yourself in the hands of the excellent locally owned and operated **ABQ Trolley Co.** (800 Rio Grande Blvd. NW, 505/240-8000, www.abqtrolley.com, Apr.-Oct., $25). Even if you're not normally the bus tour type, you'll find this one special. Not only

Breaking Bad

Walter White and Jesse Pinkman may be gone from television, but their legacy lives on in Albuquerque. The AMC show about a high school chemistry teacher turned meth cook, *Breaking Bad* was originally written for a California setting, but production moved to Albuquerque following tax incentives. It was a happy accident, and unlike other productions shot here anonymously, *Breaking Bad* was explicitly down with the 505.

Dedicated fans should book the monthly "BaD Tour" with the **ABQ Trolley Co.** (800 Rio Grande Blvd. NW, 505/240-8000, www.abqtrolley.com, Apr.-Oct., 3.5 hours, $65)—though its standard route passes a few filming locations as well.

The bike rental company **Routes** (404 San Felipe St. NW, 505/933-5667, www.routesrentals.com, $50) offers several "Biking Bad" tours every other Saturday; each route follows a different character.

A few other sights around town include:

- The **Dog House** hot-dog stand, with its exceptionally fine neon sign, is at 1216 Central Avenue Southwest, near Old Town.
- **Los Pollos Hermanos** is actually Twisters, at 4257 Isleta Boulevard Southwest, but the PH logo is painted on the wall outside.
- Walt and Skyler's **A1A Car Wash** is at Menaul and Eubank (9516 Snow Heights Cir. NE, for your GPS).
- **The Grove** (600 Central Ave. SE), where Lydia loved her Stevia too well, is a popular café downtown.

As souvenirs of your Albuquerque visit, **Great Face & Body** (123 Broadway SE, 505/404-6670) sells "Bathing Bad" blue bath salts. **The Candy Lady** (424 San Felipe St. NW, 505/243-6239), which cooked the prop "meth" for a few episodes, sells its blue hard candy in zip-top baggies.

is it in a goofy faux-adobe open-sided trolley-bus, but the enthusiastic owners give the tours themselves, and their love of the city is clear as they wave at pedestrians and tell stories about one-time Albuquerque resident Bill Gates.

All tours depart from the Hotel Albuquerque at Old Town. The 85-minute standard tour (11am and 1pm Tues.-Sat., 1pm Sun., $25) runs through downtown and some off-the-beaten-track old neighborhoods, passing many TV and movie locations. There's also a periodic *Breaking Bad* tour (3.5 hours, $65) that's hugely popular—book well in advance for this. Or join one of the monthly nighttime theme tours—such as "Albucreepy," a tour of supposedly haunted locations, or a pizza crawl—which draws locals as well. Buy tickets online to guarantee a spot; the tickets also get you discounts around town, so it's good to do this early in your visit.

ABQ BioPark

The kid-friendly **ABQ BioPark** (505/768-2000, www.cabq.gov/biopark, 9am-5pm daily, till 6pm Sat.-Sun. June-Aug.) has three components. On the riverbank just west of Old Town (2601 Central Ave. NW) is a single complex that contains, on one side, an **aquarium,** with a giant shark tank, a creepy tunnel full of eels, and displays on underwater life from the Gulf of Mexico and up the Rio Grande. The other half is **botanic gardens,** including a desert hothouse and a butterfly habitat. The most New Mexico-specific installation, and the most interesting, is the 10-acre **Rio Grande Heritage Farm,** a re-creation of a 1930s operation with heirloom apple orchards and rare types of livestock, such as Percheron horses and Churro sheep, in an idyllic setting near the river.

A few blocks away is the **zoo** (903 10th St. SW), which you can reach from the aquarium via a miniature train. The zoo is not particularly groundbreaking, but there's plenty of space for kids to run around among trumpeting elephants and screeching peacocks. The window into the gorilla nursery is probably the most fascinating exhibit. Tickets for each section (zoo or aquarium/gardens) are $12.50, and a combo ticket for entry at all three, which includes the mini-train ride, is $20.

Between the zoo and aquarium, on the east bank of the river, south of Central, so-called **Tingley Beach** (1800 Tingley Dr. SW, sunrise-sunset, free) is 18 acres of paths and ponds for fishing; you can also rent pedal boats and bicycles here.

Albuquerque Museum of Art and History

The **Albuquerque Museum of Art and History** (2000 Mountain Rd. NW, 505/243-7255, www.cabq.gov/museum, 9am-5pm Tues.-Sun., $4) has a permanent collection ranging from a few choice Taos Society of Artists members to contemporary work by the likes of Nick Abdalla, whose sensual imagery makes Georgia O'Keeffe's flower paintings look positively literal. The history wing covers four centuries, with emphasis on Spanish military trappings, Mexican cowboys, and Albuquerque's early railroad years. Free guided tours run daily around the sculpture garden, or you can join the informative **Old Town walking tour** (11am Tues.-Sun. mid-Mar.-mid-Dec.). The museum has free admission Saturday afternoon (after 2pm) and Sunday morning (9am-1pm), as well as the third Thursday night of the month, when it's open till 8:30pm.

American International Rattlesnake Museum

You'd never guess that a small storefront just off the plaza houses the **American International Rattlesnake Museum** (202 San Felipe St. NW, 505/242-6569, www.rattlesnakes.com, 10am-6pm Mon.-Sat., 1pm-5pm Sun. June-Aug., $5), the largest collection of live snakes in the world. To see the real critters, you have to wade through an enormous gift shop full of plush snakes, wood snakes, little magnet snakes, and snakes on T-shirts. You'll also see some fuzzy tarantulas and big desert lizards, and the reptile-mad staff are usually showing off some animals outside to help educate the phobic. In the off-season, September-May, weekday hours are 11:30am-5:30pm (weekends are the same).

One of the nifty secrets of Old Town, the tiny adobe **Capilla de Nuestra Señora de Guadalupe** (404 San Felipe St. NW) is tucked off a small side alley. It's dedicated to the first saint of Mexico; her image dominates the wall facing the entrance. The dimly lit room, furnished only with heavy carved seats against the walls, is still in regular use (although, unfortunately, a fire put an end to lit votive candles and required the image of the Virgin be repainted in a more modern style). Despite the building's small scale, it follows the scheme of many traditional New Mexican churches, with a clerestory that allows sunlight to shine down on the altar.

¡Explora!

A 50,000-square-foot complex adjacent to the natural history museum, **¡Explora!** (1701 Mountain Rd. NW, 505/224-8300, www.explora.us, 10am-6pm Mon.-Sat., noon-6pm Sun., adults $8, children $4) is dedicated to thrilling—and educating—children. Grown-ups may learn something too. Its colorful geodesic-dome top sets a circuslike tone, and inside, more than 250 interactive exhibits demonstrate the scientific principles behind everything from high-wire balancing to optical illusions. Kids can even build robots using Lego systems, and, since this is the desert, a whole section is dedicated to water.

Museum of Natural History and Science

The **Museum of Natural History and Science** (1801 Mountain Rd. NW,

505/841-2800, www.nmnaturalhistory.org, 9am-5pm daily) is a large exhibit space containing three core attractions: a planetarium and observatory; a wide-format theater screening the latest vertigo-inducing nature documentaries; and an exhibit of Earth's geological history. Admission is $7 to the main exhibit space or the planetarium and $10 for the theater, though there are discounts if you buy tickets to more than one.

The museum section devotes plenty of space to the crowd-pleasers: dinosaurs. New Mexico has been particularly rich soil for paleontologists, and several of the most interesting finds are on display, such as *Coelophysis* and *Pentaceratops*. In addition, the *Startup* exhibit details the early history of the personal computer in Albuquerque and elsewhere. The show was funded by Paul Allen, who founded Microsoft here with Bill Gates, *then* moved to Seattle.

San Felipe de Neri Church

Established in 1706 along with the city itself, **San Felipe de Neri Church** (2005 N. Plaza St. NW) was originally built on what would become the west side of the plaza—but it dissolved in a puddle of mud after a strong rainy season in 1792. The replacement structure, on the north side, has fared much better, perhaps because its walls, made of adobe-like *terrones* (sun-dried bricks cut out of sod) are more than five feet thick. As they have for two centuries, local parishioners attend Mass here, which is conducted three times a day, once in Spanish.

Like many religious structures in the area, this church received a late-19th-century makeover from Eurocentric Bishop Jean-Baptiste Lamy of Santa Fe. Under his direction, the place got its wooden folk Gothic spires, as well as new Jesuit priests from Naples, who added such non-Spanish details as the gabled entrance and the widow's walk. The small yet grand interior has brick floors, a baroque gilt altar, and an elaborate pressed-tin ceiling with Moorish geometric patterns. A tiny **museum** (9:30am-5pm Mon.-Sat., free), accessible through the gift shop, contains some historic church furnishings.

Turquoise Museum

The **Turquoise Museum** (2107 Central Ave. NW, 505/247-8650, tours 11am and 1pm Mon.-Sat., $10) is much more substantial than it looks from its strip-mall facade. Exhibits present the geology and history of turquoise, along with legendary trader J. C. Zachary's beautiful specimens from all over the world. But most folks can't help but think how this relates to all the jewelry they plan to buy. So come here to learn the distinction between "natural" and "real" turquoise and otherwise arm yourself for the shopping ahead. Admission is by **guided tour** only (1.5 hours).

Downtown

Albuquerque's downtown district, along Central Avenue between the train tracks and Marquette Avenue, was once known as bustling New Town, crowded with mule-drawn streetcars, bargain hunters, and wheeler-dealers from the East Coast. But in the 1950s and 1960s, shopping plazas in Nob Hill and the Northeast Heights drew business away. By the 1970s, downtown was a wasteland of government office buildings. Thanks to an aggressive urban-renewal scheme initiated in 2000, the neighborhood has regained some of its old vigor, and Central is now a thoroughfare best known for its bars.

By day, you won't see too many specific attractions, but a stroll around reveals an interesting hodgepodge of architectural styles from Albuquerque's most optimistic era. At Central Avenue and 4th Street, two versions of Route 66 intersect. When the original highway was commissioned in 1926, the road from Chicago to the West Coast ran along 4th Street; after 1937, the route was smoothed so that it ran east-west along Central.

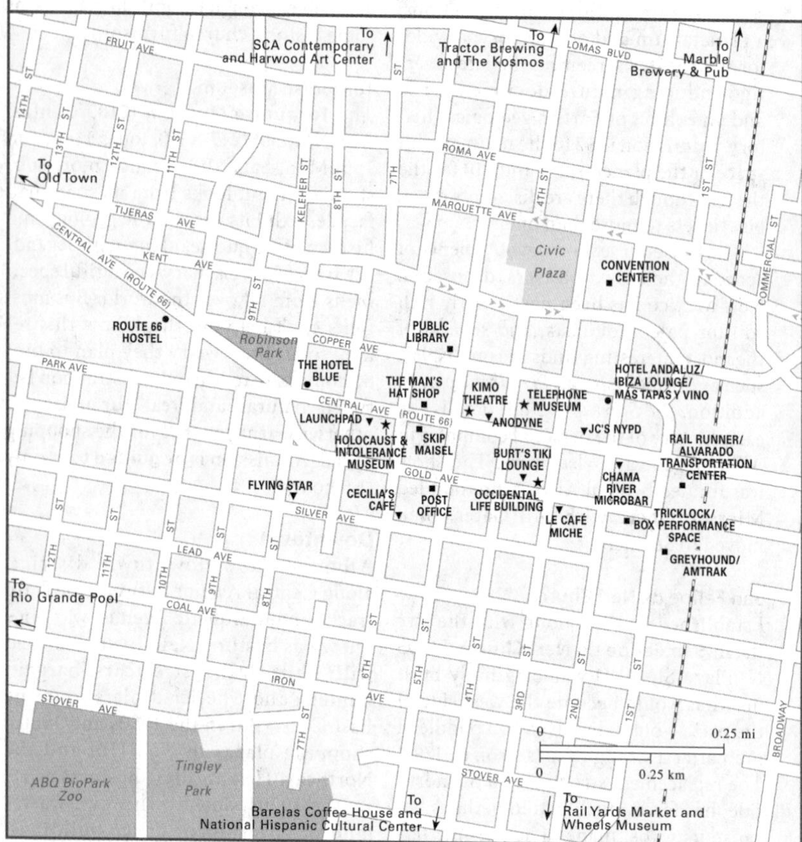

KiMo Theatre

Albuquerque's most distinctive building is the **KiMo Theatre** (423 Central Ave. NW, 505/768-3522 or 505/768-3544, www.cabq.gov/kimo). In 1927, local businessperson and Italian immigrant Carlo Bachechi hired Carl Boller, an architect specializing in movie palaces, to design this marvelously ornate building. Boller was inspired by the local adobe and native culture to create a unique style dubbed Pueblo Deco—a flamboyant treatment of Southwestern motifs, in the same vein as Moorish- and Chinese-look cinemas of the same era. The tripartite stucco facade is encrusted with ceramic tiles and Native American iconography (including a traditional Navajo symbol that had not yet been completely appropriated by the Nazi Party when the KiMo was built).

To get the full effect, take a **self-guided tour** (11am-8pm Wed.-Sat., 11am-3pm Sun.) of the interior to see the cow-skull sconces and murals of pueblo life; enter through the business office just west of the ticket booth.

Occidental Life Building

On Gold Avenue at 3rd Street, this one-story **Occidental Life Building** is another

Route 66 Gets a Makeover

Route 66 is one of the biggest repositories of American nostalgia, a little neon ribbon of cool symbolizing the country's economic growth in the 20th century. But the "mother road," on which so many Dust Bowl refugees made their way west and so many beatniks got into their grooves, officially no longer exists. The highway was decommissioned in 1985. You can still follow the brown historic-marker signs from Chicago to Los Angeles, including along Central Avenue.

But the businesses that thrived in the early highway era—especially the numerous 1940s motel courts—have fallen on hard times. As part of Albuquerque's aggressive urban-renewal program, city planners demolished a number of hotels, leaving dead neon signs standing like tombstones amid the rubble. But the city had a change of heart with the 1939 De Anza, on the east edge of Nob Hill, and bought it in 2003 to protect, among other things, beautiful interior murals by American Indian painters. In the meantime, *Burqueños* developed fresh affection for their neon-lit heritage. So when the owner of the El Vado Motel, near Old Town, threatened his vintage property with the wrecking ball, the city bought that too. Plans for redevelopment on both properties are under discussion—at press time, El Vado was slated to become a boutique hotel. Keep an eye on these icons of Route 66 history.

of Albuquerque's gems, built in 1917 by H. C. Trost, whose work defines downtown El Paso, Texas. With its ornate facade of white ceramic tile, it looks a bit like the Doge's Palace in Venice rendered in marshmallow fluff. After a 1933 fire, the reconstructing architects added even more frills, such as the crenellations along the top. The entire building is surfaced in white terra-cotta; the tiles were made in a factory in Denver, which sprayed the ceramic glaze onto concrete blocks, each individually molded and numbered, and the blocks were then assembled in Albuquerque according to an overall plan.

Museums

Production value is basic at the storefront **Holocaust and Intolerance Museum** (616 Central Ave. SW, 505/247-0606, 11am-3:30pm Tues.-Sat., free), but the message is compelling. Displays cover not just World War II, but also the Armenian genocide and actions against Native Americans. The surprisingly detailed three-story **Telephone Museum** (110 4th St. NW, 505/841-2932, 10am-1:30pm Mon., Wed., and Fri., $2) is worth a visit—if you happen to get there in its laughably narrow open time.

The **Wheels Museum** (1100 2nd St. SW, 505/243-6269, www.wheelsmuseum.org, donation) is dedicated to Western transportation, with a special focus on trains—fitting its location in the city rail yard. It displays some great interviews with former workers in the old Santa Fe workshops. The place is still being developed, so at press time did not yet have set hours. But it is reliably open during the **Rail Yards Market** (777 1st St. SW, www.railyardsmarket.org, 9am-3pm Sun. May-Oct.); model-train fans will be well rewarded.

★ Sandia Peak Tramway

The longest tramway of its type in the world, the **Sandia Peak Tramway** (505/856-7325, www.sandiapeak.com, $1 parking, $20 round-trip, $12 one-way) whisks passengers 2.7 miles and 4,000 feet up, along a continuous line of Swiss-made cables. The ride from Albuquerque's northeast foothills to the crest takes about 15 minutes. It's a convenient way to get to the ski area in winter, and in summer and fall, you can hike along the ridgeline a few miles to the visitors center. There's a so-so restaurant at the top and a small exhibit about local flora and fauna. The service runs frequently year-round (9am-9pm daily June-Aug., 9am-8pm Wed.-Mon., 5pm-8pm Tues. Sept.-May)—but check the website for periodic maintenance closures in fall and spring.

At the base of the tram, there's a small free museum about skiing in New Mexico, and even from this point, the view across the city is very good. The casual Mexican restaurant here, **Sandiago's** (38 Tramway Rd. NE, 505/856-6692, 11am-8pm daily, $13), is a bit cheesy, but it's still a nice spot for a sunset margarita (one of which, the Doogie, honors Albuquerque actor Neil Patrick Harris, who attended a nearby high school).

★ Petroglyph National Monument

Albuquerque's west side is bordered by **Petroglyph National Monument,** 7,500 acres of black boulders that crawl with some 20,000 carved lizards, birds, and assorted other beasts. Most of the images, which were created by chipping away the blackish surface "varnish" of the volcanic rock to reach the paler stone beneath, are between 400 and 700 years old, while others may date back three millennia. A few more recent examples of rock art include Maltese crosses made by Spanish settlers and initials left by explorers (not to mention a few by idle 20th-century teenagers).

Stop in first at the **visitors center** (Unser Blvd. at Western Tr., 505/899-0205, www.nps.gov/petr, 8am-5pm daily) for park maps, flyers on flora and fauna, and general orientation. From here, you will have to drive to the major trails: **Boca Negra Canyon,** a short paved loop and the only fee area ($1/car on weekdays, $2 on weekends); **Piedras Marcadas Canyon,** a 1.5-mile unpaved loop; and **Rinconada Canyon,** an out-and-back hike (2.2 miles round-trip) that can be tedious going in some spots because the ground is sandy. The clearest, most impressive images can be found here, in the canyon at the end of the trail. Everywhere in the park area, keep an eye out for millipedes, which thrive in this environment; dead, their curled-up shells resemble the spirals carved on the rocks—coincidence?

For the best overview (literally) of this area's geology, head for the back (west) side of the parkland, the **Volcanoes Day Use Area** (9am-5pm daily), where three cinder cones mark Albuquerque's western horizon. Access is via Atrisco Vista Boulevard (exit 149) off I-40; turn right (east) 4.3 miles north of the highway at a dirt road to the parking area.

From this vantage point, you can look down on the lava "fingers" that stretch east to form the crumbled edges of the escarpment where the petroglyphs are found. The fingers were formed when molten rock flowed between sandstone bluffs, which later crumbled away. The volcanoes were last reported emitting steam in 1881, though a group of practical jokers set smoky fires in them in the 1950s, briefly convincing city dwellers of an impending eruption. But the peaks are not entirely dead: Patches of green plants flourish around the steam vents that stud the hillocks, particularly visible on the middle of the three volcanoes.

Entertainment and Events

Nightlife

Because Albuquerque doesn't have enough members of any one particular subculture to pack a whole bar, the city's drinking dens can host a remarkable cross section, and even the most chic-appearing places might see an absent-minded professor and a veteran Earth Firster propping up the bar next to well-groomed professionals.

That said, the city's main bar and club scene, in a few square blocks of downtown, can feel a bit generic, with free-flowing beer specials for non-choosy students. It ends in a rowdy scene after closing time on weekends, when crowds

Albuquerque's Hot-Air History

How did it come to be that one of the most iconic sights in Albuquerque is a 127-foot-tall Mr. Peanut figure floating in front of the Sandias? Albuquerque, it turns out, enjoys the world's most perfect weather for navigating hot-air balloons. A phenomenon called the "Albuquerque Box," created by the steep mountains adjacent to the low river bottom, enables pilots to move at different speeds at different altitudes, and even to backtrack if necessary. Combine that with more than 300 days of sunshine per year, and it's no wonder that now more than 700 balloons—including "special shapes" such as Mr. Peanut—convene each October to show off their colors and compete in precision flying contests.

The city's air currents were discovered to be friendly to balloons for the first time in 1882. That was when an adventurous bartender piloted a hydrogen-filled craft into the sky as part of the New Town's Fourth of July celebrations, much to the delight of the assembled crowd, which had waited almost two days for *The City of Albuquerque,* as the balloon was dubbed, to fill. "Professor" Park Tassell, the showman pilot, went aloft alone and landed successfully; the only mishap was that a ballast sandbag was emptied on a spectator's head.

Then 90 years passed, and in 1972, Albuquerque again drew attention as a place to pursue this gentle sport. This was the year the first balloon fiesta was held, with 13 aircraft participating. The gathering, a rudimentary race, was organized as a publicity stunt for a local radio station's 50th-anniversary celebrations. The spectacle drew 20,000 people, most of whom had never even seen a hot-air balloon before—but within a few short years, the event was internationally renowned, and the **Balloon Fiesta** has been an annual event ever since.

spill out onto several blocks of Central that are closed to car traffic. So although this area does have a few good bars, you'll find more interesting entertainment elsewhere.

Downtown

The **Hotel Andaluz lobby** (125 2nd St. NW, 505/242-9090) touts itself as "Albuquerque's living room"—Conrad Hilton's original vision for the place—and it's a comfy spot to sip cocktails and nibble Spain-inspired snacks, especially if you reserve one of the private booths ("casbahs") on the weekend, when there's also live tango or salsa and a big crowd of dancers. On the second floor, the indoor-outdoor **Ibiza Lounge** (4pm-11pm Mon.-Thurs., 4pm-1am Fri.-Sat., 11am-4pm Sun.) is a chic scene on weekends. It has a good view of the mountains at sunset, and it's a cooler alternative to the mayhem just over on Central; occasional special events carry cover charges, but usually it's free to enter.

A great spot to watch the Sandia Mountains turn pink at sunset, the **Apothecary Lounge** (806 Central Ave. SE, 505/242-0040, 3pm-10:30pm Mon.-Thurs., 3pm-1am Fri.-Sun.) is the rooftop bar at the Parq Central hotel in East Downtown. Fitting with the historic atmosphere of the hotel, the bar is good at vintage cocktails, and also has a seasonal drink menu, along with finger food.

The best all-purpose casual bar downtown is the upstairs **Anodyne** (409 Central Ave. NW, 505/244-1820, 4pm-1:30am Mon.-Fri., 7pm-1:30am Sat., 7pm-11:30pm Sun.), a long, wood-floor room filled with pool tables and a younger crowd sprawled on the thrift-store sofas. Choose from more than a hundred beers, and get some quarters to plug in to the good collection of pinball machines. Happy hour is 4pm-8pm Monday to Thursday, and till 9pm on Friday.

To catch touring indie rockers or the local crew about to hit it big, head to the very professional **Launchpad** (618 Central

Ave. SW, 505/764-8887, www.launchpadrocks.com). With free live music and a pool table, **Burt's Tiki Lounge** (313 Gold Ave. SW, 505/247-2878, www.burtstikilounge.com, 8:30pm-2am Wed.-Sat.) has a funky feel and an eclectic bill, from British psychedelia to reggae.

The Arts

Albuquerque has the liveliest theater scene in the Southwest, with some 30 troupes in action. The old reliables are the black box **Vortex Theatre** (2900 Carlisle Blvd. NE, 505/247-8600, www.vortexabq.org), running since 1976 (though in a new location as of 2014), and the more standard repertory **Albuquerque Little Theatre** (224 San Pasquale St. SW, 505/242-4750, www.albuquerquelittletheatre.org), founded in 1930 and performing in a 500-seat WPA-era building.

The 70-seat **Cell Theatre** (700 1st St. NW, www.liveatthecell.com) is home to the Fusion Theatre Company, all professional union actors. It often runs recent Broadway dramas.

A more avant-garde group is the two-decade-old **Tricklock** (110 Gold Ave. SW, 505/254-8393, www.tricklock.com), which develops physically oriented shows at its "performance laboratory" downtown. It also hosts an international theater festival (in Jan. and Feb.). The neighboring **Box Performance Space** (114 Gold Ave. SW, 505/404-1578, www.theboxabq.com) hosts various improv groups and satirical comedians; the well-known absurdist comedy duo The Pajama Men often perform here when they're back home.

Also see what **Blackout Theatre** (www.blackouttheatre.com) is up to—it doesn't have its own space, but it mounts interesting shows in interesting places: improv Dickens, for instance, or an interactive zombie apocalypse in a parking

Top to bottom: KiMo Theatre; Petroglyph National Monument; hot-air balloon over Albuquerque.

lot. Other groups of note: **Duke City Repertory Theatre** (www.dukecityrep.com) and **Mother Road Theatre Company** (www.motherroad.org).

Live Music

Albuquerque's arts scene graces a number of excellent stages. The most beautiful is the city-owned **KiMo Theatre** (423 Central Ave. NW, 505/768-3544, www.cabq.gov/kimo), often hosting locally written plays and dance, as well as the occasional musical performance and film screening.

Bigger classical and folkloric acts visit the **Roy E. Disney Center for Performing Arts** at the National Hispanic Cultural Center (1701 4th St. SW, 505/724-4771, www.nhccnm.org), a modernized Mesoamerican pyramid that contains three venues, the largest of which is a 691-seat proscenium theater. This is the place to catch a performance by visiting or local flamenco artists—with the National Institute of Flamenco headquarters in Albuquerque, there's often someone performing.

The University of New Mexico's **Popejoy Hall** (UNM campus, 505/277-3824, www.popejoyhall.com) hosts the New Mexico Symphony Orchestra (which also plays at the Rio Grande Zoo in the summer).

A more intimate classical event is **Chatter Sunday** (505/234-4611, www.chatterabq.org, 10:30am Sun., $15). Originally known as Church of Beethoven, this chamber-music show aims to offer all the community and quiet of church, with none of the religious overtones. It takes place at the funky coffeehouse **The Kosmos** (1715 5th St. NW), part of a larger warehouse-turned-art-studios complex. The "service" lasts about an hour, with two musical performances, interspersed with a poem and a few minutes of silent contemplation. It's all fueled by free espresso.

Flamenco enthusiasts should check the schedule at **Casa Flamenca** (401 Rio Grande Blvd. NW, 505/247-0622, www.casaflamenca.org) in Old Town. The dance school in an old adobe house hosts a monthly *tablao,* in which local teachers and visiting experts perform.

For rock concerts, the biggest concert venue in town is **Isleta Amphitheater** (5601 University Blvd. SE, www.isleta-amphitheater.net), with space for some 12,000 people. The next step down is one of the Albuquerque-area casinos, the ritziest of which is **Sandia Casino** (I-25 at Tramway, 800/526-9366, www.sandiacasino.com), which has a 4,000-seat outdoor amphitheater. **Isleta Casino** (11000 Broadway SE, 505/724-3800, www.isleta.com), not to be confused with the amphitheater, has a smaller indoor venue, as does Laguna Pueblo's **Route 66 Casino** (14500 Central Ave. SW, 866/352-7866, www.rt66casino.com).

Also see what's on at **El Rey Theater** (620 Central Ave. SW, 505/510-2582, www.elreytheater.com) and **Sunshine Theater** (120 Central Ave. SW, 505/764-0249, www.sunshinetheaterlive.com)—both converted movie houses, they have excellent sightlines. **Outpost Performance Space** (210 Yale Blvd. SE, 505/268-0044, www.outpostspace.org) books very good world music and dance acts.

Festivals and Events

The city's biggest annual event is the **Albuquerque International Balloon Fiesta** (505/821-1000, www.balloonfiesta.com), nine days in October dedicated to New Mexico's official state aircraft, with more than 700 hot-air balloons of all colors, shapes, and sizes gathering at a dedicated park on the north side of town, west of I-25. During the fiesta, the city is packed with "airheads," who claim this is the best gathering of its kind in the world. If you go, don't miss an early-morning mass ascension, when the balloons glow against the dark sky, then lift silently into the air in a great wave. Parking can be a nightmare—take the park-and-ride bus, or ride a bike (valet parking available!).

In April is the equally colorful **Gathering of Nations Powwow** (505/836-2810, www.gatheringofnations.com), the largest tribal get-together in the United States, with more than 3,000 dancers and singers in full regalia from over 500 tribes crowding the floor of the University Arena. Miss Indian World earns her crown by showing off traditional talents such as spearfishing or storytelling.

Around November 2, don't miss the **Marigold Parade** (505/363-1326, www.muertosymarigolds.org), celebrating the Mexican Day of the Dead and general South Valley pride. The parade is a procession of skeletons, cars bedecked in flowers, and a little civil-rights activism.

Shopping

Old Town and the environs are where you can pick up traditional American Indian jewelry and pottery for very reasonable prices.

Old Town

The galleries and gift shops around the plaza can blur together after just a little bit of browsing, but the **Blue Portal Gallery** (2107 Church St. NW, 505/243-6005, 10am-4:30pm Mon.-Sat., 1pm-4pm Sun.) is a nice change, with well-priced and often very refined arts and crafts, from quilts to woodwork, by Albuquerque's senior citizens. And the **street vendors** set up on the east side of the plaza are all artisans selling their own work, at fair prices.

Just outside of Old Town's historic zone, the **Gertrude Zachary** showroom (1501 Lomas Blvd. NW, 505/247-4442, www.gertrudezachary.com, 9:30am-6pm Mon.-Sat., 10am-5pm Sun.) is the place to go for contemporary turquoise-and-silver jewelry.

If you arrived in Albuquerque unprepared for the sun, **Old Town Hat Shop** (205-C San Felipe St. NW, 505/242-4019, 10am-5pm daily) can set you right, with one of the better selections of hats in the city, for both women and men, in styles ranging from full-on cowboy to proper city slicker.

Downtown

An emporium of American Indian goods, **Skip Maisel's Indian Jewelry & Crafts** (510 Central Ave. SW, 505/242-6526, 9am-5:30pm Mon.-Sat.) feels like a relic from downtown's heyday. Whether you want a warbonnet, a turquoise-studded watch, or deerskin moccasins, it's all here in a vast, overstocked shop with kindly salespeople. Don't miss the beautiful murals above the display windows and in the foyer; they were painted in the 1930s by local Indian artists such as Awa Tsireh, whose work hangs in the New Mexico Museum of Art in Santa Fe.

Another throwback is **The Man's Hat Shop** (511 Central Ave. NW, 505/247-9605, 9:30am-5:30pm Mon.-Fri., 9:30am-5pm Sat.), just across the street. It stocks just what it promises, from homburgs to ten-gallons.

Set in the old Santa Fe workshops south of downtown, **Rail Yards Market** (777 1st St. SW, www.railyardsmarket.org, 9am-3pm Sun. May-Oct.) is a festive gathering of arts and crafts, produce, snacks, and live music. With a lot of creative Albuquerque-pride T-shirts for sale, it makes a good place to shop for offbeat souvenirs—and it's a great chance to see inside the positively majestic old buildings where locomotives for the Santa Fe line were built from the ground up.

Sports and Recreation

With trails running through several distinct ecosystems, Albuquerque gives outdoorsy types plenty to do. Late summer (after rains have started and fire danger is passed) and fall are the best times to head to the higher elevations on the Sandia Mountains. Once the cooler weather sets in, the scrub-covered foothills and the bare, rocky West Mesa are more hospitable. The valley along the

Rio Grande, running through the center of the city, is remarkably pleasant year-round: mild in winter and cool and shady in summer. As everywhere in the desert, always pack extra layers of clothing and plenty of water before you set out, and don't go charging up Sandia Peak (10,678 feet above sea level) your first day off the plane.

★ Ballooning

You don't have to be in town for the Balloon Fiesta to go up, up, and away. Take advantage of Albuquerque's near-flawless weather to take a hot-air balloon ride almost any morning of the year. A trip is admittedly an investment (and you have to wake up before dawn), but the sensation is unlike any other sort of ride, as it's slow and almost completely silent. One of the best established operations is **Rainbow Ryders** (505/823-1111, www.rainbowryders.com, $195 pp). Typically, you're up in the balloon for an hour or so, depending on wind conditions, and you get a champagne toast when you're back on solid ground.

Biking

Albuquerque maintains a great network of paved trails in the city, and the mountains and foothills have challenging dirt tracks. The most visitor-friendly bike store in town is **Routes** (404 San Felipe St. NW, 505/933-5667, www.routesrentals.com, 8am-7pm Mon.-Fri., 7am-7pm Sat.-Sun. Mar.-Oct., 9am-6pm Mon.-Fri., 8am-6pm Sat.-Sun. Nov-Feb., $15/hour, $35/day), which rents city cruisers, mountain bikes, and more at its handy location in Old Town; pickup and drop-off from hotels is free. It also runs fun daylong **bike tours,** and rents snowshoes in the winter.

City Cycling

Recreational cyclists need head no farther than the river, where the **Paseo del Bosque,** a 16-mile-long, completely flat biking and jogging path, runs through the Rio Grande Valley State Park. The northern starting point is at **Alameda/Rio Grande Open Space** (7am-9pm daily Apr.-Oct., 7am-7pm daily Nov.-Mar.) on Alameda Boulevard. You can also reach the trail through the **Rio Grande Nature Center** (www.rgnc.org, 8am-5pm daily, $3/car), at the end of Candelaria, and at several other major intersections along the way. For details on this and other bike trails in Albuquerque, download a map from the city's bike info page (www.cabq.gov/bike), or pick up a free copy at bike shops around town.

Mountain Biking

Mountain bikers can take the Sandia Peak Tramway to the **ski area,** then rent wheels to explore the 30 miles of wooded trails. Bikes aren't allowed on the tram, though, so if you have your own ride, you can drive around the east side of the mountain.

Also on the east side of the mountains, a whole network of trails lead off Highway 337 (south of I-25), through **Otero Canyon** and other routes through the juniper-studded Manzanos.

Or stay in the city and explore the foothills. Locals built a small but fun BMX terrain park at **Embudo Canyon;** park at the end of Indian School Road. For a longer cruise, head for the **foothills trails,** a web of dirt tracks all along the edge of the Northeast Heights. **Trail no. 365,** which runs for about 15 miles north-south from near the tramway down to near I-40, is the best run. You can start at either end, or go to the midpoint, at Elena Gallegos Open Space, off the north end of Tramway Boulevard at the end of Simms Park Road. Elena Gallegos in particular is very popular, so go on a weekday if you can, and always look out for hikers and other bikers. Aside from the occasional sandy or rocky patch, none of the route is technical or steep. More complex trails run off to the east; pick up a map at the entrance booth at Elena Gallegos.

Birding on the Peak

In the dead of winter, Sandia Peak does not seem hospitable to life in any form, much less flocks of delicate-looking birds the size of your fist, fluffing around cheerfully in the frigid air. But that's precisely what you'll see if you visit right after a big snowfall. These are rosy finches, a contrary, cold-loving variety (sometimes called "refrigerator birds") that migrate from as far north as the Arctic tundra to the higher elevations of New Mexico, which must seem relatively tropical by comparison.

What's special about Sandia is that it draws all three species of rosy finch, which in turn draws dedicated birders looking to add the finches to their life lists, and it's one of the few places to see them that's close to a city and accessible by car. So if you see the finches—they're midsize brown or black birds with pink bellies, rumps, and wings—you'll probably also spy some human finch fans. But they might not have time to talk, as it's not unheard-of for the most obsessive birders—those on their "big year," out to spot as many species as possible in precisely 365 days—to fly in to Albuquerque, drive to the crest, eyeball the finches, and drive right back to the airport again.

Road Biking

A popular tour is up to **Sandia Peak** via the Crest Road on the east side—you can park and ride from any point, but cyclists typically start somewhere along Highway 14 north of I-40, then ride up Highway 536, which winds 13.5 miles along increasingly steep switchbacks to the crest. The **New Mexico Touring Society** (www.nmts.org) lists descriptions of other routes and organizes group rides.

Spas

Betty's Bath & Day Spa (1835 Candelaria Rd. NW, 505/341-3456, www.bettysbath.com) is the place to get pampered, whether with a massage and a facial or with an extended dip in one of two outdoor communal hot tubs. One is coed and the other for women only; both have access to dry saunas and cold plunges—a bargain at just $12. Private reservations are available most evenings.

Closer to downtown, **Albuquerque Baths** (1218 Broadway NE, 505/243-3721, www.abqbaths.com) has similar facilities, though only one communal tub, which is solar-heated; the sauna is done in Finnish cedar. The reasonable rates ($15/two hours) include the use of robes and sandals, and massages are available too.

Spectator Sports

Minor-league baseball thrives in Albuquerque, apparently all because of some clever name: The so-so Dukes petered out a while back, but a fresh franchise, under the name of the **Albuquerque Isotopes,** has been drawing crowds since 2003. It's hard to judge whether the appeal is the cool **Isotopes Park** (1601 Avenida Cesar Chavez NE, 505/924-2255, www.albuquerquebaseball.com), the whoopee-cushion theme nights, or just the name, drawn from an episode of *The Simpsons.* Regardless, a summer night under the ballpark lights is undeniably pleasant; it helps that you can usually get good seats for $15.

Albuquerqueans also go crazy for **UNM Lobos basketball,** packing the raucous University Arena, aka **"The Pit"** (Avenida Cesar Chavez at University Blvd., 505/925-5626, www.golobos.com).

Winter Sports

Sandia Peak Ski Area (505/242-9052, www.sandiapeak.com, $50 full-day lift ticket) is open from mid-December through mid-March, though it often takes till about February for a good base to build up. The 10 main trails, serviced by four lifts, are not dramatic, but they are good and long. The area is open daily in the holiday season, then Wednesday through Sunday for the rest of the winter.

Sandia Peak also has plenty of opportunities for cross-country skiing. Groomed trails start from **Capulin Springs Snow Play Area** (9:30am-3:30pm Fri.-Sun. in winter, $3/car), where there are also big hills for tubing and sledding. Look for the parking nine miles up Highway 536 to the crest. Farther up on the mountain, **10K Trail** is usually groomed for skiers, as is a service road heading south to the upper tramway terminal; the latter is wide and relatively level, good for beginners. For trail conditions, call or visit Sandia ranger station (505/281-3304) on Highway 337 in Tijeras.

Accommodations

Because Albuquerque isn't quite a tourist mecca, its hotel offerings have languished a bit, but the scene has improved in recent years. There are still plenty of grungy places, but the good ones are exceptional values. Whether on the low or high end, you'll pay substantially less here than you would in Santa Fe for similar amenities. The only time you'll need to book in advance is early October, during Balloon Fiesta (when prices are usually a bit higher).

Under $100

Funky and affordable, the **Route 66 Hostel** (1012 Central Ave. SW, 505/247-1813, www.rt66hostel.com) is in a century-old house midway between downtown and Old Town and has been offering bargain accommodations since 1978; it's clean despite years of budget travelers traipsing through. Upstairs, along creaky wood hallways, are private rooms ($25-35) with various configurations. Downstairs and in the cool basement area are single-sex dorms ($20 pp). Guests have run of the kitchen, and there's a laundry and room to lounge. The most useful city bus lines run right out front. There have been complaints of staff not being on hand for early or late check-ins—be sure to call and confirm before you arrive.

Central Avenue is strewn with motels, many built in Route 66's heyday. Almost all of them are unsavory, except for ★ **Monterey Non-Smokers Motel** (2402 Central Ave. SW, 505/243-3554, www.nonsmokersmotel.com, $58 s, $70 d), which is as practical as its name implies. The place doesn't really capitalize on 1950s kitsch—it just offers meticulously clean, good-value rooms with no extra frills or flair. One large family suite has two beds and a foldout sofa. The outdoor pool is a treat, the laundry facilities are a bonus, and the location near Old Town is very convenient.

A fully renovated motel on the west side, just over the river from Old Town, ★ **Sandia Peak Inn** (4614 Central Ave. SW, 505/831-5036, www.sandiapeakinnmotel.com, $60 s, $70 d) is named not for its proximity to the mountain, but its view of it. It's certainly the best value in this category, offering large, spotless rooms, all with bathtubs, fridges, microwaves, and huge TVs. Breakfast is included in the rate, and the proprietors are positively sunny. There's a small indoor pool and free wireless Internet throughout.

The Hotel Blue (717 Central Ave. NW, 877/878-4868, www.thehotelblue.com, $69 s, $79 d) offers great value downtown. The rooms in this '60s block are a slightly odd mix of cheesy motel decor (gold quilted bedspreads) and bachelor-pad flair (a gas "fireplace"), and the windows don't open. But the Tempur-Pedic beds are undeniably comfortable, and the low rates include breakfast, parking, and a shuttle to the airport. There's also a decent-size outdoor pool, open in summers, and the downtown farmers market is in the park right out front. Request a room on the northeast side for a mountain view.

$100-150

The exceptionally tasteful ★ **Downtown Historic Bed & Breakfasts of Albuquerque**

(207 High St. NE, 505/842-0223, www.albuquerquebedandbreakfasts.com, $139 s) occupies two neighboring old houses on the east side of downtown, walking distance to good restaurants on Central in the EDo (East Downtown) stretch. Heritage House has more of a Victorian feel, while Spy House has a sparer, 1940s look—but both are nicely clutter-free. Two outbuildings are more private suites.

Locally owned **Hotel Albuquerque at Old Town** (800 Rio Grande Blvd. NW, 505/843-6300, www.hotelabq.com, $149 d) is a good backup in this category. Sporting a chic Spanish colonial style, the lobby is lovely and the brick-red-and-beige rooms are relatively spacious. There's a big swimming pool too. Opt for the north side (generally, even-numbered rooms) for a view of the mountains.

$150-200

A beautiful relic of early 20th-century travel, ★ **Hotel Andaluz** (125 2nd St. NW, 505/242-9090, www.hotelandaluz.com, $159 d) was first opened in 1939 by New Mexico-raised hotelier Conrad Hilton. It received a massive renovation in 2009, keeping all the old wood and murals but updating the core to be fully environmentally friendly, from solar hot-water heaters to a composting program. The neutral-palette rooms are soothing and well designed, with a little Moorish flair in the curvy door outlines. The place is worth a visit for the lobby alone; check out the exhibits from local museums on the second-floor mezzanine.

Set in the original AT&SF railroad hospital and sporting a storied past, the stylishly renovated **Parq Central** (806 Central Ave. SE, 505/242-0040, www.hotelparqcentral.com, $159 d), opened in late 2010. It makes a nice alternative to the Andaluz if you prefer your history in paler shades. The rooms are a bit smaller but feel light and airy thanks to big windows and gray and white furnishings, with retro chrome fixtures and honeycomb tiles in the bath. The hospital

Los Poblanos Historic Inn

vibe is largely eradicated, though whimsical vitrines in the halls conjure old-time medical treatments, and the rooftop bar sports a gurney. Perks include free parking, decent continental breakfast, and airport shuttle.

At Albuquerque's nicest place to stay, you don't actually feel like you're anywhere near the city. ★ **Los Poblanos Historic Inn** (4803 Rio Grande Blvd. NW, 505/344-9297, www.lospoblanos.com, $180 d) sits on 25 acres, the largest remaining plot of land in the city, and the rooms are tucked in various corners of a sprawling ranch built in the 1930s by John Gaw Meem and beautifully maintained and preserved—even the huge old kitchen ranges are still in place, as are murals by Taos artist Gustave Baumann and frescoes by Peter Hurd. In the main house, the guest rooms are set around a central patio and retain their old wood floors and heavy viga ceilings. Newer, larger rooms have been added and fit in flawlessly—Meem rooms have a very light Southwest touch, while the Farm suites have a whitewashed rustic aesthetic, accented by prints and fabrics by modernist designer Alexander Girard, of the folk-art museum in Santa Fe. There's also a saltwater pool and a gym, as well as extensive gardens and organic lavender. Included breakfast is exceptional (eggs from the farm), as is dinner at the restaurant, La Merienda.

Food

Albuquerque has a few dress-up establishments, but the real spirit of the city's cuisine is in its lower-rent spots where dedicated owners follow their individual visions. A lot of the most traditional New Mexican places are open only for breakfast and lunch, so plan accordingly. Prices given are those of the average entrée.

Old Town

Aside from the couple recommended here, the restaurants in the blocks immediately adjacent to the Old Town plaza are expensive and only so-so; better to walk another block or two for real New Mexican flavor, or drive a short way west on Central.

New Mexican

Don't waste a meal on restaurants at the Old Town plaza. Instead, walk a couple of blocks to ★ **Duran Central Pharmacy** (1815 Central Ave. NW, 505/247-4141, 9am-6:30pm Mon.-Fri., 9am-2pm Sat., $9), an old-fashioned lunch counter hidden behind the magazine rack in this big fluorescent-lit drugstore. Regulars pack this place at lunch for all the New Mexican staples: huevos rancheros, green-chile stew, and big enchilada plates. Cash only.

Fresh and Local

Founded in Santa Fe, **Vinaigrette** (1828 Central Ave. SW, 505/842-5507, 11am-9pm daily, $13) is a posh-sounding "salad bistro" that is more substantial than it sounds—and it's a welcome spot of healthy eating around Old Town.

Cafés

Inside the Albuquerque Museum, **Slate Street Café** (2000 Mountain Rd. NW, 505/243-2220, 10am-2:30pm Tues.-Fri. and Sun., 10am-4pm Sat., $8) is great for coffee and cupcakes, as well as more substantial breakfast and lunch, like a chipotle-spiked meat-loaf sandwich. Its larger, original location is at 515 Slate Avenue NW.

A 10-minute walk from Old Town, **Golden Crown Panaderia** (1103 Mountain Rd. NW, 505/243-2424, 7am-8pm Tues.-Sat., 10am-8pm Sun., $4-9) is a real neighborhood hangout that's so much more than a bakery. Famous for its green-chile bread and *bizcochitos* (the anise-laced state cookie), it also does pizza with blue-corn or green-chile crust, to take away or to eat at the picnic tables out back. And you'll want a side salad just to watch them assemble it straight from the hydroponic garden that consumes a lot of the space behind the counter. Wash it down with a coffee milk shake.

American

Built on the bones of an old fast-food joint, **Central Grill** (2056 Central Ave. SW, 505/554-1424, 6:30am-4pm Mon.-Thurs., 6:30am-8pm Fri., 8am-8pm Sat., $7) still does quick food, but with a fresher, more homemade feel. Like a good diner should, it serves breakfast all day, and real maple syrup is an option. Its daily special plate is usually a fantastic deal, with a main like barbecue chicken plus sides and a drink for $9 or so.

Italian

It's not necessarily a destination from elsewhere in the city, but **Old Town Pizza Parlor** (108 Rio Grande Blvd. NW, 505/999-1949, 11am-9pm Mon.-Sat., 11am-8pm Sun., $9) is an unpretentious, kid-friendly place to eat in the relative wasteland of Old Town, with generously topped pizzas, ultra-creamy pastas, and creative "white nachos." The back patio is a bonus.

Mexican

In a shady Old Town courtyard, **Backstreet Grill** (1919 Old Town Rd. NW, 505/842-5434, 11am-9pm Sun.-Thurs., 11am-10pm Fri.-Sat., $12) is a great place to rest your tourist feet and enjoy a New Mexican craft beer, and maybe a bowl of guacamole. For a full meal, though, you're better off elsewhere.

The big-box facade of **Pro's Ranch Market** (4201 Central Ave. NW, 505/831-8739, 7am-11pm daily, $5) hardly hints at the wonders inside. If you haven't been in one of these (it's an Arizona-based chain), step inside for a bonus travel experience, straight to Mexico. The shelves are lined with Bimbo bread and other south-of-the-border essentials, but the real action is in the food court, past the cash registers and to the left, where there's a dazzling array of quesadillas, *sincronizadas,* tamales, and more, with a separate station for fresh fruit juices.

Steak

Don't be put off by the brown, windowless cinderblock facade, with a package-liquor store in the front. **Monte Carlo Steakhouse** (3916 Central Ave. SW, 505/831-2444, 11am-10pm Mon.-Thurs., 11am-11pm Fri.-Sat., $18) is a fantastic time machine, lined with vintage Naugahyde booths and serving good, hearty food: the prime-rib special Thursday through Saturday, a softball-size green-chile cheeseburger, or marinated pork kebab, all with delicious hand-cut fries. Greek ownership means you get a tangy feta dressing on your salad and baklava for dessert. And even though there's a full bar, you're still welcome to buy wine from the package store up front and have it with your dinner, for a nominal markup.

Downtown

With so many bars in this area, there's little room left for food, beyond a couple of solid cafés.

New Mexican

Even though it's in the middle of Albuquerque's main business district, ★ **Cecilia's Café** (230 6th St. SW, 505/243-7070, 7am-2pm daily, $8) feels more like a living room than a restaurant. Maybe it's the woodstove in the corner—as well as the personal attention from Cecilia and her daughters and the food that's clearly made with care. The rich, dark red chile really shines here.

Fresh and Local

There are a number of **farmers markets** throughout the city; one of the largest is downtown at Robinson Park on Central Avenue at 8th Street (7am-noon Sat. May-Aug., 8am-1pm Sept.-Nov.). For other markets around the city, visit www.farmersmarketsnm.org.

Cafés

A branch of **Flying Star** (723 Silver Ave. SW, 505/244-8099, 7am-10pm daily, $10) occupies a hiply restored 1950 John Gaw Meem bank building.

Past the railroad tracks in EDo (East Downtown), **The Grove** (600 Central Ave. SE, 505/248-9800, 7am-4pm Tues.-Sat., 8am-3pm Sun., $12) complements its local-organic menu with big front windows facing Central and a screened-in patio. The chalkboard menu features creative salads (spinach, orange slices, and dates is one combo) as well as sandwiches and cupcakes; breakfast, with farm-fresh eggs and homemade English muffins, is served all day. It's a notch above Flying Star in price, but you're paying for the especially high-quality ingredients.

Italian

A popular hangout for urban pioneers in the EDo neighborhood, ★ **Farina Pizzeria** (510 Central Ave. SE, 505/243-0130, 11am-9pm Mon., 11am-10pm Tues.-Fri., noon-10pm Sat., 5pm-9pm Sun., $14) has exposed brick walls and a casual vibe. The pies come out of the wood-fired oven suitably crisp-chewy and topped with seasonal veggies. Make sure you get a cup of the gorgonzola-crème fraîche-chive dip for your crusts—it's the upscale version of the ranch dressing that's more commonly offered. There's usually a pasta special as well.

If you're on the go, you can grab a slice at **JC's New York Pizza Department** (215 Central Ave. NW, 505/766-6973, 11am-10pm Sun.-Wed., 11am-midnight Thurs., 11am-2:30am Fri.-Sat., $6), which specializes in thin-crust pies named after the five boroughs, like Da Bronx: pepperoni and mozzarella.

Spanish

Chef James Campbell Caruso made his name in Santa Fe as a maestro of Spanish cuisine. His Albuquerque outpost, **Más Tapas y Vino** (125 2nd St. NW, 505/923-9080, 7am-2pm and 5:30pm-9:30pm Sun.-Thurs., 7am-2pm and 5pm-10pm Fri.-Sat., $12 tapas, $28 mains), in the Hotel Andaluz, shows off many of his best dishes, but it's not quite as chummy as his other restaurants. But if you're not also visiting Santa Fe and want a creative bite of Iberian goodness (grilled artichokes, or *jamón* with poached pears), consider this a possible special-occasion meal. It also has happy hour from 4pm to 6pm daily.

Information and Services

Tourist Information

The **Albuquerque Convention and Visitors Bureau** (800/284-2282, www.visitalbuquerque.org) offers the most detailed information on the city, maintaining a kiosk on the Old Town plaza

Albuquerque to Gallup

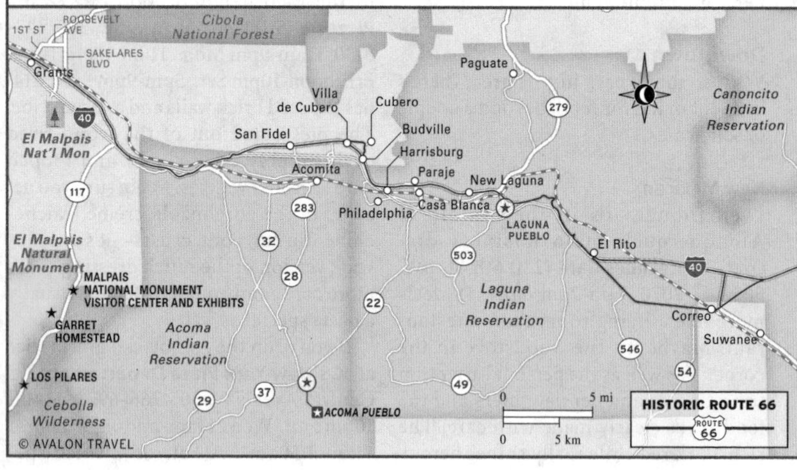

in the summer and a desk at the airport near the baggage claim (9:30am-8pm daily). The **City of Albuquerque website** (www.cabq.gov) is very well organized, with all the essentials about city-run attractions and services.

Banks

Banks are plentiful, and grocery stores and pharmacies increasingly have ATMs inside. Downtown, look for **New Mexico Bank & Trust** (320 Gold Ave. SW, 505/830-8100, 9am-4pm Mon.-Thurs., 9am-5pm Fri.).

In Nob Hill, **Wells Fargo** (3022 Central Ave. SE, 505/255-4372, 9am-5pm Mon.-Thurs., 9am-6pm Fri., 9am-1pm Sat.) is on Central at Dartmouth. Both have 24-hour ATMs.

Laguna Pueblo

About 15 miles west of Albuquerque you'll begin to pass through the 45 square miles of **Laguna Pueblo** (505/552-6654, www.lagunapueblo.org), on which 7,000 Keresan-speaking Ka-waikah (Lake People) live in six villages. You'll know you're in Laguna country when you see the huge, gleaming Route 66 Casino Hotel, reached via exit 140, 25 miles west of the city.

Getting There

As you drive west out of Albuquerque on **Central Avenue/Route 66,** look for the retro Route 66 signs and buildings, which should whet your appetite for the road. West of **Atrisco Vista Boulevard,** Central Avenue becomes I-40's **northern frontage road,** beginning around exit 149. This section runs parallel to I-40 for about 10 miles to the old **Rio Puerco Bridge,** built in 1933 (since decommissioned, though still highly desirable as a subject for photographs).

From the bridge, follow signs for **I-40 West** to join the interstate. The next easily drivable portion of Route 66 begins about 35 miles farther on at **Mesita.** Take **exit 117** off I-40 and turn right down **Mesita Road.** Take the first left to rejoin **Old Route 66.** Head west for five miles to **Laguna Pueblo,** where a sign on a traffic roundabout welcomes you to Historic Route 66 and The 66 Pit Stop gas station and fast-food café serves a mean

Ceremonial Dances

This is only an approximate schedule for ceremonial dances—dates can vary from year to year. Annual feast days typically involve carnivals and markets in addition to dances. Confirm details and start times—usually afternoon, but sometimes following an evening or midnight Mass—with the **Indian Pueblo Cultural Center** (505/843-7270, www.indianpueblo.org) before setting out.

- **January 6** - Laguna (Old Laguna): Feast of Los Tres Reyes
- **March 19** - Laguna (Old Laguna): Feast of San José
- **Easter** - Most pueblos: various dances
- **July 26** - Laguna (Seama): Feast of Saint Anne
- **August 1** - Acoma (Acomita): Feast of San Lorenzo
- **August 15** - Laguna (Mesita): Feast of the Assumption
- **September 2** - Acoma (Sky City): Feast of San Esteban
- **September 8** - Laguna (Encinal): Feast of the Nativity of the Blessed Virgin Mary
- **September 19** - Laguna (Old Laguna): Feast of San José
- **September 25** - Laguna (Paguate): Feast of Saint Elizabeth
- **October 17** - Laguna (Paraje): Feast of Saint Margaret Mary
- **October 24-27** - Laguna (Old Laguna): harvest dance
- **Late November/early December** - Zuni: Shalako
- **December 24** - Acoma (Sky City): luminaria display; Laguna: dances after evening Mass
- **December 25-28** - Acoma (Sky City): Christmas dances; Laguna: Christmas dances, all villages

green-chile burger. Follow the brown signs to continue on Historic Route 66, which is also called NM-124.

San José Mission Church

Established in 1699 when the Laguna people requested a priest (unlike any other pueblo), the **San José Mission Church** stands out for its stark white stucco coating, but this is a relatively recent addition, following a 19th-century renovation. It was mudded and whitewashed every year until the 1950s, when the boom in uranium mining in the area left no time for this maintenance; it's now sealed with stucco.

Inside, between a packed-earth floor and a finely wrought wood ceiling, the late-18th-century altar screen commands the room. It's the work of the so-called Laguna Santero, an unidentified painter who made the innovation of placing icons inside a crowded field of decorative borders and carved and painted columns, creating a work of explosively colorful folk art that was copied elsewhere in the region in subsequent decades.

If you're lucky, **Alfred Pino,** a local artist and informal guide, will be hanging around the church and offer you a personal tour and explanation of the symbols on the altar and the painted elk hides on the walls, in exchange for a tip and donation to the church. The church is officially open 8am to 4:30pm weekdays (after a 7am morning Mass), but it can be open later and on weekends if Alfred's around.

Each of the six villages of Laguna celebrates its own feast day, and then the

Acoma vs. Oñate: Grudge Match

The early history of the conquistadores with Acoma was one of brutal back-and-forth attacks, each purportedly as revenge for an earlier one. The prime Spanish actor was Don Juan de Oñate, the first governor of Spain's newest province. In a 1599 attack, after many previous skirmishes, his men killed hundreds of Acoma, more than decimating the hilltop village.

But Oñate was not content. After the battle, he brought his enemies into a makeshift court and tried them for murder. The sentence for the inevitable guilty verdict was that every male in Acoma over the age of 25 would have one foot cut off; everyone between the ages of 12 and 25 was pressed into slavery; and the children were sent to convents in Mexico.

Oñate was eventually recalled from his post and chastised for his actions. But in 1640, as if to add insult to injury, the Spanish friars presented the Church of San Esteban del Rey—built by Acoma slaves, over more than a decade—to the maimed pueblo population as "restitution" for Oñate's cruelties. As a further gift of salvation, the friars publicly purged and hanged the village's spiritual leaders in the churchyard.

Variations on this treatment happened up and down the Rio Grande, eventually inspiring the Pueblo Revolt of 1680. But Oñate's particular brand of viciousness is probably the most remembered. Shortly after a monument to the conquistador was erected north of Española in 1998, the right foot of the bronze statue turned up missing—someone had snuck in at night and sawed it clean off. An anonymous letter to newspapers stated that the act was "on behalf of our brothers and sisters at Acoma Pueblo." Rumor adds that the prankster vandals also left behind at the statue two miniature feet made of clay, attached to a shield inscribed with the words "The Agony of Defeat."

whole pueblo turns out at the church September 17-19 for the **Feast of San José,** one of the bigger pueblo events in the Albuquerque area.

★ Acoma Pueblo

About 15 miles southwest of I-40 and Paraje, New Mexico, is a flat-topped rock that juts up like a tooth. Atop the rock is the original **Acoma Pueblo,** the village known as **Sky City.**

The pueblo covers about 70 acres and is built entirely of pale, sun-bleached adobe, as it has been since at least AD 1100. Only 50 or so people live on the mesa top year-round, given the hardships of no running water or electricity, but many families maintain homes here, and the place is thronged on September 2, when the pueblo members gather for the **Feast of San Esteban.** The rest of the 2,800 Acoma (People of the White Rock, in their native Keresan) live on the valley floor, which is used primarily as ranchland.

Getting There

After a short drive along Historic Route 66 west from Laguna Pueblo to Paraje, New Mexico (about seven miles), look for the junction with Acorn Road. Turn left to get on Indian Route 23, which travels south across I-40 and on for nearly 15 miles to Acoma Pueblo and the Sky City Cultural Center, where you can book a tour of Sky City.

Sky City

The fragile nature of the windswept village accounts in part for the particularly stringent tourism policies. All visitors must stop at the **Sky City Cultural Center and Haak'u Museum** (Indian Rte. 23, 800/747-0181, www.acomaskycity.org, 9am-5pm daily Mar.-mid-Nov., 9am-5pm Fri.-Sun. mid-Nov.-Feb.) on the main road, which houses a café and shop stocked with local crafts, along with beautiful rotating exhibits on Acoma art and tradition. From here, you must join a guided tour ($23), which transports groups by bus to the village. The road to the top is the one concession to modernity; previously, all goods had to be hauled up the near-vertical cliff faces. The tour lasts about an hour and a half, after which visitors may return by bus or hike down one of the old trails, using hand- and footholds dug into the rock centuries ago. In summer, tours start at 9:30am and depart every 45 minutes or so, with the last one going at 3:30pm. In the winter, the first tour begins at 10:15am, and they go about hourly until 3pm. Definitely call ahead to check that the tours are running and verify times, as the pueblo closes to visitors periodically.

The centerpiece of the village is the **Church of San Esteban del Rey,** one of the most iconic of the Spanish missions in New Mexico. Built between 1629 and 1640, the graceful, simple structure has been inspiring New Mexican architects ever since. (Visitors are not allowed inside, however, nor into the adjoining cemetery.) As much as it represents the pinnacle of Hispano-Indian architecture in the 17th century, it's also a symbol of the brutality of Spanish colonialism, as it rose in the typical way: forced labor. The men of Acoma felled and carried the tree trunks for the ceiling beams from the forest on Mount Taylor, more than 25 miles across the valley, and up the cliff face to the village.

Acoma is well known for its pottery, easily distinguished by the fine black lines that sweep around the curves of the creamy-white vessel. On the best works, the lines are so fine and densely painted, they shimmer almost like a moiré. The clay particular to this area can be worked extremely thin to create a pot that will hum or ring when you tap it. Throughout the village, you have opportunities to buy pieces. Given the constraints of the tour, this can feel slightly pressured, but in many cases, you have the privilege of buying work directly from the artisan who created it.

Accommodations and Food

The cultural center contains the **Y'aak'a Café** (9am-4pm daily Mar.-mid-Nov., 9am-4pm Fri.-Sun. mid-Nov.-Feb., $8), which serves earthy local dishes like lamb stew, tamales, and corn roasted in a traditional *horno* oven—as well as Starbucks coffee.

Acoma Pueblo operates the small-scale **Sky City Casino & Hotel** (888/759-2489, www.skycity.com, $99 d), just off exit 102 of I-40. Its rooms are perfectly clean and functional, and there's a little pool.

Zuni Pueblo

Covering more than 600 square miles and with a population of more than 10,000, Zuni is the largest of the pueblos. For centuries, the Zuni people were spread over a wide area in several settlements. The pueblo Halona:wa (Anthill), around which the modern town of Zuni is based, was established long ago, but did not become the center of population until 1692, after the people made a peace agreement with Don Juan de Oñate and gathered here. With plenty of new, cinder-block construction, the town doesn't look immediately appealing, but if you stay overnight (it's the only pueblo where you can do so), you'll have a better appreciation for the community. If you can't spend the night, certainly take the tour of the small historic core of the village—otherwise Zuni's appeal may be lost in the dust.

Isolation from the Rio Grande-area pueblos has helped keep Zuni culture more distinct—its "*olla* maidens," for instance, perform a traditional dance with pots balanced on their heads. Zuni is also famous for its delicate inlay jewelry, called "needlepoint," in which the tiniest bits of turquoise, coral, and other stones

Zuni Pueblo and Gallup

are set in intricate patterns on a silver field; the texture almost resembles beadwork. Collectors also hold Zuni kachinas (figurines of spirit beings) and fetishes (tiny carved animals) in high esteem. If you're coming here to shop, though, avoid late June and late December, when a period of fasting called Deshkwi bans buying or selling.

Getting There

From Acoma Pueblo, take **Indian Route 38 north** to McCartys, New Mexico, about 15 miles (25 minutes), turning left onto **Pueblo Road.** After 1.5 miles, pick up **Historic Route 66/NM-124** and follow it as it rolls alongside I-40, then passes under it on the way to Grants, about 15 miles (25 minutes) more. Driving through Grants on **Route 66/Santa Fe Avenue,** look for **NM-122 E/NM-53 W** and turn left. From here, it's a 75-mile drive of about 1.5 hours to reach Zuni Pueblo.

Sights

Register first at the **visitors center** (NM-53, 505/782-7238, www.zunitourism.com, 8:30am-5:30pm Mon.-Fri., 10am-4pm Sat., noon-4pm Sun.), midway through town on the north side of the road. Here you can get information on artists' studios as well as arrange a number of tours, including the highly recommended **walking tour** around Old Zuni (Middle Village).

All tours require advance notice, but if you have a particular interest, they are a wonderful way of seeing a different side of Zuni. The visitors center can arrange a 2.5-hour **artist workshop tour** ($75 for up to four people), based on your preferred medium (silver, stone, etc.), as well as a **traditional meal** ($12 pp) featuring local tamales, bread, and more. The former requires three days' notice; the latter, seven. Archaeological site visits are also possible, to **Hawikku,** where ancestral Zuni lived and where Coronado thought one of the "Cities of Gold" might be; and to the **Village of the Great Kivas,** inhabited in the 11th century. Both are $75 for up to four people and require a week's notice.

★ Nuestra Señora de Guadalupe Church

The core of the historic area called the Middle Village is the **Nuestra Señora de Guadalupe Church,** where the walls, first erected in 1629 and rebuilt in 1692, are painted with larger-than-life Shalako figures and other elements of the Zuni tradition as they function in the four seasons. The brilliantly colored murals, created over more than 20 years beginning in 1970, are the work of one esteemed pueblo artist, Alex Seowtewa, and his sons. Together with the blankets and buffalo heads, this is one of the most syncretic churches in the state—a beautiful, fervent expression of faith over millennia.

The church is accessible only by **guided tour** (10am, 1pm, and 3pm Mon.-Sat., 1pm and 3pm Sun.), which departs from the Zuni visitors center. Theoretically, two separate tours are offered: one around the old town and one to the church, each for $10. But in practice, all visitors are usually lumped into a single tour of everything for $15. The whole combined tour takes a little over an hour.

A:shíwi A:wan Museum and Heritage Center

Zuni's small **A:shíwi A:wan Museum and Heritage Center** (2 E. Ojo Caliente Rd., 505/782-4403, www.ashiwi-museum.org, 9am-6pm Mon.-Fri., free) is fascinating. It tells the story of the Zuni people, from creation myths through more contemporary issues with archaeologists and other researchers, such as Frank Cushing, who brought the pueblo to broader attention in the 19th century and became a local hero for a time. Cushing's endeavors are portrayed in a few hilarious cartoons by a Zuni artist. Also on display are artifacts from the ancestral settlement of Hawikku, excavated in 1916. They had been whisked away to a basement in a branch of the

Smithsonian; Zuni leaders negotiated for this selection to be returned, leaving the remainder to be better preserved at the Smithsonian.

The museum is just south of Highway 53: Turn at the major stop sign on the west end of town; the museum is at the next big intersection, on the northwest corner, across from Halona Plaza.

Festivals and Events

The largest event of the year, the ritual of **Shalako** (also spelled Sha'la'ko) marks the end of the agricultural season and the beginning of winter in late November or early December. Although many of the prayers and dances take place in areas closed to visitors, it is still a remarkable time to visit the pueblo.

The Shalako, part of the extensive pantheon of kachinas, act as messengers between man and gods; when they depart the village, they are bearing the Zuni prayer for rain in the spring. For this ceremony, they are men who are elected each year to impersonate these godlike forces, and they spend the entire year preparing. The 24-hour ritual begins around noon, but the real excitement comes at dusk, when the men descend from the sacred mesa south of town. With giant eagle-feather masks with goggle eyes and wooden beaks, they are transformed into frightening, noisy, 10-foot-tall creatures; they are an awesome sight as they swoop through the crowds and the bonfires, their beaks clacking and the drums pounding behind them. As they proceed around the village, lit only by bonfires, the effect is transporting.

Shortly after Shalako, the whole community gathers for the **Give-Away,** to thank the clans involved in the ritual—preparation is a massive expense. People bring specific gifts as well as all manner of unused items, from deer meat to refrigerators, which are redistributed according to need. Again, it's a ceremony that outsiders may not entirely get, but it's a festive time to be in town.

Accommodations and Food

Unlike most pueblos, where visitors are welcome for the day or as casino customers, Zuni offers a unique opportunity to stay overnight and just soak up the atmosphere of the place: wood smoke, red dirt, and sparkling stars. The supremely comfortable ★ **Inn at Halona** (23-B Pia Mesa Rd., 505/782-4418, www.halona.com, $79) is run by a French native whose late wife had century-old roots on the reservation. The older main house has five rooms (no. 4 upstairs is beautifully sunny, while the basement no. 5 is big yet cozy-feeling), but you might prefer the side house if you like to sleep late, because the scene in the main house's breakfast room can get pretty animated. Guests dig in to what seems like an endless array of breads, eggs, meats, and the signature blue-corn pancakes. Book well ahead if you plan to be in town during any special events.

The main place to eat is the adjacent general store, **Halona Plaza,** where the deli counter serves up excellent fried chicken ($6) with smoky-hot red-chile sauce on the side—New Mexican fusion at its finest. There's a bit more of a social scene at night down at **Chu-Chu's** (1344 NM-53, 505/782-2100, 11am-10pm, Mon.-Sat., $8), on the east end of the town, where there's pizza, subs, and a nice little patio.

The seriously food-curious should also stop in to **Paywa's Bakery** (noon-5pm Wed.-Fri.), down a dirt road opposite Chu-Chu's. The operation bakes sourdough and sweet pies in a giant adobe *horno.*

Gallup

Initially just a wide spot along the railroad, Gallup took its name from the man who doled out cash in exchange for the coal that companies hauled in from the surrounding mines in the 1880s. By the 1920s, Gallup was known for its exceptionally pure coal, which meant higher wages for workers, who flooded in from Britain, China, Italy, Greece, and scores of other places, making the town a polyglot community from early on. The mining business has slowed, but at least a hundred trains still rumble through every day—it's a near-constant background noise, and as the freight loads cruise right through the center of town, you often have the disconcerting sensation of looking down a street and seeing the background in motion.

Gallup's other disconcerting effect is the sense you've stepped onto a movie set. The place was a popular Hollywood location from the 1930s on through the Route 66 heyday, and it's not hard to see why, what with the glowing neon, the red sandstone cliffs, and the jagged Hogback Mountains, which inspire visions of Wild West adventure. Less glamorously, in the 1970s and 1980s, Gallup struggled with high unemployment and astronomical rates of drunk driving and alcoholism. But one get-tough mayor started a turnaround, and now downtown is clean and lively, and the civic pride is palpable.

Getting There

The drive to Gallup from Zuni Pueblo is **40 miles,** which takes slightly under **an hour.** From the pueblo, head east on **NM-53** for about five miles. At the junction with **NM-602,** turn left and drive **north.** After 30 miles, NM-602 will deposit you directly onto **Route 66/Highway 66** in Gallup.

Sights

The railway and I-40 divide Gallup in two, but most of what visitors want is on the south side: The historic downtown area is on Highway 66 and Coal Avenue, lined with the most notable buildings and shops. The far east and west ends of town cater to through travelers on the interstate, with all the chain hotels and restaurants.

You can cover most of Gallup's attractions on foot after parking downtown. Some of the best art is outdoors, in the many murals around town, some painted by the WPA in the 1930s and others put up in the 21st century. There's one dedicated to the Navajo code talkers on South 2nd Street just south of Highway 66, as well as a great modern one on the side of the city hall (Aztec Avenue at South 2nd Street) that evokes modern life in Gallup: kids in pickup trucks, road construction, and rodeo events.

McKinley County Courthouse

Downtown is anchored by the Pueblo Revival **McKinley County Courthouse** (207 W. Hill St.), one block south of Coal Avenue. If you ask nicely and it's a slow day, you can walk around inside the courthouse and admire the tile work, the punched-tin light fixtures, and the 2,000-square-foot WPA mural in the main courtroom. Painted by Lloyd Moylan, it's the largest surviving work from that period in the state.

WWII Navajo Code Talkers Museum

Adjoining the chamber of commerce, the **WWII Navajo Code Talkers Museum** (103 W. Hwy. 66, 505/722-2228, 8am-5pm Mon.-Fri., free) is a large collection of memorabilia arranged in fluorescent-lit glass cases—ask the chamber employees to turn the lights on. No frills here: The room is mostly used for business meetings, but the collected papers, photographs, and clippings trace the use of the Navajo language as code through the fight. Given the importance of the code to the success of the U.S. campaign, it's a little depressing to realize this is one of the largest permanent exhibits on the subject (there's another inside the Burger King in Kayenta, Arizona).

Multi-Cultural Center

The old Santa Fe Rail station has been converted into a well-used community

The Navajo Code Talkers

The ingenuity and heroism of the Navajo code talkers of World War II has only come to full light in recent decades. As a result, this team of more than 300 men (and one Anglo fighter fluent in Navajo) has become a novel footnote in the history of the war, rather than a crucial element in the U.S. military's victory. In fact, the never-broken code, based on Navajo vocabulary, was an essential part of the Battle of Iwo Jima, and the code talkers were involved in every Marine battle in the Pacific.

Twenty-nine recruits formed the first team of code talkers, who also developed the code. At its core, the system used Navajo words to represent letters of the alphabet—these could be used to spell, or combined to form larger words and concepts. For instance, *w* was represented by the Navajo word for weasel, *gloe-ih*. To say "when," the code talker said "weasel" and "hen": *gloe-ih-na-ah-wo-hai;* "will" was *gloe-ih-dot-sahi,* or "sick weasel." Military terms required more creativity: a *bish-lo,* or "iron fish," was a submarine.

The advantage of Navajo was that it was a highly complex yet completely oral language, with only a handful of nonnative speakers. Moreover, it was extremely fast to transmit, because unlike previous systems, it didn't require a machine at either end. The code talkers have long been a point of pride for the Navajo, especially as symbols of the power of speaking the ancestral language.

A mural by Be Sargent on South 2nd Street in Gallup depicts the code in visual form, showing the original 29 code talkers along with the various animals and objects used as keys in the code.

arts center. Visitors will enjoy the **Storyteller Museum** (201 E. Hwy. 66, 505/863-4131, 10am-4pm Tues.-Sat., free) upstairs. The nifty collection of dioramas—scenes involving model trains, a replica trading post—are accompanied by headphones to listen to a local's explanation of the scene. You'll also find a café, a visitors info desk, a music shop, and the **Ceremonial Gallery,** which exhibits local student art.

Between Memorial Day and Labor Day, free guided **walking tours** of downtown depart from here, usually at 10am daily.

Rex Museum

Like many small-town collections, the **Rex Museum** (300 W. Hwy. 66, 505/863-1363, 9am-6pm Mon.-Fri., $2 donation) is a hodgepodge, from roller skates to programs from the Inter-Tribal Ceremonial. But perhaps it's most interesting to see the traces of the various immigrant groups that have settled in Gallup, from Chinese to Greeks.

Red Rock Park

East of town about six miles, **Red Rock Park** is Gallup's public party spot, with rodeo grounds and an outdoor amphitheater. It also has the surprisingly large **Red Rock Museum** (505/722-3839, 8am-noon and 1pm-5pm Mon.-Fri., $2 donation), which feels as though it was set up in the 1970s, then left to its own devices. The display cases, filled with information on the Zuni, Hopi, and Navajo, are a little dusty; you'll probably have to turn the lights on yourself. It houses one of the most elaborate displays of Zuni kachinas anywhere—all the figurines labeled, and their roles explained. There's also a model hogan (the traditional Navajo home) and a selection of local jewelry styles. Access the park via the frontage road (E. Hwy. 66), from exit 33 or exit 26 off I-40, then turn north on Highway 566.

Entertainment and Events

On an average day, the streets of Gallup are not exactly hopping. You will notice a significant rush on weekends, though, as people from surrounding communities come into town to do business. And expect crowds during the two big annual events, a powwow and a balloon rally. The landmark **El Morro Theatre** (110 W. Aztec Ave., 505/726-0050, www.elmorrotheatre.com) is downtown, built in 1926 in the Spanish colonial revival style. It's a venue for films as well as local theater and music.

Nightlife

Gallup's past alcohol problems mean liquor laws are strict, and few places stay open very late. Even **Coal Street Pub** (303 W. Coal Ave., 505/722-0117, 11am-10pm Sun.-Wed., 11am-11pm Thurs.-Sat.), the main bar downtown, serves only beer and wine. It's a convivial place in the evening, often with some kind of live music on the weekends.

The **49er Lounge** (1000 E. Hwy. 66, 5pm-1am daily) in the El Rancho Hotel does serve booze, but you might not need it because the setting is dizzying enough—like the rest of the hotel, this place exudes an almost overwhelming aura of decaying Western glamour. Go early, as it tends to close before the posted time if business is slow.

On weekends, you might also find mellow live music at **Angela's Café** (201 E. Hwy. 66, 505/722-7526, 9am-5pm Mon.-Thurs., 9am-9pm Fri., 11am-5pm Sat., $7).

Festivals and Events

Every night at 7pm between Memorial Day and Labor Day, Navajo, Hopi, and other dance and music groups perform in the plaza in front of the courthouse, for free.

For four days in late July or early August, Gallup hosts the **Inter-Tribal Indian Ceremonial** (www.theceremonial.com), which draws more than 20,000 participants from various tribes in Canada and Mexico, as well as all over the United States. Also on the schedule are a beauty pageant, a fashion show, and lots of music.

The other big annual event is the **Red Rock Balloon Rally** (www.redrockballoonrally.com), on the first weekend in December. With about 200 participating hot-air balloons, it has been going strong since 1981, probably because the setting, against the vibrant sandstone at Red Rock Park, is unbeatable. The balloonists often need extra volunteers, so it's a good chance to get a free ride or join a chase crew—show up early and ask around.

Shopping

With a historic trading post or overstocked pawnshop seemingly every 10 feet, Gallup can be an exciting or overwhelming place to shop, depending on your point of view. But even if you don't feel up to sifting through treasure troves of Navajo turquoise, the **trading posts,** some in business for the better part of a century and still doing business primarily with the local Indian population, are worth a visit simply as another town attraction. They're stocked with everything from hand-spun skeins of wool to crisp new blue jeans, and of course, heaps and heaps of jewelry.

One of the oldest, most respected trading posts downtown is **Richardson's Trading Co. & Cash Pawn** (222 W. Hwy. 66, 505/722-4762, 9am-6pm Mon.-Sat.), where the warren of storefronts is permeated with the smell of old leather.

Another shopping hot spot is **City Electric Shoe Shop** (230 W. Coal Ave., 505/863-5252, 10am-6pm Mon.-Sat.), where you can pick up a pair of street-ready moccasins in butter-soft suede or an embossed leather belt—both are made in a workshop in the basement.

On the south side, **Ellis Tanner Trading Co.** (1980 Hwy. 602, 505/863-4434, 8am-7pm Mon.-Sat.) has deep roots in Gallup; check inside for a huge mural by local artist Chester Kahn, honoring locals who have been good role models. You can pick up roasted piñon nuts, Diné-English children's books, vintage dance regalia, and more.

But perhaps the best shopping experience in Gallup is at the 9th Street **flea market** (505/722-7328) every Saturday on the north side of town. It's a great swap meet where you can pick up anything from a beaded necklace to a wolf-mix puppy to a bale of hay—not to mention all kinds of traditional foods. Vendors get rolling around 10am, and wind up in the mid-afternoon. To get there, head north on US 491, then cut east to North 9th Street on West Jefferson Avenue.

Sports and Recreation

The city of Gallup has developed great trails on the nearby sandstone bluffs and in the ponderosa-covered Zuni Mountains. There's a lot to do in a relatively small area, and it's all still crowd-free. For additional details to what follows, see the **Adventure Gallup website** (www.adventuregallup.org), or pick up a comprehensive map from the chamber of commerce.

Biking

The main mountain biking network is the **High Desert Trail System.** The three interconnecting loops, each rated for a different skill level, run along the mesas northwest of town. In addition to great views over cliff edges and some tricky constructed switchbacks, the trails are marked by occasional public art—so just when you think the weird rock formations are sculpture enough, you might look up to see a black steel bobcat peering down at you. The main trailhead, called Gamerco, is two miles north on US 491, then left on Chino Loop; the gravel parking lot is on the left side of the road.

For shady forest biking, head to the **Zuni Mountain Trail System,** a patch of national forest southeast of Gallup. From exit 33 on I-40, Highway 400 runs south about six miles to Hilso Trailhead, the beginning of several climbs up through ponderosa forests and aspens; nearly all intersect up on the ridgeline, so you can come back a different way.

In town, **Brickyard Park** (700 E. Aztec Ave.) is a mountain bike terrain park in Gallup's old clay quarry. Come here to practice your skills on dirt tracks and jumps.

Hiking

Hikers are also welcome on the High Desert and Zuni Mountain trails, though two-wheelers have the right-of-way. In the latter area, **Strawberry Canyon Trail** is a shady, easy 1.5-mile hike up to a lookout tower, and it runs along a rough forest road, so there's room for both bikers and hikers. Follow Highway 400 past Hilso Trailhead, up to mile marker 0; just past the entrance to McGaffey Campground is a parking area on the right.

At two accessible trails close to town, you get the whole place to yourself. They both start in Red Rock Park: **Pyramid Rock Trail** is a 1.7-mile hike up to 7,487 feet, atop an aptly named butte. **Church Rock Trail** is 2.2 miles round-trip (a stem with a loop at the end)—it's less of a climb, working around the base of some dramatic rocks. An optional connector trail (1.3 miles) links the two routes, making a full hike of three to four hours.

Rock Climbing

A well-maintained public park east of town, **Mentmore Rock Climbing Area** is frequented by only a handful of local regulars. With 31 sport routes and 50 bolted top-rope climbs spread over six different walls, along with quite a few bouldering options, there's more than enough fun to go around. At least some of the rocks get sun all the time, so it's climbable in the winter, but check the weather before heading out. The sandstone is fragile when wet, so local policy is to stay off the rocks for a couple of days after heavy rain. To get there, take exit 16 from I-40 and head west on Highway 66 for half a mile; turn north on County Road 1, then bear west as it turns into Mentmore Road, leading directly to the parking area.

Swimming

Gallup Aquatic Center (620 S. Boardman Ave., 505/726-5460, $4) is a kid's dream, with curvy slides galore, cactus-shaped sprinklers, and even a "lazy river" setup; adults get a separate competition-size pool for laps. It's all indoors, but still a lot of fun.

Accommodations

Even if you don't plan to spend the night, do stop in at ★ **El Rancho Hotel** (1000 E. Hwy. 66, 505/863-9311, www.elranchohotel.com, $92 s, $102 d). The lobby alone is a Western fantasia of rustic wood paneling, furniture made of bull horns, a giant stone fireplace, and glossy photos of all the Hollywood actors who passed through the doors back in Gallup's heyday as a movie backdrop. (It helped that the man who built the place in 1937 was D. W. Griffith's brother.) Rooms named after Kirk Douglas, Ronald Reagan, and others are kitted out with wagon-wheel headboards and vintage bathroom tile; some even have back porches.

A separate motel wing has significantly less character but perfectly clean and functional rooms—rates here start at $60. Guests at both have access to a decent swimming pool, and there's (sometimes spotty) wireless Internet access in the lobby. Practically speaking, rooms in the main hotel seem faintly overpriced. But for sheer atmosphere, this is one of the best places in the state to get a taste of what tourism must've been like back when New Mexico really was the wild frontier. Ignore the unreliable online booking engine (which doesn't show the motel rooms)—just call to reserve.

Food

All the chain places (and a couple of vintage diners) are near the freeway exits. You definitely get more local flavor, in every sense, if you venture into the center of town.

New Mexican

Family-owned, with a battered neon sign, ★ **Jerry's Café** (406 W. Coal Ave., 505/722-6775, 8am-9pm Mon.-Sat., $8) has a crowd of dedicated followers (read: addicts) who drive miles for the stuffed sopaipilla, drenched in superhot red-chile sauce. The place is tiny and often packed with courthouse employees during lunchtime, so go late or early.

It may not have the absolute best food in town, but **Earl's** (1400 E. Hwy. 66, 505/863-4201, 6am-8:30pm Mon.-Sat., 7:30am-6:30pm Sun., $8) has a timeless atmosphere that can't be beat. Since 1947, it has been serving biscuits and gravy, Navajo tacos, and enchiladas. It's conveniently close to the east-side freeway exit, and gets packed after the Saturday flea market. You'll either love or hate the fact that local artisans go table to table selling their wares.

If you're not staying at El Rancho, you could pop in for a perfectly good meal at the **El Rancho Restaurant** (1000 E. Hwy. 66, 505/863-9311, 6:30am-10pm daily, $11), where all the dishes are named after Hollywood stars. New Mexican food is your best bet, including *atole* (cornmeal mush) for breakfast; the margaritas ($7 for "top shelf" with fresh lime juice) are dangerously strong.

Cafés

The whitewashed **Coffee House** (203 W. Coal Ave., 505/726-0291, 7am-8:30pm Mon.-Sat., $6) has an old tin ceiling, contemporary photography on the walls, and a mellow atmosphere where Navajo artists and fleece-clad mountain bikers mingle. Evenings often see some local singer-songwriter. The menu ranges from fresh salads and big sandwiches to a full breakfast.

With a nice small-town diner vibe, **Angela's Café** (201 E. Hwy. 66, 505/722-7526, 9am-5pm Mon.-Thurs., 9am-9pm Fri., 11am-5pm Sat., $7), in the cultural center in the former train station, serves burgers and a good selection of craft beers to locals. Despite its opening hours, it doesn't really do breakfast—just an egg sandwich for waiting train passengers. In the evenings, there's occasionally acoustic music.

★ **Glenn's Bakery** (900 W. Hwy. 66, 505/722-4104, 6am-9pm Mon.-Sat., $3-10) is impressive first for its dazzling doughnut case, which includes wonderfully flaky cinnamon rolls. If you need more than a sugar fix, settle in alongside locals reading the morning papers for breakfast burritos, pizza, or one of the daily specials, such as lamb stew.

Aside from the fact that all burgers are served well-done, **The 505 Burgers & Wings** (1981 Hwy. 602, 505/722-9311, 11am-7pm Mon.-Fri., 11am-3pm Sat., $9) is pretty good, with hand-cut fries, pretzel-bread buns, and nice fresh sides. And, with an almost entirely local clientele, it's a good glimpse of regular life in Gallup. Look for it in a small strip mall on the south side of town.

Information

Conveniently located right downtown, the staff at the **chamber of commerce** (106 W. Hwy. 66, 505/722-2228, www.thegallupchamber.com, 8:30am-5pm Mon.-Sat. late May-early Sept., 8:30am-5pm Mon.-Fri. early Sept.-late May) can answer just about any question.

★ Petrified Forest National Park

What once was a swampy forest frequented by ancient oversized reptiles is now **Petrified Forest National Park** (928/524-6228, www.nps.gov/pefo, daily year-round, $10 per vehicle for 7 days), a blasted scrubland strewn with multicolored, quartz-wrapped logs some 225 million years old, each one possessing a smooth, multicolored splotch or swirl seemingly unique from the rest. You can walk among the logs on several easy,

Painted Desert, Petrified Forest National Park

paved trails and view a small ruin and petroglyph-covered rocks (best with binoculars, but there are viewing scopes provided). Then, while driving through the pastel-hued badlands of the **Painted Desert,** which, seen from **Tawa Point** along the park's 28-mile scenic drive, will take your breath away, stop at the **Painted Desert Inn Museum.** The historical interest in this Pueblo Revival-style structure is more modern than primordial. Redesigned by Mary Colter, the great genius of Southwestern style and elegance, the inn was a restaurant and store operated by the Fred Harvey Company just after World War II, and before that it was a rustic, out-of-the-way hotel and taproom built from petrified wood. There's a gift shop and bookstore at the inn now, and you can walk through it and gaze at the evocative, mysterious murals, full of Hopi mythology and symbolism, painted by Fred Kabotie, the great Hopi artist whom Colter commissioned to decorate the inn's walls. The park's proximity both to a major railroad stop at Winslow and Route 66 have made it a popular Southwestern tourist attraction since the late 19th century, and the lore and style of that golden age of tourism pervade the park, creating an air of pleasant nostalgia and adding an extra, unexpected dimension to the overwhelming age all around you.

Getting There

The **Painted Desert entrance** to Petrified Forest National Park is a **one-hour** drive west from Gallup, New Mexico, a distance of about **70 miles.** For about 25 miles, between Gallup and Lupton, Arizona, take **NM-118/Historic Route 66,** which runs alongside I-40. Between Lupton and the park entrance, a distance of about 50 miles, **Historic Route 66** and **I-40** mostly overlap, so the drive takes no time at all, zipping along at 75 mph. The eastern/Painted Desert entrance to the national park is at **exit 311** off I-40.

It's a 30-mile drive through the park, stopping at the sights and lookouts, to Rainbow Forest Museum on the south end. From there, pick up **US 180** to Holbrook. **Historic Route 66** pops up again here, moving through the small town's dilapidated downtown.

Visiting the Park

There are two visitors centers: Painted Desert Visitor Center, at the north entrance, and Rainbow Forest Museum, at the south end of the park road. Both show a short movie about the park and pass out free maps of all the stops. They're also both on the same operating schedule (7am-7pm daily May-Sept., 7am-6pm daily late Sept.-Oct., 8am-5pm daily Nov.-Feb.).

Park Road Driving Tour

It doesn't really matter which direction you enter the park from. To really see this understated masterpiece of a national park, you should drive the entire 30-mile

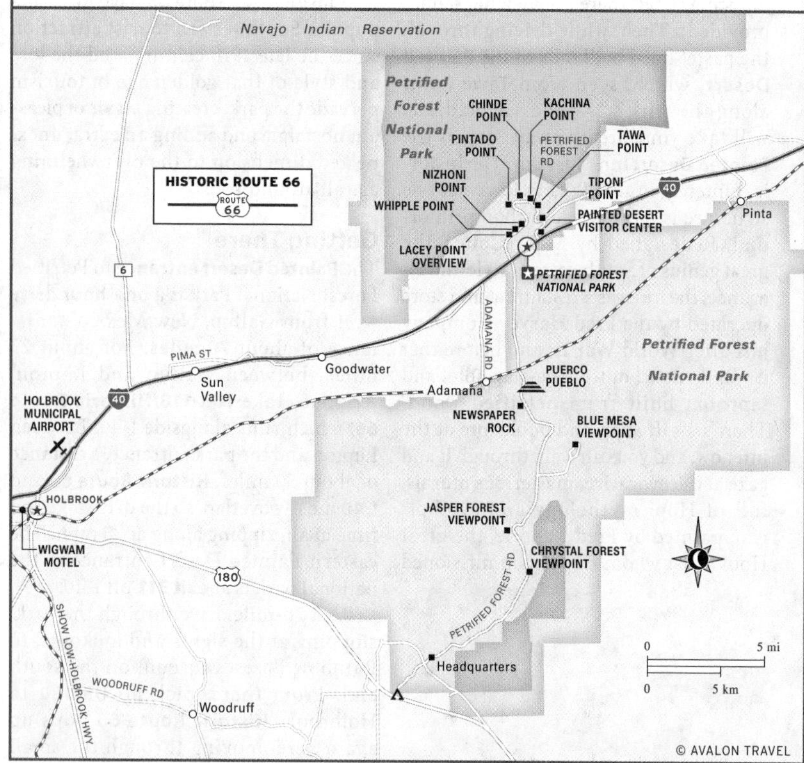

route, stopping at the pullouts along the way, with time out for short hikes into the colorful badlands.

The Painted Desert section of the park comes into view as you enter from the east off I-40, exit 311. Beginning your drive through the park from the **Painted Desert Visitor Center,** you'll first pass several viewpoints from which to view the mysterious Painted Desert, including **Tawa Point,** where the views are long, subtle, colorful, and barren. It is a wondrous, exotic landscape. Make sure to stop at the **Painted Desert Inn Museum,** where you'll see one of the most dramatic petroglyphs in the state—a large, stylized mountain lion etched into a slab of rock. After the museum, you'll pass **Pintado Point,** one of the best views of the strange land. Before you cross over the usually dry Puerco River and the Santa Fe Railroad tracks, watch out for the rusted husk of a **1932 Studebaker** sitting alone off the side of the road. This artifact marks the line that old Route 66 once took through the park, roughly visible now in the alignment of the power lines stretching west behind the car.

A few miles farther down the road, the **Newspaper Rock** petroglyphs and **Puerco Pueblo ruin** preserve the cultural leftovers of the people that once lived and thrived on this high desert plain. Continuing on through the Petrified Forest, look out for the hard-to-miss red-and-grey formations aptly named **The Tepees.** Strange, multicolored cliffs, worn and sculpted into fantastic shapes, are the main attraction of **Blue Mesa.** See it via a one-mile, fairly steep loop trail or a 3.5-mile loop road off the main road through the park. Farther south, the **Agate Bridge** pullout features a 110-foot-long bridge made of petrified logs. Nearby, there's a whole fallen petrified forest scattered around the otherwise barren stretch called **Jasper Forest,** and just up the road a bit is **Crystal Forest,** which has a paved, 0.75-mile loop trail among the petrified logs. Finally you'll reach the **Rainbow Forest Museum,** which has some amazing fossils and displays about the dinosaurs that once ruled this land. Around the museum, the **Long Logs Trail** is a 1.6-mile loop along which you'll see some of the longest petrified logs in the park, and the **Giant Logs Trail** is an easy, half-mile loop trail that features a few of the largest stone trees in the park. It's easy to combine this trail with a walk to **Agate House,** a reconstructed pueblo made of petrified wood. The combined hike is 2.6 miles round-trip.

Practicalities

Both visitors centers have excellent gift shops, and rangers are always on hand to answer your questions. The only place to get a meal in the park is the south entrance's Fred Harvey Company restaurant, ★ **Painted Desert Diner** (928/524-3756, 8am-4pm daily, $3-9), which serves delicious fried chicken, Navajo tacos, burgers, and other road-food favorites in a cool Route 66 retro dining room. The south entrance visitors center has snacks for sale, but consider bringing your own food and especially water, as the park is spread out and it is a 28-mile drive between visitors centers.

Holbrook

Long ago, by most accounts, Holbrook was a rough and violent cowboy town; then it profited, like everything else in this region, from the railroad and Route 66, back when tourists would necessarily stay a while. These days it's not much more than a convenient gateway and stopover for those visiting the nearby Petrified Forest National Park and Indian Country, offering several chain hotels and mostly fast food. The town preserves a bit of its former Route 66 scene along Hopi Drive.

Getting There

Holbrook is about **20 miles** northwest of Petrified Forest National Park's south entrance via **US 180,** a drive of less than **30 minutes.** From the park's south entrance, turn right to join **US 180 West** and drive for almost 20 miles. At **Apache Avenue,** turn right to follow the highway less than a mile into town. Historic Route 66 runs through the downtown area before meeting up again with I-40.

Sights

For those interested in the history of both the old and the modern West, a trip to the **Navajo County Historical Society's Museum** (100 E. Arizona St., 928/524-6558 or 800/524-2459, 8am-4pm daily, free) in the 1880s Navajo County Court House is a must. Donations are encouraged and rewarded with free chips of petrified wood. It's a strange, crowded place without a lot of context—you feel like you're wandering around an abandoned government building after the population has died out. Sitting in the old jail, used until the 1970s and still decorated with the graffiti and sketches of its former inmates, is an eerie, almost thrilling experience.

Accommodations and Food

American popular architecture like that employed at the **Wigwam Motel** (811 W. Hopi Dr., 928/524-3048, www.galerie-kokopelli.com/wigwam, $56-62) had its postwar heyday along Route 66, and, like the route itself, it is mostly gone from the landscape these days in favor of cookie-cutter chains. But the kitschy tradition still has a hold on these dry high-desert plains at the Wigwam Motel in Holbrook, one of the last of many similarly designed motor courts that once lined the Mother Road. It's clean and comfortable and has all the updated amenities, but a stay here is mostly about its retro appeal. It should not be missed by Route 66 enthusiasts, road-trip scholars, chroniclers of fading Americana, and the like.

Joe & Aggie's Cafe (120 W. Hopi Dr., 866/486-0021, http://joeandaggiescafe.com, 6am-8pm Mon.-Sat., $5-15) serves excellent Mexican and American food along Route 66/Hopi Drive through Holbrook's dilapidated downtown and celebrates the golden age of the Mother Road.

Winslow and Vicinity

Stop at this small, ex-Route 66, ex-railroad town if you happen to be in the area. Much of its historic downtown remains intact, if not too busy, and there are a few off-track treasures to be found if you have time to walk around. The town seems committed to celebrating the fact that its name appeared in the song "Take It Easy," an Eagles hit co-penned by Jackson Browne. There are reminders in nearly every business, and there's even **Standin' on the Corner Park** along the town's main street, featuring a statue of a man doing just that. The primary reason to stop in Winslow is to see **La Posada,** Southwestern architect Mary

Top to bottom: Painted Desert Inn Museum; Holbrook's Wigwam Motel; La Posada.

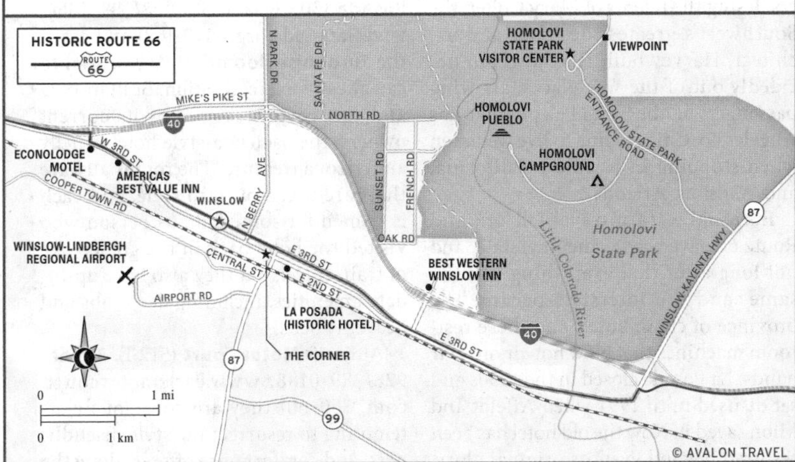

Colter's masterpiece and a place where Fred Harvey-style outback elegance is kept alive.

Getting There

From Holbrook to Winslow, **Historic Route 66** merges with **I-40,** resulting in a **35-mile** sprint (just over **30 minutes**) west toward Flagstaff. **Hopi Drive** leads out of Holbrook and takes you directly to **I-40 West.** Take **exit 255** off the interstate and join **Old Highway 66** to get into Winslow.

Sights

The **Old Trails Museum** (212 Kinsley Ave., 928/289 5861, www.oldtrailsmuseum.org, 10am-4pm Tues.-Sat., free) in downtown Winslow is a treasure trove of strange and thrilling artifacts, photographs, and stories about life in the high desert, with a special emphasis on the region's Route 66 past and its connection with the stylish railroad era of the Fred Harvey Company. The museum also has a fine collection of Navajo arts and crafts, and all kinds of weird and forgotten items that take on new historical meaning and emotional color simply by virtue of being old and saved. It's a small museum but definitely worth a stop for anyone interested in Route 66, the railroad, and Fred Harvey, and a visit here should be paired with a look around the restored Harvey House, La Posada.

La Posada

Now owned by Allen Affeldt and his wife, the brilliant painter Tina Mion (whose paintings fill the arched hallways of the hotel), **La Posada** (303 E. 2nd St., 928/289-4366, www.laposada.org) has been beautifully restored and is a reminder of the days when Indian Country was a chic travel destination for the rich and famous.

This was largely the result of the genius of Fred Harvey. He and his "Harvey Girls"—well-trained professional young women imported to the West to serve train passengers at Harvey's restaurants along the Santa Fe Railroad's right-of-way—made a trip to this barren, underdeveloped high desert an experience quite beyond merely comfortable. The Harvey Company lunch counters and hotel restaurants offered fine dining and fresh, gourmet food prepared by European chefs, and the unmatched service of the Harvey Girls, many of whom ended up marrying their customers. Using the talents of Mary Colter, the Southwest's greatest designer and architect, Harvey built fine hotels in decidedly out-of-the-way places, allowing passengers on the Santa Fe's popular Los Angeles-to-Chicago line to live well even when stopping in Needles, California, and Winslow, Arizona.

Eventually train travel fell off, and Route 66 gave way to the interstate, and not long after that everything was the same, and the interstate became the province of chain hotels and those restroom machines that blow hot air on your hands. La Posada closed in the 1950s and sat disused until 1997 when Affeldt and Mion saved it. Now the old hotel has been restored beyond even its original glory, and it's booked up often with guests from all over the world. The hotel is especially popular these days with Europeans, many of whom rent motorcycles and ride the remainders of Route 66, searching for some lost version of the "America Road." Affeldt said recently that the irony of this phenomenon was not lost on a modern-day celebrity visitor to La Posada: the "Easy Rider" himself, Peter Fonda.

Even if you aren't staying overnight, you can visit the galleries, restaurant, gift shop, and beautifully restored lobby. Never mind that there's still not much to see in Winslow: You could spend two full days exploring this hotel—walking its tiled and arched corridors and its lush green grounds, looking at co-owner and artist Tina Mion's gallery of strange and thrilling paintings, eating locally sourced, Fred Harvey-inspired meals at the Turquoise Room, or just sitting outside on the back platform, watching the trains go by.

Accommodations

There are several chain hotels and fast-food places off the interstate at Winslow for those in a hurry.

People travel to this lonely, ramshackle high-desert town just to stay at ★ **La Posada** (303 E. 2nd St., 928/289-4366, www.laposada.org, $119-169) and eat at the **Turquoise Room,** so it's essential to call ahead for a reservation. Built in 1929 and obsessively restored by its current owners, the hacienda-style hotel is truly an Arizona treasure. The rooms all have that rare touch of retro style, and each is named for some famous person who visited the hotel back in the golden age of train travel; but they also have up-to-date amenities, including deep tubs and heavenly beds.

At **Earl's Motor Court** (512 E. 3rd St., 928/289-0188, www.earlsmotorcourt.com, $50-60) they are consciously attempting to resurrect the style, friendliness, and comfort once offered along the route, and doing a pretty fair job of it too. Earl's is the best place to stay in town, besides La Posada of course.

Food

The independently operated ★ **Turquoise Room** (La Posada, 928/289-2888, breakfast, lunch, and dinner daily, $15-40, reservations required for dinner), just off La Posada's main lobby, serves "Fred Harvey-inspired" meals like prime rib and steak along with a wild blend of gourmet dishes under the heading "Native American-inspired nouvelle cuisine." Interesting, creative, and delicious is what that means. This is the best restaurant in the region and one of the best in the state.

The **Casa Blanca Café** (1201 E. 2nd St., 928/289-4191, 11am-9pm daily, $4-16) serves decent Mexican and American food in a casual setting.

Information and Services

The **Winslow Chamber of Commerce** (101 E. 2nd St., 928/289-2434, 9am-5pm Mon.-Fri., 9am-3pm Sat.) offers tourist information and advice on the region.

Flagstaff

The San Francisco Peaks, Arizona's tallest mountains and the Olympus of the Hopi kachina, watch over this highland hub. The redbrick, railroad-era downtown sits at around 7,000 feet, and the whole area is covered under about 100 inches of snow every year. In the summer it's mild, in the 70s and 80s mostly, but it gets cold from September to December. In the deep winter through early April, daytime temperatures are cold, and nighttime lows dip well below freezing.

Always a crossroads, Flagstaff is especially so these days, thriving as a tourism gateway to the Grand Canyon, Indian Country, and the Colorado Plateau. It is also a college town attracting students from all over the world, and a major pull-off along I-40. Despite all that, it has managed to retain a good bit of its small mountain-town charm and Old West-through-Route 66 character. Its picturesque qualities, combined with its myriad opportunities for outdoor adventuring, make Flagstaff a major northland tourist draw in its own right.

Getting There and Around

Car

Between Winslow and Flagstaff, **Historic Route 66** mostly follows **I-40** for a **60-mile, one-hour** straight shot of a drive. From Winslow, it's 45 miles to Winona (exit 211), a place made famous in the song "Route 66." About five miles after Winona, take **exit 204** to pick up **Historic Route 66** through the outskirts of Flagstaff and into its cool old downtown area. It's a little less than 10 miles on Route 66 before you reach **downtown Flagstaff.**

The best and, really, the only easy way to properly see Flagstaff and the surrounding country is by car. The sights closest to town are Meteor Crater, 45 miles east on I-40; Sunset Crater and Wupatki, 14 and 39 miles north on Highway 89, respectively; and Walnut Canyon, a quick, seven-mile drive east on I-40. These places attract visitors from around the world and are easy to find. You can't miss them if you follow the signs along the highway and the interstate. The Navajo Nation's reservation begins about 50 miles north of Flagstaff on Highway 89, and Lake Powell spreads across the hard land 136 miles to the north on the same route. The Petrified Forest and Painted Desert are about 115 miles east on I-40.

Train

The **Amtrak *Southwest Chief* route** (800/872-7245, www.amtrak.com), which mirrors the old Santa Fe Railway's *Super Chief* route of the grand Fred Harvey days, stops twice daily (one eastbound, one westbound) at Flagstaff's classic **downtown depot** (1 E. Route 66), the former Santa Fe headquarters and also the town's visitors center.

Long-Distance Bus

Flagstaff's **Greyhound Bus Lines** (800 E. Butler Ave., 928/774-4573, www.greyhound.com) station is located along industrial Butler Avenue. **Arizona Shuttle** (800/888-2749, www.arizonashuttle.com, $45 per person, one-way) offers several daily trips between Flagstaff's Amtrak station and Sky Harbor Airport in Phoenix.

Air

Flagstaff's small **Pulliam Airport** (FLG, 928/556-1234, www.flagstaff.az.gov), located about five miles south of downtown, offers five flights daily to and from Sky Harbor in Phoenix through **US Airways** (800/428-4322, www.usairways.com). It's a roughly 50-minute flight, as opposed to a 2.5-hour drive from Phoenix, and generally costs $150-300. This is not the best option, as you must rent a car to explore the northland properly. If you are coming

Flagstaff

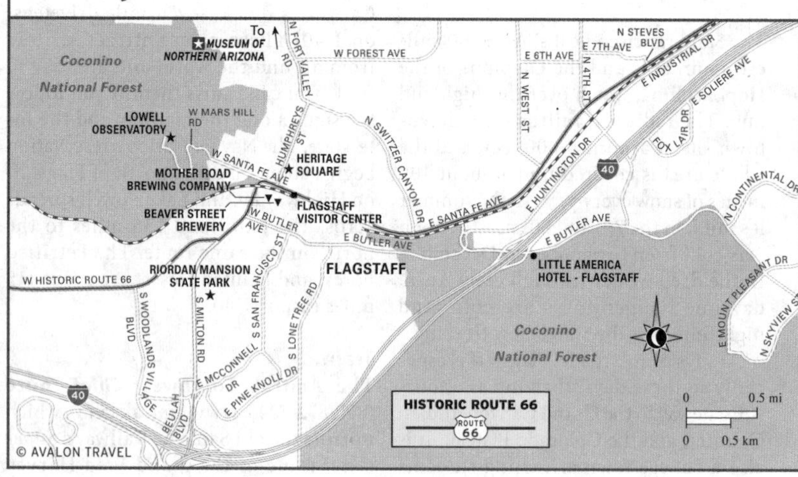

from Phoenix, it's best to rent a car there and make the scenic drive north.

Most of the major car-rental companies have a presence at Pulliam Airport. **Avis Downtown Flagstaff Car Rental** (175 W. Aspen Ave., 928/714-0713, www.avis.com, 7am-6pm Mon.-Fri., 8am-4pm Sat., 9am-1pm Sun.) is right in the middle of all the action at the corner of Aspen Avenue and Humphreys Street. **Budget** (www.budget.com) operates out of the same facility with the same hours and phone number. **Enterprise Rent-A-Car** (213 E. Route 66, 928/526-1377, www.enterprise.com, 8am-6pm Mon.-Fri., 9am-noon Sat.) is on the eastern edges of town along I-40.

If you're looking for a mythic Southwestern experience, stop by **EagleRider Flagstaff** (800 W. Route 66, 928/637-6575, www.route66rider.com, 8am-6pm daily, $159 per day, $931 per week) and rent a Harley-Davidson.

Public Transportation

Flagstaff's city bus, the **Mountain Line** (928/779-6624, www.mountainline.az.gov, $1.25 per ride or $2.50 for a day pass), runs 6am-10pm weekdays and 7am-8pm weekends to stops all over town.

Bike

Flagstaff is a relatively bicycle-friendly city, with a well-established and active bike culture. A lot of people ride mountain bikes around town, even in the winter. It's pretty easy to get around most of the town on a bike following the network of multiuse paths laid out in the **Flagstaff Urban Trails and Bikeways Map,** available for free at the Flagstaff Visitor Center downtown. Pedal from downtown to the east side of town while avoiding the traffic along Route 66 by using the popular **Route 66 Trail.** The 4.4-mile paved trail runs along the south side of Route 66 east from downtown and is popular with bike commuters. The ambitious 42-mile **Flagstaff Loop Trail** is nearly complete. It will eventually circle the town and feed smaller, spoke-like paths to various points in town.

Sights

Historic Downtown District

Flagstaff has managed to hold on to many of its historic downtown buildings, short redbrick high-rises, and quaint storefronts that served the needs of the railway and its passengers, housed and kept Route 66's argonauts, and marked the social and commercial heart of the town for generations. Its many restaurants, shops, and bars make it an ideal spot for tourists. On the National Register of Historic Places since the 1980s, many of the buildings in the downtown area date from the late 19th and early 20th centuries, including the Babbitt Brothers Building, which was constructed in 1888, and the Coconino County Courthouse, built in 1894. Just across Route 66 from the downtown area is the old Santa Fe Depot, built in the Tudor Revival style in 1926.

Downtown is a pleasant place to be any time of year, and the traveler will find myriad places to eat, drink, and hunt for all manner of artistic and handmade treasures. Take a half a day or so and walk along Humphreys Street, Beaver Street, Leroux Street, San Francisco Street, and Route 66 (also called Santa Fe) across from the train depot, ducking in and out of shops, galleries, watering holes, and eateries. **Heritage Square** (Aspen Ave. between Leroux and San Francisco Sts., 928/853-4292, www.heritagesquaretrust.org) hosts live music, outdoor movies, and arts and crafts fairs on weekends during the warmer months.

Southside Historic District

After exploring downtown, walk south of the tracks, where there are more shops, restaurants, and bars in the Southside Historic District, which is a bit shaggier than downtown and offers a look at Flagstaff's left-of-center scene. It's just south of downtown and bordered by Route 66 and the Santa Fe Railroad, the Rio de Flag, and Northern Arizona University. The neighborhood was added to the National Register of Historic Places in 2010. Check out the ruins of the **Historic Basque Handball Court** (east side of San Francisco St.) built in 1926 by tourist-home owner Jesus Garcia, who migrated to Flagstaff from Spain in 1912. The ruins of the 40-foot-high court, made of sandstone, are all that remains. It's said to be the last such court standing in Arizona and one of only a few in the nation. Route 66 enthusiasts will want to seek out the imaginative mural on a wall along West Phoenix Avenue.

Riordan Mansion State Historic Park

Riordan Mansion State Historic Park (off Milton Rd. at 409 W. Riordan Rd., 928/779-4395, www.azstateparks.com, 9:30am-5pm daily, $10 adults, $5 children 7-13) is a rock-and-log mansion sprawled amidst a stand of pines in the middle of Flagstaff's commercial section and abutting the NAU campus. Its origin is a great American success story that would have been perfectly depicted in Technicolor. Two brothers, Michael and Timothy Riordan, make it big on the Western frontier, denuding the Arizona northland of its harvestable lumber. The boys are rich, powerful, and run in Flagstaff's founding circles, helping to build a lasting American community out of a rough, arid wilderness. The close brothers marry close sisters, Caroline and Elizabeth Metz, and the two fledgling families get on so well that they decide to build a 40-room, 13,000-square-foot Arts and Crafts-style masterpiece and live in it together. They hire El Tovar Hotel designer Charles Whittlesey to design two mansions in one, each shooting off in separate directions and linked by a pool hall and communal space. They decorate their majestic home with Stickley furniture, stained glass, and enough elegant details to draw crowds of visitors for the next 100 years. And everybody lives happily ever after.

The park offers **tours** (on the hour, 10am-4pm, reservations recommended) of the Arts and Crafts treasure, one of the best examples of the distinctive architecture that left a stylish stamp on the Southwest in the late 19th and early 20th centuries. Only a small portion of the structure is included in the tour, but it's full of original furniture and displays about the family and life in Flagstaff's formative years.

Lowell Observatory

The hilltop campus of **Lowell Observatory** (1400 W. Mars Hill Rd., 928/774-3358, www.lowell.edu, 9am-9:30pm Mon., Wed., and Fri.-Sat., 9am-5pm Tues., Thurs., and Sun. Mar.-May, 9am-10pm daily June-Aug., 9am-9:30pm Mon., Wed., and Fri.-Sat., noon-5pm Tues., Thurs., and Sun. Sept.-Oct., noon-9:30pm Mon., Wed., and Fri.-Sat., noon-5pm Tues., Thurs., and Sun. Nov.-Feb., stargazing starts at 7:30pm Wed., Fri., and Sat. Sept.-May, 8pm Mon.-Sat. June-Aug., $12 adults over 17, $6 children 5-17) just west of downtown, occupied by tall straight pines and a few small white-domed structures with round concrete bases, has had a good deal of influence over the science of astronomy since its founders began searching the clear rural skies over Flagstaff in 1894. The historic viewpoint has had something to do with contemporary ideas about the beginnings of the universe as well.

It was here between 1912 and 1914 that Vesto Slipher discovered that the universe's galaxies are moving away from the Earth, a phenomenon measured by changes in the light spectrum called redshifts. This helped Edwin Hubble and others confirm that the universe is expanding, thus providing the first observable evidence for the Big Bang. Another historic distinction came a few years later in 1930, when Clyde Tombaugh discovered Pluto.

Today the campus welcomes the public with 45-minute tours offered on the hour, 10am-4pm in summer and 1pm-4pm in winter. The tours include a look through a solar telescope to view spots and flares on the sun, a duck into the Pluto Telescope building, and a look at some of fascinating historical documents and artifacts. The **Steele Visitor Center** (9am-9:30pm Mon., Wed. and Fri.-Sat., 9am-5pm Tues., Thurs., and Sun.) shows a movie about the observatory and has interesting exhibits on astronomy. If you visit at night, you can take part in galactic viewing sessions with staff astronomers.

Lowell is worth the trip for its historical import (it's one of the oldest observatories in the nation, deemed a federal Historic Landmark in 1965) and for its picturesque location in the shadowy pines at the border of Flagstaff's Thorpe Park. Don't miss checking out **Percival Lowell's tomb,** a neoclassical, observatory-shaped mausoleum that honors the observatory's founder.

★ Museum of Northern Arizona

A couple of well-educated and adventurous easterners, Mary and Harold Colton, an artist and a zoologist, respectively, who first came to northern Arizona on their honeymoon, founded the **Museum of Northern Arizona** (3101 N. Fort Valley Rd., US 180 three miles north of downtown, 928/774-5213, www.musnaz.org, 10am-5pm Mon.-Sat., noon-5pm Sun., $10 adults, $6 children 10-17) in 1928 to preserve and encourage the indigenous arts and crafts of the Colorado Plateau. Since then this essential museum has become the cultural and scientific center of the Four Corners region, collecting, interpreting, and displaying the natural history, art, and artifacts of timeless landscapes and human cultures.

The museum's main building is itself a dark-wood and river-rock work of art set among the pines along the shallow Rio de Flag, with Arts and Crafts-era touches like the handmade Hopi-tile borders around the main entrance by the famous Hopi potter Sadie Adams. Inside there are comprehensive exhibits on the Four Corners region's ancient and current biomes and its buried and blowing strata, plus one of the better introductions to Ancestral Puebloan and

Puebloan cultures you'll find, with displays on the Basketmakers through the Ancestral Puebloans and up to the Hopi of today. Volunteer docents stroll about and are eager to discuss and supplement any of the exhibits. The collection of Pueblo Indian pottery, jewelry, kachinas, and basketry is the museum's high point, and the galleries showing contemporary Hopi and Pueblo art, including oil paintings, watercolors, and sculpture, tend to open one's eyes to the vibrancy of the region's current cultural moment. Those who appreciate design should stroll into the **Branigar/Chase Discovery Center** lounge to see the Arts and Crafts flourishes in this cozy living-room setting. There's also a beautiful and relatively easy **nature trail** on the museum's forested grounds. Maps to the half-mile trail are available at the front desk.

Arizona Historical Society-Pioneer Museum

Stop at the **Arizona Historical Society-Pioneer Museum** (2340 N. Fort Valley Rd., 928/774-6772, www.arizonahistoricalsociety.org, 9am-5pm Mon.-Sat., 10am-4pm Sun., $6 adults, $3 ages 7-17) near the Museum of Northern Arizona to see how the early Anglo settlers lived in Flagstaff and northern Arizona. It's rather fascinating, after just learning about the ancient plateau lifeways of the Hopi and other tribes, to see how a completely different culture adapted to the same relatively harsh conditions. The building is something to see in itself: It's the old Coconino County Hospital for the Indigent, built in 1908. The museum has several displays on, among other things, frontier farming, education, transportation, and medicine, including a bedroom kept exactly as a hardworking nurse would have left it a century ago. There's also a retired steam train and various old farming implements parked on the beautiful forested grounds, where the museum puts on a host of events throughout the spring and summer.

Coconino Center for the Arts

Not a few artists and artisans lurk among the tall pines in Flagstaff, and many more sit atop the Hopi Mesas nearby, carving kachinas out of cottonwood root, while others walk the wide, empty roads of Navajoland and then re-create the landscape. Throughout the year the local arts group Flagstaff Cultural Partners gathers them together for a series of art exhibitions and concerts at the **Coconino Center for the Arts** (2300 N. Fort Valley Rd., 928/779-2300, www.culturalpartners.org, 11am-5pm Tues.-Sat.), a sleek, modern gallery that looks somewhat futuristic among the trees and contrasted with the historical architecture of the nearby Museum of Northern Arizona and the Pioneer Museum. Check the website for an up-to-date calendar of events at this, the "cultural hub of Flagstaff."

The Arboretum at Flagstaff

A 200-acre botanical garden and research station spotlighting the flora (and, if you're lucky, the fauna) typical of the Colorado Plateau, **The Arboretum at Flagstaff** (4001 S. Woody Mountain Rd., 928/774-1442, www.thearb.org, 9am-4pm Wed.-Mon. May-Oct., $8.50 adults, $3 children 3-17) offers 50-minute guided walking tours daily at 11am and 1pm and shows off sharp-taloned birds of prey at noon and 2pm (Sat.-Thurs.). The forested property on the volcanic lands southwest of downtown Flagstaff has easy, winding trails, tall, shaggy trees, a pond, a tree-ring maze, and much more. A few hours here and you'll be able to recognize and appreciate the unique plants and animals that flourish in the high and dry plateau country. The arboretum is about four miles south of Route 66 on Woody Mountain Road, only the first mile of which is paved, though passenger cars will have no problems making it.

Elden Pueblo Heritage Site

The **Elden Pueblo Heritage Site** (Townsend-Winona Rd. off Hwy. 89,

928/527-3452), a Sinagua ruin in the shadow of 9,280-foot Elden Mountain, on Flagstaff's eastern edge, was once a bustling trading center related to the more dramatic Wupatki and Walnut Canyon settlements to the north and east. These easily accessible volcanic-rock ruins were first studied in 1926 by the great Southwestern archaeologist and ethnologist Jesse Walter Fewkes, who also supervised digs at Casa Grande in southern Arizona and Mesa Verde in southern Colorado. The settlement in its heyday, from about AD 1100 to 1275, had 60 to 70 rooms and hosted a fairly well-connected population: archaeologists have found macaw skeletons and other evidence of trade with the far south. The site is still being studied and excavated today, often with the help of students and volunteers. Tall ponderosa pines guard the ruin along the 250-yard dirt path (ADA accessible) that circles the site. This is a perfect first stop on a daylong tour of the Sinagua ruins around Flagstaff. There's a sign for the parking lot on Townsend-Winona Road, one mile north of the Flagstaff Mall on the west side of Highway 89.

★ Sunset Crater Volcano and Wupatki National Monuments

Sunset Crater Volcano isn't really a volcano at all anymore but a nearly perfectly conical pile of cinder and ash that built up around the former volcano's main vent. Sunset Crater erupted, probably several different times, between AD 1000 and 1100. The eruptions transformed this particularly arid portion of the not exactly lush Colorado Plateau, and now huge cinder barrens, as surprising as an alien world the first time you see them, stretch out along the loop road leading through these popular national monuments. You can't climb the crater cone anymore—years of scarring by the crowds saw to that—but you can walk across the main lava field at the crater's base, a cinder field with scattered dwarfed, crooked pines and bursts of rough-rock-adapted flowers and shrubs, all the while craning up at the 1,000-foot-high, 2,550-foot-wide cone.

Along with turning its immediate environs into a scorched but beautiful wasteland, the volcano's eruptions may have inadvertently helped the Sinagua culture thrive for a brief time in this formidable environment, the subject and object of Sunset Crater's sister monument, Wupatki. The series of eruptions spewed about a ton of ashfall over 88 square miles, and closer to the source the ash created a kind of rich mulch that, combined with a few years of above-average rainfall, may have stimulated a spike in population growth and cultural influence. Archaeological findings in the area suggest that the five pueblos in the shadow of the crater, especially the large Wupatki, were at the center of a trading crossroads and the most important population hub for 50 miles or more, with about 2,000 people living within a day's walk from the sprawling red-rock apartment building by 1190. Times seem to have been good for about 150 years here, and then, owing to a variety of factors, everybody left. The Hopi and other Pueblo people consider Wupatki a sacred place, one more in a series of former homes their ancestors kept during their long migrations to Black Mesa. Today you can walk among the red and pink ruins, standing on jutting patios, looking out over the dry land, wondering what that waterless life was like and marveling at the adaptive, architectural, and artistic genius of those who came before.

Visiting the Monuments

The monuments sit side by side on an arid sweep covered with clump grass, humps of volcanic remains, pine stands, and, if you're lucky, blankets of yellow wildflowers, about 12 miles north of Flagstaff along Highway 89. Turn onto the Sunset Crater-Wupatki Loop Road, which will lead you across the cinder barrens, through the forest, out onto the red-dirt plains and the

Who Were the Sinagua and Where Did They Go?

The Sinagua left their architecture and masonry all over north-central Arizona, from the red-rock apartment buildings rising from the cinder plains below the San Francisco Peaks, the sandstone cliff hideouts of Walnut Canyon, the limestone castles in the lush, easy-living Verde Valley, to the brick-stone rooms leaning against Sedona's red walls.

We don't really know what they called themselves, but we call them, according to tradition more than anything else, the Sinagua, Spanish for "without water"—which alludes to the name used by early Spanish explorers for this region of pine-covered highlands still stuck somehow in aridity: Sierra Sin Agua ("mountains without water").

Their cultural development followed a pattern similar to that of the Ancestral Puebloans in the Four Corners region. They first lived in pit-houses bolstered by wooden beams and made a living from small-scale dry-land farming, hunting, and gathering piñon nuts and other land-given seasonal delicacies. They made strong and stylish baskets and pottery (though they didn't decorate theirs in the manner of the Ancestral Puebloans and others); they were weavers, craftspeople, and traders.

Around AD 700 a branch of the Sinagua migrated below the Mogollon Rim to the Verde Valley and began living the good life next to fish-filled rivers and streams that flowed all year around; these migrants are now called the Southern Sinagua, and the ones who stayed behind are called the Northern Sinagua. When, around AD 1000, the volcano that is now Sunset Crater, northeast of Flagstaff, erupted, there were Sinagua villages well within reach of its spewing ash and lava, though archaeologists have found evidence that nearby pit-houses had been disassembled and moved just before the eruption, leading to the assumption that they probably knew the big one was coming.

The eruption would not be the end of the Sinagua—quite the contrary. Though the reasons are debated—it could have been that crops grew to surplus because a posteruption cinder mulch made the land more fertile, or it could be that the years following the big blow were wetter than normal, or it could be a bit of both—after the eruption Sinagua culture began to become more complex, and soon it would go through a boom time. From roughly 1130 to 1400 or so, Sinagua culture flourished as the Sinagua lands became an important stop in a trade network that included Mexico to the south, the Four Corners to the north, and beyond. At pueblo-style ruins dating from this era, archaeologists have found shells, copper bells, and macaw bones, all from Mexico. Sinagua architecture became more Puebloan, and villages often had Mexican-style ball courts and kivas similar to those of the Ancestral Puebloans. It is from this era that the famous ruins protected throughout this region date.

Then it all ended. Owing to drought, disease, war, civil strife, a combination of these, or some other strange tragedy we will never learn about, by the early 1400s the Sinagua culture was on the run. By 1425, even the seemingly lucky farmers of the Verde Valley had abandoned their castles. The survivors and stragglers mixed with other tribes, their kind never to be seen again. Lucky for us they were such good builders.

To learn more about the Sinagua, check out the easy-to-read booklet *Sinagua,* written by Rose Houk, part of the Western National Park Association's series "Prehistoric Cultures of the Southwest." This and many other booklets in the series are available at Wupatki and other Sinagua sights near Flagstaff and in the Verde Valley. There are also displays on the Northern and Southern Sinagua at all of the ruins near Flagstaff and in the Verde Valley. The information above comes from various museum displays and Houk's excellent booklet.

ruins, and then back to Highway 89. One ticket is good for both monuments.

Heading north from Flagstaff, you'll get to the **Sunset Crater Volcano National Monument Visitor Center** (6082 Sunset Crater Rd., 928/526-0502, www.nps.gov/sucr, 9am-5pm daily Nov.-Apr., 8am-5pm daily May-Oct., $5 for 7-day pass, children under 16 free) first, about two miles from the junction. Take a few minutes to look over the small museum and gift shop; there are several displays about volcanoes and the history of the region. Pick up the guidebook ($1, or free if you recycle it) to the one-mile loop **Lava Flow Trail** out onto the **Bonito Lava Flow** and head up the road a bit to the trailhead. This is an easy walk among the cinder barrens, a strange landscape with a kind of ruined beauty about it—only squat pines will grow, but there are surprising flushes of life throughout, small niches in which color can find a foothold. The trail skirts the base of the great crater cone and takes about an hour or so.

Another 16 miles on the loop road and you're at the **Wupatki National Monument Visitor Center** (25137 N. Wupatki Loop Rd., 928/679-2365, www.nps.gov/wupa, 9am-5pm daily, $5 for 7-day pass, children under 16 free), a total of 21 miles from the junction, near the last of the five pueblos, the titular Wupatki. The other pueblos are before Wupatki, reached by two separate short trails, each with its own parking lot along the loop road. At Wupatki, you can purchase a guidebook ($1, or free if you recycle it) to the half-mile **Wupatki Pueblo Trail,** which leads around the village complex and back to the visitors center. If you don't have time to see all five pueblos, head straight to Wupatki, the biggest and best of them all.

★ Walnut Canyon National Monument

Not far from Wupatki, another group of Sinagua people farmed the forested rim and built stacked limestone-and-clay

Wupatki National Monument

apartments into the cliff sides of Walnut Canyon, a 20-mile-long, 400-foot-deep gathering of nearly every North American life zone in one relatively small wonderland. Near the rim, a huge island of rock juts out of the canyon innards, around which residents constructed their cells, most of them facing south and east to gather warmth. Depending on how much sunlight any one side of the island received, the Sinagua could count on several seasons of food gathering, from cactus fruit to piñon nuts and wild grapes. A creek snakes through the canyon's green bottomlands, encouraging cottonwoods and willows. The Sinagua lived in this high, dry Eden for about 125 years, leaving finally for good around 1250. This is an enchanting, mysterious place that should not be missed.

Visiting the Monument

Take I-40 east from Flagstaff for 7.5 miles to exit 204. Then it's three miles south to the canyon rim and the **Walnut Canyon Visitor Center** (928/526-3367, www.nps.gov/waca, 9am-5pm daily Nov.-Apr., 8am-5pm daily May-Oct., $5 for 7-day pass, children under 16 free), where there are a few displays, a small gift shop, and a spectacular window-view of the canyon. An hour or more on the **Island Trail,** a one-mile loop past 25 cliff dwellings (close enough to examine in detail) and into several different biomes high above the riparian bottomlands, is essential to a visit here, but it's not entirely easy; you must climb down (and back up) 240 rock-hewn steps to get to the island, descending 185 feet. Once you're on the island, though, it's an easy, mostly flat walk, and one that you won't soon forget. There's also a short trail up on the rim with some great views.

Entertainment and Events

Nightlife

Bars, Pubs, and Lounges

Most of Flagstaff's favorite nightspots can be found in and around the historic downtown, the Southside Historic District, and on the edges of the Northern Arizona University campus. The nightlife here is naturally full of college students, but you'll find plenty of older locals and tourists in the mix.

The **Monte Vista Cocktail Lounge** (100 N. San Francisco St., 928/779-6971, www.hotelmontevista.com, 1pm-2am daily) is a genial and historic place to sip cocktails or cry into your beer, with live music on the weekends, DJs on Thursdays, and pool anytime. It's in what feels like the low-ceilinged basement of the Monte Vista Hotel, built way back in 1928. On entering this little old-school joint down the steps from the hotel lobby, you can smell fourscore years of spilled beer and general revelry imprinted deeply into the walls and floor. They say there are even a few ghosts still hanging around, unwilling to go home. Also off the Monte Vista's lobby is the more modern-minded **Rendezvous Coffee House and Martini Bar** (100 N. San Francisco St.,

Side Trip to Sedona

Sedona's rare beauty is the result of geologic circumstance—the slow work of wind, rain, trickling water, and the predictable restless rocking of the Colorado Plateau. The little resort town sits at the base of the plateau, and its red-rock monuments sit dramatically alone rising into the light-blue sky. High concentrations of iron-oxide, or rust, in the sediment layers stain the rock statues many shades of red as a finishing flourish. The result is one of the most beautiful and sought-after landscapes on earth.

Only an hour or so along incredibly scenic AZ-89A, Sedona can be easily enjoyed in an unhurried day trip from Flagstaff. The creek is so inviting that you may want to stop along the side of the road and put your feet in. It's illegal to park along most stretches of the road, but there are a few pull-offs and several lodges and stores along the way where you can stop. The best and easiest place to get in the creek is at **Slide Rock State Park** (6871 N. Hwy. 89A, 928/282-3034, www.azstateparks.com, 9am-6pm daily winter, 8am-6pm daily summer, $10 per vehicle, $20 summer) where you can try out the 80-foot natural red-rock slide, walk around the short nature trails, picnic, or just soak in the creek and lie around on the warm rocks. There will likely be crowds in the summer, including many families with children. It's best to stop at Slide Rock on your way back up through Oak Creek Canyon along AZ-89A to Flagstaff, as you're going to get wet and likely a smell like a creek after you jump in the inviting water.

After a slow drive through the incredible scenery of Oak Creek Canyon (don't worry if you didn't get enough; you'll be driving back through it at the end of the day), find a place to park in Uptown Sedona and check out the shops and scenery. If you're in a shopping and people-watching mood, don't miss a stop at **Tlaquepaque Arts and Crafts Village,** which you'll find farther up the road from Uptown on AZ-179. If you're in a hiking mood, check out the various trails into the red-and-green outback at the Schnebly Hill trailheads. Or head farther south on AZ-179 toward I-17, also called the **Red Rock Scenic Byway.** Take a stroll on one of the trails around **Bell Rock,** and then stop at the **Chapel of the Holy Cross.** Next take a drive up to **Airport Mesa** for a glorious look at the buttes all spread out before you. Have lunch in Uptown before heading back into Oak Creek Canyon for some fun in the water.

Getting There

From Flagstaff, follow Milton Road south out of town and get onto I-17 South. In two miles, take exit 337 for US 89A South toward Sedona/Oak Creek Canyon. You'll be on US 89A for 25 steep and winding miles through Oak Creek Canyon, a cool green landscape. The highway will lead you directly into Uptown and then West Sedona.

928/779-6971, www.hotelmontevista.com, 6:30am-2am daily), a coffeehouse-cum-cocktail lounge with an impressive selection of spirits and creative cocktail creations. The coffee here is superior, but don't be surprised if you start drinking early after looking at all of those bottles as you sip your brew. The sleek, elegant interior and big windows that look out on bustling downtown Flagstaff encourage lounging and a "let's have another" attitude.

The State Bar (10 E. Route 66, 928/266-1282, 3pm-midnight Sun.-Thurs., noon-2am Fri.-Sat.) proves that the locavore movement is alive and well in Arizona, serving a surprisingly wide selection of beer and wine made right here in the Grand Canyon State.

Charly's Pub (23 N. Leroux St., 928/779-1919, www.weatherfordhotel.com, 8am-10pm daily), in the historic Weatherford Hotel downtown, is one of the town's favorite spot for live blues.

Charly's has live music most Friday and Saturday nights, trivia on Wednesdays, and karaoke on Thursdays.

Flagstaff Brewing Company (16 E. Route 66, 928/773-1442, www.flagbrew.com, 11am-2am daily), along Route 66 in downtown, offers expertly crafted microbrews in a pub-style setting where locals and tourists meet and mix. Try the dark-as-midnight "Sasquatch Stout" and sit on the patio, letting the strong beer and high-country air adjust your outlook on the laid-back mountain town. **Mother Road Brewing** (7 S. Mikes Pike, 928/774-9139, http://motherroadbeer.com, 2pm-9pm Mon.-Thurs., noon-10pm Fri.-Sat., noon-9pm Sun.), just across the train tracks in the Southside, has a casual tasting room, a patio with a fire pit, and a rotating menu of creative small-batch beers. Order a pizza from Pizzicletta next door, or bring your own food if you prefer.

Beaver Street Brewery (11 S. Beaver St., 928/779-0079, www.beaverstreetbrewery.com, 11am-11pm Sun.-Thurs., 11am-midnight Fri.-Sat.), on the historic Southside, serves award-winning microbrews and fantastically delicious pizzas in a bar-and-grill setting. IPA lovers should not miss the HopShot IPA served here. Connected on the inside and owned by Beaver Street Brewery, a fun atmosphere prevails at **Brews and Cues** (11am-1am Sun.-Wed., 11am-2am Thurs.-Sat.), where a few games of eight-ball provide the perfect complement to the tasty ales.

If you're looking to kick up your cowboy boots and line dance your way through an evening, check out the historic **Museum Club** (3404 E. Route 66, 928/526-9434, www.themuseumclub.com, 11am-2am daily) east of downtown. At this venerable northland institution they offer trivia (Tues.), dime beer (Wed.), country-style dance lessons, and live acts every weekend. This legendary honky-tonk, built in 1931, looks like a log-cabin hunting lodge, and it has long been a Route 66 monument. It once served as trading post, taxidermy shop, and an actual museum, but now the attractions are the big wooden dance floor and two beautiful old bars. On the list of National Historic Landmarks, the Museum Club has hosted many American music luminaries over the years and still brings in both new acts and touring immortals like Robert Earl Keen and Billy Joe Shaver.

The Green Room (15 N. Agassiz St., 928/226-8669, http://flagstaffgreenroom.com, 3pm-2am daily) has a super-fun happy hour, a big dance floor, and a party vibe nearly every night. On the weekends this dance club and live music venue brings in local and touring bands, and they have a popular karaoke program as well.

Flagstaff is a ski town, and the Southside's **Altitudes Bar & Grill** (2 S. Beaver St., 928/214-8218, www.altitudesbarandgrill.com, 11am-10pm daily) celebrates that fact with its snow-sports decor and "Skishots," a convivial way to get hammered quickly. A friendly bartender, perhaps with a full cold-weather beard and a wool cap, serves three or four shots of your favorite spirit affixed to an old ski. You and your drinking buddies must cooperate to sink them, a task that becomes increasingly tricky as the night progresses. Altitudes also offers a good selection of local beers and live music and serves a sufficiently tasty American grill-style menu until 10pm.

Collins Irish Pub & Grill (2 N. Leroux St., 928/214-7363, www.collinsirishpub.com, 11am-2am daily) downtown is a decent place to watch the game and sock back a few pints of Guinness. The emphasis here is on sports, and the menu of pub food is a strange amalgam (Irish nachos?). But if you forget that it's supposed to be an Irish pub, it turns instantly into a regular old American joint with a friendly crowd and all sorts of fun distractions.

The Wine Loft (17 N. San Francisco St., 928/773-9463, 3pm-midnight daily) is a laid-back wine bar and shop downtown with a superlative selection of wines from all over the world as well as a fairly substantial beer selection. A variety of cheeses and crackers, and oftentimes an acoustic ensemble jamming among the wine racks, contribute to a general air of relaxed sophistication. Another wine shop downtown, **Vino Loco** (22 E. Birch Ave., 928/226-1764, www.vinolocoflag.com, 11am-9pm Sun.-Wed., 11am-midnight Thurs.-Sat.), concentrates on small-vineyard wines, particularly those made in Arizona. They offer a $9 flight and other choices at their tasting bar, which also serves beer.

Live Music

Flagstaff's a pretty laid-back town, and it has its share of mountain men, bohemians, and creative types. Northern Arizona University's more than 20,000 students, many from abroad, help give the old frontier town a dash of do-it-yourself cosmopolitanism. It's not surprising, then, that the area attracts headlining acts and smaller indie favorites to its bars and theaters at a steady clip. If you're a fan of alternative pop, alt-country, classic country, bluegrass, classic rock, and just plain rock and roll, it's a good idea to check the websites of the following venues before making your travel plans. Odds are some funky act you love or have barely heard of will be playing during your visit.

The Orpheum (15 W. Aspen St., 928/556-1580, www.orpheumpresents.com), a retro-cool theater and bar that was Flagstaff's first movie house, hosts practitioners of modern music from Ozomatli to Modest Mouse and shows classic, neoclassic, and first-run movies on special nights each month. True to Flagstaff's crunchy reputation, the venue hosts a party every year on Jerry Garcia's birthday.

The **Pepsi Amphitheater** (2446 Fort Tuthill Loop, 928/774-0899, www.pinemountainamphitheater.com) out in the pines at Fort Tuthill Park is the region's best outdoor venue and attracts

The Orpheum, downtown Flagstaff

great bands from all over, many of the bluegrass and country persuasion.

Prochnow Auditorium (Knoles Dr., North Campus, Northern Arizona University, 928/523-5638 or 888/520-7214) at NAU books national and international acts into an intimate setting.

Festivals and Events

Flagstaff hosts a variety of cultural events, mostly during its cool springs and warm summers. In May, world-renowned authors come to town for lectures, signings, readings, and panel discussions at the **Northern Arizona Book Festival** (928/380-8682, www.nazbookfest.org).

The **Museum of Northern Arizona Heritage Program** (928/774-5213, www.musnaz.org) puts on several important and well-attended cultural festivals each year, featuring native arts and crafts markets, food, history displays, and entertainment: the **Hopi Festival of Arts and Culture** in early July; the **Navajo Festival of Arts and Culture** in early August; and, in late October, **Celebración de la Gente,** marking Día de los Muertos (Day of the Dead). In late May, the museum puts on the **Zuni Festival of Arts and Culture.** The second week in September, just before it starts to get cold in the north country, Flagstaff ushers in **Route 66 Days** (www.flagstaffroute66days.com), celebrated with a parade, a classic car show, and all manner of special activities along the downtown portion of the Mother Road. In October the **Flagstaff Mountain Film Festival** (www.flagstaffmountainfilms.org) screens the year's best independent films with an environmental, outdoor-adventure, and social-justice bent at the Orpheum.

If you find yourself in the northland on New Year's Eve, head over to the historic Weatherford Hotel downtown (23 N. Leroux) for the popular local party known as the **Pine Cone Drop.** Among rocking bands and general revelry, the hotel lowers a six-foot-tall, lit-up pinecone from its roof, as if this little railroad town in Arizona were Times Square. Thousands attend to meet the new year with cheer and watch the fireworks that attend the pinecone's fall. They do it twice: once at 10pm to coincide with the party on the East Coast and again at midnight.

Shopping

The best place to shop for distinctive gifts, souvenirs, decorations, clothes, and outdoor gear is Flagstaff's historic downtown. You'll find Native American arts and crafts, Western wear, New Age items, art galleries specializing in handmade objects, antiques stores, and more.

Outfitters

Babbitt's (12 E. Aspen Ave., 928/774-4775, www.babbittsbackcountry.com, 9am-8pm Mon.-Sat., 10am-6pm Sun.) sells top-notch outdoor gear from a famous old building with a famous old northland name. The store's 1880s-era, local sandstone building once housed the state's largest general store, built by a pioneer family of traders. The knowledgeable staff here can help you plan a northland backcountry adventure and will recommend the best gear for the conditions; they also have an excellent map and book section. Another locally owned outfitter downtown, **Aspen Sports** (15 N. San Francisco St., 928/779-1935, http://aspensportsflagstaff.com, 9am-7pm Mon.-Fri., 8am-7pm Sat., 10am-5pm Sun.), sells the best in outdoor, hiking, skiing, snowboarding, and trekking gear and has an experienced staff of experts, all of whom would likely rather be skiing the peaks or hurling themselves into a canyon somewhere nearby. In this wilderness those are the folks you want on your side.

Books

Bookmans (1520 S. Riordan Ranch Rd., 928/774-0005, www.bookmans.com, 9am-10pm daily), Arizona's original used-media supercenter, is the best bookstore in northern Arizona bar none, with a huge selection of used books, CDs, vinyl records, DVDs, and musical instruments.

Galleries

Stop by the **West of the Moon Gallery** (14 N. San Francisco St., 928/774-0465, www.westofthemoongallery.com, 10am-5pm daily) in Flagstaff's downtown to see the best work of contemporary painters, artists, and artisans from around the region, including both classic and experimental work from Navajo artists. This is one of several places in Arizona to see and purchase the luminous, swirling, mysterious paintings of Shonto Begay, one of the best Native American artists working today.

Sports and Recreation

Hiking

Head north on Highway 180 eight miles to the San Francisco Peaks for the best hikes in the area. There are dozens of lesser hikes around the peaks, but the most memorable, essential hike in these sylvan, volcanic lands is the **Humphreys Peak Trail** (Snow Bowl Rd./Forest Road 516, 10 miles round-trip, strenuous). The tough hike leads to the highest reaches of Humphreys Peak at 12,633 feet—the very top of Arizona and near to the sacred realms wherein the Hopi kachina dwell and watch. The 10-mile round-trip is very strenuous but beautiful and thrilling. The trail moves through a shady aspen forest and up above the tree line to a windy and rocky alpine stretch. Be careful of altitude sickness if you're a habituated lowlander. The trailhead is signed along Snowbowl Road (Forest Road 516).

The **Kachina Trail** (Snow Bowl Rd./Forest Road 516, 10 miles round-trip, moderate), which begins at the dead end of Snowbowl Road, is a less vertical walk and is popular with locals. It's a 10-mile round-trip stroll along mostly flat land—you're at 9,500 feet anyway, so why go up any more?—through thick stands of conifers and aspens with sweeping views at every corner. This is a particularly beautiful route in the fall, with fiery yellows and reds everywhere.

Contact the **Coconino National Forest** (1824 S. Thompson St., 928/527-3600, www.fs.usda.gov/coconino, 8am-4pm Mon.-Fri.) for information on hiking in the San Francisco Peaks, and see the national forest's website for other hikes in the volcanic highlands and more detailed trail descriptions.

Mountain Biking

Mountain biking is very popular in Flagstaff, and many of its trails are up-and-down exciting and technical to the point of mental and physical exhaustion. Enthusiasts will want to head straightaway to the series of moderate-to-difficult interconnected trails of the **Mount Elden Trail System** northeast of town along Highway 89. There are enough loops and mountainside single-tracks in this area to keep you busy for a while.

The **Flagstaff Biking Organization** (http://flagstaffbiking.org) offers information on northland biking events and issues. The experts at **Absolute Bikes** (202 E. Route 66, 928/779-5969, www.absolutebikes.net, 9am-7pm Mon.-Fri., 9am-6pm Sat., 10am-4pm Sun. Apr.-Dec., 10am-6pm Mon.-Sat., 10am-4pm Sun. Jan.-Mar.) keep a list of some of the best local trails on their website. They also have a store in the nearby slickrock paradise of Sedona.

Arizona Snowbowl

On the slopes of the San Francisco Peaks, the **Arizona Snowbowl** (Snow Bowl Rd. off Hwy. 180, 928/779-1951, www.arizonasnowbowl.com, lift tickets $19 adults, $10 children under 13) offers skiers and snowboarders over 2,300 feet of vertical drop and 32 scenic trails that cover 777 acres. In wet years the first snow usually falls in December, but in recent, drought-ridden years the snow has stayed away until late in the season. The resort recently prevailed in a dispute with Native Americans over artificial snow and has commenced building a system to make powder from reclaimed water when Mother Nature won't play along. The Hopi and other regional tribes consider the mountains sacred.

In the summer, the ski lift becomes the **Scenic Chairlift** (10am-4pm Fri.-Mon., $19 adults and children over 12, $10 children 8-12), lifting passengers slowly up to 11,500 feet, where you need a jacket in July and the hazy flatland stretches out for eternity. Come up here to hike around a bit and enjoy the views.

Disc Golf

The Snowbowl also has a challenging high-mountain **disc golf course** (9am-5pm daily summer, disc rental $3-8) that opens during the summer months. It takes from three to five hours to complete the 18 holes. The course has some steep climbs and, of course, gorgeous scenery.

Flagstaff Nordic Center

A complex of trails and sledding hills, the **Flagstaff Nordic Center** (Hwy. 180, mile marker 232, 928/220-0550, www.flagstaffnordiccenter.com) is a popular place for cross-country skiing, sledding, snowshoeing, and all manner of snow play as long as there's snow on the Coconino National Forest at the base of the peaks. Equipment rental, lessons, and races are available.

There's even more to do here in the summer. The high-meadow trails here offer excellent hiking and biking during the cool mountain days, and if you just can't stand to leave, camp in a **yurt or rustic cabin** ($45-65) for an unforgettable night in the star-lit forest, with the majestic San Francisco Peaks watching over your slumber.

Lake Mary and Mormon Lake

Several lakes dot the volcanic plateau south of Flagstaff, including **Mormon Lake,** the state's largest natural lake. Though shrinking and sometimes dry altogether due to drought, Mormon Lake is sometimes a beautiful body of water set amidst the green pines and junipers of the plateau. In the winter, the plateau country is popular with cross-country skiers and snowmobile enthusiasts. There are also plenty of lakeside hiking trails and mountain bike routes nearby, and myriad opportunities abound for bird-watching and wildlife-viewing, including herds of elk that call the plateau home, which can sometimes be seen from the road.

To reach Flagstaff's lake district, head south out of town on Lake Mary Road. Along the way you'll pass several smaller lakes—**Lower and Upper Lake Mary, Marshall Lake,** and **Ashurst Lake**—before reaching Mormon Lake via Forest Road 209, about 30 miles from town. Most of the lakes in northern Arizona are dependent on snowmelt and rainfall, both of which are often in short supply on this dry plateau, so don't be surprised if you find them dusty and small. The drive into the forest is worth it even if there's little water.

The **Dairy Springs and Double Springs Campgrounds** (near Mormon Lake, Coconino National Forest, 877/444-6777, www.recreation.gov, May-mid-Oct., $18 per night) offer nice forested spots with drinking water and vault toilets. Nearby, **Mormon Lake Lodge** (928/354-2227, www.mormonlakelodge.com, $54-345) has comfortable log cabins of various sizes to rent and has a 74-spot RV park as well. There's a delicious steak house with an old-fashioned mesquite pit, along with a rustic saloon that's been serving forest explorers since the 1920s. The lodge rents horses, mountain bikes, and even snowmobiles in the winter.

For more on hiking, biking, fishing, boating, and camping opportunities on the plateau, contact **The Peaks/Mormon Lake Ranger Districts** (5075 N. Hwy. 89, 928/527-3600, www.fs.usda.gov/coconino, 8am-4:30pm Mon.-Fri.).

Accommodations

Flagstaff, being an interstate town close to several world-renowned sights (not least the Grand Canyon), has all the chain hotels. A good value and a unique experience can be had at one of the historic downtown hotels like the Weatherford or the Hotel Monte Vista. Along Route 66 as you enter town from the east, there are a large number of chain and locally owned small hotels and motels, including several old-school motor inns, and a few places that are likely inexpensive for a reason. East Flagstaff, while it lacks the charm of the downtown area, is an acceptable place to stay if you're just passing through. If you're a budget traveler and don't mind students, hippies, and folks from other lands, try the hostels in Flagstaff's Southside Historic District.

Under $50

The **Grand Canyon International Hostel** (19 S. San Francisco St., 888/442-2696, www.grandcanyonhostel.com, $25-115) is a clean and friendly place to stay on the cheap, located in an old 1930s building in the Southside, in which you're likely to meet some lasting friends, many of them foreign tourists tramping around the Colorado Plateau. The hostel offers bunk-style sleeping arrangements and private rooms, mostly shared bathrooms, a self-serve kitchen, Wi-Fi, free breakfast, and a chance to join in on tours of the region. It's a rustic but cozy and welcoming hippie-home-style place to stay. The same folks operate the **Motel DuBeau** (19 W. Phoenix St., 800/398-7112, www.grandcanyonhostel.com/dubeau, $25-115), a clean and charming hostel-inn with a small dorm and eight private rooms. They offer a free breakfast, Wi-Fi, and a friendly atmosphere. Make sure to spend some time at Nomad's Global Lounge kicking back a few cold ones with your new friends.

$50-100

The ★ **Weatherford Hotel** (23 N. Leroux St., 928/779-1919, www.weatherfordhotel.com, $55-145) is one of two historic hotels downtown. It's basic but romantic, if you're into stepping back in time when you head off to bed. There are no TVs or phones in most of the rooms, the cheapest of which share a bathroom. While the whole place is a little creaky, the location and the history make this a fun place to rest. With live music at on-site Charly's Pub and the odd wedding or private party in the historic ballroom, the Weatherford can sometimes get a bit noisy. It's not for those looking for the tranquility of the surrounding pine forest.

The ★ **Hotel Monte Vista** (100 N. San Francisco St., 928/779-6971 or 800/545-3068, www.hotelmontevista.com, $70-175 Apr. 15-Nov. 5, $50-175 Nov. 6-Apr. 14), the other historic downtown hotel, is a retro-swanky, redbrick high-rise, built in 1927, that once served high-class and famous travelers heading west on the Santa Fe Railroad. These days it offers rooms that have historic charm but are still comfortable and convenient, with cable TV and private bathrooms. There's a dive-y cocktail lounge and sleek coffee bar off the lobby, and, as with many of the grand old railroad hotels, there are lots of tales to be heard about the Hollywood greats who stayed here and the restless ghosts who stayed behind.

Over $100

The **Embassy Suites** (706 S. Milton Rd., 928/774-4333, http://embassysuites3.hilton.com, $99-139) offers a cozy and tasteful compound in the center of commercial Flagstaff, with a pool and hot tub, free made-to-order breakfast, and a complimentary nightly cocktail hour in its leather-chair lounge. This place is perfect for families: A relatively inexpensive suite offers two large beds in one room, a hide-a-bed in another, TVs in both, and a refrigerator.

The Inn at 410 Bed and Breakfast (410 N. Leroux St., 928/774-0088 or 800/774-2008, www.inn410.com, $185-215) has eight artfully decorated rooms in a classic old home on a quiet, tree-lined street just off downtown. This is a wonderful little place, with so much detail and stylishness. Breakfasts are interesting and filling, often with a Southwestern tinge, and tea is served every afternoon. You certainly can't go wrong here. Booking far in advance, especially for a weekend stay, is a must.

The stately **England House Bed and Breakfast** (614 W. Santa Fe Ave., 928/214-7350 or 877/214-7350, www.englandhousebandb.com, $134-199) is set in a quiet residential neighborhood near downtown at the base of Mars Hill, where sits the famous Lowell Observatory. This beautiful old Victorian has been sumptuously restored, and its rooms are booked most weekends. If you're just passing through, the innkeepers are happy to show you around, after which you will probably make a reservation for some far future date. They pay as much attention to their breakfasts here as they do to details of the decor. This is one of the best little inns in the region.

The same can be said of the **Aspen Inn Bed and Breakfast** (218 N. Elden St., 928/773-0295 or 800/999-4110, www.flagstaffbedbreakfast.com, $129-169), an inviting Arts and Crafts-style B&B a few blocks from downtown. Wyatt Earp's cousin, C. B. Wilson, built the house in 1912, and these days it offers four comfortable rooms with televisions, Wi-Fi, and all the other comforts, plus a delicious breakfast and friendly atmosphere.

The sprawling **Little America** (2515 E. Butler Ave., 928/779-7900, http://flagstaff.littleamerica.com, $119-204) is a huge hotel complex on 500 acres near Northern Arizona University and popular with visiting parents. It has a pool, several restaurants, pine-studded grounds, and hundreds of rooms and suites. This is a good, centrally located option for families and makes a great base for skiers in the winter.

Forest Inns

The **Ski Lift Lodge** (6355 N. Hwy. 180, 928/774-0729 or 800/472-3599, www.arizonasnowbowl.com, $129-219) has simple, rustic cabins and rooms with cozy fireplaces and a good restaurant. Best of all, it's in the forest beneath the San Francisco Peaks, about seven miles northwest of downtown, right near the road up the peaks to the Snowbowl. It's dark out there, and you can see all the stars in the galaxy on many nights. This lodge is a good bet if you're skiing or engaging in other snow-related activities. Make reservations in advance for ski season, as there are few other places to stay in the immediate area. The drive from Flagstaff proper is about 10-20 minutes, longer in inclement weather. Prices are considerably lower on weekdays.

The **Starlight Pines Bed and Breakfast** (3380 E. Lockett Rd., 928/527-1912 or 800/752-1912, www.starlightpinesbb.com, $159-179) is about three miles northeast of town in the forest at the foot of Mount Elden, offering four rooms stuffed with antiques and style in a Victorian-era home. There's a porch swing, deep tubs perfect for bubble baths, and fresh-cut flowers in every room but no TVs. They'll even bring your breakfast to your room for you. This is a perfect place for couples looking for a romantic mountain getaway.

Tucked in the pines about six miles south of downtown Flagstaff, the **Abineau Lodge** (1080 Mountainaire Rd., 928/525-6212, http://abineaulodge.com, $110) has two cozy rooms in a glorious wilderness location. There's also a pet-friendly two-bedroom cabin with a kitchen ($145-160). The house itself is a stylish red-wood forest retreat built in 1997, with large decks for lounging in the cool highland air. Located in the tiny Flagstaff residential offshoot of Mountainaire, the Abineau serves a continental breakfast.

For a touch of wilderness adventure with all the comforts, try the **Arizona Mountain Inn** (4200 Lake Mary Rd., 928/774-8959, www.arizonamountaininn.com, $120-550), offering 17 rustic but comfortable family-perfect cabins ($135-550) in the pines not far from town as well as four B&B-style rooms ($120-160). Dogs are welcome in most rooms and cabins.

Food

American and Southwestern

There's something about drinking a dark, handcrafted pint of beer in the piney mountain heights that makes one feel as good as can be—maybe it's the alcohol mixed with the altitude. The best place to get that feeling is the **Beaver Street Brewery** (11 S. Beaver St., 928/779-0079, www.beaverstreetbrewery.com, 11am-11pm Sun.-Thurs., 11am-midnight Fri.-Sat., $7-18), where excellent beers are made on-site and there's delicious, hearty food of the bar and grill variety, including excellent pizzas and burgers.

For the very best burgers in the northland, head to **Diablo Burger** (20 N. Leroux St., #112, 928/774-3274, 11am-9pm Mon.-Wed., 11am-10pm Thurs.-Sat., $6-14), which serves a small but stellar menu of beef raised locally on the plains around Flagstaff. All the finely crafted creations, such as the "Cheech" (guacamole, jalapeños, and spicy cheese), or the "Vitamin B" (bleu cheese with bacon and a beet) come on Diablo's branded English muffin-style buns alongside a mess of Belgian fries. They also have a terrific veggie burger.

Brandy's Restaurant and Bakery (1500 E. Cedar Ave., #40, 928/779-2187, www.brandysrestaurant.com, 6:30am-3pm daily, $5-10) often wins the Best Breakfast honors from readers of the local newspaper, and those readers know what they're talking about. The homemade breads and bagels make everything else taste better. Try the Eggs Brandy, two poached eggs on a homemade bagel smothered in hollandaise sauce. For lunch there are crave-worthy sandwiches (Brandy's Reubens are some of the best in the business), burgers, and salads. They also serve beer, wine, and mimosas.

Buster's (1800 S. Milton Rd., 928/774-5155, 11:30am-10pm daily, $8-29) has been a local favorite for years, serving up good steaks and burgers and such, and offering the hangover-assuring Buster Bowl to any hard-drinking college student who happens in.

Josephine's Modern American Bistro (503 N. Humphreys St., 928/779-3400, www.josephinesrestaurant.com, 11am-2pm and 5pm-9pm Mon.-Fri. and 10am-2pm and 5pm-9pm Sat., 9am-2pm Sun., $9-27) offers a creative fusion of tastes for lunch and dinner, such as the roasted pepper and hummus grilled-cheese sandwich and the *chile relleno* with sun-dried cranberry guacamole, from a cozy historic home near downtown. This is one of the best places in town for brunch.

Charly's Pub and Grill (23 N. Leroux St., 928/779-1919, www.weatherfordhotel.com, 8am-10pm daily, $6-24), inside the Weatherford Hotel, serves Navajo tacos, enchiladas, burritos, and a host of other regional favorites for breakfast, lunch, and dinner. Their Navajo taco, a regional delicacy featuring fry bread smothered in chili and beans, might be the best off the reservation. Try it for breakfast topped with a couple of fried eggs. Charly's also has more conventional but appetizing bar-and-grill food such as hot, high-piled sandwiches, juicy burgers, steaks, and prime rib.

Brix Restaurant & Wine Bar (413 N. San Francisco St., 928/213-1021, http://brixflagstaff.com, 5pm-close Tues.-Sun., $18-36) operates out of a historic building a few blocks north of downtown and serves creative and memorable food using regional ingredients. The menu here changes often based on what's new at Arizona's small farms, ranches, and dairies. The New American cuisine that results is typically spectacular. They also have fine selections of wine, a slew of creative cocktails, and desserts that should not be missed.

The **Tinderbox Kitchen** (34 S. San Francisco St., 928/226-8400, www.tinderboxkitchen.com, 5pm-9pm Sun.-Thurs., 5pm-10pm Fri.-Sat., $10-30) in the Southside District serves a revolving menu of gourmet takes on familiar American favorites and has an elegant lounge (4pm-close daily) where you can wait for your table with a martini. The chef uses seasonal ingredients, and there's always something new and exciting here—like venison served with bleu cheese grits, bacon creamed corn, or jalapeño mac-and-cheese. It's one of those places where the chef is limited only by ingredients and imagination, and the chef here is lacking in neither.

For the best sandwiches in the northland, head to **Crystal Creek Sandwich Company** (1051 S. Milton Rd., 928/774-9373, http://crystalcreeksandwiches.com, 9am-9pm daily, $5-8). A Flagstaff institution, this casual order-at-the-counter joint serves high-piled delights on fresh bread and has a pool table too. Grab a couple of big sandwiches to go and head out into the pines for a picnic—the perfect way to spend a day in Flagstaff.

Diners

For a big breakfast of eggs, bacon, and potatoes, or an omelet stuffed with cheese, a hot cup of coffee, and friendly service, head over to the **Downtown Diner** (7 E. Aspen Ave., 928/774-3492, 6am-6pm daily, $3-12) right across from Heritage Square. This clean little greasy spoon also has good burgers, shakes, and hot dogs. There's similar fare at local favorite **Miz Zip's Route 66 Diner** (2924 E. Route 66, 928/526-0104, 6am-9pm Mon.-Sat., 7am-2pm Sun., $5-15) on Flagstaff's eastside. Open since the 1950s, they are still serving the same diner classics of the golden age, such as hot open-faced sandwiches smothered in rich gravy, juicy burgers, and filling breakfasts. They only take cash.

The **Crown Railroad Café** (3300 E. Route 66, 928/522-9237, http://thecrownrailroadcafes.com, 6am-9pm daily, $5-10) celebrates the golden era of the railroad. Sit among model trains, iron road memorabilia, and Navajo blankets while enjoying the huge, three-egg "Route 66 omelet," expertly prepared huevos rancheros, and a fresh homemade biscuit. They also have a location on Woodlands Village Boulevard (2700 S. Woodlands Village Blvd., Ste. 600, 928/774-6775).

Mexican and Latin American

Criollo Latin Kitchen (16 N. San Francisco St., 928/774-0541, http://criollolatinkitchen.com, 11am-10pm Mon.-Fri., 9am-10pm Sat.-Sun., $5-22), in Flagstaff's historic downtown, creates an eclectic, ever-changing menu of gourmet, Latin-inspired dishes for brunch, lunch, and dinner from ingredients grown regionally on small farms and ranches. Try the beer-battered catfish tacos and the wonderfully flavorful tortilla soup and carne asada. The sleek and refined interior, with eye-catching paintings and small tables that look out on downtown through a glass front, creates an urbane atmosphere that complements the creative food and somewhat belies the rural mountain setting.

Asian

About three miles southwest of downtown in the Wal-Mart shopping center, **Delhi Palace** (2700 S. Woodlands Village Blvd., 928/556-0019, www.delhipalaceflagstaff.com, 11am-2:45pm and 5pm-9:45pm daily, $3-17) serves all the exotic tastes of the subcontinent in a friendly, family-owned atmosphere. It's one of Flagstaff's favorite restaurants, popular for its fresh and delicious lunch buffet ($9).

Consistent with its role as a port of call for canyon-country visitors from all over the world, Flagstaff has two excellent Thai restaurants, both stars of this atypical small town's varied and cosmopolitan food scene. **Swaddee Thai** (115 E. Aspen Ave., 928/773-1122, http://swaddeethai.com, 11am-3pm and 5pm-9pm Tues.-Thurs., 11am-3pm and 5pm-9:30pm Fri.-Sat., $8-$16), in Flagstaff's historic downtown right across from the Weatherford Hotel, serves fresh and authentic Thai dishes in an elegant setting. It's a clone of a restaurant that opened in the Phoenix area in 2007 and has quickly become one of the state's most acclaimed Thai eateries. The food here is unassailable: flavorful, consistent, and filling without being heavy. They also deliver.

Just a short stroll south sits **Dara Thai** (145 San Francisco St., 928/774-0047, www.darathaiflagstaff.com, 11am-10pm Mon.-Sat., $10-25), in the Southside neighborhood. Part of a small regional chain with sister restaurants in Williams, Anthem, Santa Fe, and Taos, Dara Thai has been a beloved local institution since 1992. Close to campus, it's popular with students and locals for its rich, tasty, and perfectly spiced dishes. Both Dara Thai and Swaddee Thai offer a relatively wide range of vegetarian options.

Italian

Named Flagstaff's favorite pizza from 2002 to 2012, **Fratelli Pizza** (119 W. Phoenix Ave., 928/774-9200, www.fratellipizza.net, 10:30am-9pm daily, $7-20) swears by its "stone deck oven" and eschews the "conveyer belt" mentality of the chains. The results are sublime. Try the popular Flagstaff, with basil pesto, sun-dried tomatoes, and artichoke hearts. You can also build your own pie from among dozens of fresh toppings or stop in for a huge slice ($3). They also serve salads, antipasti, and calzones and offer a decent selection of beer and wine. They have a second location on 4th Street (2120 N. 4th St., 928/714-9700, 10:30am-9pm daily).

NiMarco's Pizza (101 S. Beaver St., 928/779-2691, http://nimarcospizza.com, 11am-9pm Sun.-Wed., 11am-10pm Thurs.-Sat., $5-20), a Southside neighborhood mainstay for decades, serves a more than decent pizza pie in a casual space with picnic tables not far from campus. This is a dependable place to call for a delivery, as long as you are downtown, Southside, or near campus. The pizza is nothing fancy, just fresh, hot, and delicious.

On the fancier side of the pizza spectrum is the wonderful **Pizzicletta** (203 W. Phoenix Ave., 928/774-3242, http://pizzicletta.com, 5pm-close Tues.-Sun., $6-15), also in the Southside neighborhood. Here they offer soppressata rather than pepperoni and prosciutto di Parma rather than ham. Among the carefully chosen, rather spare list of toppings are almonds and charred kale. But it's the dough that makes the pizza here heaven sent. They also serve fantastic bread, beer, wine, and house-made gelato.

Vegetarian

The **Morning Glory Café** (115 S. San Francisco St., 928/774-3705, 11am-2:30pm Tues.-Sat., $7-10) serves natural, tasty vegetarian eats from a cozy little spot on San Francisco Street. Try the hemp burger for lunch, and don't miss the blue corn pancakes for breakfast. With local art on the walls, free wireless Internet, and friendly service, this is an ideal place to get to know the laid-back

Flagstaff vibe. There are a lot of vegan and gluten-free options here. They don't take credit cards, so bring some cash.

Macy's European Coffee House (14 S. Beaver St., 928/774-2243, www.macyscoffee.net, 6am-8pm daily, $5-10) south of the tracks is the best place to get coffee and a quick vegetarian bite to eat, or just hang out and watch the locals file in and out.

Information

The **Flagstaff Visitor Center** (1 E. Route 66, 928/774-9541 or 800/379-0065, www.flagstaffarizona.org, 8am-5pm Mon.-Sat., 9am-4pm Sun.), housed in the old train depot in the center of town, has all kinds of information on Flagstaff and the surrounding area.

Williams

This small historic town along I-40 (what used to be Route 66), surrounded by the Kaibab National Forest, is the closest interstate town to Route 64, and thus has branded itself "The Gateway to the Grand Canyon." It has been around since 1874 and was the last Route 66 town to be bypassed by the interstate (not until 1984). As a result, and because of a resurgence over the last few decades owing to the rebirth of the Grand Canyon Railway, Williams, with about 3,000 full-time residents, has a good bit of small-town charm—the entire downtown area is on the National Register of Historic Places. It's worth a stop and an hour or two of strolling about, and there are a few good restaurants. It's only about an hour drive to the South Rim from Williams, so many consider it a convenient base for exploring the region. The drive is not as scenic as either Route 64 from Cameron or US 180 from Flagstaff, but this is the place to stay if you plan to take the **Grand Canyon Railway** to the rim, which is a highly recommended way of reaching the South Rim. It's fun, it cuts down on traffic and emissions within the park, and you'll get exercise walking along the rim, or renting a bike and cruising the park with the wind in your face.

Getting There

Historic Route 66 follows **I-40 West** from Flagstaff to Williams, a **35-mile** drive of just over **half an hour.** Take **exit 165** for **AZ-64** toward **Williams/Grand Canyon,** then turn left onto **AZ-64/Historic Route 66,** continuing for three miles into downtown Williams.

Sights

Williams Historic District

On a walk through the **Williams Historic Business District** you'll see how a typical pioneer Southwestern mountain town might have looked from territorial days until the interstate came and the railroad died. Williams wasn't bypassed by I-40 until the 1980s, so many of its old buildings still stand and have been put to use as cafés, boutiques, B&Bs, and gift shops. Walk around and look at the old buildings; shop for Native American and Old West knickknacks, pioneer-era memorabilia, and Route 66 souvenirs you don't need; and maybe stop for a beer, cocktail, or a cup of coffee at an old-school, small-town saloon or a dressed-up café. The district is bounded on the north by Railroad Avenue, on the south by Grant Avenue, and on the east and west by 1st and 4th Streets, respectively. About 250 acres, the district has 44 buildings dating from 1875-1949 and an array of Route 66-era business signs and mid-century commercial architecture worth a few snapshots. Old Route 66 is variously termed Bill Williams Avenue, Grand Canyon Avenue, and Railroad Avenue, and it splits into parallel one-way streets through the historic downtown before meeting up to the west and east.

Bearizona Wildlife Park

Don't be surprised if a big brown bear, gone lazy from living the easy life in

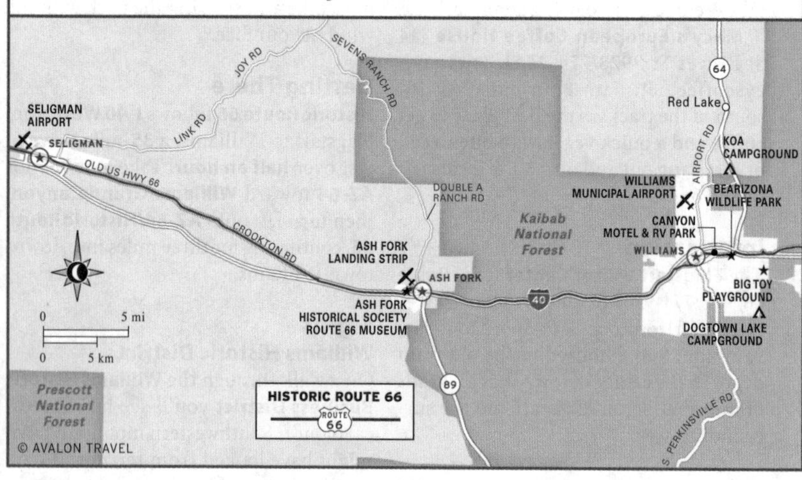

beautiful pine-covered **Bearizona Wildlife Park** (1500 E. Route 66, I-40 exit 165, 928/635-2289, www.bearizona.com, 9am-4pm daily, $20 adults, $18 seniors, $10 children 4-12), decides to lounge on his back in front of your car; it's best to drive around the old beast, one of the many rescued animals that call this family-friendly drive-through wildlife park home. Along the two-mile drive through the forested park, which the park insists be done with windows up, you'll see many brown and black bears wrestling and lounging in the meadows as well as wolves, bison, bighorn sheep, and other classic animals of North America. A walk-through section at the end of the drive called **Fort Bearizona** features adorable baby animals frolicking with innocence and wonder, along with a few regal birds of prey that would probably like to eat all those fuzzy little morsels.

Kids absolutely love this place, and it makes for an easy side trip on the way to the Grand Canyon: it's just outside of Williams near the junction of I-40 and Route 64, right on the route to the South Rim. Allow about two hours to visit this fun park; many of the animals here have a bit of personality, and you might get hooked if you stay *too* long. Bearizona is busiest in the summer, but the park is open year-round. The hours may vary according to season and weather, so call before driving out there just to make sure. As always, bring your own water no matter the season.

Shopping

There's a gathering of boutiques and gift shops in Williams's quaint, historic downtown area, between Railroad, Grant, 1st, and 4th Streets.

Don't miss **Native America** (117 E. Route 66, 928/635-4600, 8am-10pm daily summer, 8am-6pm daily winter), a Native American-owned shop with Hopi and Navajo arts and crafts.

Recreation

The alpine ski runs at the Arizona Snowbowl in the San Francisco Peaks are only a quick hour's drive from downtown Williams, so it's easy to overlook the more modest **Elk Ridge Ski and Outdoor Recreation Area** (Ski Run Rd., 928/814-5038 or 928/814-5027, www.elkridgeski.com, 10am-4pm daily, lift tickets $25-35 adults, $25-20 children) in the Kaibab National Forest about five miles from town. More laid-back and kid-friendly than the big mountains to the north, Elk Ridge allows skiing, snowboarding, and tubing whenever there's snow to slide on. They also rent equipment here—skis, tubes, and boards—and there's a decent café for warming up and resting.

Events

In mid-August, perfectly preserved classic cars and low-hung Harleys crowd Williams's narrow downtown streets for the **Cool Country Cruise-In** (928/635-1418, www.route66place.com, Aug.), a celebration of the town's prominent place along the Mother Road. The two-day festival features a car show, vendors, live music, and the **Miss Route 66 Pageant.**

Northland kids wait all year for the Grand Canyon Railway's celebration of author Chris Van Allsburg's classic holiday story *The Polar Express*. The always sold-out **Polar Express and Mountain Village Holiday** (800/848-3511, www.thetrain.com, 3:30pm, 5:30pm, and 7:30pm daily mid-Nov.-early Jan., $34-45 adults, $24-35 children 2-15) features a one-hour nighttime pajama-party train ride, complete with cookies and hot cocoa, to a lit-up Christmastown that kids ooh and ahh at from their train seats. Riders dressed up like characters in the book read the story as kids follow along in their own copies. Then Santa boards the train and gives each kid some individual attention and a free jingle bell like the one in the famous book. On the return trip, everybody sings Christmas carols, while the younger tykes generally fall asleep. This annual event is *very* popular with kids and their families from all over northern Arizona, and tickets generally sell out early (even as early as August).

Accommodations

Williams has some of the most affordable independent accommodations in the Grand Canyon region as well as several chain hotels.

It's difficult to find a better deal than the clean and basic **El Rancho Motel** (617 E. Route 66, 928/635-2552 or 800/228-2370, $90-110), an independently owned, retro motel on Route 66 with few frills save comfort, friendliness, and a heated pool open in season.

The **Canyon Country Inn** (442 W. Route 66, 928/635-2349, www.thecanyoncountryinn.com, $89-104) is an enchanting little place, home to a whole mob of stuffed bears and right in the heart of Williams's charming historic district. Its country-Victorian decor is not for everyone, but it's a comfortable and friendly place to stay while exploring the canyon country.

The **Grand Canyon Railway Hotel** (235 N. Grand Canyon Blvd., 928/635-4010, www.thetrain.com, $174-359) stands now where Williams's old Harvey House once stood. It has a heated indoor pool, two restaurants, a lounge, a hot tub, a workout room, and a huge gift shop. The hotel serves riders on the Grand Canyon Railway and offers the highest-end accommodations in Williams.

The original ★ **Grand Canyon Hotel** (145 W. Route 66, 928/635-1419, www.thegrandcanyonhotel.com, $69-185) opened in 1891, even before the railroad arrived and made Grand Canyon tourism something not just the rich could do. New owners refurbished and reopened the charming old redbrick hotel in Williams's historic downtown in 2005, and now it's an affordable, friendly place to stay with a lot of character and a bit of an international flavor. Spartan single-bed rooms go for $69 a night with a shared bathroom, and individually named and eclectically decorated double rooms with private baths are $82 a night—some of the most distinctive and affordable accommodations in the region. There are no televisions in the rooms.

The **Red Garter Bed & Bakery** (137 W. Railroad Ave., 928/635-1484, www.

redgarter.com, $160-175) makes much of its original and longtime use as a brothel (which, like many similar places throughout Arizona's rural regions, didn't finally close until the 1940s), where the town's lonely, uncouth miners, lumberjacks, railway workers, and cowboys met with unlucky women, ever euphemized as "soiled doves," in rooms called "cribs." The 1897 frontier-Victorian stone building, with its wide, arching entranceway, has been beautifully restored with a lot of authentic charm, without skimping on the comforts—like big brass beds for the nighttime and delightful, homemade baked goods, juice, and coffee in the morning. Famously, this place is haunted by some poor unquiet, regretful soul, so you might want to bring your night light along.

The Lodge on Route 66 (200 E. Route 66, 877/563-4366, http://thelodgeonroute66.com, $99-189) has stylish, newly renovated rooms with sleep-inducing pillow-top mattresses; it has a few very civilized two-room suites with kitchenettes, dining areas, and fireplaces—perfect for a family that's not necessarily on a budget. The motor court-style grounds, right along Route 66, of course, have a romantic cabana with comfortable seats and an outdoor fireplace. No pets.

Food

A northland institution with some of the best steaks in the region, ★ **Rod's Steak House** (301 E. Route 66, 928/635-2671, www.rods-steakhouse.com, 11am-9:30pm Mon.-Sat., $12-35) has been operating at the same site since 1946. The food is excellent; the staff, friendly and professional; and the menus are shaped like steers.

The **Pine Country Restaurant** (107 N. Grand Canyon Blvd., 928/635-9718, http://pinecountryrestaurant.com, 6:30am-9:30pm daily, $5-10) is a family-style place that serves good food and homemade pies. Check out the beautiful paintings of the Grand Canyon on the walls.

You'll find comforting Mexican and Southwestern food at **Pancho McGillicuddy's** (141 Railroad Ave., 928/635-4150, www.vivapanchos.com, 11am-10pm daily, $10-17). They serve satisfying burritos, enchiladas, and Navajo tacos, carne asada, New York strip, and fish-and-chips in an 1893 building that used to be the rowdy Cabinet Saloon, on Williams's territorial-era stretch of iniquity known as "Saloon Row." They mix a decent margarita, but beer is the drink of choice in this high-country burg, and they have a great selection on tap.

Cruiser's Route 66 Bar & Grill (233 W. Route 66, 928/635-2445, www.cruisers66.com, 11am-9pm Mon.-Thurs., 11am-10pm Fri.-Sun., $7-25) offers a diverse menu, with superior barbecue ribs, burgers, fajitas, pulled-pork sandwiches, and homemade chili. They have a full bar and offer live music most nights. During the summer evenings the patio is lively and fun.

The vegetarian's best bet this side of downtown Flagstaff is the **Dara Thai Café** (145 W. Route 66, 928/635-2201, 11am-2pm and 5pm-9pm Mon.-Sat., $4-10), an agreeable little spot in the Grand Canyon Hotel. They serve a variety of fresh and flavorful Thai favorites and offer quite a few meat-free dishes.

Information and Services

Stop at the **Williams-Kaibab National Forest Visitor Center** (200 W. Railway Ave., 928/635-1418 or 800/863-0546, 8am-6:30pm daily spring-summer, 8am-5pm daily fall-winter) for information about Williams, the Grand Canyon, and camping and hiking in the Kaibab National Forest.

Ash Fork

The longest remaining stretch of Historic Route 66 (about 165 miles) runs from Ash Fork, on I-40, through the dry grasslands, cholla forests, and jagged hills of northwestern Arizona west to Topock, a tiny town on the Colorado River. The tour described below ends at Kingman, about 120 miles west of Ash Fork. There are two good gas stations here that serve I-40. Consider filling up and grabbing some supplies before heading out on the 120-mile tour of this section of the old Mother Road, as there are very few services out there.

Getting There

It's a short, **20-minute, 20-mile** sprint west on **I-40** from Williams to Ash Fork. From downtown Williams, head west on **Historic Route 66.** Just after passing over the interstate, turn left to join **I-40 West.** Take **exit 146** after 15 miles, then turn right onto **Lewis Avenue,** following signs for Route 66/Ash Fork, and you'll be in the midst of Ash Fork in less than a mile.

Sights

On your way through town, follow the signs to the quirky **Ash Fork Route 66 Museum** (901 W. Old Route 66, 928/637-0204, http://ashforkrt66museum.com, 8am-4pm Mon.-Fri., donations accepted), which has fun and imaginative displays on regional and Mother Road history, and sells a variety of Route 66 souvenirs. Photographers on their way through town along Historic Route 66 should keep an eye out for **Desoto's Beauty & Barber Shop** (314 W. Lewis Ave., 928/637-9886), an old Route 66-style gas station with a hot-rod Desoto stuck on the roof. It's now a hair salon, but the building still makes a great photo subject.

Seligman

This tiny roadside settlement 87 miles east of Kingman holds on tight to its Route 66 heritage. There are fewer than

Top to bottom: downtown Williams; Grand Canyon Caverns; Rod's Steak House, Williams.

500 full-time residents living in this old ranching hub, railroad center, and Route 66 stop, but there is often, especially on summer weekends, twice that number of tourists driving through and stopping for a bite to eat and a look around the gift shops. Tour buses and large gangs of motorcycling Europeans even stop here and crowd up the one-strip town on occasion, as Seligman has become in recent years one of the top stops for a burgeoning subculture of classic car nuts, *Easy Rider* role players, and lovers of mid-20th-century commercial architecture and road culture, all of whom prefer to eschew the interstate and take to the back roads.

John Lasseter, codirector of the 2006 Disney-Pixar film *Cars*, has said that he based the movie's fictional town of Radiator Springs partly on Seligman, which, like Radiator Springs, nearly died out when it was bypassed by I-40 in the late 1970s.

Getting There

Seligman is 25 miles from Ash Fork on Historic Route 66. The drive takes about **30 minutes.** From Ash Fork, take **Lewis Avenue** west out of town for about a mile and then join **I-40 West.** After five miles, take **exit 139** toward Crookton Road, then turn right onto **Historic Route 66.** Continue for almost 20 miles, and you'll find yourself amid the kitsch of Seligman.

Sights

Stop in at the **Delgadillo's Route 66 Gift Shop** (22265 W. Historic Route 66, 928/422-3352, www.route66giftshop.com, 9am-5pm daily) to buy a Route 66 souvenir and learn about the history of the area from Angel and Vilma Delgadillo, longtime residents who are largely responsible for keeping Seligman on the map. Don't confuse this spot with the similarly named Delgadillo's Snow Cap Drive-In.

Seligman's commercial center, a three-block area off of Chino Street (Historic Route 66) that's hemmed by 1st Street on the west, Lamport Street on the east, Picacho Street on the north, and Railroad Avenue on the south, is on the National Register of Historic Places as "an important reminder of how transportation systems influenced the development of communities in the American West." Pick up a pamphlet for the self-guided tour of the **Seligman Historic District** at the Historic Seligman Sundries and other places in town, and walk the district with your camera, snapping shots of all the retro signs and buildings from the pre-interstate era.

Shopping

Inside the turquoise-and-pink 100-year-old **Historic Seligman Sundries** (22495 Historic Route 66, 928/853-0051, www.seligmansundries.com, 8am-7pm daily Apr.-Oct.), you'll find a plethora of Route 66 memorabilia as well as motorcycle- and car-culture items, Native American jewelry, cowboy kitsch, and really good coffee and malts. There's a small museum, and the walls are covered with old advertisements and other reminders of the mid-20th-century heyday of American popular culture.

That sprawling building with all the dressed-up manikins standing around on the roof, and Elvis kicking back on the bumper of a classic pink roadster, is **The Rusty Bolt** (115 E. Route 66, 928/422-0106, www.rustybolt66.com, 8am-4pm daily), where they sell the usual local Route 66 memorabilia and a large selection of items for motorcyclists.

Accommodations

There are several small, locally owned motels in Seligman, many of them with historic, retro signs and, of course, a Route 66 theme. The accommodations here are nothing special, though they are typically quite affordable.

The **Supai Lodge** (134 W. Chino St., 928/422-4153, $66-80), named for the nearby Grand Canyon-bottom village inhabited by the Havasupai, has clean and comfortable rooms at a fair price.

The **Historic Route 66 Motel** (500 W. Chino St., 928/422-3204, www.route-66seligmanarizona.com, $65-80) offers free Wi-Fi and refrigerators in clean, comfortable rooms.

The **Canyon Lodge** (114 E. Chino St., 928/422-3255, www.route66canyonlodge.com, $65-80) has free wireless Internet in its themed rooms (which means posters on the walls of James Dean, Marilyn Monroe, John Wayne, and other pop-culture icons), along with refrigerators and microwaves. They also serve a free continental breakfast.

Food

A majority of the Route 66 argonauts who slide through Seligman stop at ★ **Delgadillo's Snow Cap Drive-In** (301 E. Chino Ave., 928/422-3291), a famous food shack whose family of owners have been dedicated to feeding, entertaining, and teasing Route travelers for generations. They serve a mean chili burger, a famous "cheeseburger with cheese," hot dogs, malts, soft ice cream, and much more, but the food's not really the point. Originally built in 1953 out of found lumber, the Snow Cap has become one of the stars of the back-to-Route-66 movement. There's a lot to look at outside: a 1936 Chevy and other old cars (all of them with big eyes on their windshields, à la Disney-Pixar's 2006 homage to Route 66, *Cars*), railroad junk, and several very silly signs; and inside, the close walls are covered with the business cards of customers from all over the world. Don't go here if you're grumpy: There will likely be a stand-up wait, especially on summer weekends, and you *will* be teased, especially if you have a question that requires a serious answer.

The **Roadkill Café** (502 W. Route 66, 928/422-3554, www.route66seligmanarizona.com, 7am-9pm daily, $5-24) is more than just a funny name; it's a popular place for buffalo burgers, steaks, sandwiches, and other typical Old West-themed bar-and-grill eats. Have a few drinks in the **OK Saloon** and a look around at the cluttered interior.

The majestic, if stuffed, mountain lion that watches over diners at **Westside Lilo's Café** (415 W. Chino Ave., 928/422-5456, 6am-9pm daily, $5-23), a popular diner-style eatery (complete with counter service), was shot not far from the restaurant by a member of the owners' family. It's just one of the backcountry touches that add to the ambience here, where they serve good burgers, excellent homemade potato salad, and other standard American fare. They are famous for their carrot cake, which is moist and flavorful.

Grand Canyon Caverns

Grand Canyon Caverns (Route 66, mile marker 115, 928/422-3223, www.gc-caverns.com, 8am-6pm daily summer, 10am-4pm daily winter, $20) offers guided underground tours of North America's largest dry cave, where crystals and other strange rock formations hide in the weatherless darkness. The main tour lasts about 45 minutes and takes you about three quarters of a mile through the limestone cavern, but not before you descend 21 stories (210 feet) beneath the earth in an elevator. There's a lot of history here, too: During the Cold War the cavern served as a bomb shelter-in-waiting, packed with enough food and water to sustain hundreds of blast-weary survivors if the unthinkable occurred. The friendly folks here at this old-school combination Route 66 tourist trap (in the best sense of the phrase) and motel also offer an off-trail tour ($69) that goes much deeper into the caverns. And they'll be happy to take you out into the nearby ranch lands on horseback or in a jeep.

Getting There

Grand Canyon Caverns is **25 miles** west of Seligman on **Historic Route 66.** The drive takes about **30 minutes.** Turn left at the Caverns Inn sign to enter the parking lot for Grand Canyon Caverns.

Peach Springs

The capital of the Hualapai Reservation, Peach Springs is a tiny town of about 1,000 people, tucked in a green valley along Historic Route 66. Stop at the **Hualapai Lodge** (900 Route 66, 928/769-2230 or 928/769-2636, www.grandcanyonwest.com, $159) on the west end of town to book a tour to Grand Canyon West, which is on tribal land and features the famous Skywalk. It's also a good spot to stay the night before hiking into Havasupai Canyon, as it's only about seven miles from the trailhead.

Getting There

Peach Springs is about 30 miles from Grand Canyon Caverns on Historic Route 66. The drive takes a little more than 30 minutes. Peach Springs is right on Route 66; you can't miss it.

Truxton and Valentine

In the nearly abandoned towns of Truxton and Valentine are a few buildings dating from the 1930s to the 1950s moldering along the road. Animal-lovers will want to stop at Keepers of the Wild Nature Park in Valentine.

Getting There

Truxton is just under **10 miles** west of Peach Springs along **Historic Route 66.** Valentine is another **10 miles** farther west.

Keepers of the Wild Nature Park

Though tawny cougars are known to occasionally haunt these windy high-desert plains, and some stretches of Historic Route 66 could perhaps stand in for a sweeping African savanna, one doesn't expect to encounter a shaggy-maned lion here, or for that matter a flitting lemur or a thoughtful baboon. Except perhaps at this hospital, retirement home, and haven for abused, neglected, and abandoned exotic animals. **Keepers of the Wild Nature Park** (13441 E. Hwy. 66, milepost 87, Valentine, www.keepersofthewild.org, 9am-5pm Wed.-Mon., all-day pass $18, $12 children over 12) has tigers, several lazy cougars, a chubby black jaguar named Hope, and a whole village full of squealing, playful monkeys.

The animals live in large, fenced-in habitats, with big boulders and pools and mostly native trees and shrubs. The paths are easy, but there isn't a lot of shade, so bring a hat. The whole park is wheelchair accessible, and there's a gift shop with snacks and drinks. They encourage picnicking, so feel free to bring a basket. The last tickets are sold at 4pm. For $10 more per person, a guide will take you on a driven "safari" tour (10am, 1pm, and 3:30pm) of the park that lasts about 1.5 hours. This is an ideal stop for families with kids, most of whom might not find the barren spaces along Route 66 particularly scintillating. Most of the animals here have cute names and sad life stories, so you run the risk of falling in love.

Hackberry

The town of Hackberry is by far the most popular place to stop between Peach Springs and Kingman, owing to the carefully curated throwback that is the Hackberry General Store.

Getting There

Hackberry is about **five miles** west of Valentine on **Historic Route 66.**

Hackberry General Store

Try *not* to stop at this picture-ready old store and junkyard museum. It can't be done. Maybe it's the cherry-red, 1957 Corvette parked conspicuously out front.

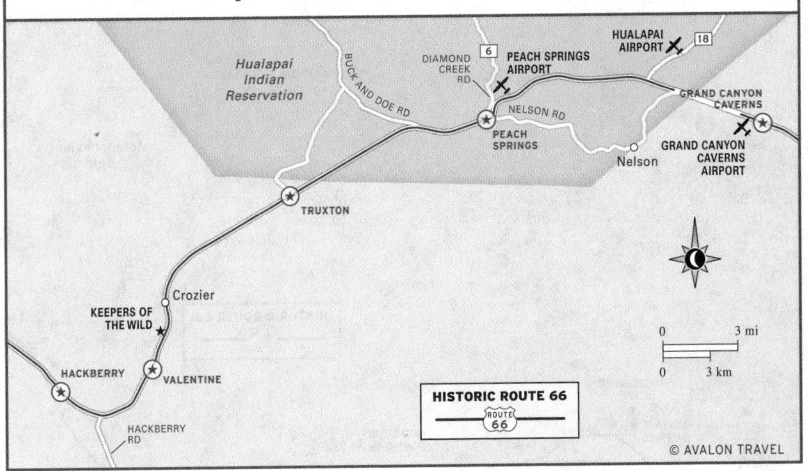

Maybe it's because it's the only sign of life for miles in either direction along this forgotten stretch of the old Mother Road. Maybe it's the root beer.

Cluttered with Route 66 and American road-culture memorabilia, including several rusting old cars that once made their way along the Route, the **Hackberry General Store** (11255 E. Hwy. 66, 928/769-2605, www.hackberrygeneralstore.com, 9am-6pm daily) looks like it belongs to another era. Inside you'll find cold sodas, snacks, souvenirs, and a lot to look at, including some really cool road-map murals on the walls by artist Bob Waldmire. The owners, who bought the place on a whim years ago while driving Route 66, encourage visitors to walk around the property, examine the memorabilia, and take pictures.

Kingman

Spread across a dry desert basin below pine-topped mountains and cut through by I-40, Kingman and its environs have long been a stopover for those traveling Route 66. Indeed, the town, mostly a transportation hub and county government center these days, has secured its place in Americana, along with a few other Arizona towns, by appearing in the song "Route 66," certainly one of the most frequently covered tunes of all time, written in 1946 by Bobby Troup and first recorded by the great Nat King Cole.

Kingman's identity, at least for the sake of tourism, is all wrapped up in being the "Heart of Route 66," and there are a few nostalgic sights here harking back to a time when cross-country travel was slower and, in a sense, more meaningful than it is today. The town, which isn't much to look at, sits near the junction of two scenic drives that will show you an unvarnished Arizona, rolling through large swaths of left-alone desert and old mining ghost towns taken over by artisans and actors, up over mountain passes held together by strange cacti, across bridges swaying high above dry arroyos, and past abandoned outposts and tourists traps, the rusted shells of long-dead vehicles, and all those tiny white roadside crosses remembering road-weary tragedies.

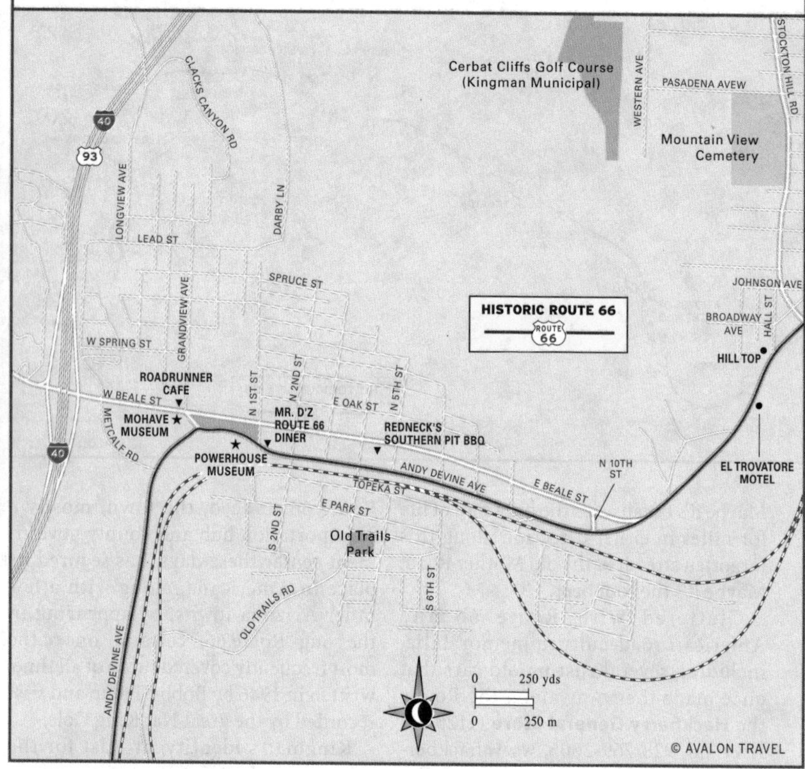

Getting There

Kingman is about **30 miles** southwest of Hackberry along **Historic Route 66.** The drive takes about **40 minutes.** Route 66 shoots directly into Kingman.

Sights

Peruse museums and stores featuring the artifacts and stories of the heyday of Route 66 travel, then hop in your car and drive the rough and lonely remains of the Mother Road, through squat cactus forests and old lost towns still pining for the region's long-gone gold- and silver-mining days.

Historic Route 66 Museum

The serious-faced manikins that populate the life-sized dioramas at the small **Historic Route 66 Museum** (Powerhouse Visitors Center, 120 W. Andy Devine Ave., 928/753-9889, www.route66museum.net, 9am-5pm daily, $4 adults, children under 13 free) are a bit unsettling, but they create an evocative picture of how Arizona was influenced, and to a major degree populated, by one long strip of road. Plastic pioneers, decked out in authentic frontier-era outfits, walk beside real wagons, while sad dust-bowl migrants gather their possessions and their children into a rickety truck and look plaintively toward a new life in the gardens of California. The curators here have stuffed a lot of history, and a good deal of local artifacts and ephemera, into a relatively small space, using detailed scenes to depict the historic movement of people and culture along the 35th Parallel—from the Native Americans to Lt. Edward Beale's 1857 trek across what was then a wagon road, at the helm of a company of 25 camels, to the well-remembered golden age of postwar car culture. One of the museum's best scenes re-creates the style and design of 1950s Route 66, the heyday of the cross-country family road trip that brought so many easterners to the still-wild West to see the Grand Canyon and the Petrified Forest. Though much of the road romance found in those eras is dead and gone now, thanks to this excellent little museum we can relive it all just a bit. Those interested in American car culture and road culture should not miss this sight.

Mohave Museum of History and Arts

A diverse local history museum, the **Mohave Museum of History and Arts** (400 W. Beale St., 928/753-3195, www.mohavemuseum.org, 9am-5pm Mon.-Fri., 1pm-5pm Sat., $4 adults, children under 12 free) has a lot to look at, including a detailed display on the life and career of Kingman's favorite son, actor Andy Devine (there are even original telegrams sent by the famous screen cowboy on display here).

About a block away from the Powerhouse Visitors Center, the museum has several rooms crowded with the history of northwestern Arizona as well as a gallery of portraits depicting each U.S. president and first lady and some stuffed examples of the region's wildlife. Other displays explain the history of mining and ranching in the area, and there are some first-rate examples of Hualapai basketry and locally mined turquoise. You could spend a few hours lost among the eclectic collections if you're not careful. Southwestern artist Roy Purcell, a former director of the museum, painted the museum's wonderful murals showing life as it used to be here in this forgotten frontier, and a gallery features the work of a rotating group of local artists.

Bonelli House

A pioneer Mormon family that settled in Kingman in the 1890s, the Bonellis built this territorial-era home after their first home burned down in 1915. They rebuilt better and stronger, using tufa stone from the rocky hills nearby to create an interior that was cool in the summer and warm in the winter. Local history buffs have restored the **Bonelli House** (430 E. Spring St., 928/753-1413, 11am-3pm Mon.-Fri., included in price of admission to Mohave Museum) with exacting detail, giving visitors an authentic look at what middle-class family and home life was like on the high-desert frontier.

Entertainment and Events

A focal point of Kingman's downtown, **The Cellar Door Wine Bar & Bottle Shop** (414 E. Beale St., http://the-cellar-door.com, 4pm-10pm Tues.-Thurs., 4pm-midnight Fri.-Sat.) adds a bit of urban class to this rural region. They offer about 120 different wines, 25 beers, and a small menu with a cheese plate, hummus, and olives. You can sit at the tasteful wine bar and listen to a laid-back local musician or take your bottle with you.

The month of May brings thousands of Route 66 nostalgics and classic-car lovers to the old stretch of the Mother Road from Seligman to Topock for the **Historic Route 66 Fun Run** (928/753-5001, www.azrt66.com, May). Far-flung drivers in a riot of old and new vehicles—many of them gorgeous and classic, and many of their owners in some kind of recycled 1950s wear—gather in Seligman for the kickoff of this popular regional event. After eating and dancing to the live bands, a host of roaring two- and four-wheelers makes its slow way along Historic Route 66 west to Kingman, where they park en masse

Who Is Andy Devine?

Kingman's favorite son was one of those great American character actors that most of us recognize but often can't name. His strained, gravelly but high voice, the result of a childhood accident that permanently damaged his vocal chords, and his size—a former football star, he was corpulent his entire adult life—make Andy Devine (1905-1977) stand out more than most.

While film buffs will remember Devine as the driver in John Ford's 1939 Western classic *Stage Coach,* John Wayne's breakout film, made partly in Monument Valley, or as one of the soldiers in John Huston's *The Red Badge of Courage* in 1951, his career was long and diverse, encompassing radio, both B- and A-grade movies, and television. He started out as a bit player in silent films during the 1920s and went on to entertain several generations.

Those of us who grew up in the 1970s and 1980s will likely remember Devine by his voice alone, which became that of the gentle and funny Friar Tuck in Disney's animated *Robin Hood* in 1973. Those who grew up in the 1950s and 1960s, on the other hand, remember Devine as "Jingle Jones" from the Western television series *Wild Bill Hickok,* or as the host of the Saturday morning show *Andy's Gang.* And, if you remember the 1930s and 1940s, you'll recognize that voice again as a regular on the Jack Benny radio show, where his greeting "Hiya, Buck!" made him famous, and of course you'll know Devine as the funny sidekick in many Roy Rogers Westerns.

Though Devine was born in Flagstaff a couple hours northeast of Kingman, where his father worked for the railroad, he moved to Kingman when he was just one year old. An on-the-job accident had taken the elder Devine's leg and a settlement with the railroad helped the family buy the Beale Hotel in Kingman, where Devine grew up and is celebrated in the local museum and during an annual festival and parade.

for show-and-tell in the parking lot of the Powerhouse Visitors Center. In downtown Kingman there's more eating, bands and other entertainment, and vendors. Come Sunday morning, hangover or not, everybody gets up, climbs back behind the wheel, and heads east to Topock and the end of the road, stopping of course to give some love to the burros in Oatman.

In late September Kingman celebrates itself and its favorite son during **Andy Devine Days Parade & Community Fair** (928/757-7919, late Sept.), which features food vendors, arts and crafts, and entertainment in the town's historic, if usually a bit desolate, downtown.

Shopping

There are two shops in the **Powerhouse Visitors Center** (120 W. Andy Devine Ave., 928/753-6106, 9am-6pm daily spring-summer, 9am-5pm Dec.-Feb.) where you'll find items you might not be able to get too many other places. For Route 66 and American road-culture gifts and souvenirs check out the **Historic Route 66 Association of Arizona Gift Shop** inside the Powerhouse.

If you're into finding the treasures that other people have given up, there are a few antiques and resale shops along East Beale Street in the historic old town area that are definitely worth wandering through.

Recreation

Hiking and Camping

If you missed north-central Arizona's pinebelt, head to northwest Arizona's answer at **Hualapai Mountain Park** (6250 Hualapai Mountain Park, 928/681-5700, www.mcparks.com), about 12 miles from Kingman. This sap-and-campfire-scented 2,300-acre mountain park is high in the pines overlooking the scrub valley. The titular mountain range rises from the plain southeast of town to heights between 5,000 and nearly 8,500 feet, cloaked in the conifers typical of such elevations in Arizona. There are 19 cabins for rent through the **Mohave County Parks Division** (877/757-0915, www.mcparks.com, $65-130), built of stacked stone and wood by the Civilian Conservation Corps in the 1930s and sleeping 2-12 people, most with rustic old fireplaces—but also with kitchens and electricity. You can camp here, too, or park your RV among the pines ($17-30); most of the camping spots don't have water and are obtained on a first-come, first-served basis.

The park's trail system leads high into the mountains for some inspiring views. The trails are well worn and forested, with huge slabs and half-buried outcroppings of granite dropped in everywhere as if there had been a rock fight among giants here long ago. The 8,417-foot **Hualapai Peak** is the highest point in the park and in the region. The 4.3-mile round-trip **Potato Patch Loop Trail** is a moderate and representative hike, running through ponderosa pines, aspens, and high stands of spruce and fir, strewn with needles and cones and watched over by boulders covered in dry lichen. Start out on the switchbacks of the **Aspen Springs Trail** and then meet up with the loop at the Aspen Springs-Potato Patch Junction after about a mile. You go up about 800 feet in the first mile and half, but it levels out on the loop. A map of the entire system, which has about 16 miles of developed and undeveloped trails, is available at the park office. There's really no time of year to stay away from this pleasant, heavily used mountain park (there will be ATV riders here, so be forewarned). It's hot in the summer, but with the breezy moderation that its elevation allows; it's cold and sometimes

Top to bottom: El Travatore Motel, Kingman; Historic Route 66; Hackberry General Store.

snowy in the winter, but not to any uncomfortable degree.

Accommodations

There are several very affordable, basic hotels located on Andy Devine Avenue, Route 66, in Kingman's downtown area, some of them with retro road-trip neon signs and Route 66 themes. There are a good many chain hotels in town as well.

The ★ **El Trovatore Motel** (1440 E. Andy Devine Ave., 928/753-6520, http://eltrovatoremotel.com, $66-100) has a fun Route 66 theme, including a charmingly illustrated map of the Mother Road painted on the outside of the sprawling complex marked and lit-up by a 100-foot neon sign. First opened in the 1930s along Route 66 in Kingman, this refurbished motor court once hosted Hollywood stars and now celebrates that fact with Hollywood-themed rooms. Aside from its attractive kitsch, El Trovatore is a good deal, with an on-site restaurant and rates that include breakfast. The rooms have refrigerators and are clean and comfortable, and there's a laundry room and free Wi-Fi.

The ★ **Hill Top Motel** (1901 E. Andy Devine Ave., 928/753-2198, www.hilltopmotelaz.com, $52-68) has character. Its 1950s-era neon sign calls out to all Route 66 road-trippers, clicking something far back in the American memory, convincing them to stop and stay. This small, affordable motel, near the top of a hill looking out on the Hualapai Mountains, has a connection to the dark side of American culture as well: Oklahoma City bomber Timothy McVeigh stayed here for a few nights in 1995 while planning his attack on the Alfred P. Murrah Building for April of that same year. The bombing killed 168 people. Built in the 1950s but refurbished since then, the Hill Top has standard, comfortable rooms with refrigerators and microwaves, and it offers free Wi-Fi. Outside there's a pool and a well-kept cactus garden.

Along Hualapai Mountain Road on the way up to the piney mountains, the **Hualapai Mountain Resort** (4525 Hualapai Mountain Rd., 928/757-3545, www.hmresort.net, $99-159) rents eight rustic but comfortable and clean rooms in a quiet, secluded setting. They have an on-site restaurant (11am-8pm Wed.-Thurs., 11am-10pm Fri., 8am-10pm Sat., 8am-8pm Sun., $6-22) serving steaks and burgers, salads, sandwiches, and other standard American fare.

At **Upton's Hidden Pines Bed & Breakfast** (935 S. DW Ranch Rd., 928/279-7394, www.uptonhiddenpines.com, $90) you can rent one of three small, tasteful, cozy rooms with big beds. Just east of town off I-40, within sight of the Hualapai Mountains, this friendly spot, on five acres and decorated with an Old West ranching theme, has a comfortable living room for chatting and lounging and a big porch for staring off into the vast distance.

Food

It is widely known throughout this flat and windy region that the retro Route 66 drive-in **Mr. D'z Route 66 Diner** (105 E. Andy Devine Ave., 928/718-0066, www.mrdzrt66diner.com, $9-18) serves the best burger in town, but they also have a large menu with all manner of delectable diner and road food, like chili dogs, pizza, hot sandwiches, baby back ribs, chicken-fried steak, and a big plate of spaghetti. Plus, breakfast is served all day. The portions are big, but save room for a thick shake or a root-beer float. Don't leave your camera in the car; the turquoise-and-pink interior and the cool old jukebox here are snapshot ready.

The **Dambar & Steakhouse** (1960 E. Andy Devine Ave., 928/753-3523, www.dambarsteakhouse.com, 11am-10pm daily, $10-30) is local favorite that serves great steaks, prime rib, lobster, cowboy beans, and burgers. The bar has excellent regionally brewed beers, and the sawdust on the floor, cowboy kitsch, and Route 66 memorabilia add a bit of character to this popular place. They offer patio seating in the summer and live country music on the weekends.

The best restaurant for miles in any direction is ★ **Mattina's Ristorante Italiano** (318 E. Oak St., 928/753-7504, www.mattinasristorante.com, 5pm-9pm Tues.-Sat., $13-25), where you can get perfectly prepared Italian food, including outstanding beef medallions and rack of lamb. It's difficult to choose among the diverse and outlandishly appetizing selection of pasta dishes, but it's equally difficult to pass up the lobster ravioli or the thick, creamy fettuccine Alfredo. Don't leave without trying the tiramisu or the key lime pie, and consider sampling liberally from their well-stocked wine cellar.

Redneck's Southern Barbecue (420 E. Beale St., 928/757-8227, www.rednecksouthernpitbbq.com, 11am-8pm Tues.-Sat., $3-10) in Kingman's small, often quiet downtown serves excellent Southern-style barbecue, with delicious baked beans and coleslaw on the side. The pulled pork and the brisket should not be missed by connoisseurs of those heaven-sent dishes.

Beale Street Brews Coffee Shop (418 E. Beale St., 928/753-4004, http://bealestreetbrews.net, 7am-6pm Mon.-Thurs., 7am-9pm Fri.-Sat., 7am-3pm Sun.) has free-trade coffee, pastries, free Wi-Fi, poetry readings, local art on the walls, local music in the air, and a few tables outside, perfect for relaxing the day away.

Information and Services

Visitors Center

Built in 1907 to supply power to the region's mines, the **Powerhouse Visitors Center** (120 W. Andy Devine Ave., 928/753-6106, 9am-6pm daily spring-summer, 9am-5pm Dec.-Feb.) has information on all the sights, accommodations, and attractions in Kingman and environs, plus a model train circling the inside perimeter.

Hospital

Kingman Regional Medical Center (3269 Stockton Hill Rd., 928/757-2101, www.azkrmc.com) has a full-service emergency room.

The Grand Canyon

The Grand Canyon must be seen to be believed. If you see it for the first time and don't have to catch your breath, you might need to check your pulse. Take your time—this view could last forever.

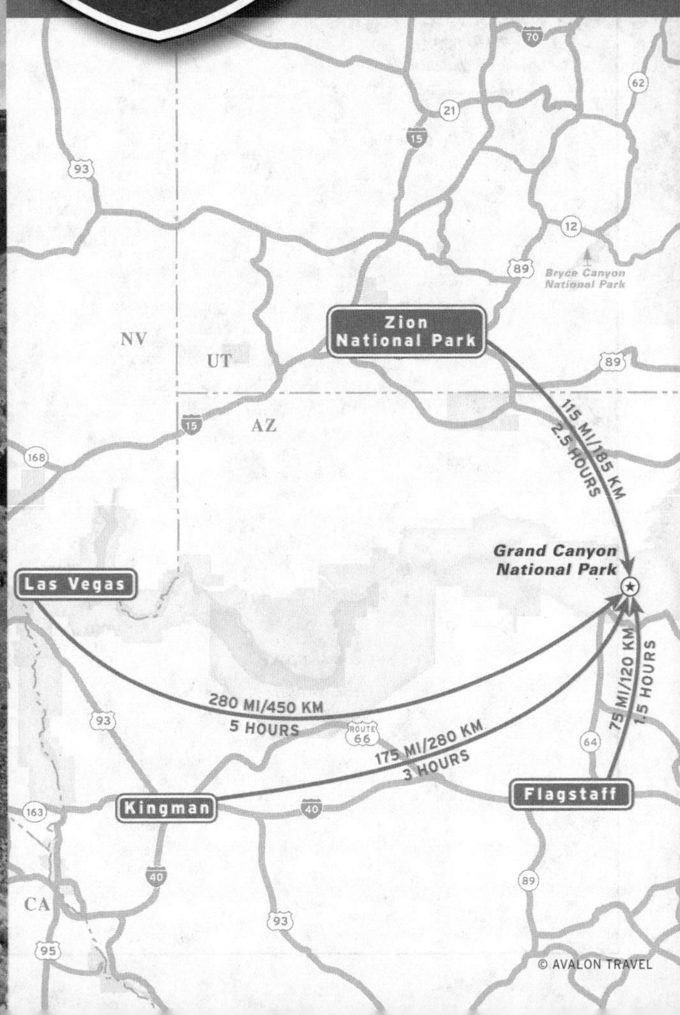

The Grand Canyon

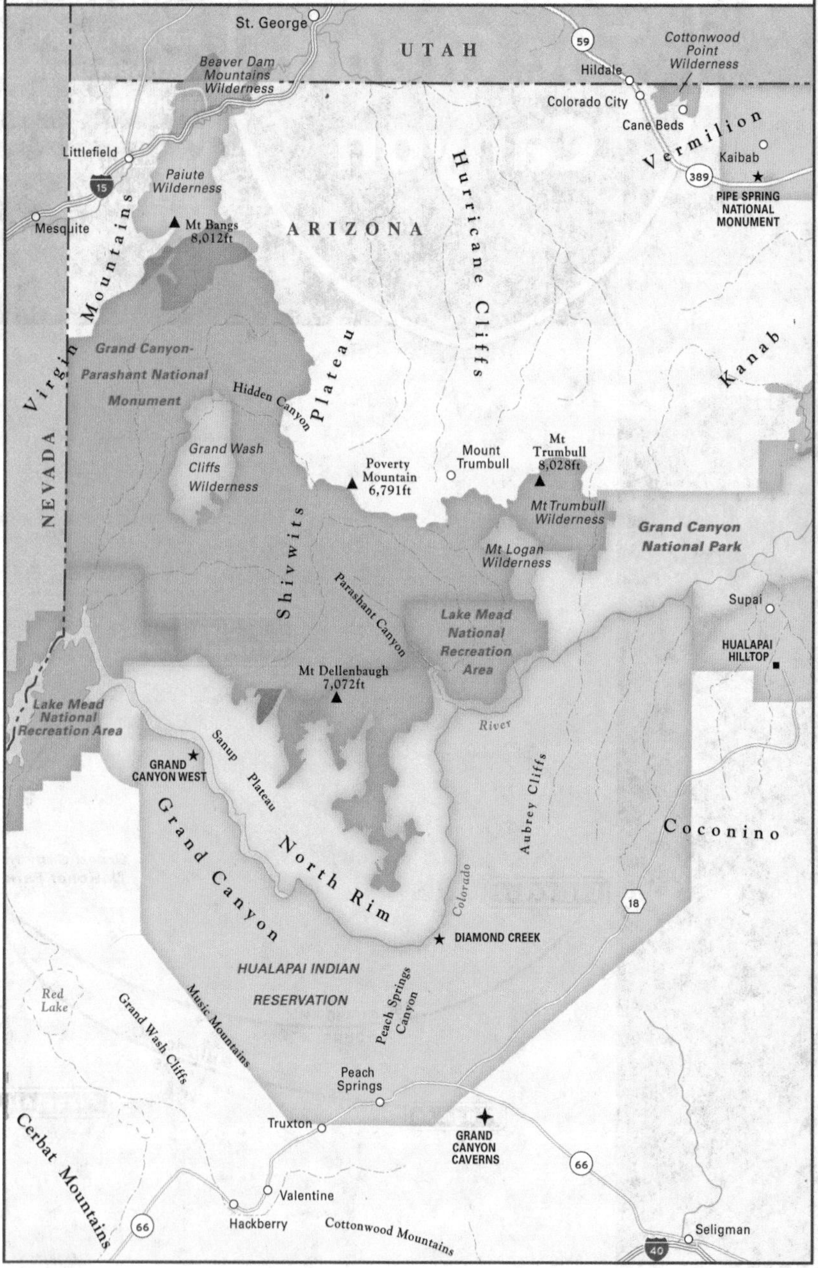

St. George
UTAH
59
Cottonwood Point Wilderness
Beaver Dam Mountains Wilderness
Hildale
Colorado City
Cane Beds
Vermilion
Kaibab
389
PIPE SPRING NATIONAL MONUMENT
Littlefield
15
Paiute Wilderness
Mesquite
Mt Bangs 8,012ft
ARIZONA
Hurricane Cliffs
Virgin Mountains
Grand Canyon-Parashant National Monument
Plateau
Kanab
Hidden Canyon
Grand Wash Cliffs Wilderness
Poverty Mountain 6,791ft
Mount Trumbull
Mt Trumbull 8,028ft
Mt Trumbull Wilderness
NEVADA
Shivwits
Mt Logan Wilderness
Grand Canyon National Park
Parashant Canyon
Lake Mead National Recreation Area
Supai
HUALAPAI HILLTOP
Mt Dellenbaugh 7,072ft
Lake Mead National Recreation Area
River
Sanup Plateau
GRAND CANYON WEST
Aubrey Cliffs
Grand Canyon
North Rim
Coconino
Colorado
18
DIAMOND CREEK
HUALAPAI INDIAN RESERVATION
Red Lake
Grand Wash Cliffs
Music Mountains
Peach Springs Canyon
Peach Springs
Truxton
GRAND CANYON CAVERNS
66
Cerbat Mountains
Valentine
Hackberry
66
Cottonwood Mountains
Seligman
40

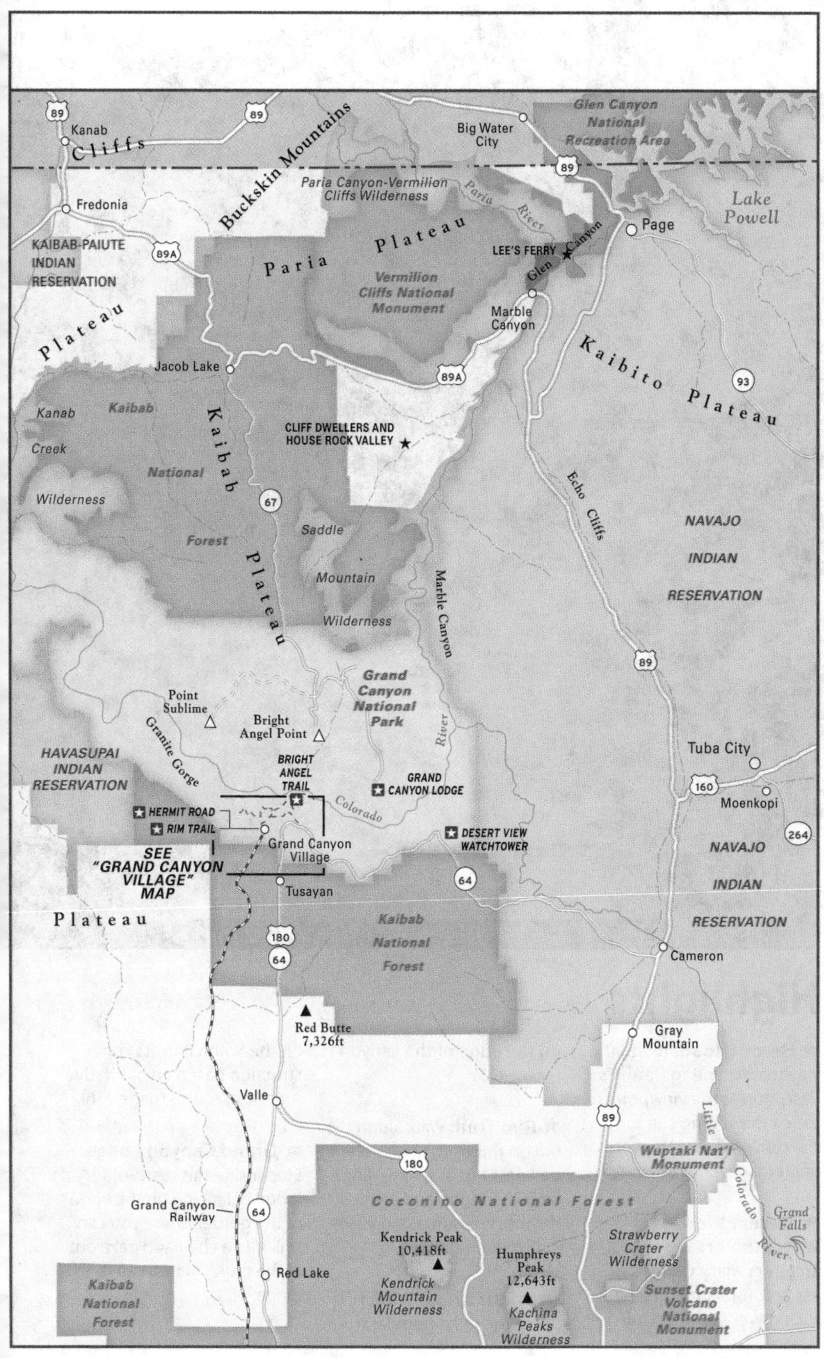

Kanab
Cliffs
Buckskin Mountains
Big Water City
Glen Canyon National Recreation Area
Paria Canyon-Vermilion Cliffs Wilderness
Paria River
Lake Powell
Fredonia
Page
KAIBAB-PAIUTE INDIAN RESERVATION
Paria Plateau
LEE'S FERRY
Glen Canyon
Vermilion Cliffs National Monument
Marble Canyon
Plateau
Jacob Lake
Kaibito Plateau
Kanab Creek Wilderness
Kaibab National Forest
Kaibab Plateau
CLIFF DWELLERS AND HOUSE ROCK VALLEY
Echo Cliffs
NAVAJO INDIAN RESERVATION
Saddle Mountain Wilderness
Marble Canyon
Grand Canyon National Park
Point Sublime
Bright Angel Point
Granite Gorge
HAVASUPAI INDIAN RESERVATION
BRIGHT ANGEL TRAIL
GRAND CANYON LODGE
Colorado River
Tuba City
Moenkopi
HERMIT ROAD
RIM TRAIL
Grand Canyon Village
DESERT VIEW WATCHTOWER
SEE "GRAND CANYON VILLAGE" MAP
Tusayan
Plateau
Kaibab National Forest
Cameron
Red Butte 7,326ft
Gray Mountain
Valle
Little Colorado River
Wupatki Nat'l Monument
Grand Canyon Railway
Coconino National Forest
Grand Falls
Kendrick Peak 10,418ft
Humphreys Peak 12,643ft
Strawberry Crater Wilderness
Red Lake
Kendrick Mountain Wilderness
Kachina Peaks Wilderness
Sunset Crater Volcano National Monument
Kaibab National Forest
89
89A
67
93
160
264
64
180

Highlights

★ **Hermit Road:** Along the way to enchanting Hermit's Rest, stop at the viewpoints to see the setting sun turn the canyon walls into works of art (page 429).

★ **Desert View Watchtower:** See one of architect Mary Colter's finest accomplishments—a rock tower standing tall on the edge of the canyon (page 435).

★ **Rim Trail:** Walk along the rim on this easy, accessible trail past historical buildings, famous lodges, and some of the most breathtaking views in the world (page 436).

★ **Bright Angel Trail:** Hike down the most popular trail on the South Rim, its construction based on old Native American routes (page 436).

★ **Grand Canyon Lodge:** Step inside this rustic old lodge balancing on the edge of the gorge, where you can sink into a chair and gaze out at the multicolored canyon (page 447).

The view from one of the South Rim's lookouts will last in your memory for a lifetime.

Travelers can make reservations, obtain a permit, and enter the desert depths of the canyon, taking a hike, or even a mule ride, to the Colorado River, or spending a weekend trekking rim-to-rim with an overnight at the famous Phantom Ranch, deep in the canyon's inner gorge. The really brave can hire a guide and take a once-in-a-lifetime trip down the great river, riding the roiling rapids and camping on its serene beaches.

There are plenty of places to stay and eat, many of them charming and historic, on the canyon's South Rim. If you decide to go to the high, forested, and often snowy North Rim, you'll drive through a corner of the desolate Arizona Strip, which has a beauty and a history all its own.

Water-sports enthusiasts will want to make it up to the far northern reaches of the state to the Glen Canyon National Recreation Area to do some waterskiing or maybe rent a houseboat, and anyone interested in the far end of American engineering prowess will want to see Glen Canyon Dam, holding back the once-wild Colorado River.

Getting to the Grand Canyon

The majority of Grand Canyon visitors drive here, reaching the South Rim from either Flagstaff or Williams and entering the park through the South or East entrances. The **South entrance** (US 180 past Tusayan) is usually the busiest, and during the summer, traffic is likely to be backed up somewhat. The quickest way to get to the South entrance by car is to take **AZ-64 to US 180** from **Williams.** It's a **55-mile, one-hour** drive across a barren plain; there are a few kitschy places to stop along the way, including Bedrock City, a dilapidated model of the Flintstones' hometown. To get to the **East/Desert View entrance** (AZ-64) from Flagstaff, take US 89 to AZ-64, a **1.5-hour, 80-mile** drive.

Best Hotels

★ **El Tovar:** The South Rim's most stylish and storied lodge, built in Arts and Crafts style, overlooks the canyon (page 441).

★ **Bright Angel Lodge:** This historic, rustic lodge is on the edge of the Grand Canyon's bustling South Rim (page 441).

★ **Historic Cameron Trading Post & Lodge:** This travelers' crossroads has sweeping views of the Navajo Nation (page 442).

★ **Grand Canyon Hotel:** This refurbished and affordable gem is in the heart of historic Williams, gateway to the Grand Canyon (page 443).

★ **Mather Campground:** Sleep under starry skies at one of 300 campsites close to Grand Canyon Village (page 443).

★ **Grand Canyon Lodge:** This grand old hotel is perched high on the edge of the canyon's wild and forested North Rim (page 449).

★ **Phantom Ranch:** Few visit this small paradise deep in the canyon's bottomlands, but those who do never forget it (page 455).

From Las Vegas

South Rim

280 miles / 5 hours

Las Vegas is **280 miles** from the Grand Canyon's South Rim; it's about a **five-hour drive,** quite breathtaking in some parts and monotonous in others. Even if you get a late-morning start and make a few stops along the way, you're still likely to arrive at the park by dinnertime. Most summer weekends, you'll find the route crowded but manageable, unless there's an accident; in that case you'll likely be stuck where you are for some time. At all times of the year, you'll be surrounded by 18-wheelers barreling across the land.

From the Strip, get to the main and most direct route, **US 93 South,** by taking **I-15 South** to **I-215 East,** then **I-515 South** for a total of about 25 miles. After you join US 93, the road passes near Lake Mead and the Hoover Dam and through a barren landscape of jagged rocks and creosote bushes. About 80 miles farther on, you'll hit **Kingman.** Here you take **I-40 East.** Drive 115 miles to **Williams,** where you pick up **AZ-64 North,** which merges with US 180 on the 60-mile shot to Grand Canyon National Park. If you feel like stopping overnight—and perhaps it is better to see the canyon with fresh eyes—do so in Williams, just an hour or so from the park's **South entrance.**

West Rim

130 miles / 2.5 hours

Driving from Vegas, you may want to stop at **Grand Canyon West** and the Hualapai Reservation's **Skywalk.** This area is only a **130-mile** drive southeast of Vegas (about **2.5 hours**). However, this will add at least a full day to your trip if you plan on also visiting the South Rim, and the view from the South Rim is better and cheaper. Grand Canyon West charges a $43 entrance fee on top of $32 for the Skywalk, and you'll probably have to ride a shuttle bus part of the way. You can purchase tickets to the Skywalk and to any of the other attractions at Grand Canyon West when you arrive.

To reach Grand Canyon West from Las Vegas, take **US 93 South** out of the city, heading south for about 75 miles to the intersection with **Pierce Ferry Road,** where you'll see signs for Meadview. Turn left (north) onto Pierce Ferry Road. In about 30 miles, turn right (east) on **Diamond Bar Road** and continue 20 miles, with about seven miles unpaved, to Grand Canyon West.

To continue on to the South Rim, retrace your steps back to **Pierce Ferry Road.** After seven miles, turn left onto **Stockton Hill Road,** which you'll follow for just over 40 miles into Kingman. Jump on **I-40 East/US 93 South** for about a mile, then take **exit 53** for **Route 66** (signs for Andy Devine Ave./Kingman Airport).

Best Restaurants

★ **El Tovar Dining Room:** Enjoy locally sourced gourmet meals in a stylishly historic atmosphere on the canyon's edge (page 444).

★ **The Arizona Room:** This quiet place amid the South Rim's bustle is perfect for a lunch with a view (page 444).

★ **Bright Angel Restaurant:** Fred Harvey-inspired, it serves pre-hike American fare right next to the Bright Angel trailhead (page 444).

★ **Rod's Steak House:** This institution in nearby Williams serves up Old West charm and juicy steaks (page 445).

★ **Diablo Burger:** This Flagstaff favorite serves one of the best burgers in the Southwest (page 445).

 Side Trip: Retro Fun on Route 66

Seligman, a tiny roadside settlement 87 miles east of Kingman, holds on tightly to its Route 66 heritage. There are less than 500 full-time residents and often, especially on summer weekends, twice that number of travelers. Don't be surprised to see European visitors, classic car nuts, and 60-something bikers passing through town. John Lasseter, co-director of the 2006 Disney-Pixar film *Cars,* has said that he based the movie's fictional town of Radiator Springs partly on Seligman, which, like Radiator Springs, nearly died out when it was bypassed by I-40 in the late 1970s.

Stop at **Delgadillo's Snow Cap Drive-In** (301 E. Chino St./Rte. 66, 928/422-3291, daily breakfast, lunch, and dinner, under $10), off Route 66 on the east end of town, a famous food shack dedicated to feeding, entertaining, and teasing Route 66 travelers for generations. They serve a mean chiliburger, a famous "cheeseburger with cheese," hot dogs, malts, soft ice cream, and much more. Expect a wait, especially on summer weekends, and you will be teased, especially if you have a question that requires a serious answer.

The **Roadkill Café** (502 W. Chino St./Rte. 66, 928/422-3554, www.route66seligmanarizona.com, daily 7am-9pm, $5-24) is more than just a funny name; it's a popular place for buffalo burgers, steaks, and sandwiches.

There are several small, affordable, locally owned motels in Seligman. The **Supai Lodge** (134 W. Chino St./Rte. 66, 928/422-4153, $66-80 d), named for the nearby Grand Canyon village inhabited by the Havasupai people, has clean and comfortable guest rooms at a fair price.

The **Historic Route 66 Motel** (500 W. Chino St./Rte. 66, 928/422-3204, www.route66seligmanarizona.com, $65-80 d) offers free wireless Internet and refrigerators in clean, comfortable guest rooms, and the **Canyon Lodge** (114 E. Chino St./Rte. 66, 928/422-3255, www.route66canyonlodge.com, $65-80 d) has free wireless Internet along with refrigerators and microwaves in its themed guest rooms. They also serve a free continental breakfast.

Continue for 45 miles to **Peach Springs** along old Route 66. Once there, you can stop for the night at the Hualapai Lodge, or continue on for about 40 miles east on Route 66 to **Seligman.** From Seligman, head another 20 miles east on **Historic Route 66** to **Ash Fork,** where you can pick up **I-40 East** to **Williams,** 20 miles farther on. From there, head north for 55 miles along **AZ-64** to reach the **South entrance.** Adding the South Rim on to a visit to Grand Canyon West will total **380 miles** and over **6.5 hours** of driving.

From Kingman (Route 66)

West Rim

75 miles / 1.5 hours

Kingman is one of the few towns of any real size along Historic Route 66. Most people who visit the West Rim and the Skywalk do so from Las Vegas. However, if you're driving the Mother Road through Kingman and want to check out this portion of the Grand Canyon, the **75-mile** drive takes about **1.5 hours.** Take **Stockton Hill Road** north for 45 miles, then turn right onto **Pierce Ferry Road.** After seven miles, turn right onto **Diamond Bar Road,** which leads to the Skywalk on the Hualapai Reservation in about 20 miles, some of which is dirt road.

South Rim

175 miles / 3 hours

It's a nearly **three-hour** drive of **175 miles** from Kingman to Grand Canyon National Park's South Rim, even if you eschew Historic Route 66 and hop right on I-40. From Kingman, it's about 120 miles on **I-40 East** to Williams. From there, take **AZ-64 North** for 55 miles into the park.

Count on adding at least another two hours to the trip if you drive the Mother Road from Kingman to Ash Fork (where you have to get on I-40). Take I-40 to Williams and pick-up AZ-64/US 180 to the South Rim, which is about an hour's drive from Williams.

From Flagstaff (Route 66)

South Rim

75 miles / 1.5 hours

To get to the **South entrance** of the South Rim from Flagstaff, it's a **1.5-hour, 75-mile** drive. From town, take **US 180 West** through the forest past the San Francisco Peaks for about 50 miles, at which point the highway merges with **AZ-64.** Continue north for about 30 miles to reach the park entrance.

To get to the **East entrance,** also known as **Desert View,** from Flagstaff, a **1.5-hour, 80-mile** drive, take **US 89 North** for just over 45 miles, then turn left onto **AZ-64 West.** From here, it's about 25 miles to the Desert View entrance. This route is recommended if you want to see portions of Navajo country on your way to the canyon. Entering here will put you right at the Desert View Watchtower and the Tusayan Museum and Ruin—sights that you'll otherwise have to travel 25 or so miles east from Grand Canyon Village to see.

From Zion National Park

North Rim

115 miles / 2.5 hours

Zion National Park is about **115 miles** from Grand Canyon National Park's North Rim. It's a **2.5-hour** drive across a forested plateau into the red rock and rolling sagebrush of the largely empty landscape around the Arizona-Utah border region.

Leaving Zion via the **Zion-Mt. Carmel Highway,** otherwise known as **UT-9,** pick up **US 89 South** after 15 miles at Mt. Carmel and head southeast for 20 miles through the small town of Kanab, Utah, where the highway becomes **US 89A.** Follow US 89A for 35 miles through the lonely Arizona Strip and into the green forests of the Kaibab Plateau to **Jacob Lake,** a small outpost with a gas station, hotel, and restaurant at the junction of US 89A and AZ-67. Turn right to get on **AZ-67 South,** the two-lane road into the park. The park entrance is about 40 miles farther on. There is no other route into the park from the north side of the canyon. **AZ-67 closes November-May,** so plan your visit accordingly.

By Air, Train, or Bus

Air

Flagstaff, Tusayan, and Williams have small airports. The **Grand Canyon Airport** (GCN) at Tusayan, just outside the park's South entrance, has flights from Las Vegas daily. From May until early September, the free **Tusayan Shuttle** runs between the Tusayan and Grand Canyon Village every 20 minutes daily 8am-9:30pm. It departs from the Imax Theater, making stops all the main drag (AZ-64) on its way into the park. You must purchase an entrance pass to the park before getting on the bus. These are available at any of the previously mentioned stops, and they cost the same as they would at the park entrance.

Flagstaff's small **Pulliam Airport** (FLG, 928/556-1234, www.flagstaff.az.gov) is about five miles south of downtown.

Las Vegas to Grand Canyon

Grand Canyon Express (800/222-6966, reservation@airvegas.com) offers daily flights from Las Vegas to the Grand Canyon Airport in Tusayan. The flight time is a little more than an hour and costs about $210 one-way. Make sure to call ahead for flight times and reservations, as flights are scheduled based on demand and don't necessarily occur every day. Much more expensive but worth it if you're looking for a one-day tour of the canyon from Vegas, **Grand Canyon Airlines** offers the 9.5-hour **Grand Canyon Deluxe Tour** (866/735-9422, $344). The tour includes hotel-to-hotel service, access to the park, and a box lunch.

Train

A fun, retro, and environmentally conscious way to reach the park, the **Grand Canyon Railway** (800/843-8724, www.thetrain.com, $65-220 round-trip per person) recreates what it was like to visit the great gorge in the early 20th century. It takes about 2.5 hours to get to the South Rim depot from the station in Williams. The train runs every day year-round. It departs from Williams at 9:30am and arrives at Grand Canyon Village at the South Rim at 11:45am. After a long day of looking at the gorge, hop back on the train at 3:30pm, and you'll arrive at Williams at 5:45pm.

It's a great option for anyone who is interested in the heyday of train travel and the Old West—or for anyone desiring a slower-paced journey. You may wonder when the train is going to speed up, but it never really does, rocking at about 60 mph through pine forests and across scrubby grassland shared by cattle, elk, pronghorn, coyotes, and red-tailed hawks, all of which can be viewed from a comfortable seat in one of the old refurbished cars. Along the way, there are ruins of the great railroad days, including ancient telegraph posts still lined up along the tracks. Kids especially enjoy the train trip, as comedian-fiddlers often stroll through the cars. You may even witness a mock train robbery, complete with bandits on horseback with blazing six-shooters.

The **Grand Canyon Railway Hotel** (235 N. Grand Canyon Blvd., 928/635-4010, www.thetrain.com, $174-359) and restaurant, just beyond the train station, makes a good base. It recreates the atmosphere of the old Santa Fe Railroad Harvey House that once stood on the same ground.

Bus

Arizona Shuttles (928/226-8060, www.arizonashuttle.com) offers comfortable rides from Flagstaff to the Grand Canyon three times daily ($60 round-trip for adults, Mar.-Oct.). The company also goes between Phoenix's Sky Harbor Airport and Flagstaff ($45 one-way) several times a day as well as from Flagstaff to Sedona, the Verde Valley, and Williams ($32-39 one-way).

Visiting the Park

Entrances

Unless you choose to ride the chugging train from Williams, there are only two ways, by road, in and out of the park's South Rim section. The vast majority of visitors to Grand Canyon National Park enter through the **South entrance** along AZ-64 from Williams, 60 miles of flat, dry, windswept plain, dotted with a few isolated trailers, manufactured homes, and gaudy for-sale signs offering cheap "ranch land." Entering through the busy South entrance will assure that your first look at the Grand Canyon is from **Mather Point,** one of the most iconic views of the river-molded gorge. The entrance stations are open daily 24 hours, including all holidays.

A less used but certainly no less worthy park entrance is the **East entrance,** in the park's **Desert View** section. About 25 miles east of Grand Canyon Village and all the action, this route is a good choice for those who want a more leisurely and comprehensive look at the rim, as there are quite a few stops along the way to the village that you might not otherwise get to if you enter through the South entrance.

The small, little-visited **North Rim entrance,** on AZ-67, is open from around May 15 through October 15.

Park Passes and Fees

The **park entrance fee** is $30 per car and includes entry and parking for up to seven days. Payment of the entrance fee at the South Rim will be honored at the

One Day at the Grand Canyon

The ideal South Rim-only trip lasts three days and two nights, with the first and last days including the trip to and from the rim. This amount of time will allow you to see all the sights on the rim, to take in a sunset and sunrise over the canyon, and even to do a day hike or a mule trip below the rim.

If you just have a day, about five hours or so will allow you to see all the sights on the rim and take a short hike down one of the major trails. But you're been warned: Once you stare deep into this natural wonder, you might have trouble pulling yourself away.

Morning

If you have just one day to see the Grand Canyon, drive to the South Rim and park your car at one of the large, free parking lots inside the park. Hop on one of the park's free shuttles or rent a bike or walk along the **Rim Trail** (page 436) and head toward Grand Canyon Village. Spend a few hours looking at the buildings and, of course, the canyon from this central busy part of the rim. Stop in at the **Yavapai Observation Station** (page 434), check out the history of canyon tourism at the **Bright Angel Lodge** (page 431), watch a movie about the canyon at the visitors center, and have lunch at **The Arizona Room** (page 444) or, better yet, **El Tovar Dining Room** (page 444).

Afternoon

After lunch, take the shuttle along the eastern **Desert View Drive** (page 430), stopping along the way at a few of the eastern viewpoints, especially at Mary Colter's **Desert View Watchtower** (page 435) on the far eastern edge of the park.

Evening

End your day by heading all the way to the western reaches of the park to see **Hermit's Rest** (page 435). If you time it right, you'll catch a gorgeous canyon sunset from one of the western viewpoints along the way. For dinner, try **El Tovar** (page 444) or one of the cafeterias before turning in early. If this is your only day at the canyon, visit Hermit's Rest first, and leave the park via Desert View Drive, stopping at the Watchtower and the **Tusayan Museum and Ruin** (page 435) on your way out.

Extending Your Stay

If you're able to spend more time in the park, hit one of the corridor trails for a day hike below the rim. Rest up after rising out of the depths, then check the park newspaper to see what's happening at the **Shrine of the Ages** (page 440), where on most nights there's an entertaining and informative talk by a ranger.

If you include a North Rim or West Rim excursion, add at least 1-2 more days and nights. It takes at least five hours to reach the **North Rim** (page 445) from the South Rim, perhaps longer if you take the daily shuttle from the south instead of your own vehicle. **Grand Canyon West** (page 456) and the **Hualapai** (page 458) and **Havasupai Indian Reservations** (page 457) are some 250 miles from the South Rim on slow roads, and a trip to these remote places should be planned separately from one to the popular South Rim.

The most important thing to remember when planning a trip to the canyon is to plan far ahead, even if, like the vast majority of visitors, you're just planning to spend time on the South Rim. Six months' advance planning is the norm, longer if you are going to ride a mule down or stay overnight at Phantom Ranch in the inner canyon.

North Rim as long as you go within seven days. The entrance fee is $15 per person for those entering on foot or bicycle, and $25 per person for those entering on motorcycle, also good for seven days.

The National Park Service offers several **annual passes** for frequent park visitors, including one for $60 that allows unlimited access to Grand Canyon National Park for a year. The **Interagency**

Annual Pass/America the Beautiful Pass allows access to all of the national parks for a year for $80; a version of this pass for seniors (age 62 or older) costs only $10. To purchase passes, inquire at the entrance station or one of the visitors centers in the park.

Visitors Centers

South Rim

Canyon View Information Plaza (daily 9am-5pm) near Mather Point, the first overlook you pass on entering the park's main South entrance, is the perfect place to begin your visit to the park. You get there by walking the short path from the Mather Point parking lot or by hopping off the free shuttle, for which the plaza serves as a kind of central hub. Throughout the plaza there are displays on the natural and human history of the canyon and suggestions on what to do, and inside the **South Rim Visitor Center,** the park's main welcome and information center, there are displays on canyon history and science. Rangers are always on duty to answer questions, give advice, and help you plan your visit. Head to the visitors center's 200-seat theater and watch the thrilling *Grand Canyon: A Journey of Wonder,* a 20-minute orientation film that takes you on a daylong journey through the canyon and around the park and explains the basics of the canyon's natural and human histories. The movie is free and starts on the hour and half hour.

Verkamp's Visitors Center (daily 8am-5pm) is near the El Tovar Hotel and Hopi House in Grand Canyon Village. Verkamp's was a souvenir shop, the park's first, from 1906 to 2008.

The farthest-flung of all the park's South Rim information centers, **Desert View Visitors Center and Bookstore** (daily 9am-5pm) is on Desert View Point about 25 miles east of Grand Canyon Village. It is staffed by helpful rangers and has information and displays on visiting the canyon; this is the natural place to stop for those entering the park from the quieter East entrance.

North Rim

The **North Rim Visitor Center and Bookstore** (daily 8am-6pm May-Oct.) near the Grand Canyon Lodge, has information, maps, and exhibits on North Rim science and history. The nonprofit Grand Canyon Association operates the well-stocked bookstore. Rangers offer a full program of talks and guided hikes throughout the day, and night programs around the campfire. The North Rim edition of *The Guide* has an up-to-date list of topics, times, and meeting places.

Reservations

Accommodations

To obtain a room at one of the lodges inside Grand Canyon National Park, you must book far in advance, especially if you are hoping to visit during the busy summer season. Reservations for all of the lodges on the South Rim, including Phantom Ranch and Trailer Village, are handled by **Xanterra Parks & Resorts** (888/297-2757, outside the U.S. 303/297-2757, www.grandcanyonlodges.com). If at first it seems like you're not going to get the room you want, keep trying right up until you arrive. Call every day and check; if you are diligent you can take advantage of cancellations.

Reservations for the North Rim's only in-park accommodations, at **Grand Canyon Lodge,** are handled by **Forever Resorts** (877/386-4383, outside the U.S. 480/337-1320, http://reservations.foreverresorts.com).

Some of the towns outside the South Rim area of the park offer more accommodations options:

- **Tusayan** (I-180): 1.5 miles (5 minutes) from Grand Canyon National Park South entrance; 7 miles from Grand Canyon Village
- **Williams** (I-40): 54 miles (1 hour) from

Grand Canyon National Park South entrance; 60 miles from Grand Canyon Village

- **Flagstaff** (I-40): 73.5 miles (1.5 hours) from Grand Canyon National Park South entrance; 79 miles from Grand Canyon Village

Campgrounds

There are two campgrounds at the South Rim. You can reserve a spot only at **Mather Campground** in Grand Canyon Village. The more rustic and undeveloped **Desert View Campground** is first-come, first-served. Spots at the **North Rim Campground** can be reserved as well. Contact the **National Recreation Reservation Service** (877/444-6777, www.recreation.gov) to reserve a spot up to six months before your trip.

Mule Rides

Mule rides are popular at the park's busy South Rim, so they book up quickly. Luckily, you can book up to 13 months in advance through **Xanterra Parks & Resorts** (888/297-2757, outside the U.S. 303/297-2757, www.grandcanyonlodges.com). To book a mule ride on the North Rim, call 435/679-8665.

River Trips

A once-in-a-lifetime trip down the mighty Colorado River through the heart of gorge takes a good deal of advance planning and booking. Make sure you start the process at least a year ahead of your preferred departure date. The best place to start your research is the website for the **Grand Canyon River Outfitters Association** website (www.gcroa.org). The GCROA is an industry group comprising the 16 companies that the Park Service allows to run trips through the canyon. The group's website has links to the websites of all 16 members, and each site has most of the information you'll need to get started making plans for your river trip. Whatever you do, do not book

river runners resting near Phantom Ranch

a trip with any company that is not listed with the GCROA.

Seasons

At about 7,000 feet, the South Rim has a temperate climate: warm in the summer months, cool in fall, and cold in the winter. It snows in the deep winter and often rains in the late afternoon in late summer. Summer is the park's busiest season, and it is *very* busy. Four or five million visitors from all over the world will be your companions, which isn't as bad as some make it out to be. People-watching and hobnobbing with fellow tourists from the far corners of the globe become legitimate enterprises if you're so inclined. During the summer months (May-September) temperatures often exceed 110°F in the inner canyon, which has a desert climate, but cool by 20-30°F up on the forested rims. There's no reason for anybody to hike deep into the canyon in summer. It's not fun, and it is potentially deadly. It is better to plan a marathon trek in the fall.

Fall is a perfect time to visit the park: It's light-jacket cool on the South Rim and warm but not hot in the inner canyon, where high temperatures during October range 80-90°F, making hiking much more pleasant than it is during the infernal summer months. October or November are the last months of the year during which a rim-to-rim hike from the North Rim is possible, as rim services shut down by the end of October. The only road to the rim is closed by late November, and often before that, due to winter snowstorms. It's quite cold on the North Rim during October, but on the South Rim it's usually clear, cool, and pleasant during the day and snuggle-up chilly at night. A winter visit to the South Rim has its own charms. There is usually snow on the rim January-March, contrasting beautifully with the red, pink, and dusty green canyon colors. The crowds are thin and more laid-back than in the busy summer months. It is, however, quite cold, even during the day, and you may not want to stand and stare too long at the windy, bone-chilling viewpoints.

Information and Services

As you enter the South Rim, you'll get a copy of ***The Guide,*** a newsprint publication that is indispensable. It's pretty comprehensive and will likely answer many of your questions. A **North Rim edition** is passed out at the North Rim entrance.

If you're driving to the park, note that the last place to fill up with gas is in **Tusayan,** seven miles from the park. The only in-park gas station is 26 miles east of the central park at **Desert View.** The park operates a **public garage** (daily 8am-noon, 1pm-5pm) near the rail depot where you can fix relatively minor car issues.

The **Canyon Village Market and General Store** (daily 7am-9pm), inside the park at **Market Plaza,** sells a variety of groceries, camping supplies, and clothing. **Chase Bank** has an ATM at Market Plaza and a bank branch that's open weekdays 9am-5pm. Market Plaza also has a **post office** (Mon.-Fri. 9am-4:30pm, Sat. 11am-1pm).

The Camper Services Building at Mather Campground has a **laundry** and **showers** (daily 6am-11pm, last load in at 9:45pm).

For 24-hour medical services within the park, **dial 911.**

The national parks, including Grand Canyon, stopped selling bottled water some time ago, so don't forget to bring along an easy-to-carry receptacle to refill at the water fountains situated throughout the park. A **water bottle, Camelback, or canteen** is necessary. You are going to get thirsty in the high, dry air along the rim. You might even take along a cooler with cold water and other drinks, which you can leave in your car and revisit as the need arises.

Getting Around

Car

The best way to tour the South Rim is to leave your car at one of the large parking lots near the park entrance, at the visitors center, or at Market Plaza. You can then pick up the park's excellent shuttle service, which will take you to each of the viewpoints. During the summer, you can even leave your car outside the park at one of the many businesses that provide stops for the Tusayan Route Shuttle. This free service runs every 20 minutes May 10-September 5 daily 8am-9:45pm. If you just can't be without your car, remember that parking is increasingly difficult to find the closer you get to the central village. Be cautious and watch for pedestrians.

Shuttle

There are three shuttle options for getting around the park and surrounding areas.

Grand Canyon National Park operates an excellent **free shuttle service** with comfortable buses fueled by compressed natural gas. It's a good idea to park your car for the duration of your visit and use the shuttle. It's nearly impossible to find parking at the various sights, and the traffic through the park is not always easy to navigate—there are a lot of one-way routes and oblivious pedestrians that can lead to needless frustration. Make sure you pick up a copy of the free park newspaper, ***The Guide,*** which has a map of the various shuttle routes and stops.

Pretty much anywhere you want to go in the park, a shuttle will get you there, and you rarely have to wait more than 10 minutes at any stop. However, there is no shuttle that goes all the way to the Tusayan Museum and Ruin or the Watchtower near the East entrance. Shuttle drivers are friendly, knowledgeable, and a good source of information about the park; a few of them are genuinely entertaining. The shuttle conveniently runs daily from around sunup until about 9pm, and drivers always know the expected sunrise and sunset times and seem to be intent on getting people to the best overlooks to view these two popular daily park events.

The **Trans Canyon Shuttle** (928/638-2820, reservations 877/638-2820, www.transcanyonshuttle.com, $90 one-way, reservations required) makes a daily round-trip excursion between the South and North Rims. Reservations are required. From the South Rim, the shuttle departs from the lobby of the Bright Angel Lodge daily at 8am and 1:30pm, bound for the North Rim. From the North Rim, shuttles depart from Grand Canyon Lodge daily at 7am and 2pm. Be there to meet the shuttle at least 15 minutes early. Travel time is 4-6 hours.

The free **Tusayan Shuttle** runs between Tusayan and Grand Canyon Village and is useful if you're staying in the small town outside the park. It runs every 20 minutes May-early September daily 8am-9:30pm. It departs from the Imax Theater, making stops along the main drag (AZ-64) on its way into the park. You must purchase an entrance pass to the park before getting on the bus. These are available at any of the previously mentioned stops, and they cost the same as they would at the park entrance. There are also signs for the shuttle along AZ-64.

Bicycle

You are strongly encouraged to bring your bicycle along on your visit to the South Rim. There are several excellent routes for bikes to the west and east of Grand Canyon Village, along which you can avoid the crowds and traffic. You'll have to get off and push through the heart of the village, but just to the west and east, it's pretty easy to navigate.

Bright Angel Bicycles and Café (928/814-8704, www.bikegrandcanyon.com, 8am-5pm daily Apr., 8am-6pm daily May-mid-Sept., 9am-5pm daily mid-Sept.-Oct., 10am-4pm daily Nov.-Mar., weather permitting, $12 per hour, $30 for 5 hours, $45 for 24 hours) rents comfortable, easy-to-ride KHS bikes as well as trailers for the tots and safety equipment. They also offer guided bike tours of the South Rim's sights for $60 per person ($45 children under 17). If you get tired pedaling through the 7,000-foot air, you can strap your bike to a shuttle and have a rest. The friendly staff members here are quick to offer suggestions about the best places to ride. The little café serves an excellent brew and sells premade sandwiches and other snacks (same hours as rentals). Bright Angel Bicycles is located right next to the Grand Canyon Visitor Center, near the South entrance and Mather Point.

Tours

Bus Tours

Xanterra, the park's main concessionaire, offers in-park **Motorcoach Tours** (888/297-2757, ww.grandcanyonlodges.com, $23-65). Sunrise tours are available, and longer drives to the eastern and western reaches of the park are offered. This is a comfortable, educational, and entertaining way to see the park, and odds are you will come away with a few new friends—possibly even a new email pal from abroad. Only pay for a tour if you like being around a lot of other people and listening to mildly entertaining banter from the tour guides for hours at a time. It's easy to see and learn about everything the park has to offer without spending extra money on a tour; as in most of the national parks, the highly informed and friendly rangers hanging around the South Rim's sites offer the same information that you'll get on an expensive tour, but for free.

Airplane and Helicopter Tours

Three companies offer helicopter tours of the canyon of varying lengths. One of the better operators is **Maverick Helicopters** (888/261-4414, www.maverickhelicopter.com, $300 for 45-minute fly-over, $420 for 3.5-hour tour from Las Vegas). Though not ideal from the back-to-nature point of view, a helicopter flight over the canyon is an exciting, rare experience and can be well worth the rather expensive price—a chance to take some rare photos from a condor's perspective.

Maverick, and four other plane and helicopter tour operators, operate out of **Grand Canyon Airport** (www.grandcanyonairport.org) along Route 64 in Tusayan. They all prefer reservations.

The South Rim

The reality of the Grand Canyon is often suspect even to those standing on its rim. "For a time it is too much like a scale model or an optical illusion," wrote Joseph Wood Krutch, a great observer and writer of the Southwest. The canyon appears at first, Krutch added, "a man-made diorama trying to fool the eye." It is *too big* to be immediately comprehended, especially to those visitors used

Grand Canyon Village

To Phantom Ranch
Mohave Point
Hopi Point
BRIGHT ANGEL TRAIL
Grand
Bright Angel Trail
To Hermit's Rest (8 miles)
POWELL POINT MEMORIAL
RIM TRAIL
Maricopa Point
HERMIT RD
TRAILVIEW OVERLOOK
SEE DETAIL
HERMIT ROAD
GATE
VILLAGE LOOP
NAVAJO
TONTO
APACHE ST
GATE
MASWIK LODGE AND CAFETERIA
BOULDER ST
CENTER RD
ROWE WELL RD
MASWIK TRANSPORTATION CENTER AND BACKCOUNTRY OFFICE
KENNELS
ALBRIGHT AVE

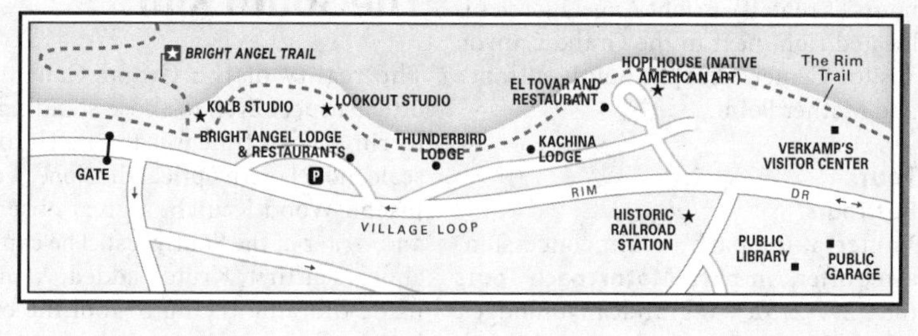

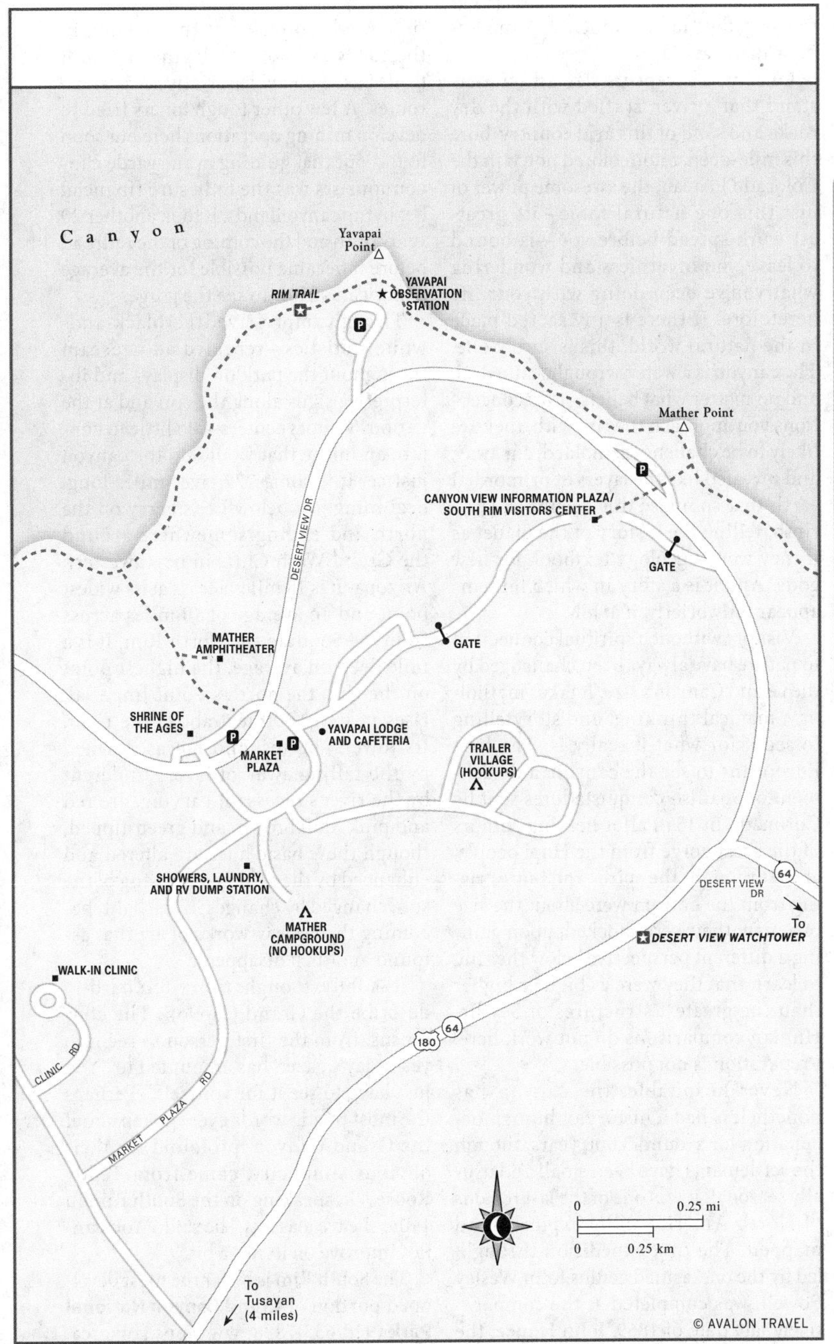
Canyon
Yavapai Point
RIM TRAIL
YAVAPAI OBSERVATION STATION
Mather Point
DESERT VIEW DR
CANYON VIEW INFORMATION PLAZA/ SOUTH RIM VISITORS CENTER
GATE
GATE
MATHER AMPHITHEATER
SHRINE OF THE AGES
MARKET PLAZA
YAVAPAI LODGE AND CAFETERIA
TRAILER VILLAGE (HOOKUPS)
SHOWERS, LAUNDRY, AND RV DUMP STATION
MATHER CAMPGROUND (NO HOOKUPS)
64
DESERT VIEW DR
To
DESERT VIEW WATCHTOWER
WALK-IN CLINIC
CLINIC RD
MARKET PLAZA RD
180
64
0
0.25 mi
0
0.25 km
To Tusayan (4 miles)
© AVALON TRAVEL

to the gaudy, lesser wonders of the human-made world.

Once you accept its size and understand that a river, stuffed with the dry rocks and sand of this arid country, bore this mile-deep, multicolored notch in the Colorado Plateau, the awesome power of just this one natural force—its greatest work spread before you—is bound to leave you breathless and wondering what you've been doing with your life heretofore. If there is any sacred place in the natural world, this is surely one. The canyon is a water-wrought cathedral, and no matter what beliefs or preconceptions you approach the rim with, they are likely to be challenged, molded, cut away, and revealed like the layers of primordial earth that compose this deep rock labyrinth, telling the history of the planet as if they were a geology textbook for new gods. And it is a story in which humans appear only briefly, if at all.

Visitors without a spiritual connection to nature have always been challenged by the Grand Canyon's size. It takes mythology, magical thinking, and storytelling to see it for what it really is. The first Europeans to see the canyon, a detachment of Spanish conquistadores sent by Coronado in 1540 after hearing rumors of the great gorge from the Hopi people, at first thought the spires and buttes rising from the bottom were about the size of a man; they were shocked, upon gaining a different perspective below the rim, to learn that they were as high or higher than the greatest structures of Seville. Human comparisons do not work here. Preparation is not possible.

Never hospitable, the canyon has nonetheless had a history of human occupation for around 5,000 years, though the settlements have been small and usually seasonal. It was one of the last regions of North America to be explored and mapped. The first expedition through, led by the one-armed genius John Wesley Powell, was completed at the comparatively late date of 1869. John Hance, the first Anglo to reside at the canyon, in the 1880s explored its depths and built trails based on ancient Native American routes. A few other tough loners tried to develop mining operations here but soon found out that guiding avant-garde canyon tourists was the only sure financial bet in the canyonlands. It took another 20 years or so and the coming of the railroad before it became possible for the average American visitor to see the gorge.

Though impressive, the black-and-white statistics—repeated ad nauseam throughout the park on displays and interpretive signs along the rim and at the various visitors centers—do little to conjure an image that would do the canyon justice. It is some 277 river miles long, beginning just below Lee's Ferry on the north and ending somewhere around the Grand Wash Cliffs in northwestern Arizona. It is 18 miles across at its widest point and an average of 10 miles across from the South to the North Rim. It is a mile deep on average; the highest point on the rim, the north's Point Imperial, rises nearly 9,000 feet above the river. Its towers, buttes, and mesas, formed by the falling away of layers undercut by the river's incessant carving, are red and pink, dull brown, and green-tipped, though these basic hues are altered and enhanced by the setting and rising of the sun, changed by changes in the light, becoming throwaway works of art that astound and then disappear.

It is folly, though, to try too hard to describe the Grand Canyon. The consensus, from the first person to see it to yesterday's gazer, has amounted to "You just have to see it for yourself." Perhaps the most poetic words ever spoken about the Grand Canyon, profound for their obvious simplicity, came from Teddy Roosevelt, speaking on the South Rim in 1903. "Leave it as it is," he said. "You cannot improve on it; not a bit."

The South Rim is by far the most developed portion of **Grand Canyon National Park** (928/638-7888, www.nps.gov/grca,

24 hours daily, $30 per car for seven-day pass, $25 motorcycles, $15 walk-ins and bikes) and should be seen by every American, as Teddy Roosevelt once recommended. Here you'll stand side by side with people from all over the globe, each one breathless on his or her initial stare into the canyon and more often than not hit suddenly with an altered perception of time and human history. Don't let the rustic look of the buildings fool you into thinking you're roughing it. The park's easy, free shuttle service will take you all over if you don't feel like walking the level rim-side trails. The food here is far above average for a national park. The restaurant at El Tovar offers some of the finest, most romantic dining in the state, and all with one of the great wonders of the world just 25 feet away.

Driving Tours

★ Hermit Road

March through November the park's free shuttle goes all the way to architect and Southwestern-design queen Mary Colter's **Hermit's Rest,** about seven miles from the village, along the park's western scenic drive, called the Hermit Road. It takes approximately two hours to complete the loop, as the bus stops at eight viewpoints along the way. On the return route, buses stop only at Mohave and Hopi Points. A few of the Hermit Road viewpoints are some of the best in the park for viewing the sunsets. To make it in time for such dramatic solar performances, get on the bus at least an hour before sunset. There is often a long wait at the **Hermit's Rest Transfer Stop** just west of the Bright Angel Lodge. The bus drivers will always be able to tell you when sunset is expected, and the times are also listed in *The Guide* newspaper handed out as you enter the park. In the winter the route is open to cars, and you can drive to most of the viewpoints and stare at your leisure.

Each of the Hermit Road lookouts provides a slightly different perspective on the canyon, whether it be a strange unnoticed outcropping or a brief view of the white-tipped river rapids far, far below.

The first stop along the route is the **Trailview Overlook,** from which you can see the Bright Angel Trail twisting down to and across the plateau to overlook the Colorado River.

The next major stop along the route is **Maricopa Point,** which provides a vast, mostly unobstructed view of the canyon all the way to the river. The point is on a promontory that juts out into the canyon over 100 feet. To the west you can see the rusted remains of the Orphan Mine, first opened in 1893 as a source of copper and silver—and, for a few busy years during the height of the Cold War, uranium.

Consider taking the 10- to 15-minute hike along the Rim Trail west past the fenced-off Orphan Mine and through the piney rim world to the next viewing area, **Powell Point.** Here stands a memorial to the one-armed explorer and writer John Wesley Powell, who led the first and second river expeditions through the canyon in 1869 and 1871. The memorial is a flat-topped pyramid, which you can ascend and stand tall over the canyon. You can't see the river from here, but the views of the western reaches of the gorge are pretty good, and this is a strong candidate for a sunset-viewing vantage point.

About 0.25 miles along the Rim Trail from Powell Point is **Hopi Point,** which offers sweeping and unobstructed views of the western canyon. As a result, it is the most popular west-end point for viewing the sun dropping red and orange in the west. North from here, across the canyon, look for the famous mesas named after Egyptian gods—Isis Temple, off to the northeast, and the Temple of Osiris to the northwest.

The next viewpoint heading west is **Mohave Point,** from which you can see the Colorado River and a few white-tipped rapids. Also visible from here are the 3,000-foot red-and-green cliffs that surround the deep side-canyon, appropriately named **The Abyss.** Right below the viewpoint you can see the red-rock mesa called the Alligator.

The last viewpoint before Hermit's Rest is **Pima Point,** a wide-open view to the west and the east, from which you can see the winding Colorado River and the Hermit Trail twisting down into the depths of the canyon.

Desert View Drive

One more Mary Colter construction—arguably her greatest—and a Puebloan ruin are located along Desert View Drive, the 25-mile eastern drive from the village. The viewpoints along this drive, which one ranger called the "quiet side of the South Rim," gradually become more desertlike and are typically less crowded.

The free shuttle goes only as far as **Yaki Point,** a great place to watch the sunrise and near the popular South Kaibab trailhead. Yaki Point is at the end of a 1.5-mile side road two miles east of Highway 180. The area is closed to private vehicles.

Along Desert View Drive, make sure not to miss the essential **Grandview Point,** where the original canyon lodge once stood long ago. From here the rough Grandview Trail leads below the rim. The viewpoint sits at 7,400 feet, about 12 miles east of the village and then a mile on a side road. It's considered one of the grandest views of them all, hence the name; the canyon spreads out willingly from here, and the sunrise in the east hits it all strong and happy. To the east, look for the 7,844-foot monument called the Sinking Ship, and to the north below look for Horseshoe Mesa. This is a heavily wooded area, so for the best view hike a bit down the Grandview Trail. The steep and narrow trail is tough, but if you're prepared to hike, you can descend three miles to Horseshoe Mesa.

Moran Point, east of Grandview, is just eight miles south of Cape Royal (as the condor flies) on the North Rim and offers some impressive views of the canyon and the river. The point is named for

the Bright Angel Trail, as seen from the South Rim

the great painter of the canyon, Thomas Moran, whose brave attempts to capture the gorge on canvas helped create the buzz that led to the canyon's federal protection. Directly below the left side of the point you'll see Hance Rapid, one of the largest on the Colorado. It's three miles away, but if you're quiet you might be able to hear the rushing and roaring.

Farther on the Desert View Drive you'll come to **Lipan Point,** with its wide-open vistas and the best view of the river from the South Rim. At Desert View, from the top of the watchtower, you'll be able to catch a faraway glimpse of sacred Navajo Mountain near the Utah-Arizona border, the most distant point visible from within the park.

Sights

Though you wouldn't want to make a habit of it, you could spend a few happy hours at **Grand Canyon Village Historical District** with your back to the canyon. Then again, this small assemblage of hotels, restaurants, gift shops, and lookouts offers some of the best viewpoints from which to gaze comfortably at all that multicolored splendor. Here is a perfect vantage from which to spot the strip of greenery just below the rim called **Indian Garden,** and follow with your eyes—or even your feet—the famous **Bright Angel Trail** as it twists improbably down the rim's rock face. You can also see some of the most interesting and evocative buildings in the state, all of them registered National Historic Landmarks. If you're just visiting for the day, you can drive into the village and park your car in the El Tovar parking lot or at a rather large, mostly dirt lot near the train depot. More often than not, especially in the summer, the lot at El Tovar will be full. You can also park at the large lot at Market Plaza and then take the shuttle bus around the park. The **Backcountry Information Center** (928/638-7875) also has a rather large parking lot, the southern portion of which can accommodate RVs and trailers.

Bright Angel Lodge

The village's central hub of activity, rustic **Bright Angel Lodge,** was designed in 1935 by Mary Colter to replace the old Bright Angel Hotel, built by John Hance in the 1890s, and the tent-city Bright Angel Camp that sat near the trail of the same name. The lodge resembles a rough-hewn hunting lodge constructed of materials found nearby and was meant to welcome not the high-toned traveler but the middle-class tourist.

In a room off the lobby there's a small museum with fascinating exhibits about Fred Harvey, Colter, and the early years of Southwestern tourism. You'll see Colter's "geologic fireplace," a 10-foot-high re-creation of the canyon's varied strata. The stones were collected from the inner canyon by a geologist and then loaded on the backs of mules for the journey out. The fireplace's strata appear exactly like those stacked throughout the

The Canyon and the Railroad

Musing on the Grand Canyon in 1902, John Muir lamented that, thanks to the railroad, "children and tender, pulpy people as well as storm-seasoned travelers" could now see the wonders of the West, including the Grand Canyon, with relative ease. It has always been easy for storm-seasoned travelers to begrudge us tender, pulpy types a good view—as if all the people who visit the canyon every year couldn't fit in its deep mazes and be fairly out of sight. Muir came to a similar conclusion after actually seeing the railway approach the chasm: "I was glad to discover that in the presence of such stupendous scenery they are nothing," he wrote. "The locomotives and trains are mere beetles and caterpillars, and the noise they make is as little disturbing as the hooting of an owl in the lonely woods."

It wasn't until the Santa Fe Railroad reached the South Rim of the Grand Canyon in 1901 that the great chasm's now-famous tourist trade really got going. Prior to that, travelers faced an all-day stagecoach ride from Flagstaff at a cost of $20, a high price to pay for sore bones and cramped quarters.

For half a century or more the Santa Fe line from Williams took millions of tourists to the edge of the canyon. The railroad's main concessionaire, the Fred Harvey Company, enlisted the considerable talents of Arts and Crafts designer and architect Mary Colter to build lodges, lookouts, galleries, and stores on the South Rim that still stand today, now considered to be some of the finest architectural accomplishments in the entire national parks system. Harvey's dedication to simple, high-style elegance and Colter's interest in and understanding of Pueblo Indian architecture and lifeways created an artful human stamp on the rim that nearly lives up to the breathtaking canyon it serves.

The American love affair with the automobile, the rising mythology of the go-west road trip, and finally the interstate highway killed train travel to Grand Canyon National Park by the late 1960s. In the 1990s, however, entrepreneurs revived the railroad as an excursion and tourist line. Today, the Grand Canyon Railway carries more than 250,000 passengers to the South Rim every year, a phenomenon that has reduced polluting automobile traffic in the cramped park by some 10 percent.

canyon walls, equaling a couple of billion years of earth-building from bottom to rim. The lodge includes a collection of small cabins just to the west of the main building, and the cabin closest to the rim was once the **home of Bucky O'Neill,** an early canyon resident and prospector who died while fighting with Teddy Roosevelt's Rough Riders in Cuba.

El Tovar

Just east of the lodge is **El Tovar,** the South Rim's first great hotel and the picture of haute-wilderness style. Designed in 1905 by Charles Whittlesey for the Santa Fe Railroad, El Tovar has the look of a Swiss chalet and a log-house interior, watched over by the wall-hung heads of elk and buffalo; it is at once cozy and elegant. This Harvey Company jewel has hosted dozens of rich and famous canyon visitors over the years, including George Bernard Shaw and presidents Teddy Roosevelt and William Howard Taft. On the rim side, a gazebo stands near the edge. While it is a wonderfully romantic building up close, El Tovar looks even more picturesque from a few of the viewpoints along the Hermit Road, and you can really get a good idea of just how close the lodge is to the gorge by seeing it from far away. Inside you'll find two gift shops and a cozy lounge where you can have a drink or two while looking at the canyon. El Tovar's restaurant is the best in the park, and it's quite pleasant to sink into one of the Mission style leather chairs in the rustic, dark-wood lobby.

Hopi House

A few steps from the front porch of El Tovar is Colter's **Hopi House,** designed and built as if it sat not at the edge of the Grand Canyon but on the edge of Hopiland's Third Mesa. Hopi workers used local materials to build this unique gift shop and Native American arts museum. The Harvey Company even hired the famous Hopi-Tewa potter Nampeyo to live here with her family while demonstrating her artistic talents, and by extension Hopi lifeways, to travelers. This is one of the best places in the region for viewing and buying Hopi, Navajo, and Pueblo art (though most art is quite expensive), and there are even items on view and for sale made by Nampeyo's descendants.

Lookout Studio

Mary Colter also designed the **Lookout Studio** west of the Bright Angel Lodge, a little stacked-stone watch house that seems to be a mysterious extension of the rim itself. The stone patio juts out over the canyon and is a popular place for picture taking. The Lookout was built in 1914 exactly for that purpose—to provide a comfortable but "indigenous" building and deck from which visitors could gaze at and photograph the canyon. It was fitted with high-powered telescopes and soon became one of the most popular snapshot scenes on the rim. It still is today, and on many days you'll be standing elbow to elbow with camera-carrying tourists clicking away. As she did with her other buildings on the rim, Colter designed the Lookout to be a kind of amalgam of Native American ruins and backcountry pioneer utilitarianism. Her formula of using found and indigenous materials, stacked haphazardly, works wonderfully. When it was first built, the little stone hovel was so "authentic" that it even had weeds growing out of the roof. Inside, where you'll find books and canyon souvenirs, the studio looks much as it did when it first opened. The jutting stone patio is still one of the best places from which to view the gorge.

Kolb Studio

Built in 1904 right on the canyon's rim, **Kolb Studio** is significant not so much for its design as for the human story that went on inside. It was the home and studio of the famous Kolb Brothers, pioneer canyon photographers, moviemakers, river rafters, and entrepreneurs. Inside there's a gift shop, a gallery, and a display about the brothers, who, in 1912, rode the length of the Colorado in a boat with a movie camera rolling. The journey resulted in a classic book of exploration and river running, Emery Kolb's 1914 *Through the Grand Canyon from Wyoming to Mexico.* The Kolb Brothers were some of the first entrepreneurs at the canyon, setting up a photography studio, at first in a cave near the rim and then in this house, to sell pictures of tourists atop their mules as early as 1902. After a falling-out between the brothers, the younger Emery Kolb stayed on at the canyon until his death in 1976, showing daily the film of the brothers' river trip to several generations of canyon visitors.

The Viewpoints

While the canyon's unrelenting vastness tends to blur the eyes into forgetting the details, viewing the gorge from many different points seems to cure this; however, there are some 19 named viewpoints along the South Rim Road, from the easternmost Desert View to the westernmost Hermit's Rest. Is it necessary, or even a good idea, to see them all? No, not really. For many it's difficult to pick out the various named buttes, mesas, side canyons, drainages, and other features that rise and fall and undulate throughout the gorge, and one viewpoint ends up looking not that different from the next.

The best way to see the canyon viewpoints is to park your car and walk along the **Rim Trail** for a few miles, if not its whole length (if you get tired you can always hop on the free shuttle at any of its many stops), seeing the gorge from developed viewpoints as well as from the trail itself.

Driving to each and every viewpoint is not that rewarding; it tends to speed up your visit and make you miss the subtleties of the different views. Consider really getting to know a few select viewpoints rather than trying to quickly and superficially hit each one. Any of the viewpoints along the **Hermit Road** and **Desert View Drive** is an ideal candidate for a long love affair. The views from just outside **El Tovar** or the **Bright Angel Lodge,** right smack in the middle of all the bustling village action, are as gorgeous as any others, and it can be fun and illuminating to watch people's reactions to what they're seeing.

There isn't a bad view of the canyon, but if you have limited time, ask a ranger at Canyon View Information Plaza or Yavapai Observation Station what their favorite viewpoint is and why. The shuttle bus drivers are also great sources of information and opinions. Try to get to at least one sunset and one sunrise at one or more of the developed viewpoints; the canyon's colors and details can get a bit monotonous after the initial thrill wears off (if it ever does), but the sun splashing and dancing at different strengths and angles against the multihued buttes, monuments, and sheer, shadowy walls cures that rather quickly.

Mather Point

As most South Rim visitors enter through the park's South entrance, it's no surprise that the most visited viewpoint in the park is the first one arrived at along that route—**Mather Point,** named for the first National Park Service director, Stephen T. Mather. While crowded, Mather Point offers a typically astounding view of the canyon and is probably the mind's-eye view that most casual visitors take away. It can get busy, especially in the summer. If you're going to the park's main visitors center, **Canyon View Information Plaza** (and you should), you'll park near here and walk a short paved path to the information plaza. At the viewpoint, you can walk out onto two railed-off jutting rocks to feel like you're hovering on the edge of an abyss, but you may have to stand in line to get right up to the edge. A good way to see this part of the park is to leave your car at the large parking area at Mather (which is often full, of course) and then walk a short way along the Rim Trail west to **Yavapai Point** and the excellent, newly refurbished **Yavapai Observation Station,** the best place to learn about the canyon's geology and get more than a passing understanding of what you're gazing at. It's a good idea to visit the Yavapai Observation Station before you hit any of the other viewpoints (unless you are coming in from the East entrance).

Yavapai Observation Station

First opened in 1928, **Yavapai Observation Station** (8am-6pm daily winter, 8am-7pm daily summer, free) is the best place in the park to learn about the canyon's geology—this limestone-and-pine museum and bookstore hanging off the rim is a must-visit for visitors interested in learning about what they are seeing. The building itself is of interest; designed by architect Herbert Maier, the stacked-stone structure, like Colter's buildings, merges with the rim itself to appear a foregone and inevitable part of the landscape. The site for the station, which was originally called the Yavapai Trailside Museum, was handpicked by canyon geologists as the best for viewing the various strata and receiving a rim-side lesson on the region's geologic history and present. Inside the building, you'll find in-depth explanations and displays about canyon geology that are fascinating and easily understood. Too much of the introductory geology found in guidebooks and elsewhere is jargon-laden, confusing, and not very useful to the uninitiated. Not here: Many of the displays are new and use several different approaches, including maps, photographs, and three-dimensional models—coupled with the very rocks, cliffs, canyons, and gorges they're talking about right outside the windows—to create fascinating and easy-to-grasp lessons. Particularly helpful is the huge topographic relief map of the canyon inside the observation center. Spend some time looking over the map in detail and you'll get a giant's-eye view of the canyon that really helps you discern what you're seeing once you turn into an ant again outside on the ledge.

Hermit's Rest

The final stop on the Hermit Road is the enchanting gift shop and rest house called **Hermit's Rest.** As you walk up a path through a stacked-boulder entranceway, from which hangs an old mission bell, the little stone cabin comes into view. It looks as if some lonely hermit stacked rock upon rock until something haphazard but cozy rose off the rim; it is a structure belonging more to the realm of fairy tales than to the contemporary world. Inside, the huge, yawning fireplace, tall and deep enough to be a room itself, dominates the warm, rustic front room, where there are a few seats chopped out of stumps, a Navajo blanket or two splashing color against the gray stone, and elegant lantern-lamps hanging from the stones. Outside, the views of the canyon and down the Hermit Trail are spectacular, but something about that little rock shelter makes it hard to leave.

Tusayan Museum and Ruin

The **Tusayan Museum** (9am-5pm daily, free) has a small but interesting exhibit on the canyon's early human settlers. The museum is located near an array of 800-year-old Ancestral Puebloan ruins with a self-guided trail and regularly scheduled ranger walks. Since the free shuttle doesn't extend this far east, you have to drive to the museum and ruin; it's about 3 miles west of Desert View and 22 miles east of the village. It's worth the drive, though, especially if you're going to be heading to the Desert View section anyway (which you should). Though it hasn't been overly hospitable to humans over the eons, the oldest human-made artifacts found in the canyon date back about 12,000 years—they include little stick-built animal fetishes and other mysterious items. The displays in this museum help put human life on the rim and in the gorge in context, and the little ruin is fascinating. Imagine living along the rim, walking every day to the great gorge, tossing an offering of cornmeal into the abyss, and wondering what your hidden canyon gods were going to provide you with next.

★ Desert View Watchtower

What is perhaps the most mysterious and thrilling of Colter's canyon creations, the **Desert View Watchtower** is an artful homage to smaller Ancestral Puebloan-built towers found at Hovenweep National Monument and elsewhere in the Four Corners region, the exact purpose of which is still unknown.

The tower's high, windy deck is reached by climbing the twisting, steep steps winding around the open middle, the walls painted with visions of Hopi lore and religion by Hopi artist Fred Kabotie. Pick up *The Watchtower Guide* free in the gift shop on the bottom floor for explanations on the meanings of the paintings and symbols. From the top of the watchtower, the South Rim's highest viewpoint, the whole arid expanse opens up, and you feel something like a lucky survivor at the very edge of existence, even among the crowds. Such is the evocative power, the rough-edged romanticism, of Colter's vision.

Recreation

Hiking

Something about a well-built trail

twisting deep into an unknown territory can spur even the most habitually sedentary canyon visitor to begin an epic trudge. This phenomenon is responsible for both the best and worst of the South Rim's busy recreation life. It is not uncommon to see hikers a mile or more below the rim picking along in high heels and sauntering blithely in flip-flops, not a drop of water between them. It's best to go to the canyon prepared to hike, with the proper footwear and plenty of snacks and water. You are, in all probability, going to want to hike a little. And since there's no such thing as an easy hike into the Grand Canyon, going in prepared, even if it's just for a few miles, will make your hike infinitely more pleasurable. Also, remember that there aren't any loop hikes here: If you hike in a mile—and that can happen surprisingly quickly—you also must hike out (up) a mile, at an oxygen-depleted altitude of 6,000 to 7,000 feet.

★ Rim Trail

Distance: 12.8 miles
Duration: all day
Elevation gain: about 200 feet
Effort: easy
Trailhead: Grand Canyon Village east to South Kaibab trailhead or west to Hermit's Rest

If you can manage a 13-mile, relatively easy walk at an altitude of around 7,000 feet, the Rim Trail provides the single best way to see all of the South Rim. The trail, paved for most of its length, runs from the South Kaibab trailhead area on the east, through the village, and all the way to Hermit's Rest, hitting every major point of interest and beauty along the way. The path gets a little tough as it rises a bit past the Bright Angel trailhead just west of the village. The trail becomes a thin dirt single-track between Powell Point and Monument Creek Vista, but it never gets too difficult. It would be considered an easy, scenic walk by just about anybody, kids included. But perhaps the best thing about the Rim Trail is that you don't have to hike the whole 13 miles—far from it. There are at least 16 shuttle stops along way, and you can hop on and off the trail at your pleasure.

Few will want to hike the entire 13 miles, of course. Such an epic walk would in fact require twice the miles, as the trail is not a loop but a ribbon stretched out flat along the rim from west to east. It's better to pick out a relatively short stretch to walk, starting from the village and ending back there after turning around. Toward the west, try walking the roughly 2.2-mile stretch from the village to Hopi Point. This would be an ideal hike toward the end of the day, as Hopi Point is a famed spot for viewing the sunset. You could then hike back in the dark, provided you have a flashlight, or take the free shuttle bus. Eastward, hike the Rim Trail from the village to Yavapai Point, a distance of about two miles one-way. This route will take you past stunning views of the canyon to the Yavapai Observation Station, where you can learn all about that which you are gaping at.

★ Bright Angel Trail

Distance: 1.5-9.6 miles
Duration: a few hours to overnight
Elevation gain: 4,380 feet
Effort: moderate to difficult
Trailhead: Grand Canyon Village, just west of Bright Angel Lodge

Hiking down the Bright Angel Trail, you quickly leave behind the twisted greenery of the rim and enter a sharp and arid landscape, twisting down and around switchbacks on a trail that is sometimes all rock underfoot. Step aside for the many mule trains that go down and up this route, and watch for the droppings, which are everywhere. Because this trail is so steep, it doesn't take long for the rim to look very far away, and you soon feel like you are deep within a chasm and those rim-top people are mere ants scurrying about.

The most popular trail in the canyon owing to its starting just to the west of

Hiking the Grand Canyon the Easy Way

One of the first things you notice while journeying through the inner canyon is the advanced age of many of your fellow hikers. It is not uncommon to see men and women in their 70s and 80s hiking along at a good clip, packs on their backs and big smiles on their faces.

At the same time, all over the South Rim you'll see warning signs about overexertion, each featuring a buff young man in incredible shape suffering from heatstroke or exhaustion, with the warning that most of the people who die in the canyon—and people die every year—are people like him. You need not be a wilderness expert or marathon runner to enjoy even a long, 27-mile, rim-to-rim hike through the inner canyon. Don't let your fears hold you back from what is often a life-changing trip.

There are several strategies that can make a canyon hike much easier than a forced march with a 30-pound pack of gear on your back. First of all, don't go in the summer; wait until September or October, when it's cooler, though still quite warm, in the inner canyon. Second, try your best to book a cabin or a dorm room at Phantom Ranch rather than camping. That way, you'll need less equipment, you'll have all or most of your food taken care of, and there will be a shower and a beer waiting for you upon your arrival. Also, for about $70 you can hire a mule to carry up to 30 pounds of gear for you, so all you have to bring is a day pack, some water, and a few snacks. This way, instead of suffering while you descend and ascend the trail, you'll be able to better enjoy the magnificence of this wonder of the world.

the Bright Angel Lodge in the village center, and considered by park staff to be the "safest" trail owing to its rest houses, water, and ranger presence, the Bright Angel Trail was once the only easily accessible corridor trail from the South Rim. As such, a $1 hikers' toll was charged by Ralph Cameron, who constructed the trail based on old Native American routes. The trail's route has always been a kind of inner canyon highway, as it has a few springs. The most verdant of these is Indian Garden, used for centuries by Native Americans, a welcome slip of green on an otherwise red and rocky land about 4.5 miles down from the trailhead. Many South Rim visitors choose to walk down Bright Angel a bit just to get a feeling of what it's like to be below the rim.

If you want to do something a little more structured, the three-mile round-trip hike to the **Mile-and-a-Half Resthouse** makes for a good introduction to the steep, twisting trail. A little farther on is **Three-Mile Resthouse,** a six-mile round-trip hike. Both rest houses have water seasonally. One of the best day hikes from the South Rim is the nine-mile round-trip to beautiful **Indian Garden,** a cool and green oasis in the arid inner canyon. This is a rather punishing day hike, not recommended in the summer. The same goes for the 12-mile round-trip trudge down to **Plateau Point,** from which you can see the Colorado River winding through the inner gorge. Unless you have somewhere you absolutely have to be, consider getting a backcountry permit and camping below the rim rather than trying to do Plateau Point or even Indian Garden in one day.

South Kaibab Trail

Distance: 1.5-7 miles
Duration: several hours to all day
Elevation gain: 4,780 feet
Effort: moderate to difficult
Trailhead: near Yaki Point

Steep but short, the seven-mile South Kaibab Trail provides the quickest, most direct South Rim route to and from the river. It's popular with day hikers and those looking for the quickest way into

the gorge, and many consider it superior to the often-crowded Bright Angel Trail. The trailhead is located a few miles east of the village near Yaki Point; it can easily be reached by shuttle bus on the Kaibab Trail Route. The 1.8-mile round-trip hike to **Ooh Aah Point** provides a great view of the canyon and a relatively easy hike along the steep switchbacks. **Cedar Ridge** is a three-mile round-trip hike down the trail, well worth it for the views of O'Neill Butte and Vishnu Temple. There is no water provided anywhere along the trail, and shade is nonexistent. Bighorn sheep have been known to haunt this trail, and you might feel akin to those dexterous beasts on this rocky ridgeline route that seems unbearably steep in some places, especially on the way back up. If you are interested in a longer haul, the six-mile round-trip hike to **Skeleton Point,** from which you can see the Colorado, is probably as far along this trail as you'll want to go in one day, though in summer you might want to reconsider descending so far. Deer and California condors are also regularly seen along the South Kaibab Trail.

Hermit Trail to Dripping Springs

Distance: 6.2 miles
Duration: 5-6 hours
Elevation gain: 1,400 feet
Effort: moderate
Trailhead: just west of Hermit's Rest

Built by the Santa Fe Railroad as an antidote to the fee-charging keeper of the Bright Angel Trail, the Hermit Trail just past Hermit's Rest leads to some less-visited areas of the canyon. This trail isn't maintained with the same energy as the well-traveled corridor trails are, and there is no potable water to be found. You could take the Hermit Trail 10 miles deep into the canyon to the river, where the first-ever below-rim camp for canyon

Top to bottom: the Desert View Watchtower; Skeleton Point, South Kaibab Trail; canyon view from the Hermit Trail.

tourists was built by Fred Harvey 10 years before Phantom Ranch, complete with a tramway from the rim, the ruins of which are still visible. But such a trudge should be left only to fully-geared experts. Not so the 6.2-mile round-trip hike to the secluded and green **Dripping Springs,** which is one of the best day hikes in the canyon for mid-level to expert hikers. Start out on the Hermit Trail's steep, rocky, almost stair-like switchbacks, and then look for the **Dripping Springs trailhead** after about 1.5 miles, once you reach a more level section dominated by piñon pine and juniper. Veer left on the trail, which begins to rise a bit and leads along a ridgeline across Hermit Basin; the views are so awe-inspiring and so unobstructed that it's difficult to keep your eyes on the skinny trail. Continue west once you come to the junction with the Boucher Trail, after about one mile; then it's about 0.5 miles up a side canyon to the cool and shady rock overhang known as Dripping Springs. And it really does drip: a shock of fernlike greenery hangs off the rock overhang, trickling cold, clean spring water at a steady pace into a small collecting pool. Get your head wet, have a picnic, and kick back in this out-of-way, hard-won oasis. But don't stay too long. The hike up is nothing to take lightly: The switchbacks are punishing, and the end, as it does when one is hiking up all of the canyon trails, seems to get farther away, not closer, as your legs begin to gain fatigue-weight. There's no water on the trail, so make sure to bring enough along and conserve it.

Grandview Trail

Distance: 8.4 miles to the river
Duration: a few hours to overnight
Elevation gain: 4,792 feet
Effort: difficult
Trailhead: Grandview Point, 12 miles east of Grand Canyon Village

A steep, rocky, and largely unmaintained route built first to serve a copper mine at Horseshoe Mesa and then to entice tourists below the forested rim, the Grandview Trail should be left to mid-level hikers and above. Though you can take the trail all the way to the river and Hance Rapid, more than eight miles in, for day hikers the 6.4-mile round-trip trek to Horseshoe Mesa, where you'll see the remains of an old copper mine, is probably as far as you'll want to go. This trail is definitely not safe for winter hiking. Hiking back up, you won't soon forget the steep slab-rock and cobblestone switchbacks, and hiking down will likely take longer than planned, as the steepest parts of the route are quite technical and require heads-up attention. Park staff members are not exactly quick to recommend this route to casual hikers. Don't be surprised if you meet a ranger hanging out along the trail about 1.5 miles in; the ranger may tell you to turn around if he or she doesn't think you have the proper gear or enough water to continue on.

Cycling

Some of us who love the Grand Canyon, innards and rim lands alike, look forward to the inevitable day when all cars will be banned from the park. Long leaps have already been made toward this goal: the Grand Canyon Railway is as popular as ever, and a fleet of natural gas-powered shuttles moves thousands of visitors around the park every day. In 2010, the National Park Service took a further stride in the green direction by awarding a long-awaited permit to a bike rental vendor. Of course, you don't have to rent. Bring your own bike: Strap it on the back of your SUV, park that gas guzzler, and pedal the rim and the forest at your own pace. There is no better way to get around the park, and you'll be helping keep emissions, traffic, and frustration to a minimum.

Bright Angel Bicycles and Café (928/814-8704, www.bikegrandcanyon.com, 8am-5pm daily Apr., 8am-6pm daily May-mid-Sept., 9am-5pm daily mid-Sept.-Oct., 10am-4pm daily Nov.-Mar., weather permitting, $12 per hour, $30 for 5 hours, $45 for 24 hours) rents comfortable, easy-to-ride KHS bikes as well as safety equipment and trailers for the tots. They also offer **guided bike tours** of the South Rim's sights ($40 adults, $32 under age 17). If you get tired pedaling in the thin air at 7,000 feet elevation, you can strap your bike to a shuttle and have a rest. The friendly staff members are quick to offer suggestions about the best places to ride. The little café serves an excellent brew and sells premade sandwiches and other snacks. Bright Angel Bicycles is right next to the Grand Canyon Visitors Center near the South entrance and Mather Point.

The **Tusayan Bike Trails** are a series of single-track trails and old mining and logging roads organized into several easy to moderate loop trails for mountain bikers near the park's South entrance. The trails wind through a forest of pine, juniper, and piñon, and there are usually plenty of opportunities to see wildlife. The longest loop is just over 11 miles, and the shortest is just under 4 miles. At the beginning of the trails is a map of the area showing the various loops. Pick up the trails on the west side of AZ-64 north of Tusayan, about one mile south of the park entrance.

Lectures and Programs

The staff at the South Rim does an above-average job keeping guests comfortable, informed, and entertained. Rangers seem to be always giving lectures, leading walks, and pointing out some little-known canyon fact—and such activities at the Grand Canyon are typically far more interesting than they are at other, less spectacular places. It will be worth your time to attend at least one of the regularly illuminating lectures held most nights at the **Shrine of the Ages** during your visit to the South Rim. Check *The Guide* for specific times and topics. Every day prior to late October there are at least 10 ranger programs offered at various sites around the rim. Typically these programs last between 15 minutes and an hour and are always interesting.

Shopping

There are more than 16 places to buy gifts, books, souvenirs, supplies, and Native American arts and crafts at the South Rim. Nearly every lodge has a substantial gift shop in its lobby, as do Hermit's Rest, Kolb Studio, Lookout Studio, and the Desert View Watchtower.

For books, the best place to go is **Books & More** at the Canyon View Information Plaza, operated by the nonprofit Grand Canyon Association. You'll find all manner of tomes about canyon science and history for both adults and children. All of the gift shops have a small book section, most of them selling the same selection of popular canyon-related titles. If you're in need of camping and hiking supplies to buy or rent—including top-of-the-line footwear, clothes, and backpacks—try the general store at the **Canyon Village Market Plaza.** You'll also find groceries, toiletries, produce, alcoholic beverages, and myriad other necessities, like "I hiked the Grand Canyon" T-shirts and warm jackets in case you forgot yours.

Whether you're a semi-serious collector or a first-time dabbler, the best place on the South Rim to find high-quality Native American arts and crafts is inside Mary Colter's **Hopi House,** where pottery, baskets, overlay jewelry, sand paintings, kachina dolls, and other treasures are for sale. Don't expect to find too many great deals—most of the best pieces are priced accordingly.

Accommodations

The South Rim of Grand Canyon National Park has some of the best accommodations in the national park system, but it's not always possible to get reservations. The park's lodging rates are audited annually and compare favorably to those offered outside the park, but you can sometimes find excellent deals at one of several gateway towns around canyon country. Using one of these places as a base for a visit to the canyon makes sense if you're planning on touring the whole of the canyon lands and not just the park.

Inside the Park

There are six lodges within Grand Canyon National Park at the South Rim, most of them operated by **Xanterra** (www.grandcanyonlodges.com). Over the last decade or so most of the rooms have been remodeled and upgraded, and you won't find any of them too much more expensive than those outside the park, as the rates are set and controlled by an annual review comparing the park's offerings to similar accommodations elsewhere.

A stay at ★ **El Tovar** (303/297-2757, www.grandcanyonlodges.com, $210-340), more than 100 years old and one of the most distinctive and memorable hotels in the state, would be the secondary highlight—after the gorge itself—of any trip to the South Rim. The log-and-stone National Historic Landmark, standing about 20 feet from the rim, has 78 rooms and suites, each with cable TV. The hotel's restaurant serves some of the best food in Arizona for breakfast, lunch, and dinner, and there's a comfortable cocktail lounge off the lobby with a window on the canyon. A mezzanine sitting area overlooks the log-cabin lobby, and a gift shop sells Native American art and crafts as well as canyon souvenirs. If you're looking to splurge on something truly exceptional, there's a honeymoon suite overlooking the canyon.

When first built in the 1930s, the ★ **Bright Angel Lodge** (303/297-2757, www.grandcanyonlodges.com, $95-210) was meant to serve the middle-class travelers then being lured by the Santa Fe Railroad, and it is still affordable and comfortable while retaining a rustic character that fits perfectly with the wild canyon just outside. Lodge rooms don't have TVs, and there is generally only one bed in each room. The inexpensive "hikers" rooms have shared baths, so if that bothers you, make sure to ask for a room with a private bath. It's the perfect place to stay the night before entering the canyon's inner depths; you just roll out of bed onto the Bright Angel Trail. The lodge's cabins just west of the main building are a little better equipped, with private baths, TVs, and sitting rooms. There's a gift shop; drinking and dining options include a small bar; a family-style restaurant offers breakfast, lunch, and dinner; and a more upscale eatery serves lunch and dinner.

Standing along the rim between El Tovar and Bright Angel, the **Kachina Lodge** (303/297-2757, www.grandcanyonlodges.com, $198-232), a more recent addition to the canyon's accommodations list, offers basic, comfortable rooms with TVs, safes, private baths, and refrigerators. There's not a lot of character, but its location and modern comforts make the Kachina an ideal place for families to stay. The **Thunderbird Lodge** (303/297-2757, www.grandcanyonlodges.com, $198-232) is in the same area and has similar offerings.

Maswick Lodge (303/297-2757, www.grandcanyonlodges.com, $95-205) is on the west side of the village about 0.25 miles from the rim. The hotel has a cafeteria-style restaurant that serves just about everything you'd want and a sports bar with a large-screen TV. The rooms are basic and comfortable, with TVs, private baths, and refrigerators.

Yavapai Lodge (11 Yavapai Lodge Rd., 928/638-4001 or 877/404-4611, www.visitgrandcanyon.com, $132-176), the only in-park accommodation not run by Xanterra, is east of the village and offers nice rooms with all the comforts but little character or artistic value, though you don't really need any of that when you've got the greatest sculpture garden in the world a few hundred yards away.

Outside the Park

Tusayan

About a mile outside Grand Canyon National Park's South entrance, along AZ-64/US 180, Tusayan is a collection of hotels, restaurants, and gift shops that has grown side by side with the park for nearly a century. The village makes a decent, close-by base for a visit to the park, especially if you can't get reservations at any of the in-park lodges.

Most of Tusayan's accommodations are of the chain variety, and though they are clean and comfortable, few of them have any character to speak of, and most of them are rather overpriced for what you get. Staying in Williams is a better choice if you're looking for an independent hotel or motel with some local color, and you can definitely find better deals.

The **Red Feather Lodge** (300 AZ-64, 928/638-2414, www.redfeatherlodge.com, $126-199), though more basic than some of the other places in Tusayan, is a comfortable, affordable place to stay with a pool, hot tub, and clean rooms in separate hotel and motel complexes. The **Grand Hotel** (149 AZ-64, 928/638-3333, www.grandcanyongrandhotel.com, $179-220), resembling a Western-themed ski lodge, has clean and comfortable rooms, a pool, a hot tub, a fitness center, and a beautiful lobby featuring a Starbucks coffee kiosk. The **Best Western Grand Canyon Squire Inn** (74 AZ-64, 928/638-2681, www.grandcanyonsquire.com, $188-289) has a fitness center, a pool and spa, a salon, a game room, a bowling alley, and myriad other amenities.

Before you reach Tusayan, you'll pass through Valle, a tiny spot along AZ-64/US 180, where you'll find one of the better deals in the whole canyon region. The **Red Lake Campground and Hostel** (8850 N. AZ-64, 928/635-4753, $20 pp/night), where you can rent a bed in a shared room, is a basic but reasonably comfortable place sitting lonely on the grasslands next to a gas station; it has shared baths with showers, a common room with a kitchen and a TV, and an RV park ($25) with hookups. If you're going super-budget, you can't beat this place, and it's only about 45 minutes from the park's South entrance.

Cameron

Along US 89, near the junction with AZ-64 east of the park, the nearly 100-year-old ★ **Historic Cameron Trading Post & Lodge** (800/338-7385, www.camerontradingpost.com, $69-189) is only about a 30-minute drive from the Desert View area of the park, a good place to start your tour. The lodge is a charming and affordable place to stay. It has a good restaurant (6am-9:30pm daily summer, 7am-9pm daily winter, $3-27) serving American and Navajo food, including excellent beef stew, heaping Navajo tacos, chili, and burgers. There's also an art gallery, a visitors center, a huge trading post-gift shop, and an RV park (no restroom or showers, full hookup $25). A small grocery store has packaged sandwiches, chips, and sodas. The rooms are decorated with a Southwestern Native American style and are clean and comfortable, some with views of the Little Colorado River and the old 1911 suspension bridge just outside the lodge. There are single-bed rooms, rooms with two beds, and a few suites that are perfect for families. The stone-and-wood buildings and the garden patio, laid out with stacked sandstone bricks with picnic tables and red-stone walkways below the open-corridor rooms, create a cozy, history-soaked setting and make the lodge a memorable place to stay. The vast, empty red plains of the Navajo Nation spread out all around and create a lonely, isolated atmosphere, especially at night. The rooms have cable TV and free Wi-Fi. In the winter, the lodge drops its prices significantly. In January and February, you can get one of the single-bed rooms for about $59 d.

Williams

This small historic town along I-40, formerly Route 66, is the closest interstate town to AZ-64, and thus has branded itself "The Gateway to the Grand Canyon." It's only about an hour's drive to the South Rim from here. Williams has some of the most affordable independent accommodations in the Grand Canyon region, as well as several chain hotels. This is the place to stay if you plan to take the Grand Canyon Railway to the South Rim. This selection of accommodations in Williams represents the best options available. For more in-depth information on Williams accommodations, please see page 397.

The **Grand Canyon Railway Hotel** (235 N. Grand Canyon Blvd., 928/635-4010, www.thetrain.com, $174-359) serves riders on the Grand Canyon Railway and offers the most upscale accommodations in Williams.

The original ★ **Grand Canyon Hotel** (145 W. Rte. 66, 928/635-1419, www.thegrandcanyonhotel.com, $69-185) is an affordable, friendly place to stay with a lot of character and an international flavor with some of the most affordable accommodations in the region.

The Lodge on Route 66 (200 E. Rte. 66, 877/563-4366, http://thelodgeonroute66.com, $99-189) has stylish, modern rooms. Pets are not allowed.

Flagstaff

Flagstaff, 80 miles southeast of the park's main South entrance, was the park's first gateway town. To reach the Grand Canyon from Flagstaff, take US 180 northwest for about 1.5 hours, and there you are. Historic hotels downtown offer both good value and a unique experience. East Flagstaff, as you enter along Route 66, has a large number small hotels and motels, including chains and several old-school motor inns. It lacks the charm of downtown but is an acceptable place to stay if you're just passing through. If you're a budget traveler, try the hostels in the Historic Southside District. This selection of accommodations in Flagstaff represents the best options. For more in-depth information on Flagstaff accommodations, please see page 390.

The Grand Canyon International Hostel (19 S. San Francisco St., 888/442-2696, www.grandcanyonhostel.com, $25-115) is a clean and friendly place to stay on the cheap. The same folks operate the **Motel DuBeau** (19 W. Phoenix St., 800/398-7112, www.grandcanyonhostel.com/dubeau, $25-115), a clean and charming hostel-inn with a small dorm and eight private rooms.

The Weatherford Hotel (23 N. Leroux St., 928/779-1919, www.weatherfordhotel.com, $55-145) is one of two historic hotels downtown. It's basic but romantic. **The Hotel Monte Vista** (100 N. San Francisco St., 928/779-6971 or 800/545-3068, http://hotelmontevista.com, mid-Apr.-early Nov. $70-175 d, early Nov.-mid-Apr. $50-175 d), the other historic downtown hotel, is a bit swankier. There's a hip cocktail lounge downstairs.

Camping

Inside the Park

★ **Mather Campground** (877/444-6777, www.recreation.gov, $18 Mar.-Nov., $15 Dec.-Feb.) takes reservations up to six months ahead through November 20 and thereafter operates on a first-come, first-served basis. It is near the village and offers more than 300 basic campsites with grills and fire pits. It has restroom facilities with showers, and laundry facilities are available for a fee. The campground is open to tents and trailers but has no hookups and is closed to RVs longer than 30 feet. Even if you aren't an experienced camper, a stay at Mather is a fun and inexpensive alternative to sleeping indoors. Despite its large size and crowds, the campground gets pretty quiet at night. Even in summer, the night takes on a bit of chill, making a campfire not exactly necessary but not out of the question. Bring your own wood or buy it at the store nearby. A large, clean restroom and shower facility is located within walking distance from most sites, and they even have blow-dryers. Everything is coin operated, and there's an office on-site that provides change. Consider bringing bikes along, especially for the kids. The village is about a 15-minute walk from the campground on forested, paved trails, or you can take the free tram from a stop nearby.

About 25 miles east of the village, near the park's east entrance, is **Desert View Campground** (first-come, first-served, May-mid-Oct. depending on weather, $12), with 50 sites for tents and small trailers only, with no hookups. There's a restroom with no showers and only two faucets with running water. Each site has a grill but little else.

If you're in a rolling mansion, try **Trailer Village** (888/297-2757, www.xanterra.com, $35) next to Mather Campground, near the village, where you'll find hookups.

Food

Inside the Park

★ **El Tovar Dining Room** (928/638-2631, ext. 6432, 6:30am-11am, 11:30am-2pm, and 5pm-10pm daily, $17-35, reservations required) truly carries on the Fred Harvey Company traditions on which it was founded more than 100 years ago. A serious, competent staff serves fresh, creative, locally inspired dishes in a cozy, mural-clad dining room that has not been significantly altered from the way it looked back when Teddy Roosevelt and Zane Grey ate here. The wine, entrées, and desserts are all top-notch and would be appreciated anywhere in the world—but they always seem to be that much tastier with the sun going down over the canyon. Pay attention to the specials, which usually feature some in-season local edible; they are always the best thing to eat within several hundred miles in any direction. If you only have one nice dinner planned for your trip, choose El Tovar over the Arizona Room. El Tovar has greater historical and aesthetic interest and is not that much more expensive than the Arizona Room.

★ **The Arizona Room** (928/638-2631, www.grandcanyonlodges.com, 11:30am-3pm and 4:30pm-10pm daily Mar.-Dec., $14-32), next to the Bright Angel Lodge, serves Southwestern-inspired steak, prime rib, fish, and chicken dishes in a stylish but still casual atmosphere. There's a full bar, and the steaks are excellent—hand-cut and cooked just right with unexpected sauces and marinades. The Arizona Room is closed for dinner in January and February and closes to the lunch crowd November-February.

★ **Bright Angel Restaurant** (928/638-2631, www.grandcanyonlodges.com, 6:30am-10pm daily, $9-22), just off the Bright Angel Lodge's lobby, is a perfect place for a big, hearty breakfast before a day hike below the rim. It serves all the standard, rib-sticking dishes amid decorations and ephemera recalling the Fred Harvey heyday. At lunch there's stew, chili, salads, sandwiches, and burgers, and for dinner there's steak, pasta, and fish dishes called "Bright Angel Traditions," along with a few offerings from the Arizona Room's menu. Nearby is the **Bright Angel Fountain** (11am-5pm daily in season), which serves hot dogs, ice cream, and other quick treats.

Maswik Food Court (928/638-2631, www.grandcanyonlodges.com, 6am-10pm daily, $3-9) is an ideal place for a quick, filling, and delicious meal. You can find just about everything—burgers, salads, country-style mashed potatoes, french fries, sandwiches, prime rib, chili, and soft-serve ice cream, to name just a few of the dozens of offerings. Just grab a tray and pick your favorite dish, and you'll be eating in a matter of a few minutes. There's a similar cafeteria-style restaurant at the Yavapai Lodge to the east of the village.

Outside the Park

Tusayan

A lot of tour buses stop in Tusayan, so you may find yourself crowded into waiting for a table at some places, especially during the summer high season. Better to eat in the park, or in Williams, which has many charming and delicious local restaurants worth seeking out. It's only about an hour's drive to Williams, so you might be better off having a small snack and skipping Tusayan altogether.

Nobody would go to Tusayan specifically to eat, but it makes for a decent emergency stop if you're dying of hunger. With one exception: **We Cook Pizza & Pasta** (125 E. AZ-64, 928/638-2278, www.wecookpizzaandpasta.com, 11am-10pm daily Mar.-Oct., 11am-8pm daily Nov.-Feb., $10-30) makes an excellent, high-piled pizza, served in slices or whole pies. It calls you just as you enter Tusayan coming from the park. They have a big salad bar with all the fixings, plus beer and wine. It's a casual place, with picnic tables and an often-harried staff. It gets busy during the summer.

One of the better places in Tusayan is the **Canyon Star Restaurant** (149 AZ-64, 928/638-3333, 7am-10am and 11:30am-10pm daily, $10-25), inside the Grand Hotel, which serves Southwestern food, steaks, and ribs, and features a saloon in which you can belly up to the bar on top of an old mule saddle (it's not that comfortable).

The Coronado Room (74 AZ-64, 928/638-2681, 5pm-10pm daily, $15-28), inside the Grand Canyon Squire Inn, serves tasty steaks, seafood, Mexican-inspired dishes, and pasta.

Williams

There are a few good restaurants in Williams, which is located along I-40 near the junction with AZ-64, about an hour's drive south of the park. This section represents the best choices in town. For more in-depth information on dining options in Williams, please see page 398.

A northland institution with some of the best steaks in the region, ★ **Rod's Steak House** (301 E. Rte. 66, 928/635-2671, www.rods-steakhouse.com, 11am-9:30pm Mon.-Sat., $12-35) has been operating at the same site since 1946. The food is excellent, the staff is friendly and professional, and the menus are shaped like steers.

The **Pine Country Restaurant** (107 N. Grand Canyon Blvd., 928/635-9718, http://pinecountryrestaurant.com, 6:30am-9:30pm daily, $5-10) is a family-style place that serves good food and homemade pies. Check out the beautiful paintings of the Grand Canyon on the walls.

Flagstaff

This section represents the best dining choices in town. For more in-depth information on food options in Flagstaff, please see page 392.

For the best burgers in the northland, head to ★ **Diablo Burger** (20 N. Leroux St., Ste. 112, 928/774-3274, 11am-9pm Mon.-Wed., 11am-10pm Thurs.-Sat., $8-14), which serves a small but stellar menu of beef raised locally on the plains around Flagstaff.

The best place for a beer is the **Beaver Street Brewery** (11 S. Beaver St., 928/779-0079, www.beaverstreetbrewery.com, 11am-1am Sun.-Wed., 11am-midnight Thurs.-Sat., $7-18), and there's delicious, hearty food.

At **Brandy's Restaurant and Bakery** (1500 E. Cedar Ave., #40, 928/779-2187, www.brandysrestaurant.com, 6:30am-3pm daily, $5-10), the homemade breads and bagels make everything else taste better, and the Reubens are some of the best in the business.

The North Rim

Standing at Bright Angel Point on the Grand Canyon's North Rim, crowded together with several other gazers as if stranded on a jetty over a wide, hazy sea, blurred evergreens growing atop great jagged rock spines banded with white and red, someone whispers, "It looks pretty much the same as the other rim."

It's not true—far from it—but the comment brings up the main point about the North Rim: Should you go? Only about 10 percent of canyon visitors make the trip to the North Rim, which is significantly less developed than the South; there aren't many activities other than gazing, unless you are a hiker and a backcountry wilderness lover. The coniferous mountain forests of the Kaibab Plateau, broken by grassy meadows painted with summer wildflowers, populated by often-seen elk and mule deer, and dappled with aspens that turn yellow and red in the fall and burst out of the otherwise uniform dark green like solitary flames, are themselves worth the trip. But it is a long trip, and you need to be prepared for a land of scant services and the simple, contemplative pleasures of nature in the raw.

It's all about the scenery here at 8,000 feet and above. The often misty canyon, and the thick, old-growth forest along its rim, command all of your attention. Some of the people you'll meet here are a bit different from the South Rim visitors, a good portion being hard-core hikers and backpackers waiting for early morning to hit the North Kaibab Trail for a rim-to-rim trek.

That's not to say that there's nothing to do on the North Rim. Spend some time on the lodge's back porch, have an overpriced beer at the cantina, and hike through the highland forest on easy trails to reach uncrowded viewpoints. There are similarly lonely lookouts (at least compared to the often elbow-to-elbow scene at some the South Rim's spots) at the end of a couple of scenic drives. Only a rare few see the North Rim covered in snow, as it often is past November. The park here closes in mid-October and doesn't open again until mid-May.

The **North Rim Visitor Center and Bookstore** (8am-6pm daily May-Oct.), near the Grand Canyon Lodge, has information, maps, and exhibits on North Rim science and history. The nonprofit Grand Canyon Association operates the well-stocked bookstore. Rangers offer a full program of talks and guided hikes throughout the day and night programs around the campfire. The North Rim edition of *The Guide* has an up-to-date list of topics, times, and meeting places. Try to attend at least one or two—they are typically interesting and entertaining for both kids and adults, and it tends to deepen your connection with this storied place when you learn about its natural and human history from those who know it best. For the kids, the visitors center has the usual super-fun and educational Junior Rangers program.

Getting There

Although it's only an average of about 10 miles across the canyon from points on the South Rim to points on the North Rim—but only if you're a hawk or a raven or a condor—it's a **215-mile, five-hour drive** for those of us who are primarily earthbound. The long route north is something to behold, moving through a corner of the Navajo Nation, past the towering Vermilion Cliffs, and deep into the high conifer forests of the Kaibab Plateau. On the plateau, which at its highest reaches above 9,000 feet elevation, **AZ-67** from Jacob Lake to the North Rim typically **closes to vehicles by late November until May.** In the winter, it's not uncommon for cross-country skiers and snowshoe hikers to take to the closed and snow-covered highway, heading with their own power toward the canyon and the North Kaibab Trail.

Between the hotel, restaurant, and gas station at Jacob Lake on the Kaibab Plateau and the entrance to Grand Canyon National Park on the North Rim, there's not much more than high mountain forest scenery. However, in case you forget anything before venturing into this relative wilderness, you can always stop at the well-stocked **North Rim Country Store** (AZ-67, mile marker 605, 928/638-2383, www.northrimcountrystore.com, 7:30am-7pm daily mid-May-early Nov.), about 43 miles along AZ-67 from Jacob Lake. The store has just about anything you'll need, from snacks to gas to camping supplies. There's also a small auto shop. The store closes for winter, as does the whole region, around the beginning of November.

It takes at least five hours to drive from the South Rim to the North Rim, through an empty land with scant services. Take the **Desert View Drive (AZ-64)** out of the park's **East entrance** near Cameron. Turn left onto **US 89** and head north to Bitter Springs, where US 89 splits off into **US 89A** going west. You'll cross over the Colorado River at **Navajo Bridge,** where you can stop at a visitors center and learn about the area's history and culture. Continue on US 89A past the Vermilion Cliffs National Monument, Cliff Dwellers, and the House Rock Valley. The highway eventually starts to rise to the Kaibab Plateau. At **Jacob Lake,** which is not a lake at all but a small lodge and service center with a great restaurant, take **AZ-67** about an hour through the forest to the park entrance.

The **Trans Canyon Shuttle** (928/638-2820, www.transcanyonshuttle.com, $90 one-way, reservations required) makes a daily round-trip excursion between the North and South Rims, departing the North at 7am and arriving at the South Rim at 11:30am. The shuttle then leaves the South at 1:30pm and arrives back at the North Rim at 6:30pm.

Driving Tours

Cape Royal Scenic Drive

You can reach Point Imperial and several other lookout spots on the Cape Royal Scenic Drive, one of the most scenic, dramatic roads in the state. From the lodge to Cape Royal it's about 30 miles round-trip on a paved road that wends through the mixed conifer and aspen forests of the **Walhalla Plateau.** There are plenty of chances for wildlife spotting, plus short trails to viewpoints offering breathtaking views of the canyon off to the east and even as far as Navajoland. Plan to spend at least half a day, and take food and water. Go to **Point Imperial** first, reached by a three-mile side road at the beginning of the Cape Royal Road. The best way to do it would be to leave the lodge just before sunrise, watch the show from Point Imperial, and then hit the scenic drive for the rest of the day, stopping often along the way. Binoculars would be of use on this drive, as would, of course, a camera. Along the way, **Vista Encantadora** (Charming View) provides just that, rising above Nanokoweap Creek. Just beyond that is **Roosevelt Point,** where you can hike the easy 0.2-mile loop trail to a view worthy of the man who saved the Grand Canyon for all of us. When you finally reach the point of the drive, **Cape Royal** at 7,865 feet, you'll walk out on a 0.6-mile round-trip paved trail for an expansive and unbounded view of the canyon—one of the very best, from which, on a clear day, you can spot the South Rim's Desert View Watchtower way across the gorge and the river far below. Along the short trail you'll pass **Angel's Window,** an unlikely rock arch that seems designed by some overly ambitious god trying to make an already intensely rare and wonderful view even more so.

Sights

★ Grand Canyon Lodge

Even if you aren't staying at the **Grand Canyon Lodge** (www.grandcanyonlodgenorth.com), a rustic log-and-stone structure built in 1927-1928 and perched on the edge of the rim at the very end of the highway, don't make the trip to the North Rim without going into its warm Sun Room to view the gorge through the huge picture windows. You may want to sink into one of the comfortable couches and stare for hours. At sunset, head out to the Adirondack chairs on the lodge's back patio and watch the sun sink over the canyon; everybody's quiet, hushed in reverence, bundled up in jackets and sweaters, and wondering how they came to such a rare place as this. Right near the door leading out to the patio, check out sculptor Peter Jepson's charming life-size bronze of **Brighty,** a famous canyon burro whose story was told in the 1953 children's book *Brighty of the Grand Canyon* by Marguerite Henry. A display nearby tells the true-life aspects of Brighty's story, and they say if you rub his bronze nose you'll have good luck. The book, along with a movie based on the story, is available at gift shops and bookstores on both the North and South Rims.

Viewpoints

There are three developed viewpoints at the North Rim, each of them offering a slightly different look at the canyon. **Bright Angel Point,** about a half-mile round-trip walk outside the lodge's back door, looks over Bright Angel Canyon and provides a view of Roaring Springs, the source of Bright Angel Creek and the freshwater source for the North Rim and the inner canyon. **Point Imperial,** at 8,803 feet, is the highest point on the North Rim and probably has the single best view from the rim, and **Cape Royal,** a view toward the South Rim, is a 15-mile one-way drive across the Walhalla Plateau.

Recreation

Hiking

It's significantly cooler on the high, forested North Rim than it is on the South, making hiking, especially summer hiking and even more so summertime hiking below the rim, much less of a chore. There are a few easy rim trails to choose from and several tough but unforgettable day hikes into the canyon along the North Kaibab Trail.

Easy trails lead to and from all the developed scenic overlooks on the rim, their trailheads accessible and well marked. *The Guide* has a comprehensive listing of the area's trails and where to pick them up. The three-mile round-trip **Transept Trail** is an easy hike along the forested green rim from the Grand Canyon Lodge to the campground that provides a good overview of the park. Hiking along the rim is an excellent way to see the canyon from many different points of view.

Uncle Jim Trail

Distance: 5 miles round-trip
Duration: 3 hours
Elevation gain: about 200 feet
Effort: easy
Trailhead: North Kaibab Trail parking lot, 3 miles north of Grand Canyon Lodge on the main park entrance road

Take this easy, flat trail through the pine forest, from which you can watch backpackers winding their way down the North Kaibab Trail's twisting switchbacks and maybe see a mule train or two along the way. The Uncle Jim Trail winds through old stands of spruce and fir, sprinkled with quaking aspen, to Uncle Jim Point, where you can let out your best roar into the side notch known as Roaring Springs Canyon.

Widforss Trail

Distance: 10 miles round-trip
Duration: 5-6 hours
Elevation gain: negligible
Effort: easy
Trailhead: 4 miles north of the lodge; look for the sign

The mostly flat and easy Widforss Trail leads along the rim of the side canyon called Transept Canyon and through ponderosa pine, fir, and spruce forest, with a few stands of aspen mixed in, for five miles to Widforss Point, where you can stare across the great chasm and rest before heading back.

North Kaibab Trail

Distance: varies; 9.4 miles to Roaring Springs
Duration: a few hours to overnight

Elevation gain: 5,961 feet from Phantom Ranch
Effort: moderate to difficult
Trailhead: North Kaibab Trail parking area

The North Kaibab Trail starts out among the coniferous heights of the North Rim. The forest surrounding the trail soon dries out and becomes a red-rock desert, the trail cut into the rock face of the cliffs and twisting down improbable routes hard against the cliffs, with nothing but your sanity keeping you away from the gorge. This is the only North Rim route down into the Inner Canyon and to the Colorado River. Sooner than you realize, the walls close in, and you are deep in the canyon, the trees on the rim just green blurs now. A good introduction to this corridor trail and ancient native route is the short, 1.5-mile round-trip jog down to the **Coconino Overlook,** from which, on a clear day, you can see the San Francisco Peaks and the South Rim. A four-mile round-trip hike down will get you to **Supai Tunnel,** blasted out of the red rock in the 1930s by the Civilian Conservation Corps. A little more than a mile onward you'll reach **The Bridge in the Redwall** (5.5 miles round-trip), built in 1966 after a flood ruined this portion of the trail. For a tough, all-day hike that will likely have you sore but smiling the next morning, take the North Kaibab five miles in to **Roaring Springs,** the source of life-giving Bright Angel Creek. The springs fall headlong out of the cliff side and spray mist and rainbows into the hot air. Just remember, you have to go five miles up and out too. Start hiking early, and take plenty of water.

The North Kaibab trailhead is a few miles north of the Grand Canyon Lodge, the park's only accommodations on the North Rim. To get from the lodge to the trailhead, take the **hiker's shuttle** (1st person $7, each additional person $4), which leaves every morning from the lodge at 5:45am and 7:10am. Tickets must be purchased the day before at the lodge.

North Rim Mule Rides

The mules at the North Rim all work for **Canyon Trail Rides** (435/679-8665, www.canyonrides.com, May 15-Oct. 15), the park's northside trail-riding concessionaire. Guides will take you and your friendly mule on a one-hour rim-side ride ($40) or a half-day ride to Uncle Jim Point ($80). You can also take a mule down into the canyon along the North Kaibab Trail to the Supai Tunnel ($80). Kids have to be at least 7 years old to take part in a one-hour ride, at least 10 for the half-day, and 12 for the full-day rides. There's a 220-pound weight limit. Call ahead for a reservation if this is something you're set on doing. You might be able to hop on at the last minute, though probably not in June, which is the busiest time at the North Rim.

Accommodations

Built in the late 1930s after the original lodge burned down, the ★ **Grand Canyon Lodge** (928/638-2611 or 888/297-2757, www.grandcanyonlodgenorth.com, mid-May-mid-Oct., $130-190) has the only in-park accommodations on the North Rim. The rustic but very comfortable log-and-stone lodge has a large central lobby, a high-ceilinged dining room, a deli, a saloon ($6 for a beer), a gift shop, a general store, and a gas station. There are several small, comfortable lodge rooms and dozens of cabins scattered around the property, each with a bathroom and most with a gas-powered fireplace that makes things very cozy on a cold night. The lodge is open from mid-May through mid-October. You must book far in advance (at least six months), though there are sometimes cancellations that could allow for a last-minute booking.

The **Kaibab Lodge** (928/638-2389, www.kaibablodge.com, mid-May-early Nov., $95-185) is a small gathering of rustic, cozy cabins behind the tree line at the edge of a meadow along AZ-67, about five miles north of the park boundary. You can rent cabins of varying sizes and enjoy

beneath the shady trees at Indian Garden, you face a mere 4.9-mile hike to the rim.

From the **North Rim,** the **North Kaibab** is the only trail to the river and Phantom Ranch.

Rim to Rim

For an epic, **20-plus-mile** rim-to-rim rim hike, you can choose, as long as the season permits, to start either on the north or south. Starting from the South Rim, you may want to go down the **Bright Angel** to see beautiful Indian Garden; then again, the **South Kaibab** provides a faster, more direct route to the river. If you start from the north, you may want to come out of the canyon via the South Kaibab, as it is shorter and faster, and at that point you are probably going to want to take the path of least resistance. Remember, though, while it's shorter, the South Kaibab is a good deal steeper than the Bright Angel, and there is no water available.

It doesn't matter who you are or what trail you prefer, the hike out of the Grand Canyon is, at several points, a brutal trudge. It's even worse with 30-40 pounds of stuff you don't really need on your back. But when you finally gain the rim, and you will get there, a profound sense of accomplishment, nearing on glory, washes away a least half of the fatigue. The other half typically hangs around for a week or so.

Guides

You certainly don.'t need a guide to take a classic backpacking trip into the Grand Canyon along one of the corridor trails. The National Park Service makes it a relatively simple process to plan and complete such a memorable expedition, and, while hikers die below the rim pretty much every year, the more popular regions of the inner canyon are as

Top to bottom: Indian Garden, midway down Bright Angel Trail; riding mules into the canyon; River Trail, inner canyon.

safe as can be expected in a vast wilderness. Then again, having some friendly, knowledgeable and undoubtedly badass canyonlander plan and implement every detail of your trip sure couldn't hurt. Indeed, it would probably make the whole expedition infinitely more enjoyable. As long as you're willing to pay for it—and it is never cheap—hiring a guide is an especially good idea if you want to go places where few visitors and casual hikers dwell.

There are more than 20 companies authorized, through a guide permit issued by the National Park Service, to take trips below the rim. If your guide does not have such a permit, do not follow him or her into the Grand Canyon. For an up-to-date list, see www.nps.gov/grca.

The **Grand Canyon Field Institute** (928/638-2481, www.grandcanyon.org, $560), which is operated by the nonprofit Grand Canyon Association, offers several three- to five-day guided backpacking trips to various points inside the canyon, including trips designed specifically for women, for beginners, and for those interested in the canyon's natural history.

Operating out of Flagstaff, **Four Season Guides** (1051 S. Milton Rd., 928/779-6224, www.fsguides.com, $799-1,450) offers more than a dozen different backpacking trips below the rim, from a three-day frolic to Indian Garden to a weeklong, 45-mile expedition one some of the canyon's lesser-known trails. The experienced and friendly guides tend to inspire a level of strength and ambition that you might not reach otherwise. These are the guys to call if you want to experience the lonely, out-of-the-way depths of the canyon but don't want to needlessly risk your life doing it alone.

Hiking

Day Hikes Around Phantom Ranch

Some people prefer to spend their time in the canyon recovering from the hard walk or mule ride that brought them here, and a day spent cooling your feet in Bright Angel Creek or drinking beer in the cantina is not a day wasted. However, if you want to do some exploring around Phantom Ranch, there are a few popular day hikes from which to choose. When you arrive, the friendly rangers will usually tell you, unsolicited, all about these hikes and provide detailed directions. If you want to get deeper out in the bush and far from the other hikers, ask one of the rangers to recommend a lesser-known route.

River Trail

Distance: 1.5 miles round-trip
Duration: 1-2 hours
Elevation gain: negligible
Effort: easy

This rather short hike is along the precipitous River Trail, high above the Colorado just south of Phantom Ranch. The Civilian Conservation Corps (CCC) blasted this skinny cliff-side trail out of the rock walls in the 1930s to provide a link between the Bright Angel and the South Kaibab Trail. Heading out from Phantom, it's about a 1.5-mile loop that takes you across both suspension bridges and high above the river. It's an easy walk with fantastic views and a good way to get your sore legs stretched and moving again. And you are likely to see a bighorn sheep's cute little face poking out from the rocks and shadows on the steep cliffs.

Clear Creek to Phantom Overlook

Distance: about 1.5 miles
Duration: 1-2 hours
Elevation gain: 826 feet
Effort: easy to moderate
Trailhead: about 0.25 miles north of Phantom Ranch on the North Kaibab Trail

Another popular CCC-built trail near Phantom, the 1.5-mile Clear Creek Loop takes you high above the river to Phantom Overlook, where there's an old stone bench and excellent views of the canyon and of Phantom Ranch below.

The rangers seem to recommend this hike the most, but, while it's not tough, it can be a little steep and rugged, especially if you're exhausted and sore. The views are, ultimately, well worth the pain.

Ribbon Falls

Distance: 11 miles round-trip
Duration: 5-6 hours to all day
Elevation gain: 1,174 feet
Effort: easy to moderate
Trailhead: look for the sign 5.5 miles north of Phantom Ranch on the North Kaibab Trail

If you hiked in from the South Rim and you have a long, approximately 11-mile round-trip day hike in you, head north on the North Kaibab from Phantom Ranch to beautiful Ribbon Falls, a mossy, cool-water oasis just off the hot, dusty trail. The falls are indeed a ribbon of cold water falling hard off the rock cliffs, and you can scramble up the slickrock and through the green creek-side jungle and stand beneath the shower. This hike will also give you a chance to see the eerie, claustrophobic "Box," one of the strangest and most exhilarating stretches of the North Kaibab.

Mule Rides

For generations the famous Grand Canyon mules have been dexterously picking along the skinny trails, loaded with packs and people. Even the Brady Bunch rode them, so they come highly recommended. A descent into the canyon on the back of a friendly mule—with an often taciturn cowboy-type leading the train—can be an unforgettable experience, but don't assume because you're riding and not walking that you won't be sore in the morning. One night at Phantom Ranch, meals included, and a ride down on a mule costs $548 per person or $960 for two. Two nights at Phantom, meals, and a mule ride costs $745 per person or $1,229 for two. For reservations call 888/297-2757 or visit www.grandcanyonlodges.com. Call six months or more in advance.

River Trips

People who have been inside the Grand Canyon often have one of two reactions—they either can't wait to return, or they swear never to return. This is doubly true of those intrepid souls who ride the great river, braving white-water roller coasters while looking forward to a star-filled evening camped—dry, and full of gourmet camp food—on a white beach deep in the gorge. To boat the Colorado, one of the last explored regions of North America, is one of the most exciting and potentially life-changing trips the West has to offer.

Because of this well-known truth, trips are neither cheap nor easy to book. Rafting season in the canyon runs from April to October, and there are myriad trips to choose from—from a 3-day long-weekend ride to a 21-day full-canyon epic. An Upper Canyon trip will take you from River Mile 0 at Lee's Ferry through the canyon to Phantom Ranch, while a Lower Canyon trip begins at Phantom, requiring a hike down the Bright Angel with your gear on your back. Furthermore, you can choose between a motorized pontoon boat, as some three-quarters of rafters do, a paddleboat, a kayak, or some other combination. It all depends on what you want and what you can afford.

If you are considering taking a river trip, the best place to start is the website of the **Grand Canyon River Outfitters Association** (www.gcroa.org), a nonprofit group of about 16 licensed river outfitters, all of them monitored and approved by the National Park Service, each with a good safety record and relatively similar rates. After you decide what kind of trip you want, the website links to the individual outfitters for booking. Most of the companies offer trips between 3 and 18 days, and have a variety of boat styles. It's a good idea to choose two or three companies, call them up, and talk to someone live. You'll be putting your life in their hands, so you want to make sure that you

Lee's Ferry: River Mile 0

Lee's Ferry (www.nps.gov/glca) is the only spot in hundreds of miles where you can drive down to the Colorado River. Located in the Glen Canyon National Recreation Area, Lee's Ferry provides the dividing line between the upper and lower states of the Colorado River's watershed, making it "river mile 0," the gateway and crossroads to both the upper and lower Colorado, and the place where its annual flows are measured and recorded. It's also the starting point for river-trippers who venture into the Grand Canyon atop the Colorado every year. It's a popular fishing spot, though the trout have been introduced and were not native to the warm muddy flow before the dam at Glen Canyon changed the Colorado's character. For guides, gear, and any other information about the area, try **Lee's Ferry Anglers** (928/355-2261 or 800/962-9755, www.leesferry.com) located at the Cliff Dweller's Lodge.

This lonely spot is named for a man who occupied the area rather briefly in the early 1870s, Mormon outlaw John D. Lee, who was exiled here after his participation in the infamous Mountain Meadows Massacre in Utah. He didn't stay long, escaping as a fugitive before his capture and execution. One of Lee's wives, Emma Lee, ended up running the ferry more than Lee ever did. The Lee family operated a small ranch and orchard near the crossing, the remnants of which can still be seen on a self-guided tour of the **Lonely Dell Ranch Historic Site.** There's a nice **campground** (no hookups, $12), a ranger station, and a launch ramp.

Accommodations and Food

Cliff Dweller's Lodge (928/355-2261 or 800/962-9755, www.cliffdwellerslodge.com, $75-85) offers charming, rustic-but-comfortable rooms with satellite television, and the restaurant serves good breakfasts, lunches, and dinners ($10-25), everything from fajitas and ribs to falafel and halibut. They also serve beer and wine, which you can sip on the little patio at what seems like the end of the world. There's also a gas station.

The **Lee's Ferry Lodge at Vermilion Cliffs** (US 89A near Marble Canyon, 928/355-2231 or 800/451-2231, www.leesferrylodge.com, $63) has romantic little rooms in a rock-built structure that blends into the tremendous background. A delicious restaurant (breakfast, lunch, and dinner daily, $10-20) serves hearty fare like hand-cut steaks and ribs, as well as a diverse selection of beer.

Getting There

Lee's Ferry is located in the vast, empty regions along the road between the South and North Rims, about 60 miles from the North Rim. Just after crossing over **Navajo Bridge** at Marble Canyon, along **US 89A,** turn on **Lee's Ferry Road.** The river is about seven miles along the road from the Navajo Bridge Visitors Center.

like the spirit of the company. Also consider the size of the group. These river trips are very social; you'll be spending a lot of time with your fellow boaters. Talk to a company representative about previous trips so you can get a gauge of what kind of people, and how many, you'll be floating with.

If you are one of the majority of river explorers who can't wait to get back on the water once you've landed at the final port, remember that there's a strict one trip per year per person rule enforced by the National Park Service.

Accommodations and Food

Designed by Mary Colter for the Fred Harvey Company in 1922, ★ **Phantom Ranch** (888/297-2757, www.grandcanyonlodges.com, dormitory $47 pp, 2-person cabin $135, $13 each additional person), the only noncamping accommodations inside the canyon, is a shady, peaceful place that you're likely to miss and yearn for once you've visited and left it behind. Perhaps Phantom's strong draw, like a siren wailing from the inner gorge, is less about its intrinsic pleasures and more about it being the only sign of civilization in a deep wilderness that can feel like the end of the world, especially after a 17-mile hike in from the North Rim. But it would probably be an inviting place even if it were easier to get at, and it's all the better because it's not.

As such, it is difficult to make a reservation. Some people begin calling a year out and still can't get a room, while others show up at the South Rim, ask at the Bright Angel Lodge, and find that a cancellation that very day has left a cabin or bed open. This strategy is not recommended, but it has been known to work. Phantom has several cabins and two dormitories, one for men and one for women, both offering restrooms with showers. The lodge's center point is its cantina, a welcoming, air-conditioned, beer- and lemonade-selling sight for anyone who has just descended one of the trails. Two meals a day are served in the cantina—breakfast, made up of eggs, pancakes, and thick slices of bacon ($20), and dinner, with a choice of steak ($45), stew ($28), or vegetarian ($28). The cantina also offers a box lunch ($13) with a bagel, fruit, and salty snacks. Reservations for meals are also difficult to come by.

Most nights and afternoons, a ranger based at Phantom Ranch will give a talk on some aspect of canyon lore, history, or science. These events are always interesting and always well attended, even in the 110°F heat of summer.

Phantom is located near the mouth of Bright Angel Canyon, within a few yards of clear, babbling Bright Angel Creek, and is shaded by large cottonwoods planted in the 1930s by the Civilian Conservation Corps. There are several day hikes within easy reach, and the Colorado River and the two awesome suspension bridges that link one bank to the other are only about 0.25 miles from the lodge.

Camping

There are three developed campgrounds in the inner canyon: **Cottonwood Campground,** about seven miles from the North Rim along the North Kaibab Trail; **Bright Angel Campground,** along the creek of the same name near Phantom Ranch; and **Indian Garden,** about 4.5 miles from the South Rim along the Bright Angel Trail. To stay overnight at any of these campgrounds you must obtain a permit from the **South Rim Backcountry Information Center** (928/638-7875, $10 plus $5 pp per night). All three campgrounds offer restrooms, a freshwater spigot, picnic tables, and food storage bins to keep the critters out. There are no showers or other amenities.

The best campground in the inner canyon is Bright Angel, a shady, cottonwood-lined setting along cool Bright Angel Creek. Because of its easy proximity to Phantom Ranch, campers can make use of the cantina, even eating meals there if they can get a reservation, and can attend the ranger talks offered at the lodge. There's nothing quite like sitting on the grassy banks beside your campsite and cooling your worn feet in the creek.

Grand Canyon West

Since the Hualapai Tribe's Skywalk opened to much international press coverage in 2007, the remote western reaches of the Grand Canyon have certainly gotten more attention than in the past. Though as remote as ever, there has been an uptick in tourism to the Hualapai's portion of the rim, which is about two hours of dirt-road driving from the Hualapai Reservation's capital, Peach Springs, located along Route 66 east of Kingman. At the same time, all that press has led to a little confusion. At the South Rim Visitor Center, one can usually hear the question, "How do we get to the Skywalk?" a few times an hour, followed by moans of disbelief and the cancellation of plans when the answer comes that it's about 250 miles away. If you want to experience Grand Canyon West, it's a good idea to plan a separate trip, or else carve out at least two extra days to do so. Along the way, you can drive on the longest remaining portion of Route 66, and, if you have a few days on top of that, hike down into Havasupai Canyon and see its famous, fantastical waterfalls.

Havasupai Indian Reservation

Havasu Creek is heavy with lime, which turns the water an almost tropical blue-green. It passes below the weathered red walls of the western Grand Canyon, home these many centuries to the Havasupai (Havasu 'Baaja), the "people of the blue-green water."

The creek falls through the canyon on its way to join the Colorado River, passing briefly by the ramshackle, inner-canyon village of Supai, where it is not unusual to see horses running free in the dusty streets, and where reggae plays all day through some community speaker, and where the supply helicopter alights and then hops out again every 10 minutes or so in a field across from the post office. Then, about two miles on from the village, the creek plunges 120 feet into a misty turquoise pool, and it does it again after another mile, but not before passing peacefully through a cottonwood-shaded campground.

Thousands of people from all over the world (the tribe says 20,000; other sources say half that) visit **Havasupai** (928/448-2731, www.havasupai-nsn.gov, entry $35 pp plus $5 environmental-care fee) every year just to see these blue-green waterfalls, to swim in their pools, and to see one of the remotest hometowns in America. The trip is all the more enticing and memorable because it's rather an expedition, or near to it. Still, there are those who return year after year, as if going home.

Getting There

A visit to Havasupai takes some planning. It's unbearably hot in the deep summer, and you can't hike except in the very early morning; the best months to visit are September-October and April-June. If you aren't a backpacker, you can hire a **packhorse** ($190 round-trip) or take the **helicopter** ($85 one-way). A popular way to visit is to hike in and take the helicopter out. It's a five-minute thrill-ride through the canyon to the rim, and the helipad is only about 50 yards from the trailhead parking lot.

Most visitors stay the night at one of the motels along Historic Route 66 the night before hiking in. Get an early start, especially during the summer. It's a **60-mile drive** to the trailhead at Hualapai Hill from Route 66. The closest hotel is the **Hualapai Lodge** (900 Rte. 66, 928/769-2230 or 928/769-2636, www.grandcanyonwest.com, $159) in Peach Springs, about seven miles west of Highway 18, which leads to the trailhead. You'll find cheaper accommodations in **Seligman** (see page 400), about 30 miles east. The tribe requires a reservation to visit Supai and the falls; call at least six months in advance.

The **eight-mile one-way hike** to the village of Supai from Hualapai Hilltop is one of the easier treks into the Grand Canyon. A few miles of switchbacks lead to a sandy bottomland, where you're surrounded by eroded humps of seemingly melted, pockmarked sandstone. This is not Grand Canyon National Park: You'll know that for sure when you see the trash along the trail. It doesn't ruin the hike, but it nearly breaks the spell. When you reach the village, you'll see the twin rock spires, called Wii'Gliva, that tower over the little farms and cluttered-yard homes of Supai.

The Waterfalls

What used to be Navajo Falls, just down the trail from the village, was destroyed in a 2008 flash flood. Now there's a wider set of falls and a big pool that sits below a flood-eroded hill. Perhaps the most famous of the canyon's falls, **Havasu Falls** comes up all of a sudden as you get closer to the campground. Few hikers refuse to toss their packs aside and strip to their swimming suits when they see Havasu Falls for the first time. The other major waterfall, **Mooney Falls,** is another mile down the trail, through the campground. It's not easy to reach the pool below; it requires a careful walk down a narrow rock-hewn trail with chain handles, but most reasonably dexterous people can handle it. **Beaver Falls,** somewhat underwhelming by comparison, is another two miles of creek-sloshing toward the river, which is seven miles from the campground.

Accommodations and Food

The **Havasupai Lodge** (928/448-2111 or 928/448-2201, up to 4 people $145) has air-conditioning and private baths. The village also has a small café that serves decent breakfast, lunch, and dinner, and a general store. Most visitors pack in and stay at the primitive **campground** (first-come, first-served, $17) not far from the main waterfall, which is another 1.5 miles from the village.

Hualapai Indian Reservation

Although Peach Springs is the capital of the Hualapai (WALL-uh-pie) Nation, there's not much there but a lodge and a few scattered houses. The real attractions are up on the West Rim about 50 miles (two hours' drive) away. Peach Springs makes an obvious base for a visit to the West Rim, which has several lookout points, the famous Skywalk, and a kitschy Old West-style tourist attraction called Hualapai Ranch. The tribe's **Hualapai River Runners** (928/769-2219) will take you on a day trip on the river, and there are several all-inclusive package tours to choose from. Check out the tribe's website (www.grandcanyonwest.com) for more information.

The Skywalk

Tour Packages

To visit Grand Canyon West, the Hualapai Tribe requires you to purchase one of its rather overpriced **Legacy Packages** ($40-75 pp), and only the most expensive "Gold" package includes the Skywalk. The lesser packages allow you to ride a shuttle from **Eagle Point,** where the Skywalk juts out, to **Guano Point,** an unobstructed view of the western canyon, and **Hualapai Ranch,** where fake cowboys will entertain you with Old West clichés and take you on a ride in a wagon or on a horseback ride in a corral or to the canyon rim ($10-75). You can stay the night in one of the ranch's rustic cabins ($100). A couple of the packages include a meal, or you can add one for $15 per person. You can also add the Skywalk to your package for $30 if you get up there and decide you really must try it. Frankly, the packages that don't include the Skywalk are definitely not worth the price or the drive. The views from the South and North Rims are much more dramatic and memorable, and it costs only $30 (the park entrance fee) to see those.

The Skywalk

The Skywalk (928/769-2636, www.grandcanyonwest.com, tours $90 and up) is as much an art installation as it is a tourist attraction. A horseshoe-shaped glass and steel platform jutting out 70 feet from the canyon rim, it appears futuristic surrounded by the rugged, remote western canyon. It's something to see, for sure, but is it worth the long drive and the high price tag? Not really. If you have time for an off-the-beaten-path portion of your canyon trip, it's better to go to the North Rim and stand out on Bright Angel Point—you'll get a somewhat similar impression, and it's cheaper. There is something of the thrill ride to the Skywalk, however. Some people can't handle it: They walk out a few steps, look down through the glass at the canyon 4,000 feet below, and head for (seemingly) more solid ground. It's all perfectly safe, but it doesn't feel that way if you are subject to vertigo. Another drawback of this site is that they won't let you take your camera out on the Skywalk. If you want a record of this adventure, you have to buy a "professional" photo taken by somebody else. You have to store all of your possessions, including your camera, in a locker before stepping out on the glass, with covers on your shoes like a surgeon entering the operating room.

Recreation

Though the Skywalk may not be worth the high price of admission and the long drive to reach it, the Hualapai Tribe offers one adventure that is worth the steep price tag: the canyon's only **one-day river rafting experience** (928/769-2636, www.grandcanyonwest.com, May-Oct., $330 pp). It generally takes up to a year of planning and several days of roughing it to ride the river and the rapids through the inner gorge, making a Colorado River adventure something

The Hualapai

Before the 1850s, northwestern Arizona's small Hualapai Tribe didn't really exist. It was the federal government's idea to group together 13 autonomous bands of Yuman-speaking Pai Indians, who had lived on the high dry plains near Grand Canyon's western reaches for eons, as the "People of the Tall Pines."

Before the colonial clampdown and the Hualapai Wars of the 1860s, the Pai bands were independent, though they "followed common rules for marriage and land use, spoke variations of one language, and shared social structures, kin networks, cultural practices, environmental niches, and so on," according to Jeffrey Shepherd's *We Are an Indian Nation: A History of the Hualapai People,* which the scholar spent 10 years researching and writing.

The U.S. Army nearly wiped out the bands during the land wars of the 1860s, and the internment of the survivors almost finished the job. But the bands persisted, and in 1883 the government established the million-acre Hualapai Reservation, with its capital at Peach Springs. Then it spent the next 100 years or so trying to take it away from them for the benefit of ranchers, the railroad, and the National Park Service.

These days the Hualapai Nation, though still impoverished, is a worldwide brand—Grand Canyon West. How did this happen?

The small, isolated tribe has always been willing to take economic risks, one of the many ways, as Shepherd argues, that the Hualapai have twisted colonial objectives for their own survival. A few years ago they partnered with Las Vegas entrepreneur David Jin and built the Hualapai Skywalk, a 70-foot-long glass walkway hanging from the Grand Canyon's western rim. Now you can't walk two steps along the Vegas Strip without a tour guide offering to drive you to one of the most isolated sections of Arizona.

Throughout their relatively short history as a nation proper, the Hualapai have consistently tried to make their windy and dry reservation economically viable, sometimes with the assistance of the government but often in direct contradiction to its goals. For generations they were cattle ranchers, but they could never get enough water to make it pay. They successfully sued the Santa Fe Railroad over an important reservation spring in a landmark case for indigenous rights. For a time in the 1980s they even hesitantly explored allowing uranium mining on their reservation. Now, they have bet their future on tourism.

that the average tourist isn't likely to try. Not so in Grand Canyon West. For about $330 per person, Hualapai river guides will pick you up in a van early in the morning at the Hualapai Lodge in Peach Springs and drive you to the Colorado via the rough Diamond Creek Road, where you'll float downstream in a motorboat over roiling white-water rapids and smooth and tranquil stretches. You'll stop for lunch on a beach and take a short hike through a watery side canyon to beautiful Travertine Falls. At the end of the trip, a helicopter picks you out of the canyon and drops you on the rim near the Skywalk. It's expensive, yes, but if you want to ride the river without a lot of preplanning and camping, this is the way to do it. Along the way the Hualapai guides tell stories about this end of the Grand Canyon, sprinkled with tribal history and lore.

You can drive to the river's edge yourself along the 19-mile **Diamond Creek Road** through a dry, scrubby landscape scattered with cacti. The road provides the only easy access to the river's edge between Lee's Ferry, not far from the North Rim, and Pearce Ferry, near Lake Mead. The route is best negotiated in a high-clearance SUV; they say you can do it in a regular sedan, but you have to cross Diamond Creek six times as the dirt road winds down through Peach Springs

Canyon, dropping some 3,400 feet from its beginning at Peach Springs on Route 66. The creek is susceptible to flash floods during the summer and winter rainy seasons, so call ahead to check **road conditions** (928/769-2230). At the end of the road, where Diamond Creek marries the Colorado, there's a sandy beach and an enchanting, lush oasis, and, of course, there's that big river rolling by.

Accommodations and Food

The **Hualapai Lodge** (900 Rte. 66, 928/769-2230 or 928/769-2636, www.grandcanyonwest.com, $159) in Peach Springs has a small heated saltwater pool, an exercise room, a gift shop, 57 comfortable newish rooms with soft beds, cable, free wireless Internet access, and train tracks right out the back door. The lodge is a good place to stay the night before hiking into Havasupai, as it's only about seven miles west of the turnoff to Hualapai Hill and the trailhead.

The lodge's restaurant, **Diamond Creek** (6am-9pm daily, $7-17), serves American and Native American dishes. They offer a heaping plate of delicious spaghetti if you're carbo-loading for a big hike to Havasupai; the Hualapai taco (similar to the Navajo taco, with beans and meat piled high on a fluffy slab of fry bread) and the Hualapai stew (with luscious sirloin tips and vegetables swimming in a delicious, hearty broth) are both recommended. They also have a few vegetarian choices, good chili, and pizza.

More food and lodging options are available in **Kingman** (see page 408) and **Seligman** (see page 400) along Old Route 66.

Getting There and Around

The best way to get to **Grand Canyon West** is to take **I-40** to the **Ash Fork exit** and then drive west on **Route 66.** Starting at Ash Fork and heading west to Peach Springs, the longest remaining portion of Route 66 runs through **Seligman,** a small roadside town that is a reminder of the heyday of the Mother Road. The route through Seligman, which is worth a stop and a walk around if you have the time, is popular with nostalgic motorcyclists, and there are a few eateries and tourist-style stores in town. Once you reach Peach Springs, take **Antares Road** 25 miles, then turn right on **Pearce Ferry Road** for 3 miles, then turn east onto **Diamond Bar Road** for 21 miles, 14 of it on dirt. Diamond Bar Road ends at the only entrance to Grand Canyon West. The 49-mile trip takes about two hours. For **park-and-ride reservations,** call 702/260-6506.

To reach **Havasupai Canyon,** turn north on Highway 18 just before Peach Springs and drive 68 miles north to a parking area at Hualapai Hilltop. From there it's an eight-mile hike in to Supai and the lodge, and another two miles to the campground. The trail is moderate and leads through a sandy wash with overhanging canyon walls. For the first two miles or so, rocky, moderately technical switchbacks lead to the canyon floor; then it's easy and beautiful the rest of the way. If you don't want to hike in, you can arrange to **rent a horse** (928/448-2121, 928/448-2174, or 928/448-2180, www.havasupaitribe.com, $120 round-trip to lodge, $150 round-trip to campground), or even hire a **helicopter** (623/516-2790, $85 pp one-way).

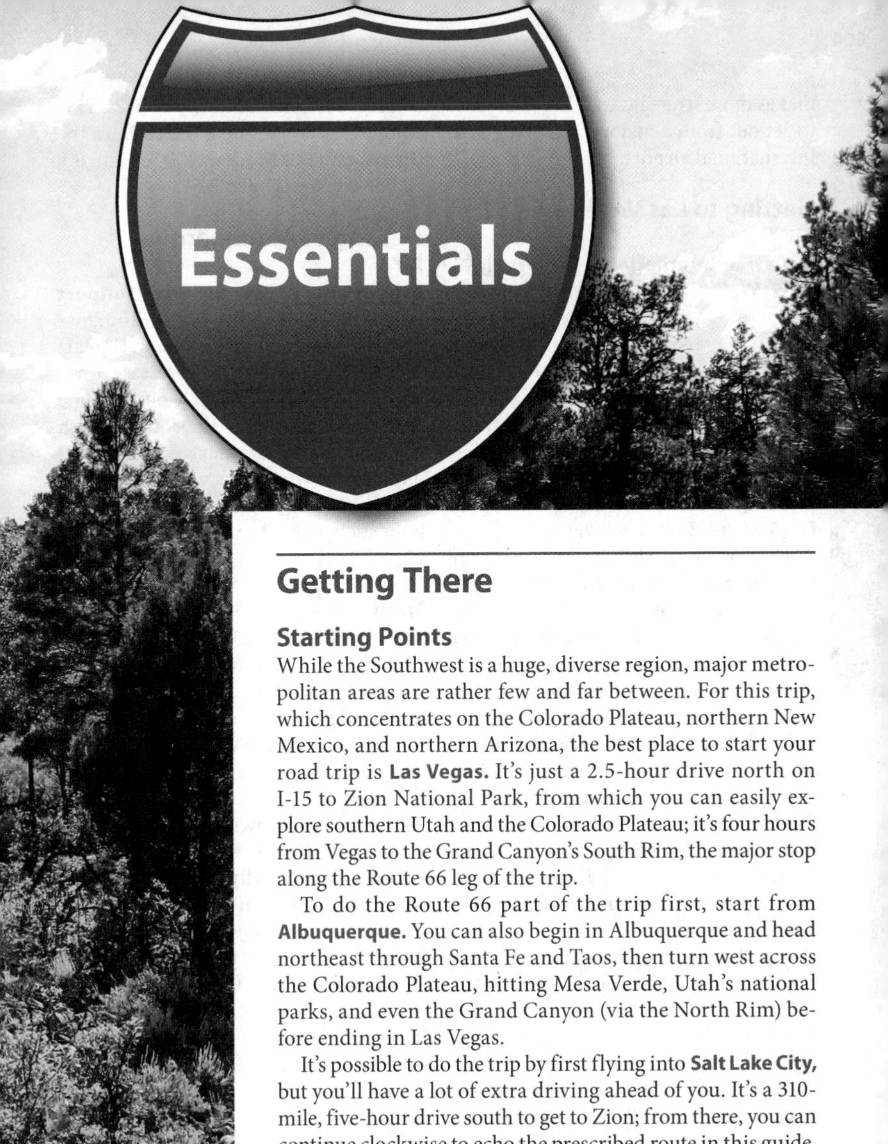

Getting There

Starting Points

While the Southwest is a huge, diverse region, major metropolitan areas are rather few and far between. For this trip, which concentrates on the Colorado Plateau, northern New Mexico, and northern Arizona, the best place to start your road trip is **Las Vegas.** It's just a 2.5-hour drive north on I-15 to Zion National Park, from which you can easily explore southern Utah and the Colorado Plateau; it's four hours from Vegas to the Grand Canyon's South Rim, the major stop along the Route 66 leg of the trip.

To do the Route 66 part of the trip first, start from **Albuquerque.** You can also begin in Albuquerque and head northeast through Santa Fe and Taos, then turn west across the Colorado Plateau, hitting Mesa Verde, Utah's national parks, and even the Grand Canyon (via the North Rim) before ending in Las Vegas.

It's possible to do the trip by first flying into **Salt Lake City,** but you'll have a lot of extra driving ahead of you. It's a 310-mile, five-hour drive south to get to Zion; from there, you can continue clockwise to echo the prescribed route in this guide.

If you're moving from south to north, start out in **Phoenix.** Sky Harbor International Airport is one of the largest hubs in the region (and where you'll get to see the famous saguaro cacti, a southwestern icon that you won't encounter anywhere else on the trip). Rent a car at Sky Harbor and drive north on I-17 for 3.5 hours to the Grand Canyon's South Rim, and then head north to Utah or east to Colorado and New Mexico from there.

Flagstaff and Tusayan, Arizona; Santa Fe, New Mexico; and St. George, Utah, all have small, regional airports, but it makes more strategic and financial sense to set out from a major city with a large international airport.

Getting to Las Vegas

Air

McCarran International Airport (LAS, 5757 Wayne Newton Blvd., 702/261-5211, www.mccarran.com) is the airport for Las Vegas. The big airlines (Delta, American Airlines, United) fly into Las Vegas, but many smaller airlines (Allegiant, Spirit, Volaris) sometimes offer better deals. Vision Airlines flies into the significantly less crowded **North Las Vegas Airport** (VGT, 2730 Airport Dr., 702/261-3801, www.vgt.aero).

The Las Vegas Strip and its hotels are just three miles from the airport. Ten taxicab companies pick up from the airport, including the **Desert Cab Company** (702/568-7700, https://desertcabinc.com) and the **Lucky Cab Company** (702/732-4400, www.luckycablv.com). The three-mile ride will cost around $15. Shuttles are also an option. **SuperShuttle** (800/258-3826, www.supershuttle.com) and **Airline Shuttle Corp.** (702/444-1234, www.airlineshuttlecorp.com) pick up at the airport. Of course, this is Las Vegas, so a limo service is not out of the question. **Las Vegas Limousines** (702/888-4848, www.lasvegaslimo.com) can get you from the airport to where you need to be in style.

Train

Believe it or not, there is no **Amtrak** (800/872-7245, www.amtrak.com) train stop in Las Vegas. But passengers who take the train to Kingman, Arizona, can catch an Amtrak shuttle bus to the **Las Vegas Curbside Bus Stop** (6675 Gilespie St.). In addition, Amtrak reserves a number of seats on Greyhound buses from Los Angeles to Las Vegas, which can be booked through Amtrak.

Bus

Greyhound (800/231-2222, www.greyhound.com) and **Megabus** (http://us.megabus.com) both have buses traveling to Las Vegas. Like the casinos, the **Greyhound Bus Station** (200 S. Main St., 702/384-9561) is open 24-7.

Getting to Albuquerque

Air

Albuquerque International Sunport (ABQ, 505/244-7700, www.cabq.gov/airport) is served by all major U.S. air carriers, including Southwest Airlines and JetBlue. Fares fluctuate on the same schedule as the rest of the country, with higher rates in summer and over holidays; in the winter, it's wise to choose a connection through a more temperate hub, such as Dallas (American) or Salt Lake City (Delta).

Train

Amtrak (800/872-7245, www.amtrak.com) runs the *Southwest Chief* daily between Chicago and Los Angeles, stopping in New Mexico at Raton, Las Vegas, Lamy (18 miles from Santa Fe), Albuquerque, and Gallup.

Arriving in Albuquerque, you're in the middle of downtown, in a depot shared with Greyhound. There are lockers here (occasionally full), and city bus service and taxis are available just up the block. From Chicago, Amtrak pads its schedule heavily between Lamy and Albuquerque—so if the train is running behind, you'll be late arriving in Lamy but generally will still get to Albuquerque on schedule.

Bus

Greyhound (800/231-2222, www.greyhound.com) connects New Mexico with adjacent states and Mexico. Routes run roughly along I-40 and I-25, with little service to outlying areas. If you're coming from elsewhere in the Southwest, you may want to investigate **El Paso-Los Angeles Limousine Express** (505/247-8036, www.eplalimo.com), the biggest operator of bargain bus service for the Mexican immigrant population. It connects Denver and Albuquerque and is both less expensive and more comfortable than Greyhound.

Getting to Salt Lake City

While Las Vegas is a better option for international travelers, Salt Lake City has a major airport and is an interesting sight as well. To get to Zion and Bryce from Salt Lake City, simply take I-15 south; driving time is about five hours. It's a long 240-mile drive to Moab, the center for exploring Arches and Canyonlands National Parks. The fastest route takes you south from Salt Lake City on I-15, cutting east at Spanish Fork on US 6/US 89 to Price, south to Green River and I-70, and then to Moab on US 191. Dramatic scenery highlights the entire length of this four-hour drive.

Air

Salt Lake City is a hub for **Delta Airlines** (800/221-1212, www.delta.com), and all other major airlines have regular flights into **Salt Lake City International Airport** (SLC, 776 N. Terminal Dr., 801/575-2400, www.slcairport.com). You'll find all of the major car rental companies at the Salt Lake City airport.

Getting to Phoenix

Phoenix is a good starting point for travelers who are concentrating on the Grand Canyon, Monument Valley, and Route 66. One of the largest cities in the region, the Valley of the Sun is about 3.5 hours of scenic roads north on I-17 to the Grand Canyon's South Rim. From the South Rim, drive northeast across the vast and beautiful Navajo Nation to reach Moab, Canyonlands, Arches, Mesa Verde, and New Mexico. If you are concentrating on the southern Utah sights like Zion, Bryce, Capitol Reef, and others, Las Vegas is a better starting point.

Air

If you're flying into Arizona, you'll likely find yourself at **Phoenix Sky Harbor International Airport** (3400 E. Sky Harbor Blvd., 602/273-3300, www.phoenix.gov/skyharborairport). One of the Southwest's largest airports, Sky Harbor has three terminals served by many domestic and international airlines. The airport is just three miles east of downtown Phoenix and easy to find. There's a free shuttle system that will take you between terminals.

Getting to Santa Fe

Air

Small **Santa Fe Municipal Airport** (SAF; 505/955-2900), west of the city, receives direct flights from Dallas and Los Angeles with American Eagle, and from Denver with United and Great Lakes.

Train

Amtrak (800/872-7245, www.amtrak.com) runs the *Southwest Chief* daily between Chicago and Los Angeles, stopping in New Mexico at Raton, Las Vegas, Lamy (18 miles from Santa Fe), Albuquerque, and Gallup. Lamy (the stop nearest Santa Fe) is no more than a depot—though it is a dramatic and wild-feeling place to get off the train. Amtrak provides an awkwardly timed shuttle service to Santa Fe hotels: Passengers arriving on eastbound trains must wait for passengers from the westbound train, an hour later.

Road Rules

Driving the Route

Throughout this trip you'll often find yourself far from the interstate. Instead, you'll negotiate mostly rural two-lane highways across the vast Colorado Plateau, through the sprawling Navajo Nation, and up and down the mountains and mesas of Colorado and New Mexico. In southern Utah's Dixie Country, around Zion and Bryce, and on to Capitol Reef National Park, UT-9, US 89, UT-12, and UT-24 are all incredibly scenic and well-traveled highways. US 191 runs south from I-70 in eastern Utah, past the entrances to Canyonlands and Zion, and Moab, which is the perfect base camp for exploring these must-see parks.

US 160 crosses the Navajo Nation, branching off US 89 about an hour outside Grand Canyon National Park South Rim's eastern entrance. At Kayenta on Navajoland, US 163 branches off US 160 and heads north to Monument Valley—a wonderfully scenic route that should not be missed.

US 160 continues east through the high pine forest of southern Colorado, passing Cortez, Mancos, and the entrance to Mesa Verde National Park, and then moves past Durango and Pagosa Springs.

From there, an equally scenic forest highway, US 64/US 84, heads south into New Mexico and passes the routes to Taos and Santa Fe. From Santa Fe to Albuquerque it's a short sprint on I-25.

Between Albuquerque and Kingman, Arizona, there are several portions of Historic Route 66 that more or less follow the route now dominated by I-40. The South Rim of the Grand Canyon can be reached from Flagstaff via US 180, or from Williams via AZ-64 and US 180.

You'll find most of the roads on this trip somewhat crowded during the summer high season, especially near the national parks. It gets cold and snowy in this region during the winter, but the roads are generally kept clear and safe.

Car and RV Rental

All the major airports in this region have large rental-car facilities, and they all provide transportation to their lots. It's best to reserve your car in advance of your trip. Call Budget Rent A Car (800/218-7992, www.budget.com), Hertz (800/654-3131, international 800/654-3001, www.hertz.com), or Enterprise (800/261-7331, www.enterprise.com).

You must be at least 21 years old to rent a car in Utah, Nevada, Arizona, Colorado, and New Mexico, and in most

a lonely Nevada highway

places you'll have to pay a surcharge ($30) if you are under 25.

Check with your credit card company and your car insurance provider before booking to see if you need to purchase **additional insurance.** Most of the time it's not worth the extra money (at least $10 per day) because the coverage is redundant. Rental car agents will try to up-sell you, so it's best to go into it with knowledge of your existing coverage. Expect to pay between $45-75 per day during the high season, depending on the size of your car, and $11-13 per day to add an extra driver.

Conventional wisdom says that it's usually cheaper to rent a car at an inland lot rather than at the airport, but this is not always true. Spend some time researching for the best price far in advance of your trip.

This is definitely **RV country,** and you'll be in good company if you decide to rent your own house on wheels. Expect to pay about $1,300 per week. Many of the RVers out on these roads rent from **Cruise America** (800/671-8042, www.cruiseamerica.com). Another good option is a campervan from **Jucy Rentals** (800/650-4180), which are easier to drive than an RV but still have small kitchens, tables, beds, and other amenities. You can rent a campervan in Las Vegas for an average of $40 per day.

Road Conditions

While it snows in the high country along this route in the winter, storms don't usually shut down the major roads in the region. Well traveled by tourists in all seasons, the highways covered by this guide are usually kept clear and open year-round.

Occasionally roads in the canyonlands north and east of Grand Canyon will close due to rock slides. Always be on the lookout for wildlife and livestock, especially early in the morning and in the evening.

Always check road conditions before traveling. To get information on road conditions via phone, call 511.

Summer heat in the desert puts an extra strain on both cars and drivers. It's worth double-checking your vehicle's cooling system, engine oil, transmission fluid, fan belts, and tires to make sure they are in top condition. Carry several gallons of water in case of a breakdown or radiator trouble. Never leave children or pets in a parked car during warm weather—temperatures inside can cause fatal heatstroke in minutes.

At times the desert has too much water, when late-summer storms frequently **flood** low spots in the road. Wait for the water level to subside before crossing.

Dust storms can completely block visibility but tend to be short-lived. During such storms, pull completely off the road, stop, and turn off your lights so as not to confuse other drivers.

If stranded, either on the desert or in the mountains, stay with your vehicle unless you're positive of where to go for help, then leave a note explaining your route and departure time. Airplanes can easily spot a stranded car (tie a piece of cloth to your antenna), but a person walking is more difficult to see. It's best to carry emergency supplies: blankets or sleeping bags, a first-aid kit, tools, jumper cables, a shovel, traction mats or chains, a flashlight, rain gear, water, food, and a can opener.

Roadside Assistance

In an emergency, **dial 911** from any phone. The American Automobile Association, better known as **AAA** (800/222-4357, www.aaa.com), offers roadside assistance—free to members; others pay a fee.

Be aware of your car's maintenance needs while on the road. The most frequent maintenance needs result from **summer heat.** If the car gets hot or overheats, stop for a while to cool it off. Never open the radiator cap if the engine is steaming. After the engine cools, squeeze the top radiator hose to see if there's any pressure in it; if there isn't, it's safe to open. Never pour water into a hot radiator because it could crack the engine block. If you start to smell rubber, your tires are overheating, and that's a good way to have a blowout. Stop and let them cool off.

Parking

Parking is at a premium in Las Vegas. Most hotels will charge guests $50 or more per night for parking. Remove any valuables from your vehicle for the evening, because some hotel valets just park your car in an adjacent public parking deck.

Parking is strictly regulated at national parks. At all of the national parks, **park entrance fees** include entry and parking for up to seven days. Visitors are encouraged to park their cars at the outer edges of the parks and use the extensive network of **free shuttles** to get around **Zion National Park** and **Grand Canyon National Park.**

International Drivers Licenses

If you are visiting the United States from another country, you need to secure an International Driving Permit from your home country before coming. It can't be obtained once you're here. You must also bring your government-issued driving permit.

Visitors from outside the United States should check the **driving rules of individual states online** (www.usa.gov/Topics/Motor-Vehicles.shtml). Among the most important rules is that traffic runs on the right side of the road in the United States. Note that Nevada bans the use of handheld cell phones while driving. If you get caught, expect to pay a hefty fine. In Utah you can use your cell phone while driving, but texting while driving could earn you a $750 fine. Outside of Phoenix and Tucson, there are no rules for using a cell phone or texting while driving in Arizona. Texting while driving in Colorado is subject to a $50 fine for the first offense. There are no restrictions on cell phone use while driving in New Mexico.

Maps and Visitor information

The American Automobile Association, better known as **AAA** (800/222-4357, www.aaa.com), offers free maps to its members. The **Thomas Guide Road Atlas** (866/896-6277, www.mapbooks4u.com) is a reliable and detailed map and road guide and a great insurance policy against getting lost. Almost all gas stations and drugstores sell maps.

Nevada

The website **Travel Nevada** (www.travelnevada.com) has downloadable visitor guides, including the US-95 Adventure.

Utah

The **Utah Department of Transportation** (801/965-4000, www.udot.utah.gov) prints and distributes a free, regularly updated map of Utah. Ask for it when you call for information or when you stop at a visitor information office. If you're planning on extensive backcountry exploration, be sure to ask locally about conditions. Backcountry enthusiasts or back-road explorers should also pick up Benchmark Maps' *Utah Road and Recreation Atlas.*

Obtain literature and the latest information on all of Utah's state parks from the **Utah State Parks and Recreation** (801/538-7220 or 877/887-2757, http://stateparks.utah.gov). If you're planning a lot of state park visits, ask about the $75 annual state park pass. Reservations for campgrounds and some other services can be made at 800/322-3770 or www.reserveamerica.com; a reservation fee of $9 applies.

General tourist literature and maps are available from the **Utah Travel Council** (800/200-1160, www.utah.com). Utah's many chambers of commerce also have free material and are happy to help with travel suggestions in their areas.

New Mexico

For pre-trip inspiration, the New Mexico Tourism Board publishes the monthly ***New Mexico Magazine*** (www.nmmagazine.com), which covers both mainstream attractions and more obscure corners of the state.

If you plan to do a lot of hiking, you can order detailed topographical maps from the **National Forest Service** office in New Mexico (505/842-3292) or from the Bureau of Land Management's **Public Lands Information Center** (www.publiclands.org). Santa Fe's **Travel Bug** (839 Paseo de Peralta, 505/992-0418, 7:30am-5:30pm Mon.-Sat., 11am-4pm Sun.) bookstore also stocks maps. Many smaller towns' chambers of commerce can be extremely helpful.

Arizona

The **Arizona Office of Tourism** (1110 W. Washington St., Ste. 155, Phoenix, 602/364-3700 or 866/275-5816, www.arizonaguide.com) will send you a free print or electronic version of the official state guide, and its website is full of information and lists of accommodations, events, and restaurants throughout the state. If you're planning to spend a lot of time in the state's national forests, you can get maps and information beforehand from the **National Forest Service, Southwestern Region** (333 Broadway SE, Albuquerque, NM, 505/842-3292, www.fs.fed.us/r3), or from the websites for the individual forests, listed in the chapters in which they appear. The **Arizona BLM State Office** (1 N. Central Ave., Ste. 800, Phoenix, 602/417-9200, www.blm.gov/az/st/en.html) also has a lot of information on the state's wildlands, and the **Arizona State Parks Department** (1300 W. Washington, Phoenix, 602/542-4174, www.azstateparks.com) has information on all the parks managed by the state. Passes and reservations for state and federal parks can be obtained and made online or at the parks themselves.

Visas and Officialdom

Passports and Visas

Visiting from another country, you must have a **valid passport** and a **visa** to enter the United States. If you hold a current passport from one of the following countries, you may qualify for the **Visa Waiver Program:** Andorra, Australia, Austria, Belgium, Brunei, Chile, Czech Republic, Denmark, Estonia, Finland, France, Germany, Greece, Hungary, Iceland, Ireland, Italy, Japan, Latvia, Liechtenstein, Lithuania, Luxembourg, Malta, Monaco, the Netherlands, New Zealand, Norway, Portugal, San Marino, Singapore, Slovakia, Slovenia, South Korea, Spain, Sweden, Switzerland, Taiwan, and the United Kingdom. To qualify, you must apply online with the Electronic System for Travel Authorization at www.cbp.gov and hold a **return plane or cruise ticket** to your country of origin dated less than **90**

days from your date of entry. Holders of Canadian passports don't need visas or visa waivers.

In most other countries, the local U.S. embassy should be able to provide a **tourist visa.** The application fee for a visa is US$160, although you will have to pay an issuance fee as well. While a visa may be processed in as little as 24 hours on request, plan for at least a couple of weeks, as there can be unexpected delays, particularly during the busy summer season (June-Aug.). For information, visit http://travel.state.gov.

Embassies and Consulates

If you should lose your passport or find yourself in some other trouble while visiting this region, contact your country's offices for assistance. The website of the **U.S. State Department** (www.state.gov) lists the websites for all foreign embassies and consulates in the United States. A representative will be able to direct you to the nearest embassy or consulate.

Customs

Before you enter the United States from another country by sea or by air, you'll be required to fill out a customs form. Check with the U.S. embassy in your country or the **Customs and Border Protection website** (www.cbp.gov) for an updated list of items you must declare.

If you require medication administered by injection, you must pack your syringes in a checked bag; syringes are not permitted in carry-ons coming into the United States. Also, pack documentation describing your need for any narcotic medications you've brought with you. Failure to produce documentation for narcotics on request can result in severe penalties in the United States.

You'll also be asked about fruits and veggies on your U.S. Customs form, which you'll be asked to fill out on the airplane or ship before you reach the United States.

Travel Tips

Visiting Reservations and Pueblos

When visiting pueblos, remember that you are not at a tourist attraction—you are walking around someone's neighborhood. So peeking in windows and wandering off the suggested route isn't polite. If you want to take photos, you'll usually need a camera permit, for an additional fee. Always ask permission before taking photos of people, and ask parents, rather than children, for their consent. Virtually all pueblos ban alcohol.

Some pueblos are more welcoming than others. Some are open year-round, whereas others are completely closed, except for some feast days. So it's flawed logic to seek out the less-visited places or go in the off times in order to have a less "touristy" experience. In fact, the most rewarding time to visit *is* on a big feast day—you may not be the only tourist there, but you have a better chance of being invited into a local's home.

Some Pueblo Indians find loud voices, direct eye contact, and firm handshakes off-putting and, by the same token, may not express themselves in the forthright way a lot of visitors are used to. Similarly, a subdued reaction doesn't necessarily mean a lack of enthusiasm.

Don't drive off road for any reason—that's somebody's land and livelihood. It's a good idea to hire a guide to take you around, as there are can be places that are off limits without one.

Accessibility

If you'll be visiting a lot of wilderness areas, you should get the **National Park Service's Access Pass** (888/467-2757, www.nps.gov), a free lifetime pass that grants admission for the pass-holder and three adults to all national parks, national forests, and the like, as well as discounts on interpretive services, camping fees, fishing licenses, and more. Apply in person at any federally managed park or wilderness area; you must show medical documentation of blindness or permanent disability.

The **Las Vegas Convention and Visitors Authority** (www.lvcva.com) provides for information on the assistance available in **Las Vegas.**

Travelers with disabilities will find **Utah** quite progressive when it comes to accessibility issues, especially in the heavily traveled national parks in southern Utah. Most parks offer all-abilities trails, and many hotels advertise their fully accessible facilities.

Wheelchair access can be frustrating in some historic properties and on the narrower sidewalks of **Santa Fe** and **Taos,** but in most other respects, travelers with disabilities should find no more problems in New Mexico than elsewhere in the United States. Public buses are wheelchair-accessible, an increasing number of hotels have ADA-compliant rooms, and you can even get out in nature a bit on paved trails such as the Santa Fe Canyon Preserve loop or the Paseo del Bosque in Albuquerque.

Many of the best sights in **Arizona** are accessible in one way or another. **Grand Canyon National Park** operates wheelchair-accessible park shuttles and the park's **website** (www.nps.gov/grca) has a downloadable accessibility guide. The Grand Canyon and most of the other major federal parks have accessible trails and viewpoints. For advice and links to other helpful Internet resources, go to www.disabledtravelers.com, which is based in Arizona and is full of accessible travel information, though it's not specific to the state. The **National Accessible Travelers Database** may also be helpful. For questions specific to Arizona, you may want to contact the state Department of Administration's **Office for Americans with Disabilities** (100 N. 15th Ave., Ste. 361, Phoenix, 602/542-6276 or 800/358-3617, or TTY 602/542-6686, www.azada.gov).

Traveling with Children

Hispanic and American Indian cultures are typically very child-friendly, so your little ones will be welcome in most environments, including restaurants and hotels. The only exceptions would be some of the more formal restaurants in **Santa Fe** and **Albuquerque.** Kids are sure to be fascinated by ceremonial dances at the **pueblos,** but be prepared with distractions, because long waits are the norm. Prep children with information about American Indian culture, and brief them on the basic etiquette at dances.

Kids will also enjoy river rafting. In particular, relaxing floats along placid sections of the **Rio Grande** and **Rio Chama** are good for younger ones. For skiing, **Taos Ski Valley** has a very strong program of classes for youngsters.

Senior Travelers

Senior discounts are available nearly every place you go, including restaurants, golf courses, major attractions, and even some hotels. The minimum age ranges 50-65. Ask about discounts and be prepared to produce ID if you look younger than your years. You can often get additional discounts on rental cars, hotels, and tour packages as a member of **AARP** (888/687-2277, www.aarp.org). If you're not a member, its website can also offer helpful travel tips and advice. **Road Scholar** (800/454-5768, www.roadscholar.org), formerly known as Elderhostel, is another great resource for senior travelers. Dedicated to providing educational opportunities for older travelers, Road Scholar provides package trips to beautiful and interesting destinations. Called Educational Adventures, these trips are generally 3-9 days long and emphasize nature, history, art, and music. **Senior Discounts Las Vegas** (http://seniordiscountslasvegas.com) has an online directory of businesses with senior discounts.

The best thing those 62 years old or older can do before a trip to this region is to purchase an **America the Beautiful—National Parks and Federal Recreational Lands Senior Pass.** This golden ticket will get you and up to three adults into every national park and monument for the rest of your life, as well as a 50 percent discount on activities such as camping and boat-launching. It costs just $10, paid one time in person at any federal park. For more information, contact the **National Park Service** (888/467-2757, www.nps.gov).

Gay and Lesbian Travelers

The **International Gay and Lesbian Travel Association** (www.iglta.org) has a directory of gay- and lesbian-friendly tour operators, accommodations, and destinations.

Las Vegas has some gay-friendly fixtures, whether it's the glamorous entertainers on stage or the Fruit Loop, a cluster of gay bars along Paradise Road, north of the airport.

Santa Fe is one of the major gay capitals in the United States, second only to San Francisco in the per-capita rates of same-sex coupledom, and particularly popular with lesbians. There are no designated "gay-borhoods" (unless you count RainbowVision Santa Fe, a retirement community) or even particular bar scenes—instead, gay men and lesbian women are well integrated throughout town, running businesses and serving on the city council. Two weeks in June are dedicated to Pride on the Plaza, a festive time of gay-pride arts events and parades.

Albuquerque also has a decent gay scene, especially if you want to go clubbing, which is not an option in quieter Santa Fe. As for smaller towns and pueblos, they're still significantly more conservative.

Gay culture in New Mexico isn't all about cute shops and cabarets. One big event is the annual **Zia Regional Rodeo,** sponsored by the **New Mexico Gay Rodeo Association** (505/720-3749, www.nmgra.com). It takes place every June in Albuquerque, with all the standard rodeo events, plus goat dressing and a wild drag race.

Traveling Without Reservations

During the busy summer months, accommodations can be hard to come by. If you find yourself without reservations, many online travel services, including **Hotels.com,** can set you up with a last-minute room.

It's also not unusual for national park lodgings and campgrounds to be full during high season. It may be possible to find a last-minute campsite at one of the nearby national forests. The **Kaibab National Forest** (www.fs.usda.gov/kaibab) is near the Grand Canyon.

Discount hotel chain **Super 8** (800/454-3213, www.super8.com) has locations in Las Vegas and Williams, Arizona, gateway to the Grand Canyon. Slightly more upscale, **La Quinta** (800/753-3757, www.lq.com) has hotels in Las Vegas. There are many affordable chain hotels in Moab, near Canyonlands and Arches, and in Cortez, near Mesa Verde National Park.

Alcohol and Smoking

The legal **drinking age** everywhere in the United States is 21. Expect to have your ID checked if you look under age 30, especially in bars and clubs, but also in restaurants and wineries. Smoking is generally not permitted in any of the restaurants and bars in this region, though some hotels offer a few smoking rooms. Vegas is the exception, allowing smoking in most casinos, strip clubs, and standalone bars. Restaurants within casinos are nonsmoking.

Money

Nevada, Utah, New Mexico, and Arizona use the **U.S. dollar ($).** Most businesses also accept the **major credit cards** Visa, MasterCard, Discover, and American Express. ATM and debit cards work at many stores and restaurants, and ATMs are available throughout the region.

Utah's Drinking Laws

The state's liquor laws can seem rather confusing and peculiar to outsiders. Changes to Utah's once prohibitive rules have made it easier to buy and consume alcohol. Note that it's no longer necessary to be a member of a private club in order to consume alcohol in a bar—no more buying a temporary membership or signing in on someone else's membership just to enjoy a drink.

Several different kinds of establishments are licensed to sell alcoholic beverages:

Taverns, which include brewpubs, can sell only 3.2 percent beer (beer that is 3.2 percent alcohol by volume). Taverns can't sell wine, which is classed as hard liquor in Utah. Stronger beer is available in Utah, but only in bottles, and this beer is also regulated as hard liquor. You don't need to purchase food to have a beer in a tavern. With the exception of brewpubs, taverns are usually fairly derelict and not especially cheery places to hang out.

Licensed restaurants are able to sell beer, wine, and hard liquor, but only with food orders. In many parts of Utah, you'll need to specifically ask for a drink or the drink menu to begin the process. In Salt Lake City, Moab, and Park City, most restaurants have liquor licenses. In small towns, few eating establishments offer alcohol.

Cocktail bars, lounges, live music venues, and nightclubs, which once operated on the private club system, can now serve alcohol without asking for membership. However, some continue the income flow by demanding a cover charge for entry. Depending on which county you are in, you may still be required to order some food to have a drink.

Nearly all towns will have a state-owned **liquor store,** though they can be difficult to find, and 3.2 percent beer is available in most grocery stores and gas station minimarts. Many travelers find that carrying a bottle of your favorite beverage to your room is the easiest way to enjoy an evening drink. The state drinking age is 21.

You can **change currency** at McCarran International Airport in Las Vegas, but by far the best way to keep yourself in cash is by using bank, debit, or cash cards at **ATMs** (automated teller machines). Not only does withdrawing funds from your own home account save on fees, but you also often get a better rate of exchange.

Most ATMs at banks require a small fee to dispense cash. Most **grocery stores** allow you to use a debit or cash card to purchase food, with the option of a cash withdrawal. These transactions are free to the withdrawer.

ATMs

As with anywhere, traveling with a huge amount of cash is not recommended, which may make frequent trips to the bank necessary. Fortunately, most destinations have at least one major bank. Bank of America and Wells Fargo have a large presence throughout the region. **Banking hours** tend to be Monday-Friday 8am-5pm, Saturday 9am-noon. Never count on a bank being open on Sunday or on federal holidays. If you need cash when the banks are closed, there is generally a **24-hour ATM** available. Furthermore, many cash-only businesses have an ATM on-site for those who don't have enough cash ready in their wallets. The unfortunate downside to this convenience is a fee of $2-4 per transaction. This also applies to ATMs at banks at which you don't have an account.

Tax

Nevada sales tax is 6.85 percent and can reach up to 8.1 percent, depending where you are. **Arizona sales tax** is 5.6 percent but can reach as high as 10.7 percent, depending on the municipality.

Utah sales tax varies from 5.95 to 7.95

percent and is added to most transactions on goods, food, and services. Additional room taxes are added; these vary by community and can be quite steep. **New Mexico sales tax** starts at 5.1 percent but can range as high as 8.8 percent in some areas.

Tipping

Tipping is expected and appreciated, and a **15 percent tip** for **restaurants** is the norm. When ordering in bars, tip the bartender or wait staff $1 per drink. Cafés and coffee shops often have tip jars out. There is no consensus on what is appropriate when purchasing a $3 beverage. Often $0.50 is enough, depending on the quality and service. For **taxis,** plan to tip **15-20 percent** of the fare, or simply round up the cost to the nearest dollar.

Time Zones

Nevada is in the **Pacific time** zone (PST and PDT) and observes daylight saving time (advanced one hour) March-November. Utah and New Mexico are in the **mountain time** zone (MST) and go on daylight saving time March-November. Arizona is also in the mountain time zone (MST), but only the Navajo Nation observes daylight saving time.

Electricity

As in all of the United States, electricity is 110-120 volts, 60 hertz. Plugs have either two flat prongs or two flat prongs plus one round prong. Older homes and hotels may only have two-prong outlets. If you're traveling with computers or appliances that have three-prong plugs, ask your hotel or motel manager for an adapter. You may need to buy a three-prong adapter, but the cost is small.

Health and Safety

Medical Services

For an emergency anywhere in Nevada, Utah, New Mexico, or Arizona, **dial 911.** Inside hotels and resorts, check your emergency number as soon as you get to your guest room. In urban and suburban areas, full-service hospitals and medical centers abound, but in remoter regions, help can be more than an hour away.

Wilderness Safety

Backcountry Travel

If you're planning a backcountry expedition, follow all rules and guidelines for obtaining **wilderness permits** and for self-registration at trailheads. These are for your safety, letting the rangers know roughly where you plan to be and when to expect you back. National park and state park visitors centers can advise in more detail on any health or wilderness alerts in the area. It is also advisable to let someone outside your party know your route and expected date of return.

If you're hiking in the canyon country in the Southwest, you'll spend most of your time at the bottom of narrow and twisting canyons. It's easy to get lost, or at least disoriented. Always carry adequate and up-to-date **maps** and a **compass** (a GPS unit may not work in canyon country)—and know how to use them if you're heading off into the backcountry. Always plan a route. Planning usually saves time and effort. Tell someone (like a family member or a ranger) where you are going and when you'll be back, so they know where and when to start looking for you in case you get into trouble. Always take at least one other person with you: Do not venture into the desert alone. Parties of four people (or two vehicles) are ideal, because one person can stay with the person in trouble, while the other two escort each other to get help. It's a good idea to carry your cell phone in case you need to make an emergency call or send an email.

Thunderstorms can wash hikers away in the canyons and washes of the Southwest. **Flash floods** can happen almost any time of year but are most prevalent in the summer months. Before entering slot canyon areas, check with rangers or local authorities for weather reports. And while you're hiking, read and heed the clouds. Many washes and canyons drain large areas, with their headwaters many miles away. The dangerous part is that sometimes you just can't tell what's coming down the wash or canyon because of the vast number of acres that these canyons drain, and because the cliff walls are too high to see out to any storms that may be creating flood potential upstream. At any sign of a threat, get out of the canyon bottom—at least 60 vertical feet up—to avoid water and debris. Since many of these canyons are narrow, there are places where it's not possible to get out of the canyon on short notice. Never drive a vehicle into a flooded wash. Stop and wait for the water to recede, as it usually will within an hour.

Extreme Temperatures

Being out in the elements can present its own set of challenges. The least of what the sun can do to you is not to be taken lightly. A **sunburn,** which comes on quicker than you'd think, can lead to skin cancer, and that can lead to death. If you get a sunburn, there's little you can do, save try to make yourself more comfortable. Stay out of the sun, of course, and try to keep cool and hydrated. There are dozens of over-the-counter balms available, but simple aloe works as well as anything. A popular home remedy is to gently dab the burned areas with vinegar.

Heat exhaustion and **heatstroke** can affect anyone during the hot summer months, particularly during a long strenuous hike in the sun. Common symptoms include nausea, light-headedness, headache, or muscle cramps. **Dehydration** and loss of electrolytes are the common causes of heat exhaustion. The risks are even higher in the desert regions. If you or anyone in your group develops any of these symptoms, get out of the sun immediately, stop all physical activity, and drink plenty of water. Heat exhaustion can be severe, and if untreated can lead to heatstroke, in which the body's core temperature reaches 105°F. Fainting, seizures, confusion, and rapid heartbeat and breathing can indicate the situation has moved beyond heat exhaustion. If you suspect this, call 911 immediately.

Similar precautions hold true for **hypothermia,** which is caused by prolonged exposure to cold water or weather. This can happen on a hike or backpacking trip without sufficient rain gear, or by staying too long in a cold body of water without a wetsuit. Symptoms include shivering, weak pulse, drowsiness, confusion, slurred speech, or stumbling. To treat hypothermia, immediately remove the wet clothing, cover the person with blankets, and feed him or her hot liquids. If symptoms don't improve, call 911.

Altitude Sickness

The high country in this region frequently rises up to 10,000 feet. Though most visitors won't be going that high, you should be aware that a few of the mountain towns sit between 5,000 and 8,000 feet above sea level. Lowlanders in relatively good shape may get headaches, a little dizziness, and shortness of breath while walking around Flagstaff, Grand Canyon, Mesa Verde, or Bryce Canyon, but very few will experience serious altitude sickness—the result of not getting enough oxygen, and therefore not enough blood flow to the brain. Still, take it easy in the higher elevations if you begin to feel tired and out of breath, dizzy, or euphoric. If you have heart or lung problems, you need to be more aware in the higher elevations; the best thing to do is to get a prescription for oxygen from your doctor and carry it with you if you plan on spending a lot of time in the mountains.

Dangerous Animals and Plants

In this region, **poisonous rattlesnakes** and **scorpions** are a threat. When hiking or climbing in desert areas, never put your hand onto a ledge or into a hole that you can't see. Both are perfect lairs for snakes and scorpions. While snakebites are rarely fatal anymore, they're no fun either. If you are bitten, immobilize the affected area and seek immediate medical attention.

A scorpion's sting isn't as painful as you'd expect (it's about like a bee sting), and the venom is insufficient to cause any real harm. Still, it's not what you'd call pleasant, and experienced desert campers know to shake out their boots every morning, as scorpions and spiders are attracted to warm, moist, dark places.

Tarantulas and **black widow spiders** are present across much of the Colorado Plateau. Believe it or not, a tarantula's bite does not poison humans; the enzymes secreted when they bite turn the insides of frogs, lizards, and insects to a soft mush, allowing the tarantula to suck the guts from its prey. Black widow spiders, on the other hand, have a toxic bite. Although the bite is usually painless, it delivers a potent neurotoxin, which quickly causes pain, nausea, and vomiting. It is important to seek immediate treatment for a black widow bite; although few people actually die from these bites, recovery is helped along considerably by antivenin.

If you do much hiking and biking in the spring, there's a good chance you'll encounter **ticks.** While ticks in this part of the United States don't usually carry Lyme disease, there is a remote threat of Rocky Mountain spotted fever, spread by the wood tick. If a tick has bitten you, pull it off immediately. Grasp the tick's head parts (as close to your skin as possible) with tweezers and pull slowly and steadily. Do not attempt to remove ticks by burning them or coating them with anything. Removing a tick as quickly as possible greatly reduces your chance of infection.

This region is home to **black bears,** which aren't as menacing as their grizzly bear cousins. However, black bears weigh more than most humans and have far sharper claws and teeth. An encounter with a black bear is rarely fatal, but it's something to be avoided.

If you encounter a bear, give it plenty of room and try not to surprise it. Wearing a fragrance while in bear country isn't a good idea because it attracts bears, as do strong-smelling foods. Always store food items outside the tent, and if you're in bear territory, sleep well away from the cooking area. Waking up with a bear clawing at your tent is to be avoided. Hanging food in a bag from a tree is a long-standing and wise precaution. If a bear becomes aggressive, try to drop something that will divert its attention while you flee. If that isn't possible, the next best bet is to curl up into a ball, clasp your hands behind your neck, and play dead, even if the bear begins to bat you around. Taking precautions and having respect for bears will ensure not only your continued existence, but theirs as well.

In recent years, as humans have increasingly moved into **mountain lion** habitat (and as their numbers have increased), they have become a threat to humans, especially small children. Never leave children unattended in forests, and never allow them to lag far behind on a family hike. Nearly every summer, newspapers in the western states carry tragic stories of children stalked and killed by mountain lions. Safety is in numbers.

Illness and Disease

West Nile virus from mosquitoes and **hantavirus** from rodents are the long-shot threats to your health in this region, and both can be avoided by taking precautions. Use a DEET-based insect repellent to ward off mosquitoes and simply stay away from rodents. Hantavirus is an airborne infectious disease agent transmitted from rodents to humans when rodents shed hantavirus particles in their saliva, urine, and droppings and humans inhale infected particles. It is easiest for a human to contract hantavirus in a contained environment, such as a cabin infested with mouse droppings, where the virus-infected particles are not thoroughly dispersed.

Simply traveling to a place where the hantavirus is known to occur is not considered a risk factor. Camping, hiking, and other outdoor activities also pose low risk, especially if steps are taken to reduce rodent contact.

The very first symptoms can occur anywhere between five days and three weeks after infection. They almost always include fever, fatigue, and aching muscles (usually in the back, shoulders, or thighs) and other flu-like conditions. Other early symptoms may include headaches, dizziness, chills, and abdominal discomfort (such as vomiting, nausea, or diarrhea). These are shortly followed by intense coughing and shortness of breath. If you have these symptoms, seek medical help immediately. Untreated infections of hantavirus are almost always fatal.

Giardia, a type of protozoa that has become common in even the remotest mountain streams, is carried in animal or human waste that is deposited or washed into natural waters. When ingested, it begins reproducing, causing an intestinal sickness in the host that can become very serious and may require medical attention.

You can take precautions against giardia with a variety of chemicals and filtering methods or by boiling water before drinking it. The various chemical solutions on the market work in some applications, but because they need to be safe for human consumption, they are weak and ineffective against the protozoan in its cyst stage of life (when it encases itself in a hard shell). Filtering may eliminate giardia, but there are other water pests too small to be caught by most filters. The most effective way to eliminate such threats is to boil all suspect water. A few minutes at a rolling boil will kill giardia even in the cyst stage.

Crime

In both rural and urban areas, **theft** can be a problem. Don't leave any valuables in the car. If you must, place them out of sight, either in a locked glove box or in the trunk. Don't leave your wallet, camera, or other expensive items accessible to others, for example in a backpack or purse. Keep them on your person at all times if possible.

Take some **basic precautions** and pay attention to your surroundings, just as you would in any unfamiliar place. Carry your car keys in your hand when walking out to your car. Don't sit in your parked car in a lonely parking lot at night; just get in, turn on the engine, and drive away. When you're walking down a city street, be alert and keep an eye on your surroundings and on anyone who might be following you. In case of a theft or any other emergency, **call 911.**

Internet Resources

Spend some time on the Internet before your trip to find out about current conditions in the areas you are visiting. You also may be able to find out about some places to visit that you never knew existed.

General Information

National Park Service
www.nps.gov
The National Park Service offers pages for all its areas at this site. You can also enter this address followed by a slash and the first two letters of the first two words of the place (first four letters if there's just a one-word name); for example, www.nps.gov/brca takes you to Bryce Canyon National Park and www.nps.gov/zion leads to Zion National Park.

Public Lands Information Center
www.publiclands.org
Buy USGS, Forest Service, and other topographical maps online from the Bureau

of Land Management's well-organized website. Good stock of nature guides and other travel books too.

Recreation.gov
www.recreation.gov
If a campground is operated by the federal government, this is the place to make a reservation. You can expect to pay close to $10 for this convenience.

Reserve America
www.reserveamerica.com
Use this website to reserve campsites in state campgrounds. It costs a few extra bucks to reserve a campsite, but compare that with the cost of being skunked out of a site and having to resort to a motel room.

Arizona

Travel Information

Arizona Department of Transportation
www.azdot.gov
For information about the conditions of Arizona's roadways, visit this site.

Arizona Office of Tourism
www.arizonaguide.com
The official site for the state's Office of Tourism has basic information on the state's regions and lists various possible itineraries.

Flagstaff Convention and Visitors Bureau
www.flagstaffarizona.org
This site has general information on visiting Flagstaff, the northland, and the Grand Canyon along with helpful listings.

Grand Canyon National Park
www.nps.gov/grca
The Grand Canyon's official website has basic information on the park; go here for information about backcountry permits. For reservations and information on the park's accommodations, go to the **Xanterra South Rim** site at www.grandcanyonlodges.com.

News and Culture

Arizona Republic
www.azcentral.com
The state's largest newspaper is free online every day, and the site has a robust Arizona travel guide and a useful dining and entertainment section.

Nevada

Travel Information

Las Vegas.com
www.lasvegas.com
"The only official website of Las Vegas" has hotel deals, show deals, and a downloadable visitors guide.

Nevada Department of Transportation
www.nevadadot.com
Nevada Department of Transportation's website has a map detailing current road conditions.

New Mexico

Travel Information

Albuquerque Convention and Visitors Bureau
www.visitalbuquerque.org
The official intro to the city and surrounding areas, with events listings as well as hotel-booking services.

Fiber Arts Trails
www.nmfiberarts.org
A guide to the wool-loving state via the work of ranchers and artisans, both traditional and modern. The North Central route covers Albuquerque, Santa Fe, and Taos.

Hiking in the Sandia Mountains
www.sandiahiking.com
Mike Coltrin hiked every trail in the Sandias over the course of a year, covering about 250 miles. He detailed each hike, complete with GPS references, here.

New Mexico Board of Tourism
www.newmexico.org
The best of the official sites, this one has thorough maps, suggested itineraries,

and background info like weather. Includes the Green Chile Cheeseburger Trail and the Breakfast Burrito Byway, as well as routes based on Hollywood filming locations, among other suggested itineraries.

New Mexico Department of Transportation
http://dot.state.nm.us
For information about getting around New Mexico, visit this site.

Santa Fe Convention and Visitors Bureau
www.santafe.org
Near-exhaustive listings of tourist attractions and services on this slickly produced site.

Santa Fe Creative
www.santafecreativetourism.org
The Santa Fe Arts Commission's listings of arts classes, workshops, and other special events in this creative hub.

Taos Vacation Guide
www.taos.org
A thorough directory and events listings.

News and Culture

Albuquerque Journal
www.abqjournal.com
The state's largest newspaper is available free online after answering survey questions.

Alibi
www.alibi.com
This free weekly has been cracking wise since 1992, taking a critical look at politics and culture. Its annual "Best of Burque" guide is usually reliable.

Chasing Santa Fe
www.chasingsantafe.blogspot.com
The glamorous Santa Fe lifestyle, lovingly documented: local chefs, new shops, and fashion spotting.

Duke City Fix
www.dukecityfix.com
This Albuquerque-centric discussion forum covers everything from politics to gossip about the restaurant scene.

New Mexico Magazine
www.nmmagazine.com
Not everything from the print edition of the excellent state magazine is online, but it's rounded out with video, a dedicated food blog, and a general travel guide.

New Mexico Politics with Joe Monahan
www.joemonahan.com
Analyst Monahan's obsessive, snarky blog charts the circus that is state politics.

Santa Fe New Mexican
www.santafenewmexican.com
Santa Fe's main newspaper. The gossip column *El Mitote* documents celebs in Santa Fe, and the Roundhouse Roundup does roughly the same—but with politicians.

Santa Fe Reporter
www.sfreporter.com
Santa Fe's free weekly is politically sharp and often funny. Get opinionated reviews and news analysis here.

Smithsonian Folkways
www.folkways.si.edu
Prep for your road trip at this enormous online music archive, which has a number of traditional treasures from the state, including the excellent *Music of New Mexico: Hispanic Traditions* and *New Mexico: Native American Traditions.*

Taos News
www.taosnews.com
The town paper is a weekly, but its website has daily updates and an events calendar.

Utah

Travel Information

The American Southwest
www.americansouthwest.net/utah
Utah Guide provides an overview of national parks, national recreation areas, and some state parks.

Canyonlands Utah
www.canyonlands-utah.com
Good source for information on Moab and the surrounding areas, including Canyonlands and Arches National Parks.

Desert USA
www.desertusa.com
Desert USA's Utah section discusses places to visit and what plants and animals you might meet there. Here's the best part of this site: you can find out what's in bloom at www.desertusa.com/wildflo/wildupdates.

Moab Area Travel Council
www.discovermoab.com
Upcoming events, mountain bike trails, local restaurants and lodging, and outfitters are all easy to find at this comprehensive site.

State of Utah
www.utah.gov
The official state of Utah website has travel information, agencies, programs, and what the legislature is up to.

Utah Department of Transportation
www.udot.utah.gov
For information about the conditions of Utah's roadways, visit this site.

Utah Mountain Biking
www.utahmountainbiking.com
Details mountain biking routes listed in this book as well as other local trails.

Utah's Dixie
www.utahsdixie.com
The southwestern Utah city of St. George is the focus of this site, which also covers some of the smaller communities outside Zion National Park.

Utah State Parks
www.stateparks.utah.gov
The Utah State Parks site offers details on the large park system, including links to reserve campsites.

Utah Travel Council
www.utah.com
The Utah Travel Council is a one-stop shop for all sorts of information on Utah. It takes you around the state to sights, activities, events, and maps, and offers links to local tourism offices. The accommodations listings are the most up-to-date source for current room rates and options.

Zion Park
www.zionpark.com
This site will point you to information on Springdale and the area surrounding Zion National Park, with links to lodging and restaurant sites.

INDEX

A

Abe's Cantina y Cocina: 16, 328
Abiquiu: 296
ABQ BioPark: 339-340
ABQ Trolley Co.: 333, 338-339
Abyss, The: 430
accessibility: 470-471
accommodations: Albuquerque 350-353; Bryce Canyon National Park 112-113, 122-126; Capitol Reef National Park 148-151; Grand Canyon National Park 415, 421, 440-444, 449-450, 455-456, 458, 461; Las Vegas 63-67; Moab 182-186; Santa Fe 259, 279-282; Taos 321-325; Zion National Park 104-108; *see also specific place*
Aces of Comedy: 58
Acoma Pueblo: 333, 358-359
adobe: 266
Adventuredome Theme Park: 61
Agate Bridge: 371
Agate House: 371
Agathla Peak: 235
Agua Canyon: 116
Airport Mesa: 384
air travel: 10, 464, 465; Albuquerque 335; Flagstaff 375-376; Grand Canyon 418-419; *see also* flightseeing; helicopter tours; *specific place*
Alameda/Rio Grande Open Space: 349
Albuquerque: 8, 10, 16, 332-356, 463, 464-465, 471, 472; accommodations 350-353; entertainment 344-348; food 353-355; getting there/around 334-338; information/services 355-356; maps 337, 342, 348, 356; recreation 348-351; shopping 348; sights 333, 338-344
Albuquerque Convention and Visitors Bureau: 355-356, 478
Albuquerque International Balloon Fiesta: 345, 347
Albuquerque International Sunport: 335, 464
Albuquerque Isotopes: 350
Albuquerque Little Theatre: 346
Albuquerque Museum of Art and History: 340
Alcove Spring Trail: 213
Allan Houser Gallery: 274
All Shook Up: A Tribute to the King: 58
altitude sickness: 475
American International Rattlesnake Museum: 340
Anasazi State Park Museum: 21, 133
Andy Devine Days Parade & Community Fair: 406
Angels Landing: 85, 92, 99
Angel's Window: 447
Anthony Cools—The Uncensored Hypnotist: 39
Anticline Overlook: 214-215
Arboretum at Flagstaff: 379
Arches National Park: 8, 14, 15, 18, 20, 153-156, 189-201; maps 154, 190; *see also* Moab
Aria: 19, 26, 40
Arizona Department of Transportation: 13, 478
Arizona Historical Society-Pioneer Museum: 379
Arizona Office of Tourism: 469, 478
Arizona Room: 20, 416, 420, 444
Arizona Snowbowl: 389
Arizona State Parks Department: 469
Arroyo Hondo: 304
Arroyo Seco: 304, 324, 328-329
art galleries: 274; *see also specific place*
Artist Point Overlook: 241
Arts Factory: 48
Ash Fork: 19, 20, 398-399
Ash Fork Route 66 Museum: 399
A:shíwi A:wan Museum and Heritage Center: 361-362
Ashurst Lake: 389
Aspen Springs Trail: 406-407
Aspen Vista: 278-279
Atalaya Mountain: 278
ATMs: 472-473
atomic bomb: 294
Atomic Testing Museum: 25, 51-52
ATVs: 178-179
automotive care: *see* driving tips
Aztec: 246-247
Aztec Butte Trail: 211-212
Aztec Ruins National Monument: 246-247

B

backcountry permits/travel: 474-475; *see also specific park*
backpacking: 451-452; *see also* hiking
Badger House Community Trail: 251
Balanced Rock: 193
Balcony House: 245, 250
Bali Hai golf course: 62
Balloon Fiesta: 345, 347
ballooning: 333, 345, 347, 349, 364
B&B Burger & Beer: 31
banks/banking: 473; Albuquerque 356; Bryce Canyon National Park 113; Santa Fe 289; Zion National Park 91-92; *see also specific place*
Barney's Trail: 102
baseball: 321, 350
basketball: 350

Bearizona Wildlife Park: 395-396
bears: 476
Bear's Best: 62
Beaver Falls: 458
Behind the Rocks: 169
Behunin Cabin: 136
Believe: 42
Bellagio: 14, 26, 37-38
Bellagio Conservatory: 38
Bellagio Gallery of Fine Art: 38
Bell Rock: 384
Best Western Canyonlands Inn: 14, 20, 156, 184
Big Apple Coaster: 41
Big Bend: 94-95
Big Elvis: 34
Big Spring Canyon Overlook: 204, 216, 217
Big Spring Canyon Trail: 218-219
biking: Albuquerque 336-338, 349-350; Arches National Park 200; Canyonlands National Park 207; Capitol Reef National Park 147-148; Flagstaff 376; Gallup 366; Grand Canyon 425, 439-440; Moab 171-175; Santa Fe 277-278; Taos 318; Zion National Park 103; *see also* mountain biking
Binion's: 44
birds/bird-watching: 350
Bitter Creek Divide: 140
Blackbird Studios: 48
Blackout Theatre: 346-347
Blackrock Springs: 320
Blue Coffee Pot Café: 20, 243
Blue Man Group: 53
Blue Mesa: 371
Blue Rain Gallery: 274
Bluff to Monument Valley Scenic Byway: 160
Blumenschein, Ernest: 305
boating: 175-177
Boca Negra Canyon: 344
Bodies...the Exhibition: 50
Bond House: 292
Bonelli House: 405
Bonito Lava Flow: 382
Boulder Mountain Loop: 147-148
Boulevard Mall: 75
boxing: 63
Box Performance Space: 346
Boyd Gaming 300 Xfinity Series: 62-63
Bradbury Science Museum: 294
Brad Garrett's Comedy Club: 58
Branigar/Chase Discovery Center: 379
Breaking Bad: 339
Brickyard Park: 366
Bridge in the Redwall: 449
Bright Angel Campground: 451, 456
Bright Angel Lodge: 20, 415, 420, 431-432, 434, 444
Bright Angel Point: 448
Bright Angel Trail: 18, 19, 414, 431, 436-437, 451-452
Bristlecone Loop Trail: 116, 120
bristlecone pine: 119
Broken Arch: 198
Brooklyn Bowl: 59
Brown, Gordie: 58
Bryce Canyon National Park: 8, 11, 14, 15, 18, 19, 84, 109-127; accommodations 122-126; food 126-127; getting there/around 109-110, 114; maps 86, 111; recreation 116-122; sights 14-116
Bryce Canyon Shuttle: 114
Bryce Canyon Winter Festival: 121
Bryce Point: 115
Buck Canyon Overlook: 209
Bullfrog Marina: 141
Burning of Zozobra: 272, 273
Burrow Wash: 140
Burr Trail Road: 139, 140-141
bus travel: 464-465; Flagstaff 375; Grand Canyon 419; Las Vegas 79; *see also specific place*

C

Caesars Palace: 25, 28, 35
Cafe Diablo: 134, 151
Café Pasqual's: 16, 260, 282-283
Caineville: 151
Camel Butte: 241
Camel Rock: 290
Cameron: 442
camping: Arches National Park 200-201; Bryce Canyon National Park 113, 122-124, 125-126; Canyonlands National Park 207-208, 213, 215, 221; Capitol Reef National Park 134-135, 139, 148-149, 151; Grand Canyon National Park 422, 443-444, 450, 456; Kingman 406-408; Mesa Verde National Park 248, 252; Moab 185-186; Monument Valley Navajo Tribal Park 242; reservations 478; Zion National Park 91, 104-106, 108; *see also specific place*
canoeing/kayaking: 176-177; *see also specific place*
Canyonlands Field Institute: 168
Canyonlands Half Marathon: 181
Canyonlands National Park: 8, 14, 15, 18, 20, 153, 156, 201-229; maps 154, 202-203; *see also* Moab
Canyonlands PRCA Rodeo: 181
Canyonlands Utah: 480
Canyon Lodge: 401-417
Canyon Overlook Trail: 95, 101
Canyon Rims Recreation Area: 214-215, 221
Canyon Road: 256, 257, 264, 267, 274, 287
Canyon View Information Plaza: 421, 434

Cape Royal: 447, 448
Cape Royal Scenic Drive: 447
Capilla de Nuestra Señora de Guadalupe: 340
Capitol Art Collection: 267
Capitol Gorge: 14, 18, 131, 134, 137, 147
Capitol Reef Inn and Café: 14, 149, 151
Capitol Reef National Park: 8, 14, 15, 18, 20, 129-151; accommodations 148-151; food 151; getting there/around 132-133, 135; maps 130, 138; recreation 142-148; sights 131, 135-142
Capitol Reef Scenic Drive: 131, 137-138; map 138
Capulin Springs Snow Play Area: 351
car care: *see* driving tips
Carnaval Court: 34
car rental: 10, 466-467; Flagstaff 376; Santa Fe 290
Carrot Top: 43, 53, 58
Carson, Kit: 307, 309
Carson National Forest: 317
Casa Flamenco: 347
casinos: 30-45
Cassidy Arch: 146-147
Castillo Gallery: 300
Castle Creek Winery: 187
Cataract Canyon: 176, 229
Cathedral Basilica of St. Francis of Assisi: 16, 264-265
Cathedral Valley Campground: 139, 149
Cathedral Valley Loop: 148
Cave Spring Trail: 216
CBS Television City Research Center: 41-42
Cedar Mesa Campground: 140, 149
Cedar Ridge: 438
Celebración de la Gente: 387
cell phone service: 13; *see also specific place*
Cell Theatre: 346
Center Strip: 28, 32-37
ceremonial dances: 293, 315, 316, 357
Ceremonial Gallery: 364
Chama: 245-246
Chapel in the Clouds: 30
Chapel of the Holy Cross: 384
Chapin Mesa: 249
Chapin Mesa Archeological Museum: 16, 245, 248, 249
Chasing Santa Fe: 479
Chatter Sunday: 347
Checkerboard Mesa: 95
Chesler Park: 219
children, tips for traveling with: 471
Chimayó: 297-299
Chimayó Museum: 298-299
Chimayó Trading Post: 292
Chimney Rock Trail: 131, 134, 143
Chinatown Plaza: 75
Chippendales: 53
Chocolate Drops Trail: 224
Christ in the Desert Monastery: 296
Chuck Jones Studio Gallery: 274
Church of San Esteban del Rey: 359
Church Rock Trail: 366
Circus Circus: 30
Cirque du Soleil: 54-55
Classical Gas Museum: 295
Clear Creek Loop: 453-454
Cliff Palace: 16, 234, 245, 250
climate: 10, 12
climbing: Arches National Park 200; Capitol Reef National Park 148; Gallup 366; Moab 179-180; Santa Fe/Taos 321; Zion National Park 103-104
clothing: 12
Cly Butte: 241
Cockroach Theatre Company: 60
Coconino Center for the Arts: 379
Coconino National Forest: 388
Coconino Overlook: 449
code talkers: 364
Cohab Canyon Trail: 145-146
Colorado Department of Transportation: 13
Colorado Overlook 4WD Road: 220
Colorado pikeminnow: 228
Colorado River: 176
Colter, Mary: 369, 374, 414, 420, 429, 430, 431, 432, 433, 440, 450, 455
comedy shows: 58-59
communes: 313
Community Gallery: 274
Confluence Overlook Trail: 217-218
consulates: 470
Cool Country Cruise-In: 397
Cools, Anthony: 39
Copperfield, David: 59
Copper Ridge Dinosaur Trackways: 161
Córdova: 300
Cordovas Handweaving Workshop: 300
Corona Arch and Bowtie Arch Trail: 169-170
Corona Arch Trail: 164, 169-170
Cortez: 16, 252, 253
Cosmopolitan: 19, 26, 28, 40
Cottonwood Campground: 456
Cottonwood Wash: 140
Courthouse Wash: 166
Court of the Patriarchs Viewpoint: 14, 15, 85, 93-94
Couse-Sharp Historic Site: 309
Cowabunga Bay: 61
crafts: *see* shopping
Crater View Trail: 209
Cravings Buffet: 31
Crawford, Stanley: 303

credit cards: 472
crime: 477
Crystals at City Center: 75
CSI: The Experience: 42
Cuba: 334-335
Culinary Dropout: 19, 27, 72
Cumbres & Toltec Scenic Railroad: 245
currency: 472-473
customs regulations: 470
cycling: *see* biking

D

Dairy Springs Campground: 390
Dark Angel: 199
datura: 144
David Copperfield: 59
Davis Canyon: 220
Dead Horse State Park: 155, 162-163, 174, 186
dehydration: 475
Delgadillo's Snow Cap Drive-In: 401, 417
Delicate Arch Trail: 18, 20, 155, 191, 194, 197-198
Delicate Arch Viewpoint: 196
DeMotte Campground: 450
Desert Bistro: 14, 20, 157, 187-188, 191
Desert USA: 480
Desert View Campground: 422, 444
Desert View Drive: 420, 430-431, 434
Desert View Visitors Center and Bookstore: 421
Desert View Watchtower: 414, 420, 435
Desoto's Beauty & Barber Shop: 399
Devils Garden: 195
Devils Garden Campground: 200
Devils Garden Loop: 155, 191, 198-199
Devine, Andy: 406
Dewey Bridge: 167
Diamond Creek Road: 460
dinosaur tracks: 164
dirt bikes: Moab 178-179
disabilities, tips for travelers with: 470-471
Divas Las Vegas: 58
Dixie National Forest: 110
Dixon: 295
Dixon Studio Tour: 295
Dodge Luhan, Mabel: 308
Dolphin Habitat: 25, 49
Donna Beam Fine Art Gallery: 60
Don Quixote Distillery: 290
Double Down Saloon: 59
Double O Arch: 199
Double Springs Campground: 390
Downtown Arts District: 48
Downtown Container Park: 76-77
Dream Racing: 62
drinking laws: 472, 473
Dripping Springs: 438-439
drivers licenses: 468
driving directions: to Albuquerque 334-336; to Arches National Park 189; to Bryce Canyon National Park 109-110; to Canyonlands National Park 201; to Capitol Reef National Park 132-133; to Four Corners Monument 243-244; to Grand Canyon 415-418; to Las Vegas 24-27; to Mesa Verde National Park 244-247; to Moab 157-160; to Monument Valley Navajo Tribal Park 235-237; to Santa Fe 258-260; to Taos 302; to Zion National Park 84-89
driving tips: 12-13, 78-79, 465-469
Druid Arch: 219
Duke City Fix: 479
Duke City Repertory Theatre: 347
dust storms: 467

E

Eagle Point: 459
Earthships: 313
Easter Jeep Safari: 181
East Mesa Trail: 100
East Mitten Butte: 241
Echo Canyon Trail: 100
Eddie McStiff's: 20, 157, 180, 187, 204
Edge of the Cedars State Park Museum: 21, 161
Egg & I, The: 14, 27, 68
Egyptian Temple: 137
Eight Modern: 274
E. L. Blumenschein Home: 305-306
Elden Pueblo Heritage Site: 379-380
electrical current: 474
Elephant Butte: 241
Elephant Hill 4WD Loop Road: 220-221
Elephant Rock: 210
Elk Ridge Ski Area: 396-397
El Meze: 260, 264, 327
El Morro Theatre: 364
El Rancho Hotel: 16, 367
El Rey Theater: 347
El Salto Falls: 18, 319-320
El Tovar Dining Room: 20, 416, 420, 444
El Tovar Hotel: 19, 20, 415, 416, 420, 432, 441, 444
embassies: 470
Embudo: 295
Embudo Canyon: 349
Emerald Pools: 14, 18, 85, 98-99
emergencies: 467-468, 474; *see also specific place*
Enchanted Circle Century Tour: 318
Encore: 30
entertainment/events: Albuquerque 344-348; Flagstaff 383-387; Las Vegas 52-63; Moab 180-181; Santa Fe 271-273; Taos 313-316; *see also specific place*
Escalante: 110

Escalante Interagency Visitor Center: 110
Española: 292-295
Esplanade: 76
events: *see* entertainment/events
Everything Coca-Cola: 49-50
Excalibur: 28
exchanging currency: 473
Exotics Racing: 62
¡Explora!: 340
Explore Navajo Interactive Museum: 237
Eye of the Whale Arch: 196

F

Fairyland Canyon: 14, 115
Fairyland Loop Trail: 14, 112, 115, 117, 118
Fairyland Point: 115
Fairyland Ski Trail: 121
Fall of Atlantis: 35
Fantasy: 42-43
Far View Lodge: 16, 248, 252
Farview Point: 115-116
Fashion Show: 74-75
Fator, Terry: 53
Feast of San Esteban: 358
Feast of San Geronimo: 315-316
Fechin, Nicolai: 307
Festival Fountain Show: 35
Fiber Arts Trails: 478
Fiery Furnace: 191, 195, 198
Fiesta de Santa Fe: 272
Fiestas de Taos: 315
Film Museum: 165
Fin Canyon: 199
First Friday: 48
fish/fishing: 228, 320
Fisher Towers: 165-167, 171
Five Mile Wash: 140
Flagstaff: 16, 336, 375-395, 422, 443, 445; map 376
Flagstaff Convention and Visitors Bureau: 478
Flagstaff Film Festival: 387
Flagstaff Loop Trail: 376
Flagstaff Nordic Center: 389
Flamingo: 36
Flamingo Wildlife Habitat: 36
flash floods: 13, 467, 474-475
flightseeing: 114, 155, 179, 425
Flint Trail 4WD Road: 210, 225
food: Albuquerque 353-355; Bryce Canyon National Park 126-127; Grand Canyon National Park 416, 444-445, 450, 455-456, 458, 461; Las Vegas 67-74; Moab 186-188; Santa Fe 260, 282-289; Taos 325-329; Zion National Park 108-109; *see also specific place*
Forum Shops: 35, 75
Fountains at Bellagio: 38
Four Corners National Monument: 8, 15, 16, 231, 243-244; map 232-233
four-wheeling: Arches National Park 194-195; Canyonlands National Park 210, 220-221, 225; Moab 176; *see also specific place*
Franco, Mat: 36
Fremont Gorge Overlook Trail: 145
Fremont petroglyphs: 136
Fremont River Trail: 18, 20, 134, 146
Fremont River Waterfall: 136-137
Fremont Street Experience: 25, 45-46
French Pastry Shop: 16, 283
Fruita: 134, 137, 150
Fruita Campground: 14, 134-135, 148
Fruita Schoolhouse: 135-136, 137
Fuller Lodge Art Center: 294

G

Gallup: 16, 362-368; map 360
Gallup Aquatic Center: 367
Garden of Eden Viewpoint: 193
gas stations: 13; Bryce Canyon National Park 113; Route 66 332; Zion National Park 91-92; *see also specific place*
Gathering of Nations Powwow: 348
Gavilan Trail: 18, 319
gay/lesbian travelers, tips for: 472
Gemini Bridges Trail: 155, 173
geology: 194, 217
Georgia O'Keeffe Home: 296
Georgia O'Keeffe Museum: 265-266
Gerald Peters Gallery: 274
Ghost Ranch: 296
Giant Logs Trail: 371
giardia: 477
Gifford Farmhouse: 134, 137
Give-Away: 362
Golden Nugget: 26, 44-45
Golden Stairs: 224
Golden Throne Trail: 147
golf: Las Vegas 62; Moab 180
gondola rides: 25, 48
Gonzo Inn: 14, 20, 156, 184
Gooseberry Trail: 211
Goosenecks Overlook: 15, 135
Goosenecks State Park: 21, 236
Goss, Matt: 35, 53-54
Governor Bent House and Museum: 306
Grand Bazaar Shops: 77
Grand Canal Shoppes: 33, 76
Grand Canyon Airport: 418, 425
Grand Canyon Caverns: 19, 336, 401-402
Grand Canyon Field Institute: 453
Grand Canyon Lodge: 414, 415, 421, 447-448, 450

Grand Canyon National Park: 8, 10, 15, 18, 19, 20, 54, 411-461, 471, 478; accommodations 415, 440-444, 449-450, 455-456, 458, 461; food 416, 444-445, 450, 455-456, 458, 461; getting there/getting around 415-419, 424-425, 446-447, 461; information/services 421, 423-424, maps 412-413, 426-427; recreation 422-423, 435-440, 448-440, 451-455, 450-461; reservations 421-422; sights 414, 425-435, 447-448, 457-459; tours 54
Grand Canyon Railway: 19, 395, 419
Grand Canyon Village Historical District: 20, 431
Grand Canyon West: 416, 417, 420, 457-461
Grand Staircase-Escalante National Monument: 110
Grand View Picnic Area: 209
Grand View Point (Canyonlands): 14, 15, 204, 209
Grandview Point (Grand Canyon): 430
Grand View Trail (Canyonlands): 14, 18, 20, 155, 209, 211
Grandview Trail (Grand Canyon): 439
Grand Wash Trail: 131, 137, 145
gratuities: 474
Greater World Earthship Development: 312-313
Great Gallery Trail: 226
Great White Throne: 94
Green River: 176, 209
Green River Overlook: 14, 15, 209
Green River State Park: 228
Grotto, The: 94
Guadalupe: 268
Guano Point: 459
guest ranches: 185

H

Hacienda de los Martinez: 305, 309-310
Hackberry General Store: 19, 336, 402-403
Halls Creek Overlook: 141
Hamburger Rock Campground: 221
Hanksville: 141, 157-160
Hans Flat Ranger Stations: 204, 205, 222, 225
hantavirus: 476-477
Hard Rock: 40-41
Harrah's: 14, 26, 34
Harrell House of Natural Oddities: 277
Harwood Museum of Art: 305
Hatch Point Campground: 215, 221
Hat Shop: 120
Havasu Falls: 458
Havasupai Canyon: 461
Havasupai Indian Reservation: 420, 458-461
Hawikku: 361
health: 474-477
heat exhaustion/heatstroke: 475
helicopter tours: 54, 80, 81, 121, 425, 460, 461
Hermit Road: 414, 429-430, 434
Hermit's Rest: 420, 429, 435
Hermit Trail: 438-439
Hickman Natural Bridge: 144
Hidden Canyon Trail: 85, 92 100-101
Hidden Lake: 30
Hidden Valley Trail: 168, 169
High Road: 15, 16, 260, 264, 278, 290, 295-301, 302
High Road Art Tour: 297
High Roller: 25, 49, 35
hiking: 18; Arches National Park 196-200; Bryce Canyon National Park 117-121; Canyonlands National Park 210-213, 216-219, 224-225, 226; Capitol Reef National Park 141-148; Dead Horse Point State Park 162-163; Flagstaff 388; Gallup 366; Grand Canyon National Park 12, 435-439, 448-449; Kingman 406-408; Mesa Verde National Park 251-252; Moab 168-171; New Mexico 478; Santa Fe 278-279; Taos 319-320; Zion National Park 96-103
Historic Basque Handball Court: 377
Historic Cameron Trading Post & Lodge: 415
Historic Fruita School: 137
Historic Route 66: *see* Route 66
Historic Route 66 Fun Run: 405-406
Historic Route 66 Hotel: 401, 417
Historic Route 66 Museum: 19, 404-405
Historic Tuba City Trading Post: 237
Hittle Bottom Recreation Site: 176
Holbrook: 371-372
Hole 'n the Rock: 161
Holocaust and Intolerance Museum: 343
hoodoos: 113
Hoover Dam: 19, 80
Hopi Festival of Arts and Culture: 387
Hopi House: 20, 433, 440
Hopi Point: 429
Hopper, Dennis: 311
horseback riding: Bryce Canyon National Park 121; Moab 180; Monument Valley Navajo Tribal Park 241; Santa Fe/Taos 296; Zion National Park 103; *see also specific place*
Horse Canyon 4WD Road: 220
Horseshoe Canyon Unit: 206, 225-226
Horsethief Campground: 186
hostels: Las Vegas 66-67; *see also specific place*
hot-air ballooning: *see* ballooning
Hotel La Fonda de Taos: 304
hot springs: 320
House of Blues: 43
Hualapai Indian Reservation: 420, 457-458
Hualapai Mountain Park: 406-407
Hualapai Peak: 407
Hualapai Ranch: 459

Hualapai Tribe: 460
Hub, The: 241
humpback chub: 228
humpback sucker: 228
Humphreys Peak Trail: 18, 388
Hunters Canyon: 168-169
hunting: 320
Hyde Memorial State Park: 279
hypothermia: 475

I

Illusions: 59
Improv, The: 58
Indian Creek: 214
Indian Garden: 431, 437, 451, 452, 456
Indian Pueblo Cultural Center: 293
Indian reservations: 13, 470; *see also specific place*
Indian Ruins Viewpoint: 163
Indigenous Fine Art Market: 272
Inspiration Point (Bryce Canyon): 19, 85, 115
insurance: 467
International Folk Art Market: 272
Internet resources: 477-480
Inter-Tribal Indian Ceremonial: 364
Intrepid Trail System: 163, 172, 173-174
Island in the Sky District: 20, 201, 204, 205, 206, 208-213
Island Trail: 383
Isleta Amphitheater: 347
Isotopes Park: 350
itineraries: 14-21; Arches National Park 191; Bryce Canyon National Park 112; Canyonlands National Park 205; Capitol Reef National Park 134; Grand Canyon National Park 420; Las Vegas 31; Mesa Verde National Park 245; Route 66 336; Santa Fe/Taos 264; Zion National Park 92

J

Jana's RedRoom: 48
Jasper Forest: 371
Jean Cocteau Cinema: 264, 273
jeep rentals/tours: 178, 195-196; *see also specific place*
Jersey Boys: 54
Jesus Nazareno Cemetery: 311
jimsonweed: 144
John Ford's Point: 241
John Wesley Powell River History Museum: 228
Joint Trail: 219
Jug Handle Arch: 164

K

Kà: 54-55
Kachina Trail: 388
Kaibab Camper Village: 450
Kaibab National Forest: 472
Kanab: 87-88
Kane Creek Scenic Drive: 167, 168
kayaking: *see* canoeing/kayaking
Kayenta: 16, 20, 237, 243
Kayenta Campground: 186
Keepers of the Wild Nature Park: 402
KiMo Theatre: 342, 347
King Creek Campground: 124
Kingman: 8, 10, 19, 19, 20, 403-409; map 404
Kit Carson Home and Museum: 16, 309
Kit Carson Park and Cemetery: 307-308
Klondike Bluffs: , 191, 195
Kobalt 400 Sprint Cup: 62-63
Kodachrome Basin State Park: 125
Kokopelli's Trail: 174
Kolb Studio: 433
Kolob Canyons: 91, 92, 96, 102-103
Kolob Reservoir: 96
Kolob Terrace: 95
Kolob Terrace Road: 101-102, 103

L

La Chiripada: 295
L.A. Comedy Club: 58
La Fonda: 16, 257, 259, 266-267, 281
Laguna Pueblo: 356-358
Lake Mary: 389-390
Lake Mead National Recreation Area: 24, 86
La Loma Plaza: 306
Lamy: 270-271
Lamy, Jean-Baptiste: 303, 305
Lamy Railroad & History Museum: 270-271
Land of Standing Rocks: 223-224
Landscape Arch: 199
La Posada: 336, 372, 373-374
La Sal Mountains Loop Road: 165
Las Trampas: 300
Las Vegas: 8, 10, 12, 14, 15, 19, 23-81, 463, 464, 471, 472; accommodations 26, 63-67; casinos 30-45; entertainment 52-63; food 27, 67-74; getting there/around 24-28, 78-81; information/services 77-78; maps 29, 46; orientation 28-30; shopping 74-77; sights 25, 45-52; transportation 24-28, 78-81
Las Vegas Advisor: 77
Las Vegas Ballet Company: 60
Las Vegas Chamber of Commerce: 77
Las Vegas Convention and Visitors Authority: 77
Las Vegas Little Theatre: 60
Las Vegas Magazine: 77
Las Vegas Monorail: 79
Las Vegas Motor Speedway: 62-63
Las Vegas Natural History Museum: 46-47

Las Vegas Perspective: 78
Las Vegas Philharmonic: 60
Las Vegas Springs Preserve: 25, 51
Las Vegas Weekly: 78
Laugh Factory: 58-59
Laughternoon: 59
Lava Flow Trail: 382
Lava Point: 95-96, 105
Lava Point Campground: 105
Lavender Canyon: 220
Lawrence, D. H.: 301, 304, 308-309
Le Boulevard: 39, 77
Lee Pass: 96
Lee's Ferry: 455
Legends in Concert: 55
Lensic Performing Arts Center: 272
Le Rêve: 55
LewAllen: 274
LGBT travelers, tips for: 472
Lied Discovery Children's Museum: 47
limousines: 80
Linq, The: 31, 35-36, 77
Lions Park: 180
Lipan Point: 431
Lipshtick: 58
liquor laws: 473
Lodge at Bryce Canyon: 14, 19, 88, 89, 112, 122, 126
Lodge on Route 66: 16
Lonely Dell Ranch Historic Site: 455
Long House: 251
Long Logs Trail: 18, 371
Lookout Studio: 20, 433
Loretto Chapel: 265
Los Alamos: 294
Los Alamos Historical Museum: 294
Lost Canyon Trail: 218
Love: 14, 25, 31, 34, 55
Lowell Observatory: 378
Lower Muley Twist Canyon: 141-142
Lower Red Lake Canyon Trail: 219
Lower Strip: 28
Low Road: 16, 264, 291, 302
Luxor: 28, 42-43

M

Mabel Dodge Luhan House: 257, 308-309
Mac King Comedy Magic Show: 58
Madame Tussauds Las Vegas: 33, 48
magic shows: 59
Manby Springs: 320
Mancos: 16, 252, 253
Mandalay Bay: 19, 26, 43-44
Mandalay Place: 43, 77
Mandarin Bar: 15, 64
Mandarin Oriental Las Vegas: 26, 64
M&M's World: 49
Manzanita Trail: 321
maps: 13, 468, 474; *see also specific place*
Marching Men: 195
Maricopa Point: 429
Marigold Parade: 348
Marjorie Barrick Museum of Natural History: 52
Marriage Can Be Murder: 60
Marshall Lake: 389
Martinez, Antonio: 303, 305
Martin, George R. R.: 273
Mather Campground: 415, 422, 443-444
Mather Point: 15, 419, 434
Maynard Dixon Living History Museum: 21, 87
Maze District: 204-205, 206, 221-225
Maze Overlook Trail: 224
McCarran International Airport: 27-28, 464
McKinley County Courthouse: 363
Meadows Mall: 75
medical services: 474; Bryce Canyon National Park 113; Capitol Reef National Park 135; Las Vegas 78; Moab 188; Zion National Park 92; *see also specific place*
Mentmore Rock Climbing Area: 366
Mesa Arch Trail: 155, 204, 211
Mesa Top Loop Road: 234, 245, 250
Mesa Verde National Park: 8, 11, 15, 16, 18, 231, 244-253; map 232-233
Mesa Verde Visitor and Research Center: 247-248
Metate Room: 245, 252
Mexican Hat: 16, 237, 242-243
MGM Grand: 28, 41-42
Michael Jackson ONE: 43
Mile-and-a-Half Resthouse; 437
Millard Canyon Overlook: 224
Mill Canyon Dinosaur Trail: 161
Millicent Rogers Museum: 311-312
Million Dollar Quartet: 34, 55
Mineral Canyon: 228
Miracle Mile: 75
Mirage, The: 34
Misión Museum: 292
Miss Route 66 Pageant: 397
Mitchell Mesa: 241
Mitten View Campground: 242
mixed martial arts: 63
MJ Live: 30
MMA: 63
Moab: 14, 20, 156-188; accommodations 156, 182-186; food 157, 186-188; entertainment 180-181; getting there/around 157-160; maps 158-159, 164; recreation 167-180; shopping 181-182; sights 160-167
Moab Area Travel Council: 480

Moab Arts Festival: 181
MOAB Brand Trails: 172
Moab Canyon Pathway: 174
Moab Century Tour: 181
Moab Dock: 228
Moab Fault: 192-193
Moab Folk Festival: 181
Moab Golf Club: 180
Moab Information Center: 167, 188
Moab Music Festival: 181
Moab Recreation and Aquatic Center: 180
Moab Rim Trail: 168, 169
Moab Salt Plant: 164-165
Moab Skinny Tire Festival: 181
Mob Museum: 25, 31, 47-48
Mohave Museum of History and Arts: 405
Mohave Point: 429-430
Mon Ami Gabi: 27, 31, 71
money: 472-473; *see also* banks/banking
Monitor and Merrimac Trail: 174
monorail: 79
Monument Valley Navajo Tribal Park: 8, 15, 16, 18, 20, 231-243; map 232-233
Monument Valley Navajo Tribal Park Visitor Center: 15, 237, 238-239
Mooney Falls: 458
Moran Point: 430-431
Morefield Campground: 252
Mormon Fort: 47
Mormon Lake: 389-390
Morning Glory Natural Bridge: 170-171
Mossy Cave Trail: 112, 120-121, 127
Mother Road Theatre Company: 347
Mount Elden Trail System: 388
mountain biking: 173; Albuquerque 349; Canyonlands National Park 210-211, 220-221; Flagstaff 388-389; Gallup 366; Moab 171-175; Santa Fe 278; *see also* biking
mountain lions: 476
Mr. D'z Route 66 Diner: 20, 408
Muir, John: 432
mule rides: 12, 422, 449, 454
Muley Twist Canyon: 141-142
Museum Association of Taos: 305
Museum of Indian Arts & Culture: 269-270
Museum of International Folk Art: 257, 270
Museum of Moab: 160-161
Museum of Natural History and Science: 340-341
Museum of Northern Arizona: 333, 378-379
Museum of Northern Arizona Heritage Program: 387
Museum of Organized Crime and Law Enforcement: 25, 31, 47-48
Museum of Spanish Colonial Art: 269
Mystère: 55

N

Nambé Falls Recreation Area: 297
Nambé Pueblo: 297
Nathan Burton Comedy Magic: 59
National Forest Service: 469, 477
Native American ceremonial dances: 293, 315, 316
Natural Bridge: 116
Natural Bridges National Monument: 21, 161
Navajo Arch: 199
Navajo Bridge: 455
Navajo code talkers: 363, 364
Navajo County Historical Society's Museum: 371
Navajo Festival of Arts and Culture: 387
Navajo Loop Trail: 14, 18, 85, 112, 115, 118-119
Navajo Parks and Recreation Department: 239
Navajo sandstone: 94
Neck Springs Trail: 204, 211
Nedra Matteucci Galleries: 274
Needles District: 201, 204, 205, 206, 213-221
Needles Outpost: 215, 221
Needles Overlook: 214
Negro Bill Canyon: 170
Neon Museum and Boneyard: 31, 47
Nevada Ballet Theatre: 60
Nevada Conservatory Theatre: 60
Nevada Department of Transportation: 12, 13, 478
Nevada State Museum: 51
New Mexico Board of Tourism: 478-479
New Mexico Culture Pass: 265
New Mexico Department of Transportation: 13, 479
New Mexico History Museum: 261
New Mexico Museum of Art: 16, 261-264
New Mexico State Capitol: 267
New Mexico Touring Society: 350
Newspaper Rock Historical Monument (Canyonlands): 155, 214
Newspaper Rock (Petrified Forest): 370
New York New York: 41
Nichols, John: 303
nightlife: *see* entertainment
N9NE: 19, 27, 72
Nordebskiold Site No. 16 Trail: 252
Norski Trail: 279
North Campground: 14, 113, 122
Northern Arizona Book Festival: 387
Northgate Peaks Trail: 102
North Kaibab Trail: 448-449
North Las Vegas Airport: 464
North Point: 224
North Rim: 418, 419, 420, 421, 445-450
North Rim Campground: 422, 450
North Rim Visitor Center and Bookstore: 421, 446

INDEX

North Window Overlook: 241
Notom-Bullfrog Road: 131, 134, 139-141
Notom Ranch: 140
Nüart Gallery: 274
Nuestra Señora de Guadalupe Church: 333, 361
Nuestra Señora del Rosario de las Truchas Church: 300

O

O: 19, 55-56
Oak Creek: 140
Observation Point Trail: 99-100
Occidental Life Building: 342-343
O'Keeffe, Georgia: 265-266, 296
Old Santa Fe Trail: 267
Old Town Albuquerque: 338, 353-355
Old Trails Museum: 373
Old Wagon Trail Loop: 134, 147
Oñate, Juan de: 358
O'Neill, Bucky: 432
Onion Creek Road: 165
Onyx Theatre: 60
Ooh Aah Point: 438-439
Oo-oonah Art Center: 311
Orilla Verde Recreation Area: 295
Osmond, Donny and Marie: 53
Otero Canyon: 349
Outpost Performance Space: 347
Overton: 26
Owl Rock: 235

P

packing: 12
Pagosa Springs: 16, 21, 258-259
Painted Desert: 369-370
Painted Desert golf course: 62
Painted Desert Inn Museum: 369, 369
Palace of the Governors: 261, 276
Palazzo, The: 33
Palms, The: 37
Pancho McGillicuddy's: 19, 398
Panguitch: 112, 125-126
Panorama Point: 15, 135
Paria Ski Trail: 121
Paria View: 115
Paris Las Vegas: 39
Paris Theatre: 39
Park Avenue Trail: 191, 193, 196
parking: 468
park passes/fees: *see specific park*
Partition Arch: 199
Pa'rus Trail: 97, 98
Paseo de Peralta: 260
Paseo del Bosque: 349
passports: 12, 469-470
Peach Springs: 402
Pearl Concert Theater: 37
Pecos League: 321
Pecos Wilderness Area: 301
Peekaboo Loop Trail: 115, 118, 119
Peekaboo Trail: 218
Peñasco: 301
Peñasco Theatre: 301
Penn & Teller: 56, 59
Peppermill Restaurant & Fireside Lounge: 31
Petrified Forest National Park: 16, 333, 336, 368-371
Petroglyph National Monument: 16, 333, 344
Petroglyph Point Trail: 16, 18, 234, 245, 251
petroglyphs: 136, 163-164, 166, 344
Peyton Wright: 274
Phantom Overlook: 453-454
Phantom Ranch: 415, 451, 453-454, 455-456
Phoenix: 10, 463, 465
Phoenix Sky Harbor International Airport: 465
pictographs: 166
Picurís Pueblo: 301
Piece of Me: 56
Piedras Marcadas Canyon: 344
Pilar: 295
Pima Point: 430
Pine Cone Drop: 387
Pine Country Restaurant: 19, 398, 445
Pine Lake Campground: 123-124
Pine Tree Arch: 199
Pintado Point: 370
Pin Up: 30
Plateau Point: 437
Plaza Café: 264, 283
Pleasant Creek: 140
Pleasant Creek Road: 138
Poeh Museum: 290
Point Imperial: 447, 448
Pojoaque: 290
Polar Express and Mountain Village Holiday: 397
Ponderosa Canyon: 116
Popjoy Hall: 347
Porcupine Rim Trail: 173
Portal Overlook Trail: 169
postal services: Santa Fe 289
Post Corral: 141
Potash Dock: 228
Potato Patch Loop: 407
Pothole Point Nature Trail: 216-217
Powell Point: 429
Powerhouse Visitors Center: 409
Pritchett Canyon: 169
Public Lands Information Center: 469, 477-478
Pueblo of Tesuque Flea Market: 276
pueblos: 293, 315, 316, 470, 471; *see also specific place*

Puerco Pueblo: 370
Pulliam Airport: 418
Pyramid Rock Trail: 366

QR

Queen's Garden Trail: 18, 19, 85, 115, 118, 119
Questa Dome: 321
rafting: 471; Canyonlands National Park 207, 226-229; Grand Canyon 12, 422-423, 451, 454-455, 458, 459-460; Moab 175-177; Santa Fe/Taos 320-321
Raiding the Rock Vault: 42
Railyard: 268
Railyard Artisan Market: 276
Rail Yards Market: 343
Rainbow Forest Museum: 371
Rainbow Point: 85, 112, 116, 119
Rain God Mesa: 240, 241
Rancho de las Golondrinas: 270
Ranchos de Taos: 303, 324-325, 328
Rat Pack Is Back: 31, 57-58
rattlesnakes: 475-476
razorback sucker: 228
recreation: Bryce Canyon National Park 116-122; Capitol Reef National Park 142-148; Grand Canyon National Park 422-423, 435-440, 448-440, 451-455, 450-461; Moab 167-180; Santa Fe 277-279; Zion National Park 96-104; *see also specific place*
Red Canyon Campground: 124
Red Dot Gallery: 274
Red Ledge Campground: 105-106
Red Rock Balloon Rally: 364
Red Rock Grill: 92, 108
Red Rock Museum: 364
Red Rock Park: 364
Red Rock Scenic Byway: 384
rental cars: 10, 466-467; Flagstaff 376; Las Vegas 78-79; Santa Fe 290; *see also specific place*
reservations: 10-12, 472; Bryce Canyon National Park 112-113; Grand Canyon National Park 421-422; Zion National Park 91; *see also specific place*
restaurants: *see* food
Rex Museum: 364
Ribbon Falls: 454
Richard Petty Driving Experience: 61-62
Riggs Spring Loop Trail: 116, 120
Rim Overlook Trail: 144-145
Rim Route (Capitol Gorge): 142
Rim Trail (Bryce Canyon): 112, 115, 117, 118, 121
Rim Trail (Grand Canyon): 18, 19, 20, 414, 420, 433-434, 436
Rinconada Canyon: 344
Rio: 36-37
Rio Chama: 471
Rio Chama Campground: 296
Rio Grande: 471
Rio Grande Gorge: 15, 257, 312, 325
Rio Grande Gorge Visitors Center: 295
Rio Grande Heritage Farm: 339
Rio Grande Nature Center: 349
Riordan Mansion State Historic Park: 377-378
Rivers District: 205, 206, 226-229
Riverside Walk: 19, 92, 101
River Trail: 453
road conditions: 467-468; *see also* driving tips
Roadkill Café: 401, 417
roadside assistance: 468
Roadside Ruin Trail: 216
Roaring Springs: 449
Robert Nichols Gallery: 274
rock climbing: *see* climbing
Rockville: 91, 106
Rod's Steak House: 19, 398, 416, 445
Rogers, Millicent: 311-312
Roosevelt Point: 447
Rose.Rabbit.Lie: 14, 27, 40, 73
Rotary Park: 180
Route 66: 8, 15, 16, 18, 19, 20, 330-409, 417; maps 334-335, 356, 370, 396, 403; *see also specific place*
Route 66 Casino: 347
Route 66 Days: 387
Route 66 Trail: 376
Roy E. Disney Center for the Performing Arts: 347
RVs: 67, 79, 466-467

S

safety: 474-477
sales tax: 473-474
Salt Creek Canyon 4WD Road: 220
Salt Lake City: 463, 465
Salt Lake City International Airport: 465
Sand Bench Trail: 97-98
Sand Dollar: 59
Sand Dune Arch: 198
Sandia Casino: 347
Sandia Peak: 350
Sandia Peak Ski Area: 350-351
Sandia Peak Tramway: 16, 333, 343-344
sandstone: 94
Sandy Ranch Junction: 140
San Felipe de Neri Church: 341
San Francisco de Asis Church: 257, 310
San Geronimo Church: 310-311
San José de Gracia Church: 300
San Lorenzo de Picurís Church: 301
San Miguel Mission: 268
Santa Cruz de la Cañada Church: 292

INDEX

Santa Fe: 8, 15, 16, 18, 255-290, 465, 471, 472; accommodations 259, 279-282; entertainment 271-273; food 260, 282-289; getting there/around 258-260, 289-290; information/services 289; maps 258, 262-263; recreation 277-279; shopping 273-277; sights 257, 260-271
Santa Fe Canyon Preserve: 278
Santa Fe Chamber Music Festival: 272
Santa Fe Children's Museum: 277
Santa Fe Convention and Visitors Bureau: 289, 479
Santa Fe Creative: 479
Santa Fe Downs: 276
Santa Fe Flea: 276
Santa Fe Municipal Airport: 465
Santa Fe Opera: 264, 272
Santa Fe Plaza: 16, 261
Santa Fe Pro Musica: 272
Santa Fe Wine and Chile Festival: 272-273
Santo Tomás de Abiquiu Church: 296
Santuario de Chimayó: 257, 297-298
Santuario de Guadalupe: 268-269
scorpions: 475-476
seasons: 10, 423
Secret Garden: 25, 49
Sedona: 384
Sego Canyon: 166
Seligman: 19, 336, 399-401, 417, 461
senior discounts: 471-472
Shafer Canyon Overlook: 20, 209
Shafer Trail Road: 209
Shalako: 362
Shark Reef: 51
Sheets Gulch: 140
Shidoni: 275
shopping: Albuquerque 348; Flagstaff 387-388; Grand Canyon 440; Las Vegas 74-77; Moab 181-182; Santa Fe 273-277; Taos Pueblo 316-317; *see also specific place*
Showcase Mall: 49
Showstoppers: 56
Shrine of the Ages: 420, 440
shuttle bus: Bryce Canyon National Park 114; Grand Canyon National Park; 424-425; Zion National Park 93
Siena Golf Club: 62
Sinagua people: 381
SITE Santa Fe: 269
Skeleton Point: 438
skiing: Albuquerque 350-351; Flagstaff 389; Santa Fe 279; Taos 313, 321; Williams 396-397
Ski Santa Fe: 279
Sky City: 358-359
Sky City Cultural Center and Haak'u Museum: 336, 358-359
skydiving: 179
Sky Harbor International Airport: 10
Skyline Arch: 195
Skywalk: 416, 459
Slickrock Bike Trail: 172-173
Slickrock Trail (Canyonlands): 217
Slide Rock State Park: 384
SlotZilla: 61
SLS: 30, 31-32
Smith Center for the Performing Arts: 59-60
Smithsonian Folkways: 479
smoking: 472
snakes: 475-476
Soda Canyon Overlook Trail: 251
Soldiers' Monument: 261
South Campground: 14, 104-105
South Kaibab Trail: 437-438, 451
South Rim: 20, 416, 417-418, 421, 425-445
South Rim Backcountry Information Center: 456
South Rim Visitor Center: 421
Southside Historic District: 377
Sovereign Single-Track Trail: 174
Spanish Bottom Trail: 225
Spanish Market: 272
Spanish Trail Arena: 181
Spanish Valley Vineyards and Winery: 187
spas: Albuquerque 350; Santa Fe 279
Spearhead Mesa: 241
Spears, Britney: 56
spiders: 476
Spring Canyon Route: 143
Springdale: 12, 14, 89, 91, 106, 108-109
Springs Resort, The: 16, 250
Spruce Canyon Trail: 251
Spruce Tree House: 16, 234, 245, 249-250
Spruce Tree Terrace: 245, 253
Square Tower House: 250
Squaw Canyon Trail: 218
Squaw Flat Campground: 205, 221
Stagecoach Springs: 320
Standin' on the Corner Park: 372
Starr Springs Campground: 141
Step House: 251
Stoney's Rockin' Country: 59
Storyteller Museum: 364
Stratosphere Casino, Hotel, and Tower: 30
Stratosphere Tower: 15, 30, 60-61
Strawberry Canyon Trail: 366
Streetmosphere: 33
Strike Valley Overlook Trail: 142
Strip, The: 28-30; map 29
Sulphur Creek Route: 143-144
sunburn: 475
Sun Point View: 15, 250
Sunrise Point: 15, 85, 112, 115

Sunset Campground: 14, 113, 122
Sunset Crater Volcano National Monument: 333, 380-382
Sunset Point (Bryce Canyon): 85, 115
Sunset Point (Capitol Reef): 135
Sunshine Theater: 347
Sun Temple: 250
Supai Lodge: 400-401, 417
Supai Tunnel: 449
Super Ticket: 305
Surprise Canyon: 141
Swamp Canyon Loop: 120
Syncline Loop Trail: 212-213

T

Taos: 8, 15, 16, 18, 255-257, 301-320, 471; accommodations 321-325; entertainment 313-316; food 325-329; getting there/around 302-303; information/services 329; maps 258, 304; recreation 317-321; shopping 316-317; sights 257, 303-313
Taos Art Museum at Fechin House: 16, 257, 307
Taos Blizzard: 321
Taos Center for the Arts: 314-315
Taos County Courthouse: 304
Taos Fall Arts Festival: 315
Taos Inn: 309
Taos Plaza: 16, 264, 303-309; map 304
Taos Pueblo: 16, 257, 264, 303-304, 310-311
Taos Pueblo Powwow: 315
Taos Ski Valley: 304, 313, 318, 319, 321, 329, 471
Taos Solar Music Festival: 315
Taos Vacation Guide: 479
Taos Visitors Center: 329
Taos Wool Festival: 316
Taos Youth and Family Center: 317
Tapestry Arch: 198
tarantulas: 476
Tawa Point: 15, 370
taxes: 473-474
taxis: 79-80, 474
Taylor Creek Trail: 96, 102
Teasdale: 134, 149-150
Telephone Museum: 343
temperatures: 475; *see also* weather
Temple of Sinawava: 95
Tepees, The: 371
Tesuque: 290-291
Tesuque Glassworks: 275
theft: 477
Thelma and Louise Half Marathon: 181
Three-Mile Resthouse: 437
Three Sisters: 241
Thumb, The: 241
Thunderbird Mesa: 241
thunderstorms: 474
Tia Sophia's: 16, 260, 264, 282
ticks: 476
Timber Creek Overlook Trail: 96, 102-103
time zones: 474
tipping: 474
Titanic exhibit: 50-51
Tlaquepaque Arts and Crafts Village: 384
Tony 'n Tina's Wedding: 56-57
Top-of-the-World Road: 167
Torrey: 134, 149-151
Totem Pole: 241
Tournament of Kings: 57
tours: Bryce Canyon National Park 114; Grand Canyon National Park 54, 425, 459, Las Vegas 80-81; Monument Valley Navajo Tribal Park 239; Zion National Park 92; *see also specific place*
Tower Arch: 191, 195, 199-200
Town Square: 75
Trail no. 365: 349
Trailview Overlook: 429
train travel: 464, 465; Albuquerque 335-336; Flagstaff 375; Grand Canyon 419; Santa Fe 260
Trampas Lakes: 300
Transept Trail: 448
transportation: 10, 463-469; *see also specific place*
Travel Bug: 469
Travel Nevada: 468
Tricklock: 346
Tropic: 12, 19, 112, 124-125, 127
Tropicana: 28, 42
Truchas: 300
Truxton: 402
Tuba City: 236-237
tubing: *see* rafting
Tunnel Arch: 199
Turquoise Museum: 341
Turquoise Room: 16, 336, 374
Tusayan: 12, 421, 442, 445
Tusayan Bike Trails: 440
Tusayan Museum and Ruin: 420, 435
24 Hours of Moab: 181
Twin Bridges: 119

U

Uncle Jim Trail: 448
Under-the-Rim Trail: 115, 116, 119-120
UNLV Performing Arts Center: 60
Upheaval Dome: 209
Upheaval Dome Viewpoint Trail: 212
Upper Cathedral Valley Trail: 139
Upper Muley Twist Canyon: 142
Upper Strip: 30-32
Utah Department of Transportation: 13, 468-469, 480

Utah Guide: 480
Utah Mountain Biking: 480
Utah State Parks and Recreation: 469, 480
Utah Travel Council: 469, 480

V

Valentine: 402
Valley Drive: 234, 240-241
Valley of the Gods: 21, 236
Vegas Live Show: 77
Venetian, The: 32-33
Verkamp's Visitors Center: 421
Village of the Great Kivas: 361
Virgin River: 24
Virgin River Canyon Recreation Area: 28
Virgin River Gorge: 21, 24, 28
Virgin River Gorge Nature Trail: 28
visas: 12, 469-470
visitor information: 468-469; *see also specific place*
Vista Encantadora: 447
Vista Verde Trail: 295
Vivác Winery: 295
Volcanoes Day Use Area: 344
Vortex Theatre: 346

W

Walhalla Plateau: 447
Wall Arch: 199
Walnut Canyon National Monument: 333, 382-383
Warehouse 21: 277
Warner, Edith: 303
Watchman Campground: 14, 104-105
Watchman Trail: 97
Waterpocket Fold: 139, 140
weather: 10, 12-13, 423, 474-475
websites: 477-480
Weeping Rock: 92, 94, 99
Westgate: 30
West Mitten Butte: 241
West Nile virus: 476
West Rim (Grand Canyon): *see* Grand Canyon West
West Rim Trail (Rio Grande Gorge): 312, 318
West Rim Trail (Zion): 85, 92, 99
West Rim Viewpoint (Zion): 99
Westwater Canyon: 167, 176
Wetherill Mesa: 245, 250-251
Wet 'n' Wild: 61
Whale Rock Trail: 212
What's On: 77
wheelchair accessibility: 470-471
Wheeler Peak Summit Trail: 319
Wheels Museum: 343
Wheelwright Museum of the American India: 270
White Cliffs: 95
White Rim Overlook Trail: 211
White Rim Road: 210-211
White Wash Sand Dunes: 179
Widforss Trail: 448
Wildcat Canyon Trail: 102
Wildcat Trail: 16, 18, 234, 241
wilderness safety: 474-475
Williams: 16, 19, 20, 336, 395-398, 421-422, 443, 445
Williams Historic District: 395
Williams Lake Trail: 319
Willow Flat Campground: 205
Windows, The: 14, 20, 191, 193, 196-197
Windwhistle Campground: 215, 221
wine/wineries: 187
Wingate Formation: 148
Winslow: 16, 336, 372-374; map 373
Wolfe Ranch: 193-194
Wupatki National Monument: 333, 380-382
Wupatki Pueblo Trail: 382
WWII Navajo Code Talkers Museum: 363
Wynn Las Vegas/Encore: 19, 26, 30, 32

XYZ

X Rocks: 37
XS: 31
Yaki Point: 430
Yavapai Observation Station: 15, 420, 434-435
Yavapai Point: 434
Yei Bi Chei: 241
Yovimpa Point: 85, 116
Zia Regional Rodeo: 472
Zion Canyon: 93, 97-101
Zion Canyon Field Institute: 92
Zion Canyon Scenic Drive: 103
Zion Canyon Shuttle: 93
Zion Canyon Visitor Center: 85, 91
Zion Human History Museum: 93
Zion Lodge: 14, 19, 91, 94, 104
Zion National Park: 8, 11, 14, 15, 18, 19, 83-109; accommodations 88, 104-108; food 89, 108-109; getting there/around 84-89, 92-93; maps 86, 90; recreation 96-104; sights 85, 93-96
Zion Nature Center: 93
Zumanity: 57
Zuni Festival of Arts and Culture: 387
Zuni Mountain Trail System: 366
Zuni Pueblo: 359-362; map 360

LIST OF MAPS

Front map
The Southwest: 2-3

Discover the Southwest
route overview: 10

Las Vegas
mileage map: 23
The Strip: 29
Downtown Las Vegas: 46

Zion and Bryce
mileage map: 83
Zion and Bryce Canyon National Parks: 86
Zion National Park: 90
Bryce Canyon National Park: 111

Capitol Reef National Park
mileage map: 129
Capitol Reef National Park: 130
The Scenic Drive: 138

Arches and Canyonlands
mileage map: 153
Arches and Canyonlands National Parks: 154
Moab: 158-159
Vicinity of Moab: 164
Arches National Park: 190
Canyonlands National Park: 202-203

Monument Valley, Four Corners, and Mesa Verde
mileage map: 231
Monument Valley, Four Corners, and Mesa Verde: 232-233

Santa Fe and Taos
mileage map: 255
Santa Fe and Taos: 258
Downtown Santa Fe: 262-263
Between Santa Fe and Taos: 291
Taos Plaza: 304

Route 66
route overview: 331
Route 66: 334-335
Albuquerque: 337
Old Town Albuquerque: 338
Downtown Albuquerque: 342
Albuquerque to Gallup: 356
Zuni Pueblo and Gallup: 360
Petrified Forest National Park to Holbrook: 370
Winslow: 373
Flagstaff: 376
Williams to Seligman: 396
Grand Canyon Caverns to Hackberry: 403
Kingman: 404

The Grand Canyon
mileage map: 411
The Grand Canyon: 412-413
Grand Canyon Village: 426-427

PHOTO CREDITS

Discover the Southwest page 1 © Chee-Onn Leong/123rf.com; pages 5, 4, 7 (bottom), 12, 17 (top left), 21 © Tim Hull; pages 9 (top right), 11 (top left), 17 (top right, bottom) © Zora O'Neill; pages 7 (top), 11 (top right) © Julian Smith; page 18 © Judy Jewell; page 9 (bottom) © Miroslav Liska/123rf.com; page 11 (bottom) © Varina and Jay Patel/123rf.com; page 9 (top left) © Steve Collender/123rf.com **Las Vegas** page 22 © Caesars Entertainment/Denise Truscello; page 38 © MGM Mirage; page 50 (top) © MGM Mirage; page 56 © Caesars Entertainment; page 50 (middle) © Caesars Entertainment/Erik Kabik; pages 25, 50 (bottom) © donyanedomam/123rf.com; page 76 © Harrah's Entertainment; page 44 © Kobby Dagan/123rf.com **Zion and Bryce** pages 82, 85, 98 (top), 100, 106, 105 (middle, bottom), 116, 118 (top, bottom), 126 © Judy Jewell; pages 98 (middle, bottom), 105 (top) © Paul Levy; page 118 (middle) © Tim Hull **Capitol Reef National Park** pages 128, 131, 136 (top, bottom), 146 © Judy Jewell; page 136 (middle) © Paul Levy **Arches and Canyonlands** page 152 © kravka/123rf.com; pages 155, 162, 171 (top), 178, 182, 192, 197 (top), 212, 215 (middle, bottom) © Bill McRae; pages 171 (middle, bottom), 197 (middle), 215 (top), © Paul Levy; pages 197 (bottom), 222 © Judy Jewell; page 226 © Tim Hull **Monument Valley, Four Corners, and Mesa Verde** page 230 © Tim Hull; page 234 © Julian Smith; page 240 (all) © Tim Hull; page 246 (top) © Visions of America LLC /123rf.com; page 246 (middle) © Alexey Kamenskiy/123rf.com; page 246 (bottom) © Tim Hull; page 238 © Julian Smith **Santa Fe and Taos** pages 254, 257, 268, 275 (all), 284, 298, 306, 308 (all), 318, 322, 327 (all) © Zora O'Neill **Route 66** pages 330, 407 (bottom) © Candacy Taylor; pages 333, 346 (all), 352 © Zora O'Neill; pages 368, 372 (top, bottom), 382, 386, 399 (middle), 407 (top, middle) © Tim Hull; page 372 (middle) © Julian Smith; page 399 (top, bottom) © Elizabeth Jang **The Grand Canyon** pages 410, 414, 438 (all), 452 (top, bottom) © Kathleen Bryant; pages 422, 430, 452 (middle) © Tim Hull; page 458 © Robert Wilson/123rf.com **Essentials** pages 462, 466 © Stuart Thornton